H. Mortimer Franklyn

A Glance at Australia in 1880

Or, food from the South, showing the present condition and production of some of its leading industries, namely, wool, wine, grain, dressed meat, etc. The amounts of each produced and exported

H. Mortimer Franklyn

A Glance at Australia in 1880
Or, food from the South, showing the present condition and production of some of its leading industries, namely, wool, wine, grain, dressed meat, etc. The amounts of each produced and exported

ISBN/EAN: 9783337315788

Printed in Europe, USA, Canada, Australia, Japan

Cover: Foto ©Andreas Hilbeck / pixelio.de

More available books at www.hansebooks.com

A GLANCE

AT

AUSTRALIA IN 1880:

OR,

FOOD FROM THE SOUTH:

SHOWING THE PRESENT CONDITION AND PRODUCTION OF SOME
OF ITS LEADING INDUSTRIES, NAMELY,

WOOL, WINE, GRAIN, DRESSED MEAT,

ETC. ETC.,

THE AMOUNTS OF EACH PRODUCED AND EXPORTED.

TO WHICH IS APPENDED

THE RISE AND PROGRESS OF SOME OF THE LEADING MERCANTILE HOUSES

IN MELBOURNE, SYDNEY, AND ADELAIDE.

AND ALSO A

PASTORAL & AGRICULTURAL DIRECTORY

OF THE WHOLE OF AUSTRALIA.

By H. MORTIMER FRANKLYN,

Editor of "The Victorian Review."

Melbourne:
THE VICTORIAN REVIEW PUBLISHING COMPANY LIMITED.
1881.

MELBOURNE:
M'CARRON, BIRD AND CO., PRINTERS,
FLINDERS LANE WEST.

CONTENTS.

	Page
PREFACE	xi
INTRODUCTION	xv

CHAPTER I.
VICTORIA.

First Settlement of the Colony	1
Its Area and Salubrity	2
Its Soil and Productions	4
Progress of Agriculture	5
Commerce of Victoria	6
Manufactures	7
Industry of the People	7
Why there is Poverty in the Country	7
Nine hundred thousand People spend £3,700,000 in Drink and Smoke	8
Thrifty Habits of the Present Classes	9
Mining in Victoria	9
Provision for Religious Worship	9
Educational Institutions of the Colony	11
Literary, Scientific, and Recreative Associations	11
The Melbourne Race Course on the Cup Day	13
Parks and Pleasure Grounds of the Metropolis	13
The Fitzroy Gardens	14
Benevolent Institutions of Victoria	15
Transitory Nature of its Political Troubles	16
Conservative Influences at work	16
Distribution of the Population	18
Rates of Wages on Farms and Stations	18
Prices of Provisions	19
Wages of Artisans and Labourers	19
Concluding Remarks	21

CHAPTER II.
NEW SOUTH WALES.

Discovery, Settlement, Extent and Physical Features of the Colony	22
Its Natural Resources	24
Its Political and Social Advantages	28
Aspect of Sydney	29
Its beautiful Situation and lovely Surroundings	30

CHAPTER II.—NEW SOUTH WALES—continued.

	Page
Port Jackson	31
The Blue Mountains	33
Provincial New South Wales	34
Providence and Improvidence	35
Australia the Paradise of Domestic Servants	36
A Country Town and its Features	36
The future Aristocracy	38
Political Transformations which the Colony may undergo	39
Its Government	40
Its Railways	40
Its wonderful Progress during the last Decade	41
Its Prosperity under the fostering influences of Free-trade	41
Its External Commerce far greater in proportion to its Population than that of Great Britain, Canada, or the United States	42
Wages, Hours of Labour, and Cost of Provisions in the Metropolis of New South Wales, and in seven of the Principal Towns of the Interior	43

CHAPTER III.
QUEENSLAND.

Area of the Colony	47
Its Geographical Divisions and Topographical Features	48
Its Vegetation and Meteorology	48
Its Grazing Capabilities	50
Mistakes of the Early Pastoral Settlers	50
Inaccurate Statistics	51
Stock and Prices	52
At what Rates Meat can be Raised for Exportation	53
Area of Land held under Pastoral Leases	54
Nature of the Country	55
Mineral Wealth of Queensland	56
Its Principal Goldfields and their Product	57
Tin, Copper, and other Metals	61
Coal Measures of the Colony	63
Agriculture, and its relatively Slow Progress	63
Liberal Land Laws	64
Sugar-planting: its Extent and Productiveness	64
Vine-growing	66
Other Crops	67
Small Area under Wheat	67
Cultivation of Cotton, Arrowroot, Tobacco, and Tropical Fruits	67
Timber and Miscellaneous Products	69
Condition of the People	70
Statistics	71

CHAPTER IV.
SOUTH AUSTRALIA.

Foundation of the Colony	72
Its Land Laws and their Operations	73
Eligibility as a Field of Settlement for Emigrants	74
Large Exports of Staple Products	75

CHAPTER IV.—SOUTH AUSTRALIA—*continued*.

	Page
German Colonists and the Secret of their Success	75
Commerce of South Australia greater per head than that of either of the other Colonies	77
Lightness of Taxation	78
Devotion of its Population to Rural Industries	78
Mineral Resources	79
Flora of South Australia	79
Small Industries which may be profitably pursued there	80
Special Facilities offered by the Legislature for the Cultivation of the Olive	80
Manufacturing Industries of the Colony	81
Statistics	81
Births, Marriages, and Deaths, 1879	82
Census	82
Immigration and Emigration	83
Imports and Exports	83
Live Stock	85
The Wallaroo and Moonta Mines, and their Management	86

CHAPTER V.
TASMANIA.

Its Settlement from New South Wales	97
The Capua of Australia	98
Its Mountains and Lakes	98
Its Eligibility as a Place of Residence	99
Its Picturesque Scenery	100
Its thoroughly English Character	100
Mount Wellington, and the Prospect from its Summit	100
Launceston and its Environs	101
Population of the Island	101
Its Agricultural Products	102
Imports and Exports of the Island	102
General and Widely Diffused Prosperity of its Inhabitants	103
Well-to-do Condition of the Great Mass of the People throughout the whole of Australia	103
Mineral Wealth of Tasmania	103
Large Yield of One of its Tin Mines	103
Total Live Stock on the Island	103
Accumulations of the People	103
Public Instruction	104
Places of Worship	104
Vital Statistics of Tasmania, as an Evidence of its Extreme Salubrity	104

CHAPTER VI.
WESTERN AUSTRALIA.

Area of the Colony	105
British Statesmanship should direct its efforts to promote systematic Colonisation	106
Capabilities of the Australian Colonies for absorbing the surplus Population of the Mother-Country	106
The Impetus it would give to her Commerce	107

CHAPTER VI.—WESTERN AUSTRALIA—*continued.*

	Page
Sparseness of People in Western Australia	107
Its Liberal Land Regulations	108
A Farm for Nothing	108
Productions of the Colony	109
Its Climate and general Salubrity	109
Freedom from Epidemics	110
Mineral Resources	111
Want of Capital and Labour	111
Who should Emigrate	112
Governments of the Colony	112
Current Rates of Wages and Prices of Provisions	113

CHAPTER VII.

NEW ZEALAND.

"The Great Britain of the South"	114
Its Salubrity and Beauty	115
Brief Sketch of its History	116
Its Political Life	118
Why it is Free from Demagogism	119
Vital Statistics of the Colony	119
Robustness of its Inhabitants	122
The Land System in Force	123
Free Trade in Land	126
How Farmers get on	126
Cost of Cultivation	127
Stock Raising	128
Special Settlements	128
Yield of Wheat per Acre	129
Agricultural Statistics	130
Its diversified Industries	131
Mineral Resources of the Country	132
Population of New Zealand	132
Provision for their Education	132
Trade and Commerce of the Colony	133
Religion and Sects	134
The Present and Future of New Zealand as portrayed by a local writer	134

CHAPTER VIII.

THE FUTURE OF AUSTRALIA.

The Probable Achievements of Science in expediting and facilitating Inter-Communication	136
Their Effects upon Civilised Mankind generally	137
General Levelling-up of Society, and its Advantages	137
Australia will largely participate in the Prosperity that is occasioned	138
A Population of Fifteen or Twenty Millions, under Free Institutions, in a Country teeming with Wealth	138
Expansion of Trade with Great Britain, and Increased Productiveness of Australia	139
Federation of the Colonies	140
Its Probable Results	140
The Great Northern Port of the Future	140

CONTENTS. vii

CHAPTER IX.

THE EXPORT TRADE IN FROZEN MEAT.

	Page
The *Strathleven* Experiment	141
Tepid Enterprise	141
Limitations of the supply available	142
Stock of Cattle and Annual Increase	143
American Competition	143
Our Opportunities of Building up a Colossal Trade	144
Unoccupied and Understocked Country	144
Best Quality of Stock required	145
The Future of British Agriculture	145
A Change of System	145
Great Britain and the Australian Colonies will both Benefit in an equal degree by this Trade	146

CHAPTER X.

RAILWAYS AS FACTORS IN THE AUSTRALIAN EXPORT TRADE IN MEAT.

The Railways of Victoria, and the Districts to which they give access	148
Her Live Stock	149
Similar Information with respect to New South Wales and Queensland	149
Projects for a Trans-Continental Line, and the Routes it is proposed they should adopt	150
Distances from the various Capitals to the Gulf of Carpentaria	150
Railways and Live Stock in South Australia	150
Another Trans-Continental Project	151
Splendid Pastoral Country in Western Australia	153
Tasmania and its Railways	153

CHAPTER XI.

AUSTRALIA THE VINEYARD OF THE WORLD.

Great variety of Wines it is capable of producing	154
The Vineyards of South Australia	155
One of them described	155
A Frenchman's visit to St. Hubert's, in Victoria	157
The Vine in Western Australia	158
The Pioneer of the Industry in New South Wales	159
Character and diversity of the Wines of that Colony	159
Cultivation of the Vine in Victoria and Queensland	160
The dying-out of the French Vineyards should act as a Stimulus to the extension of the Industry in Australia	161
Ravages of the Phylloxera in France	161
The Vineyards of Australia contain mines of undeveloped Wealth	162
The Anglo-Australians, being a Wine-producing people, will probably be a Sober Population	162
Some French Statistics bearing on the subject	162

CHAPTER XII.
IMMIGRATION TO AUSTRALIA.

	Page
Apathy on the Subject in England	163
Systematic Colonisation Wanted	164
A Career for all in Australia	165
Its Attractions and Advantages	165
A Land of Promise to the Manual Labourer	166
The Diversified Resources of the Colonies	167
Their Healthfulness	169
Each of them reproduces some of the Best Features of the Mother-Country	170
Sketches of Victorian Life and Scenery	170
Melbourne on the Eve of the Cup-day	170
One of the Suburbs of the Victorian Metropolis	171
Up among the Vineyards at Yering and St. Hubert's	172
The Future belongs to Australia, as the Past does to the Old World	174

CHAPTER XIII.
ADVANTAGES OF AUSTRALIA AS A PLACE OF RESIDENCE.

The Classes of Persons who Should and Should Not Emigrate	176
The Colonies and their Products	177
Room and Abundance for All	177
Natural Endowments of the Country	178
Its Social Life as Attractive as that of the Old World	179
A Salubrious, Bright, and Exhilarating Climate	180
Opportunities for Husbandmen	182
Condition of the Wage-earning Classes	182
Temptations to Dissipation and Discontent	183
Those who Succumb to Them	184
Anglo-Australians the Spoiled Children of Nature	185
Productive forces of Society in a New Country	186
Wealth of the Population	187
A Self-made Territorial Magnate	187
The Story of some Fortunate Diggers	187
Conclusion	190

STATISTICS.

"Where England Buys her Breadstuffs," Quantities of Wheat and Flour Imported into the United Kingdom, 1861-1876	191
Statistical Summary of Population, Agriculture and Live Stock in the Australian Colonies, 1874 to 1878 inclusive	192-3
Statistical Summary of the Principal Exports, the Produce or Manufactures of each Colony, from 1874 to 1878, inclusive	194-5

SOME OF THE LEADING MERCANTILE HOUSES IN MELBOURNE.

Allan and Co.	298
Alston and Brown	281
Apollo Stearine Candle Company, Limited	247
Australasian Mortgage and Agency Company	206
Australasian Agency and Banking Corporation, Limited	216

CONTENTS.

LEADING MERCANTILE HOUSES IN MELBOURNE—*continued*.

	Page
Balfour (James) and Co.	222
Briscoe and Co.	240
British and Australasian Trust and Loan Company, Limited	212
Colonial Mutual Life Assurance Society, Limited	286
Craig, Williamson and Thomas	288
Cuningham (Hastings) and Co.	206
Dalgety, Blackwood and Co.	245
De Castella and Rowan	261
Derham and Co.	275
Exchange, The	271
Fanning, Naukivell and Co.	214
Goldsbrough (R.) and Co.	196
Harper (Robert) and Co.	291
Kilpatrick and Co.	302
Mullen, S.	316
Munro (David) and Co.	294
M'Arthur, Morrow and Brind	410
M'Culloch (William) and Co., Limited	266
M'Ewan (James) and Co.	237
M'Lean Bros. and Rigg	243
M'Meckan, Blackwood and Co.	226
National Mutual Life Association	249
New Zealand Loan and Mercantile Agency Company, Limited	203
Nicholson and Co.	301
Paterson, Laing and Bruce	257
Peninsular and Oriental Steam Navigation Company	228
Permewan, Wright and Company, Limited	269
"Red Cross" Preserving Company	283
Rocke (W. H.) and Co.	263
Rowlands, E.	306
Singer Sewing Machine Company	313
Sloane (William) and Co.	210
Smith (William Howard) and Sons	232
Stanway, John	309
Swallow and Ariell	278
Synnot (Monckton D.) Bros.	223
Toohey (Thomas) and Co.	311
Trustees, Executors, and Agency Company	234
Turner (James) and Son	219
Victoria Ice Company, Limited	304
Welch (Henry P.) and Company	255

SOME OF THE LEADING BANKS IN MELBOURNE.

	Page
Bank of Australasia	321
Bank of Victoria	326
Colonial Bank of Australasia	330
London Chartered Bank of Australia	328
National Bank of Australasia	325
Oriental Bank Corporation	324
Union Bank	319

SOME OF THE LEADING BANKS IN SYDNEY.

	Page
Australian Joint Stock Bank	337
Bank of New South Wales	332
City Bank	340
Commercial Banking Company	335

SOME OF THE LEADING MERCANTILE HOUSES IN SYDNEY.

Alderson and Sons	412
Farmer and Co.	346
Goodlet and Smith	368
Hardie and Gorman	364
Hoffnung (S.) and Co.	352
Hudson Brothers	358
Maiden, Hill and Clark	350
Maddock, William	373
M'Arthur and Co.	410
Prince, Ogg and Co.	343
Vickery, E.	362
Wright, Heaton and Co., Limited	371
Young and Lark	344

SOME OF THE LEADING MERCANTILE HOUSES IN ADELAIDE.

Darling (John) and Son	389
Dunn (John) and Co.	393
Elder, Smith and Co.	376
Faulding (F. H.) and Co.	400
Fowler, D. and J.	381
Gordon (W.) and Co.	408
Kent Town Brewery	403
Murray, D. and W.	386
Peacock (Wm.) and Son	396
Smith, E. T.	403
Stilling (Joseph) and Co.	379
Wigg (E. S.) and Son	405

Pastoral and Agricultural Directory of Australia . . . i—lvii

PREFACE.

THE year 1880 promises to constitute what may be called an epochal year in the history of the Australian colonies. We shall be greatly disappointed if it does not mark a new departure in the industrial development in all, or in the greater part of them. The International Exhibition in Sydney closed and that in Melbourne opened, during the currency of that period. Both are events of no ordinary importance to the inhabitants of this part of the world, and are calculated to exercise no inconsiderable influence upon our future welfare. It is not alone that they have furnished the best of all evidences of what we are capable of producing; it is not alone that they have shown us the progress of other nations in the arts and sciences, in manufactures, and in the useful pursuits of daily life; but that they have had the effect of making these colonies known to the rest of the world. Hitherto the word "Australia" has been little more than an unmeaning sound to millions of people in Europe and America. They knew that it was a large island situated somewhere in the South Pacific; that some portion of it had been a penal settlement; that gold was being, or had been, found there in large quantities; that there were quantities of sheep and cattle roaming over the face of the country; and that people sometimes went out there and returned, in the course of a few years, with large fortunes. But, beyond this, the sum of popular information on the subject was extremely limited. Ask a college don, who could tell you all about the Troad, and the Amphictyonic Council, and the Achaian League and the route of Xenophon, what he knows concerning Australia, and he would probably quote Sydney Smith's description of it, as a region in which nature has been so capricious that "she makes cherries with the stone on the outside, and a monstrous animal as tall as a grenadier, with the head of a rabbit, and a tail as big as a bed-post, hopping along at the rate of five hops to a mile, with three or four young kangaroos looking out of its false uterus to see what is passing. Then comes a quadruped as big as a large cat, with the eyes, colour, and skin of a mole, and the bill and web-feet of a duck—puzzling Dr. Shaw, and rendering the latter half of his life miserable, from his utter inability to determine whether it was a bird or a beast. Add to this a parrot with the legs of a sea-gull; a snake with the head of a shark; and a real bird of such monstrous dimensions that a side-bone of it will dine three real carnivorous Englishmen." Ask an ordinary man of letters, more addicted to reading books than newspapers, what are his impressions about Australia, and he will very likely make answer:—"Australia; ah! yes; Botany Bay, you know. The 'Hades of Thieves,' as Charles Lamb described it in his letter to Barron Field. Wait a moment, while I turn to the passage in his *Essays of Elia*, and I'll tell you all about it. Look! Here it is:—' I see Diogenes prying among you with his perpetual fruitless lantern. What must you be willing by this time to give for the sight of an honest man? You must almost have forgotten how *we* look. The Kangaroos—your aborigines—do they keep their primitive simplicity un-Europe tainted, with those little short forepads, looking like a lesson formed by nature to the pickpocket? We hear the most improbable tales at this distance. Pray is it true that the young Spartans among you are born with six fingers, which spoils their scanning? It must look very odd; but use reconciles. For their scansion, it is less to be regretted, for, if they take it into their heads to be poets, it is odds but they turn out, the greater part of them, vile plagiarists. Do you bleach in three or four generations? I have many questions to put, but ten Delphic voyages can be made in a shorter time than it will take to satisfy my scruples. Do you grow your own hemp? What is your staple trade—exclusive of the natural profession, I mean? Your locksmiths, I take it, are some of your great capitalists.'" Ask a humourist his opinion of social life in Australia, and it is more than probable he will assure you that it is a country in which the sexes are so unequal in number that when a ship-load of female immigrants arrives in Port Jackson, or Hobson's Bay, or the Derwent, the shores are lined with eager bachelors, provided with telescopes and speaking trumpets, and bawling out offers of marriage to the fortunate fair ones long before a single passenger has left the deck of the vessel. And then, in confirmation of his statement, he will refer you to Thomas Hood's "Letter from a Settler for Life in Van Diemen's Land," wherein Susan Gale writes as follows, to Mary, at No. 45 Mount-street, Grosvenor Square :—"As soon as ever the Botes rode to Land I don't agrivate the Truth to say their was half a duzzen Bows apeace to Hand us out to shoar, and sum go as far as say they was offered to thro Speeking Trumpits afore they left the Shipside. Be that as it may or may not I am tould We maid a Verry pretty site all wauking too and too in our bridle wite Gounds with the Union Jacks afore Us to pay humbel Respex to Kernel Arther who behaived very Gentlemanny and Complemented us on our Hansom appearances and Perlitely sed he Wisht us All in the United States. The Salers was so gallaunt as giv three Chears wen We left there Ship and sed if so be they had not Bean without Canons they wood have saluted us all round. Servents mite live Long enuff in Lonnon without Being sich persons of Distinkshun. For my hone Part cumming among strangers and Pig in Pokes prudence Dicktated not to be askt out At the very fust cumming in howsumever All is settled And the match is approved off by Kernel Arther and the Brightish government who as agread to giv me away. thems wot I call Honners as we used to say at wist."

These effusions of mere fun are, after all, no very great exaggerations of the notions which were at one time widely prevalent, and which still obtain considerable currency in England with respect to these colonies ; and we think the time is opportune for the publication of a work which shall present, as far as possible, a faithful glance at "Australia in 1880." In its preparation, the author has received the valuable co-operation and assistance of writers conversant with some of the special subjects treated of in its pages ; and it has been his endeavour to combine accuracy of statement with agreeableness of narrative. Whether he has succeeded, he must leave the reader to determine.

INTRODUCTION.

There is a very old, a very solemn, and a very impressive injunction, which warns us against hiding our light under a bushel. And if to do so is censurable in the individual, it is still more so in the nation, which is, after all, but an aggregation of individuals. Publicity is at once the soul of business and the safeguard of political freedom. The shopkeeper who does not advertise might as well put up his shutters; and the Government which has anything to conceal from the people over which it has been appointed to rule, may be justly regarded with suspicion by those who have entrusted it with supreme power. Thanks to the printing press and to the electric telegraph, the affairs of the whole world are now being publicly transacted in the presence of the whole world. And as nothing is sacred to the French sapper, so also no seclusion is proof against invasion by the indomitable, the inevitable and irrepressible interviewer or reporter. He penetrates to the cabinet of the statesman, the council chamber of the sovereign, the tent of the commander-in-chief, the study of the successful author, the boudoir of the reigning beauty, the laboratory of the scientist, the dressing-room of the actress, the atelier of the artist, and the condemned cell of the murderer. Publicity, then, is one of the conditions of modern existence. Formerly to be out of the fashion was to be out of the world. *Nous avons changé tout cela.* Now-a-days to be unnoticed is to be unknown; and to be unknown is to be *non ens*. Communities can as little afford to be overlooked as individuals can, and we acknowledge, with the utmost frankness, that our end and aim in writing this book, is to advertise the Australian colonies, and to endeavour to present in it as faithful a picture as possible of their present economic position, as well as to shadow forth their future prospects. By showing the really wonderful results which have been accomplished in this part of the world during the last half-century, we shall enable readers at a distance to forecast the enormous strides which Australia is bound to make during the succeeding one. Here, for example, are a few figures which will prove to be more eloquent than any words. In the year 1830 the total population of the Australian colonies—which then consisted of New South Wales and Tasmania exclusively (for Western

Australia had only been settled the year before and contained a mere handful of pioneers) was 70,581 all told. To-day it is two millions and a quarter. Fifty years ago, the entire commerce of Australia with other countries was of the value of £1,000,000 sterling; in 1880, it exceeded the value of £80,000,000 sterling. Other items illustrative of progress may be conveniently exhibited in the subjoined form:—

	1830.	1880.
Land in Cultivation...	110,000 acres	4,000,000 acres
Live Stock, Horses ...	18,000	840,000
,, Cattle ...	390,000	6,400,000
,, Sheep ...	1,300,000	46,000,000
Exports of Wool, value	£65,000	£16,000,000
Shipping ...	57,000 tons	6,000,000 tons
Public Revenue ...	£155,000	£14,000,000
Miles of Railway ...	Nil	2,600 miles

These statistics, taken from official records, tell their own story, they bear testimony alike to the bounty of Providence, and the untiring industry and invincible enterprise of the race to which we belong. And it must be remembered that during the half century embraced by these returns, cities have been built, towns and villages innumerable have been established and enlarged; docks and harbours, bridges and piers constructed; churches and schoolhouses erected; and all the means and appliances of a complex civilisation brought hither from the other end of the world. Fifty years ago, Victoria, South Australia, the greater part of Queensland, all the Northern Territory, and the centre of the continent, were little better than solitudes over which various tribes of aborigines roamed; and where any map of the period would have exhibited an utter blank. To-day all this is changed, and to-morrow——! Who shall venture to predict the extent of its advancement, or to estimate the magnitude of the resources which science and industry will combine to develop within the four corners of the island-continent? But in order to achieve these splendid possibilities, Australia wants more and more of the two great factors of wealth—men and money. For both, she offers illimitable opportunities of enterprise, and it is to indicate these, and also to make known to the people of the old world the magnitude and importance of the markets which these colonies open up for the manufactures and the art products of Great Britain and the Continental nations, that the compilation of this work has been undertaken.

Let us bring into juxtaposition two groups of contrasted facts. The first of these may be formulated thus: The continent of Europe having an estimated area of 3,800,000 square miles, supports a population of 500,000,000. It does so on a soil which, in so far as the countries peopled by the Latin and Teutonic races are concerned, has been partially exhausted by centuries of incessant culture, while its productiveness has been diminished by the destruction of many of its mountain forests, and by the disastrous climatic and meteorological changes to which this devastation has given rise. The whole of its principal rivers are more or less tainted by drainage, and many of its cities were originally constructed and continue to be built in utter disregard of the principles of political science. Not only so, but the aggregation of human beings, in numbers ranging from 100,000 to four millions, within the limits of a single town or capital, under conditions eminently unfavourable to health, is productive of alarmingly high rates of mortality. Moreover, in the immediate neighbourhood of all these centres of population are graveyards, in which have been buried, only a few feet below the surface of the soil, generations upon generations of decomposing corpses, the emanations from which rising through the porous earth, must taint the air so that the living are being poisoned by the dead. Then again, the enormous national debts of Europe, amounting, in the whole, to upwards of £2,000,000,000 sterling, and the maintenance of several millions of men under arms, involve so vast an annual expenditure upon interest and upon military and naval establishments, as to necessitate the imposition of so heavy a load of taxation by the various governments as to fall with crushing weight on the great mass of the people; and wherever these are most numerous, relatively to the area of the country they inhabit, there is found to prevail a large amount of poverty and wretchedness. These induce drunkenness, disease, vice, physical, moral, and mental degeneration, insanity and crime, until the ingenuity of the legist and the benevolence of the philanthropist are taxed to the utmost in their endeavours to cope with the evils by which they are confronted; and thus the highest developments of a complex and artificial civilisation are found to coexist with the most serious of social dangers, the most alarming of political discontents, so that, as Macaulay once said of the United States, the day may come when some of the fairest regions of Europe will be plundered and laid waste, not by foreign barbarians, but by the Huns and Vandals who have been engendered within their own political and geographical limits.

Let us now turn to the other group of facts. Here is an island-continent with an area of 3,000,000 square miles, or only one-sixth less than that of the United States, with a population which scarcely reaches 2,250,000, or below that of Switzerland, and not more than half that of Ireland. Within its wide range of surface it includes an equally wide range of climate, from that of the north of France, in the southern portion of Victoria, to that of Egypt, Algeria, and Morocco, in Queensland, and in the Northern Territory of misnamed South Australia. It is a virgin soil girdled by the ocean, which tempers the heat of the tropical regions of Australia, and increases the natural healthfulness of all. It contains some of the finest pastures in the world; it is exceedingly rich in mineral wealth; its wheat, its wine, and its wool have no superiors; it could clothe and feed sixty millions of people within its own limits, supposing the density of population to be no greater than it is in Turkey at the present time, and still leave a surplus available for export, adequate to the wants of a hundred millions of people in the old world. Its public indebtedness, *i.e.*, that of the whole of the colonies, excluding New Zealand, does not exceed £50,000,000, and has been chiefly incurred in the execution of reproductive works such as railways, docks, harbours, reservoirs, &c., and there are no standing armies to constitute a permanent drain upon the earnings of the people, and to draw from the pursuits of industry the very flower of the population. Inconsiderable, in point of numbers, as that population is, its wealth is very great indeed; it raises a revenue of upwards of seventeen millions sterling, of which, however, rather more than a third only is obtained by taxation. It owns 70,000,000 acres of land, of which 6,000,000 have been brought under cultivation. It does a total trade with other countries of the value, in round numbers, of £95,000,000 sterling. It has constructed upwards of 4000 miles of railway, and 2600 miles of electric telegraph. Its commerce is transported by 16,000 vessels, with an aggregate tonnage of seven millions. It possesses one million horses, seven millions and a half of cattle, sixty-one millions of sheep, and 800,000 pigs; and these accumulations and achievements have all been the work of half a century only, as will be apparent from some comparative figures which we have given above. What, therefore, may not be accomplished during the next fifty years, especially if we should receive any large accession to our population by immigration? Hitherto, our net gain in this respect has averaged something like 50,000 per annum; an altogether insignificant number as compared with the magnitude of the human tide which pours upon the shores of the United States. Only once since the year 1845 has this fallen as low as 91,800 in any one period of twelve months; while in 1872 it reached its maximum of 449,483, and it is not improbable that this will have been equalled, if not exceeded, in 1880. Between the years 1819 and 1876, America received 9,726,455 persons from Europe, who carried with them a capital, *en gros*, of £112,000,000 sterling, while their value to the country as wealth producers has been estimated at £1,800,000,000 by some statists, and at £2,700,000,000 by others. The Australasian colonies could easily absorb 200,000 immigrants per annum, especially if such immigration were systematically conducted, and were, as it ought to be, a matter of imperial concern in Great Britain, and of federal action in Australia. Unhappily, at this end of the world, the very classes which would benefit most by immigration, the operative masses who would be raised in the social scale by the introduction of workers, of whom they would become the employers, are so unenlightened, so little conversant with the principles of social science, and so much accustomed to regard every fresh arrival as a competitor and not as a co-operator, as an enemy to be feared, and not as a friend to be welcomed, that State immigration has been stopped for many years in the most populous of the colonies, namely, Victoria; and the result is that the other colonies are rapidly overtaking it in population, and that New South Wales will probably shoot ahead of it in two or three years' time. As all political power is in the hands of the numerical majority, that majority dictates the policy of the country, and instead of government by the people, we have government by the populace, in so far as this particular colony is concerned; hence the establishment of protection and the discontinuance of immigration. The evil, however, is not incurable; because, as agricultural settlement extends, a countervailing political power will grow up, opposed to the short-sighted selfishness and ignorant prejudices of urban democracies, and impelled, by their own interests, to demand freedom of exchange, and to insist upon the resumption of immigration.

To the uneasy classes in the mother-country, to British workmen out of employment, and to all who feel that they are "cribb'd, cabin'd, and confined" in the United Kingdom, or in France, Belgium, the Netherlands, or Italy, we say, "Come." In one or other of the colonies you may confidently calculate upon obtaining better remuneration for yourselves, and a much more hopeful and prosperous career for your children, than is possible in the overcrowded continent of Europe. There is room for all—for the man with money, for the man with brains, and for the man of muscle. You will not pick up gold in the streets. You must not suppose that the conditions of success—industry, application, sobriety, frugality, and perseverance—can be dispensed with here, any more than they can elsewhere. You must not expect to find the employment or opening you desire, immediately on arrival. You must have patience, courage, and determination; and with these you are bound to "get on" and to rise in life. And it must be remembered as one of the advantages held out by the Australian colonies, that not only are wages higher and living cheaper here than they are in America, but that the hours of labour are shorter, and the days in the year during which a man can work at his trade, more numerous than they are in the United States.

For the information of all classes in the mother-country, it has been our anxious endeavour to present, in the following pages, a truthful and trustworthy photograph of "Australia in 1880," exaggerating and concealing nothing. We believe that each colony possesses special advantages, and that all offer a desirable field for immigration. We have not consciously exhibited any bias towards one or the other, because we regard them as integral portions of one great whole, and believe that their prosperity is so interrelated and inter-dependent, that whatever increases the population and stimulates the progress of a single constituent of the group must conduce to the benefit of all. We are firmly convinced that this portion of the British Empire has a magnificent future before it, and the writer of this work has no higher ambition than to co-operate, in however humble and insignificant a degree, in contributing to proclaim its resources and to promote its welfare.

A GLANCE AT AUSTRALIA IN 1880.

Chapter I.

VICTORIA.

FIRST SETTLEMENT OF THE COLONY—ITS AREA AND SALUBRITY—ITS SOIL AND PRODUCTIONS—PROGRESS OF AGRICULTURE—COMMERCE OF VICTORIA—MANUFACTURES—INDUSTRY OF THE PEOPLE—WHY THERE IS POVERTY IN THE COUNTRY—NINE HUNDRED THOUSAND PEOPLE SPEND £3,700,000 IN DRINK AND SMOKE—THRIFTY HABITS OF THE PRUDENT CLASSES—MINING IN VICTORIA—PROVISION FOR RELIGIOUS WORSHIP—EDUCATIONAL INSTITUTIONS OF THE COLONY—LITERARY, SCIENTIFIC, AND RECREATIVE ASSOCIATIONS—THE MELBOURNE RACECOURSE ON THE CUP DAY—PARKS AND PLEASURE GROUNDS OF THE METROPOLIS—THE FITZROY GARDENS—BENEVOLENT INSTITUTIONS OF VICTORIA—TRANSITORY NATURE OF ITS POLITICAL TROUBLES — CONSERVATIVE INFLUENCES AT WORK—DISTRIBUTION OF THE POPULATION—RATES OF WAGES ON FARMS AND STATIONS—PRICES OF PROVISIONS—WAGES OF ARTISANS AND LABOURERS—CONCLUDING REMARKS.

VICTORIA has not yet reached the fiftieth year of its age as a British settlement, nor the fortieth anniversary of its elevation to the dignity of a separate existence as a colony, nor the thirtieth of its accession to the responsibilities and troubles of self-government. It is true that as far back as 1828 Mr. William Dutton landed at Portland Bay, and afterwards built a house there, established a whaling station at that place, and planted the first garden; but the first permanent settlement was effected in this part of the Australian continent, by Mr. Edward Henty, in the year 1834. In the year following, an association was formed in Van Diemen's Land for colonising a tract of country surrounding Port Phillip. Batman, one of the party, ascended the River Yarra Yarra as far as the site of the present city of Melbourne; and in the same year five acres of land were planted with wheat on a spot which is now covered with warehouses, wharves, and railway lines. Next year, Mr. John Pascoe Fawkner, one of the founders of the settlement, issued the first newspaper—a manuscript sheet entitled *The Melbourne Advertiser*; and, in the course of the same year, Major (afterwards Sir Thomas) Mitchell, crossed the Murray from Sydney, explored the whole of the country lying between that stream and the sea coast in the south-west, and retraced his steps by a more easterly route to Port Jackson. In the year following the infant settlement numbered 177 persons, all of whom had migrated thither from Van Diemen's Land, and by this time many of the settlers were pushing out in all directions with the sheep and cattle which they had brought with them in order to occupy the fine pastoral country which was found to exist in the interior. On the 30th of April, 1837, the first child was baptised in Melbourne, and the town was laid out with marvellous foresight by Mr. Hoddle, who is still living, and the principal streets were marked out 99 feet wide; the first land sale was held, and the average price realised was at the rate of £70 an acre. Each acre now is worth a king's ransom. In the year after, a fortnightly mail was established overland between Melbourne and Sydney; and in 1839, two adventurous gentlemen started—the one in a tandem, and the other on horseback—overland to Adelaide, successfully accomplishing the journey in 27 days. From this time until the gold discoveries in 1851, the settlement continued to make steady and rapid progress, although this was chequered at times by seasons of adversity, resulting from drought, or from fluctuations in the price of sheep and cattle, wool and tallow. The year before those remarkable discoveries, the population of Port Philip, as the province was then called, had risen to 76,162; the revenue was, in round numbers, £260,000; and the general expenditure, £200,000; there were 52,341 acres of land under cultivation; the imports and exports were of the aggregate value of one million and three quarters sterling; and the live stock in the country amounted to 21,219 horses, 378,806 head of cattle, 6,032,783 sheep, and 9,260 pigs.

The settlement of Port Phillip was detached from New South Wales and formed into a separate colony in 1851, and in that year the auriferous wealth of the new colony—which had been named Victoria, in honour of Her Majesty—was first brought to light, and led to the influx of scores of thousands of adventurers from all parts of the world, allured to the country by the most potent of all attractions—gold. Towards the close of the year 1855, the new Constitution was proclaimed in Victoria, and in the year following, the first Parliament, elected under a system of responsible government, was opened on the 21st of November. There have been nine Parliaments since then, and a total of eighteen administrations.

This brief sketch of the history of the colony may suffice as an introduction to some account of the country and its resources. Its area in square miles is 88,198, or very little more than that of England and Wales and Scotland; whilst its population may be set down, in round numbers, at 900,000, of whom nearly one-third are congregated in Melbourne and its suburbs. Lying within the same isothermal lines as the countries of Southern Europe, it is favoured with a beautiful climate, the natural salubrity of which is greatly increased by the peculiar character of the flora of the country, the eucalyptus predominating. Of this singular tree—probably the most swiftly growing in the world—upwards of a hundred varieties have already been figured and described, and the chemical contents of each are more or less rich in a volatile oil, which, on being liberated by the combined agencies of the plant and the atmosphere, exercises a most beneficial influence on the latter. Not only so, but the eucalyptus is a preventive of marsh fevers and miasma, because planted, or growing naturally, in places where stagnant water would collect, and decayed vegetation might taint the air, its roots absorb all such moisture, and the marvellous alchemy of nature transforms these pestilential elements into health-giving foliage; therefore, the agues, which are so prevalent in the North American forests, are almost unknown in the Australian bush. The leaves of this tree yield to the chemist an essential oil, which is valuable as a febrifuge, and for its antispasmodic and anti-asthmatic uses; and we feel justified in asserting that the eucalyptus will prove to be a greater boon to mankind than even the far-famed chinchona tree. It is being planted, for sanitary purposes, by millions in Italy, in the South of France, in Algeria, and in California, and the important hygienic *rôle* which it plays in Victoria may be inferred from the following extract from a paper read before the Royal Society of Victoria by Mr. Bosisto, M.L.A., a chemist of some local eminence. He said :—"The mallee country plays a very important part in the climatic influences of Australia. . . . The whole of these dwarf eucalypts consequently retain in their leaves at one time 4,843,872,000 gallons of oil. . . . If we now take into consideration the extent of the mallee country in the territory of New South Wales and South Australia, we have 96,877,440,000 gallons of oil held at one and the same time in a belt of country massed together, over which the hot winds pass; and considering also that the same condition exists throughout the major part of Australia with the other eucalypts as that which exists in Victoria, we cannot arrive at any other conclusion than that the whole atmosphere of Australia is more or less affected by the perpetual exhalation of these volatile bodies." The leaves of one variety—the *E. amygdalina*—are so rich in this essential oil, that as much as 500 ounces have been obtained from 1000lbs. of fresh leaves, with their stalklets and branchlets. And the activity of the respiration and transpiration of the leaves of this remarkable tree is indicated, perhaps, by the amazing number of stomata which they possess. These, in the *E. Cloëziana*, reach the very high figure of 310,000 to the square inch; and of eighteen varieties, microscopically examined by Baron von Mueller, the distinguished botanist, only one was found to contain as low as 100,000 air holes. In upwards of a hundred other varieties, the stomata were found on both sides of the leaves, sometimes in equal quantities, and sometimes with a preponderance on the lower surface. The eucalyptus is found in all parts of the Australian continent, and its economic value is second only to its hygienic importance. It often grows at the rate of from 12 to 18 feet per annum, and a plantation of these trees in Algeria was found to have attained an average altitude of 45 feet, and a circumference of three feet— measured a yard above the ground—in the space of six years.

Geologically speaking, Victoria belongs to one of the older formations, in proof of which it may be mentioned that its forests contain some fifty or sixty genera of living plants resembling those which are fossilised in the Eocene beds of the Tyrol. The bed rock, upon which the country rests, dates from the Silurian epoch, and this bed rock is veined by auriferous quartz, to the attrition of which, we are in all probability indebted for the rich deposits of alluvial gold which have been found in this colony. Most of the best land in Victoria is the product of a decomposition of the upper volcanic rock. This soil is either of a dark chocolate colour, or of a deep black; it often extends to a great depth, and its fertility can scarcely be exaggerated. According to a competent authority, who formed his estimate from a personal inspection of the country, it contains about twenty-three millions of acres of rich loams and alluvial flats; eight millions of acres of rich black and chocolate-coloured soils, and five millions of acres of light and sandy soils. The choicest portions of this territory have no doubt passed into private ownership already, but there are still 20,000,000 acres of lands unalienated from the Crown, from which any person is free to select 320 acres, upon conditions which are almost equivalent to a free gift. Other colonies, with a more spacious territory, can offer larger areas to the individual settler on equally, or still more favourable terms; but, on the whole, the indirect advantages which he acquires in regard to proximity to the largest markets in Australia, and to the country being furnished with a railway system which will soon bring every portion of it into connection with the seaboard, are such as to compensate the farmer for the restrictions imposed upon him as a selector; and probably the day will come when his own personal experience will convince him that an intensive method of husbandry applied to a limited area is more profitable in the long run than a slovenly mode of culture applied to a much larger one.

As the climate and soil of Victoria vary with the latitude and altitude of the country, and with the proximity of the region to, or its distance from, the Southern Ocean, the colony is well adapted for the production of an exceedingly wide variety of plants. Besides the whole of the cereals, the vine, the olive, the hop, the tea-plant, the orange and lemon, the numerous fruits and the tubers and pulse familiar to the husbandmen of the mother-country, the following plants may be enumerated, as suitable for cultivation in Victoria:—The algaroba tree, arrow-root, bananas, bamboos, broom corn and buckwheat, the butter-nut, camphor, candlenut and carob trees, the caper plant, chicory, the castor oil plant, the cottonwood tree, the date palm, the earth chesnut and egg plant, flax, gamboge, ginger, gram, guavas, the senna bush, hickory trees, Indian corn, ipecacuanha, jute plants, the kumquat, lavender, liquorice, the mastic tree, mustard, the nut pine, the paper mulberry, the chinchona tree, plantains, the poppy, the quandong, saffron, sumach, the tallow-tree, wormwood and yams. In process of time, there is every reason to anticipate that the rural population of the country, who generally own the land they till, will devote their attention to those *petites industries* in the pursuit of which, their wives and children will find light, pleasant and remunerative occupations, and that Victoria will present something of the garden-like appearance of the mother-country, especially when steps have been taken to store the annual rainfall of the colony for irrigation purposes, which is now felt to be a national want.

An almost unerring indication of the nature of the soil is presented by the timber which grows upon it, and the old settler can tell at a glance the character of the country by the indigenous trees which it produces. Where the red gum flourishes, cattle may generally find good pasturage, although if it be low-lying land on the banks of a creek the probabilities are it will be subject to floods in the rainy season. Where the blackwood thrives, the husbandman may expect to see his shining ploughshare open a rich furrow of deep black soil, while the natural grasses will be succulent and fattening for cattle. In districts where the curiously misnamed he-oak and she-oak prevail, the soil is generally too poor and sandy to repay tillage. The honeysuckle tree is also an unfavourable omen, as it is everywhere the product of a comparatively barren and positively hungry soil. The habitat of the Murray pine should be likewise shunned by the farmer and grazier. So, too, each of them would be wise to avoid the ridges or ranges which appear to be most congenial to the stringy and iron bark trees, while the "prospector" hails the appearance of the last-named tree as one of the indices of a rocky soil which is probably rich in auriferous quartz. Where the silver wattle grows, the land is usually light in quality, and it may be suitable for grazing purposes, if only sparsely timbered. As to the forests which clothe most of the ranges, and in which the trunks of the trees rise like gigantic columns to a height of two, three, and even four hundred feet, with a plume of foliage on their lofty crests, they are frequently immensely rich in vegetable humus, the gradual accumulation of thousands of years ; but the cost of clearing a few acres of land under such circumstances is enormous, and in nine cases out of ten the settler finds he has made a serious mistake in selecting such a spot for his homestead.

Of the progress made by agriculture in Victoria, the following figures will serve to give a good general idea. On the 31st of March, 1880, there were in round numbers, 50,000 land owners whose holdings exceeded one acre in extent; so that it may be fairly asserted that one adult male in every five is a freeholder, or is in process of becoming so, as soon as he shall have complied with the conditions of the Land Act, and be entitled to claim a Crown grant of the land he occupies as a licensee or a lessee. But this is altogether exclusive of the many thousands of townsfolk, both in Melbourne and its suburbs, and in the country districts, who own the houses or cottages they inhabit, and we do not think we are forming an extravagant estimate if we put these down at another 50,000, so that this would give us 100,000 real property owners in a population of 900,000. There are 16,614,967 acres of land alienated from the Crown, which are being occupied for agricultural or pastoral purposes—rather more than one-tenth of that area, or 1,687,400 acres, being under tillage.

Of this extent 708,738 acres were under wheat, 167,721 under oats, 41,600 under potatoes, and 201,169 under hay; the gross produce being 9,407,503 bushels of wheat, 4,024,962 bushels of oats, 167,986 tons of potatoes, and 291,781 tons of hay. Barley, maize, rye, peas and beans, turnips, mangel wurzel, beet, carrots and parsnips, onions, chicory, grass seeds, hops, and tobacco also figure in the list of products. Gardens are returned as covering 12,841 acres, and orchards 7464. The vineyards of the colony comprise 4285 acres, yielding 89,890 cwt. of grapes, converted into 574,143 gallons of wine, and 3284 gallons of brandy, while those consumed as fruit are set down at 16,295 cwt.

Of the principal crops raised by the farmers, the average yield per acre was 13·3 bushels of wheat, 24·0 bushels of oats, 4·0 tons of potatoes, and 1·5 tons of hay. This is rather above the average as regards every item but wheat. From the foundation of the colony up till the year 1877, the colony expended upwards of eleven millions sterling for the purchase of imported breadstuffs; but, from this time forth, it is pretty certain that there will be a large surplus of wheat and flour available for export. In 1879, 321,809 centals of Victorian wheat were thus disposed of, and a much larger quantity will be exported this year. Up to the 9th August our shipments were as follows:—530,173 bags of wheat, containing 4¼ bushels each, equal to 2,278,077 bushels; and 154,896 bags of flour, equal to 516,653 bushels; in all about 2,794,675 bushels.

It may be convenient in this place to speak of the external commerce of the colony in connection with its productive interests generally. Its imports for the year 1879 were of the value of £15,035,538, while the exports were of the value of £12,454,170, showing an apparent balance of upwards of £2,500,000 in favour of Victoria. But as wool of the value of £1,700,000 grown in New South Wales, and gold of the value of £367,244 produced outside the colony, were shipped from the port of Melbourne, it brings down the profit in the year's barter to half-a-million only. The principal items exported were these :—

Gold, of the value of	£857,294
Apparel and slops	188,113
Wheat	132,314
Leather	227,312
Specie	1,386,858
Wool	3,564,721

Articles of Victorian manufacture also make a creditable figure in these returns. Under free trade, there had commenced a considerable export of locally-fabricated commodities, and the statistics for 1863 show that Victoria was then exporting seventy-two distinct articles of her own manufacture, including furniture, carriages, agricultural implements, boots and shoes, candles, wearing apparel, machinery, etc., etc. In fact, these industries were so well established that it was out of the power of protection to retard their progress and development. Consequently, we find the following items of Victorian manufacture figuring in the exports for 1879 :—Agricultural implements, apparel and slops, bags, sacks and woolpacks, biscuits, steam boilers, boots and shoes, brushware, candles, carriages, carts and waggons, confectionery, cordage, steam engines, flour, furniture and upholstery, hardware and ironmongery, felt hats, jams and preserves, jewellery, leather, agricultural machinery, malt, wrought marble, preserved meats, oilmen's stores, paper bags, saddlery and harness, soaps, stationery, stearine, wine, wooden ware, woollen piece goods. The articles thus enumerated will suffice to show the diversified forms which manufacturing industry has assumed, and the varied occupations provided for its people. No doubt, protection has retarded the growth of enterprise in this direction, as all such artificial obstacles necessarily do; but it is extremely improbable that this will long continue the policy of a country which must look abroad for outlets for the yearly increasing surplus of its agricultural produce, and where the good sense and practical experience of its population will convince them that every barrier erected by legislative enactment against imports must also operate as a barrier against the emission of exports.

In the mean time, the precise phase of industrial development, reached by the colony is denoted to some extent by the occupations of the people; and these indicate that sub-division of labour which is only found in highly-organised societies, possessing a complex civilisation, combined with the enjoyment of a reasonable amount of security for the pacific pursuit of labour, and the enjoyment of its accumulations, known as property. In a colonial community of comparatively recent origin, it may be said that all but an insignificant percentage of the population are workers—that is to say, all who are not too young, or too old, or too feeble, to be so among the male sex. And their industry is immensely productive; because, in a country where the soil is of great extent, and in many instances, exceedingly fertile, and where the superabundance of light and warmth—the two great elements of plant growth—stimulates the productiveness of the earth, nature co-operates so powerfully with human labour in the creation of wealth as to ensure to every unit of the population such an amount of the necessaries and comforts of life, as is necessarily unattainable in old and thickly-peopled countries. And, *therefore*, paradoxical as the statement may appear, there is a great deal of poverty and distress in Victoria. For wherever there is abundance, there also is improvidence. Prudence and frugality are to be found in the cottage of the French peasant farmer, whose life is one of prolonged and persevering toil. If you want to see waste and profusion, you must descend into the kitchen of any of the mansions of Mayfair, where you will find as much excellent food daily consigned to the waste-butt, by domestics who have been brought up on coarse fare, and not too much of it, as would supply the wants of a poor man's family. And so, too, in Victoria, and in the colonies generally, there is an immense amount of that unthrift and self-indulgence which accompanies the state of things popularly known as "light come, light go."

Thus the account of the population—barely 900,000—for fermented liquors, tobacco and snuff, and malt stood as follows for the year 1879, exclusive of what was expended upon spirits, malt, wine, and malt liquors manufactured in the colony, and of the tobacco grown there :—

	Value.	Duty.	Total.
Ale and Porter	£193,262	£26,591	£219,853
Malt	67,698	12,346	80,044
Spirits	386,813	444,542	831,355
Tobacco and Cigars	177,017	87,891	264,908
Snuff	775	306	1,081
Wines	91,600	31,617	123,217
			£1,520,458

If we add only 33½ per cent. to this, for importers' and vendors' profits, we reach a total of two millions sterling disbursed for the above-named articles. But during the same year there were 15,370,745 gallons of beer brewed in the colony; and supposing this to average to the consumer no more than two shillings a gallon, we have thus one million and a-half expended in this way. Then, there were 410,333 gallons of wine made; of which one-half at the very least would find its way into consumption; and the market value of this may be put down at one tenth of a million; while the 15,662 cwt. of tobacco grown in the colony, may be put down as costing the smokers £75,000. Here, then, is a total of £3,700,000 spent by a community of less than 900,000 men, women, and children upon drink and smoke; and these figures, we submit, are both an evidence of prosperity, and an explanation of the destitution that prevails. For, inasmuch as it is not an intemperate community, and inasmuch as the various temperance and total abstinence associations, are both numerous and strong in members, and inasmuch as moderation may be said to be very generally practised among the well-to-do classes of society, it follows that there must be a section of the community which is given to hard drinking, and the smaller this is in number the greater must be its habits of self-indulgence. And this, we contend, sufficiently accounts for the poverty which is often met with in the large towns; and for much of the insanity which fills our lunatic asylums with patients.

On the other hand, it is gratifying to point to the thrifty habits of the better class—morally speaking—of the Victorian population. These are shown by the deposits in the savings banks, amounting to £1,510,273, by the income of the friendly societies, which reaches the sum of £78,863, and by the annual payments to the building societies, which are given at £1,097,475. But this is far from representing the total savings of the people, much of which is lodged on deposit with the ordinary banks, and with numerous financial associations, which lend money on mortgages of real estate, while other sums are paid to life assurance companies, as annual premiums upon policies, and numerous accumulations are applied to the clearance, fencing, and cultivation of land taken up by free selectors. So that while a strict regard for truth has led us to mention the existence of a large amount of poverty, which is too often the result of personal misconduct, we are bound to exhibit the per contra accounts, and to show the virtues of the majority, while not concealing the vices of the minority.

Besides agriculture, commerce, and manufactures, Victoria has long been celebrated for her mining industries, albeit these have suffered a steady and gradual decadence, owing to the fiscal policy of the Legislature, which by taxing the machinery and implements, the oil, candles, and cordage, of the miner, as well as everything he wears, from his felt hat to his heavy boots, has imposed a heavy handicap upon this peculiarly native industry. Hence, it is greatly to be regretted, that between 1871, when the Customs duties were doubled, and 1879, the number of miners in Victoria decreased from 58,279 to 37,553, while the yield of gold fell from 1,368,942 ounces to 758,948 ounces during the same space of time. But as the area of auriferous territory in the colony is known to be not less than 25,000 square miles, of which only 1,234 square miles have been worked over, and as deep mining is only in its infancy, and there is every indication that there are "leads" of gold—ancient river beds, in point of fact—lying many hundreds of feet below those which were first discovered comparatively near the surface, and were found to be richer in the precious metal than the famous sands of Pactolus, we may anticipate a revival of this important branch of industry in Victoria. Of metals and minerals other than gold, the colony contains silver, tin ore, and black sand, copper, antimony, lead, iron, gypsum, lignite, kaolin, granite, sand-stone, marble, slate, and coal ; but, hitherto, the last-named mineral has not been found to exist in seams of sufficient thickness to render the "winning" of it profitable.

Having thus glanced at the material resources of the colony, we will proceed to speak of its religious, moral, and social aspects. Most people who have "ever been where bells have knoll'd to church," and who may be meditating the transference of themselves and their families to one of the Australian colonies, in the well-founded hope of bettering their circumstances, and of providing their children with a career less crowded by competition than that which is open to them in the mother-country, will naturally feel some anxiety as to the opportunities of spiritual and mental instruction which are available in the new land. Well, in Victoria, no less than in the old country, such opportunities are ample, and, as a general rule, readily accessible. Although there is no State Church in any part of Australia, and all denominations rest upon the voluntary principle, each is liberally supplied with churches, and with ministers of religion. Thus, in the colony under notice, there are 2,815 churches or chapels, or other edifices used as places of worship, affording accommodation for 420,000 persons; the average attendance being close upon 300,000. Of these buildings 657 belong to the Presbyterians, 653 to the Wesleyan Methodists, 482 to the Church of England, 454 to the Church of Rome, 116 to the Primitive Methodists, 101 to the Bible Christians, 93 to the Independents, and 78 to the Baptists, while the Jews have seven synagogues. Sixteen other denominations possess 178 places of worship. There are also 1557 Sabbath schools in Victoria, with 13,450 teachers, and an average attendance of 116,142 children. Taking them altogether, the colonial clergy will be found to maintain a high average of ability, personal character, and ministerial zeal. It is not to be expected that they should reach so elevated a standard as in the old country, where the State Church holds out so many and such brilliant prizes to those who enter holy orders, and where there is nothing to prevent the poor curate from rising to be Archbishop of Canterbury; but, *en revanche*, we think we may claim for the Australian clergy a greater breadth of view, superior liberality of sentiment, and a greater disposition to break down the artificial barriers which separate sect from sect, and to co-operate with their reverend brethren in other denominations, than is to be met with in countries where tradition, caste, pride, and prejudice, are such potent forces. In a word, there is a not inconsiderable element of "broad" churchmanship in most of the Protestant churches, and notably in the Episcopalian, Presbyterian, and Independent denominations. Large sums of money are raised for church building purposes, and good sites have been presented, upon which to erect ecclesiastical structures, by the Government. The Roman Catholic Cathedral of St. Patrick, in Melbourne, occupies one of the best of these, and promises, when completed, to be one of the most prominent and imposing monuments of architecture in the city. The most capacious Presbyterian and Independent churches are also finely situated, and are standing evidences of the liberality of their respective congregations; and the Wesleyan Church, in Lonsdale-street, almost assumes the dimensions of a cathedral. The inland towns and cities can also point to their places of worship as among the handsomest buildings in the place; and every little village has usually one or more edifices in which the population assemble on a Sunday, as their forefathers for generations back were accustomed to do, in the time-hallowed churches and chapels of the mother-country.

And while abundant provision has been thus voluntarily made for spiritual instruction and refreshment, the educational institutions of the country open the avenues to intellectual culture to the poorest child in the colony without money and without price. The State expends every year upwards of half a million sterling upon elementary education, employing for that purpose 3906 masters and mistresses, assistants and pupil teachers, in 1664 schools. There are 231,169 children on the rolls of the State schools, and the average attendance is 116,608. Then there are 596 private schools in the colony, attended by 37,582 pupils; six colleges and grammar schools, containing 1099 students, and above these is the Melbourne University, with its staff of able professors, its library, museum, and school of medicine, its faculty of law, its 529 graduates, and its 252 matriculated, and six non-matriculated students attending lectures. Nor must we omit to mention the schools of mines, at Ballarat and Sandhurst respectively, with their seventeen lecturers, and 250 students; and the 51 schools of art and design scattered over the whole of the colony, and numbering upwards of 1600 pupils, to say nothing of the Industrial and Technological Museum in Melbourne, where there are 27 students attending the class lectures on chemistry and mineralogy, 23 those on engineering, and 50 those on telegraphy. Even this enumeration would be incomplete were we to avoid referring to the National Museum, visited on an average by 2000 persons a week, and the National Gallery, with its 226 art students, and the Melbourne Public Library, with its 100,000 volumes of books, and its annual visits amounting to 256,400. This is open daily for unrestricted use to the people, and similar institutions have sprung up in the country districts, to which loans are made from the Melbourne one. Now, remembering that the population of the whole of Victoria is only double that of the town of Liverpool, and that during the first half-century of a colony's existence an immense amount of money and energy has to be expended in rough preliminary work—in making piers and harbours, in constructing roads, railways, and bridges, in laying out and building towns, in clearing forests, and preparing land for cultivation, and, in short, in acquiring hundreds of things indispensable to civilisation—all of which England has inherited from bygone generations; we think the colony may be justly proud of what it has accomplished with respect to the studies which inform the mind, and the arts which beautify our daily lives. And before passing on to speak of her works of charity, it will not be out of place to state that there are 168 mechanics' institutes, or kindred bodies in Victoria, with an annual income of £25,589, and with 322,649 volumes of books in their possession. Only 95 of these institutions keep a record of the number of visits paid, but these give a total of 1,698,880 for the year 1880. The population of the colony is undoubtedly a reading one. In proportion to its numbers we have the authority of experts for saying that more books are bought in Victoria, year by year, than in any part of Her Majesty's dominions. In 1879, for example, 6297 packages were imported, of the value of £193,235, and deducting from these the £76,798 worth exported to the adjoining colonies, we have the sum of £116,437 as the net amount, plus 25 or 30 per cent. received by the vendors as profit, expended upon books by the people of Victoria. To be sure nearly eight times as much was dissipated upon foreign spirits; but we believe the same painful disproportion between the sums spent upon food for the mind and those wasted upon stimulants for the body will be found to exist in most civilised countries.

All the newest books are to be found upon the counters of the leading booksellers, such as Messrs. George Robertson, S. Mullen, M. L. Hutchinson and others; and the newest music may be found at Messrs. Nicholson and Ascherberg and Messrs. Allan and Co., and the latest changes in fashion, the freshest designs in furniture, are to be obtained in the greatest variety at Messrs. W. H. Rocke and Co., as well as glass, china, and so forth. There is nothing in Melbourne but the broader streets, the warmer atmosphere, the brighter sun, and the newness of the public and private buildings, to efface the impression that you are in an English city. Lines of omnibuses converge upon two centres of traffic adjacent to the railway station; carriages, with their liveried coachmen and footmen, are drawn up outside the principal linendrapers, jewellers and music-sellers. Showy posters on the dead walls and hoardings announce such and such operatic and dramatic performances for the evening at the four theatres, with a concert at the Town Hall, perhaps, in which some distinguished vocalist, pianist, or violinist, who has made the tour of Europe and the United States, will exchange his or her foreign notes for Victorian gold. Then, there are three or four concert halls, besides spacious lecture rooms, and other places of public assembly. The associated trades have their hall, the Oddfellows theirs, the Horticulturists theirs, the Freemasons theirs, the Medical Society theirs, the Christian Young Men's Association theirs, the Temperance Society theirs, the Presbyterian Assembly theirs, the St. Patrick's Society theirs, the Congregational Union theirs, and the Royal Society theirs. The architects of Victoria have an Institute, the artists an Academy, and the two branches of the legal profession an Institute. There are associations of anglers, of Australian natives, of canary and pigeon fanciers, of cricketers, of rowers, of bicyclists, of oarsmen, of licensed victuallers, of manufacturers, of old colonists, of pharmaceutists, of riflemen, of old blues, and of the promoters of acclimatisation. There are in Melbourne and its suburbs seven rowing clubs, fifteen cricket clubs, one hunt club, a coursing club, two or three amateur dramatic clubs, two yacht clubs, several football clubs, besides bowling, lacrosse, base ball, tennis, and rifle clubs. The study and practice of music are promoted by a philharmonic society, two Liedertafels, three musical associations, and a musical union. There are debating associations for those who are ambitious to become orators, or to acquire facility and fluency in public speaking, eight temperance societies, and eight organisations of a missionary character; so that almost every form of religious, mental and physical activity is encouraged by specific combinations of men and women.

In few communities are holidays so frequent, or out-of-door recreations so popular all the year round, for each season has its sports, and although these are liable to be somewhat intermittent in the winter months, yet, in a climate where evaporation is so rapid, twelve hours of sunshine will usually suffice to make the bowling-green, the football ground, the wicket, or the bicycle course firm enough for use. Melbourne admittedly possesses one of the finest race courses in the world, and the spectacle which it presents on the "Cup day," which usually takes place on the 9th of November, or thereabouts, and brings together 70,000 people from all parts of Victoria and from the neighbouring colonies, excites the admiration and surprise of tourists fresh even from Epsom, Ascot, and Goodwood. The spectacle from any point of the natural amphitheatre, by which about two-thirds of the course is environed, seen from such a commanding position is a really imposing one. The grand stand, thronged with a variegated mass of human beings; the hill behind, black with its swarming thousands; the lawn, bright with the summer costumes of the ladies as they pace up and down the green sward; the dark fringe of people lining each side of the course for upwards of half a mile, and the strange-looking encampment which covers so large an area of the flat, are the constituents of a scene upon which you look down as upon an enormous formicary. And when a race has been run, and the crowd breaks in upon the track of the horses and follows them up, and the whole of the immense concourse of people on the hill, in the saddling paddock, on the lawn, and on the level, becomes suddenly disintegrated, and falls into what looks like anarchical disorder, the sight is a very curious one to witness, and enables you to comprehend what must be the confusion and disorder of a great army which has undergone a total rout and *débâcle* in the supreme moment of defeat, when the cry of *Sauve qui peut* runs shuddering through its demoralised ranks. The roar, too, of fifty thousand voices, when an outsider is landed winner of the Cup, as it is borne in upon you at your "coign of vantage," is as weird and uncanny a sound as you can well imagine.

On Saturdays, business is suspended in the middle of the day, and in the summer months the river Yarra is populous with boats, the cricket grounds are alive with competitors, and bowlers, football players and bicyclists enter into their respective sports with the utmost zest.

Melbourne and its suburbs are abundantly supplied with "lungs." There are no less than nine parks or public gardens in and around the city. Of these, the most beautiful are the Botanical Gardens, which are prettily situated, and, under the skilful direction of Mr. Guilfoyle, have been rendered a charming place of resort, both for the botanist and the lover of landscape gardening. These are a mile distant from the city; but the

Fitzroy Gardens are only separated from the best thoroughfare in Melbourne by the equally bowery Treasury Gardens, adjoining which are most of the public offices. A stroll through the former when the deciduous trees are in full leaf, is, as the present writer has elsewhere observed, like taking a refreshing bath. The elm avenues have just put forth a wealth of foliage, and underneath are rich masses of shadow, into which the eye plunges with a delightful sense of coolness and refreshment on a day of cloudless sunshine; and the sward hard by is green as an English meadow in a genial spring. In the opposite direction the footpath embowered by the sycamores resembles a splendid mosaic, with golden pencils of radiance dropping through the lightly-woven leaves and branches, and tesselating the ground with interspaces of gloom and lustre that flicker and waver as a light breeze gently stirs the rustling canopy. Sometimes, as a female figure flits across the path from one of the walks that bisect it, you catch a glimpse of blue, orange, or crimson, that lends a new element of picturesqueness to the scene, and you cannot help wondering why some of the students in the public gallery do not desist from perpetually copying the works of landscape artists, and do as Claude, and Constable, and Gainsborough, and Turner did—come out into the open air, and endeavour to reproduce some of the charming pictures of which the Fitzroy Gardens would be found to offer an inexhaustible variety. For, besides the innumerable objects which present themselves for study, it is to be remarked that their aspects are constantly changing as the sun shifts his position in the heavens, or as a passing cloud throws a tender veil over some portion of the scene, or as a fitful wind lifts the leaves of the lightly-stirred poplar, and causes them to glitter with an almost metallic sheen as they shiver in response. Here is another avenue of elms, slower in growth than the other, and of inferior altitude, but no ray of light penetrates the closely-matted leaves, and you recognise the accuracy of Milton's observation of nature when he wrote the lines—

"Under the shady roof
Of branching elms, star-proof;"

for they construct by means of their over-arching boughs an impervious cluster, through which no planet could send a luminous message to the lover or the dreamer seated beneath this pillared aisle.

The Fern Tree Gully, which has been formed of a natural watercourse, traversing the gardens from north to south, is a perfect thicket of trees and shrubs, flowers and creepers—a sort of congress of the vegetation of many countries and of many epochs, for the arborescent ferns, the araucariæ, and the tree-like varieties of the liliaceæ, belonging to the carboniferous period, flourish side by side with plants of the geological age in which we live. The place is the chosen haunt of the songbirds which have established themselves in this locality, and they build there and rear their young in perfect security. If you want to hear the music of the wind you can turn into the pine-tree avenue, where the sombre giants wear quite a funereal aspect, by comparison with the vivid foliage and the brightly-coloured flowers in close proximity to them. If there is any motion in the air, a dirge-like moan, rising at times to a shrill cry, and occasionally subsiding into a low sob, goes shuddering through the multitudinous spikes and spires of these grim organs. In the neighbourhood of the great fountain and of the music pavilion, the parterres are tapestried with flowers as fresh of hue as they are diversified in form and character, and at times the air is heavily laden with the scent of the heliotrope and the mignonette, while the plash of the water, as it descends in glittering drops from the *jet d'eau* above the stone giant, falls pleasantly upon the ear, especially on a hot day. Altogether, Melbourne has every reason to be proud of and grateful for such a charming *rus in urbe* as the Fitzroy Gardens, and in laying them out and planting them, Mr. Clement Hodgkinson established his indefeasible title to be held in affectionate remembrance by after generations as one of our public benefactors.

The benevolent institutions of the colony are both numerous and liberally supported. It contains thirty-three hospitals, the income of which from Government aid, private contributions and other sources, is £100,000, per annum in round numbers. There are six benevolent asylums, with an aggregate expenditure of £40,000 per annum, and seven orphanages, which cost £20,000 for their maintenance. In addition, there are five lunatic asylums, containing (we regret to say) 2816 inmates ; and the yearly outlay upon these institutions exceeds £100,000. A private retreat for the insane affords accommodation to an average number of 47 patients. To the foregoing must be added nine industrial and reformatory schools, with 870 inmates ; a deaf and dumb institution ; an eye and ear hospital ; an asylum and school for the blind ; five female refuges ; four medical dispensaries ; a free hospital for sick children ; a sailors' home ; a retreat for inebriates ; a home and institute for governesses ; and thirty-seven benevolent societies, which afford temporary relief to about ten thousand persons in the course of the year, at an outlay of £13,000. There is, moreover, a society for the assistance of persons of education in distressed circumstances, which is doing much excellent work with very limited means.

We have thus endeavoured to show that in its religious, moral, social and industrial aspects, Victoria is a reproduction of the mother-country, a copy of its institutions, and a transcript of much that is best and most distinctively English in the organisation of society. And the same remark will apply with equal force to all the other Australian colonies. Each bears the strong impress of the race which founded it. Each exhibits the unmistakable characteristics of its parent. Each maintains the habits, usages and traditions of the old stock. Each, as a naturalist would say, is true to species. And if there has been a disposition on the part of one or two to run into political excesses, and to dishonour the sacred cause of political freedom, it is attributable to the fact that power has sometimes fallen into the hands of undisciplined men, unaccustomed to its exercise, intoxicated by its possession, and without an adequate, or without any, sense of the responsibility which accompanies it; that the political adventurer has occupied the position which belongs of right to trained statesmen in older countries; and that in Australia, as in the United States, the demagogue who appeals to the passions, flatters the vanity, fosters the prejudices, and foments the class jealousies and antipathies of the multitude, is in a much more favourable position to gratify his ambition, and fill his purse at the public expense, than the patriotic citizen who addresses himself to the reason, judgment and experience of the educated and thoughtful minority. These, however, are transitory evils, and incidental to a period of national uncertainty, just as the eruption of measles or the small-pox is incidental to the early life of the individual. To the people of England, it would appear almost incredible that the first Minister of the Crown, in any British dependency, should publicly declare to a crowded meeting that a civil war was indispensable to the execution of his policy, and should hold up to the ridicule of an excited throng the heads of all the principal denominations; that another should announce it to be the intention of the Government to "burst up" all the large estates in the colony; that a third should advocate the abolition of the offices held by the heads of the public departments; and that a fourth should boast that he and his colleagues had their hands upon the throat of the capitalist, and this, too, in a country where nine-tenths of the population are capitalists; but the political ascendancy of men of this stamp marks a transitional stage of society, when the basis of power resides in the democracy of the capital and a few large towns, and when a policy of centralisation of bureaucracy, and of a lavish expenditure of money upon public works, combine to enable a "people's Ministry" to become autocratic for the time being. Not many years will elapse, however, before an entirely different state of things will prevail in Victoria, which has been the chief offender in this respect. The rapid settlement of the soil by tens of thousands of freeholders is steadily creating a powerful body of permanent colonists who are Conservatives in the best sense of the word; and who will be sufficiently strong in numbers to offer a successful resistance to the policy, hitherto in force, of making the country tributary to the towns. The centre of political gravity will shift from the latter to the former. Most of the costly public edifices which have been erected at so large an outlay of money in Melbourne, chiefly to provide employment for the operative classes, who are so influential at the polls, are either complete or approaching completion; and "decentralisation" is pretty sure to be the watchword of our Victorian "franklins," who want roads, railways, bridges, schoolhouses and other local improvements. Hence, while a feeling of candour compels us to acknowledge the existence of a dangerous amount of demagogism in that colony; we are bound, on the other hand, to point out that it is one of those diseases of political childhood which, although painful and debilitating for the time being, passes away sooner or later, and, if the patient possesses a robust constitution, leaves no *sequelæ*. And Victoria is undoubtedly endowed with vigorous stamina. Less stalwart communities would have sustained lasting and irreparable injuries by the political events of 1877-8-9; but although the effects were undoubtedly severe, there is an amount of elasticity and resiliency in the sufferer, which has enabled her to advance towards recovery with gratifying speed. She has escaped the "broken heads" and "flaming houses" by which she was menaced by the head of the then Government; and a majority at the next general election pronounced in favour of law and order, peaceful reform and constitutional progress. And although the "reds" have since returned to power, their claws have been pared, and their sinister influence diminished. Then, again, the resources of any one of the Australian colonies are so vast and so rich, that it is almost out of the power of any amount of misrule to do more than temporarily retard their development. For while the demagogue is making incendiary speeches on the platform, or proposing additional taxes of an oppressive character in Parliament, for the purpose of providing himself and his party with the means of corruption, or of a prodigal expenditure in order to propitiate political support out of doors; boon nature is actively engaged in preparing wealth for the whole community, in total disregard of human ignorance, perversity and folly. Upon millions of acres of pasturage cattle are transforming the succulent grasses into beef and hides; and innumerable sheep are accumulating mutton and wool by the same subtle alchemy. Upon hundreds of thousands of acres of arable land, crops of wheat, barley, oats, potatoes and turnips are gathering from the soil, the sunshine, and the atmosphere, the materials of man's future sustenance in measureless abundance; and the sea, with its boundless harvest of fish, the forests, the quarries, the vineyards, the gold and copper mines, and the gardens and orchards, yield up their several contributions to the sum of public wealth with unstinted liberality. So that, just as desolating wars, followed by the exaction of enormous indemnities, have altogether failed to destroy the prosperity of a country like France, so neither has the temporary reign of demagogism in Victoria done more than partially arrest the progress of a country, to which may be fairly applied the lines in which Lord Byron apostrophised Portugal :—

>Oh, Christ ! it is a goodly sight to see
>What Heaven hath done for this delicious land !
>What fruits of fragrance blush on every tree !
>What goodly prospects o'er the hills expand !

At the present time, half the population of the colony resides in cities, towns and boroughs, and half in the shires. There are about sixty of the former, and about 110 of the latter, each having its local governing body, elected by the ratepayers. The aggregate value of the rateable property in the colony falls little short of £80,000,000, yielding a revenue of £1,000,000 in round numbers. Outside of Melbourne, there are four cities—Ballarat, one of the handsomest in the colony, Collingwood, Prahran and Sandhurst; and there are fifteen towns, each containing upwards of 4000 inhabitants.

Out of a population of 900,000, 103,520 persons are employed on farms and stations, 708 in flour mills, 897 in breweries, 817 in woollen mills, 1531 in tanneries and fellmongeries, 922 in brickyards and potteries, 480 in stone quarries, and 28,403 in other manufactories and works. The average rates of wages on farms in 1879 were as indicated below. It must be remembered that they are also accompanied by liberal rations, which generally include meat three times a day :—

Ploughmen	20s. 10d. per week.
Farm labourers	17s. 6d. do.
Married couples	25s. 10d. do.
Females	10s. 3d. do.
Mowers	28s. 6d. do.
Reapers	29s. 4d. do.
Threshers	6d. per bushel.

On stations, that is to say land held exclusively for grazing purposes, the wages paid last year were as follows, also including rations :—

	£	s.	d.	
Stockmen	47	5	0	per annum.
Boundary riders	40	9	0	do.
Shepherds	34	1	0	do.
Hutkeepers	28	3	0	do.
Married couples	61	2	0	do.
Females	27	16	0	do.
Station labourers		17	8	per week.
Sheep washers		21	2	do.
Shearers		14	1	per 100 sheep shorn.

The average price of machine labour on the different farms throughout the country in 1879 was 4s. 10d. per acre for reaping, 4s. 8d. per acre for mowing, and 24s. 4d. per 100 bushels for threshing. The average price of agricultural produce was 4s. 2d. per bushel for wheat, and the same price for maize, 4s. 1d. for barley, and 3s. 6d. for oats; 75s per ton for hay, 92s. 4d. for potatoes, and 25s. 6d. for mangel wurzel. The average weight of crops being from 60 lb. per bushel for wheat, 40 for oats, 50 for barley, and 56 for maize.

There were in the colony, on the 31st of March, 1880, the following quantities of live stock :—

Horses	216,710
Milch cows	278,360
Other cattle	850,998
Sheep	8,651,775
Pigs	144,733

The quantity slaughtered for food in each year may be set down at 2,000,000 sheep and lambs, 200,000 cattle and calves, and 100,000 pigs. These figures indicate the large consumption of meat by a population of 900,000, just as the following will serve to show the cheapness of articles of food in general :—

Bread, per 4lb. loaf	4d. to 6d.
Beef, per lb., retail	1½d. ,, 6d.
Mutton, do. do.	1d. ,, 4d.
Veal, do. do.	4d. ,, 5d.
Pork, do. do.	7d. ,, 8d.
Butter, do. do.	6d. ,, 10d.
Cheese, do. do.	7d. ,, 10d.
Milk, per quart, retail	4d. ,, 6d.
Eggs, per dozen, do.	7d. ,, 10d.
Potatoes, per ton	60s. ,, 80s.
Tea, per lb.	2s. ,, 3s.
Coffee, do.	1s. 6d. ,, 2s.
Sugar, do.	2½d. ,, 7d.
Rice, do.	4d. ,, 5d.
Soap, do.	5d. ,, 6d.
Candles, do.	6d. ,, 1s.
Coals, per ton	30s. ,, 35s.
Firewood, do.	10s. ,, 12s.

Domestic servants command high wages; general servants receive from £30 to £35, housemaids from £25 to £30, nursemaids from £20 to £25, laundresses £30, and cooks from £35 to £60 per annum. Hotel waiters obtain from 25s. to 35s. per week, grocers' assistants from 15s. to 30s., and assistants in general stores from 20s. to 40s. per week. Nursery governesses find engagements at from £30 to £40, and finishing governesses from £60 to £80 per annum; but in Victoria, as elsewhere, there is a plethora of educated persons seeking employment. What the country chiefly wants is workers.

The following are the latest quotations in other branches of industry :—

Building Trades.—Stonemasons, 10s. per day; plasterers, bricklayers, slaters, 10s. per do.; carpenters, 10s. per do.; labourers, 7s. per do.; pick-and-shovel men, 6s. 6d. per do. The day's work is eight hours.

Bootmakers.—The following are the nominal rates : —For making children's peg boots the rate is 6d. per pair; boys', 10d.; women's, 1s.; and men's, 1s. 3d.; the same rates are paid for finishing. In some of the best order shops the rates paid are :— Wellingtons, 10s.; elastics, 7s. 6d.; closing. 8s. Higher rates are paid in first and second class "bespoke shops."

Bakers.—First-class workmen (foremen) average £3 per week; second hands, £2 to £2 2s. In inferior shops the rates are slightly lower.

Butchers.—Shopmen receive from 35s. to 40s. per week; boys, 15s. to 20s. per week; slaughtermen receive from 40s. to 50s. per week; small-goods men (pork buchers) receive 30s. to 40s. per week, all with rations.

Brassfinishers and Coppersmiths.—In the engine-fitting shops there is a fair supply of workmen; the wages are from 9s. to 12s. per day. The same rates are paid in the fine brass-finishing shops.

Cabinetmakers.—The earnings of the men employed in this trade are very variable. In some of the best shops in Melbourne the wages paid are as high as £3 10s. per week, while in inferior establishments the men receive from £2 10s. to £3 per week. In the country the wages paid are still less.

Clothing Factories.—Where the work is done on the premises, the wages earned are as follows :—Tailoresses, £1 to £1 15s. per week ; pressers, £2 to £2 15s., and upwards. From 12s. to £1 is earned at shirt-making in factory hours, but the greater portion is taken home. Clothing machinists earn from 15s. to 30s. per week in factory hours.

Coopers. — Most of the work in this trade is done by the piece; the wages fixed by the trade are 10s. per day of 10 hours. Tallow casks are made at 5s. to 5s. 6d. for thirds, and 4s. 6d. for fourths.

Coachbuilders.—Smiths receive from £2 10s. to £3 5s. per week. Bodymakers—Most of this work is done by the piece ; the average earnings of good hands are from £2 10s. to as high as £3 per week. Wheelers—Most of this work is done by the piece; the wages made are from £2 10s. to £3 per week. Painters receive from 8s. to 10s. per day. Trimmers get from £2 10s. to £3 10s. per week. Vycemen earn from £1 5s. to £1 10s. per week. The rate of labour in this trade is 10 hours per day.

Drapers.—In all the best establishments well-qualified drapers' assistants earn from £2 10s. to £4 per week. Carpet salesmen obtain about the same rates. Upholsterers, £2 10s. to £3 and £4 per week. Mantlemakers, 15s. to 20s. per week. Milliners, from 35s. to £3 10s. per week. Needlewomen and dressmakers from 15s. to 20s. per week.

Farriers.—First-class firemen get £2 15s. per week ; door-men receive from £1 10s. to £2 per week. Farriers for the country receive from 20s. to 30s. per week, with their board and lodging.

Grooms in livery stables get from 30s. to 40s. per week ; coachmen receive from 35s. to 50s. per do.

Gardeners.—The men in this trade are not well paid. In situations near town the rates are from 30s. to 40s. per week without rations. The rates with rations are 15s. to 20s. Very good men get 25s. per week.

Hatters.—Bodymakers get 18s. to 20s. per dozen for regulars, and 12s. to 14s. per dozen for low crowns. Finishers get 22s. to 24s. per dozen for silk hats ; 20s. per dozen for pullover ; and 12s. to 14s. per dozen for low crown.

Iron Trades.—Fitters receive from 9s. to 12s. per day ; turners from 10s. per do.; boilermakers and platers, from 11s. to 13s. per do.; riveters from 9s. to 11s. per do.; blacksmiths, from 10s. to 13s. per do.; hammermen from 7s. to 8s. per do.; and moulders from 10s. to 12s.

Jewellers.—In the manufacturing jewellers' establishments the workmen receive from £2 15s. to £3 15s. For the finer work the wages range higher. Good tradesmen can get full employment.

Miners.—The average rates for miners are £2 per week for surface miners, and £2 5s. for underground work. In some outlying districts higher rates are obtained, but only by a few men.

Navvies.—The rate paid the men employed on the Government railways is 6s. 6d. per day.

Painters and Glaziers.—Fair tradesmen receive 9s. per day.

Plumbers and gasfitters receive £3 per week of eight hours per day.

Printers, &c.—The rate paid in this trade is 1s. per 1000. In manufacturing stationers' establishments lithographers are paid £2 10s. to £3 15s. per week ; binders, £2 to £3 per week ; paper rulers, £3 to £3 10s. per week. The demand for labour in these trades is limited, and is at present fully supplied ; good head men get higher rates in the binding and lithographing departments.

Stevedores' Men, &c.—Lumpers' wages are 12s. per day at present. Engineers in tug-boats and donkey-engine drivers receive £18 per month.

Ship Carpenters.—The rate paid in this trade is 13s. per day of eight hours. Work is irregular.

Sailors on board ocean-going ships and steamers receive £4 10s. per month. In coasting vessels the rate is £5 per month. Men receive £6 per month in coasting steamers. Trimmers get £7, and firemen £9, in coasting steamers.

Saddlers.—The earnings are about £2 15s. per week. The commoner sorts of work are not paid for so well, and wages vary from 25s. to 35s. per week. The work in this trade is nine hours per day.

Tanners and Curriers.—Beamsmen receive 40s. to 50s. per week; shedsmen, 42s. to 45s. per do.; tanners, 38s. to 45s. per do.—Time, 10 hours per day. Curriers, at piecework, can earn from 50s. to 70s. per week.

Tailors.—In all order shops the rate paid is 10d. per hour. In second-class shops the earnings are from £2 10s. to £3 per week. In factories the rates vary, the men being often paid by the piece. Where wages are paid, the rate is 40s. per week in factory hours.

Tinsmiths earn from £2 to £3 per week; ironworkers, £2 10s. to £3 per do.; galvanisers, £3 per do. Most of the work in this trade is done by the piece.

Watchmakers earn from £3 10s. to £5 per week. The demand for labour in this trade is fully supplied.

With these facts and figures before them, all of which have been derived from official sources, our readers in England will be enabled to form a pretty accurate estimate of the advantages which Victoria holds out to the capitalist and the industrious man, who may be dissatisfied with their position and prospects in the mother-country, and who may contemplate bettering their circumstances by emigration. That emigration is not synonymous with exile, we think, will be apparent to everyone who will diligently examine the social condition of any one of these colonies. And that there must be a much better career open to a man's children in a young country, richly endowed by nature, than in an old one, where the growth of population outruns the means of subsistence, and half the supplies of food have to be drawn from abroad, must be patent to every reflective mind. Money is not to be picked up in the streets in any part of Australia, and the same conditions of success—industry, sobriety, application, and self-denial—have to be observed here as elsewhere; but what we confidently assert is this, that by the exercise of these qualities any man may safely calculate upon achieving a competence, if not upon making a fortune, in either of these dependencies of the British Crown. And he may also calculate, with ordinary temperance and prudence, upon enjoying better health, experiencing more cheerfulness of mind, and having more frequent opportunities for rest and recreation in Australia, than would be possible for him in the mother-country. The owner of a few thousands who does not wish to invest it in real property or in business, can lend it on the very best security at seven or eight per cent., and if house rent, wages, and wearing apparel are dearer here than in England, he will find the account more than balanced by the superior cheapness of all the necessaries, and many of the comforts of life.

Chapter II.

NEW SOUTH WALES.

DISCOVERY, SETTLEMENT, EXTENT, AND PHYSICAL FEATURES OF THE COLONY—ITS NATURAL RESOURCES—ITS POLITICAL AND SOCIAL ADVANTAGES—ASPECT OF SYDNEY, ITS BEAUTIFUL SITUATION, AND LOVELY SURROUNDINGS—PORT JACKSON—THE BLUE MOUNTAINS—PROVINCIAL NEW SOUTH WALES—PROVIDENCE AND IMPROVIDENCE—AUSTRALIA THE PARADISE OF DOMESTIC SERVANTS—A COUNTRY TOWN AND ITS FEATURES—THE FUTURE ARISTOCRACY—POLITICAL TRANSFORMATIONS WHICH THE COLONY MAY UNDERGO—ITS GOVERNMENT—ITS RAILWAYS—ITS WONDERFUL PROGRESS DURING THE LAST DECADE—ITS PROSPERITY UNDER THE FOSTERING INFLUENCES OF FREE TRADE—ITS EXTERNAL COMMERCE FAR GREATER IN PROPORTION TO ITS POPULATION THAN THAT OF GREAT BRITAIN, CANADA, OR THE UNITED STATES—WAGES, HOURS OF LABOUR, AND COST OF PROVISIONS IN THE METROPOLIS OF NEW SOUTH WALES, AND IN SEVEN OF THE PRINCIPAL TOWNS OF THE INTERIOR.

THE colony of New South Wales, the parent of the group of settlements founded on this island-continent, dates its existence from 1788, just eighteen years after its having been taken possession of, on behalf of Great Britain, by Captain Cook, as the discoverer of the great *Terra Australis*. Upon the 26th of January in that year, Captain Phillip landed on the shores of Port Jackson and disembarked a thousand souls—the humble beginnings of what will one day prove to be a mighty nation. In 1862, there died at Launceston, in Tasmania, at the age of 102, an out-pensioner of Chelsea Hospital, named John Dill, who came out as a private soldier in the 102nd regiment of foot with that expedition, and whose memory of the incidents connected with it was sound to the last. His animated description of them, as given, reminded one, in substance, although not in form, of Livy's narrative of some of the circumstances associated with the foundation of Rome. It constitutes a dark chapter in the history of colonisation, and it may be passed over accordingly. The land was an earthly paradise, and the Imperial Government committed the deplorable mistake of transforming it, for a time at least, into a social pandemonium. But with the increase of voluntary immigration, and the abolition of transportation, the evils thus inflicted upon this fair and fertile region were gradually effaced, and just as there arose upon the seven hills of the Latin city a magnificent community, renowned alike in arts and arms, in statesmanship and jurisprudence, in social polity and civic grandeur, which exhibited no trace of its base beginnings, so, also, in New South Wales there is growing up a race of Anglo-Australians who are pursuing, with distinguished success, the industries that enrich, and the arts that adorn and beautify humanity. From Sydney, the superbly-situated capital of New South Wales, geographical explorers have struck out in all directions, and the discoveries of men like Hume, Sturt, Mitchell, Strzelecki, Leichhardt and Kennedy were the forerunners of pastoral settlement, which was succeeded in due time by the formation of fresh centres of population; and these, after the lapse of a few years, assumed such dimensions as to justify their erection into separate political communities. It was thus that the colonies of Tasmania, Victoria and Queensland were detached from the mother settlement, and started in life on their own account, while South Australia and Western Australia, on the other hand, were planted by Great Britain.

Originally, nearly one-third of the continent of Australia, or New Holland, as it was then called, was included within the limits of New South Wales; but its present territory may be roughly described as having an extreme length of 900 miles, with an average breadth of 500; its total area being 323,427 square miles. In other words, it is larger than England and Wales, Scotland and Ireland, Belgium and the Netherlands, and Switzerland put together. It is nearly three times as great as Italy, and half as large again as the empire of Germany. With a population no denser than that of France, it could carry 48 millions of people; while, if there were as many to the square mile as there are in Belgium, New South Wales would support 142 millions. But as it is, the estimated number of its inhabitants is 750,000 all told.

With a coast-line of about 800 miles, indented by eighteen bays and inlets, one of which has no superior in the world, the colony contains three regions—that of the coast, the soil of which is alluvial, and runs back about thirty miles from the sea; that of the plateau, which traverses the country from north to south, and rises to a considerable elevation, besides being embossed by a grand chain of mountains; and the vast plains of the interior, which are thinly timbered and heavily grassed, and afford pasturage to countless herds of sheep and cattle. Writing of the general configuration and economic capabilities of these divisions of the country, Mr. Reid remarks, in his excellent *Essay on New South Wales*, that fourteen rivers discharge their water-shed into the sea, while the more important of the streams—the Murray, which is 1120 miles long, the Murrumbidgee, which is 1350, and the Darling, which is 1160—take their rise on the western side of the Great Dividing Range. Speaking of the soil, he says:—"That of the flats of the coast district is alluvial, of remarkable richness near the watercourses, and upon which there is a variety of heavy timber and scrub. The soil of the immense western and interior slopes available for agriculture is composed chiefly of red and chocolate loam, well grassed but thinly timbered, generally with a species of the eucalyptus known as box. The saltbush country succeeds, stretching to our western and north-western boundaries. It consists of red, loamy plains, of the same character as the slopes, but without timber; except in those parts which are liable to floods in winter. The soil of the plains is loose, and in very dry weather the grass nearly disappears; but as the country becomes stocked the tread of the animals binds the surface; the grass acquires closeness and strength, and the saltbush gives way to the characteristics of the slopes. As a consequence, the rain that falls begins to form watercourses, waterholes become creeks, and the streams increase in volume."

The climate is, upon the whole, a very fine one, bright, exhilarating and salubrious. Along the coast line of country, the sea breeze tempers the heat of summer; and on the table-lands, where the altitude ranges from 2000 to 3000 feet above the sea level, the temperature is agreeable during the hottest months of the year, and decidedly bracing and invigorating in the winter. The town of Goulburn, for example, is 2071, that of Bathurst 2153, and that of Orange 2843 feet above the sea; and hence they enjoy, in a latitude corresponding with that of Syria and Persia, a climate as pleasant as that of the Riviera. In the coast line of country, the vine, the olive, and the sugar-cane are cultivated with success—the latter yielded 18,278,736 lbs. in 1879—as well as wheat, barley, oats, maize and the ordinary root and fodder crops. Oranges, pine-apples, bananas, loquats, lemons, peaches, nectarines and apricots thrive luxuriantly; while the plateaux yield all the hardier fruits with which we were familiar in the orchards and gardens of the mother-country. On an average, something like 800,000 gallons of wine are annually made; and as the vineyards were originally planted with the choicest varieties selected from the most famous wine-growing districts in Europe, the produce is of the choicest quality, and will one day astonish the world by the exquisite delicacy of its flavour, its purity, and its fragrant bouquet.

The pastoral wealth of the country is enormous. It contains more sheep than the whole of England (23,962,373), nearly three million head of horned cattle, upwards of 330,000 horses, and nearly 220,000 pigs. It raised in 1879 4,000,000 bushels of maize, 3,400,000 bushels of wheat, and barley and oats in proportion. And under the fostering influences of free-trade, the development of its manufacturing industries has been both sound and rapid. These include iron and engineering works, woollen and boot factories, ship and boat building, breweries, meat and fruit preserving establishments; chemical, glass, and smelting works; distilleries, sugar refiners, potteries; carriage and waggon, ice, soap and candle, salt, confectionery, kerosene oil, cordials, rope and cordage, basket, brush and comb, mast and block, maizena, starch, glue, metallic paint, furniture, and many minor factories. Exposed to free competition with the commodities imported from Great Britain, America, and the neighbouring colonies, the energetic and self-reliant manufacturers of New South Wales have gone on extending their operations, and increasing their products year by year, and the gratifying result has been strikingly set forth by Mr. Reid, in a comparison which he has instituted between the trade of the colony in the first five years of the last decade and the corresponding half of the present one; the net import for each period being arrived at by deducting the exports. Here are the figures:—

THE GROWTH OF THE HOME INDUSTRY OF NEW SOUTH WALES.

Articles.	Net import, 1860–4. Mean pop., 369,168.	Net import, 1870–4. Mean pop., 541,157.	According to population. net import, 1870–4, should have been	Probable growth of Home Industry.
	£	£	£	£
Agricultural implements	50,262	47,357	73,382	26,025
Apparel and slops, haberdashery, linen and drapery, millinery, hats, caps, and bonnets	6,532,140	5,914,390	9,536,924	3,622,534
Beer	1,030,549	1,029,902	1,504,602	474,700
Cordage and rope	130,437	51,545	190,438	138,893
Furniture	163,692	165,297	238,990	73,693
Flour, grain, and bread	1,794,748	1,397,935	2,620,332	1,222,397
Fruit (dried and bottled)	212,772	196,722	310,647	113,925
Hay	40,625	769	59,313	58,544
Leather, boots, and shoes	1,325,276	235,943	1,934,903	1,698,960
Oilmen's stores	421,601	141,151	615,538	474,387
Provisions	91,791	*	134,015	134,015 *482,587
Saddlery and harness	209,159	163,000	305,372	142,372
Rum	270,915	163,749	395,536	231,787
Sugar	1,782,940	2,443,296	2,603,092	159,796
Treacle and molasses	4,183	*	6,107	6,107 *127,708
Timber	240,503	*	351,135	351,135 *72,501
Tobacco (manufactured)	298,128	95,736	435,267	339,531
Vinegar	33,918	28,828	49,520	20,692
Wine	545,461	311,393	796,373	484,980
	15,179,100	12,387,013	22,161,486	10,457,269
Less actual excess of exports.				
Provisions	...	482,587*	...	...
Molasses and treacle	...	127,708*	...	...
Timber	...	72,501*	...	...
	15,179,100	11,704,217	22,161,486	10,457,269

"This shows," he observes, "that although our population increased by nearly half, say 46 per cent., our import of the 19 lines specified decreased in actual amount by £2,792,087, and according to population by no less a sum than £10,457,269. This is an evidence of progress in its best sense, for being brought about by the free play of private enterprise, it means advantage to all."

The mineral resources of New South Wales, in so far as they are known, which is but very imperfectly, are exceedingly rich and diversified. They include gold, silver, copper, lead, iron, tin, coal, antimony, cinnabar, lime-stone, and fire-clay; to say nothing of diamonds, emeralds, rubies, amethysts, opals, sapphires, and garnets; and as the geological surveyor has officially declared, the mineral wealth of New South Wales " is practically inexhaustible." The area of its coal measures is simply enormous. It has been traced for hundreds of miles along the coast, and has been worked at various levels from 450 feet below, to 1500 feet above the sea. The lower beds are geologically older than any that have been yet worked in Europe, and the quality of the coal which is taken from these inferior strata is therefore unsurpassed. Not only so, but in certain districts, immense seams of this mineral are found in immediate juxtaposition with an abundance of iron ores, lime-stone, and fire-clay. Hence nature seems to have indicated New South Wales as the great manufacturing colony of the group. Up to the present time, coal has been ascertained to exist over an area of something like 25,000 square miles of country; and it is almost everywhere within easy reach of water or railway communication. Now, when it is remembered that the coalfields of Britain only cover one-twentieth part of the area of the country, or about 4000 miles, and that nevertheless the output of this mineral in the parent State is upwards of 120,000,000 tons per annum, the export alone having been over 15,400,000 tons in 1878, it would be difficult to over-estimate the magnitude of the proportions to which the coal trade of New South Wales may be expected to grow hereafter.

"Without any exaggeration," writes the Chief Inspector of Colleries in that colony, "we can undoubtedly claim to be in possession of the richest, most accessible, and most extensive coalfields in the Southern Hemisphere, which must ultimately make New South Wales the greatest and richest of all the Australian colonies; and we know the value of them and how much as a nation Great Britain has to depend upon her collieries for her great national prosperity. Our bituminous, semi-bituminous, splint, anthracite, and cannel coals are equal in thickness and in quality to any found in other parts of the world, and we have numerous deposits of petroleum oil cannel coal, some of them superior to any yet found elsewhere. During the last few years the growth of our coal trade has most satisfactorily and rapidly increased; and when the proposed extra shipping appliances are completed at Newcastle, and vessels can have rapid dispatch, our trade will undoubtedly increase at a much greater rate than it is even now doing."

The forests of New South Wales cover the whole of her mountain ranges, only a few of which rise above the snow line, as well as many of the rich valleys which slope downward to the coast. The variety of the timber they produce is not less remarkable than its magnitude and beauty.

Unhappily, with the spread of settlement, the work of destruction by axe and fire has proceeded with indiscriminating energy; and furniture and building woods of great value have been swept away with as much unconcern as if they were only so much worthless scrub. For constructive purposes in dock yards, piers, bridges, house carpentry, coachmakers' and wheelwrights' work, railway building, fencing, and piles, nearly the whole of the *Myrtaceæ*, of which New South Wales possesses something like fifty varieties, are extremely valuable, and certain of them incomparably so. For the uses of the cabinetmaker and the house decorator, the timber familiarly known as the black-apple, the Moreton Bay pine, the red cedar, coachwood, Clarence light-yellow wood, turnip-wood, rose-wood, Illawarra mountain-ash, tulip-wood, myall, cypress-pine, and others, is capable of being worked up into furniture and panelling, beautiful in grain, rich in colour, and susceptible of a high polish. The timber of the prickly-leaved ti-tree *(Melaleuca styphelioides)* is said to be incapable of decay; that of the white tea-tree *(Melaleuca leucadendron)* is said to be imperishable under-ground; that of the Turpentine tree *(Syncarpia laurifolia)* resists the attacks of the *teredo navalis* in salt water ; and that of the brush-bastard, or white-box *(Tristania conferta)* has been known to preserve its soundness, when employed in building the ribs of a ship, for a period of thirty years. To the carver and wood engraver the corkwood *(Duboisia myoporoides)*; the rose-wood *(Dysoxylon Frasernum)*, and the pittosporum *(undulatum)* commend themselves as a serviceable substitute for European box ; while the cooper finds in the native ash *(Flindersia Australis)*, the silky oak *(Grevillea robusta)*, the stave-wood *(Tarrietia actinodendron)*, the green and silver wattle *(Acacia decurrens* and *Acacia dealbata)*, and the swamp-oak *(Casuarina quadrivalvis)* excellent material for staves. Other kinds of timber are specially adapted for oars, spokes and naves, tool-handles, telegraph poles and turners' work. And thus it will be seen that the economic value of the indigenous trees of New South Wales can scarcely be over-estimated. To the medical botanist the forests present an almost virgin field of exploration. Of the ascertained properties of the eucalyptus it would be almost superfluous to speak. Partially discovered by Australian chemists, like Mr. Bosisto, of Melbourne, they have been more fully revealed by men of science in France, who have demonstrated the efficacy of its leaves for the healing of wounds, and of preparations from it, as local stimulants, as astringents, as disinfectants, as anti-septics, as a remedy for certain uterine diseases, and as an anti-catarrhal agent. A dwarf shrub commonly known as the wild hop, is stated to be an infallible specific for dysentery; and the tonic qualities of the bitter principle contained in the bark of the sassafras are well known and highly appreciated. Thence it would be quite safe to predict that the *Materia Medica* of the civilized world will be enriched, in years to come, by discoveries made in the Australian flora to an extent undreamed of at the present time.

Let us now briefly review the industrial resources of New South Wales, considered as a field of enterprise for the capitalist, and for the skilled or manual labourer. The extent of country comprised within its limits, we have shown to be enormous. Its pastoral wealth is on a scale of commensurate magnitude; its agriculture embraces the cultivation both of the cereals of the temperate regions and the plants which flourish under a sub-tropical climate; its horticulture is equally comprehensive; its manufactures repose upon the solid basis of an unlimited supply of coal, iron, and limestone, all lying in close juxtaposition, as also of the finest wool in the world; its commerce promises to cover the whole of the South Pacific, and has already found profitable relations with the adjoining colonies, with the island of Tasmania, with Fiji, with New Zealand, and with New Caledonia, and the position of its capital and of its unrivalled harbour seems to mark it as one of the chief entrepots of the Southern Seas.

All these advantages are enjoyed under the beneficent protection of political institutions which guarantee the utmost freedom to every citizen, which admit the poorest man in the community to a share of power, and which do not debar him from entering the Legislature, or from aspiring to and achieving the highest position in the State. There is no Established Church; there are no poor laws; and, if everybody was sober and provident there would be no poverty, and very little disease; there is no privileged class or caste; and there is that freedom of transfer and bequest, in relation to land, which the agrarian reformers of the mother-country set down as the ideally perfect system of dealing with the soil. Education, free of cost to the very poor, is within the reach of all; and the higher schools of the colony are the succursals of a University which has been built and endowed at a cost of £200,000, and receives £5000 a year from the State; while its funds have just been augmented by the munificent bequest of £100,000 from the late M. Challis, who was formerly a resident in Sydney, where he laid the foundations of the fortune which enabled him to devise this princely gift to so noble an object. The graduates of the University are entitled to the same rank, title, and precedence, as graduates of British Universities; and there are three colleges affiliated to it. The professors are men of the highest attainments and distinction, and the standard of instruction is an elevated one. Thus it will be seen that the educational advantages enjoyable in New South Wales are such as will bear favourable comparison with those which are accessible to rich and poor in England; while social life presents much the same attractions in Sydney, as it does in most cities of a corresponding size in Great Britain. A colonial capital resembles, in fact, a block of civic England, detached from the parent mass, and planted on a virgin soil, beneath a brighter sky, and in a far more genial atmosphere. The public and private amusements are the same. The opera house, the theatre, the concert room, the flower-show, the garden-party, and the ball-room, are as popular in the new as in the old country.

There is nothing to differentiate George-street, Sydney, from one of the principal thoroughfares of York, or Liverpool, or Exeter, but the brighter aspect of the buildings and the warm and lustrous quality of the air. The highway is full of omnibuses, coaches, private carriages, cabs, drays, and waggons. The pavement is alive with foot passengers; and the shop windows display the latest fashions in jewellery and dress, the newest books and engravings, the freshest designs in furniture and ironmongery, and the most recent novelty in quack medicines or cosmetics. Perhaps the one point of dissimilarity between an Australian and an English, or indeed any European city, is the absence of that extreme poverty and squalor which cast such a dark and ominous shadow upon the chief centres of population in the old world. Not that poverty and squalor are unknown in the new; but penury and wretchedness do not obtrude themselves upon your notice, and it is tolerably certain that, in ninety-nine cases out of a hundred, they are the result of misconduct and not of misfortune. Drink and improvidence lie at the root of the evil; and these contribute to fill the gaols and to provide inmates for the lunatic asylums.

As to the out-of-door life in the neighbourhood of a city like Sydney, it is altogether unique, because the surroundings of the place are also unique. It would be difficult to exaggerate their loveliness. A recent visitor from Victoria, who combines a quick perception of the beauties of nature with the skill of a master of word-painting, has permitted us to incorporate with the present chapter, the following description of his first impressions of the capital of New South Wales, on approaching it from the sea:—

"Port Jackson is one of a few choice spots upon the earth's surface, which amply fulfil your expectations, and justify the praises of preceding visitors. It is, as Sannazaro said of Naples, '*Un pezzo di cielo, caduto in terra.*' Other places, of which the beauty has been incessantly lauded to you, frequently disappoint you, when you come to see them for the first time. Perhaps you look at them, under the influence of different emotions to those experienced by your informant. Perhaps you see them at a different season of the year, or under a different aspect, or arrive at them by a different approach. Or perhaps they have been over-praised, and, in resentment of the mild fraud that has been practised upon you, you are tempted to depreciate what has failed to charm you to the degree you had anticipated. But you are under no such temptation with respect to Sydney Harbour and its environments. The first sight of it is like the first sight of Venice from the lagunes, the first sight of the Bernese Alps between Baden and Basle, the first sight of Florence and the Val d'Arno from the gallery of the monastery at Fiesole, or the first sight of Mount Cook at sunrise, when steaming down the west coast of New Zealand. You hang it up, as it were, in the picture gallery of your memory, as one of your permanent treasures, there to be recurred to, as often as ' in the silent sessions of sweet thought,' you desire to refresh your mind with pleasant remembrances of the past. And its beauty grows upon you; for you find that it has that quality which Anthony attributed to Cleopatra's beauty—'Age cannot wither it, nor custom stale its infinite variety.' Nature, indeed, possesses the precious gift of eternal youth, and nowhere has she exhibited her 'infinite variety' with a more lavish prodigality than in this favoured spot of earth, with the climate of Sicily, and with more than the beauty of the Bay of Naples, or the shores of Amalfi and Sorrento.

"Of the city itself, the impression produced upon a visitor, fresh from the rectangular formality of a younger capital in a neighbouring colony, is that it is uncolonial, and free from the dreadful newness and the garish rawness which characterise most Australian centres of population. It reminds you, in fact, of an English city, or rather of many such. It is like a bit of Bristol and Clifton, of Bath, Exeter, and Southampton, with here and there a reminiscence of Genoa and Spezzia, welded together in one harmonious whole under the most picturesque conditions; and interspersed with spaces of luxurious greenery, to say nothing of leafy avenues, into which the eye can plunge for the sweet solace of umbrageous shadow, with the certainty of finding it, while there are, in the gardens and shrubberies, a loveliness of colour, a diversity of plant structure, and a redundance of leaf and flower which convince you of what the botanical taste and skill of three generations of colonists have accomplished in seconding the bounty of the 'boon mother.' Let me add that, to a lover of old English cities, and of curved lines in nature and art, there is something agreeable in the irregular outlines of Sydney, and in the wayward directions taken by some of its thoroughfares, although this liking may not be so liberally accorded to the unevenness of its foot pavements, which are anything but 'primrose paths of dalliance.'

"As compared with those of Melbourne, a city fifty years its junior, the principal streets of Sydney are narrow, because it was originally laid out by English surveyors, without any forecast, in all probability, that, in less than a century, a quarter of a million of inhabitants would be congregated on the shores of Sydney Harbour. And we are not at all sure that, for the comfort of the inhabitants, and leaving out of sight such thoughts as convenience of traffic and architectural effects, narrow thoroughfares are unsuitable to a warm and brilliant climate. In high latitudes you want as much as possible of the sun at all periods of the year, but in Australia, where it may be said of that luminary, that it is 'unchangingly bright'—

> Shining on, shining on, by no shadow made tender,
> Till love falls asleep in its sameness of splendour—

you need shadow, and are glad to escape from the dazzling glare of an almost vertical sun, and refresh your eyes with the half light, lying at the bottom of a narrow street flanked by lofty warehouses, offices, or shops."

The public buildings of Sydney are not unworthy of its matchless position. They are mostly constructed of a bright and easily-worked sandstone, which is often quarried on the spot, and they comprise two cathedrals, with numerous churches, and a Jewish synagogue; the vice-regal residence, the town hall, and general post-office; the university, hospital, and museum; the banks, and the various public offices. To these must be added the International Exhibition building, with a dome resembling that of the cathedral at Florence, occupying a commanding position in the Domain overlooking the harbour, and constituting one of the chief ornaments of the city. But after all, the environs of Sydney are its supreme distinction, and its never failing charm. And these have been so vividly described by the writer we have previously laid under contribution; that we cannot do better than transfer to these pages his graphic picture of the scene:—

"The visitor who explores a small portion of the waters of Port Jackson for the first time is bewildered by the complexity and variety of their shore outline, and fascinated by the never-ending beauty of the apparently innumerable coves and inlets into which it breaks. It is a succession of surprises, and the comparatively small area into which this astonishing diversity of surface is crowded, is, perhaps, the greatest wonder of the whole. The late Sir William Don once told me that he had seen nearly all the most famous harbours and bays in the world, including Naples, Genoa, Constantinople, San Francisco, and Rio Janeiro, and that each of them must yield the palm to Sydney. 'It stands alone,' he said, 'peerless and unapproachable.' Dunedin is picturesquely situated, and one must not undervalue the noble position of Hobart Town, with the waters of the Derwent lying at its feet, with the majestic form of Mount Wellington rising behind it, and dwarfing all the neighbouring eminences by its gigantic bulk and lofty altitude. But the unique charm and supreme distinction of Port Jackson is the gracious amenity and perpetual variety of its surroundings. There is a picture in the French gallery of the Fine Arts collection, entitled '*Hymne au Createur*': a young girl, in the infancy of the world, is so impressed with the exquisite loveliness of fruit and flower, of bird and blossom, is so full of a delicious sense of the preciousness of existence, in the midst of so much sunshine and fragrance, abounding life and delicious colour, that, feeling the utter impotence of speech to express the adoring emotion of her full heart, she spreads forth her hands towards heaven, with a thank-offering of flowers in them, to the beneficent Creator of all things. A feeling akin to hers takes possession of the mind, in some of the more sequestered recesses which are accessible from so many points in the neighbourhood of Sydney. For there are some spots upon which the unsullied freshness and delicate bloom of virgin nature still rest, and where you are conscious of influences such as Virgil felt, and Wordsworth described; while they enable you to fully comprehend the strength and simple piety of the sentiment which actuated the primitive nations in erecting altars to the personified agents of the Divine bounty. Looking down, for example, upon two arms of the Middle Harbour from a rocky platform at a considerable elevation above the Spit, the scene which meets the eye is one that is primeval in its wild beauty; and that, in one direction at least, breathes nothing but peace and tranquillity. The undulating contour of the hills, and the graceful curve of the shores; the sea of foliage, brightened in places by the spring leaves which have lingered upon the young wood; the silent motion and soft shadows of the clouds, that flit across the landscape; the picturesque greys and browns of the weather-stained boulders which crop out of the herbage, richly tapestried, as this is, with wild flowers; the calm surface of the water, which ranges in colour from a pale green to a Tyrian purple; and the changing aspect of cove and promontory, as the sun varies his position, or shines out with summer splendour, or veils his lustrous face in vapour, combine to make you feel that there is a nearness and a dearness in nature—a power to soothe, to elevate, to purify, and to delight, to which we are, as a general rule, strangely and calamitously indifferent in this age of great cities.

"And scenes of this kind are so immediately accessible in Sydney. Half-an-hour's ride by land or water conducts you to sylvan haunts as secluded from observation as those in which the melancholy Jacques moralized upon the wounded deer; or in which Titania fell in love with Bottom the weaver, or in which Una rode forth upon her lion, 'in maiden meditation, fancy free.' Some of these, with their tangled underwood, their fern brakes, their charming waterfalls, and their natural bowers, remind one of certain portions of the New Forest and of Fontainebleau. In all, there are endless themes for the Australian artists of the future. And what motives for poems and pictures in the sinuous coves of the harbour, and in the massive headlands and romantic bays along the ocean beach! At Manly, at South Head, and at Coogee, in the course of an hour or two's saunter along the shore, you are presented with a whole gallery of sea-pieces, exhibiting such charming accidents of light and shade, such fluctuations of colour, such grandeur of form and romantic beauty of outline, such incessant changes in the aspects of shifting cloud and restless wave, of creamy ripple and foaming breaker, of shimmering surface or dark expanse, that you are tempted to break the Tenth Commandment, and to covet the possession of artistic gifts like those displayed by Herr Weber in his splendid picture of the iron-bound coast of Canada; by Mr. Mogford in his 'Eastern Broad;' by Mr. Brierly in his grand 'Whaleboats Saving a Wrecked Crew;' and by Herr Eschke, in the lovely 'Sunrise at Whatcombe,' which adorn the walls of the art gallery of the Exhibition.

"In the Middle Harbour, in Lane Cove, and in Mossman's Bay, you are surrounded by sylvan scenery, of which the predominating characteristic is the gracious amenity spoken of above, and upon which peace broods like a heavenly benediction. There are tracts of forests, spreading from the water's edge to the undulating ridges of the hills, which are rendered august by their indefinite antiquity. During thousands of years, they may be conceived of, as having worn their robes of verdure just as they wear them now. During countless centuries, the spring has quickened the sap in those stately trees; the summer has flushed their plumed crests with its luminous glory; the autumn has mellowed their foliage; and the winter has brought its interval of repose to their vital activity. They are the witnesses and monuments of a past that has no history in their secluded quietude, save that of the silent processes, the divine order, and the perpetual beneficence of nature. And hence the impression produced upon the mind, in contemplating this glorious scenery, is of a twofold character. It fascinates you by its beauty of form and colour, and at the same time it awakens a series of emotions of a meditative character, inspired by the consciousness that you are brought face to face with the silent inheritors of an immense antiquity; that you, the spectator, are but a fugitive shadow—

> 'A poor player,
> That struts and frets his little hour upon the stage,
> And then is seen no more;

whereas those giants of the forest have been pursuing their calm growth in these virgin solitudes during whole ages of time, while on the other side of the globe, countless generations of human beings have come and gone, empires have risen and fallen, dynasties have been established and swept away, war, famine and pestilence have devastated some of the fairest regions of the globe, and the sites of once vast and populous cities have relapsed into the desert, where the lizard basks among the ruins of sumptuous palaces, and the hyæna prowls among the graves of forgotten kings and heroes, or drags from their tombs the crumbling bones of beauties, as renowned in their day as was that famous Helen of Troy, whose alluring face, as an old poet says—

> 'Launched a thousand ships
> And burnt the topless towers of Ilium.'

"To live within half-an-hour's ride of landscapes and seascapes so various and beautiful as these, so endless in diversity and so full of contrasts in their loveliness, seems to me to be an advantage of which it would be difficult to over-estimate the magnitude or the value. To look upon them for the first time is an event in the life of the person who is so fortunate as to do so; and to remember them hereafter will certainly be a pleasure, comparable with that which the owner of a large picture gallery, filled with the works of the best *paysagistes*, derives from the contemplation of his art-treasures."

Sydney enjoys the advantage of being only forty miles distant from the commencement of a chain or labyrinth of mountains not less remarkable for their specific grandeur and beauty than is the harbour. A railway climbs up their shaggy summits, and then winds around their majestic shoulders, for a distance of sixty or seventy miles, presenting the tourist with a rapid succession of landscapes of the most romantic character; the enjoyment of which is heightened by the fact that you are overlooking pathless forests and virgin solitudes.

Mr. Henry James, in his recent monograph on Hawthorne, when speaking of nature in the western world, remarks:—"The very air looks new and young, the light of the sun seems fresh and innocent, as if it knew as yet but few of the secrets of the world and none of the weariness of shining. The vegetation has the appearance of not having reached its majority. A large juvenility is stamped upon the face of things, and in the vividness of the present, the past which died so young, and had time to produce so little, attracts but scanty attention." And this air of primitive freshness characterises the scenery of the Blue Mountains, as they are called. The exquisite vapoury bloom which lies upon them, and from which they have derived their name, appears to be so very delicate that a touch might be expected to efface it, just as in the case of the down that covers the surface of a purple plum or grape. When the railway has reached an elevation of a thousand feet or so above the level of the sea, the air—in the hottest months of summer—grows crisp and fresh, and possesses a transparency and purity which render its respiration delightful; while the foliage of the saplings is singularly bright and green, and new kinds of vegetation meet the eye. You obtain glimpses of depressions in the mountains so heavily timbered as to present "a boundless contiguity of shade." Their outlines heave and sink, like the waves of the sea when a heavy swell is on it, just after the subsidence of a fierce tempest. On cleared plateaux near the line of railway, some of the leading citizens of Sydney have erected sylvan dwellings in which they keep their *villegiatura*, and these little slabs of cultivation tesselating the enormous wilderness of primeval forest, are in striking contrast with their majestic surroundings. In places, the deep, silent, solitary valleys are flanked on either side by walls of rock rising sheer up to the height of many hundred feet, but clothed with timber to the very summit. Only here and there, where two jutting headlands confront each other and seem to have constituted the gateway of some long-forgotten inland sea, masses of laminated stone crop out, weather-stained and often rich in colour, owing to the oxydisation they have undergone by exposure to the atmosphere. Through these stupendous cliffs, the eye is carried on into a magnificent amphitheatre of verdure, covered with that exquisite veil of blue gauze, which is the never-failing charm of this noble range of mountains. At Blackheath, you look across just such a foreground to a pastoral valley of great extent, with an imposing background of undulating ranges, rising tier on tier, until their faint outlines almost blend with the delicate azure of the distant horizon. But everywhere, the prospects combine grandeur with loveliness, and remind you now of the Pyrenees and now of the Appenines.

Provincial New South Wales differs from provincial England only as provincial America does, namely, in its newness and brightness, and in the absence of that extreme poverty in the lower strata of society, which seems to be inseparable from a thickly peopled and highly civilized community, in which, it is to be feared, habits of improvidence and intemperance have been highly fostered by the poor law system on the one hand, and by a superabundance of hospitals, almshouses, "doles," and other demoralising forms of relief, on the other. Not that either of the Australian colonies is free from the reproach of thriftlessness and of inebriety; although the latter is not so much an indigenous as an imported vice, for the rising generation in all parts of Australia, is more temperate than that which emigrated from the mother-country. The chief danger to both the mental and physical stamina of the Anglo-Australian race lies in its immoderate addiction to tobacco, which insidiously poisons the sources of life in the heart and brain, gives the face a pale and bloodless look, and impairs the energy of the nervous system. The consumption of the weed in the whole of the Australian colonies is enormous, and the waste of health and money it entails is one of the most serious social and economic phenomena of the day. The expenditure of the population of New South Wales upon tobacco, is not less than one pound per head per annum, or three-quarters of a million sterling. This would give an average of something like five pounds per head for each smoker. At least it would do so, if smoking were only indulged in by male adults. This, however, is very far from being the case. Children begin to smoke at from ten to twelve, and you will see little urchins standing at street corners, puffing away at a short pipe or a cheap cigar, with pallid countenances and meagre forms, and busily laying the foundations of dyspepsia, and a host of resultant ailments in later life, by ejecting the saliva which is so essential to the efficient performance of the processes of deglutition and digestion.

Of the improvidence which prevails, it may be remarked, that while it is to be regretted under any circumstances and in any country, its effects are not felt in a young and thinly-peopled country, as they are in an old and densely-populated one. Nature is the chief, and human labour only a very subordinate, factor in the production of wealth, and the rewards of industry being so large, the consequent abundance prevents the absence of frugality from being attended by its customary penalties. The weekly "rations" of an Australian farm labourer would suffice to maintain the entire family of a French peasant proprietor for a month. We have known cases in which harvestmen have regarded it as a serious grievance that they have had to sit down to a *cold* forequarter of lamb or saddle of mutton for breakfast, instead of having hot rump-steaks provided for them at that meal. And it may be remarked in passing that the most fastidious of complainants in this respect are usually immigrants who have come out to Australia from districts of Great Britain, in which the farm hand considered himself extremely fortunate, if he could procure a dinner of rusty bacon on weekdays, and some "butcher's meat" on Sundays. Female domestics are likewise improvident and extravagant, although many of them, and this is more particularly the case with the Irish, will regularly remit a portion of their earnings for the support of their aged parents in the mother-country, or in order to enable their brothers and sisters to join them in Australia. A girl who has been accustomed to receive an annual wage of £5 in Ireland, or of £10 in England, and who earns, or rather is paid, £30 or £36 per annum in the colonies, will think nothing of giving a couple of guineas for a bonnet or hat of the latest fashion, and will array herself on her "Sunday out" in a velvet mantle, for which she has given seven or eight pounds, and which is liable to be ruined by a sudden dust-storm, followed by an equally sudden downfall of rain.

Australia is, indeed, the paradise of Bridget and Sarah Jane. Not only are wages very high, but household labours are pursued under conditions much more favourable than those which prevail in a cold and and gloomy climate, like that of England. Numbers of the Australian houses are of one story only, and few exceed two. Excepting in the towns, where there is a good deal of dust, and very little smoke, the air is pure and clear, and there is relatively little domestic cleansing to be performed. For eight or nine months in the year there are no fires required, except for domestic purposes, and in the principal cities the gas stove is beginning to supersede the kitchen-range. There is no creeping down stairs in the cold and darkness of a winter morning with blue fingers and shivering limbs to light a fire, thaw the frozen water-pipes, and holy-stone a flight of front doorsteps, while everything is icy to the touch, and gloomy to the vision. And there are very few of the restraints, wholesome or otherwise, which are imposed upon the freedom of the female domestic in most well-ordered households in Great Britain. In Australia, the mistress's authority is exercised on sufferance, as it were, and she is obliged to temper it with extreme discretion, lest her cook or housemaid should abruptly leave her. But, in any case, the practice prevails pretty extensively at Christmas time, when Bridget and Sarah Jane feel that they would like a fortnight's holiday. There are the pantomimes at the theatres, there are the outdoor sports which are held on Boxing-day, there is a succession of pic-nics and *al fresco* festivities at this midsummer season, and many a mater-familias finds herself compelled to cook her own Christmas dinner, and to do her own "chores," because her cook and parlourmaid gave her a week's notice to leave on the 17th of December. By the end of the first week in January, however, there are plenty of applicants for situations, and the holiday-makers prepare to settle down to work again, until the approach of Easter causes them to become restless once more.

A country town in New South Wales reproduces most of the architectural features of an English country town; wanting only the charm of antiquity. There are no time-worn and weather-stained buildings; because they are all apparelled, like Macbeth with his honours, "in their newest gloss." There are no ancient inns, with balustraded staircases and intricate corridors and passages, such as Washington Irving and Nathaniel Hawthorn loved to describe; no old gabled houses, no mouldering market cross, no ruinous and ivygrown bridges, and nothing to link the present with the past. Australia is the country of the future, with a history to make, and its face set forward to the coming ages. In the place of endearing memories, it cherishes large and glowing hopes. The ancestry of its population has to be sought for in another land, and it looks to posterity to achieve the distinctions by which it may be rendered famous.

A provincial centre of population usually grows up either at some halting place upon a main line of traffic, or in the heart of an agricultural district, or on the edge of a good harbour, or in the midst of a gold-field. A blacksmith's shop, two or three general stores, one or more public-houses, a baker's shop, and a butcher's, form the nucleus of a hamlet which grows into a village, and soon expands into a town. Commodious inns replace the rude shanties in which liquors were formerly sold; substantial brick structures supersede the wooden zinc-roofed stores, and the place undergoes a complete transformation in the course of a very few years. A municipality is formed, a town-hall is built, and a police station erected. Meanwhile, each of the leading religious denominations has raised a place of worship for itself; the State-school has opened its doors to all comers; one or two branch banks have been established; a solicitor has settled down and is gradually feeling his way into a good practice; a couple of doctors have set up a big lamp, with crimson bull's eyes, before their respective doors, and each of them has started a buggy; two newspapers have been struggling into existence, and are advocating diametrically opposite views in politics; there is a circulating library, which has some difficulty in competing with the mechanics' institute over the way; and, in due time, the iron-horse reaches the growing town; and the opening of the railway is celebrated by a public dinner, at which two or three members of the Ministry are present, and as the district returns one of their supporters to the Legislative Assemby, the Chief Secretary proposes the toast of "prosperity to the town of Boonamundra," and prophesies that it will one day become a place second only in importance to the capital, and that with a population so energetic, so intelligent, so enterprising, and so far-seeing, as that represented by the gentlemen he sees around him, there are no limits to the greatness and no bounds to the prosperity which await the spirited inhabitants of Boonamundra in the near future.

Rhetorical exaggerations apart, there is an element of truth in prognostications of this kind. What political economists call the "unearned increment" in the value of real property, increases very rapidly in a new country; so that the pioneers of settlement may calculate, by the exercise of ordinary prudence and sagacity, upon arriving at independent circumstances, if not at affluence, in twenty or thirty years, by the mere operation of natural causes, such as the steady growth of population, improved methods of intercommunication, and the development of the resources of the district. It is, at the same time, unfortunately true, that prosperity is occasionally a great calamity to some of those who have been most successful in life. It leads to the formation of habits of extreme parsimony on the one hand, or of the most destructive dissipation on the other. Many a strenuously industrious man, after having amassed a fortune and retired from active life, has proceeded to "knock it down" in drink, has died in a fit of *delirium tremens*, or ended his days in a lunatic asylum, bequeathing to his widow and offspring a heritage of poverty and shame. Nor is the reason far to seek; for it may be found in the unfortunate man's destitution of mental resources, resulting from his neglected education in the mother-country. So long as he was occupied in the business of life, he was tolerably happy; but when he had earned the means to "rest and be thankful," he had no intellectual pleasures and employments to fall back upon. The vacuity of his mind must be filled, and he flew to the stimulation which spirits are capable of affording it. The habit once acquired, grew upon him with terrible celerity, speedily mastered, and eventually slew him.

But it must be recorded to the credit of what are sometimes contemptuously called "the wealthy lower orders" in the Australian colonies, that they are by no means unconscious of the defects of early training, and of the inconveniences and disadvantages resulting from want of culture, and that, as a general rule, they are liberal in their expenditure upon the education of their children, and it may be anticipated that the inheritors of a position of affluence will, in very many instances at least, impress it with a due sense of the responsibilities which its possession entails; while we may also expect to witness the effect of that refining process alluded to by the author of "The Autocrat of the Breakfast Table," in the following passage:—"Money kept for two or three generations transforms a race. I don't mean merely in manners and hereditary culture, but in blood and love. Money buys air and sunshine, in which children grow up more kindly, of course, than in close back streets; it buys country places to give them happy and healthy summers, good nursing, good doctoring, and the best cuts of beef and mutton . . . As the young females of each successive season come on, the finest specimens among them, other things being equal, are apt to attract those who can afford the expensive luxury of beauty. The physical character of the next generation rises in consequence. It is plain that certain families have in this way acquired an elevated type of face and figure, and that in a small circle of city connections one may sometimes find models of both sexes which one of the rural counties would find it hard to match from all its townships put together."

Thus a steady levelling upwards is going on in New South Wales, as in all the Australian colonies, and we should not be at all surprised, if it eventually modifies the political institutions of each. These are democratic in the first instance, *e necessitate*. Where there is no territorial aristocracy, no State church, no old families, and nothing to connect the present with a grand and imposing past, a theoretical equality is bound to prevail, especially so long as the fluid elements of society are in a state of ferment, and before they have begun to solidify. But when the crystallising process commences, those institutions will undergo a change corresponding with the social mutations. Human nature will assert itself in spite of political theories and systems; and human nature, in all English speaking countries, is fond of titles and decorations, and distinctions. It loves superiority, sometimes in others, always in itself. The "Druid," the Oddfellow, the Good Templar, the Rechabite, the volunteer, and the member of almost any association, likes to prefix an honorary epithet to his name, and to put some initials after it. It gives him pleasure to wear a collar, badge, scarf, medal, or symbol, and to fill a prominent position in his lodge or club. Ridicule is impotent to destroy or weaken predilections of this kind, because they appear to be innate and ineradicable. The colonial legislator covets the appellation of "Honourable" to which he will be entitled on obtaining a seat in the Upper House, or on his becoming a member of the Government, and very few have been found capable of refusing a knighthood, when it is offered them. When it is declined, it is probably owing to the same feeling which induced Diogenes to trample on the carpet—because his pride was greater than that of the monarch to whom it belonged.

Looking, therefore, at what may be called the aristocratic tendencies of human nature, and at the many causes which conspire to render equality impossible—causes such as differences of mental and physical capacity, differences of *morale* and habit, differences of circumstance and opportunity—we might almost venture to predict that in less than a century, the political institutions of the Australian colonies, will be found to have undergone a remarkable transformation; and that they will exemplify the operation of that law in virtue in which societies pass through certain stages of development, which may be accelerated or retarded in their progress, but cannot be affected in their order. As the elder colony, New South Wales may be expected to take the lead in instituting the changes referred to; we need not now stop to speculate upon the precise direction they are likely to adopt.

It remains to say a few words with respect to the finances and the trade and commerce of this colony. Its revenue in 1878 amounted, in round numbers, to £5,000,000 sterling, and this more than covered the expenditure; but of this amount little more than one-fourth was raised by taxation; the principal part of the residue being derived from the sale and rental of Crown lands, and the Government railways and other sources. On the 31st of December, 1878, it had a credit balance of no less than £3,872,783. Its imports are close upon £15,000,000 per annum, and its exports a little over £13,000,000; so that its external commerce shows an annual profit of £2,000,000.

The colony is governed by its own Legislature, consisting of two Chambers; the one a nominee Council, of which the members are appointed for life by the Government for the time being; and they number thirty-seven at the present time. The Second Chamber, or Legislative Assembly, consists of seventy-three members, who are elected by manhood suffrage, under the protection of the ballot. No property qualification is required on the part of candidates for a seat in the Assembly; and most of the members of the Ministry are selected from that body.

The railways of New South Wales are the property of the Government, and are substantially constructed and admirably equipped. The Southern line is in operation from Sydney to Gerogery, a distance of 368 miles and will be opened before the end of the present year to Albury, where it will effect a junction with a line which is already completed from Melbourne to the river Murray. A branch is also being pushed on from Junee to Narrandra and Hay in a westerly direction. The Western line, which crosses the Blue Mountains previously referred to, is open to Wellington, 248 miles distant from Sydney, is being extended to Dubbo, and will eventually reach Bourke, on the river Darling. A suburban line runs to Richmond and Parramatta; while from the important sea-port of Newcastle there is railway communication to Tamworth, a distance of 182 miles, and to Gunnedah, a distance of 196; while extensions are projected to Tenterfield in a northerly, and to Narrabri in a north-easterly direction.

These great undertakings have been executed with money borrowed on the security of the Government of the colony; and it is surely unnecessary to point out to English investors in Australian securities, the superiority of these over those of Continental nations, or of Central or South American Republics. Here such loans are expended upon reproductive works, which open up the country, stimulate the development of its resources, distribute population, encourage agricultural industry, and promote trade and commerce; whereas most of the national debts of other countries have been contracted for the purpose of enabling the people of adjoining nations to butcher each other; to waste, ravage, and destroy; to consume and dissipate the thrifty accumulations of years; and to "make a solitude and call it peace." As a general rule, colonial railways defray pretty nearly the interest on their original cost, besides covering all the working expenses; and where they fail to do this, the indirect advantages they confer upon the community far outweigh any demand they may happen to make upon the revenue. But hereafter, with the growth of population and the rapid expansion of every description of industry, these important undertakings may be expected to yield a handsome profit to the public exchequer, or to enable the Government for the time being to make material reductions in passenger fares and goods freight.

What New South Wales may be expected to become in 1888 may be inferred from its progress during the last decade, which has been truly astonishing. The following figures, however, may be left to speak for themselves:—

	1868.	1878.
Population	466,765	693,743
Schools	1,254	1,744
Scholars	66,835	118,788
Mills and manufactories	3,743	14,057
Acres under crop	434,756	613,642
Horses, sheep, and cattle	17,122,854	27,075,104
Coal raised (value)	£954,231	£1,575,497
Shipping (tonnage)	724,193	1,267,371
Wool (lbs.)	25,721,632	111,833,017
Do. (value)	£1,879,751	£5,723,316
Imports	£8,051,377	£14,768,873
Exports	£7,192,904	£12,965,879
Revenue	£2,476,700	£6,708,047

We submit that, outside of Australia, there is no country in the world, not even the United States, which can show so wonderful a progress in all the elements of material well-being as is disclosed by the above statistics taken from the official records. In a single decade, the population of New South Wales has increased nearly 50 per cent., the number of children receiving instruction has more than doubled, the number of mills and manufactories has been quadrupled, agriculture has greatly expanded, nearly ten millions have been added to the live stock of the colony, there has been an increase of about 66 per cent. in the output of coal, the clip of wool is four times as great as it was ten years ago, the external commerce of the country is nearly double what it was then, and its revenue has risen "by leaps and bounds." Truly, a wonderful record, as well as an impressive testimony to the lavish bounty of Providence, and to the industry and enterprise of the Anglo-Australian race settled in that part of this great island-continent.

New South Wales has been additionally fortunate in having had, at the head of its political affairs, statesmen who were fully impressed with the inestimable advantages which free-trade is capable of conferring upon the nascent industries of a young country. As Mr. G. H. Reid has observed in the Essay previously quoted from:—"Differing on most other points, our Parliaments have always agreed that the best training for manufacturing industry is free competition, and its best support that earned by the sweat of its own brow. We have the sense to perceive that in trade as in politics a free condition is the only healthy one; and that to make industry the creature of legislation is to unnerve and degrade it.

We believe that in this, as in every country inhabited by Englishmen, profitable openings for enterprise cannot long be neglected. We know, too, that our advantages for commerce and manufactures are so great that we need not distress ourselves by forced efforts to anticipate them. Such will be the view of all able to see the true bearings of national policy, much more is it the conviction of those who can see what is really the interest of manufacturing industry itself. . . . Free trade is considered to be now on its trial in New South Wales, and protection in Victoria. Public opinion in the other colonies has not been clearly pronounced. By a strange perversity, the colony which has fixed upon herself the trammels of the restrictive policy, had the better start in commerce, but the less chance in manufactures, because destitute of coal, except as geological specimens, and, compared with New South Wales, poor in all the other essential minerals. Were it not for the Riverina trade, the evils of the policy of Victoria would already be too obvious to be disputed. But the increase in the wool in the pastoral districts of New South Wales on her south-west border conceals the full significance of the change. The public of this colony can have no reason to be pleased by the errors of a neighbour. Victoria is one of our best customers, and her welfare is therefore our interest. Taking a broader view, every colonist ought to look upon colonial topics as an Australian. The communities settled upon this continent, and contending so zealously for their own advancement, are really hastening the unification of the group as much as their own progress. In this light we rejoice at the emulations which animate them, and deplore divergences of policy which tend to dim the prospect of federation."

New South Wales is reaping the rich reward of her loyal attachment to sound principles of political economy, and her manufacturing industries, resting upon more solid bases than the shifting quicksands of protection, have a grand future before them. Sydney promises to become, in these seas, what Tyre and Carthage, Genoa and Venice formerly were in the Mediterranean. The palaces of her merchant princes will adorn the shores of a harbour compared with which, that of Genoa herself "pales its ineffectual fires;" and the commerce of this new Queen of the South will cover half the surface of the globe. Its magnitude at the present moment will be apparent from the following table of figures:—

Countries.		Population at last enumeration.		Trade.	Per head.
Austria and Hungary	(1869)	35,904,435	(1872)	£97,462,246	£2 14 3
France	(1872)	36,102,921	(1873)	320,000,000	8 17 9
Russia in Europe	(1867)	63,658,934	(1872)	113,875,000	1 15 9
Great Britain	(1871)	31,817,108	(1873)	682,292,137	21 8 10
The United States	(1870)	38,558,371	(1874)	230,737,876	5 19 8
Canada	(1871)	3,602,321	(1873)	44,923,240	12 9 2
New South Wales	(1878)	693,743	(1878)	27,734,752	40 18 1¾

In other words, this young colony has an external trade, according to population, upwards of three times that of Canada, nearly five times that of France, nearly eight times that of the United States, more than sixteen times that of Austria and more than twenty-five times that of Russia; and its average is already nearly double that of the mother-country, the greatest of all commercial nations.

What, it may be asked, are the prospects held out to the immigrant to New South Wales? We will not answer this question by the ordinary method of drawing an alluring picture of its attractiveness as a place of residence, and of the advantages it offers to the manual labourer and the artisan: for, although these are very great indeed, they are liable to be over-estimated by the power of imagination; and as they are seldom immediately secured by the new-comer, his disappointment is sometimes as unreasonable as his expectations were exaggerated. We shall therefore submit for the information of our readers in the mother-country, the following tables of wages and prices; and leave them to tell their own story:—

IN THE METROPOLIS.

WAGES.

Occupation.	Wages per day.
Building trades (8 hours of labour).	
Carpenters and joiners	8s. to 10s.
Bricklayers	10s. ,, 11s.
Stonemasons	10s. ,, 11s.
Plasterers	10s. ,, 11s.
Painters	8s. ,, 9s.
Plumbers and gasfitters	9s. ,, 10s.
Shinglers and Slaters (any hours of labour)	4s. ,, 6s. per square of 100 ft.
Excavating labourers (10 hours of labour)	6s. ,, 7s.
Brickmakers' labourers	8s. ,, 10s.
Plasterers' labourers	7s. ,, 9s.
Iron trades (8 hours of labour).	
Fitters and turners	8s. to 10s. 8d.
Boiler-makers	8s. ,, 12s.
Pattern-makers	8s. ,, 10s. 8d.
Blacksmiths	8s. ,, 12s.
Coppersmiths	10s. ,, 12s.
Iron-moulders	8s. ,, 10s.
Iron-trade labourers	5s. ,, 7s.
Brass-founders	10s. ,, 12s. 6d.
Shipwrights	11s. ,, 12s.
Carriage trades (8 to 10 hours of labour).	per week.
Wheel-makers	35s. to 65s.
Body-makers	35s. ,, 65s.
Trimmers	40s. ,, 60s.
Painters	40s. ,, 60s.
Smiths	35s. to 70s.

Occupation.	Wages per week.
Leather trades.	
Bootmakers (9 to 10 hours of labour)	36s. to 70s.
Boot-finishers (10 to 13 hours of labour)	36s. ,, 70s.
Tanners (8½ to 10 hours of labour)	36s. ,, 40s.
Curriers (8½ to 9 hours of labour)	63s.
General.	
Saddlers (piecework)	50s.
Tailors (piecework)	60s. to 100s.
Drapers' assistants (8 hours of labour) *	40s. ,, 100s.
Grocers' assistants	15s. ,, 50s.†
Milliners' ,,	15s. ,, 50s.
Barbers' ,,	20s. ,, 60s.†
Ostlers	40s.‡
Coachmen	40s.
Waiters	15s. ,, 30s.‡
Cooks	16s.§
Laundresses	16s.§
Housemaids	12s.§
General servants	10s. ,, 16s.§
Labourers, ordinary (8 hours of labour)	8s. per day.
Labourers, wharf (8 hours of labour)	8s. ,,

* Half-holiday on Saturday in the large shops. † With board, and sometimes lodging
‡ With board and perquisites. § With board and lodging.

Rents of Cottages for Mechanics.

N.B.—All taxes paid by landlord.

In the City.

	Per week.
House of 3 rooms	7s. to 12s.
,, 4 ,,	10s. ,, 15s.
,, 5 ,,	12s. ,, 17s.
,, 6 ,,	14s. ,, 20s.

One or two miles from the City.

	Per week.
House of 3 rooms	5s. to 7s.
,, 4 ,,	6s. ,, 9s.

One or two miles from the City (cont.)

	Per week.
House of 5 rooms	8s. ,, 12s.
,, 6 ,,	12s. ,, 15s.

Three miles from the City.

	Per week.
House of 3 rooms	4s. to 6s.
,, 4 ,,	5s. ,, 7s.
,, 5 ,,	7s. ,, 10s.
,, 6 ,,	10s. ,, 14s.

Prices.

Beef, per lb.	4d.
Mutton ,,	3½d.
Corned beef, per lb.	3¼d.
Pork, ,,	6d.
Bacon, ,,	1s.
Cheese, ,,	1s.
Flour, ,,	1¾d.
Bread, ,,	1¾d.
Sugar, ,,	3d. to 4d.
Tea, ,,	1s. 6d. to 2s. 6d.
Coffee, ,,	1s. to 1s. 6d.
Butter, ,,	2s.
Milk, per quart	8d.
Rice, per lb.	3d.
Oatmeal, per lb	3d.
Candles, ,,	5d.
Kerosene oil, per quart	8d.
Tobacco, per lb.	3s. to 5s.
Beer (English), per pint	6d.
Beer (Colonial) ,,	3d.
Rum, per pint	2s.
Brandy ,,	2s.
Gin, ,,	2s.
Prints, per yard	4½d.
Calico, ,,	6d.
Mole trousers, per pair	7s. 6d.
Rough jackets, each	15s.
Twilled shirts, ,,	2s. 11d.
Men's boots, per pair	5s. 6d. to 9s.
Women's boots, per pair, from	6s.
Children's boots, per pair	4s. to 4s. 6d.

Mining Industry in the Interior.

Occupation.	Wages per day.
Gold mines (8 hours of labour)	7s. 6d. to 8s. 4d.
Coal mines (5 hours of labour)*	9s. 5d.
Copper mines (8 hours of labour)	8s. 4d. to 10s. 10d.
Tin mines (8 hours of labour)	7s. to 8s. 4d.
Iron mines (9 hours of labour)	7s. to 14s.

* Average all the year round. The miners receive 5s. a ton for hewing. When the mine is in full work the average earnings are 15s. a day. It is right to state that the coal miners complain just now of slackness of employment.

TOWNS IN THE INTERIOR.—WAGES.

Occupation.	Hours of Labour.	Young, 215 miles S. from Sydney.	Albury, 351 miles S. from Sydney.	Maitland, 95 miles W. from Sydney.	Goulburn, 134 miles S. from Sydney.	Bathurst, 144 miles W. from Sydney.	Mudgee, 168 miles N.W. from Sydney.	Armidale, 313 miles N. from Sydney.
		s. d. s. d.	s. d. s. d.	s. d. s. d.	s. d. s. d.	s. d. s. d.	s. d. s. d.	s. d. s. d.
Carpenters (wages per day)	8	12 0 b —	10 0 —	9 0 to 10 0	12 0 d —	11 0 —	9 0 to 12 0	10 0 d —
Bricklayers do.	8	12 0 —	12 0 —	11 0 ,, 13 0	10 0 —	11 0 —	10 0 ,, 12 0	12 0 d —
Masons do.	8	12 0 —	12 0 to 14 0	10 0 ,, 12 0	12 0 —	11 0 —	12 0 ,, 14 0	12 0 d —
Blacksmiths do.	8	10 0 —	10 0 ,, 11 8	8 0 ,, 12 0 b	8 4 to 11 8	11 0 d —	10 0 ,, 12 0	10 0 d —
Saddlers do. (piece work)	—	10 0 —	6 9 ,, 11 8	6 8 ,, 10 0 b	5 0 ,, 8 4	9 0 —	7 9 ,, 13 4	10 0 d —
Shoemakers do. do.	—	9 0 d —	8 4 ,, 19 0	7 6 ,, 10 0 b	6 8 ,, 13 4	7 0 to 13 0	6 0 ,, 8 4	11 8 to 16 8
Tailors do. do.	—	10 0 d —	7 6 —	11 0 ,, 12 0	6 8 ,, 13 4	10 0 —	6 0 ,, 9 0	11 8 —
Labourers do.	10	8 0 —	6 0 to 8 0	6 0 ,, 7 0 f	6 0 ,, 8 0 d	8 0 —	7 0 ,, 9 0	6 0 —
Milliners' assistants (wages ⅌ wk.)	10	60 0 c —	40 0 ,, 60 0	20 0 ,, 40 0 c	20 0 ,, 50 1 g	42 0 —	29 0 ,, 32 0 c	20 0 —
Drapers' do. do.	10	60 0 c —	60 0 ,, 80 0	30 0 ,, 60 0	30 0 ,, 90 0 g	42 0 to 72 0	40 0 ,, 60 0 c	40 0 —
Grocers' do. do.	10	48 0 —	50 0 ,, 70 0	20 0 ,, 60 0	20 0 ,, 70 0 g	42 0 ,, 60 0	40 0 ,, 60 0 c	40 0 —
Draymen do.	8	48 0 b —	25 0 c —	42 0 —	35 0 h —	36 0 —	25 0 ,, 30 0	20 0 —
Waiters (per week, with board) a	—	14 0 —	15 0 to 20 0	40 0 —	15 0 —	20 0 —	14 0 ,, 18 0	15 0 —
Ostlers do. a	—	36 0 —	20 0 ,, 30 0	15 0 —	15 0 —	15 0 —	15 0 ,, 20 0	20 0 —
Shepherds (per week, with rations and lodging)	—	10 0 —	25 0 —		10 0 to 20 0	12 0 —	16 0 —	20 0 —
Domestic servants (per week, with board and lodging)	—	10 0 —	8 0 to 15 0	7 0 to 12 0	8 0 ,, 12 0	10 0 to 15 0	10 0 to 15 0	15 0 —
Agricultural labourers (per week, with board and lodging) e	—	20 0 to 25 0	20 0 ,, 25 0	16 0 ,, 25 0	12 0 —	18 0 ,, 20 0	14 0 ,, 16 0	18 0 —

a Exclusive of perquisites.　*b* 9 hours.　*c* With board.　*d* 10 hours.　*e* At harvest time rates are very much higher.　*f* 8 hours.　*g* 11 hours.　*h* 12 hours.

TOWNS IN THE INTERIOR.—RENTS AND PRICES.

		Goulburn.	Bathurst.	Mudgee.	Armidale.	Young.	Albury.	Maitland.
		Rents per week.						
Cottage of four rooms		10s.	9s. to 10s.	8s. to 12s.	8s.	10s. to 15s.	9s. to 15s.	5s. to 7s.
		Prices.						
Beef	℔ lb.	4d. to 5d.	4d.	4d.	4½d.	4d.	4d. to 5d.	4½d. to 5d.
Mutton	,,	,,	,,	,,	,,	3d.	3½d. to 5d.	4d.
Corned Beef	,,	4d.	3½d.	3d.	4d.	3½d.	4d.	3½d.
Pork	,,	6d.	5d.	6d.	5d.	6d.	6d.	6d.
Bacon	,,	10d.	7d.	6½d. to 8d.	9d.	8d.	1s.	1s.
Cheese	,,	11d.	8d. to 1s.	7d. to 9d.	,,	8d. to 1s.	1s. 3d.	9d.
Flour	,,	1½d.	2d.	2d.	2d.	2½d.	2½d.	1½d.
Bread	,,	2d.	,,	,,	,,	2½d.	2d.	1½d. to 1¾d.
Potatoes*	,,	1d.	¾d.	1d.	¾d.	1½d.	....	½d.
Sugar	,,	4d.	3½d. to 5½d.	3½d. to 6d.	5d.	4d. to 4½d.	4d. to 6d.	4d.
Tea	,,	2s. to 2s. 6d.	1s. 6d. to 2s. 6d.	1s. 6d. to 2s. 6d.	2s.	2s. to 2s. 6d.	2s. to 3s.	1s. 9d. to 2s.
Coffee	,,	1s. 6d.	1s. 4d. to 1s. 6d.	1s. 5d. to 1s. 8d.	1s. 6d.	1s. 6d.	1s. 3d. to 2s. 6d.	1s. 4d.
Butter*	,,	1s. 8d.	2s.	2s. 3d.	......	2s. 6d.	1s. 9d.	1s. 6d.
Milk*	℔ quart	6d.	6d.	4d.	6d.	6d.	6d.	6d.
Rice	℔ lb.	4d.	3½d.	,,	5d.	4d.	4d.	3d.
Oatmeal	,,	5d.	6d.	4½d.	,,	6d.	4d.	4d.
Eggs*	℔ doz.	2s.	2s.	1s. to 2s.	1s. 6d.	1s.	1s. 9d. to 2s.	1s. 4d.
Candles	℔ lb.	6d.	6d.	6d.	7d.	6d.	1s.	6d.
Kerosene oil	℔ gal.	2s. 6d.	4s.	3s.	4s. 6d.	3s. 6d.	3s. 6d.	2s. 8d.
Tobacco	℔ lb.	3s. to 5s.	2s. to 4s. 6d.	2s. 6d. to 6s.	,,	4s. to 5s.	4s. 6d. to 5s.	from 1s. 4d.
Prints	℔ yard	4½d. to 9d.	5d. to 8½d.	5d. to 9d.	7d.	7d.	4d. to 1s.	6d. to 8d.
Calico	,,	3½d. to 7d.	2½d. to 1s.	3½d. to 9d.	6d.	4d.	4d. to 2s. 6d.	4d. to 8d.
Mole trousers	℔ pair	6s. 6d.	5s. 6d. to 8s. 6d.	5s. 6d. to 9s. 6d.	7s. 6d.	8s.	9s. 6d.	5s. 6d. to 7s. 6d.
Rough jackets	each	10s.	10s. 6d. to 21s.	12s. 6d. to 20s.	20s.	from 15s.	15s. to 20s.	from 14s.
Twilled shirts	,,	2s.	2s. to 3s.	2s. 6d. to 4s.	3s. 6d.	from 3s.	2s. 6d. to 4s. 6d.	2s. 9d. to 4s.
Men's boots	℔ pair	9s.	7s. 6d. to 15s.	6s. 6d. to 10s. 6d.	9s.	8s.	from 7s. 6d.	7s. 6d. to 8s. 6d.
Women's do.	,,	5s. to 10s.	5s. 6d. to 12s. 6d.	6s. 6d. to 8s. 6d.	,,	7s.	from 5s. 6d.	5s. 6d. to 7s. 6d.
Children's do.	,,	2s. 6d. to 5s.	2s. 6d. to 7s.	1s. 6d. to 5s.	5s.	4s.	from 3s. 6d.	4s. to 6s.

* Very scarce at present; ordinary prices from 50 to 100 per cent. less. The ordinary price of butter is from 10d. to 1s. per lb.

CHAPTER III.

QUEENSLAND.

AREA OF THE COLONY—ITS GEOGRAPHICAL DIVISIONS AND TOPOGRAPHICAL FEATURES—ITS VEGETATION AND METEOROLOGY—ITS GRAZING CAPABILITIES—MISTAKES OF THE EARLY PASTORAL SETTLERS—INACCURATE STATISTICS—STOCK AND PRICES—AT WHAT RATES MEAT CAN BE RAISED FOR EXPORTATION—AREA OF LAND HELD UNDER PASTORAL LEASES—NATURE OF THE COUNTRY—MINERAL WEALTH OF QUEENSLAND—ITS PRINCIPAL GOLDFIELDS, AND THEIR PRODUCT—TIN, COPPER, AND OTHER METALS—COAL MEASURES OF THE COLONY—AGRICULTURE, AND ITS RELATIVELY SLOW PROGRESS—LIBERAL LAND LAWS—SUGAR-PLANTING, ITS EXTENT AND PRODUCTIVENESS—VINE-GROWING—OTHER CROPS—SMALL AREA UNDER WHEAT—CULTIVATION OF COTTON, ARROWROOT, TOBACCO, AND TROPICAL FRUITS—TIMBER AND MISCELLANEOUS PRODUCTS—CONDITION OF THE PEOPLE—STATISTICS.

QUEENSLAND is the youngest daughter of New South Wales, and the dower she has received from nature is a most opulent one. Separated from the mother colony in 1859, and endowed with the privileges and responsibilities of self-government, this portion of the Australian continent has advanced in material prosperity "by leaps and bounds" during the one-and-twenty years which have elapsed since then. Its area is 669,520 square miles, with an extreme length of 1550 miles, an average breadth of 800, and a coast-line of 2550 miles. Although the larger half of the territory lies within the tropics, the climate of Queensland is tempered and modified by two important and providential causes. A great part of the interior consists of elevated downs, or plateaux, stretching inland from the Dividing Range, while the coast-line of country is exposed to the influences of the sea breezes. As this question of climate is an important one in relation to immigration from the temperate regions of Europe, which it is one of the objects of this work to promote, by an honest and truthful picture of the present position and future prospects of each of the Australian colonies, we shall best discharge our duty to our readers by stating, upon the testimony of residents of the most trustworthy character, that it is not only healthy, but is such as to permit of out-of-door labour being pursued by Europeans throughout the greater part of its extensive territory.

In describing that territory, it is absolutely necessary to make divisions corresponding roughly to the wide differences in character of country, soil, and climate found in different parts of it, and the most convenient separation will be into the interior, the tropical, and the sub-tropical coast districts. The core, or interior of the colony, contains, at a rough estimate, about 300,000 square miles, and includes the districts of North and South Gregory, Mitchell, Warrego, and part of the Maranoa. The remaining 369,000 square miles fall into the other two divisions. Of these, the sub-tropical part includes the smaller moiety, consisting of part of the district of Maranoa, the Darling Downs, East and West Moreton, Burnett, Wide Bay, Leichhardt, Port Curtis, and part of South Kennedy. In the tropical division are included the remainder of South and the whole of the North Kennedy district, having a seaboard on the east coast of the continent. There is in it also the huge district of Cook, including the Cape York Peninsula, and with a seaboard on the east coast as well as on the Gulf, and the still larger district of Burke, entirely on the coast of Carpentaria.

In the core, or interior of the colony, the climate is dry, the temperature high in summer, but cool in the winter months, when sharp frosts occur, the thermometer often ranging several degrees below freezing point during the night and early morning. The surface of the country is generally open, very little of what is called forest—*i.e.*, country covered with trees not growing close enough to be designated scrub—being found in it. At the heads of the main watercourses, the surface of the ground rises into long rolling downs; in other places, it sinks into vast flat plains, both downs and plains being nearly, if not quite, treeless. What timber is found there, is generally confined to the main watercourses or the ranges. The scrubs, which are extensive in some places, consist mainly of stunted, gnarled trees of brigalow and gidya, yielding small logs of a very hard heavy timber, the latter especially being of a dark colour, showing a pretty golden grain. These scrubs are "open," having no entangling vines and lianas, which are only found in the coast districts, and the salt and other bushes growing thickly among the trees, are greedily devoured by stock. The downs and plains are thinly covered with grasses growing for the most part in tufts, capable of retaining vitality through very prolonged droughts, and affording most excellent pasturage for stock, even when apparently dry and withered. In a good—*i.e.*, a moist—season, this permanent pasturage is supplemented by an endless variety of nutritious herbs, of which the seeds lurk in the ground, and which spring into existence with almost miraculous rapidity after rain. What is known strictly as "herbage" country is generally very thinly grassed, and occurs among the plains bordering the lower courses of the rivers, but herbs grow freely among the green tufts on the highest downs and all over the interior of Queensland. Saline herbs and plants abound everywhere. The rivers and creeks are in all cases fed only by surface drainage, and there are consequently no constantly running streams. The main defect of the interior is the absence of a reliable water supply. Even in a moderately dry season tracts measuring hundreds of square miles are left entirely destitute of water. These are barren, sandy, and worthless stretches of country, but as a rule the downs and plains are covered to the depth of several feet with brown or black earth, rich in vegetable matter. Whenever a wet season occurs, or wherever, as in gardens, the ground is regularly watered, its great fertility is made evident by the abundance of its produce.

In the sub-tropical part of Queensland the rainfall is more evenly distributed throughout the year, and the moisture of the atmosphere increases as the coast is approached. In that portion of it which is nearest the interior, open plains are still numerous, but "forest" is the rule, almost without exception, in the districts near the sea. In a similarly gradual manner the scrubs change their character till they become closely grown jungles, filled with a great variety of tall trees, and thickly interlaced with vines and parasitical creepers. Water is more abundant. Running streams are often met with inland, and the rivers on the eastern slope of the main range, as well as most of the creeks that feed them, are constantly running. The soil varies greatly, but the greater part is good. The scrub soil everywhere is excellent, and so is the chocolate and black soil of the Darling Downs, Burnett, Leichhardt, and Port Curtis districts. Great metalliferous tracts occur, and many large coal basins. Timber is abundant, both cedar and the various descriptions of pine, and the ordinary colonial hardwoods. Throughout this region the temperature is more equable than in the interior, the sun heat is lower in summer, and greater in the winter, but frosts are everywhere experienced. Near the coast, however, and in the northern part of this division, the winter frosts are very slight, so that sugar cane and other tropical plants grow freely. As a rule the winter months are dry, clear, and bracing, but on the whole the coast climate is rather oppressive, the damper heat of summer being more enervating than the dry sunshine of the interior.

In tropical Queensland the winter frosts disappear altogether, although there is a well-marked cool season. On the east coast, the strong trade winds temper the heat of the sun wherever they penetrate, while inland, much of the country is at some considerable elevation above the level of the sea, so that on the whole the average temperature is not so high as might be expected from the latitude. The climate is distinctly healthy though hot. In its general characteristics the country very much resembles sub-tropical Queensland, with this exception, that the average rainfall being much greater, there are many more running streams. In fact, it may fairly be said that this part of Queensland is abundantly watered. The scrubs partake more decidedly of the character of jungles, and palms and other distinctly tropical trees are more frequently met with. Much of the soil is extremely rich. Great basaltic table lands occur inland, covered with strong, tall, succulent grasses, and the soil of the cleared jungle is a rich vegetable mould. Almost all the ranges are metalliferous, and gold is to be found in so many places that it would not be inaccurate to describe northern Queensland as one great goldfield.

This general description of the colony must be taken merely as a rough outline sketch. The areas described are so great that no general description can be literally accurate. It is in the interior that the greatest uniformity prevails; in both tropical and sub-tropical Queensland, the differing elevation of the land and the occurrence of great mountain ranges create wide climatic differences. This feature ought, however, to be noticed in any description of the colony. In spite of its huge extent, very little of the country is absolutely worthless, the sterile patches are few in number and of no great extent. Nearly the whole of it is valuable for agriculture, grazing or mining.

The progress that Queensland has made in rearing sheep is not what it ought to have been. On its separation from New South Wales, at the end of 1859, the colony possessed a total stock of 3,166,802 sheep. For the first few years of its existence, the squatters of Queensland devoted themselves to rearing sheep with far more zeal than knowledge. This description of stock was put upon country, even in the purely tropical coast districts—in fact, what is now known to be the best sheep country was then hardly explored. A great number of young men from the old country, younger sons of country gentlemen and others accustomed to out-door pursuits, came to the colony intent upon becoming Queensland squatters. After a hasty training on the established sheep stations, they pushed out north and west, taking sheep to stock the country they acquired. The legislature of the young colony enacted that leases should not be issued for bush tracts until a certain proportion of stock to the square mile had actually been placed upon it, and also prohibited the importation of sheep from across the border. This compelled the pioneers, who would only take sheep, to purchase from the established stations. The demand, acting on a limited market, raised prices to an extraordinary height—as much as 20s. and 25s. being occasionally paid for ewes. The high prices created a perfect *furore* for sheep, and numbers rose rapidly. Wool also maintained a good price during these years. The collapse inevitable from the purely artificial nature of the industrial structure which the squatters were building up, was still further delayed by a constant succession of purchasers, ready to buy newly-formed stations at a price calculated per head of stock. The aim therefore of every pioneer was to multiply sheep without regard to quality, so that, as numbers increased, the breed degenerated. In 1866 the first note of destruction was sounded, the numbers in the beginning of that year having been 7,278,778. The process of multiplication still went on, and in 1867 they were 8,665,757. Then the evil day began to come swiftly down on the squatters. In the beginning of 1868 there was a slight increase in the numbers recorded, but that year one of the severest droughts known in the colony prevailed over the sheep districts. The whole speculative fabric collapsed, and a wave of ruin passed over the pioneer sheep farmers. From that year the sheep stock of the colony began to decline in numbers, the declension being due to a rigorous culling out of inferior animals for the boiling-down pots in the true sheep districts, and a progressive falling-off among the flocks, still kept in the worst and unsuitable pastures of the coast districts. The decline continued till 1872, when the numbers showed a decrease of over two million sheep, and the export of wool an average increase in weight, all over, of between four or five ounces—a very considerable proportion in fine merino fleeces. Then a turn became noticeable, and the recorded numbers disclosed an increase. But at the same time a general movement westward set in. Not only were the sheep removed entirely from the unsuitable coast lands, but the flock owners pushed out into the far west—the country which experience had shown them to be most suitable for their stock. The change has undoubtedly been beneficial. But, as one minor effect, it has rendered the official statistics of the colony absolutely worthless as a record of the flocks. The Registrar-General complains yearly to Parliament of the inefficient means at his disposal for collecting returns in the far interior. In a footnote attached to the sheep returns in the Statistics of the Colony for 1878, he explains that the figures from townships which are the official centres for the whole interior of the colony, are imperfect, and in his report laid before Parliament in 1879, he estimates the error for the previous year at something like 700,000. The official sheep statistics are therefore worthless. But the *Courier* and *Queenslander*, the leading papers of the colony, give as the result of careful calculation, based on the export of wool, their belief that the sheep stock of the colony has been gradually increasing since 1873, although it experienced a check in the prolonged drought of 1877-78. If the lambing of this year be as good as that of last, Queensland will probably possess a stock of sheep at the close of it not far inferior in numbers to the maximum of 1878—about 8,600,000—the whole being of much higher average quality.

The sheep country of the colony includes the whole of what has been spoken of as the core or interior, besides much of the inland portion of the sub-tropical division. Throughout the whole of this territory, about half as large again as the colony of New South Wales, the frosts are sufficiently sharp in winter to ensure the growth, and maintain the quality, of the wool, while the native vegetation, largely intermixed with the saline herbs, affords the most excellent pasturage for sheep.

If the squatters of Queensland have not used all their opportunities for rearing sheep, they cannot be accused of neglecting cattle.

The Registrar-General in his official statistics for the year 1878 gives the number of horned cattle at 2,469,555. This total is admittedly imperfect, although it is not considered to be so much under the mark, as the recorded number of sheep. But the imperfection of the record is, in being less than the real number; there are certainly all the cattle figured in the statistics and more. And the increase in the total number has been progressive since the first separation of the colony of New South Wales—Queensland started in 1859 with 432,890 head. By 1870 the annual increase remaining over and above all used for home consumption and exportation was about 140,000 head. In 1877-8, in spite of general drought, it had risen to 240,000. It is thought that in 1879, when the season was unusually favourable for breeding, Queensland must have added at least 300,000 head to her horned stock. And, if so, allowing for the imperfect record of our statisticians, it is probable that she began in 1880 with a stock of not much less than three million head of cattle.

All Queensland is well adapted for cattle breeding; every part of it has advantages for the purpose, peculiar to itself. In the interior, or the core of the colony, bullocks put on volumes of hard fat, and it is fat that will "travel," suffering little diminution in a journey of many hundred miles. As the coast districts of the southern part of the colony are reached, the fat cattle do not attain such extreme weights, but on the other hand butchers prefer the meat, alleging that the fat and lean are more evenly mixed than in the western monsters, clothed as they are with an armour of adipose matter. But coast cattle must be slaughtered near their stations—they lose condition rapidly on a long journey. In the tropical part of the colony, cattle thrive splendidly right to the shores of Carpentaria, and on the peninsula of Cape York. The great basaltic plateaux of the Kennedy, clothed with thick, springing, sweet grass, ought alone to support a cattle stock equal to the whole of that now in the colony, and cattle country has been taken up along the shores of the Gulf to the boundary of the northern territory of South Australia. We know of no part of the colony of Queensland unsuitable for cattle, and nowhere has any natural impediment to their increase been found. If no other stock were kept, we believe that Queensland could easily "run" from thirty to forty million head of cattle without cultivating an acre of ground for fodder, or spending sixpence in the improvement of the natural pasturage. In this direction its capabilities may fairly be spoken of as unlimited. Prices of stock:—The average price of fat cattle in Brisbane market for the last six months has been from £3 10s. to £4 10s. per head for bullocks giving from 750 to 900 lbs. of dressed meat. It would be more correct to say that the price is from 10s. to 12s. per 100 lbs. dressed. Lower figures have to be accepted by sellers in the more northern towns. It is difficult to say what the fair value of a fat bullock is in Queensland. The capital is situated at one end of a long coast line, and can only claim to be at present the most considerable of many commercial towns, each one the post and trading centre for a large tract of country. Prices in each place are affected by a number of purely local causes, and the markets being small the manner and cost of supplying them vary considerably. In fact, the price of fat cattle depends mainly upon the demand, altogether outside of the colony. Western bullocks, when fit for market, were almost always travelled down to the southern colonies in search of the high prices ruling there. When two or three years ago those prices began to fall, and Queensland graziers were compelled to fall back on the local markets, the prices ruling in Brisbane quickly gave way. During the last two or three years they have fallen from £8 and £12 to £3 10s. and £4 10s. And this figure is necessarily not the minimum. With a total population of about 230,000 souls, of whom perhaps 20,000 are Chinese and Polynesians—all adults, and not great consumers of meat—it is evident that the annual output of fat cattle from all the stations and selections with their total stock of about three million head, must largely exceed the demand. Experienced salesmen have told us that an annual demand for from 250,000 to 300,000 fats, in addition to the quantity required for home consumption, would probably do no more than ward off a glut, and would not raise the price to more than 12s. to 14s. per 100 lbs. of dressed beef. We think the calculation a moderate one. There ought to be from 400,000 to 600,000 fats annually, according to the season. We do not think the consumption is 75,000 head in the year, and the excess of fat stock will increase year by year.

The average weight of prime bullocks in the colony, dressed, is from 750 to 900 lbs., those fattened in the interior averaging about 100 lbs. heavier than those prepared for market in the southern coast districts. We think we are justified in saying that with a *certain* market at the ports 12s. per 100 lbs. will pay graziers very fairly, and that at even lower prices those whose runs are not too remote can make both ends meet. A price equal to 13s. or 14s. per 100 lbs. would leave an ample margin of profit on cattle-breeding. The cost of travelling fat cattle, in average mobs of say 200, is about 2s. 6d. per head for each 100 miles. A mob was lately brought into Brisbane from Tambo—the head of the Barcoo, a distance of about 600 miles—for 13s. per head, but this was an exceptionally low price. From the Barcoo to Deniliquin the cost of travelling is about 25s. a head. The centre of the Barcoo or Mitchell District is in about latitude 24, longitude 146, and the greater part of the cattle country lies to the north and west of it. The Queensland Government is engaged in constructing lines of railway running due west from Brisbane, Rockhampton, and Townsville. These lines will collect the traffic from the interior, that from Brisbane taking all between the 29th and 25th parallels of latitude, from Rockhampton between the 25th and 22nd, and the Townsville line all north of it, except so much as will go to the Gulf, and the Cape York Peninsula. From some portions of the first-named belt, the cost of travelling cattle to Deniliquin would be less than the sum named, 25s. per head. From the second it would be that and more, and from the third the charge would probably be double in some cases. At present cattle are not trucked on the railways, the Government having made no effort to secure this kind of traffic, probably because the bulk of the fat cattle have been driven south, and not eastward, to the coasts. But, if necessary, cattle could be quickly and cheaply brought to the coast by these railways. The line from Brisbane is being made to a point 137 miles inland, and that from Rockhampton 230 miles, but the Townsville railway is only just begun. The mob of fat cattle which were driven from Tambo to Brisbane for 13s. per head could have been placed at the present inland terminus of the Rockhampton railway for 2s. or 2s. 6d.

The price of sheep in the Queensland markets is maintained at a high figure, although quite recently, it has shown signs of a falling-off. At present the values are from 7s. 6d. to 10s. for wethers giving from 48 to 60 lbs., dressed carcases varying according to the value of the pelt. Most of the fat sheep have followed the track of the cattle down south, but they are likely to fall back on the local markets, and, although the stock is proportionately far smaller than that of cattle, it is still largely in excess of home requirements. There is much difficulty in arriving at the cost of travelling sheep, but we should put it, at from one penny to two pence each for every hundred miles, according to the season and the size of the mobs travelled. There is a considerable profit on sheep-breeding at the prices quoted for fat wethers, and lower prices even would pay. Any large demand on her sheep stock would however speedily raise prices.

We take from the last report of the Under-Secretary for Lands, presented to Parliament in May, 1879, the following particulars. It should be remarked that very little additional country was taken up last year, in fact, except in the great Burke District, lying round the Gulf of Carpentaria, there is not much good country left to take :—

Interior.						Square Miles.
Gregory North	...	...	...	...	...	77,800
Gregory South	...	...	...	...	...	48,712
Mitchell	...	...	...	...	...	42,869
Warrego	...	...	...	...	...	58,660
(Part) Maranoa	...	...	...	...	...	16,838
						244,879

All this country is available for sheep breeding, but it is equally suitable for cattle.

Sub-tropical Division.						Square Miles.
Burnett	...	...	...	...	...	9,755
Darling Downs	...	...	...	...	...	14,714
Leichhardt	...	...	...	...	...	23,111
(Part) Maranoa	...	...	...	...	...	16,838
(Part) South Kennedy	...		...	...	...	5,763
						70,181

Of this the greater part is suitable for sheep, and the whole will run cattle.

Tropical Division.	Square Miles.
(Part) South Kennedy	5,763
North Kennedy	9,628
Cook	4,069
Burke	40,048
	59,508

The whole of this is cattle country, none of it suitable for sheep.

Of this total area of 374,568 square miles, there are 99,640 miles classed as "unavailable." A squatter is entitled to a considerable reduction in rent for country so classed, although included in the area for which he holds a license. It is supposed to be thick scrub or broken country, but as the runs are taken up in a wholesale manner, as much as 1000 square miles being often included in a lease, and as the applicants' own description is generally taken without verification in the remote districts, it may fairly be supposed that not more than half the country classed as unavailable, is unfit to depasture stock. In fact, the existence of scrub by no means indicates barren country. In the interior, the scrubs are full of saline bushes which afford the most excellent pasturage. Nearer the coast, and especially in the north, the scrubs are fertile tropical jungles which, if unavailable at present, could, if cleared, be turned into pasture land of the best description. The word "scrub" is applied to every stretch of thick-growing timber, from a thicket of bushes to a forest of stately timber trees.

Besides the area held under lease, there are large tracts of inferior country for which no person has applied, and many thousands of square miles hardly yet explored in the Burke and Cook districts. There are also the Settled Districts, near the coast, so called because within their boundary the pastoral leases are held subject to the right of free selection. In these districts there is an area of 87,220 square miles, divided, according to the plan we have adopted, thus:—

Sub-tropical.	Square Miles.
East Moreton	3,030
West Moreton	4,490
Darling Downs	6,080
Wide Bay	7,740
Fraser's Island	520
Port Curtis	14,560
	36,420

Tropical.	Square Miles.
Kennedy	11,800
Cook	30,800
Burke	8,200
	50,800

Of all this country, only a small portion of the Darling Downs is available for sheep, the rest is cattle country. The area actually held under pastoral lease is difficult to ascertain, as, owing to the expiry of one term and some political complications concerning the rates at which they are renewed, much of the country is occupied without any definite arrangement. The area in 1877 was 6,599,596 acres, five-sixths of it being in the sub-tropical division. About 5,718,206 acres had been selected and sold, and of this nine-tenths was in the southern division. This accounts, in round numbers, for about 20,000 out of the 36,000 square miles in the southern part of the settled districts, as being in actual occupation for the purpose of agriculture or pasturage. Of the 50,800 square miles in the north, it is impossible to say how much is taken up by mountain and dense scrub, but it may fairly be reckoned, that half of it is fitted for cattle. It should be explained, that the line, dividing the settled from the unsettled districts, runs at a distance of about thirty miles from the coast in the north. In the south it is carried so far inland as to include the greater part of the Darling Downs.

Summing up these, we have in actual occupation—

	Square Miles.
Settled Districts (about)	20,000
Unsettled Districts ...	374,568
	394,568

Of this the whole is good cattle country, and about two-thirds is well suited for sheep. There are about 274,952 square miles in the colony not occupied at all. Of this probably a third is actually available for cattle-breeding, although from its remoteness it has hardly even yet been properly explored. Of the remainder, some is no doubt sterile—actual desert—but a good deal is merely second-rate, and not occupied because good country is too abundant to render it worth even the small rent asked for a pastoral lease.

In Queensland the metalliferous belts of country are of great extent, and widely distributed throughout the sub-tropical and tropical divisions of the colony. With the exception of the interior, or core of the colony, we know of no district in which metallic ores have not been found. Here, as elsewhere, pre-eminence must be given to gold. This has been found in the southern part of the Darling Downs, but nowhere in quantity. Small " rushes " have taken place, and one or two reefs have been, and are being, worked in the neighbourhood of Warwick. Gold has also been found in East Moreton, the district in which the capital of the colony, Brisbane, is situated. These finds have been unimportant, although some little work is going on at Ennogera. " Colours," as miners call the indications of gold, have been found in many places, and there are people who yet hope that a good reefing field may be found in the scrub-covered ranges at the head of the Brisbane River.

It is on the northern side of that same mass of broken country that the first discovered goldfield of importance in Queensland, Gympie, was found. This field is small, but rich. Discovered by accident in 1867, its rich alluvial deposits attracted a considerable rush from the neighbouring colonies, who, after working out the circumscribed patch, discovered and exhausted other alluvial patches in the neighbourhood. It was soon found that Gympie possessed a more permanent attraction than alluvial gold in its reefs, and although these have maintained up to the present time a population of three or four thousand souls, there is no appearance of exhaustion about the field. Its return of gold for 1877 was 43,854oz.; for 1878, 40,435. The average per ton in the first year was 2oz. 5dwt. 8gr.; in the second, 1oz. 16dwt. 1gr.; and the ordinary value of the gold is about £3 15s. per ounce. Besides the field at Gympie, reef gold has been found in many other parts of the same district (Wide Bay), and its neighbour, the Burnett. But the Queensland miners are accustomed to such high returns from quartz, and have such an enormous extent of country over which to select their field of operations, that second and third rate stone does not receive any attention.

Going northward, we come to the Port Curtis district, where, in the neighbourhood of Gladstone, some highly metalliferous, but very disturbed country exists. Auriferous quartz has been worked in several places, but the erratic manner in which the metal is distributed in the stone, and the numerous dislocations of the lodes or reefs themselves, discourage miners. Some exceedingly rich stone has been found, and a good deal of money has been spent at intervals in the locality, but the industry has only a doubtful and flickering existence. It produced 2000oz. in 1877, and 1285oz. in 1878. Near Rockhampton, a little further to the northward, are several small reefing patches, which are worked with a fair amount of steadiness. They contain no great bodies of stone, and are not rich, but they add an average of about 2000oz. yearly to the gold production of the colony. West of Rockhampton, and about two hundred miles inland, is the Peak Downs goldfield, one of the first to be discovered and worked in the colony. It was never a field of much importance, and it has only been mined in a very desultory fashion for many years past, serving apparently as a resource for miners when work at the great copper mines of the district is slack. It yielded 3000oz. in 1877, and 4000oz. in 1878.

Finally, we come to the main gold-producing areas of Queensland, those of the north or tropical part of the colony. It might almost be said that all Northern Queensland is auriferous, gold is so widely and generally distributed throughout the country. The goldfields, that we are about to enumerate, are in most cases provinces seamed with quartz reefs, and they do not include many gold-producing areas which have not proved attractive enough to induce miners to overcome the danger and difficulty attendant on opening new workings in remote and inaccessible wild country.

Of those the best established, are the fields known as Charters Towers and Ravenswood. The latter was the first opened, and at one time the most important; the former is now the main field. Both are situated in the Kennedy District. In those fields there has been no alluvial found of any importance, mining has, therefore, been from the first a comparatively settled industry; and in Charters Towers particularly it is carried on with all the latest scientific appliances.

The town, which is of considerable size, and is about to have railway communication with its port, Townsville, may be regarded as the mining centre of this part of Northern Queensland. But gold-mining is carried on for hundreds of miles to the west and north-west of the plain. The Cape River, Etheridge, Gilbert, and Cloncurry are the principal subsidiary mining centres, but it can hardly be said that the localities known by these names are mined. Small groups of miners are congregated round favourite points in wide-stretching areas of auriferous country, of which the greater part will some day be made to yield a profitable return. The output of gold, for the districts which we have thus grouped, was 106,708 oz. in 1877, and 95,153 oz. in 1878. It is as well to explain here that the difference between the gold-yield of 1877 and 1878, was due in a great measure to the prevalence of an extremely dry season, which circumscribed the operations of miners in the latter year. Besides, as often happens, the "luck," which is such an important factor in the success of mining operations, was bad in the chief mining centres, several well-known reefs happening to come on poor stone. However, 1879 has made up the deficiency, we believe, especially in Charters Towers, although no official statistics are attainable as yet. The question of exhaustion cannot possibly arise in the northern goldfields, during any period of time that is worth taking into calculation. The fields known as the Etheridge and Gilbert cover about 12,000 square miles, and scattered over this expanse of country, there are about 400 lines of reef proved to be auriferous. The workings are only carried on in little selected spots, leaving the greater part of the auriferous country untouched. Besides, while the present high rate of wages and high price of working capital continues, it does not pay to work any but rich reefs. The field for mining operations would be practically unlimited, if less than one ounce per ton were accepted as a sufficient yield. The average yield per ton of quartz on Charters Towers was 1oz. 10dwt. 1gr. in 1878, and 1oz. 17dwt. 22gr. in 1876.

Last, but perhaps most important of all, there are the goldfields of the Cook District. Of these, the first opened, generally known as the Palmer, includes a great district, 2000 square miles in extent, officially divided into the Palmer, Maytown, Byerstown and Lukinville districts. The gold yield for 1878 was 120,233 ounces, being a considerable reduction on that of the previous year. This is due to a natural and inevitable cause. The Palmer is the most important alluvial field found in the colony, and it is undergoing the usual process of exhaustion. It was opened in 1874, and the yield from alluvial workings is officially estimated as follows:—

	ounces.
1874	150,000
1875	250,000
1876	185,000
1877	167,760
1878	112,000

The return for 1879 is not attainable yet, but it is known that the decrease in alluvial continues. It should be noted, that the returns, in the earlier years, do not probably account for all the gold won. The miners, especially the Chinese, were very negligent in registering the amount of gold taken away by them, and a large proportion always came down to port, by private hands and not by Government escort. The most unsatisfactory feature in the history of this field, is the absence of any development in quartz-mining, for the alluvial workings are everywhere shallow and were never expected to last long. But although the fields abound in auriferous reefs, hardly any work has been done on them, the yield of gold in 1877 from quartz being only 15,800 ounces, and this small amount having decreased to 10,000 ounces in 1878, and a still smaller sum in 1879. This falling-off is remarkable in face of the fact officially reported by the warden, that the average yield of gold is $2\frac{1}{2}$ ounces per ton, the metal being of the unusual average value of £4 2s. 6d. It is probably due to the isolation of the Palmer, its distance from port, the rough rugged country, and the rival attraction of its more accessible neighbour, the Hodgkinson. These disadvantages have deterred the few moneyed strangers, who penetrate so far north, from going to the Palmer, and the locally produced capital, the gold won from the alluvial, has been for the last two or three years monopolised by the Chinese, who send it all to China, and never re-invest a penny in quartz-mining. As an instance of the kind of difficulty that impedes the progress of the field, we may mention the case of one reef, the Queen of the North, which was being worked by a party of miners, who found that although they were raising stone containing over two ounces of gold from a fairly large vein, they made no profit whatever. Their imperfect pumping and other machinery, and the distance—two miles of rough country—from the nearest crushing machine, caused expenses which swallowed up all the proceeds. It was reckoned that about £6000 would supply them with efficient machinery, and place a crushing-mill on their ground, thus halving the cost of working, which would of course leave a large profit. They endeavoured to float a company in order to raise this modest capital but failed. The handful of miners working on the claim subscribed £1000; but the small European community was too poor to raise the balance, and not enough outsiders could be interested in the speculation. It should be noted that this was a " proved " reef. It had given a small fortune from surface stone to the first proprietors, and they had, with the usual improvidence of miners, spent the money, leaving themselves destitute when, on the the shaft reaching water-level, proper mining machinery was needed. The reef or lode was well defined, the stone steadily productive, and the mine presented every appearance of permanence. This incident, which occurred at the commencement of the present year, will explain why a rich quartz field should be almost abandoned. The few European residents have no capital, they can obtain none from outside, and the mines, though rich, are so situated that they can only be worked profitably by the aid of proper appliances.

In this respect, the Hodgkinson field is better off; situated to the south of the Palmer, it is nearer the coast, and has comparatively cheap and easy communication with the two little ports of Cairns and Port Douglas. The country also is more level and far less rugged and rocky than the Palmer. When first discovered, the amazing number of reefs astonished even the northern miners, and quite a considerable rush took place, although there was no alluvial ground. The over-sanguine expectation of the first comers led to a reaction. It was found that although the reefs were large, especially on the surface, the payable gold was often limited to "pipes" or shoots of stone running through them. Therefore, although about 350 lines of reef have been proved to be auriferous, and about 800 distinct claims taken up, yet no great progress has been made.

The reefs or lodes were attacked by men with very little capital who, when disappointed by the capricious distribution of the gold, had not the means to encounter the chances of following down the reef. The value of the gold also, was much lower than that found on the Palmer. Notwithstanding these disadvantages, the output of gold is increasing. It was 33,818 ozs. in 1877, and 44,435 ozs. in 1878. In course of time the erratic reefs that have been thrown up will, no doubt, be again explored by moneyed men, and a large proportion will, no doubt, prove payable at a moderate depth, for as yet the sinking on the field can only be described as surface scratching. The immense number of reefs guarantees the future prosperity of the field, as among so many there may be a considerable number of what miners call "duffers," and yet enough permanent workings remain to support a very large population.

In concluding this short sketch of the goldfields of Queensland, we must repeat that we take no notice of innumerable localities in which the precious metal has actually been found, though not in sufficient quantity to induce miners to search or "prospect" thoroughly. Besides, Northern Queensland is so generally auriferous, that it is believed that systematic prospecting must discover many deposits not yet known. As it is, there are scores of gullies or "likely plains" where a prospector, hurrying to a rush, or otherwise prevented from remaining, may have noticed promising "colours," and which he may any day return to examine, and thus disclose the existence of a new and rich field. The fact is that the northern miners suffer from an *embarras de richesses*. Promising fields are abandoned simply because the men will not stay and persevere in the facing of difficulties, knowing that they can go elsewhere and earn the same money more easily. And on the whole they earn a great deal. The average yield of quartz gold, per miner engaged, in 1878, was 57 ozs. 11 dwts. $8\frac{1}{2}$ grs., which, calculated at an average of £3 10s. per oz., represents a very handsome return for labour; and this, in spite of a general absence of mining appliances and rough machinery, which must have made the proportion very much less than it might have been. The field of operations is too large, and the capital and labour engaged on it are frittered away over too many points. But this, though a present disadvantage, is, of course, a guarantee of future productiveness. In Queenland there are two fields, Gympie and Charters Towers, where mining is carried on with adequate capital and proper appliances, although in both places there are numerous lines of reef not yet properly explored, and in neither would anything like really poor stone be thought worth raising. In Northern Queensland at the close of 1878, there were only 2245 quartz miners; but if all the known reefs in the established fields in that part of the colony were worked, as the two places we have mentioned are worked, at least twenty thousand miners would be constantly and profitably employed. And, if all the disregarded patches were searched, and the profitable reefs contained in them worked, the number of miners would have to be greatly increased. And, as there is no reason to suppose that the lodes would be less permanent there than elsewhere, while there is good cause to believe that not half, we may say not a tenth-part, of the auriferous veins in the country has as yet been even seen, gold mining in the north must be a progressive industry for very many years to come.

Queensland is very rich in metallic ores of all descriptions. Copper is found in a great many places, and worked in two or three districts. Some large rich lodes were discovered on the Peak Downs, in the Kennedy District, in 1862, soon after the formation of the colony, and the mine of that name, of which the metal is well known on the market, is still being worked. Although large quantities of metal have been produced, the mine has not been very profitable to the shareholders, the long land-carriage to port, and the necessity of smelting with wood, having consumed much of the profit. During the mining excitement of 1871-2-3, caused by the high price of copper, the management paid a very large dividend—75 per cent. on the whole large capital stock; but this was obtained by working out all the ore "in sight," and neglecting exploration. The result has been that when the speculative fever died out, and the price of copper fell, the workings languished. They have never been worked with much energy since. The mine is still kept open by tributors, and is said to contain plenty of good ore yet.

Mount Perry, in the Burnett District, is the name of another mine, opened during the excitement of 1872, and although also hampered by long land-carriage, it produced a large quantity of copper, and repaid in dividends about two and a-half times the cash capital invested in it. When the price of copper fell, it ceased to pay dividends, and work is nearly suspended now. The mine is, however, not worked out. In the neighbourhood of Mount Perry, there is a great deal of country intersected with copper lodes, and during the mining excitement some score of mines were opened there, as well as at Kilkivan, near Gympie. These undertakings were for the most part rather stock-jobbing than mining enterprises, and although most of the lodes opened appeared to be payable, the cash capital subscribed was in no case sufficient to put the mines in proper working order. The fall in copper stopping all speculation, also put an end to the mining operations, and, indeed, most of the companies exhausted their scanty capital in preliminary work. The lodes, however, were many of them sufficiently promising, and some could no doubt be profitably worked with adequate capital and proper appliances even at the present price of copper.

Copper has also been found and worked near Rockhampton and Gladstone. A mine about twenty miles from Mackay, has only recently been closed, owing to the low price of the metal. Copper ore is known also to exist in several places near the north-eastern coast of the colony. On the Cloncurry, a river emptying itself into the Gulf of Carpentaria, one of the most remarkable deposits of native copper found in Australia, was discovered by Captain Henry, in 1868. Attempts were made to work it and the surrounding lodes, but although the deposits were exceptionally rich, the long distances from port, and the high rates of provisions and labour in that remote part of the colony, rendered it impossible for the miners to make any profit by their work.

The greatest value of copper exported from the colony was £257,723 in 1872; it had sunk to £35,126 in 1878.

Tin was discovered on the New South Wales border of the colony in 1872, and the alluvial deposits attracted quite a rush, which resulted in the foundation of the town of Stanthorpe. The productiveness of the field reached its greatest height in 1873, when stream tin to the value of £370,912 was exported. The rapid fall in the price of the metal and the exhaustion of the more accessible deposits, changed the character of the mining, which was ultimately abandoned to a few capitalists, who had the means to counteract the decrease in value by improved mining appliances. The productiveness of the field was greatly diminished by the severe drought of 1877-78, but it is again on the increase. There is yet a great deal of stanniferous ground to be worked. Tin has also been found in a part of the Palmer field, and at the foot of the coast range near Cairns. The deposits in both places are said to be extensive, but are only being worked on a small scale. The low price of tin, and the high rates of wages and carriage in the north, militate against the successful prosecution of the industry.

Antimony and cinnabar have both been found and worked in the Wide Bay District, the first at Neardie, and the second at Kilkivan. The antimony lodes are productive, and the ore of good percentage; but the profits to be derived from working a low-priced metal did not seem sufficiently attractive to Queensland miners or mining speculators. Good antimony ore has also been found in the Burnett. The cinnabar lodes have been worked on a small scale, but they were not found till after the mining excitement had died away, and it had become difficult to attract capital to any mining enterprise.

Silver, zinc, lead, plumbago, and bismuth have been found. The silver ore is apparently not very rich anywhere. A vein is now being worked on a small scale at Ravenswood. Opals of good quality have been found in one or two places—in the Mitchell district especially. Iron abounds in a great many places, and the ore is said to be very good in some localities. It has nowhere been worked.

Coal is very abundant, or, at least, coal beds abound. The mineral is worked pretty extensively in pits near the Brisbane River and its tributary, the Bremer. These raised 50,000 tons in 1878, and the output is yearly increasing. Coalfields exist further inland, but this mineral cannot, of course, be worked, except in places where very cheap and easy transport is possible. Another great coal basin extends from the May to the Burnett Rivers in the Wide Bay district. This is being successfully worked near the Burrum, a small stream emptying itself into the sea between the two rivers mentioned above, and some New South Wales speculators are now negotiating with the Government for the construction of a short line of railway to connect the pits with the town of Maryborough, the Burrum having only a shallow and very tortuous channel. Coal has been found on the Dawson, near Bowen, and in several other localities; but these basins have not been tested in any way.

The progress of agriculture in Queensland has not been very great. At the end of 1878—the latest date which the corrected official returns reach—the area of land alienated, either conditionally, that is subject to the payment of instalments of purchase-money and fulfilment of certain specified conditions, or granted in fee simple, was 5,935,496 acres. Of this large area only 117,489 acres were broken up for cultivation, and 111,746 acres actually in crop. A further deduction should be made of about 18,000 acres under sown grasses and other fodder plants cultivated solely for feeding cattle. All the remainder of the alienated land was simply used by the holders to depasture stock, just in the same manner as a pastoral lessee uses his run. No attempt had been made to increase the productiveness of this land, except in a few instances, by thinning the timber, although much of it had been enclosed by fences, and in some places water had been stored. This neglect of agriculture does not arise from any want of fertility in the soil, which is often very rich, nor is it due to the climate in the coast districts, for the rainfall is usually abundant and fairly distributed throughout the year. The backward condition of agriculture is certainly not due to any lack of encouragement from the Government. Land is sold at very reasonable rates, and the purchaser has ten years over which to spread the payment. A very fair quantity is always left open to selection in the various coast districts, and the selector may choose a holding wherever he pleases in the areas set apart for the purpose. And for years past there has been a homestead law in operation by which a selector may take up a limited holding and secure the grant in fee simple, on the sole condition of five years' personal residence together with the payment of sixpence an acre yearly. No intending selector could desire easier conditions, and the charge of half-a-crown an acre, in five annual instalments, is almost equivalent to a free grant of the land. The limit of a homestead used to be eighty acres, but it was increased last year to 160 acres. The reason why settlers in Queensland do not cultivate, is probably to be found in the variety of profitable openings for the employment of labour during the decade—between 1868 and 1878—in which the colony made its greatest progress. A succession of goldfields, the excitement of "flush times," consequent on the rage for mining speculation, which occurred during the period, and the constant and large expenditure of loan money on public works, have served to keep up the price and demand for labour. Only a small proportion of the labouring class, who elsewhere form the pioneer agricultural settlers of a colony, have therefore turned to the land for a living. They found that they could earn money more rapidly and surely by taking the high wages offered than by engaging in the irksome, monotonous, and isolated toil of the selector who wins with axe, hoe, and plough a farm from the wild bush. The continuance of the same "good times" has had an unfortunate effect even on those who have settled on the soil. Queensland agricultural settlers have been in the habit of expecting quick and large returns. They have, therefore, confined themselves mainly to the production of crops which could be quickly grown, and for which they could get an immediate payment; neglecting many products for which the soil and climate of the colony is suitable, but which are not rapidly matured.

Among the agricultural products of the colony, sugar undoubtedly takes first rank. As far back as 1862, a patch of twenty acres of sugar cane was recorded in the official statistics. At first the pioneers of the industry had much to contend with. The cane grew well enough, but the growers were inexperienced, and they had all to learn in the art of making sugar. Labour was also a great difficulty. European labourers were not only dear, but they could not be depended on. They disliked the hot troublesome task of hoeing and trashing, *i.e.*, stripping dead leaves among the tall growing rows of cane, sheltered from the breeze and exposed to the moist summer heat of the coast districts. They therefore were ready to abandon the work whenever an opportunity offered, and opportunities were frequent, as has already been explained. This led to the introduction of South Sea Islanders, engaged for three years, who proved quite capable of performing the simple work of cane cultivation, and were found to be fairly docile and industrious labourers. Experience was gained in the art of sugar-making, and the industry prospered for a while to be met by another unexpected difficulty. The Bourbon variety of cane, which grew freely and yielded large quantities of juice, was generally planted, and it was suddenly smitten with a disease, called rust, which destroyed field after field. For a while the check was very disheartening, but it was overcome. Varieties of cane from all sugar-growing countries were introduced, and it was found that a great many species were proof against the disease. The difficulty was completely overcome. So many descriptions of cane are now grown, that a disease attacking one kind cannot cause any important check. The planters have found out by experience how to adapt their cultivation to the soil and climate. Men skilled in every department of cane-growing and sugar-making abound, the best machinery is used, and local machinists are constantly making improvements and experiments which will doubtless lead to improvements. In fact, the industry is prosecuted with energy, it has attracted and is attracting a good deal of capital, and those engaged in it are constantly on the alert, to make or adopt any promising improvements. Substantial progress has therefore been made. In 1878 there were 68 sugar mills in operation, and those crushed the produce of 10,702 acres, which yielded 13,525 tons of sugar; and the 12 distilleries at work turned out 216,395 gallons of rum. The rapidity with which the industry was progressing was indicated by the breadth of land put under cane, amounting to 16584 acres, an increase of 1364 acres on the previous year, in spite of the prevalence of a severe drought from which Queensland, in common with New South Wales, was suffering. The returns for last year, 1879, are not complete, but it is believed that over 16,000 tons of sugar were produced, and a very large additional area of land was prepared for cane. The production of sugar, besides supplying the local demand, gave rise to an export trade which is fast increasing. Queensland exported, in 1878, sugar and rum to the value of about £130,000, and the export of 1879 was probably of not less a value than £200,000.

The main centres of sugar cultivation are the districts of Mackay, Maryborough, and Brisbane, their importance being in the order of their names. In the two last-named districts the coolness of the winter and the occurrence of occasional frosts are disadvantages. The cane does not make any growth for at least two months out of the twelve, and the stools are sometimes killed by the hoar frosts. These disadvantages are, however, not great enough to make the industry unprofitable in localities where suitable

F

soil is to be found. But Mackay is evidently destined to be the main sugar district of the colony. Fairly within the tropics, it escapes winter frosts, and the cane grows throughout the year. The rainfall is so distributed as to be peculiarly advantageous to the planters. There is a pretty well-defined rainy season, commencing in January, but instead of the year being divided, as it is in many places further north, into about four months of incessant downpour, followed by eight of almost unbroken drought, the showers are prolonged till about August. From that month to December the planters can depend on dry weather, and can carry on crushing operations under the most favourable conditions. The soil also, a deep, rich, friable loam, is very suitable for the growth of cane. The area of cultivation, already considerable, is about to be largely increased, some land in the neighbourhood having been recently thrown open to selectors, and seized upon with avidity by intending canegrowers. Cane has also been grown for many years on the Herbert River, near the little northern port of Cardwell, but the industry has languished. The cause of its want of success is probably to be found in the fact, that the pioneers under-estimated the amount of capital required, and the difficulties attendant on establishing such an industry in a remote locality, far from any considerable centre of population. One or two plantations, however, are carried on, and it is probable that cane-growing will again spread. There are a great many rivers on the north-east coast having suitable soil on their banks, and affording the necessary facilities for punting the bulky crops of cane to the mills. On one of these, the Johnstone, a considerable area of land has recently been taken up, and an old Queensland planter is about to establish a large sugar-mill. In several other places in the southern part of the colony cane-growing has been, or is about to be, commenced, and the development of the industry has received a great impetus from the high prices lately ruling for sugars.

Viticulture in Queensland is not in a satisfactory condition. In 1878 there were 188 wine makers, who produced 64,407 gallons of wine. Of these 158 were in the neighbourhood of Toowoomba, Warwick, and Brisbane, and they produced about 55,000 gallons of the wine made. Ipswich comes next as a wine-producing place, and there is one vineyard of some importance in its neighbourhood. Not much can be said for Queensland wine as yet; it is generally crude and ill-made, although one or two vignerons have succeeded in winning prizes at the Sydney Exhibition. Not only is the wine of indifferent quality, but it is dear, the vignerons having the full advantage of a duty of 10s. and 6s. per gallon levied on all wines, according to alcoholic strength, imported into the colony. An attempt made by the Government about three years ago to enter into a reciprocity treaty with South Australia was rigorously resisted by them, and they succeeded in working up an agitation that discouraged the Ministry, who gave up the attempt. The gradual increase in the quantity of wine produced, and competition among vine growers, is beginning to reduce the price, and will probably improve the quality of the wine made. The southern part of the colony is well suited for the growth of vines, and it has been found that they flourish vigorously, and produce most excellent fruit in the neighbourhood of the inland town of Roma, on the boundary of the interior or core of the colony. It is believed, and the belief seems to be well founded, that this will be one of the main wine-producing districts of the colony. The grape vine will mature its fruit far within the tropics in Queensland; but, of course, the grapes are not equal to those grown in the more temperate regions. In fact, it is probably the sharp winter frosts of the southern interior, that serve to invigorate the vines and cause them to produce such excellent fruit.

Queensland settlers grow maize, potatoes, pumpkins, sweet potatoes, oats, and lucerne for hay, besides other crops, such as are grown in temperate and sub-tropical climates. Wheat is grown, but at present its cultivation is confined to a very small locality—the Darling Downs. In 1878 there were 9617 acres under wheat, cut for grain, according to the official statistics, and 2114 acres cut for hay. In 1879 the breadth of land under wheat was more than doubled, but the crop was almost entirely destroyed by an unprecedented outbreak of rust. This calamity is attributed to the unusually moist, "muggy" winter and spring season, and there is a general conviction that the country, lying further to the westward, will be better suited to wheat as it has a climate which is drier and more similar to that of South Australia. The Darling Downs farmers are endeavouring to meet these difficulties, as the sugar planters did, by introducing different varieties of grain, and also by adopting different methods of cultivation. The soil of the district is extremely fertile—in fact, it has been called the garden of Southern Queensland—and it is a pity that wheat cultivation should have received a severe check just when it appeared about to expand. It is a comparatively recent industry in the colony, only about 1100 acres being returned as under wheat in 1870. The average yield had been, up to 1879, over 20 bushels to the acre on land free from rust. Experimental patches of wheat have been found to thrive in a great many parts of Southern Queensland.

Cotton cultivation was established in the first year of the separate existence of the colony, and stimulated by Government bonuses; but it never took root. While the bonus was paid, it was a favourite crop in West Moreton, and some thousands of acres were devoted to it; but when the Government grants were withdrawn, it was found that growing cotton for the open market did not pay well enough to suit Queensland expectations of profit. In 1878 only 37 acres were under this crop, and it is now probably entirely given up. Both soil and climate were, however, found very suitable for the production of cotton.

Arrowroot was attempted some years ago in the Southern Coast districts, and partly given up because the local storekeepers were not ready to take the roughly got up product at once, and the farmers were not inclined to spend the time or money necessary to perfect it. Some cultivators, however, in the country immediately south of the capital, noticing with what luxuriance the plant grew, persevered, and succeeded in producing a merchantable article, equal in quality and "get up" to any imported. The industry proved profitable, and the cultivation of the tuber is again increasing. In 1878, there were 124 acres devoted to arrowroot, and 232,388lbs. of prepared product sent to market. In the same year 178,672lbs. were exported, and as the export has been found profitable, and a great deal of suitable land exists in the coast districts, it is probable that this branch of agricultural industry will assume greater importance.

Tobacco cultivation does not progress. Only 71 acres were devoted to it in 1878, and there is not much sign of any marked increase. The plant thrives, but the cultivators are ignorant of the proper method of preparing it for market.

No other field crops are grown in the colony. In fruits, Queensland produces many bananas and pineapples, about 462 acres being devoted to the former, and 184 acres to the latter, in 1878. The cultivation of bananas received a severe check some years ago, the trees being attacked by a worm that destroyed whole plantations. Some bananas grown in the Far North have lately attracted attention, being of unusually fine flavour and, for the species, large size. It may be mentioned that the blacks in the Cook District were found by the whites to use the fruit of an indigenous banana growing in the river-side scrubs. The list of Queensland fruits is likely to be greatly increased, as the Brisbane Acclimatisation Society is introducing a great variety of tropical and sub-tropical trees, and distributing them among its members scattered throughout the colony. By far the greater proportion are found to thrive. The custard apple and mango are to be seen in the local fruit-shops now, and those grown in the latitude of Bowen are very fine. In Southern Queensland the tropical fruits are matured, but not in the full perfection of their flavour. Cocoa-nut palms are now growing in quantity near Mackay and Bowen, and are being planted in several localities. In fact, palms were found growing on some of the islands that cluster inside the Barrier reef, off the coast of the Cook District, and sound nuts are occasionally washed ashore on the mainland. It has been stated as a reason why the palms were not found on the northern coast, that the aborigines dig up the young plants whenever they see them sprouting in the sand, and use the roots and shoots as food, cooking them as they do native game. Such fruits as apples, pears, and plums are only grown in the cooler districts of the extreme southern part of the colony, and do not attain any remarkable perfection there. Peaches are largely grown, and the trees bear profusely; but that is about all that can be said for them.

Olives grow well in Southern Queensland wherever tried. Coffee-bushes are growing vigorously in gardens in many parts of the colony. Experimental patches of rice thrive. There has been no attempt, however, to produce any of these things for market. The *sida retusa*, introduced originally because it yields a useful fibre, has never been grown for that purpose, but has spread itself over the coast districts, becoming a dreaded pest to the farmers, and destroying even the pasturage in places. The agricultural capabilities of Queensland appear, in short, to be almost unlimited, but there is as yet not much disposition on the part of the settlers to avail themselves of the power, which nature has bestowed upon them, of growing a wide variety of crops, and thus securing themselves against the danger of overstocking their markets.

The timber forests of Queensland are large and valuable, and lumbering has been a thriving industry in some localities since the formation of the colony. Very little prudence has, however, been displayed in dealing with the timber stock; in fact, the lumberers have just cleared all before them and wasted as they pleased, the only condition imposed on them being the payment of a small annual license fee. In this manner the valuable pencil cedar has been almost extirpated on the Southern Rivers, and the process is in full swing in the far north, where it is abundant. Besides cedar, hardwood and pine of two varieties, known as the Hoop and Kauri pine, are cut. The timber-getters, beside supplying the needs of the colony, give rise to a considerable timber export. It is simply impossible to give the actual amount of cedar sent away, as it is shipped in the log at the mouths of remote northern rivers, where no accurate official returns are procurable. The official returns for 1878 record the shipment of 3,916,010 feet of log cedar valued at £28,271, but this is an under-estimate. The recorded exports of sawn pine may be relied on, as this is shipped at the southern ports of Bundalery, Maryborough, and Brisbane, where the whole can be accurately checked. In the year above mentioned, 3,421,422 feet, valued at £25,920, were exported to the other colonies.

The pearl-shell fishery, carried on in the north, may be spoken of as an industry *in*, but not of, Queensland, as it is mainly in the hands of Sydney firms. The official value of shell exported in 1878 is given at £54,149, but the amount is believed to be under-estimated. The resident magistrate at Thursday Island, the head-quarters of the fishery, gives a much higher value. Bêche-de-mer is also gathered on the nothern reefs and exported to the value of about £10,000 annually. A Chinese junk, built in Cooktown, is engaged by the Chinese fishermen to gather the dried slug from their fishing stations.

The dugong is caught in Moreton and Wide Bay by parties of fishermen provided with nets and harpoons, and a good deal of medicinal oil—said to be superior to cod-liver oil—prepared from it. Despite the facts that good leather of extraordinary thickness can be made from the hide of the dugong, and that the bones of the skeleton are of unusual density, which, together with the oil procured by boiling down the fat, make the animal of considerable value, the fishery has never been prosecuted on any considerable scale. The dugong is found on all parts of the coast of the colony.

The estimated population of Queensland on the 31st December, 1878, was 210,510. There has been no estimate published yet of the population at the end of 1879, but there is reason to believe that the increase was very slight, as although immigrant ships continued to arrive, the great depression prevailing throughout the colony led, as is generally supposed, to a considerable exodus. It should be remarked, however, that up to the last recorded date, the official calculations showed a gain to the colony in the interchange of people by steamers trading along the coast. Out of this number, 60,458 were returned as living in municipalities. As yet, therefore, we have not the disproportionately large town population to be found in Victoria. There are no great manufactories in Queensland. A woollen mill recently established in Ipswich and some large foundries in Brisbane and Maryborough, are our principal industrial establishments, other than those connected with the natural products of the soil. There are several large saw-mills cutting up timber for export, and besides the sugar-mills there is a large establishment at Gargarie, near Maryborough, where cane juice is manufactured directly into high-class refined sugar. A considerable number of small industrial establishments exist in the towns, including breweries, tanneries, soap works, fellmongeries, biscuit factories, ropeworks, brickworks, potteries, cooperage works, boat-building yards, and so on, but these are not on a large scale. As yet "protection" is not the policy of Queensland. The principle has never been admitted in the arrangement of the Customs tariff, and although there is a protectionist party, it is very small, and has not been able to attract sufficient popular support to be a factor in local politics.

In the official statistics, the Chinese and Kanakas, amounting probably to over 20,000 souls, nearly all adult males, are included in the general population. The value of much of the Vital and Social Statistics, is therefore destroyed. The existence of so large a number of adult males, who are necessarily unmarried, affects both the births and marriage rates, and the large number of deaths among the Kanakas, a race that is vitally very feeble, swells abnormally the official death-rate. These facts must be remembered in connection with the figures about to be quoted.

Proportion of births, marriages and deaths to every 1000 of the population:—

	Births.	Marriages.	Deaths.
1870	43.51	7.79	14.59
1871	43.25	8.06	14.83
1872	40.70	8.69	14.97
1873	40.82	9.66	16.06
1874	41.15	8.62	18.01
1875	38.89	8.62	23.80
1876	37.48	7.57	18.82
1877	36.74	7.57	17.29
1878	35.77	6.98	20.41

It will be perceived that the effect of the "rush" to the North in 1874-75, attracted by the Palmer Gold Fields, had a speedy effect in diminishing the proportion of births and marriages and increasing that of deaths. This was due to the incoming of so many unmarried men, followed by a flood of Chinese, when the northern fields were first opened; also, the reckless exposure of the gold-seekers to the tropical sun, and more especially to the tropical wet season, without either a shelter or a sufficiency of food, caused a great mortality, which told on the returns. But, about 1875, a "wave" of disease passed over the colonies generally. As bearing on the effect produced by the opening of the northern goldfields on the death-rate of the colony, it may be noted that what are grouped as "Miasmatic Diseases" in the Registrar-General's returns, including fevers, caused the following proportion of cases treated in the hospitals of the colony:—

1870	...	440	1873	...	487	1876	...	1140
1871	...	313	1874	...	754	1877	...	1497
1872	...	537	1875	...	1781	1878	...	1913

Primary education in Queensland is "free, secular, and compulsory," although the last provision is not actually enforced. Grants to non-vested schools—*i.e.*, schools not under the control of the Minister of Education, mainly Roman Catholic institutions—are to be discontinued at the end of the present year, 1880. The average daily attendance of children at the primary schools in 1878 was—

	Boys.	Girls.	Total.
State Schools	9,178	7,782	16,960
State Provisional Schools	824	758	1,582
State, Non-vested	981	1,471	2,452
	10,983	10,011	20,994
Private Schools	848	1,569	2,417
Grammar Schools			290

The endeavour to follow up the scattered population of the colony with schools is vigorously and persistently maintained, and with a fair measure of success. The annual expenditure on State education is now over £100,000 annually, and the Roman Catholics raise considerable sums to maintain their own schools, most of those included under the head of "private" belonging to that church.

In 1878, 197 persons were convicted of serious crimes before the higher courts, and 6153 individuals were found guilty of lesser offences by the magistrates. This last total is greatly swelled in the Queensland, as in all colonial statistics, by the habit of counting, as a separate charge, each detail of a drunkard's misdoings. A drunken man is generally violent, and uses obscene language, and often assaults the policeman and tears his coat. If he succeed in accomplishing all these exploits, he counts in the statistics as three or four separate offenders. As 1947 cases of drunkenness were punished in 1878, it will be seen how large a portion of the 6153 convictions may be accounted for in this manner.

CHAPTER IV.

SOUTH AUSTRALIA.

FOUNDATION OF THE COLONY—ITS LAND LAWS AND THEIR OPERATION—ELIGIBILITY AS A FIELD OF SETTLEMENT FOR IMMIGRANTS—LARGE EXPORTS OF STAPLE PRODUCTS—GERMAN COLONISTS AND THE SECRET OF THEIR SUCCESS—COMMERCE OF SOUTH AUSTRALIA GREATER PER HEAD THAN THAT OF EITHER OF THE OTHER COLONIES—LIGHTNESS OF TAXATION—DEVOTION OF ITS POPULATION TO RURAL INDUSTRIES—MINERAL RESOURCES—FAUNA OF SOUTH AUSTRALIA—SMALL INDUSTRIES WHICH MAY BE PROFITABLY PURSUED THERE—SPECIAL FACILITIES OFFERED BY THE LEGISLATURE FOR THE CULTIVATION OF THE OLIVE—MANUFACTURING INDUSTRIES OF THE COLONY—STATISTICS—BIRTHS, MARRIAGES AND DEATHS, 1879—CENSUS—IMMIGRATION—EMIGRATION—EXPORTS—IMPORTS—LIVE STOCK—THE WALLAROO AND MOONTA MINES AND THEIR MANAGEMENT.

UNLIKE Victoria and Tasmania, South Australia was settled by a number of enterprising gentlemen, who had formed themselves into an association, under the authority of the Imperial Legislature, for the colonisation of the country, upon the broad and liberal principle that it should not cost a penny to Great Britain; that there should be no state church, and no transportation to its shores. The first settlers landed in Holdfast Bay, on the 28th of December, 1836; and soon afterwards, the site of the future capital was selected, on the banks of the Torrens, and the incipient city received the name of the then Queen, Adelaide. The infant settlement passed through the usual vicissitudes incidental to young countries; but the first colonists were composed of men of no ordinary force of character. They were not daunted or disheartened by temporary reverses. They had an invincible faith in the country, in its fine resources, and in its splendid future; and most of them lived to witness the fruition of their hopes, and to participate in the prosperity, which rewarded their energy, their perseverance, and their dogged determination to succeed. And at this moment, forty-four years after the foundation of the colony, it may be confidently asserted that there is no portion of Her Majesty's dominions, in which the average standard of welfare is higher than it is in South Australia.

The first Constitution of the colony was granted in 1851, and the second in 1856. The latter conferred upon it the amplest powers of self-government; and it must be recorded to the credit of its politicians, that these powers have been exercised, as a general rule, with credit and discretion, and to the advantage of the community. As the late Mr. Harcus wrote, in his valuable work on South Australia:—"The bitter rancour of political antagonism, which is seen in some countries, is comparatively unknown in South Australia. It is not, that our public men do not feel strongly on political questions, but we are so closely mixed up in social and business life, that we cannot afford to allow political asperities to pass beyond the region of politics." There, as elsewhere, the mere adventurer, with a glib tongue, a face of brass, and an unlimited supply of impudent assurance, will sometimes struggle to the surface of political life, and will make a great disturbance, for the sake of attracting attention, but the notoriety and self-importance of such persons are always short-lived, and they are betrayed, sooner or later, into the commission of the sin which is unpardonable,—that of being found out. They then drop out of sight, and are speedily forgotten.

South Australia is essentially an agricultural and pastoral country, and much of its progress and prosperity is attributable to the facilities offered by the Legislature to intending settlers for the acquisition of land, and to the absence of any enactments—like the fiscal laws of Victoria—to prevent the distribution of the people over the country, and to favour their concentration in a few centres. Any person is at liberty to select 640 acres, that is to say a square mile of land, on any surveyed areas south of the 26th parallel of south latitude, at the upset price of £1 an acre; upon which he pays a deposit of ten per cent. as interest for the next three years, during which no demand is made upon him. At the end of that term, a further sum of ten per cent. is required from him, as interest for the succeeding three years. If he should be then unable to pay the whole of the purchase money, his credit will be enlarged for a period of four years, on paying half the amount; interest at the rate of four per cent. per annum being charged on the balance. It is needful to add that purchasers on credit must reside upon the land they take up for nine months in the year, as an evidence of their *bona fides* as settlers, and are called upon to make substantial improvements upon the land, to the extent of 5s. per acre before the end of the second, of 7s. 6d. per acre before the end of the third, and of 11s. per acre before the expiration of the fourth year. These regulations have been framed with a view to prevent the Crown lands from falling into the hands of mere speculators and "land sharks," and to promote genuine and beneficial settlement. The improvements may consist either of the erection of a dwelling-house, or farm buildings, or the sinking of wells, the formation of water tanks or reservoirs, or of fencing, draining, clearing, or grubbing the land. We believe there are hundreds of farmers in Great Britain, with a moderate capital at their disposal, who must be wholly unacquainted with the easy terms upon which they can acquire estates in these colonies; or else there would surely be a large migration of persons of this class to Australia, where a few years of strenuous exertion would place themselves and their families in a condition of comparative affluence. Let us take the case of a yeoman, with three grown-up sons and daughters. By taking up four contiguous sections they could secure 2560 acres in a ring fence, in South Australia, New South Wales, or Queensland, or half that quantity in Victoria. The whole of their available capital could be expended in bringing a portion of the block into cultivation, in building a homestead, in fencing and stocking the farm, and in permanent improvements; and it would go hard indeed, if they could not pay the whole of the purchase money out of the profits of cultivation in the course of six years.

According to the testimony of a trustworthy writer, the present land law of South Australia has worked with singular success. "Immense areas of land in the north," he tells us, "have been surveyed and offered for sale on credit. Half-a-dozen years ago, most of this land was used as sheep runs, supporting a dozen or a score of persons, now it is covered with smiling homesteads, and prosperous farms, in which many hundreds of families are settled, with every prospect of future success. In the course of a few years these farms will be the freehold estates of a steady and intelligent class of farmers, farming their own land, who will constitute the pith and strength of the colony. A few thousands of farmers, each farming his own freehold estate of a square mile, or a thousand acres, would form an independent and prosperous class, of which any country may well feel proud. The amount of money due to the Government for these lands purchased on credit, which will be due within the next six years, amounts to over £2,225,000. There is reason to believe that most of the purchases will be completed; but if they are not, the land, greatly improved by the erection of buildings and cultivation during the six years, will revert to the Government, and can be sold again. I had an opportunity of visiting these northern areas just before the last harvest, when they were loaded with magnificent crops of golden grain. I had seen the country three years before, when only a small portion was devoted to agriculture; the rest was still immense sheep-runs. I travelled for miles, day after day, amongst the finest crops of wheat I ever witnessed. In some places the reaping had commenced, and the farmers were cleaning up from fourteen to eighteen bushels per acre. In other more favoured spots, it reached from twenty-five to thirty bushels. I saw several towns which had sprung up as if by magic, on sites where three years before there was not a soul to be seen, and where my companions and I lighted a fire, boiled our 'billy,' and made tea for our midday refreshment. A fine port in Spencer's Gulf, for the outlet of the produce of the district, had risen up from what used to be something like a dismal swamp. Wharfs were erected, large stores built, banks and churches founded; and all this was the work of less than three years! And as far as can be seen, we are just tapping that great agricultural district which lies to the north of the Burra and Clare. The squatter has to give place to the agriculturist and move backward."

This was written four years ago, at which the latest agricultural statistics then available showed that there were 1,330,484 acres of land under cultivation. But, in the interim, this has increased to 2,011,319 acres, being an average of eight acres per head of population, no other Australian colony reaching half that proportion. In the year 1878, the exports of domestic produce in three items alone reached the magnificent total of, in round numbers, four millions and a half, namely:—

Breadstuffs	£1,672,628
Wool	2,417,398
Minerals	409,749
Total	£4,499,774

And two years previously, the exports of breadstuffs were within a fraction of two millions in value; this surplus remaining after abundant provision had been made for the sustenance of the population of the colony. Henceforth, it may be confidently asserted that the yearly exports of South Australia will be equivalent in value to £20 per head of the population. In other words, they are much greater relatively to the number of inhabitants than the entire trade—*both imports and exports*—of Great Britain! Talk of a land flowing with milk and honey; here is one which is exuberant with the staff of life, with the golden fleece, and the juice of the grape. And its flour deservedly enjoys the reputation of being some of the best in the world, so that it is much sought after in the neighbouring colonies for the manufacture of the choicer kinds of biscuits, the different varieties of fancy bread, and the most delicate *patisserie*. We believe it enjoys the same high repute in the mother-country.

South Australia alone could absorb the whole population of Great Britain, and yet continue sparsely peopled. Its area is, in round numbers, 900,000 square miles; that is to say, it is thirty times as large as Scotland or Ireland, nearly sixteen times as large as England and Wales; four times as large as Austria-Hungary, or as the whole of Germany, with Belgium, Switzerland, and the Netherlands thrown in; and nearly as large as the whole of British India. At present, however, it contains fewer inhabitants than the town of Birmingham, or the city of Dublin; and its vast area invites settlement by all the disinherited of fortune in the old world, who have strong arms, stout hearts, and willing minds. A few years of persevering effort, combined with sobriety and prudence, will suffice to transform the farm labourer into a well-to-do land-owner; and the skilful artisan into a master tradesman. This, indeed, is the history of hundreds of successful men in this, as in the other colonies. Many a German peasant and many a *bauer*, has exchanged a life of struggle and privation in his Fatherland, for one of comfort, competence, independence, and even affluence in South Australia, where there are whole communities of them, settled in districts upon which they have bestowed such names as Hahndorf, Lobethal, North and South Rhine, Grünthal, Blumberg, Rosenthal, etc., in affectionate remembrance of the country from which they migrated. We allude to these German colonists more particularly because they exhibit, as a general rule—almost invariably, indeed—the best qualities of a settler in a new country. The conditions of life are necessarily hard, at the outset, just as the rewards of pertinacious industry and application are most liberal in the sequel. The immigrant must "rough it" at first. He must work very strenuously; practise vigorous self-denial; and meet temporary difficulties and unforeseen reverses, if not with cheerfulness, at any rate without despondency or dismay. His lot is not one of easy self-indulgence, while he is grubbing his land, building his hut, fencing in his "cultivation paddock," and getting together a cow, some pigs, and some poultry. Until he has "turned the corner," and the proceeds of his first or second crop have placed him in secure possession of the means of subsistence for the next twelvemonth, he is not unfamiliar with anxiety, nor unaccustomed to arduous struggles. But the German, with his quiet perseverance, his stolid submission to the inevitable, his patient and plodding habits, and his steady determination to succeed, rarely fails to do so. He is frugal, even to penuriousness. His wife and children, as soon as the latter are old enough, labour with him, and their joint exertions contribute to the well-being of the family. The English immigrant is not unfrequently an unreasonable malcontent; and the poorer his circumstances were in the old country, the greater are his expectations and the more unreasonable his demands, in the new one. The farm labourer who has been accustomed to earn two shillings, or, at the utmost, half-a-crown, a day, in Hampshire or Sussex, will refuse an offer of five or six shillings a day in one of the colonies, and will prefer to "loaf" about the towns until his last earnings have been spent, and then he will join in a meeting of "the unemployed," and will clamour for work to be provided for him by the State, at six shillings a day, and "the Government stroke." Of course, we are not speaking of a whole class, but of individual members of it; and what we say will be readily borne out by employers of labour in the various colonies, who have experienced how difficult it is to procure hands in some parts of the country, at the very time that men were walking about the metropolis, in a condition of self-impossd idleness, and of actual or pretended destitution.

Now the German, and, indeed, the Continental immigrant generally, will take whatever work he can find, at the current rate of wages; and he will endeavour to support his family, while his crops are growing, by taking a job of fencing, or sheep-washing, or shearing, or shepherding, or dam-sinking, from the neighbouring squatter or estate-owner. He does not care much for political or social agitation. Everything the most advanced liberal could have wished and striven for in the Fatherland, he enjoys as a rational right in Australia. There is no privileged class—outside of Victoria; no standing army, and therefore no compulsory service in the *landwehr* and the *landsturm*; no bureaucratic tutelage and direction; no liability to see his little property devastated by war, or his crops requisitioned by an invading army; no heavy taxes imposed to defray the interest on a national debt, incurred to gratify the sanguinary ambition of military rulers, and to meet the annual outlay upon bloated armaments; and none of the evils incidental to old and thickly peopled countries. He is entitled to exercise the franchise, under protection of the ballot; there is nothing to impede him from becoming a member of the Legislature, if he is a naturalized subject of Her Majesty, nor to prevent him from rising to the highest distinction which the colony can offer. He can purchase, sell, encumber or release, real property, with as much ease as if it were a chattel; and at a very trifling cost. The protection of the law follows him wherever he goes, but does not, as in Germany, limit his freedom of action, by a multitude of petty and irritating restraints; and in every settlement, the State takes care that the schoolmaster shall not be far distant from it. The German appreciates these manifold advantages, more warmly than the average Englishman does, with his national propensity to grumble, and his dissatisfaction with what is undeniably "better," because it does not happen to be the ideally "best." He can bear adversity with a noble fortitude; but prosperity is apt to demoralise him.

South Australia is a really wonderful colony. It is not yet fifty years of age; while its population is about a quarter of a million only. Nevertheless the annual value of its trade, relative to the number of its inhabitants, is greater than that of either New South Wales, Victoria, New Zealand, or Queensland, the figures for 1878 being these:—

	Total trade.	Imports per head.			Exports per head.			Total value per head.		
	£	£	s.	d.	£	s.	d.	£	s.	d.
South Australia...	11,074,632	23	11	1	22	1	0¼	45	12	1¼
New South Wales	27,734,752	21	15	8	19	2	6	40	18	2
Victoria............	31,087,587	18	11	11¼	17	3	6	35	15	5¼
New Zealand	14,771,188	20	15	3½	14	5	4	35	0	7½
Queensland.........	6,626,496	16	12	3¾	15	8	6¾	32	0	10½

It will be observed that the colony of Victoria, which formerly stood at the head of the list, now occupies the third place only. This is attributable to her protectionist policy, which, by artificially lessening imports, diminishes exports *pro tanto*. And as it necessarily contracts the consuming powers of the people, there is a falling-off in the imports, on this account also. The South Australian legislature, which shapes its fiscal policy in accordance with the principles of economic science and with a view to promote the interests of the whole community, and not that of certain privileged classes, aggregated in one or two centres of population, imposes Customs duties for revenue purposes only, and the colony reaps the reward of so patriotic and judicious a system, in the enjoyment of general and widely distributed prosperity. During the cycle of depression, from which the whole civilised world is now emerging, South Australia almost escaped its contagious influences; and there can be no question that there are in that country, reserves of wealth to draw upon, like those which enabled

France to recover with such miraculous celerity from her unparalleled reverses. For the same causes are at work in both countries to produce a durable prosperity. In each a very large percentage of the population is engaged in the pursuits of husbandry; and those who till the soil are also its owners. But while the peasant proprietor in France is heavily taxed, the burdens of the South Australian wheat grower or vigneron are comparatively light. They are only about £2 per head per annum in the colony, as compared with £2 12s. in the former country; while the local taxation in France is very onerous as compared with what it is in South Australia. Taking into consideration the difference in the value of money in the two countries, and that wages are at least four times as high in the colony as they are in France, where the workman rarely makes more than 280 clear days in the year, we shall be within the mark when we say that the French husbandman, or *ouvrier*, is taxed five times as heavily as the corresponding agriculturist or workmen in South Australia.

And this dedication of so much of the capital and industry of the colony to the raising of flocks and the cultivation of the soil, is not merely conducive to the material welfare of the population, but also to its morality and virtue. Men who are engaged from morning till night in out-door pursuits, have not the leisure even if they have the inclination to be vicious; and the occupation they follow induces a fatigue which makes sleep desirable, without occasioning that exhaustion which drives men and women to the use of stimulants; while, on the other hand, any industry which brings people into close and constant contact with the processes and phenomena of nature, tends to awaken and to cause the exercise of the faculties of observation and reflection; so that the natural intelligence of the husbandman is being educated and expanded by the object-lessons of his daily life. At the same time his business is a healthy one, and when pursued under conditions of independence, as it is by the yeomen of these colonies, it is calculated to promote the physical development of the Anglo-Australian race. "Compare," observes a French writer who has never ceased to extol the advantages of a rural, over those of an urban life, "compare a troop of children issuing from a factory with a troop of children brought up in the country and accustomed to field labours; their fresh animated complexions, their somewhat stumpy but robust and agile bodies; their too sonorous voices springing from well-filled lungs; the health, gaiety, and carelessness of their countenances. The work they perform is proportioned to their age and strength, and is, besides, effected in the free and open air. They learn almost unconsciously the duties they have to discharge, and are already engaged in them. Entrusted with the care of animals, they contract an intimate acquaintance with them. Employed in weeding, they begin to distinguish the different characters of plants and soils. Young as they are, they interest themselves in the signs of the weather; and apply themselves to prognosticate its changes according to the symptoms which their elders have taught them to observe. They see the corn germinate and the grape ripen. They are interested in the progress of cultivation, and comprehend the necessity for that toil of which the result is so immediate. They play in the grass, while the factory children play in the mud." And the habits of industry acquired in early life grow with their growth, and strengthen with their strength.

That South Australia has a magnificent future before it, no one can doubt who considers its magnitude; its position, stretching from ocean to ocean; and its exceedingly rich and diversified resources. Besides its wheatfields, its vineyards, and its vast pastures, it possesses stores of mineral wealth, of which the extent and variety can only be matter for conjecture at present. Some of its copper mines have yielded almost fabulous returns. One mine, the Moonta, upon which no capital whatever was expended by the fortunate shareholders, paid them £928,000 in dividends during the fourteen years succeeding its discovery; and the returns from the Burra Burra, are as well-known in Lombard-street as they are in Adelaide. Gold, silver, iron, silver lead, plumbago, bismuth, manganese, antimony, cobalt, kaolin clay, marble, magnesia, nickel, ochre, platinum, native sulphur, shale, dolomite, amethysts, emeralds, opals, sapphires, topazes, and diamonds have also been found; and in the Northern Territory, gold is known to exist over an area of 1700 square miles; from many parts of which, large quantities have been taken, with very imperfect appliances.

Dr. R. Schomburgk, the highly accomplished Director of the Botanical Gardens in Adelaide, describes the predominant orders of the South Australian flora to be the *Leguminosæ, Myrtaceæ, Compositæ, Proteaceæ, Cruciferæ, Rubiaceæ,* and *Gramineæ*; the eucalyptus and the acacia being everywhere predominant. The same excellent authority remarks:—

"The South Australian cereals are considered to be the finest grown in the world; and it is a fact that, with the exception of the intra-tropical, all fruits from other parts of the globe thrive most luxuriantly in South Australia, and come to a perfection, in size and flavour, in the different localities of the colony, hardly known in other countries; and most fruits, vegetables, and useful plants are found to improve materially by the change, as the climatic conditions often succeed in modifying and improving their condition. The finest grapes are grown on the plains; here they ripen to great perfection, and the South Australian wine must soon obtain a high character in the foreign markets. On the plains also grow apricots, peaches, nectarines, oranges, citrons, lemons and shaddocks, plums, cherries, figs, almonds, mulberries, olives, &c., &c., &c.; while in the hills and gullies are grown strawberries, raspberries, currants, walnuts, chestnuts, filberts, &c., &c., of the best quality. In such gullies are also raised the finest vegetables and other culinary herbs, at all seasons, in great abundance, as also on the plains during the rainy season; cauliflowers, often two feet in diameter, are not seldom seen; cabbage, turnips, asparagus, artichoke, leeks, onions, beet, carrots, potatoes, endive, lettuce, radish, celery, &c.; cucumbers, the luscious fruits of the sweet and water melon, pumpkins, &c., growing to a flavour and size which at home would be considered an exaggeration when described."

In fact, we have seen, at horticultural shows in Melbourne and Adelaide, vegetables and fruit of such dimensions as, if stated, would only subject us to the suspicion of wishing to impose upon the credulity of readers at a distance.

With respect to the products capable of being raised with profit by immigrants who are disposed to embark in what the French call small industries, the following are enumerated on the authority of Dr. Schomburgk:—Silk, flax and hemp, beet-root, hops, tobacco, almonds, Zante currants, Sultana and other raisins, olives, the castor-oil plant, mustard, sunflowers, canary seed, grain and maize, caper, chicory, liquorice, osiers, broom millet, esparto grass, opium, cochineal, and perfumes. With respect to the cultivation of olives, for which the soil and climate of South Australia are particularly well-adapted, we may mention that the latest Land Act contains this clause for the encouragement of that branch of horticulture :—

"46. If any selector shall be desirous of engaging in the cultivation of osiers, olives, mulberries, vines, apples, pears, oranges, figs, almonds, or hops, or such other plants as the Governor-in-Council may define by proclamation in the *Gazette*, the planting and cultivating in a husbandlike manner of one acre of land with any of the above trees or plants shall, for all the purposes of this Act, be deemed to be equivalent to the cultivation of six acres of such land as hereinbefore defined : Provided that such cultivating be *bonâ fide* continued and kept up to the satisfaction of the Commissioner until full payment of the purchase-money, but not otherwise : Provided that if such selector shall wish to grow artificial grass, as a rotation of crops, he may, every third year, plant and cultivate lucerne or artificial grass for such purpose, and in that case the planting of three acres of land with lucerne or artificial grass during such third year shall be deemed to be equivalent to the cultivation of one acre of cereal or root crops."

On the subject of growing flowers for perfumes, Dr. Schomburgk has not omitted to point out that nearly all the flowers which yield the necessary material for them, such as mignonnette, verbena, jasmine, rose, laurel, lavender, heliotrope, rosemary, peppermint, violets, wallflowers and oranges, grow luxuriantly in South Australia, to say nothing of the wattle, myallwood, and other native plants, which yield valuable scents.

And this reminds us that we have omitted to mention oranges and lemons as among the choicest products of South Australian orchards. Trees, upwards of forty years old, are to be seen in the neighbourhood of Adelaide and elsewhere, laden with hundreds of dozens of these luscious fruit, while the air is heavy with their faint perfume; and it is pretty certain, that, at no very distant period, a very large trade will spring up between this colony and New South Wales on the one hand, and New

Zealand and Tasmania on the other, in these fruits, which will not grow in the cooler latitudes of these islands.

The manufacturing industries of South Australia are numerous and various, and they possess that stability which results naturally and necessarily from their having escaped being forced into a sickly growth, under favour of a fiscal hot-house. Flour mills, meat-preserving establishments, tanneries, ironfoundries, agricultural implement works, coach and carriage, woollen, hat, boot and shoe, and brush factories, breweries, wine-making establishments, olive oil, jam, dried fruits, tobacco, blacking, sauce and pickle, salt, and confectionery manufactories, afford constant employment, at good wages, to about 7000 persons. Upwards of 3000 are engaged in mining, and nearly 25,000 in husbandry. As the adult male population of the colony is very little over 50,000 persons, of whom 4000 are occupied in trade, 3000 in the conveyance of men and goods, 2700 in personal offices, and 1600 as dealers in food and drinks, it will be seen that there are very few idlers in a community like this, except those who are too young or too old, or are otherwise unable to participate in the active business of life. In fact, the term "working classes" embraces every grade of the community in a young country, and probably none labour more strenuously, or more advantageously, for the whole community than those who do not come within the category of what popularity-hunting demagogues call "the horny-handed sons of toil."

With respect to the vital statistics of South Australia, it will suffice to say that the excess of births over deaths is higher than in any other colony, save that of New Zealand, and that the climate generally is favourable to health and longevity, while even the tropical regions appear to possess a salubrity for Europeans, which regions lying within the same isothermal lines in other parts of the world do not enjoy. The religious and intellectual instruction of the people of the colony is abundantly provided for. It contains 938 places of worship belonging to the various denominations, 580 Sunday schools, besides 420 ordinary schools, to which Government aid is afforded, and in which 34,491 children are receiving instruction during the year, at an annual cost of £150,000. Adelaide, the capital, can boast of its University and its Literary Institute, the latter containing a library of 21,600 volumes, while there are also 78 country institutes.

In conclusion, the live stock statistics of the colony furnish us with the following figures:—

Horses	121,553
Cattle	251,802
Sheep	6,377,812
Pigs	103,422

Thus it will be seen that there is upwards of one head of cattle and twenty-five sheep to every man, woman, and child in South Australia.

We give the following information as matter of interest, not only to those of our readers whose lives have been laid in the Australian colonies, but for the advantage of those who, in other countries of the world, are interested in the progress of the British dependencies.

The following vital statistics with which we have been favoured, show the number of births, marriages, and deaths which were registered in South Australia in the year 1879, and the proportion of births, marriages and deaths to every thousand persons living. They are arranged under the heads of metropolitan, that is Adelaide, and extra-metropolitan, that is the whole of the colony exclusive of the metropolis:—

TOTAL NUMBER OF

DISTRICTS.	Births.	Marriages.	Deaths.
Metropolitan	1394	737	909
Extra-metropolitan	8508	1501	2671
Total	9902	2238	3580

PROPORTION TO EVERY THOUSAND OF THE POPULATION.

DISTRICTS.	Births.	Marriages.	Deaths.
Metropolitan	40·32	21·31	26·30
Extra-metropolitan	35·58	6·80	12·11
Total	38·81	8·77	14·04

From this we see, that the proportion of births in the whole population is nearly three times as many as that of deaths, and that the death-rate is something like a small fraction over fourteen per thousand of the population in the year. This speaks volumes for the climate, and nothing, we venture to say, could be so great an incentive, combined with the temporal advantages which are held out to new settlers, to the emigration of our surplus population from home.

The following table will show at the date of the census of 1871 and of 1876 respectively, the number of persons of each nationality in South Australia:—

	1871.	1876.
South Australia	102,676	128,400
England and Wales	46,752	47,346
Scotland	4,547	8,246
Ireland	14,255	14,053
Other British Possessions	3,469	4,592

FOREIGN STATES.

Germany	8,309	7,659
France	162	247
Other Foreign States	1,194	2,045
Born at sea, ditto	519	503
Unclassified	123	180
Total	185,626	213,271

We thus see that in half a decade there has been an increase in the population of 27,645. We doubt not but that the next census will discover a much larger proportionate increase, more particularly as the great natural wealth of the colony is becoming more widely known. It is gratifying to know that so many nationalities are represented, and the several proportions are not excessive one over the other. According to the population of those countries which are known as Great Britain and Ireland, the emigration is fairly representative; that of Scotland being a little in arrear. The sons of the Fatherland are considerably in excess of those of *La Belle France*; but the cultivation of the vine, which has so largely developed during the last few years, will bring up the average more evenly, and the next census will show a much larger advent of Frenchmen. However, we are glad to see our German brothers in such large numbers, and we trust that those numbers will go on increasing. They are thrifty, hard-working, and sober, and the introduction of this modern Teutonic element deserves the greatest encouragement.

The following table showing the estimated population of South Australia at the end of the year 1879, as well as the increase during the year, will, to a great extent, verify our prognostications of what the increase will be at the next census:—

	Males.	Females.	Total.
Population 1st January, 1879	130,001	118,794	248,795
Increase by excess of births over deaths to end of year	2,922	3,350	6,322
Increase by excess of immigration over emigration by sea to end of year	2,082	2,088	4,170
Population on 31st December	135,055	124,232	259,287
Increase during the year, 1st Jan. to 31st Dec.	5,054	5,438	10,492

There is, according to the two tables we have given, an estimated increase in population in four years of something like 46,016 souls, or nearly double the increase shown by the census taken in 1876, including a period of five years. In this way, when the increase of another year is added, the colony will most certainly be able to record during the five years intervening between 1876 and 1881 more than double the increase which was recorded at the census previously taken, *i.e.*, between 1871 and 1876.

The following return of immigration and emigration by sea during the year 1879, shows the excess of the former over the latter:—

	Males.	Females.	Total.
Immigration	8,962	4,518	13,480
Emigration	6,737	2,400	9,137
Immigration in excess of emigration	2,225	2,118	4,343

From the table of returns showing the general imports into South Australia for 1879 we find the value of the total amounting to the enormous sum of £5,014,149 18s., while the gross amount of duty payable on this sum was £502,839 13s. 11d. This, of course, includes the imports from nearly every civilised country in the world. In enumerating some of these, which will give a general idea of the progress of the colony in commerce, trade, and the various industries, we will give the value as well as the duty payable, and although it may give an approximate idea, yet we must not forget that many of the articles are manufactured in the colony itself.

The value of the agricultural implements proper imported from Victoria was £23, upon which no duty was payable. Here we notice a feature which distinguishes South Australia from its sister colony—Victoria, that while in the latter all agricultural implements are heavily burdened with duty, in the former colony no duty is payable. Hence the great advantage of South Australia over Victoria to those engaged in agricultural pursuits. The value of imports in apparel and slops was £290,635, on which there was a duty charged of £29,023. An interesting feature of the imports is the number of books which, during the year, have found their way into South Australia, showing that while the commerce and trade are flourishing, there is no lack of literary pabulum, and that the number of readers is as large in proportion to the population as in any other country in the civilised world. The value of the books was, in round numbers, £52,000, upon which no duty was payable. Butter valued at £25,025, and cheese at £25,879 2s., no duty being payable on the former article, while the duty paid on the latter amounts to £6327 8s. 6d. These are two natural productions which, with the increase of population and the development of the agricultural resources, must soon cease to be an import, and in a short time present, after supplying the demand of the colony, a sufficient surplus to constitute a large export trade. The imports in grain are gradually decreasing, showing that this branch of commerce is largely cultivated, and will soon itself be a source of wealth through the export trade, which only requires encouragement to be developed to the largest proportions. Many more articles, too numerous to mention, are at present imported which can be grown or supplied to an almost unlimited extent by the colony itself, and which, in a few years, will cease to appear in the table of imports into the colony. We now turn to a more interesting feature, viz., the export trade, presenting to us a fair estimate of the prosperity of the colony, as well as the progress of the development of its own resources. We will start with agricultural instruments manufactured in the colony itself. The value of these articles exported in the year 1879 amounted to £262, or over £200 more than the value of the imported article. The export of apparel amounted in value to £1313, which was manufactured solely in the colony. The amount of beef exported from the colony was valued at £1424; while the value of the exported butter was £2195, and of cheese £220. The amount of barley exported was 2215 bushels, the whole of which was grown in the colony, while its value was £495. One of the most gratifying items in the export trade is that of flour produced and manufactured in the colony itself. There were 70,518 tons, valued at £809,028. This export trade has been rapidly increasing, and is likely soon to be of great importance in a commercial point of view. There were 9258 bushels of oats exported, which were the produce of the colony, the value of which was £1687. The produce of the colony in wheat, which was exported, was 3,376,917 bushels, valued at £818,679 5s. Another gratifying feature in the export trade is the great increase of wine over previous years, viz., 2068 gallons, the total value of which was £984 10s. The growth of the vine is, in all probability, destined to be a great feature amongst the natural productions of South Australia. The total value of the goods exported from the colony during 1877, and which were the productions of, and manufactured in the colony, amounted to £3,957,853 14s. The increase of the exports of the produce of the colony during the nine years intervening between 1870 and 1879, was as follows:—

1870	£2,123,297
1871	3,289,861
1872	3,524,087
1873	4,285,192
1874	3,868,275
1875	4,442,100
1876	4,338,959
1877	3,922,962
1878	4,198,034
1879	3,957,854

So that the increase of 1879 over 1870 was exactly £1,834,557.

The following is a return of the number of life stock imported into and exported from the province of South Australia (overland) during the year ended 31st December, 1879:—

Colony.	Sheep.	Cattle.	Horses.
Imported from			
New South Wales	221,596	8,790	455
Queensland	—	19,632	360
Victoria	38,101	7,659	1,173
Total imported	259,697	36,081	1,988
Exported to			
New South Wales	65,476	234	—
Queensland	—	—	—
Victoria	25,766	—	—
Total exported	91,242	234	—
Excess of imports	168,455	35,847	1,988

The great increase between 1870 and 1879 of imported and exported sheep, cattle, and oxen, may be seen from the following figures:—

	Sheep.		Cattle.		Horses.	
	Imported.	Exported.	Imported.	Exported.	Imported.	Exported.
1870	85,470	88,555	6,348	1,038	275	704
1879	259,697	91,242	36,081	234	1,988	—
Increase	174,227	2,687	27,733	—	1,713	—
Decrease	—	—	—	804	—	704

On the 31st December, 1879, there were 559 miles of railway lines opened out, with a rolling stock valued at £551,446 8s. 9d., and a total of machinery and plant valued at £39,739 19s. The expenditure on these items, including, at the same time, what is known technically as way works and buildings, amounted in all to the enormous sum of £4,103,501 4s. 10d.

The Savings Bank of South Australia, which was opened in 1848, consequently giving it an existence of 31 years, is as flourishing an institution as there is in the colony. The following returns for the years 1848 and 1879 will show the wonderful increase in the savings of the people. In the first-named year, *i.e.*, 1848, the number of accounts opened during the year was 293; while in the year 1879 'the number was 7246. The amount deposited in 1848 was £6473 18s. 3d., while in 1879 it had increased to £583,209 11s. 11d.

We were much interested in the Wallaroo and Moonta copper mines, and as they are of some importance, and are developing a great natural wealth in South Australia, we purpose giving a somewhat full account of our visit.

They are situated on the eastern side of Spencer's Gulf, at the northern end of Yorke Peninsula. The Wallaroo copper mine is about six miles east of Port Wallaroo, while the Moonta copper mine is about twelve miles to the south of the same place. A tramway laid down by the Government connects each mine with the port, and a railway connects the district with Adelaide.

The Wallaroo smelting works at Port Wallaroo, and the Hunter River copper works at Newcastle, New South Wales, are both the property of the " proprietors of the Wallaroo mines," which we may remark is a mining and smelting company, while the "proprietors of the Moonta mines" is a mining company only. A better idea may be formed of the locality, and of its adaptability for copper mining purposes, by a succinct description of its natural features. The Peninsula lies between Spencer's Gulf and the Gulf of St. Vincent, and is about 100 miles in length, with an average breadth of a little more than 20 miles. Some twenty years ago, before the mines were discovered, the northern part of the district, embracing within it the principal mines of South Australia, was occupied by Mr. Walter Watson Hughes as an outlying sheep run. The land for pastoral purposes was inferior, and, in fact, much below the average. There is a level sweep of country, gradually rising towards the centre, which is slightly elevated above the surrounding plain. Some sandhills have been formed in some places by the drifting of the surface soil, which is of the nature of a light sandy loam. The subsoil is a limestone crust of varying thickness, which in a solid mass stretches over the entire district. We were led to suppose that the sea had at no remote period covered this tract of country. Of course, the usual characteristics of Australian scenery known as scrub were to be found there, such as box, dwarf eucalyptus, and wattle, and this was varied by open flats at intervals, extending in some cases to only a few hundred yards, while in others they extended to several miles, and except during a few months in the rainy season, the herbage is as a rule dry and scant, the rainfall being below the average. The primeval character of the country still remains, except in those places which are in the immediate neighbourhood of the mines and the townships, or where agricultural settlement has taken place. Here the country has been denuded of its timber and larger scrubs, for mining or fuel purposes, and presents those features peculiar to the advance of civilisation.

The mines were discovered, in 1860, by two shepherds in the employ of Mr. Hughes. Mr. Hughes had long been convinced from certain surface indications that extensive and valuable deposits of copper ore would be found, and that this great source of wealth was simply waiting exhumation. Stones of copper ore had been found on the sea beach, evidently washed down by the rains from the low cliffs near the head station, and though attempts were made to trace them inland, these attempts were unsuccessful. Mr. Hughes had not only noticed, but drawn attention to the fact that the wood, which was cut from a particular spot and used for fuel in a shepherd's hut, burned with a greenish-hued flame, such as might have arisen from the presence of copper in the sap, and he consequently instructed his men to bring to him any likely-looking stones which might be found. The hopeful and enthusiastic spirit of Mr. Hughes stimulated his men, and this, seconded by the hope of substantial benefit to themselves, caused a keen watch to be kept, and small heaps of ore and ore-stained limestone were found from time to time without, however, resulting in any discovery of importance, until one day a shepherd, named James Boor, came across a mound which had been thrown up by a native rat, and, on observing it, discovered that it was strewn with small stones of ore. Taking the matter somewhat coolly, he did not, until a day or two afterwards, whilst on a visit to the head station, mention the fact of his discovery to Mr. Duncan, the manager, who at once had a hole dug on the spot, and forwarded to Mr. Hughes samples of the ore which was found. This resulted in Mr. Hughes at once securing mineral leases, and testing the discovery, and this beginning has now developed into what has since that time been known as the Wallaroo mine. The Moonta mine, which is much more valuable, was discovered some months later. This mine was found by another of Mr. Hughes's shepherds named Patrick Ryan. The mineral wealth which lay hid in this mine was evidenced by surface indications much more extensive than at the Wallaroo.

The development of the mines has been greatly facilitated by their proximity to Port Wallaroo, where there is an excellent harbour. There smelting works were at once erected for the purpose of converting the ore into copper. The construction and economical working of tramways between the mines and the port were considerably facilitated by the level nature of the country. Separate joint-stock companies were formed. The Moonta Mining Company undertook the working of the later discovery, while the first discovery was developed by the Wallaroo Mining and Smelting Company, by whom smelting works were erected to reduce the ores of both mines. It is a matter deserving of honourable mention that both companies were carried on without the necessity of subscribing capital, although not with such ease and facility in the one case as in the other, for while in the case of the Moonta mine, one lode after another was discovered revealing almost fabulous richness, and so making the working of it comparatively easy, it was only through the indomitable perseverance and unwavering faith of the principal proprietor, Mr. Hughes, and through the pecuniary aid which was provided for him by the well-known commercial firm of Elder, Stirling and Co. (now Elder, Smith and Co.), that the Wallaroo was successfully brought through its first difficulties. The building of smelting works at Port Wallaroo was followed some years afterwards by the erection of similar works, but on a smaller scale, at Newcastle, New South Wales. The works at Newcastle were erected because of the want of coal or other suitable fuel in South Australia, and in this way a great saving was effected in the cost of reducing the ores, a coal fleet being constantly employed in bringing coal to Wallaroo to smelt the richer ores, and carrying back the poorer ores to be smelted at Newcastle, which was facilitated by the fact that the coal for that purpose could be procured on the spot.

The mining leases are held from the South Australian Government, and comprise 2098 acres in respect of the Wallaroo mine, and 2691 acres in respect of the Moonta mine. These leases were granted originally for the period of 14 years, at a low rental, with a right of renewal for the same period on payment of a fine. However, they have now been exchanged and consolidated under the Crown Lands Consolidation Act into leases for 99 years, at an annual rental of 1s. per acre, and a royalty of $2\frac{1}{2}$ per cent. on the realised or declared profits.

Although the proprietaries of the two mines are entirely distinct, it has been found a matter of expediency and convenience to place them under the superintendence of one and the same manager, with distinct sets of subordinate officers. The combined management of the two mines has been entrusted to Mr. H. R. Hancock, who was the superintendent of the Moonta mine, and who proved himself in every way so able, as well as so successful, in that position. We are glad to record that the present arrangement works well and satisfactorily. The communication between the various parts of the extensive works at the Moonta mine is facilitated by the use of the telephone, and for the convenience of the management a wire has lately been connected with the Wallaroo mine, a distance of 12 miles.

With regard to the nature of the copper ore, and ore-bearing strata of the Moonta mine, we may mention that the lodes are formed as near as possible in a line running in a northerly and southerly direction, and traverse a porphyritic rock formation. The green ore (hydrous oxychloride of copper) is not only found near the surface, but also from the surface to a depth from 10 to 15 fathoms, and often in large masses. Below that depth, only small quantities are occasionally found, which may, in fact, be regarded as mere specimens. Native copper is found at a depth ranging from seven to twenty fathoms, and is frequently to be found in company with rich black ore in somewhat large quantities. Below that depth only occasional patches are found. The red oxide of copper in a crystallised and massive state is only to be found in occasional places at a depth of twelve fathoms, where the lodes are intersected by cross courses. The grey sulphide is usually found under the oxides, while the purple sulphide, and copper pyrites of various classes, are found at all depths below the shallow levels. We are told that some very rich copper pyrites, yielding 30 per cent. of pure metal, and some very rich purple sulphide, yielding 50 per cent., have recently been disclosed at the deepest level in the mine, viz., 200 fathoms. The ores, we understand, when dressed, average 20 per cent. of fine copper.

A similar order respecting the ores obtains at the Wallaroo mines, but they are not so rich in metal, the ores, when dressed, averaging only ten per cent. of fine copper. In this mine there are altogether five ore-producing lodes, some of which are nearly parallel, being however somewhat connected by cross courses and oblique branches, which to a certain extent may be regarded as a complete chain of mineral veins. They run in a direction east and west, and the rock through which they pass may be chiefly characterised as a chloritic schist.

With regard to the treatment of the ores in the Wallaroo mines, we may state that the average of the output is about ten per cent., and the treatment consists in greater part of classification, very little being done in the way of dressing them to a higher standard. This arises chiefly from the difficulties presented by the too nearly approaching specific gravities of the ore and the gangue with which it is associated. The ores are hand picked and broken to a size such as to admit of their passing through a three inch ring, and in that form sent to the smelting works. Here they are prepared for smelting by calcination and crushing.

At the Moonta mine a very small proportion of the ore as raised is worth 20 per cent., the great bulk of it being vein-stuff of a very poor quality as broken, which can only be profitably worked through the very fine dressing machinery which is erected on the mine, a part of which, the well-known Hancock's jigger, was invented and patented by the present superintendent. Nearly the whole of the vein-stuff has to be lifted by means of inclines and tram-waggons to what are called stonebreakers. It passes through the jaws of these to the crusher-rolls, and thence to the jiggers, from which it is discharged in different qualities, varying from 16 to 25 per cent. The labour cost is reduced to a minimum, through the apparatus, both for crushing and jigging, being for the most part automatic. One very remarkable feature in the appearance of the mine, and which is worthy of notice, is the immense hills of what are known as "tailings," which are the results of years of accumulation from the various sets of crushing and jigging machinery. We noticed that the largest of these piles was in the neighbourhood of Richman's engine-house, and that its height varied from 30 to 60 feet, the outside portion of the hill averaging about 59 perpendicular feet. This hill alone covers an area of about three and one-third acres. The hills consist of small pieces of quartz and other vein-stuff, being, as stated, the waste from the jiggers, and present to the eye a pinkish hue of great beauty, arising from the presence of the porphyritic rock. These vast accumulations may be accounted for through much of the veinstone raised from underground consisting of quartz and other waste, being in great part intermixed with copper pyrites, with an occasional mixture of purple sulphide. The stuff, however, is sometimes so poor that 20 tons, and even 30 tons, have to be crushed and jigged to obtain one ton of dressed ore of 20 per cent. This, through the admirable arrangement of the operations, can be done profitably, which is a great desideratum. These piles of tailings have been carefully sampled and tried by different assayers, one pile giving three-quarters per cent. of fine copper, another pile one-half per cent., while a third gave at the rate of one-fourth per cent. Occasionally, assays have been made which have given over one per cent. of fine copper. When the waste is found to contain as much as this, it is so placed in the pile as to be convenient for further pulverising and turning to account in the event of an advance in the price of copper rendering it profitable to do so. Although the jigging machinery effectually separates in most cases all the solid ore from the crushed veinstone, it is sometimes mixed up with the rock in such minute particles that nothing but a thorough pulverising of the waste will effect a separation. For this purpose, a battery of stamps is used, and the copper remaining in the waste is extracted by an elaborate and very perfect system of buddles, both Cornish and German. Water, led from an artificial reservoir, feeds both the jigging machinery and buddles, so that the stoppage of pumping operations does not cause a corresponding stoppage of the dressing operations.

About 100 to 150 tons of stuff per diem can be worked by one of the patent jiggers. We were given to understand that, a short time ago, an experiment was made in the way of extracting copper from the waste by the process of precipitation, with certain satisfactory results.

With regard to the buildings and machinery, we noticed that at both the mines the offices, engine-houses, and surface appliances were, as a rule, of the most complete and substantial character. Extensive workshops for the mechanical department have been erected, and these are, at the Moonta mine especially, on a most complete scale. All the latest and most approved appliances for economising labour are to be found, and we noticed that all the requirements for the mine, which it was found could be economically turned out on the spot, were manufactured under the superintendence of Mr. Hancock, ranging from the largest castings and machinery, to the candle and safety-fuse of the miner. A perfect forest of pulley-stands studs the grounds, carrying the wire-hauling ropes from the winding-engines to the various shafts from which the vein-stuff is drawn, and by which the miners ascend and descend to their work. The pit work is maintained in most efficient order both underground and on the surface. The men are conveyed to and from their work underground by means of what are known as man-skips, running between timber fitted in the shafts. In this way, a great amount of energy and time is economised, which was formerly wasted in climbing up and down the ladders. These man-skips are provided not only with self-acting breaks, which are put into operation by the breakage of the rope, but also with a powerful lever, which can be worked by the men inside and made to grip the skip road on the least sign of danger. The water is drained from the mines by powerful and well-acting machinery. At the Wallaroo mine, there are three Cornish pumping-engines, each having a 60 inch cylinder and 10 feet stroke, one of which only is required to work ordinarily at anything approaching its capability. These are supplemented by various engines of less power, which are also used for hauling the vein-stuff, and supplying the mechanical shops with steam power. As there is less influx of water at the Moonta mine, it has been found necessary to erect only one large pumping engine, the pumping from the various shafts throughout the mine being accomplished mainly by connection with this one, as well as with the engines which are used for other purposes. Three large crushing engines, with from 32 to 35 inch cylinders, do the crushing of all the vein-stuff in connection with the dressing machinery. In addition to these, there are six principal hauling engines, with others of less power, in the shops and elsewhere. We were glad to observe that Darlington's rock-boring machinery, which is worked by compressed air, has been introduced at the Moonta mine in connection with the sinking of the deepest of the main shafts, and has been successfully used for that purpose for the last 40 fathoms of sinking. Some driving, we are told, has also been done with it, simultaneously with the sinking, and with equal advantage. The average rate of speed of sinking and driving has been double that which could be obtained from hand-drills and manual labour. It is in contemplation, we understand, to introduce the same kind of rock-boring machinery at the Wallaroo mine.

During the past two or three years, the superintendent of the Wallaroo and Moonta mines has introduced, in connection with their working, a system of submitting all the underground work to public tender, including such of the surface work as the system could be advantageously applied to. Some of these contracts have embraced 50 or 100 fathoms of driving, or the removal by stoping of an entire block of ore lying between the levels, or the sinking of a considerable portion of a shaft. To complete each of these sometimes requires a period of from 12 to 18 months. The advantages of this system both to employer and employed are obvious, and it has been found to work much more satisfactorily than the old system of letting short contracts to the men. One proof of its superiority is that it is more popular among efficient miners than among those who are less so. A percentage of the work done, generally $12\frac{1}{2}$ per cent., is retained by the company from each monthly pay of the men as a guarantee of the due fulfilment of the contracts, which are all entered into by the tenderers, subject to the general rules of the mine. These rules, we are glad to say, reflect great credit upon the proprietaries, inasmuch as they are stringent in prohibiting any acts or modes of working on the part of the men which might tend to endanger either their own or the lives of others. No one, we are told, against whom a breach of the rules can be proved, can, in cases of injury received, claim relief from the club-fund. Accidents, especially fatal ones, are very few in number. The wages earned by the miners under such a system as this are, of course, unequal, varying according as the men are good or inferior workmen, and as the contracts may go in their favour or otherwise. Miners average from £1 15s. to £2 10s. per week, and surface men from 5s. to 6s. per day, while mechanics receive full rates of wages, in proportion to their calling and skill. In judging of these wages, we must bear in mind that nearly all the men employed on the mines, by the circumstance of their residence on the mineral section, are exempt from rent, as well as corporation rates.

One very interesting feature of the mines is what may be called the provident institutions. A doctor fund and club fund have been established from the commencement of the mines by both the companies, and are exclusively for the benefit of the workmen, who are required by the mine rules to subscribe to them, the deductions being made from their wages by the mines' office, and credited to the funds. These funds are administered by the mine authorities, payments being made from them with all necessary precaution. Married men subscribe 1s. per week to the doctor fund; single men, 6d.; and boys, 3d. In return, they have free medical attendance and medicine. One advantage is that the men can choose their own medical man. The contributions to the fund are paid once a month to the doctors in exact proportions, and this duty belongs to the accountant. The subscriptions to the club fund are 6d. weekly by all adult members, and 3d. per week by the boys. In return, they are entitled to draw—the men 2s. and the boys 1s. per day, in case of sickness. In addition to this, in case of the death of the subscriber, or any of his family, he is entitled to an amount sufficient to pay the funeral expenses. There is a provision that no one can remain on the fund, in case of sickness, more than 12 months. The men and boys are also members of one or more of the friendly societies, from which sick pay and other benefits are derived. Many of the workmen have a considerable amount of money in the Savings Bank, proved from the fact that at the close of last year the deposits in the Moonta Savings Bank alone amounted to £18,296, while thousands of pounds are known to be out at interest on other securities. The whole of these moneys are the savings of the miners.

In referring to the social and moral condition of the people, we can scarcely dissociate them from the condition under which the settlement of the district has taken place. At the last census, in 1876, the total population of those depending almost wholly on these two mines, and some smaller ones, combined with a small agricultural element, was 15,899. About 5000 of these are resident in the Government towns of Moonta and Kadina, adjacent to the Moonta and Wallaroo mines respectively, and at Port Wallaroo, leaving 10,000 as the number resident on the mineral sections of the various mining companies, the balance being farmers and others. In consequence of the leases containing a clause prohibiting the carrying on of any other business on the section than mining, the rapid development of the mines led, as a matter of course, to the laying out and sale by the Government, of townships in the neighbourhood, for the purposes of business operations. But in spite of this, the greater proportion of those employed on the mines preferred to squat on the mineral leases in close proximity to them. This they did without any title other than the tacit consent of the Government and the lessees, and thus the mining townships have gradually sprung up. Very little was done in the early days to preserve regularity in the way in which these townships were grouped, and consequently they present an appearance wanting in order. The favourite building materials of the miners were pines and battens, cut from the adjoining scrub, formed into a framework, and filled in with mud and stones, all of which were to be found close at hand. The covering of the cottage is of palings, and the whole presents a certain homeliness of appearance and comfort, which are added to by small plots of garden ground, tastefully laid out and carefully cultivated. The interior of the houses is, for the most part, ceiled and plastered, and comfortably furnished, far beyond what one might expect from their external appearance. This somewhat original mode of settlement has had a most marked effect upon the social and moral well-being of the people, especially from the fact that this population of 10,000 souls is living under what is virtually a prohibitory liquor law, at least so far as public-houses are concerned, the result of which has been most satisfactory. The evidence of local magistrates, clergymen, and medical men, given before a commission which was recently appointed by the Government to inquire into the working of the liquor laws, is unanimous and most conclusive as to the benefits which have resulted from it. The Government townships adjacent, with the usual number of public-houses, furnish instances of drunkenness sufficiently numerous, while such cases in the mining townships are not only rare, but so much so, that we heard that hundreds of the children have never seen a drunken man. The calendar of crime is lighter in this district than any other in South Australia, the convictions for crime in Moonta being 1 to 100 of the population, as against 1 to 25 for the whole of the province. Convictions for drunkenness are 1 to 180, as against 1 to 60 for the whole of the colony. One policeman is found sufficient for the whole of the Moonta mine population, while at Kadina and Wallaroo mine there has never been more than one policeman for the whole population of both Government and mining townships. Besides the usual proportion of churches, chapels, and an institute in each of the corporate towns, there are on the mining townships numerous chapels, some of them capable of seating more than 1000 people. Centrally situated on each mine, are a reading-room and library, supported by the voluntary contributions of the men, the proprietors having made a free gift of the building and furniture. The libraries are only excelled by those in Adelaide.

Sanitary matters have not been altogether so satisfactory as could be wished. Since the appointment, however, of a local board of health, and the construction of drains to carry off flood-waters, as well as the surplus waters drawn from the mines, to such a distance as to render it innocuous, the general health has much improved. No water other than that which is very brackish or purely salt being procurable in the district, the water supply has been for long a source of much anxiety. The miners depended entirely on the rain-water, which was led from the surface of the ground, or from the roofs of the houses, into rudely-constructed tanks, and the result was sickness arising from its impurity, or a water famine in seasons of drought. The usual resource was the water distilled from the engines, but now a number of tanks or dams have been constructed by Government, where rain water flowing into them over a clean surface is now stored for general use and for contingencies.

Since the new Education Act has been in force, we noticed that good schools had been erected in central positions on the mineral sections. The one at Moonta mine is the largest State-school in the colony, and, judging by the official returns, one of the most ably conducted. Another important and interesting feature is the night schools, which are available for those whose occupation does not admit of attendance at day schools. We must not omit to mention that in this district the compulsory clauses of the Act are in force.

The following statistics refer to the mines only, except in the case of the dividends paid by the Wallaroo Company, which include the profits of the smelting works as well:—

	Wallaroo Mine.	Moonta Mine.
Total ore raised from 1860 to 1879 inclusive	348,437 tons.	357,864 tons.
Average percentage	10 per cent.	20 per cent.
Representing in fine copper	33,250 tons.	71,572 tons.

	Wallaroo Mine.	Moonta Mine.
Average yearly production of ore	17,422 tons.	18,834 tons.
The maximum output in one year	29,076 tons.	23,608 tons.
Total expenditure	£1,489,649	£2,727,700
Average annual expenditure	£74,482	£143,563
Average cost per ton of raising the ore, including the amounts written off yearly for depreciation of buildings, plant, &c.	£4 2s. 9d.	£7 1s. 11d.
Number of hands employed when in full work	800	1267
Maximum number in one year	1003	1687
Total amount divided amongst the shareholders	£372,256	£1,024,000

The Wallaroo Smelting Works have twenty-one calcining kilns, one Oxland and Hocking's mechanical calciner, and thirty-four reverberatory furnaces, including six for refining. There are also two crushing engines, with machinery and mechanical workshops, besides offices and a complete laboratory. The ores smelted are those, as we have said, which are the production of the Wallaroo and Moonta mines. The process employed is a modification of the ordinary Welsh method of smelting. A portion of the ore is calcined either in the mechanical calciners or in the kilns, the *smalls* being treated in the former and the roughs in the latter. A mixture of raw ore and calcined, with slag in proper proportion, is charged into the smelting furnaces. When the charge is smelted, the slag is skimmed off, and the regulus or metal is tapped out into moulds formed in sand. The slag is thrown away, and the regulus is ready for further treatment. It is charged into another furnace, and after suitable treatment by the combined action of heat and air the result is attained in the form of rough copper, which only requires to be refined and ladled into suitable moulds to render it ready for shipment. The average number of charges per week for each furnace in the first smelting operation, as described above, is 22 of about three tons each, and for the second operation four charges of about seven tons of regulus. For the refining process the charge is about nine tons of rough copper per 24 hours. The regulus contains about 48 per cent. and the rough copper about 81 per cent. of fine copper respectively. Nearly all the furnaces work through a large culvert into one chimney 120 feet high and 15 feet square.

The process employed at the Hunter River copper works is the ordinary Welsh method, with but a few minor modifications. The ore treated consists almost entirely of copper pyrites from the Wallaroo and Moonta mines, intermixed more or less with iron pyrites, quartz, etc. A portion of the ore is calcined in the ordinary single-bed calcining furnace, the charge being about six tons, which remains in the furnace 24 hours. The charge for the reducing furnace is made up of raw and calcined ore, slag, etc. The result of the first smelting process is slag and metal in regulus, the slag being thrown away. The regulus contains about 30 per cent. of copper. The process of roasting which this now undergoes is, at this establishment, conducted in two operations, the final result being rough copper of about 93 per cent. This is then ready for refining, after which process it is ladled out into ingot or cake moulds, and is then ready for shipment. The charge for each reducing furnace is about three tons of ore, and 25 such charges are smelted per week. The furnaces here for the most part work into separate small chimneys.

Finally, we may state that the total number of men employed at both smelting works is about 300, the maximum being in one year about 383. The quantity of ore which has been treated in them since their erection has been 618,081 tons, with a maximum in one year of 61,458 tons. The quantity of copper which has been made is 84,802 tons, with a maximum in one year of 7280 tons. All the copper is of one quality, chiefly made into cakes weighing about 100lbs., and ingots weighing 14lbs.; the brand "Wallaroo."

We strongly recommend all visitors to South Australia to inspect these works, which will astonish, instruct, and interest.

CHAPTER V.

TASMANIA.

ITS SETTLEMENT FROM NEW SOUTH WALES—THE CAPUA OF AUSTRALIA—ITS MOUNTAINS AND LAKES—ITS ELIGIBILITY AS A PLACE OF RESIDENCE—ITS PICTURESQUE SCENERY—ITS THOROUGHLY ENGLISH CHARACTER—MOUNT WELLINGTON, AND THE PROSPECT FROM ITS SUMMIT—LAUNCESTON AND ITS ENVIRONS—POPULATION OF THE ISLAND—ITS AGRICULTURAL PRODUCTS—IMPORTS AND EXPORTS OF THE ISLAND—GENERAL AND WIDELY DIFFUSED PROSPERITY OF ITS INHABITANTS—WELL-TO-DO CONDITION OF THE GREAT MASS OF THE PEOPLE THROUGHOUT THE WHOLE OF AUSTRALIA—MINERAL WEALTH OF TASMANIA—LARGE YIELD OF ONE OF ITS TIN MINES—TOTAL LIVE STOCK IN THE ISLAND—ACCUMULATIONS OF THE PEOPLE—PUBLIC INSTRUCTION—PLACES OF WORSHIP—VITAL STATISTICS OF TASMANIA, AS AN EVIDENCE OF ITS EXTREME SALUBRITY.

TASMANIA may be called the eldest daughter of New South Wales, from whence it was originally colonised, as an auxiliary settlement, in the year 1803; so that, like its parent, it has a very respectable antiquity—as antiquity goes in a part of the world where time is so pregnant with events, and so fruitful of progress, that decades are equivalent to centuries elsewhere. The garden-island—as it is affectionately termed by those who are most familiar with its beauty, fertility, and salubrity—was discovered by Tasman, in 1642, who named it in honour of the then Governor-General of Batavia, "Antoni Van Diemen's Landt." Painful and humiliating associations eventually came to be associated with this appellation, and it was exchanged for the more euphonious one of Tasmania, by which, also, an appropriate compliment was paid to its adventurous discoverer. Captains Furneaux and Cook both visited the island; but no attempt was made to explore the interior until the date of its settlement, seventy-seven years ago; at which time Lieut. Bowen landed at Risden, on the Derwent, when that river was surveyed in the south, as the Tamar was soon afterwards in the north. As we are not writing a history of the island, we need not trace the progress made in its colonisation, nor follow the fluctuations of its political and social annals. Enough to say that it was, at a very early period, constituted a separate colony, and placed under a governor of its own; that

H

representative institutions were conferred upon it in 1850; and that three years afterwards, it was relieved of the reproach, and saved from the further injury, of being a penal settlement, to the extreme delight, although to the temporary injury, of the great bulk of the inhabitants, who had necessarily benefited as well by the large expenditure of the Imperial Government upon the convict establishments, as by the labour of the convicts themselves, most of whom were employed in roadmaking, and in the execution of other equally useful public works. As nearly thirty years have passed away since the abolition of transportation to what was then Van Diemen's Land, the convict element has been almost, and will soon be altogether, eliminated from the population. Some day its very existence will have become a vague tradition, like that which made the Capitoline hill at Rome a sort of Alsatia for the fugitive rogues and vagabonds of the thirty towns of Latium.

The capital of Tasmania may never become another Rome, but in all likelihood it will stand, hereafter, in the same relation to such cities as Sydney, Melbourne, Adelaide, and Brisbane, which Pompeii and Baiæ once did to the metropolis of Italy. An English tourist has denominated the island "The Capua of the Australias;" but accurate and felicitous as the epithet is in some respects, it is inapplicable in others. A memorable incident in the life of Hannibal has caused us to associate languid and enervating influences with the place at which he wintered after annihilating the Roman legions, but the inhabitants of the colonies on the mainland repair to Tasmania, to be fortified and invigorated by its pure and bracing air, as well as to delight their eyes with its picturesque and charmingly diversified scenery.

The area of the island is nearly equal to that of Ireland, and its climate is not unlike that of the Isle of Wight and Jersey. Its mountains resemble those of Scotland, while its lake scenery will recall to the recollection of the English tourist, similar features in the landscapes of Cumberland and Westmoreland. Of the mountains, the more conspicuous are Ben Lomond in the north, and Mount Wellington in the south. The former attains an altitude of 5010 feet, which is only 59 feet less than that of the Cradle Mountain, the loftiest peak of Tasmania; while Mount Wellington only reaches a height of 4166 feet. But what the ranges of this island want in altitude they make up for in massiveness of bulk and grandeur of outline; and this applies more especially to the huge giant which overlooks Hobart Town, and to the grand mass which rises up from the valley of the South Esk, much as Mount Soracte does from the surrounding plain, although it can only be occasionally said of Ben Lomond that *Stet nive candidum*.

Most of the lakes of Tasmania are to be found in the depressions of elevated plateaux, where they form so many natural reservoirs, which will prove of incalculable value for the irrigation of the more low-lying country, hereafter. That which is known as the Great Lake is nearly thirteen miles long; and with an average width of about three miles, it sometimes broadens into eight. Its superficial area is estimated at 28,000 acres. It is encircled by forests, and the line of the horizon is broken by the undulating silhouettes of a tier of mountains to the west. Lakes Sorell and Crescent, which are connected by a stream, cover about 17,000 acres, while Lake St. Clair, the next in magnitude, is roughly estimated to comprise 10,000 acres within its limits. In point of picturesqueness, it may be said, perhaps, to bear away the palm from all its rivals, as upon one side rises the august form of Mount Olympus, and upon the other Mount Ida confronts the eye; and a little to the northward of this isolated eminence, a grand range of unexplored mountains lends additional beauty to the scene.

We do not know any part of Australia more eligible as a place of residence for the half-pay officer; the annuitant; the invalid who wishes to escape from the cruel east winds, the fogs and the inclemency of English winters; the Anglo-Indian, debilitated by a long residence in Hindostan; the British farmer, with a limited amount of capital and a large family; or the possessor of a modest competence, who finds himself unable to adjust his income to the high standard of expenditure, which the growth of wealth in the mother-country has imposed upon all persons in independent circumstances, than the island of Tasmania. Its picturesque scenery, its salubrious climate, its natural products, the cheapness of living, the many points of resemblance which it offers to Old England, and the numerous opportunities of recreation it offers to the sportsman and naturalist, combine to render it peculiarly attractive to immigrants of the better class. Its towns and villages, its country mansions and farmhouses, its highroads and green lanes, its orchards and its hop gardens, are all redolent of the mother-country. "There is a green lane at New Norfolk," a village so called, "than which," writes Mr. James Smith, "I know of nothing more thoroughly English in the pages of Mary Russell Mitford; or on the canvas of Gainsborough, Constable, or Creswick; or in the beautiful county of Kent itself. All the elements of the picturesque are there—the lofty hedgerows, white with blossom in the spring, and crimson with berries in the autumn; the luxuriant foliage, the winding lane, the sweet breath of the new-mown hay, the sweep of the scythe through the long grass, and the rustic bridge spanning a brawling brook. The hop-gardens, with their long-drawn aisles of vivid green, the delicate curves and spiral movements of the graceful vine, the sunshine dropping in golden rifts, and the shadows falling in dark brown lines: all hint of good old Saxon Kent. So do the gurgling runnels, that wind away in the secrecy and darkness among the pollard willows, until they empty their waters into a stream, cool, shadowy, transparent, and impetuous—such as Sir Humphrey Davy or Christopher North would have delighted to angle in, and old Isaak Walton would have loved to have written about. But the blue over-arching sky, and the bright bland, balmy air are redolent of Italy; while the glorious mountains which enclose and frame this charming picture recall to recollection some of the softer parts of Switzerland." Essentially English, too, are the names of the counties; for these include another Kent, as beautiful as its prototype, containing like it a seaside Ramsgate, Hythe, and Folkestone; another Devon, Dorset, Somerset, and Cornwall; another Buckingham, Lincoln, and Westmoreland; and another Pembroke, Monmouth, and Glamorgan; while the names of British worthies are commemorated by the counties of Wellington, Russell, and Franklin.

What Mr. Martineau says of the island* is perfectly true :—" Without a large income, Arcadian luxury of climate, scenery, and quiet may be enjoyed in Tasmania. It is the perfection of retired country life. If there is in general not much wealth, there are almost always comfort and plenty." And after describing the really magnificent scenery to be met with in all directions in the immediate neighbourhood of Hobart Town, the southern capital the same impartial writer proceeds to ask, " Can any country be more perfectly delightful ? Once mounted (and, rich or poor, there are few who cannot possess or borrow a horse of some sort in Tasmania), one is free with a freedom known only in dreams to dwellers in the old country of hedges and Enclosure Acts, where to quit the dreary flinty roads is to trespass and to break the law. One's first reflection is on the astonishing folly of humanity in neglecting to inherit it. Surely there must be many wearied with the crowd, and strife, and ugliness of English cities, who, brought to a virgin forest such as this (on the banks of the Huon), would be ready to sing their *Nunc Dimittis* in thankfulness that it had been permitted them to exist in such beauty, to have their dreams helped to the imagination of the glory of the new heavens and the new earth."

Strangers to the scenery of Tasmania might suspect Mr. Martineau of exaggerating its natural beauty, but every one who has explored the localities he has described, who has watched the sun rise from the summit of Mount Wellington, and has followed the course of one of the springs which are formed on its table top, through its stony channel, and alongside its sounding cataract, and through its sylvan outfall into the Huon, will acknowledge "the glory" of the varying landscape, and the wonderful variety and freshness of its never-failing charms. The view from the cairn erected by the trigonometrical surveyors—the pinnacle, as it is called—of Mount Wellington has been thus described by a Victorian visitor :—" Of the magnificence of the prospect from Mount Wellington one may say as Mark Antony said of Cleopatra's beauty,

> Age cannot wither it,
> Nor custom stale its infinite variety.

The vastness of the field of vision, the lucid transparency of the atmosphere, and the interchange of mountain, valley, sea, and river combine to fascinate

---

* *Letters from Australia* : By John Martineau. London, 1869.

your gaze at the time, and to haunt your memory for ever afterwards. And the very clouds which occasionally blur the scene confer additional beauties on it; for sometimes as they break away to seaward they disclose one of the islands in the estuary so completely detached from the line of the horizon as to appear as if suspended in the heavens; and sometimes a strong sunbeam striking on the valley of the Huon, while all around is mist and purple shadow, kindles the tract of country it illuminates into such a lustre that it appears to be absolutely transfigured, and recalls to your recollection the light which abode upon the Land of Goshen when impenetrable darkness had settled upon the rest of Egypt. As it flashes in the sunlight, or fades in the shadow, the Derwent gleams like a sheet of burnished silver, or assumes the colour of a turquoise; while the undulating country inland seems to advance towards, or to recede from you, according as it vividly reveals itself in the light, or grows indistinct in transitory gloom. The city itself, sloping to the water's edge, looks like the collection of the tiniest of toy houses dropped by a child in careless play; and the altitude at which you stand, coupled with the amazing extent of country comprehended in the view, enables you to realise the prospect visible from a balloon."

Mount Wellington, Mount Nelson, and Mount Knocklofty, are all within walking distance of Hobart Town. Other points, remarkable for their natural beauty, such as the Salvator Rosa Glen, the Fern Tree Valleys, the Bower, and New Town, are equally easy of access to the pedestrian; while the equestrian can visit Brown's River, the Thorn, Rokeby, Richmond, New Norfolk, Glenorchy, and the Salmon Ponds.

Launceston, the northern capital, has also some exceedingly romantic and picturesque scenery in its immediate vicinity; such as the Rocky Gorge of the South Esk River, the Devil's Punch Bowl, and Corra Linn, a spot which recalls, in many of its features, the famous cataract it is named after, and described by Sir Walter Scott as having been the scene of the interview between Morton and Balfour of Burley, in one of the concluding chapters of "Old Mortality." The coast scenery of the island is full of grandeur and sublimity, owing in a great measure to the columnar formation and huge dimensions of the basaltic cliffs which form, in places, its massive sea-wall.

The electoral district of Hobart Town contains a population in round numbers of 20,000, while that of Launceston is nearly 11,000; and there are nearly 70,000 persons distributed in the towns and villages of the interior; so that an island which, as we have said, is almost as large as Ireland, contains fewer inhabitants than the county of Kilkenny, or than the town of Belfast, although it could with ease support a population of three or four millions at the very least. Of the seventeen millions of acres comprised within its geographical limits, less than one-fourth has been alienated from the Crown. About two millions and a-quarter of acres are held by pastoral or other tenants, under licenses or leases. There are 355,403 acres under cultivation for cereals, root crops, artificial grasses, orchards, hop gardens, and otherwise. The average produce of the soil under anything but scientific methods of farming, was as under, during the last five years:—

Wheat	...	17·68 bushels per acre.	
Barley	...	24·07	,, ,,
Oats	...	24·67	,, ,,
Potatoes	...	3·42 tons	,,
Hay	...	1·26 ,,	,,
Hops	...	1318 lbs.	,,

The orchard produce, in so far as it is enumerated, ranges from 130,000 to 170,000 bushels of apples, and from 10,000 to 30,000 bushels of pears per annum; but a large amount of the smaller varieties of fruit is converted into jam every year, and the export of this article, and of fruit and vegetables, in 1878, was of the value of £172,000. To European readers these figures—like Australian statistics generally—may appear small, by comparison with those which express the magnitude of national transactions in the old world; but, as all measures and dimensions are relative, so the productive industries and the commercial exchanges of a new country must be measured in relation to the number of its inhabitants; and, when this is done, it will be found that both are very considerable when they come to be divided by the number of persons engaged in them.

The total value of the imports of Tasmania for the year 1878, reached the respectable figure of £1,324,812, while that of the exports amounted to £1,315,695; the excess of the former over the latter, showing a much smaller profit than might have been anticipated; but during the five previous years, the totals had shown thus:—

Imports	£5,992,568
Exports	5,452,815

Showing a profit balance of £539,753

And it is not improbable that, as the year 1878 was one of great mercantile depression in every part of the civilised world, when there was everywhere a considerable shrinkage of values, Tasmania's dealings with other countries did not diminish so much in volume as in value.

We may also remark, in this place, that while the external commerce of a colony is pretty satisfactory evidence of its general prosperity, it by no means tells the whole story. A complete and accurate picture of the well-being of any one of the Australian communities could only be drawn with the aid of such information as is collected by the Bureau of Statistics at Washington, for example, which are so comprehensive and minute as to cover the whole field of domestic industry, so that an American knows what is the manufacturing output of the country, as well as the annual produce of its husbandry, its mines, its fisheries, and its forests; and can form an approximate estimate of the consuming powers of the whole of the people. These particulars are wanting in the Australian colonies; admirable as, in other respects, the system is which has been adopted by their leading statists. But we are justified in asserting that, in no English-speaking country, does the great mass of the people command a greater abundance of nutritious food, wear better clothing, take more holidays, or spend a greater sum of money, week by week, upon amusements, than they do in Australia. In many respects, the condition of the colonies presents a close parallel to that of the mother-country when it was known far and wide as "merry England." The hours of labour for artisans and labourers are limited to eight per diem; Saturday afternoon is observed as a half-holiday; New Year's Day, Easter Monday, Whit Monday, St. Andrew's, St. Patrick's and Boxing-day are devoted to recreations; and it is observed that, as a general rule, the pit, gallery, and upper circles of the theatres, or, in other words, those portions of them which are frequented by the operative classes, are habitually the most numerously attended. And the numbers of well-dressed, well-nourished, and well-behaved persons who turn out in each centre of population to witness horse races, regattas, cricket matches, football contests, or public ceremonials, offer the most convincing testimony that could be afforded of the generally flourishing condition of the great mass of the people. These remarks apply with the greatest force, perhaps, to the colonies on the mainland, where the pulse of industrial life beats quicker than it does in Tasmania; but in that island there is an immense amount of solid, steady-going, safe and sure prosperity which makes no great show, but is very real, and promises to be very durable, for the resources of the country are exceedingly rich and varied. Its product of gold in 1878 was of the value of £100,000, irrespective of what left the island by private hands and escaped official record at the Custom-house. The yield of tin was 6192 tons, one mine alone furnishing 2160 tons of this amount, which is said to be the largest quantity yielded by any one mine in the world, during the same period of time. From the coal mines in seven different localities 12,311 tons were obtained; while from the various freestone quarries which are of so frequent occurrence in the island, 88,350 cubic feet and 800 tons of this valuable building material, so highly prized by architects, was hewn in the year 1878; not to speak of blue-stone, flag-stone, lime and lime-stone, of which there are large deposits.

The returns of live stock for the year just mentioned give the following totals:—

Horses.	Cattle.	Sheep.	Pigs.
24,107	126,276	1,838,831	39,595

Five banks, with numerous branches, transact the financial business of the island, and have deposits to the amount of £1,873,003; and the savings banks returns show that 12,764—or one person in every eight of the population—have a total of upwards of £300,000 standing to their credit, the average balance being £24 3s. 2d. per head.

There are 164 public schools in Tasmania, with an average daily attendance of 6032 male and female children; and the colony devotes £23,000 per annum to the laudable work of instructing the young. Thirty-five lodges belonging to the various friendly societies have 3755 members enrolled on their books, and an accumulated capital stock of £24,642. The island contains 316 places of worship, and Hobart Town is the residence of a Bishop of the Episcopal, and of a Bishop of the Roman Catholic Church; the former denomination comprehending 53, and the latter 22 per cent. of the population.

The vital statistics for 1878 show the birth rate to have been 32·27 per thousand of population, the marriage rate 7·98 per thousand, and the death rate 15·66 per thousand. This is a lower average as regards the deaths than that of any of the other Australian colonies; and is only about half that of Austria, Spain, and Italy; while it is much below that of Sweden, Denmark, and Great Britain, which are the healthiest parts of Europe. With the exception, perhaps, of New Zealand, Tasmania is entitled to be designated one of the most salubrious countries in the world.

Chapter VI.

WESTERN AUSTRALIA.

AREA OF THE COLONY—BRITISH STATESMANSHIP SHOULD DIRECT ITS EFFORTS TO PROMOTE SYSTEMATIC COLONISATION—CAPABILITIES OF THE AUSTRALIAN COLONIES FOR ABSORBING THE SURPLUS POPULATION OF THE MOTHER-COUNTRY—THE IMPETUS IT WOULD GIVE TO HER COMMERCE—SPARSENESS OF PEOPLE IN WESTERN AUSTRALIA—ITS LIBERAL LAND REGULATIONS—A FARM FOR NOTHING—PRODUCTIONS OF THE COLONY—ITS CLIMATE AND GENERAL SALUBRITY—FREEDOM FROM EPIDEMICS—MINERAL RESOURCES—WANT OF CAPITAL AND LABOUR—WHO SHOULD EMIGRATE—GOVERNMENTS OF THE COLONY—CURRENT RATES OF WAGES AND PRICES OF PROVISIONS.

WESTERN AUSTRALIA is the largest of the group of colonies to which it belongs, for it comprises an area of 1,000,000 square miles : so that twenty Englands, or a hundred Belgiums, or fifty Netherlands, or five Germanys, or as many Frances could be carved out of its magnificent territory; and yet its population numbers less than 30,000, or not quite half that of the borough of Plymouth. What painful reflections do figures and comparisons like these give rise to. In one corner of the empire millions of human beings swarm like ants in an ant-hill; the increase of population has long ago outstripped the growth of the food supplies in the British Islands, and the struggle for existence is yearly becoming fiercer and fiercer. In another portion of Her Majesty's dominions there are countries which offer a home, industrial employment, and abundance to all who can reach their shores; yet there is so little statesmanship at either end of the empire, that nothing whatever is done to transfer the surplus population of the parent-hive to the surplus food available for their sustenance, in the colonial dependencies of Great Britain. This is the great colonising people of modern times; but beyond the discovery and occupation of virgin regions she does nothing whatever, as a nation, to colonise them. She has the largest navy in the world, and it is ready to transport her forces to any points at which the honour or the interests of the country may happen to be assailed; but if the First Lord of the Admiralty—be he Sir Joseph Porter, K.C.B., or anybody else—were asked to put a number of ships into commission for the transfer of an industrial army from the over-crowded markets of Great

Britain to the sparsely-peopled colonies of Australia, and to employ her naval officers in organising new settlements, and superintending the first beginnings of new societies, the official mind would probably stand aghast at such a proposition. Yet it would relieve the tax and rate-payers of many of their burdens; it would lighten the pressure of competition for employment; it would diminish crime, vice, and disease; and it would convert tens of thousands of unprofitable consumers into beneficial producers. England would have fewer paupers and petty larcenists to support at home, and more customers for her manufactures abroad. For such a policy, like the quality of mercy, would be "twice blessed." It would bless the emigrants, and bless the country which would send them forth from penury and scarcity to prosperity and abundance. Not only would every pound spent in this way be saved in poor and police rates; but it would be eventually returned tenfold, by the augmentation of England's external commerce, which would necessarily follow. Have our countrymen at home sufficiently pondered over the fact that every man, woman, and child in the Australian colonies annually consumes imports of the value, in round numbers, of £20; most of these imports being drawn from Great Britain? Think of it, ye statesmen, ye journalists, ye chambers of commerce, ye poor-law guardians, ye influential men and woman in every grade of life! An Australian family of five persons, expends close upon £100 per annum upon commodities, which are mostly of British manufacture; and for these they pay you in gold, tin, and copper, in wheat and meat, in wool and wine. We can produce these so much more cheaply than you can; and you can manufacture many articles so much more reasonably than we can; and the exchange of these furnishes employment to fleets of merchantmen, in which are to be found the materials wherewith to man your navy in the event of a maritime war. But perhaps it may be said that the conduct of systematic emigration is no part of the duty of the British Government. The question, at any rate, is an arguable one; and the special circumstances of Great Britain are such as to demand exceptional legislation. In no part of the world is population so dense as it is in England and Wales, with the single exception of Belgium; and no nation of modern times, unless it were Holland, when her commercial greatness and political power had reached their culminating point, has ever been so largely dependent upon foreign countries for the food of her people. This is surely a position of insecurity, if not of danger, especially when it is associated with a land system by which the great mass of the people is dissociated from the soil on which, but not by which, they live. Would it not be sound wisdom and patriotic policy for the mother-country to organise emigration, to be the leader of her own people into her own vacant territories, there to build up under her own guardianship, tutelage, counsel, and direction, communities which should reproduce all that is best worthy of reproduction in her political, social, and industrial life? The six colonies of Australia and New Zealand could alone absorb 250,000 persons annually, without taking into account the capabilities of Canada and South Africa in this respect, which are probably quite equal to those of Australasia. Now, this total of half-a-million would be equivalent to the natural increment of population in Great Britain, and thus any increase of the pressure of population upon the means of subsistence would be effectually guarded against; and we may venture to affirm, with the utmost confidence, that the prosperity of all classes would undergo a steady augmentation. Wages would rise, no doubt; but so they did during that period of mercantile and manufacturing prosperity which was brought to a close in the year 1873; and at the same time the profits of employers increased in a still greater ratio. And so it would be, if half-a-million of English people were annually transferred to the colonial possessions of Great Britain; for this would mean an addition of £10,000,000 to the export trade of the mother-country, and of £15,000,000 or £20,000,000 to her import trade. For these emigrants whose productiveness—assuming them to have been all producers—could not probably have been appraised at a higher value than £50 per head, per annum—averaging agricultural with mechanical labour—representing in the aggregate £25,000,000, would produce with the co-operation of nature in a new country at least treble those values, or £75,000,000; and of this amount a fifth or a fourth, consisting either of breadstuffs, or wool, or wine, or meat, or timber, or tallow, or minerals, would be available for export to England, from whence these colonists would draw, in return, the manufactured commodities which can be fabricated at a lower price, and of a better quality, there than elsewhere. And supposing a scarcity of labour to arise in Great Britain, which we regard as extremely improbable, inasmuch as there is the neighbouring continent to draw upon, the inventive genius of her mechanicians would come to her rescue, and would provide mechanical substitutes for the handicraftsmen who would be no longer available.

We have been led to indulge in these remarks by reflecting on the vastness of the area of Western Australia, and the ludicrous disproportion of its population to that area. It would sustain tens of millions; and it contains 28,166 persons of European birth or descent, all told. It is larger than British India; and its population is only 3000 in excess of that of the wretched little island of Aden. It could feed and clothe whole nations; and it has only 51,674 acres under cultivation, out of an estimated acreage of 626,111,323! There are hundreds of thousands of persons in England, Ireland, and Scotland who are hungering after a little freehold of their own, and who cannot acquire one even by purchase; and yet here are millions of acres of fertile land which can be literally had for the mere asking. In order that we may not be suspected of trifling with the credulity of our readers in the mother-country, to whom the free gift of a fifty-acre farm, on the simple condition of fencing the whole and cultivating a portion of it within a given time, may appear to resemble a traveller's story, we will append two clauses of the Land Regulations of Western Australia as issued by the Government in 1879:—

112.—Any immigrant on first arriving in this colony, whether introduced wholly or partially at the expense of the Imperial or Colonial Government, or at their own cost and expense, may select from any unimproved rural Crown Lands open for selection, if of the age of 21 years or over, 50 acres; or between the ages of 14 and 21, 25 acres; or under such age, if with parents, 12½ acres. Provided that no greater quantity than 150 acres be allotted to one family, and that every selection be made within three years after the arrival of the selector.

113.—When selected, such lands may be allotted to such immigrants as may immediately then occupy them, by occupation certificates, which shall only be deemed transferable in case of death of the holder on application of the executors or administrators and on payment of a fee of ten shillings. These certificates may be exchanged for Crown Grants after five years from date of each, provided that the land described in such has been enclosed with a good and substantial fence, and at least one-fourth shown to be in cultivation, and that if at the end of the said term of five years the above conditions, or any of them, be not fulfilled to the satisfaction of the Commissioner of Crown Lands, the lots in which default shall have been made shall revert to the Crown, with any or all improvements that may be thereon. Provided, however, that if the conditions as above mentioned, in regard to cultivation and fencing, be complied with, at any time prior to the above term of five years, the Crown Grants shall be issued.

The waste lands of the colony are divided into four classes—town, suburban, country, and mineral lands. The two first can be purchased at auction, an upset price for each being fixed upon by the Government. Country lands are sub-divided into agricultural and pastoral lands, either of which can be purchased for ten shillings an acre, or leased—the former for eight years, at the nominal rental of one shilling per acre, with a pre-emptive right of purchase; and the latter for one year, at an annual rental of two shillings per hundred acres, with the privilege of renewing the tenure; or for eight years at an annual rental of £5 per thousand acres with certain pre-emptive rights attached. Mineral lands are leased in blocks of not less than 80 acres, at £3 per acre, payable by three annual instalments. Licenses for cutting timber are issued at £20 per annum for any quantity not exceeding 640 acres of land; and at £40 per acre for any area of not less than 640, and not more than 1280 acres. The forests of Western Australia, we may here remark, are exceedingly rich in timber, some of it being almost unique in value. Chief among the trees of this colony are the jarrah *(eucalyptus marginata)*, which possesses the valuable property of resisting the attacks of the white ant on land, and of the *teredo navalis* under water, some of it having been exposed to the latter for nearly half a century and having been found to remain intact; the sandal-wood, so well known for its strong perfume throughout the East; and the white gum or tuart. The latter is an exceedingly close-grained, hard and heavy wood, and capable of sustaining great pressure. Besides these, there is the Kauri, which nearly reaches the height of the *eucalyptus amygdalina*, and is so hard that it is used, washed with iron, for driving piles; the raspberry jam wood, so called on account of its scent resembling that of raspberry jam;

the casuarina, red-gum, she-oak, wattle, and many trees whose bark is very rich in tannin.

With respect to the capabilities of the soil in a country embracing twenty degrees of latitude, it is enough to say that they are exceedingly diversified. Mr. W. H. Knight, to whom we are indebted for a great deal of the information to be found in this chapter, writes:—"In the southern, and more settled portion of the colony, plants, fruits, and cereals indigenous to cool and temperate climates, thrive best—grapes, peaches, apricots, nectarines, oranges, lemons, apples, figs, plums, loquats, bananas, and in some places, gooseberries, currants, strawberries, and cherries, *cum multis aliis*, grow in the greatest luxuriance, while kitchen vegetables of every description are produced in great abundance. Wheat, barley, oats, maize, and tobacco, also grow well in nearly all parts of the colony. Much more flour is now produced than is sufficient for home consumption, and should the increased and less expensive means of transport from the agricultural districts, now projected, be carried out, a considerable quantity of flour will be exported in the course of a few years." The vine flourishes luxuriantly in Western Australia, and excellent raisins are furnished by the grapes. Ultimately, too, the production of wine may be expected to become an important article of industry when capital, skill, and experience shall have been brought to bear on it. New Zealand flax thrives vigorously in the soil of this colony, while the olive grows luxuriously, and the castor-oil plant is almost obnoxious, owing to the rapidity of its development.

With respect to the climate of Western Australia, it is necessary to observe that it is modified by causes peculiar to the Southern Hemisphere. For, as the researches of the scientists connected with the *Challenger* Expedition have shown, the Antarctic Ocean is an immense reservoir of cold, the influence of which upon the immense body of water which "tumbles round the world" in these latitudes is very great indeed, and it is scarcely too much to assert, that just as the gulf-stream is believed to temper the inclemency of the atmosphere during the winter months in the British Islands and in the north-east coast of Europe, so the otherwise tropical heat which would prevail during the summer months over a very large portion of the Australian continent, is materially moderated by a cold sub-surface stream flowing up towards the Equator from the South Pole.

"Speaking generally," writes Mr. Knight, whose assertions are confirmed by the testimony of many trustworthy persons, "the climate of Western Australia may be said to be one of the most healthy, invigorating, and delightful climates in the world.

"In the northern portion of the colony, which falls within the torrid zone, the average temperature is of course high, and the summer heat excessive; yet even there, the climate possesses the peculiar Australian characteristic of extreme dryness of atmosphere, which renders it so unlike, and so superior to, most tropical climates.

"A temperature such as the thermometer frequently indicates in the northern settlements would utterly incapacitate Europeans for all out-door work in other tropical countries, yet there men are enabled to perform the most laborious work, exposed to the fierce rays of an unclouded sun, with perfect impunity, though of course the summer temperature of that district, notwithstanding that it has no injurious effect on the constitution, is far too hot to be agreeable.

"Towards the southern part of the colony, however, the climate is superb; as compared with an English climate, that of Australia throughout is, as might be expected, hot, yet the heat is of a kind which produces no unpleasant effect. The emigrant from England soon becomes accustomed to it, and after a short time learns to bear, not only without inconvenience, but even with a large amount of positive gratification, a temperature which in England, with its humid atmosphere, would be extremely enervating and depressing.

"It is only during three months of the year that any unpleasantly hot weather is experienced; during that period hot land-winds occasionally prevail, and during their continuance the air gets intensely heated, though nothing like the hot winds known as 'brickfielders,' so common and so oppressive in the other Australian colonies, is ever felt in Western Australia.

"The prevailing winds in summer blow from the eastward and southwest, the former being known as 'land winds,' and the latter as 'sea-breezes.' They generally occur alternately—the land winds prevailing at night, and sea-breezes during the day; the heat of one being counteracted by the cool refreshing influence of the other.

"The nights and mornings are nearly always cool, and there being so little moisture in the atmosphere during the summer months, shepherds and others frequently sleep in the open air for a great portion of the year without suffering the slightest ill-effects."

The surgeon of H.M. Sloop *Sulphur*, which was stationed there for three years, has placed on record the following statement :—" Small-pox, measles,* scarlatina, are unknown; dysentery is a rare disease; diarrhœa is also unfrequent; disease of the liver is extremely rare." Vice-Admiral Sir James Sterling, formerly Governor of Western Australia, was of opinion that it was very suitable as a sanitarium for the Indian army, and remarked that the climate "is formed and governed by a constant cause—the prevailing westerly winds; that it is essentially a sea-climate, fresh and invigorating, temperate in point of heat, equable in point of temperature, free from sudden chills, and with this remarkable circumstance attaching to it, that the season of greatest heat is also the driest season, and consequently malaria is not produced to any appreciable extent. Hence, therefore, fever, dysentery,

---

* This immunity is no longer enjoyed, as the measles have been imported into the colony.

cholera, and liver-complaints are almost unknown in Western Australia. The causes which produce these diseases in India do not exist in the colony —their climates are essentially and entirely the reverse of each other."

At present, the vast territory comprised within the limits of Western Australia has only been partially explored, and the latest map of the country offers as many blanks as that of Africa did at the commencement of the present century. But the expeditions of Messrs. John and Alexander Forrest have done much to open up the interior of the continent, and a journey which the latter undertook last year, and of which he contributed an interesting narrative to the *Victorian Review*, was the means of discovering the watershed of the Fitzroy, and other large rivers, as well as an available pastoral country of not less than 20,000,000 acres in extent, well-grassed, abundantly watered, and very suitable in places for the cultivation of sugar, coffee, and rice.

As a matter of course, the extent and variety of the resources of Western Australia, have been, as yet, but inadequately estimated. In a report transmitted to the Secretary of State for the Colonies by Governor Weld, in 1874, that gentleman writes :—" The colony is extraordinarily rich in lead, silver, copper, iron, plumbago, and many other minerals are found in various localities, and indications of coal and petroleum are not wanting. What is wanting is energy and enterprise to develop these riches." The forests, the pearl and pearl-shell fisheries, the cultivation of silk, tobacco, and hops, of coffee and cotton, and the preparation of dried fruits and preserves, are all capable of adding very materially to the wealth of this little community, which raises a revenue of £163,344, and maintains a civil establishment costing £113,212 per annum, and has an import trade of £379,049, and an export one of £428,491.

But the two great wants of Western Australia are capital and labour; for both of which there is a boundless field. To the industrious and sober man it offers plenty of employment and liberal pay in the present, and every opportunity of reaching an independence before he has passed the prime of life. The rate of wages for carpenters, blacksmiths, saddlers, coachbuilders, and painters is from 7s. to 10s. per day; for brewers and printers, 6s. to 8s.; for boat-builders, 8s. to 10s.; for gardeners, 6s.; for masons and navvies, 7s.; and for domestic servants, from £18 to £50 per annum. The colony ceased to be a penal settlement upwards of ten years ago, and many of the convicts who have been engaged as "predial" servants have turned out satisfactorily. Western Australia offers the same religious and educational advantages to the settler, which the other colonies do, and the intending emigrant who is steady and self-reliant, need not hesitate for a moment in exchanging privation at home for abundance here. But, as has been well-observed:—He must give up the notion of looking to others for the supply of his ordinary wants, and learn to depend wholly and entirely upon his own exertions. No one should emigrate to

Western Australia who is not prepared to work, and to work hard—to undertake, that is, solid bodily labour, to put forth his muscular powers, to call his thews and sinews into action—to earn his living, in fact, by the "sweat of his brow," and to forego, for some time at least, the superfluities and luxuries of life. These are not to be found in the bush, or at any rate, not until the preliminary labours of the first few years of toil, have legitimately prepared the way for them. There is, of course, a limited opening for the employment of intellectual as well as of physical labour, and the demand for the former will no doubt increase as population extends, and the various social wants of a community growing in intelligence and refinement call for its more extended employment; but, at present, the great demand is for manual labour and handicraft skill, shepherds and herdsmen, farm labourers, artisans of every description;—carpenters, masons, sawyers, smiths, wheelwrights, tanners, bricklayers, and others—together with domestic servants, are the classes which constitute the most useful emigrants. These are the men that are wanted—not such as come with the idea of making a fortune, or of saving their earnings merely to move on to some other part of the world, or to return to the mother-country to spend their gains—but such as come with a determination to settle down permanently, and fully resolved to attain a position of prosperity.

Western Australia was formerly a "Crown Colony," governed by Her Majesty's representative, an Executive, and a Legislative Council, the latter enacting laws, imposing taxes, and voting their expenditure. Half its members were nominated by the Crown, and half by the people. But a partly elective and partly nominee Council was substituted for that body about ten years ago. It now consists of twenty-one members, two-thirds of whom represent eleven electoral districts, while the other owe their appointments to the Crown. Up to the present time, the colony seems to have escaped the curse of the professional politician and the mercenary demagogue, who are the bane of some of the more populous colonies, and it is free from "crises" and deadlocks accordingly.

Perth, the capital, is picturesquely situated on the banks of the Swan River, twelve miles inland from the port of Fremantle, and its aspect is thus described by a resident:—"Cape lilac or neme trees have been planted along the sides of some of the principal streets, after the manner of the Boulevards of Paris, and they add greatly to the beauty of the place; indeed the view, looking up St. George's Terrace, when these trees are in full leaf and blossom, is one of the most lovely that can be conceived. The bright green leaves glittering in a brilliant sunlight, the beautiful and fragrant lilac flowers thickly interspersed through the foliage, and the exquisite combination of light and shade, form a scene which attracts the attention of every stranger. Many of the large native trees have been left standing, and though they add much to the picturesque beauty of the place, they hide many of the buildings, and shut out from view a large portion of the town, the full extent of which can only be seen from the top of Mount Eliza—a hill on the western side of the town, about 300 feet high. There are, within the limits and in the outskirts of the town, some fine gardens which yield an abundance of fruit and vegetables, and almost every house in the town has more or less garden-ground attached to it."

Fremantle is the chief shipping port of the colony; but Champion Bay is also becoming a place of great importance, on account of its increasing exports of wool and grain. Large quantities of timber find their way down to Port Vassi; and King George's Sound is the coaling station of the P. and O. Company's steamers. York, Bunbury, Northam, Newcastle, Beverley, and Guildford are all rising places; although their growth is necessarily slow when compared with that of townships in more populous colonies.

Western Australia exports wool of the value of £150,000, timber of the value of £180,000, guano of the value of £66,000, lead ore of the value of £43,000, pearls and mother-of-pearl shells of the value of £36,000, and sandal-wood of the value of £35,000 per annum. It contains 32,701 horses, 56,158 head of cattle, 869,325 sheep, and 16,762 horses. Subjoined are the average prices of various articles in general use:—

			£ s. d.
Wheaten Flour	per bag of 200lbs. ...	...	1 15 0
Wheat ...	... per imperial bushel	...	0 6 6
Wheaten Bread	... per lb. ...	...	0 0 2
Horned Cattle	... ,, ...	...	0 0 3
Horses ...	... each ...	...	£5 to 25 0 0
Sheep ...	... each ...	...	0 13 0
Goats ...	... each ...	...	1 0 0
Swine ...	... per lb. ...	...	0 0 6
Milk ...	... per gall. ...	...	0 2 0
Butter, Fresh	... per lb. ...	...	0 2 0
,, Salt	... ,, ...	...	0 1 8
Cheese ...	... ,, ...	...	0 1 6
Beef	... ,, ...	...	0 0 6
Mutton	... ,,	...	0 0 5
Pork	,,	...	0 0 10
Rice	... ,,	...	0 0 3
Coffee	... ,,	...	0 1 6
Tea	... ,, ...	...	0 2 0
Sugar	... ,, ...	...	0 0 5
Salt ...	... ,, ...	...	0 0 1
Wine, Imported	... per gall. ...	...	£1 and upward
,, Colonial	... ,, ...	...	4s. and ,,
Brandy ...	... ,, ...	...	1 10 0
Beer, Imported	... ,, draught, 4s.; bottled	...	0 7 0
,, Colonial	... ,, ...	...	0 3 0
Tobacco ...	... per lb. ...	...	0 4 0

CHAPTER VIII.

NEW ZEALAND.

"THE GREAT BRITAIN OF THE SOUTH"—ITS SALUBRITY AND BEAUTY—BRIEF SKETCH OF ITS HISTORY—ITS POLITICAL LIFE—WHY IT IS FREE FROM DEMAGOGISM—VITAL STATISTICS OF THE COLONY—ROBUSTNESS OF ITS INHABITANTS—THE LAND SYSTEM IN FORCE—FREE TRADE IN LAND—HOW FARMERS GET ON—COST OF CULTIVATION—STOCK-RAISING—SPECIAL SETTLEMENTS—YIELD OF WHEAT PER ACRE—AGRICULTURAL STATISTICS—MINERAL RESOURCES OF THE COUNTRY—ITS DIVERSIFIED INDUSTRIES—POPULATION OF NEW ZEALAND—PROVISION FOR THEIR EDUCATION—TRADE AND COMMERCE OF THE COLONY—RELIGION AND SECTS—THE PRESENT AND FUTURE OF NEW ZEALAND AS PORTRAYED BY A LOCAL WRITER.

No more felicitous, appropriate, or, we may venture to add, prophetic epithet was ever bestowed upon a group of islands than that which the illustrious Peel conferred upon those which constitute the colony of New Zealand, when he designated them as the "Great Britain of the South." If there is any part of the empire in which it may be expected that the youth of the old country will renew itself, and where it is almost certain that some of the best features of English life and character will be faithfully reproduced, and indefinitely perpetuated, that portion of the British dominions is New Zealand. Soil, climate, geographical position, and configuration, mineral wealth, and agricultural resources, all point to these islands as the home of a race which will be as famous for its enterprise and progress as the energetic peoples from whom it has descended, and whose best qualities will be blended and commingled in its future population. The inhabitants of New Zealand will be seafarers and mercantile adventurers in distant countries from sheer necessity, even if they were not impelled thereto by their inherited instincts. With so enormous a coast-line, and with their shores indented by so many noble harbours and inlets, these islands seem to have been marked out by the hand of nature for occupation by the descendants of the old vikings of the far north. Writing of the mother-country, Emerson says:—
"As soon as the land thus geographically posted got a hardy people into it,

they could not help becoming the sailors and factors of the globe. From childhood they dabbled in water; they swam like fishes; their playthings were boats." And Fuller, more than two hundred years ago, was also struck by the influence of insularity of position on the national character. "England being an island," said he, "the very midland shores therein are all to be accounted maritime; the genius even of land-locked counties driving the natives with a maritime dexterity." And if this was so in the land of Drake, and Hawkins, and Frobisher, of Blake, and Cook, and Nelson; how much more so is it likely to be the case in the long and comparatively narrow islands of New Zealand, upon either of which it is impossible to get so far as a hundred miles away from the sea.

Then again, its coal mines, its large deposits of iron ore and iron sands, its masses of limestone, its mineral oils and shales, its lead, zinc, copper and antimony ores, and the nearness of every district to the sea, combine to indicate, that this colony has a great manufacturing future before it, so soon as capital and labour shall be more abundant than they are at present. As we shall have occasion to show, by-and-bye, industries of this kind have been already commenced; and those persons who are acquainted with the climatic conditions of the islands will agree with us that, in so far as the middle one more particularly is concerned, they are pre-eminently favourable to the production of those textile fabrics, for the manufacture of which, a certain amount of humidity in the atmosphere seems to be almost indispensable.

We believe, too, that in a bracing and invigorating climate, like that of New Zealand, the Anglo-Saxon will flourish vigorously, and will attain a very high degree of mental and physical development. It is contended by Buckle—and the facts of history lend a powerful countenance to his argument—that climate, food, soil, and the general aspect of nature, are highly important factors of civilisation; that they have been attended with the most important consequences in regard to the general organisation of society; and that they have been productive of "those large and conspicuous differences between nations which are often ascribed to some fundamental difference in the various races into which mankind is divided." Now, in each of these particulars, New Zealand is exceptionally fortunate. It is no exaggeration to say that the climate is one of the finest in the world, as temperate as, but more equable than, that of Great Britain. There is only an average range of 20° throughout the year; the mean temperature during the season of spring being 55°, of summer 63°, of autumn 57°, and of winter 48°; while the total rainfall varies from 36 to 59 inches,* according to locality, in the North Island, and from

---

* For most of the statistics we shall have occasion to introduce we are indebted to Dr. Hector's excellent *Handbook of New Zealand*, prepared for the Melbourne International Exhibition of 1880.

25 to 111 inches per annum in the South Island. Hence the rich verdure of each, and hence also, in some degree, the great number and volume of the rivers which discharge their waters into the sea on each side of both islands. As regards food, it will suffice to say that the country produces large crops of excellent cereals, and that its pastures carry extensive flocks, and herds of sheep and cattle of the choicest quality. With respect to soil, its general richness is sufficiently attested by the magnificence of the timber composing its indigenous forests. In many places, it is composed of fluviatile drifts; in others, of volcanic deposits; in others, of decomposed calcareous marls; and in others, of stiff clay. As to the general aspect of the country, it would be difficult to exaggerate its grandeur and beauty. Its mountain scenery presents most of the imposing features of the more romantic portions of Switzerland; while the various sounds, on the west coast of the South Island, exceed in sublimity the finest of the Norwegian fiords. There is one inlet—known as Milford Sound—to which it would be difficult for the pencil of the artist, or the pen of the most skilful word-painter, to do adequate justice. It is a chasm, ploughed by a stupendous glacier, which gradually cut its way through a mountainous mass, leaving a vast wall standing on either side, many hundreds of feet above, and as many hundreds of feet below, the present level of the sea. Cataracts, fed by existing glaciers, lying far up in the snowy recesses of the alps which girdle this awful recess, plunge into its shattered waters; and after a heavy shower of rain, thousands of glittering streams gush out from all the surrounding eminences, and send down their tribute to the sea. Higher up, on the same coast, the Mount Cook range rises up from the very edge of the sea, crowned with eternal snows, and attaining an altitude, in some places, of between 11,000 and 13,000 feet. It enfolds within its icy boundaries the famous Tasman glacier, extending for a distance of eighteen miles, and having a breadth of nearly two miles at its terminal face; while four other glaciers of grand dimensions serve as tributaries to this enormous sea of ice. In the North Island are the wonderful geysers, and the no less wonderful terraces of silicious deposits; the brilliantly yellow, pure white, and bright scarlet hues of which contrast so vividly with the intensely blue colour of the basins of boiling water, poured from the seething cauldron above. But travel in almost any direction you will, in New Zealand, you cannot fail to be charmed with the amazing beauty and the equally amazing variety of its landscape scenery; and the lakes alone—those in the province of Otago more particularly—possess all the characteristics of grandeur and beauty, of amenity in themselves, and of sublimity in their surroundings, which are to be found in those of Switzerland and the Tyrol.

A brief sketch of the history of New Zealand may suffice to introduce some account of its social and industrial development. Discovered by Tasman, in the year 1642, these islands were found to be inhabited by a fine race of men, presenting many points of resemblance to the ancient

Britons. They were not indigenous, however, and they seem to have migrated thither, by accident or design, about the beginning of the fifteenth century. In all probability they displaced an autochthonic and inferior race. Tasman met with such a hostile reception from the Maoris that he refrained from landing and taking possession of the country, which remained unnoticed until Captain Cook visited it in the month of October, 1769, and discerning in it a splendid field for colonisation, he added it to the British dominions, and revisited it in 1773 and 1777. At a later period, it was resorted to by whaling vessels from New South Wales, and trading ports were established at the Bay of Islands, Hokianga, Tauranga, and other places. It also become a favourite field of missionary enterprise, as the Maoris were cannibals, and the risk of being killed and eaten seemed to lend a certain zest to the adventurous efforts of the reverend gentlemen who endeavoured to Christianise the Maoris. By the year 1833 a good many white people had settled at various points along the coast of New Zealand, and the Imperial Government considered it advisable to appoint a commissioner to reside among them, watch over their interests, and administer their public affairs. Six years afterwards, an influential company was organised in London for the systematic colonisation of these islands; and on the 7th of February, 1840, New Zealand was proclaimed a British colony, and the native chiefs signed a treaty, ceding the sovereignty of the country to the Queen of England. In the meantime, some shiploads of immigrants from Great Britain had reached Port Nicholson; and almost simultaneously two emigrant vessels from France had arrived in the colony, for the purpose of taking possession of the South Island. They intended to form a settlement on the shores of Akaroa Bay, but a British gun-brig, under the command of Captain Owen Stanley, seizing time by the forelock, hastened thither before the Frenchmen, hoisted the union-jack on a flagstaff, and proclaimed the territory to be the property of Her Majesty. Thenceforth the whole of New Zealand was recognised as constituting an integral portion of the British Empire. Auckland was selected as the seat of government and the future capital; and Wellington was chosen, at the same time, as the nucleus of another province. A third settlement was formed at Wanganui, and a fourth at New Plymouth. In due time, the New Zealand Company extended its operations to the neighbouring island, and Nelson was founded in one of the most charming districts of New Zealand. We may pass over the native wars, which soon afterwards threw a cloud over the prosperity of the settlers, and darkened their prospects. It will be enough to say that we are still too near those disastrous events, in point of time, to enable us to speak of them with judicial impartiality. Let us proceed, therefore, to trace the progress of civilisation. During the governorship of Sir George Grey, he divided the islands into six provinces—Auckland, Taranaki, Wellington, Nelson, Canterbury, and Otago; but Hawke's Bay was subsequently carved out of Wellington,

Marlborough out of Nelson, and Southland out of Otago. The Canterbury settlement was established by a body of English churchmen in 1850, and that of Otago by members of the Free Church of Scotland, two years prior to that date, the capital of the latter province having been fixed at Dunedin, and that of the former at Christchurch. In the year 1852, constitutional government was conferred upon the inhabitants of New Zealand, and between 1857 and 1865 such important gold discoveries were made as had the effect of attracting a large influx of population, and of giving a marked and permanent impulse to the progress of the whole colony, which is now governed by a single Legislature, having its seat at Wellington, instead of by numerous provincial councils, and is one of the most important possessions of the British Crown; peopled by immigrants who are not surpassed in intelligence and enterprise by the inhabitants of any other portion of Her Majesty's dominions. The only occasion of misgiving is that, which arises in connection with the public debt, amounting as it does to £20,000,000, or upwards of £44 per head of the population; but large as this appears, we must not overlook the fact that a considerable portion of it has been expended upon works, which, if not immediately reproductive, may be expected to become so a few years hence, and that if successive administrations resolutely adhere to an honest determination to maintain an equilibrium of income and expenditure, and to conduct the affairs of the country with as rigorous an economy as is consistent with efficiency, the natural increase of population—which nearly doubles itself in ten years—will lighten the public burdens, in so far as the individual tax-payer is concerned, one-half during the next decade; while the same circumstance may be expected to double the returns from the various railways constructed by the Government; so that some of these which at present do not yield a sufficient surplus after paying working expenses to cover the interest on the loans contracted to build them with, will not only do so hereafter, but yield a margin of profit to the State.

Thus, then, the only small cloud which darkens the bright prospects of New Zealand is likely to be dissipated in a few years, and it may be confidently asserted that the 1200 miles of railway, which have been constructed with borrowed money will be increasingly powerful auxiliaries to the development of the economic resources of New Zealand for all time to come. And with respect to the financial administration of that country, it is right to point out that there are not the temptations to extravagant expenditure, jobbery and corruption, which exist in some of the other colonies. Take the case of Victoria, for example, where one-fourth of the whole population is concentrated in the capital and its suburbs, and 25 out of the 86 members of the Assembly are elected by the metropolitan and suburban constituencies. As the wage-earning classes are in a majority in most of the districts, this class controls the stipendiary branch of the Legislature, and that branch makes and unmakes Ministries. Now, these are, more often than not, mainly or exclusively composed of professional politicians, with no other means of support than their wages as members, or their salaries as Ministers supply; and accordingly, office is opulence to them, and exclusion from it is relative poverty. Therefore it must be obtained and retained, at all hazards and at any cost. A majority must be kept together, and this is effected by the Government of the day securing them a salary of £300 per head per annum as the price of their fidelity. Such an income is sufficient to attract into the political arena needy stump-orators and ambitious adventurers, who, from want of industry or of principle, may have failed to make a reputable living in any of the ordinary pursuits of life. And the easiest method of obtaining the votes of the numerical majority in every constituency, where the wage-earning classes predominate, is, by supporting a policy of lavish expenditure upon public works, and by pledging the future credit of the colony in order to raise the means of profusion in the present. The country districts may, and do, resent and protest against an extravagant and centralising policy of this kind; but rural populations are scattered and unorganised; whereas the artisans and labourers of the metropolis and its environs are compact and associated, and no candidate would stand the slightest chance of election if he had the courage, or the hardihood, to propose a material curtailment of the annual expenditure on public works. Besides, he is urgently in want of £300 per annum, and the perquisites attaching to a seat in the Legislative Assembly; and instead of thwarting the popular will, he acquiesces in it with the utmost alacrity.

Fortunately for New Zealand, for the cause of good government, and for the prudent and honest administration of its public finances, population is more diffused than it is in Victoria. Strictly speaking, it contains no great capital, for Wellington, which is the seat of the Legislature, resembles Washington, in that it is not thickly-peopled when compared with the other centres, of which there are eleven. The total number of Europeans in New Zealand is estimated at 445,563, and this was the population of the principal towns according to the census of 1878 :—

Dunedin and suburbs	35,026
Christchurch and suburbs	26,653
Auckland and suburbs	24,772
Wellington	18,953
Nelson	6,604
Oamaru	4,927
Invercargill	3,761
Timaru	3,381
Hokitika	3,202
Greymouth	2,921
New Plymouth	2,680

Thus it will be seen, that the largest place in New Zealand contains less than one-twelfth of the entire number of inhabitants in the colony, while Melbourne and its suburbs comprise one-fourth of the total population of the colony of Victoria. We cannot help regarding this excessive aggregation of people in one centre as a source of political and social danger in any country in which supreme power resides in the hands of the numerical majority, and we have given some prominence to the phenomenon in this chapter, because we are of opinion that the absence of it in New Zealand will conduce to the stability of its institutions, to the maintenance of its credit, to the preservation of a higher tone of political morality, to the promotion of its industrial progress, and to a more equable distribution of wealth. For nowhere do affluence and poverty exhibit such a tendency to run into extremes as in great cities, nowhere do vice and crime flourish in such rank luxuriance, nowhere do epidemics find so congenial a habitat, nowhere is the rate of mortality so high, and nowhere do the evils which seem to be inseparable from a high civilisation manifest themselves so nakedly and offensively as in a populous capital.

Of the eleven towns or cities enumerated above, the last five may be fairly reckoned country places, so that we have something like three-fourths of the inhabitants of New Zealand resident in localities where the conditions may be said to be favourable to health and morality; while, as regards the situation and structure of Auckland, Dunedin, Wellington and Nelson, they may both be compared to those of some of the most beautiful sea-side resorts in Great Britain, or on the shores of the Mediterranean. Christchurch, which lies inland, resembles a cathedral city in England, and recalls in some of its features that famous Warwickshire town in which the greatest poet of all time first saw the light. The romantically-picturesque situation of each of the other provincial capitals must be seen to be appreciated; while the towns of New Plymouth, Timaru, Hokitika, and Greymouth, all lie on the sea coast.

In confirmation of what has previously been said with respect to the healthfulness of New Zealand, it will be necessary to quote some of the vital statistics of the colony. The birth-rate may be put down at 46 per thousand of the population, which is nearly 11 per thousand higher than that of Great Britain, while the marriage-rate is somewhat lower. The death-rate is barely 11 per thousand of the population, or about half the death-rate in England, taking the average of a decade. According to the census of 1878, the total number of persons of fifteen years of age and upwards, returned as suffering from sickness, accident, debility, or infirmity, was 2673, or 111·63 per 10,000 persons living. Distinguishing between the sexes, the proportion was greater of males, mostly on account of their greater liability to accident, being 125·37 per 10,000 of males, and 91·38 per 10,000 of females. Of these, the sick males amounted to 87·03, and the sick females to 80·63 per 10,000, respectively; the males suffering from accident to 31·19, and the females suffering from accident to 3·93 per 10,000.

The following figures, being proportions per 10,000 persons, males, and females, show the relative prevalence of sickness, accidents and debility for the years 1874 and 1878:—

		Total 15 Years and upwards.	Sickness.	Debility and Infirmity.	Accident.
Persons	1874	126·45	98·64	6·55	21·26
	1878	111·63	84·45	7·01	20·17
Males	1874	137·03	99·40	6.83	30·80
	1878	125·37	87·03	7·15	31·19
Females	1874	109·35	97·41	6.12	5·82
	1878	91·38	80·63	6·82	3·93

Let us now proceed to speak of the area and resources of the three islands, which constitute the colony of New Zealand. These are the North, South and Stewart's Islands. The first contains 44,000 square miles, or 28,000,000 acres; the second, 55,000 square miles, or 36,000,000 acres; and the third, 1000 square miles, or 640,000 acres. We have thus a total of 100,000 square miles, or 64,000,000 statute acres, or about 13,000,000 less than the area comprised within the boundaries of Great Britain and Ireland. From Cape Maria Van Diemen, in the north, to South-West Cape, at the extremity of Stewart's Island, the distance is about 1100 miles, and the islands have an average breadth of 140 miles. They lie between the same isothermal lines as France, but their geographical configuration necessarily exercises a marked influence on the climate, which resembles that of the south of Italy in the neighbourhood of Auckland, and does not differ from that of Scotland during the winter months in Stewart's Island. To be more circumstantial, Dunedin lies in the same parallel as Lyons, Geneva, Odessa, and Astrakan in the northern hemisphere. Oamaru corresponds with Venice; and Auckland with Syracuse, Pekin, and San Francisco; and although, as Mr. John Bathgate has pointed out, "changes of weather and temperature are often sudden, the range is limited, the extremes of daily temperature only varying throughout the year by an average of 20°; whilst in Europe, in places of corresponding latitude, the variation extends to 30° and upwards. London is 7° colder than the North Island, and 4° colder than the South Island, and less moist. The mean annual temperature of the South Island is 52°; that of London and New York being 51°, and Edinburgh 47°. In summer, the heat is tempered by cooling breezes, so that a fine day in summer is most enjoyable. A New Zealand fine day has become proverbial, as something peculiarly pleasant and agreeable. In 1877, the rainfall in Dunedin was 37 inches; Christchurch, 24; Wellington, 52; and Auckland, 40. The greatest rainfall was at Hokitika, on the west coast, 136 inches; and the least at Cape Campbell, on the east coast, 16 inches. The west coast may be described as a wooded fringe of the great Alpine Range, and is chiefly occupied by a mining population. In New Zealand there is no suspension of work, either from the heat or from the cold. Cattle do not require protection as in Italy during the heat of summer, and in many places no shelter is deemed necessary even for the work-horses during night in the middle of winter. It is stated, by Surgeon-major Thompson, to be the opinion of persons who have sojourned in different parts of the world, that the Anglo-Saxon race can work and expose themselves to the climate of New Zealand, without injury, during more days in the year, and for more hours of the day, than in any other country."

One of the results of the salubrity of the climate, and of the relative humidity of the atmosphere, is, that the inhabitants of New Zealand, both male and female, are "rounder and rosier" than those of the people on the Australian continent, where the air is drier and the natural juices of the system seem to be diminished by the dry heat of the summer, in Victoria and South Australia more particularly. In a collection of photographs of European settlers of all ages, displayed in the New Zealand court of the Melbourne International Exhibition, we could not help being struck by the fresh beauty of the young girls, the maturer charms of the matrons, and the conformity of both to the British type. Nathaniel Hawthorne has remarked upon the tenacity with which English ladies retain their personal beauty until a late period of their lives; and this, we have good grounds for believing, will be one of the characteristics of the ladies of New Zealand, owing to the climatic influences previously alluded to. In the Australian colonies, we may expect the British race to undergo some important modifications, and to develop into something akin to the Anglo-American. But no such change is probable in New Zealand, where the descendants of English, Scottish and Irish settlers are likely to continue "true to species," if not to exhibit still higher types of the old stock. And as with the higher, so with the lower animals. Imported horses, sheep, oxen, poultry, ground game and song birds thrive and increase mightily, and appear to be singularly free from disease.

If it should be asked, what are the causes of this special salubrity, the answer would be, that they are numerous. In the first place, the geographical configuration of the two principal islands has to be taken into account. They are, as we have said, long and narrow, and consequently from one direction or the other, volumes of atmosphere charged with life-giving or energising elements are being constantly blown inland from the circumjacent ocean. In the next place, the extensive forests which still clothe so many parts of the country, and especially its lower ranges, are so many reservoirs of oxygen, which are being incessantly poured into the air. And, thirdly, the vast masses of snowy sierras, which lift up their icy peaks to so great an altitude in both the north and south islands, temper the heat of the summer by cooling the successive layers of air, which bathe their slopes; while the heat waves, by their action on the glaciers, provoke that evaporation, which fills the air with clouds, and occasions that humidity to which reference has previously been made. If our readers were to imagine England and Scotland drawn out so as to cover twelve instead of nine degrees of latitude, and shifted to a position a thousand miles due west of Spain; if they would picture England and Scotland as separated by a sea as narrow as the Straits of Dover; and if they would suppose both these islands to be ridged by chains of mountains, equalling the Alps in massiveness and altitude; they would be able to form an approximate idea of the form, situation, character, and climate of the "Great Britain of the South." It is a possession of which the mother-country may be justly proud, and the day will come when its inhabitants will be able to declare, that in this highly-favoured region England has renewed her youth, and that her adventurous children have founded another nation with the promise of a grandeur and a glory equal to her own.

As a field of settlement, New Zealand vies with the colonies of Australia in offering special advantages to men of enterprise and men of means. On the 30th June, 1879, there were open for selection upwards of thirteen millions of acres of land, irrespective of a much larger area at the disposal of the local boards. The position of this land may be learned from the following table :—

Locality.	Open for Selection, 30th June, 1879.	Remaining at disposal of Land Boards, exclusive of Native Lands.	Total.
NORTH ISLAND.	Acres.	Acres.	Acres.
Auckland...	15,417	2,370,744	
Hawke Bay	33,800	284,883	
Taranaki...	5,139	1,337,623	
Wellington	22,244	1,125,977	
	76,600	5,119,227	5,195,827
SOUTH ISLAND.			
Nelson	5,847,004		
Marlborough	1,096,593	1,056,547	
Canterbury	4,458,653	840,000	
Westland...	246,145	2,657,700	
Otago	206,978	10,928,915	
Southland	1,551,701	218,487	
	13,407,074	15,701,649	29,108,723

The mode by which land may be obtained, and the very liberal terms conceded by the Legislature, are matters upon which we may naturally anticipate, that our readers in the mother-country will desire the fullest and latest information, and we may preface what follows by remarking that the colony of New Zealand is divided into ten land districts, in each of which there is a Land Board, and a Resident Commissioner, representing the Government, and acting under the instructions of a responsible minister. In 1877 a Land Act was passed, applicable to the whole colony, and its leading provisions are these :—

Clauses 4-6 give power to the Governor to declare residence optional on bush land taken up on deferred payments; also to fix the price at which any allotments of rural or suburban land, open for sale on deferred payment, may be disposed of, the price, however, being not less, in any case, than

20s. per acre for Rural land, and 90s. per acre for Suburban land,

and may increase the price of any allotments which he may consider to be of special value.

Clause 6 provides that several small sections, contiguous to one another, may be grouped in one allotment.

Clauses 17 and 19 enable two or more selectors of land on deferred payment to hold an allotment as tenants in common.

One very important section of the Act is that which makes provision for the formation of village settlements, and to this we would call particular attention, because it seems to us to offer such special facilities for systematic colonisation upon the old Greek plan, as described by Sismondi, when a body of emigrants, comprising a complete epitome of the body politic in the parent state—a microcosm, as it were, of the microcosm—went forth and planted a new community—a little model of the old—in some favoured spot upon the shores of the Mediterranean. Each class of society was represented in it, and the colony reproduced, on a small scale, all the best features of the social and industrial life of the mother-country.

Are there no younger sons of good family in Great Britain gifted with sufficient enterprise to organise the constituents of a complete village, and to charter a vessel to bring out four or five hundred immigrants, with their furniture, tools, implements and household gods, and with habitations ready to put up as soon as they reach their southern home? Such a community might embrace two or three farmers, the village butcher, baker, grocer, shoemaker, tailor, blacksmith and wheelwright, a carpenter, bricklayer, brickmaker, slater and glazier, a number of farm labourers, and last, though not least, a minister of religion, a doctor and a schoolmaster. If all these had been neighbours and associates from childhood, they would naturally pull together in a new country, where they would prolong the feelings of good fellowship which they had cherished towards each other in the old one. They would be mutually helpful, and knowing each other so well, they would be mutually trustful.

For such a body of colonists, the following clauses of the New Zealand Land Act seem to us to be particularly well adapted:—

20. The Governor, by proclamation, may from time to time set apart out of any Crown lands, such blocks or allotments of land contiguous to any line of railway or main lines of road, as he shall think fit, and declare the same open for sale as village settlements; and he may from time to time alter, amend, or revoke any such proclamation.

21. The Governor in Council may fix the terms and conditions upon which the lands comprised in any village settlement shall be disposed of, and the mode of payment for the same, subject to the rules following:

(1.) Every village settlement shall be surveyed, and divided into village allotments not exceeding one acre each, and small farm allotments not exceeding fifty acres each; or, if the Governor so direct, a village settlement may be divided into village allotments only, or into small farm allotments only.

(2.) The Governor may fix a day on which any allotments within a village settlement shall be open for application, and may appoint that any such allotments shall be sold for cash immediately on purchase, or on deferred payments subject to the conditions of the said Act ["Land Act, 1877."]

(3.) The price of village allotments shall be not less than Five pounds per allotment, and of small farm allotments not less than One pound per acre: Provided that in the case of inland districts not opened up by railway communication, it shall be lawful to the Governor to proclaim a district a special district for the opening of blocks of land as village settlements, and from time to time to alter, amend, or revoke such proclamation; and, in the case of village settlements included within the boundaries of any such special district, the price of village allotments shall be not less than Two pounds Ten shillings per allotment, and of small farm allotments not less than Ten shillings per acre.

(4.) All applications for land in village settlements shall be made in the same manner as other applications for land are directed to be made under the said Act.

(5.) If more persons than one apply for the same allotment on the same day, the right to occupy the allotment shall be determined by lot amongst the applicants in respect of small farm allotments; but, in respect to village allotments, the same shall be disposed of by public auction amongst the applicants at an upset price of not less than Five pounds for each allotment.

Land obtained upon such reasonable terms is bound to rise in value, partly owing to the rapid increment of population, and partly to the large expenditure by the Government upon local public works, such as roads, bridges and railways. The latter have already, it is estimated, more than doubled the value of real estate in the colony, while in some districts it has quadrupled, and even decupled it. According to a very good authority on this subject, "first-class agricultural land, fenced and improved, and conveniently situated, must be regarded as low in price estimated at £20 an acre. £3 per acre, per annum, of clear profit is under the average. We know of an instance of a settler purchasing 200 acres improved land at £15 an acre, and clearing his whole purchase price from his first crop. But, taking the low average mentioned, it is highly improbable that good land will remain at its present value. As society progresses in population and wealth, and as new branches of industry develop and prosper, so will the value of land steadily increase. As has been well observed, land is the natural deposit bank into which all the savings of the community gravitate. Every improvement of a public nature, in the way of harbours, roads and railways, goes to add to its value without effort on the part of the owner. There is every reason to expect that land in New Zealand will touch a far higher price than has yet been dreamt off. No one can believe that land in a country occupied by less than half-a-million of people, will be purchasable at present current prices when the country contains a population of several millions. A capitalist is therefore dealing in safety when he advances money, or becomes the actual owner of land, on the basis of present values. In the one case his margin of security is always widening; and in the other he is certain to find that in the course of twenty years he has at least doubled his capital, while in the meantime he has been in the enjoyment of a reasonable annual return.

"There is also a specialty in land in New Zealand which ought not to be overlooked, and it is this—the area is limited in extent. There is none of the boundless back-country which exists in the neighbouring colonies. No part of New Zealand is above 100 miles from the sea-board; in the South Island, 75; and when the Crown shall have parted with the last acre of its waste lands, then the value of freehold throughout the colony will rise with a bound, to an amount to which it is difficult to assign a limit."

Nor must we omit to remind our readers in England that, under the Land Transfer Act, which is almost a transcript of the admirable measure introduced into South Australia by Sir Robert Torrens, and afterwards adopted by the Legislature of Victoria, real estate can be bought, sold, or encumbered by a very simple and inexpensive process. The Government guarantees an indefeasible title, and all transactions relating to land are so expeditiously and cheaply effected, that in the year ending the 30th of June, 1879, the cost of each of 17,422 registrations, purchases, sales and mortgages, covering property of the value of £7,585,291, was only 22s. 9d. Let any one who knows anything of conveyancers' bills in the mother-country ponder well upon the full force and meaning of these highly significant statistics. By the New Zealand system of transfer, as has been well observed, "the principles of feudal law are set aside, and land can be dealt with as easily as a share in a ship or a joint-stock company, and with the same security as regards title. Trusts are not recognised. Instruments declaring trusts may, however, be deposited with the registrar for safe custody. These deeds are binding between the parties to them, but they in no way affect persons dealing with trustees who are registered proprietors. Under the Land Transfer Act, it is not necessary to examine the deeds in the abstract of title. These no longer exist. They have been delivered up to the registrar, and when a certificate of title is issued they are cancelled. An investor, therefore, does not run the risk of a mistake or blunder of his solicitor. Every transaction has in it finality and complete security guaranteed by the State."

Not long ago the proprietors of the *Otago Witness*, a weekly newspaper, issued from the office of the *Otago Daily Times*, instituted an inquiry into the condition of agriculture in that province, and collected a mass of valuable information illustrative of the enterprise and prosperity of the farming class, no small proportion of whom are shrewd, thrifty, intelligent and persevering Scotsmen. The story of one successful man's career will suffice as a very fair sample of the whole :— He had been a shepherd in Roxburghshire, and arrived in Dunedin with his wife and eight children in 1860. He found that the best of the land about Dunedin had been bought up, and he visited Southland. He bought 60 acres at Ryal Bush, at £2 per acre. There were neither roads nor bridges, and the butter, eggs and other produce were taken to Invercargill, a distance of twelve miles, by the settler, in a large bag slit in the centre, slung over a horse; often, when the streams were high, at the risk of his life. He made money, however; butter selling as high as 4s. 6d. per pound, and eggs at 4s. 6d. per dozen, prices being raised at that time, owing to the great rush of miners into the country in consequence of the discovery of gold. Eighteen months after he started, he bought 60 acres more, at £2 5s. an acre. In two and a-half years more, he secured 133 acres at £4 11s. 6d. an acre, and continued to make additional purchases from time to time. The land became his savings-bank, and it has yielded him rich interest. He and his sons, who are settled near him, now possess 2628 acres of freehold, worth at a moderate estimate £25,000. The whole farm is managed judiciously, great care being exercised in the breeding of stock. His 30 cows are noted for their excellent frames and their milking qualities; and he sends to market beef which commands the highest price. His wife and daughter are famous for their butter and Dunlop cheese. Two or three years ago, one season's cheese at a shilling per pound brought in £450. This season (1878-79) three tons sold at sevenpence-halfpenny per pound. In connection with the dairy, a number of pigs are fed yearly for the market. The sheep are the Leicester-Lincoln breed, which yield a large carcase and a heavy fleece. Hoggets' fleeces average 11 lbs., and ewes 8 lbs., in the grease. His shorn hoggets have been sold averaging 68 lbs. weight. The machinery employed is of the most improved kind, and the whole operations are conducted with spirit and intelligence. This instance is but one of many which might be quoted to illustrate the fact that New Zealand is a country in which a man with small means for a start may in a few years by industry and thrift push his way into a comfortable independence. All this has been the work of less than twenty years, and it is quite competent for hundreds of others to go and do likewise.

With respect to the profits of wheat growing, we may have recourse to the estimates of a gentleman living in the district of Oamaru, one of the finest grain-producing tracts of country in New Zealand:—

"1. Cultivation—namely:

	£ s. d.
Ploughing, double-furrow, done by contract, per acre	£0 9 0
Three harrowings at 10d., usual rate 30 acres per day	0 2 6
Rolling once	0 1 6
Seed, 1¼ bushels per acre	0 5 0
	£0 18 0
2. Harvesting: Cutting, binding, stooking and stacking, per acre	1 0 0
3. Threshing: Average crop of 32 bushels per acre, contract price for machine, including all charges	0 15 0
4. Carting to railway station	0 5 0
Say an average of £3 per acre."	£2 18 0

We now come to the returns, which are given as under:—

"Charges on wheat: Railway charges are at present 3d. per mile per ton. Taking 40 bushels of 60 lbs., equal to 10 bags to the ton, the grain can be placed on board a vessel for London for—railway carriage, 3s.; harbour dues, 2s. per ton—say 5s.

"The total charges to London, including the cost of putting on board at Oamaru, amount to 1s. 8d. per bushel. If wheat in London brings 45s. per quarter, this allows the grower 4s. at the station on the land. Forty bushels to the acre is an ordinary good crop, but 65 have been reaped. Assuming 30 bushels as a low average, this at 4s. per bushel gives a return of £6 an acre. Deducting £3 an acre as the expense of cultivation, harvesting, &c., a free profit of £3 an acre is left at low prices. In some seasons, £15 an acre has been cleared by settlers. This last year, a farmer adjoining Elderslie has threshed out the crop of barley from a field of 60 acres. The yield was 80 bushels an acre. The market price is from 6s. to 6s. 6d. per bushel. He will gross, say, £25 an acre, and after deducting all expenses, will net of clear profit at least £21 an acre."

With respect to a combination of wheat-growing with the breeding and grazing of stock on a farm of 500 acres, the following calculations are believed to be trustworthy, and if so they will be found to leave a handsome balance of profit, namely, £1145 :—

"The tenant should have a capital of £3 per acre ; or, in all, £1500. This is a full allowance for stocking. Divide the farm into 10 paddocks of 50 acres each. Keep 150 acres in white crop, 50 acres in roots, and 300 in grass. The flock of sheep should consist of 1000 Lincolns or Leicester ewes. The tenant may begin with three-quarter bred for the ordinary flock, which may be obtained at 8s. a head. Improve the stock by keeping 15 pure rams, which may be got at £5 a head.

These sheep would average 10 lbs. wool per head. This, at the low average price in the colony of 9d. per lb., would yield 7s. 6d. each. This gives a total for wool of	£375
The usual average increase is 120 per cent.; but, say, only 100 per cent., or 1000 lambs. One-third of these may be used to replace a third of the flock culled and fattened. This leaves 700 lambs to sell fat, after using the roots, say, 700 lambs at 10s.	350
300 ewes sold fat at 12s.	180
Average profit of 100 acres wheat, at £3 per acre	300
50 acres oats, at £2	100
All straw and part of the turnips to be used for fattening off 40 head of cattle to yield an average profit of £3	120
Total yearly income	£1425

DEDUCT EXPENSES—NAMELY :

1. White crop : Only the profit on this crop has been credited.	
2. Root crop: If sown broadcast, say 15s. an acre ; but if drilled it may be stated thus: 50 acres at 40s.	£100
3. Sheep-shearing : At the high cost of £20 per 1000 ; say with extras	25
4. Wages : The cost of the white crop has been already allowed for. The cost of the root crop is charged above. Cost of one shepherd—£60 wages, £25 rations	85
5. Repairs to fences, &c.	50
6. Rates and insurances	20
Total expenses	£280

A good deal has already been done by public companies in the mother-country in the way of purchasing large tracts of land in New Zealand, and then breaking them up into farms of suitable size and convenient situations, which are offered on easy terms to intending settlers. Twenty years are allowed for the repayment of principal and interest, during which period the purchaser will have paid twenty shillings per acre, per annum, and as it is estimated that the annual average profit is £3 per acre, the arrangement must be regarded as highly beneficial to the investor.

Special settlements have been also formed in this colony by private gentlemen, and by incorporated societies. As a sample of these we may refer to what is known as the Feilding Settlement, organised in 1871, when 100,000 acres of bush land were taken up in the Manawata district, in the northern island, at 10s. per acre. Under the conditions of this settlement, writes Mr. Bathgate, "the immigrants have the right to take up 40 acres of rural land at a rental of £5 per annum, or 2s. 6d. an acre, with a right to purchase at £3 per acre at the end of seven years.

On landing they were placed in possession of a two-roomed cottage and an acre of town land, for which they paid a rent of seven shillings a week, the payment of which for three years conferred a freehold right upon them. The first settlers arrived in January, 1874. The settlement has had to encounter various difficulties, many of the immigrants having arrived with exaggerated expectations, which led them to be dissatisfied with the hard bush-work, and a Maori tribe in the neighbourhood having made heavy exactions for a right-of-way over their reserve. The settlement is nevertheless making good way, and the immigrants who have settled on their rural land are rapidly improving it. In August, 1877, there was a settled population on the block of 1600, and the corporation had sold 21,501 acres for the total sum of £67,563, being an average price of £3 2s. 10d. an acre. If to this average be added the cost of clearing the land, each acre may be estimated to have cost the settler from £6 to £10 an acre. While we write (1879) the corporation have a large extent of their land still to dispose of, affording an opportunity to any hard-working labourer to obtain possession of 40 acres, and by his own industry eventually to attain to a position of comparative comfort. Population now 3000."

Owing to the exceptional advantages of soil and climate, which are enjoyed by New Zealand, wheat can be grown in any district possessing cheap and ready access to the sea-board at 1s. 8d. per bushel, and as the average yield is higher than in any of the Australian colonies, farming is much more profitable in the "Great Britain of the South" than in either of the latter. Subjoined are the maximum yields of each between the years 1869 and 1879 inclusive :—

New Zealand, 1876	32 bushels per acre.
Queensland, 1875	27 ,,
Tasmania, 1864	24 ,,
Victoria, 1870	20 ,,
New South Wales, 1877	20 ,,
South Australia, 1876	11½ ,,

The American average during a series of years is, we may remind our readers, only twelve bushels per acre. It may be interesting to give the minima of the various colonies compared, during the same decade. They were as follows :—

New Zealand, 1869	23 bushels per acre.
Queensland, 1878	11 ,,
Tasmania, 1872	16 ,,
Victoria, 1879	8½ ,,
New South Wales, 1871...	7 ,,
South Australia, 1877	6 ,,

Thus it will be seen that the minimum yield of wheat per acre in New Zealand between 1869 and 1879 was considerably higher than the maximum yield of either Victoria, New South Wales, or South Australia, during the same period. But in order to enable our reader to form a more accurate estimate of the agricultural capabilities and progress of the country we subjoin the accompanying table, which we borrow from the latest volume of statistics published by the Government at Wellington.

ACCOUNT OF LAND IN CULTIVATION AND AGRICULTURAL PRODUCE—SEASON 1878-9.
(February 1879.)

Provincial Districts.		Numbers of Holdings over 1 Acre in Extent.			Extent of Land broken up, but not under Crop.	In Wheat.				In Oats.			In Barley.		In Potatoes.		In Other Crops.	Total Number of Acres under Crop, exclusive of Land under Grasses.	In Hay.		In Sown Grasses.		Grass-sown lands not previously ploughed (including such as in Hay).	
		Freehold.	Rented.	Part Freehold, Part Rented.	Acres.	Acres.	Estimated Gross Produce (in bushels).	For Green Food or Hay.	For Grain.	Estimated Gross Produce (in bushels).	Acres.	Estimated Gross Produce (in bushels).	Acres.	Estimated Gross Produce (in bushels).	Acres.	Estimated Gross Produce (in tons).	Acres.		Acres.	Estimated Gross Produce (in tons).	In Grasses after having been broken up (including such as in Hay).	Acres.	Acres.
Auckland	1879	3,980	618	318	34,922	6,635	158,293	7,800	4,018	100,437	369	8,721	4,170	17,737	6,407	29,429	11,927	14,135	213,655	227,723				
"	1878	3,705	681	277	25,138	5,073	118,357	3,965	3,229	66,470	198	4,571	4,580	22,713	4,637	21,691	10,560	12,564	173,121	231,613				
Taranaki	1879	562	197	194	2,153	2,205	57,786	141	1,797	59,602	170	4,812	534	1,965	350	5,257	1,854	2,904	24,542	69,392				
"	1878	496	212	143	1,451	2,069	45,628	88	690	22,210	91	2,470	518	2,194	240	3,705	1,962	2,999	20,717	64,952				
Wellington	1879	1,628	595	270	7,270	7,670	187,698	1,026	10,852	314,528	299	7,417	1,333	7,144	1,319	22,499	7,100	10,630	91,450	657,061				
"	1878	1,544	549	216	38,068	5,891	159,121	673	6,523	182,907	367	9,687	1,324	7,113	402	25,180	5,826	8,217	77,298	500,354				
Hawke's Bay	1879	458	150	97	14,446	1,668	27,555	1,115	3,830	68,909	483	8,856	608	2,041	1,904	7,973	5,460	4,564	70,305	446,238				
"	1878	436	165	93	9,729	673	16,596	631	2,955	51,272	334	9,456	617	3,441	707	5,022	3,646	4,159	57,504	379,094				
Marlborough	1879	313	76	86	3,012	2,503	69,588	1,127	2,591	84,204	2,757	89,778	450	2,456	727	10,215	1,177	1,691	17,297	37,836				
"	1878	315	74	64	4,394	3,017	74,380	897	1,068	45,448	2,865	72,528	410	2,349	332	9,108	718	885	15,227	29,205				
Nelson	1879	774	481	241	5,499	3,224	61,955	3,465	3,013	75,133	2,345	56,585	1,008	4,036	2,563	15,558	3,802	4,733	36,039	67,068				
"	1878	725	459	230	2,867	2,794	45,817	2,529	1,422	28,010	2,074	37,683	1,033	5,473	1,013	10,870	2,500	2,737	21,161	37,421				
Westland	1879	161	106	15	314	..	..	373	8	180	..	..	208	789	68	657	182	249	2,581	5,437				
"	1878	124	163	6	463	1	10	193	9	458	..	..	285	1,257	57	545	209	297	2,122	2,852				
Canterbury	1879	2,996	1,124	503	120,483	173,895	3,621,830	15,183	128,384	3,237,462	17,062	371,000	4,614	26,767	97,161	436,304	11,749	10,864	479,725	115,354				
"	1878	3,055	1,408	600	123,060	147,255	3,400,953	9,638	86,315	2,398,943	13,757	335,733	4,419	26,786	64,294	326,173	10,126	14,288	418,000	163,038				
Otago	1879	2,895	1,561	635	77,404	66,941	1,885,904	19,073	123,503	4,416,690	5,131	161,287	4,390	22,651	70,825	289,918	10,237	14,330	315,557	100,651				
"	1878	2,778	1,388	554	67,430	76,028	2,475,498	12,737	57,924	3,134,244	3,027	104,605	4,360	23,152	64,294	249,444	9,453	12,555	292,304	89,726				
Totals	1879	13,762	4,938	2,348	265,512	264,861	6,070,599	49,187	278,031	8,357,150	28,666	700,465	17,315	86,186	181,264	819,445	53,503	64,520	1,251,151	1,646,758				
"	1878	13,178	5,102	2,239	272,605	243,406	6,336,369	31,351	190,344	5,929,062	22,713	576,823	17,564	94,478	136,452	641,833	45,090	58,671	1,077,454	1,488,385				
Increase in	1879	584	..	109	..	21,455	..	17,836	87,687	2,427,188	5,953	132,642	..	..	44,800	177,612	8,413	5,849	173,697	158,373				
Decrease in	1879	..	184	..	7,093	..	265,770	..	..	..	..	..	249	8,292	..	..	..	..	..	..				

NEW ZEALAND: ITS DIVERSIFIED INDUSTRIES. 131

Every description of industry that can be legitimately and profitably pursued in a new country, has already found a firm footing in New Zealand, and the following table exhibits the diversified employments of its population, as well as the number of persons engaged in the various manufactories and works, in the month of March, 1878:—

Description of Manufactory, Work, &c.	Total Number of Establishments.	Hands Employed.	Approximate Value of Land and Buildings.	Approximate Value of Machinery and Plant.
			£	£
BOOKS AND STATIONERY—Printing Establishments	77	1,268	101,000	112,528
MUSICAL INSTRUMENTS—Pianoforte Manufactories	1	7	..	..
MACHINES, TOOLS, IMPLEMENTS—Agricultural Implement Manufactories	8	208	13,050	9,710
Machine Manufactories	8	111	8,970	4,920
CARRIAGE AND HARNESS—Coachbuilding, Painting	49	433	41,477	13,955
Railway Carriage	1	10	..	..
SHIPS AND BOATS—Ship, Boat Builders	43	322	10,313	20,073
Block, Pump Manufactories	2	5	..	..
Patent Slips	5	42	11,200	37,200
HOUSES, BUILDINGS, &c.—Lime Works	34	68	5,755	1,429
FURNITURE—Furniture Makers	11	87	12,950	4,485
Chair and Washboard Makers	1	3	..	..
CHEMICALS—Chemical Works	3	25	3,150	1,700
Cleaning and Dyeing	2	8	..	..
TEXTILE FABRICS—Woollen Mills	3	78	7,500	18,000
DRESS—Boot Manufactories	18	747	29,185	8,140
Clothing Factories	2	120	..	..
Oilskin Manufactories	2	9	..	..
Stocking Weaving	1	4	..	..
FIBROUS MATERIALS—Rope, Twine Works	19	109	11,695	20,373
Sail Factory	1	3	..	..
ANIMAL FOOD—Meat Preserving (included with boiling down)—see Animal Matters—				
Bacon Curing Establishments	6	35	1,100	550
Fish Curing	2	17	..	..
VEGETABLE FOOD—Biscuit Manufacturers	6	52	4,170	4,075
Grain Mills	102	325	166,611	126,274
DRINKS AND STIMULANTS—Breweries	91	513	228,965	81,315
Aerated Water, Cordial Manufactories—Steam, Gas	7	52	14,050	8,835
Coffee, Spice Works	10	40	10,800	4,650
Malt Houses	25	100	40,350	5,465
Sauce, Pickle Manufactories	2	8	..	..
Colonial Wine ,	4	9	9,075	1,700
ANIMAL MATTERS—Boiling Down and Meat Preserving	32	443	73,775	39,875
Bone Cutting Mills	8	21	3,350	3,400
Brush Manufactories	1	18	..	..
Glue	2	5	..	..
Portmanteau	1	3	..	..
Soap, Candle Works	13	70	12,285	9,700
Fellmongery, Tanning, Currying, Woolscouring	100	671	78,995	42,758
VEGETABLE MATTERS—Chaff Cutting	6	10	10,180	980
Saw Mills, Sash and Door Factories	204	4,114	407,418	354,055
Paper Mills	2	23	..	..
Flax Mills	31	202	..	..
COAL—Collieries	40	518	224,888	51,055
Gasworks	12	145	45,149	175,144
STONE, CLAY, EARTHENWARE—Brick, Tile, Pottery Manufactories	124	620	57,775	25,908
Stone Quarries	14	90	5,190	3,325
METALS—Mining (Manganese)	1	11	..	..
Iron Foundries	28	855	81,042	75,308
Spouting and Ridging Manufactories	1	13	..	..
	1166	12,710	1,754,604*	1,289,028

* These amounts represent the total values, including the values of certain industries the particulars of which are left blank in the table, not being published for sufficient reasons.

With respect to the live stock of the colony, it amounted, at the latest date, to 137,768 horses, 578,430 cattle, and 13,069,338 sheep, besides the animals in possession of the Maori population, of which no account can be taken. Of wool, in the year 1878, there were 59,270,256lbs. exported, of the value of £3,292,807; but this was below the export of 1877, and will probably be found to have been exceeded in 1879.

The mineral resources of New Zealand are great and diversified. They include coal, of which thirty mines are being worked—in one of which the seam is 55 feet in thickness—with an annual output of 162,218 tons; gold, of which 9,246,946 ounces, of the value of £36,110,490, had been exported up to the end of December last; silver, of which the gross export has been 338,581 ounces, valued at £90,457; iron ores, containing from 63 to 97 per cent. of iron; iron sands, containing from 28 to 70 per cent. of iron; chrome ore, of great richness, which is being largely exported from Nelson; copper, lead, zinc, antimony and manganese ores; mineral oils, oil shales and graphite; while the building stones and materials include basalts, trachytes, and granites, numerous varieties of limestone and sandstone, natural cement stones, or septaria, the materials for Portland cement, and for bricks, pottery, porcelain and terra-cotta.

The population of the colony on the 3rd of March, 1878, when the last census was taken, was 414,442, exclusive of 42,819 Maoris. This showed an increase since March, 1874, of 114,898, or 38·36 per cent. The rate of increase was, therefore, much greater in the 4 years from March 1, 1874, to March 3, 1878, than in the previous period from February, 1871, to March, 1874, the increase during that period having only been at the rate of 16·82 per cent.

Of the above increase of 114,898 the natural increase by excess of births over deaths amounted to 40,844, or at the rate of 13·64 per cent. for the period. The balance, 74,054, consists of the excess of immigration over emigration during the same period. With a natural increase at the rate of 13·64 per cent. every four years, the population of the colony, if during the period there should be no excess of immigration over emigration, would in 1886 amount to about 535,000.

With respect to the educational status of the people, the census returns give much useful information. They show that the proportion of those who cannot read to every 100 living at the various ages, is least at the ages 13-14. At 9-10, 5·88 per cent. of those living at that age cannot read. The proportion diminishes year by year, till at the age 13-14, 1·60 per cent. cannot read. After that the proportion increases. At the age 20 to 21, 2·19 per cent. cannot read; and at each age-period afterwards the percentage of those living who cannot read is greater: at 70-75 it is 6·58 per cent. The proportion of those who can read and write is greatest at the period 15-20 years, amounting to 96·03 per cent., the proportion lessening with age. At 65-70 only 85·61 per cent. could read and write, and the proportions were again less with the older people.

From childhood to 21 years of age there was not much difference between the proportions of males and females who were able to read and write. After 21 the proportion of females able to read and write diminishes steadily, until at 55-60 the proportions are—males 90·65, and females 83·75; at 65·70, males 89·28, and females 80·34. Of the population at all ages 72·11 of the males could read and write, and 66·33 of the females. These are higher proportions than in 1874, when they were—males 71·40, and females 63·94. In 1874, however, only 18·61 per cent. of the population were between 10 and 21, but in 1878, 20·99 per cent. were at those ages—the ages at which the proportions who can read and write are greatest.

The colony expends upon public instruction something like £350,000 per annum, and besides the provision which is made for education in the common schools there are colleges in Christchurch, Wellington, Auckland and Nelson, the University of Otago, having its local habitation at Dunedin, the New Zealand University, which exists only as an examining body, a school of agriculture at Christchurch, the New Zealand Institute, which has its headquarters at Wellington, various Roman Catholic seminaries, and 271 public libraries. In fact, it may be truthfully affirmed that in point of intelligence and culture the people of New Zealand have no superiors in any of the Australian colonies.

With respect to trade and commerce, the latest statistics, which come down to the end of last year, exhibit the astonishing progress, which both have made since the colony was first established. Figures like these speak for themselves:—

Period.	Imports.	Exports, the Produce of the Colony.
	£	£
1841-5, average for 4 years...	139,000	33,000
1845-9 ,, 5 ,,	193,000	77,000
1853-5 ,, 3 ,,	766,000	330,000
1856-60 ,, 5 ,,	1,188,000	438,000
1861-5 ,, 5 ,,	5,352,000	2,718,000
1866-70 ,, 5 ,,	5,168,000	4,335,000
1871-5 ,, 5 ,,	6,367,000	5,276,000
1876-7 ,, 2 ,,	6,939,000	5,783,000
1878 ...	8,755,663	6,015,525
1879 ...	8,373,233	5,563,245

The great bound exhibited in the above table, as taking place in the quinquennial period 1861-5, was caused by the gold discoveries. The first considerable export of this metal occurred in 1861, the value being £752,657, increasing in the following year to £1,591,389; and the year subsequent, 1863, to £2,431,723. A more than corresponding large increase in the imports took place in the same period, due to the great influx of miners and immigrants from all parts of the world.

The total import and export trade of the colony for the year 1878, in proportion to population, stood thus:—

Imports —per head	£20 13 6¼
Exports ,,	14 4 1¼
Total	£34 17 7½

The great bulk of this large trade is transacted, we may add, with the mother country, although there is, simultaneously, a considerable expansion of the commercial relations of New Zealand with the United States.

From 1870 to 1878, £12,652,739 was expended on public works in the colony, and there were on the 30th of June, 1879, 1140 miles of railway in operation, and 142 in course of construction, besides 2356 miles of electric telegraph.

Last, but not least, the spontaneous liberality of the people has made abundant provision for places of public worship, and for the means of religious instruction; and it may be interesting to mention that the members of the Church of England in New Zealand amount to 176,337, or 42·55 per cent. of the population; the Presbyterians number 95,103, or 22·95 per cent., and the Methodists number 37,879, or 9·40 per cent. of the population; the Roman Catholics number 58,881, or 14·21 per cent. of the population. Of the principal denominations, the proportions to the 100 of population were respectively in 1878 and 1874 as follows:—

	1878.	1874.
Church of England	42·55	42·46
Presbyterians	22·95	24·20
Roman Catholics	14·21	13·48
Methodists	9·40	8·42

The various religious bodies have erected about 600 churches, and make use, in addition, of 156 schools for the purposes of public worship.

We cannot conclude this chapter better than by quoting the words of the district judge of Dunedin, with which our own knowledge of New Zealand enables us fully to concur:—

" In a country where self-government is of the freest and most popular kind, there is no impediment in the way of ability taking any place to which its possessor desires to attain. A family can be reared in comfort and refinement. The means of excellent primary and high-class education are scattered broadcast throughout the colony, under the administration of a special department of the general government. Although there is no State church, the blessings of religious ordinances are not wanting, numerous churches, through the zeal of different denominations, having been erected in every district, the members of which live in harmony with one another. The days of hardship and difficulty have passed away. There is no exile. The dreary six months' voyage has been superseded by an enjoyable six weeks' passage in well-appointed steamers. We are linked to the world by the ocean telegraph, and have the latest news and prices on our breakfast tables every morning. The monotony of ordinary life can be varied by ample sources of amusement. The sportsman has abundance of game to follow in the season, and the streams are now well filled with large trout rising readily to the fly. Every township has its racecourse, and at the principal meetings the population musters by thousands. The amount of added money run for in the colony in 1878 was £30,500. Coursing matches are now common, and the provinces strive together for victory on the cricket ground. Our harbours have their annual regattas, and our volunteers their encampments and prize-firing, at which the champion wins £100. A keen spirit of competition is manifested at our cattle shows, where animals of the purest strain are exhibited. Numerous choral societies exist for the practice of high-class music.

"With a climate which renders life positively enjoyable, with a fertile and grateful soil to cultivate, with a country having all the elements necessary to build up a free, a prosperous and a happy nation, the labours of the colonist are a pleasure to him. There is no vista before him shrouded with the dark shadows of an overgrown, under-fed population. There are no political animosities rending friendships asunder. On every side he perceives manifold signs of the rapid development of the varied resources of his adopted country, and he is nerved for greater exertions by the knowledge, that the fortunes of himself and his children must advance with its increasing progress. There is no strife, no crowding out, from the multitude of competitors in the struggle for existence. There is room for all comers of the right sort for many generations. He rejoices in his independence, and in feelings previously unknown to him. Much as we love the land of our birth and manhood, numerous as are the kind friends to whom we are attached, prickly as some of the thorns in colonial life we have had to encounter have been, we candidly declare we have never regretted for a single instant the choice of New Zealand as a new home."

CHAPTER VIII.

THE FUTURE OF AUSTRALIA.

THE PROBABLE ACHIEVEMENTS OF SCIENCE IN EXPEDITING AND FACILITATING INTER-COMMUNICATION—THEIR EFFECTS UPON CIVILISED MANKIND GENERALLY—GENERAL LEVELLING UP OF SOCIETY, AND ITS ADVANTAGES —AUSTRALIA WILL LARGELY PARTICIPATE IN THE PROSPERITY THAT IS OCCASIONED—A POPULATION OF FIFTEEN OR TWENTY MILLIONS UNDER FREE INSTITUTIONS IN A COUNTRY TEEMING WITH WEALTH—EXPANSION OF TRADE WITH GREAT BRITAIN, AND INCREASED PRODUCTIVENESS OF AUSTRALIA—FEDERATION OF THE COLONIES—ITS PROBABLE RESULTS— THE GREAT NORTHERN PORT OF THE FUTURE.

IN forecasting the future of Australia, we have very little guidance from the past history, either of this group of colonies themselves, or of the United States of America, for the twentieth century will resemble none of its predecessors. We have entered upon an era of discoveries in science, altogether without precedent, and the wildest predictions of the most imaginative writer might altogether fall short of the most prosaic facts which will be actually realised during the next fifty years. Steam may be altogether superseded as a motive power. A fortnight may suffice for the journey from London to Sydney, or Melbourne. It may be assumed, as a matter of certainty, that a transcontinental line will connect the whole of the southern or eastern cities of this continent with some northern port, and that there will be a direct and uninterrupted line of overland railway communication from Madras to Calais, and thence by submarine tunnel to the capital of the British Empire. London will be in speaking communication with every city in the civilised world. The ideas of space and time, as we now conceive, or receive, them, will be no longer current. The globe itself, as a mental concept, will have shrunk into very small dimensions. A voyage round it will have contracted to the proportions of a pleasure excursion. The history of the whole world, as it is written day by day, in the columns of its myriads of newspapers, will be epitomised each evening in the great centres of intelligence, and published next morning by the journals of all the principal cities of the earth. Science will have perfected engines of destruction and implements of warfare, to such an extent that the choice of two alternatives will be offered to makind—the abandonment of war, or its pursuit under circumstances, which would involve something like the mutual extermination of the peoples who engage in it. But before that time arrives, in all probability, the huge military and naval establishments of the great European powers will have broken down by their own inherent weight and massiveness. States will have been rendered bankrupt by the joint operation of these two causes—the stupendous cost of maintaining those establishments, and the absorption into them of the productive forces of the country. In the great political and social cataclysms, which will result from these national insolvencies, the three military empires of Continental Europe will probably collapse, and conservative republics will be erected on their ruins. These will be federated, and Victor Hugo's dream of the United States of Europe will be realised. All international custom-houses will be abolished, and free-trade will cement and consolidate the union brought about by financial ruin and political convulsion. The national bankruptcies just spoken of will involve the extinction of national debts; and as there will be no interest to be defrayed on these, and no armies and navies to be maintained, taxation will be light, and capable of being met by a small and inoppressive impost on the incomes of all classes of society. And this will be borne with the utmost ease, because the ten millions of men in the prime of life and the flower of their strength, who are now withdrawn from the ranks of industry, and are being maintained by the toil of their fellow-subjects in vicious idleness, while peace prevails, and as slaughtermen and agents of destruction, when war commences, will be then devoted to the pursuits of industry, and will be co-operators with, instead of a burden upon, the rest of the community. The drunkenness and disease which spring from ignorance, and the insanity, vice, and crime, which are the results of drunkenness, will have undergone a material diminution owing to the spread of knowledge, and the growth of the masses in intelligence and self-control. With the abolition of protection, a heavy blow will have been administered to that new form of feudalism, known as a manufacturing plutocracy; and the diffusion, by popular education, of sound principles of political economy and social science among the handicraftsmen of each community, will prove an effectual antidote to the pernicious teachings of the demagogue, the professional agitator, and all such obnoxious parasites of society.

In the process of levelling up, which will necessarily follow these great and, as we believe, inevitable changes, the condition of the great body of the people will be approximate to that of the middle classes of to-day. Scores of millions of pounds sterling will not be annually wasted, as at present, upon the formation and maintenance of armaments, organised for the purposes of human butchery,* and hundreds of millions will no longer

---

* The military and naval establishments of Europe are maintained at an annual cost of £145,000,000 sterling, while the yearly interest upon the national debts of the Continental States and of Great Britain—mostly contracted for the purposes of mutual destruction—amounts, in round numbers, to £120,000,000 sterling.

be dissipated in drink. Instead of constructing barracks and fortifications, Governments will found schools and colleges, libraries and industrial museums, public parks and pleasure grounds, art galleries and popular gymnasia. The ingenuity and inventive powers, which are now perverted to the discovery of implements and machines for the wholesale destruction of human life, for blowing up citadels, and for sending to the bottom of the sea, at one mighty blow, an armoured vessel, which has cost half-a-million sterling to construct, will then be directed to the preservation of human life, to the extension of its term, to the removal or alienation of its ailments, to the sanitation and improvement of people's dwellings, and to rendering existence more beautiful, fuller of happiness, and in every way more desirable. Science will banish epidemics; peace, industry, and temperance will diffuse prosperity through all classes of society, and wherever population increases beyond the capacity of the soil to sustain it in abundance, Governments will feel it to be their duty to promote, direct, and superintend systems of colonisation resembling those of old Greece.

In the prosperity thus occasioned, Australia will largely participate. The raw materials she produces in such great quantities and of such choice qualities, will be more and more sought after by the manufacturers of the old world; and the markets of Europe will be supplied, in addition, with her cattle and sheep, her wheat and her wine, and with the cotton, sugar, rice, tea, coffee, fruits, and spices, grown in her southern latitudes. Commerce will be as free as the air, and a generation of statesmen will look back with wonder and incredulity upon the strange freaks and follies of amateur politicians and ignorant experimentalists in Victoria and elsewhere, during the third and fourth quarters of the nineteenth century. The stump-orator will have become a relic of the past, and the protectionist will be as obsolete as the witch-finder. The idea of government by count of noses, and of legislation by fluent gabble, will be classed among the other delusions and hallucinations which mankind have outgrown, and the theory, that the intellect of the body politic is lodged in its toes and not in its head, and that the latter should be placed in subjection to the former, will be discarded by all rational men, and scouted by even the least instructed members of the community.

Fifteen or twenty millions of Anglo-Australians, living under political institutions, which will guarantee freedom of conscience and freedom of speech, freedom of commerce and freedom of person, freedom of the press and freedom of public meeting, may be reasonably expected to develop a high degree of material prosperity, and to reach an equally high stage of moral and intellectual progress. Half-a-century hence, the "common sense of most" will, in all human likelihood, have arrived at the conclusion, that the concentration of great masses of people in a few large cities is anything but conducive to public health, morality, or happiness; as also, that no wise and benevolent government has the right, or should exercise the power, of offering by class legislation special inducements to certain highly-favoured capitalists to establish large manufactories, in which are congregated large bodies of workmen, pursuing unhealthy occupations, attended with this additional disadvantage, that they necessarily tend to degrade the operative into a bit of human mechanism—a living wheel, or screw, or pinion, in a vast and complicated machine, useful enough in its particular place, and fulfilling its appointed function with methodical regularity and creditable efficiency, but nothing more.

To promote the decentralisation and distribution of those huge aggregations of men and women which are now to be met with in all metropolitan cities; to minimise the causes of excessive competition; to lessen the prevalence of those diseases, and of that vice, poverty, insanity, crime, and misery, which flourish so rankly in populous places; to encourage the growth of a feeling in favour of rural life, of the pursuits of husbandry, and of country sports and pastimes; and to popularise the fact, that those industries are necessarily the most productive, and, therefore, the most advantageous to be followed, in which nature is the chief co-operant—these will form an essential portion of the policy of the true statesmen of the future, when the provincial politics of the nineteenth century shall have passed away, and when the enlargement of the political horizon in Australia, resulting from the federation of the whole of the colonies, shall have been attended by a commensurate and correlative expansion of the intellectual outlook, mental grasp, and range of thought of those who shall then be called to the administration of Australian affairs.

In the year 1930 it may be confidently predicted that the import and export trade of Great Britain and Ireland with the Australian colonies, will be of the annual value of £300,000,000 sterling, furnishing employment to an enormous mercantile marine, and conducing in as remarkable a degree to the welfare of the outlying portions of the Empire, as to that of the mother-country. Pastoral settlements will have extended to every acre of the interior of this continent suitable for occupation by flocks and herds; and large areas, that are now sterile, will have been made available for cultivation by means of artificial irrigation, for science will have detected and defined the course of the subterranean rivers, which now discharge their waters into the Southern Ocean, and will have tapped those rivers at innumerable points so as to ensure perpetual verdure to tracts of country, which are periodically desiccated by drought, and to cause the desert to blossom like the rose. It will have been discovered, that the annual rainfall of the Australian continent, when prevented from running to waste, is as productive of wealth as if it poured down gold instead of water; and that, what Valencia was under the wise and beneficent rule of the Moors, these countries will become by the agency of reservoirs, aqueducts, artificial canals, and artesian wells.

Melbourne will have become the Paris, and Sydney the Pompeii or Baiæ of the island-continent. Both will reproduce the refined enjoyments of the more populous cities of the old world. Art and music will be cultivated with enthusiasm by a race of people, endowed with that nervous, impressionable, and emotional temperament, which is so peculiarly susceptible to, what is commonly called, the inspiration of genius; and possibly the operatic 'managers of the old world will seek in Australia for the tenors, contralti, and soprani, whom they will require for the lyric stage in Paris, London, Milan, Naples, Berlin, Vienna, and St. Petersburg.

In place of parish vestries and parish vestrymen at each provincial capital, there will be a Federal Parliament, composed of real statesmen drawn from each of the federated colonies. The trade of the professional politician will have become extinct; and those, who formerly pursued it, will probably be dealt with summarily as rogues and vagabonds, and compulsorily taught some honest occupation inside the walls of a prison. To talk of the "great heart of the people," and to appeal to mere numbers in proof of the wisdom of a given proposition, will be held to justify the incarceration of the speaker in a lunatic asylum; and gutter journalism will have become obsolete.

Each colony will be careful to elect to the Federal Legislature its ablest publicists, so as to maintain the credit of the people, whom they will represent, to take an honourable and influential part in the debates, which may arise, and to be qualified to enter the administration of a country which will have an annual budget of fifty millions sterling, and will send to the Parliament of the Empire, as many representatives as England herself. And, in the year 1930, it may be fairly anticipated, that a great commercial entrepôt will have been established on the northern shores of this continent, to which may be prophetically applied the lines which Erasmus Darwin penned concerning Sydney, at the commencement of the present century :—

> There shall broad streets their stately walls extend,
> The circus widen, and the crescent bend:
> There ray'd from cities o'er the cultured land,
> Shall bright canals and solid roads expand.
> There the proud arch, colossus-like, bestride
> Yon glittering stream, and bound the chafing tide;
> Embellished villas crown the landscape scene,
> Farms wave with gold, and orchards blush between;
> There shall tall spires and dome-capt towers ascend,
> And piers and quays their massy structures blend;
> While with each breeze approaching vessels glide,
> And northern treasures dance on every side.

Chapter IX.

THE EXPORT TRADE IN FROZEN MEAT.

THE "STRATHLEVEN" EXPERIMENT—TEPID ENTERPRISE—LIMITATIONS OF THE SUPPLY AVAILABLE—STOCK OF CATTLE AND ANNUAL INCREASE—AMERICAN COMPETITION—OUR OPPORTUNITIES OF BUILDING UP A COLOSSAL TRADE—UNOCCUPIED AND UNDER-STOCKED COUNTRY—BEST QUALITY OF STOCK REQUIRED—THE FUTURE OF BRITISH AGRICULTURE—A CHANGE OF SYSTEM—GREAT BRITAIN AND THE AUSTRALIAN COLONIES WILL BOTH BENEFIT IN AN EQUAL DEGREE BY THIS TRADE.

RARELY, indeed, in the history of these colonies, has the electric cable flashed to them an item of intelligence of greater moment and importance than that, which was received some months ago, announcing the safe arrival of the *Strathleven* in England, with the first experimental shipment of Australian meat, in excellent condition. No doubt the almost enthusiastic feelings of satisfaction, which were excited by the gratifying success of the preliminary enterprise, cooled down after a time; and the timid, the penurious, the croakers and the prophets of evil found occasion to suggest doubts as to the remunerative character of the undertaking. And it must also be admitted, that a good deal of hesitation and lukewarmness was exhibited by some of those, who were very properly appealed to, to subscribe the capital requisite to organise a company, for the purpose of prosecuting the business of preparing and exporting frozen meat, systematically, and on a sufficiently large scale. In the United States, under similar circumstances, an influential syndicate would have been immediately formed, the necessary funds would have been provided in a very few hours, and operations would have been commenced at once. But owing, perhaps, to an excess of caution on the part of the large cattle-owners, who are chiefly interested in this new branch of business; or to a desire, on the part of some, to see others incur the risk of launching an association for the purpose, while they themselves would wait until its prosperity should have been assured, before embarking their money in it; the formation of a public company for the exportation of frozen meat, proceeded much more slowly than the more sanguine friends of this promising industry could have wished. Ultimately, however, the project assumed a concrete form. A capital of £100,000 was subscribed, in one thousand shares of £100 each; and, as we write, a large refrigerating machine is approaching completion at the Melbourne Meat Preserving Company's works, and it is expected that a cargo of frozen meat will be despatched from Hobson's Bay, in sufficient time to enable it to appear in company with "the roast beef of old England," upon many a table, at the Christmas festival, in the mother-country. What the supply, available for export from these Australian colonies, will be for the time to come, must be, to a considerable extent, contingent upon the demand. For, although this continent is only one-fifth less in area than the United States, and is more than three-fourths the size of Europe, the quantity of cattle grazing on its almost measureless pastures, is limited, by comparison with the herds of other countries. This will be seen by the subjoined figures derived from Maurice Block's *L'Europe Politique et Sociale*, and from other sources:—

France	494	head of cattle to every 1000 inhabitants.
Great Britain	514	,, ,,
Prussia	540	,, ,,
Bavaria	803	,, ,,
Wurtemberg	685	,, ,,
Saxony	345	,, ,,
Cis-Leithan Austria	552	,, ,,
Trans-Leithan Austria	718	,, ,,
Spain	367	,, ,,
Portugal	316	,, ,,
Italy	291	,, ,,
Russia in Europe	693	,, ,,
Sweden	650	,, ,,
Norway	760	,, ,,
Denmark	1,202	,, ,,
Netherlands	492	,, ,,
Belgium	402	,, ,,
Switzerland	500	,, ,,
Australasia	2,500	,, ,,

Now, when we take into consideration the density of population in all the European countries enumerated above, and its sparseness in these colonies, it will be seen, that our stock of cattle bears no proportion whatever to the magnitude it is capable of assuming, if, as we anticipate, a large demand should spring up in Great Britain and elsewhere for the frozen meat of Australia. In the United Kingdom, in some parts of Germany, in the Netherlands, and in Belgium, there are, on the average, two head of cattle to every acre of land in the country. In Australasia, on the other hand, there are 27,000 acres of land to every head of cattle; the total number, at the present time, not exceeding 7,500,000. This includes the herds of South Australia, West Australia, Tasmania and New Zealand. But, as a writer on this question in the *Argus*, to whom we are under considerable obligations for the statistics we shall make use of in this chapter, observes, the supplies of frozen meat for exportation are likely to be drawn, for some time to come, from Queensland, New South Wales, and

Victoria chiefly, if not exclusively; and it is interesting, therefore, to trace the increase of cattle in each during the last six years. This is shown in the annexed table, from which it will be seen that the increase has been very unequally divided, it having been greatest in Queensland, and smallest in New South Wales; notwithstanding the fact, that the latter colony is two and a-half times larger than Victoria. The extent of such increment will be apparent by the subjoined statement:—

INCREASE OF CATTLE IN VICTORIA, NEW SOUTH WALES, AND QUEENSLAND BETWEEN 1873 AND 1878 :—

VICTORIA.
1878—Number of cattle	1,184,843
1873—Do. do. ...	883,763
Increase in 1878...	301,080

NEW SOUTH WALES.
1878—Number of cattle	2,771,583
1873—Do. do. ...	2,710,374
Increase in 1878...	61,209

QUEENSLAND.
1878—Number of cattle	2,433,567
1873—Do. do. ...	1,343,093
Increase in 1878...	1,090,474
Increase in the three colonies during the six years	1,452,763

The rates of increase have therefore been 10,000 a-year for New South Wales, 50,000 a-year for Victoria, and 180,000 a-year for Queensland.

But as there are millions of acres of splendid natural pastures in the interior of this continent, which could be stocked with cattle, if there were an export market for them; and as these could be transported overland from their grazing grounds to the port of shipment at Melbourne, Sydney, or Brisbane, there is abundant room for an immense expansion of this trade. And we are appropriately reminded by the writer above referred to, that if Australia does not secure the supply of the British market, the energetic Americans will; for they are now exporting in fresh meat and live bullocks, the annual equivalent of 200,000 cattle, as appears from the latest returns :—

BEEF AND BULLOCKS EXPORTED FROM THE UNITED STATES FOR THE YEAR ENDED JUNE 30, 1879.

Quantity.	Value in dollars.
54,025,832 lbs. fresh beef	4,832,080
136,720 bullocks ...	8,379,200
Total value ...	13,262,280

"Nor should we," it is observed, "while scanning the foregoing figures, overlook either of these facts: first, that this is a comparatively new enterprise in the United States—not of more than five years' standing; secondly, that the Americans are pushing it not only in England, but on the continent of Europe, especially since the arrival of the *Strathleven* in London with frozen meat from Australia; and thirdly, that we have as great facilities for the prosecution of the trade as the Americans have, particularly since fast-steaming vessels of large tonnage have begun to trade constantly and regularly between England and the Australian colonies. During the quarter ended the 30th March, 1876, the Americans exported 24,080 cwt. of fresh meat to England, which would be equivalent to 2,697,408 lbs., or at the rate of 8,789,632 lbs. a year. But during the year ended the 30th June, 1879, they exported in fresh meat and live bullocks what would be equivalent to 162,000,000 lbs. of fresh meat—a prodigious increase in so short a time! Why should we not then go and do likewise in proportion to our supply? What is there to hinder us?"

Nothing—it may be answered—but a lack of energy, a want of foresight, and an indisposition to provide the capital necessary for establishing the export trade in frozen meat, upon a sound and durable basis. But we cannot think so disparagingly of the people of these colonies, of the pioneers of their pastoral settlement, of their merchants and capitalists, and of all those, who have contributed by their enterprise, their industry, and their courage, to build up the splendid fabric of their material prosperity, as to assume, that they will allow a great undertaking of this kind to fail of its accomplishment, by any deficiency of money or determination. The opportunity of founding a literally colossal trade, is now presented to them; a trade, which will transform the pastures of this continent to a vast manufactory of food for the teeming millions of Europe, who will send us the products of their looms, their mills, their foundries, their workshops, and their ateliers in exchange, and the transport of these commodities will furnish employment to whole fleets of merchantmen, and to tens of thousands of shipwrights, sailors, stevedores, wharfingers, porters, carriers, and operatives on both sides of the world; so that it would be the height of folly—it would be almost an act of criminality on our part—if we failed to embrace the opportunity thus afforded, and to take, at its flood, that tide in our affairs, which must inevitably lead on to fortune. The time will come, we trust, when not one, but a dozen companies will find lucrative employment for their capital in this particular branch of commercial enterprise; and when it will have grown to dimensions more than equalling the magnitude of the export of wool from these colonies.

Meanwhile, let us glance for a moment at the stock-raising capabilities of some portions of this continent, which pastoral settlement has scarcely reached, and in others, where it has been but imperfectly developed. In North-western Australia, a tract of country has been recently discovered by Mr. Alexander Forrest, containing an area of 20,000,000 acres, well grassed and abundantly watered, with a navigable river flowing through it, for upwards of 200 miles. On the plateaux of Queensland there are also vast cattle runs, which cannot be fully stocked, for want of an outlet for the natural increase, and the same state of things prevails, we are informed, in many parts of Central Australia. Let a steady demand be once established, and the production of meat for export will be engaged in, on a far larger scale than at present, and run-holders will continue to improve their breeds of cattle, well knowing that, inasmuch as the cost of refrigerating and transporting a ton of beef of the best quality, is no more, than would be incurred by freezing and conveying to Europe a ton of inferior meat, it will pay better to raise the first than the second. According to the writer previously quoted, Durhams or shorthorns are most suitable for the purpose, and we are told "the age at which they can most profitably be slaughtered is from 18 to 24 months old, when they can easily be made fully ripe, and will weigh from 1200 lb. to 1500 lb. Still, they may be kept till they are three years old, when they will weigh 2000 lb. or more, or even till they are five or six years old, when they will attain, in some instances, the extraordinary weight of from 3000 lb. to 4000 lb. But the meat is not then so tender and juicy, nor are the growers' profits so large, owing to the extra fodder required, and other expenses in connection with them. Next to Durhams or shorthorns, preference is given to Herefords, which make as good beef, but have thicker hides and more bone and offal. Moreover, they do not mature so early as the Durhams or shorthorns, and are, consequently, less profitable to their breeder. For both these descriptions of cattle, there is ample room in the vast prairie lands in the United States. And they are produced in great perfection in the Western District of Victoria, and in some other parts of the colony. The late Hon. Niel Black's noted NB brand of Durhams, or pure shorthorns, is known all the colonies over; and so is the Messrs. Robertson Bros.' FF brand of pure Herefords, not to mention those of other breeders of the same description of cattle. Devons are also spoken of, as suitable for this trade, and they are said to make excellent beef if killed at the proper age."

At present these colonies have an annual surplus of about a quarter of a million head of cattle available for export, but it would not be long before this increased to a million, and a trade of this magnitude would necessarily involve an export of British manufactures of corresponding value; for we need not repeat the hackneyed truism, that all commerce implies an exchange of commodities, and that Australian meat would be paid for by British merchandise.

Perhaps some of our English readers will say, " But what is to become of our own pastures and our own graziers, if the colonies flood the home markets with cheap meat?" We reply, that British farmers will have to adapt themselves to the altered condition of the time, just as the New England farmers have done. Wheat and meat can be raised in the Western and North-western States of the Union, and transported to the Atlantic seaboard so cheaply, that the corngrowers and graziers of the Eastern States have found it impossible to compete with their rivals on the other side of the continent. At first, that is to say, soon after railway communication was perfected with the west, many farms were parted with in Massachusetts, Vermont, and Connecticut, at a great sacrifice, to Irish and German immigrants, while others actually went out of cultivation. But, after awhile, Brother Jonathan began to "calculate," and to "figure it out," and he very soon made the discovery, that corn-growing belonged to an early stage of agricultural development; and that, as population became denser, it was more profitable to devote land to market-gardening, orchards and the growth of dairy produce. This has been done with great advantage to all parties concerned in the United States; and we venture to predict, that it will have to be done in Great Britain. Surely a country which imported the following quantities, and values of the undermentioned articles, in the year 1876, ought to be able to produce them at home, and thus save what is now paid for them:—

Bacon and hams	...	...	3,181,569 cwts.	of the value of	£8,611,329
Butter	...	...	1,659,492 ,,	,,	9,718,226
Cheese	...	...	1,531,204 ,,	,,	4,237,763
Eggs ...	...	...	753,026,040 No.	,,	2,620,306
Lard ...	...	...	562,174 cwts.	,,	1,579,721
Potatoes	...	...	6,023,926 ,,	,,	1,740,749
	Making a total of	...		...	£28,508,184

And it must be remembered, that when the nominal price of the four-pound loaf ranges, as it will do in England for the future, at from fourpence to sixpence, and when the top price of excellent meat will not exceed sixpence per pound, the great bulk of the community will have more money to spend upon the articles, which are enumerated above, and which are still, in a vast number of families, unattainable luxuries at present. Not only so, but the producers of them will share in the increased prosperity of the country, which will necessarily result from her steadily-expanding exports to Australia. Half-a-century hence, the population of these colonies will have risen to fifty millions. The discoveries of science will have abridged the distance between the heart of the empire and her extremities, to a fortnight, in all probability; and no man would be daring enough to predict, to what dimensions the commerce of the old country and the new, will have swollen by that time. But, in the meanwhile, it will suffice to say, that that commerce must go on increasing year by year, and that, for every million's worth of wheat, or wine, or wool, which Great Britain imports from Australia, she will export its value in those manufactures, which can be prosecuted most advantageously in a densely-populated and highly-civilised community. She can produce these with a much smaller expenditure of capital and labour than we can, and therefore it is to our interest to buy them from her. We can produce the great staples, we have just enumerated, at a smaller outlay of capital and labour than she can, and it is therefore to her interest to obtain them from us. Each benefits by the exchange, which also sets in motion a mass of industrial machinery in its transaction.

In conclusion, it is not unreasonable to anticipate, that an opening will be found for the frozen meat of Australia, in some of the countries of Western Europe, where the consumption per head of this kind of food, is at present extremely limited. As free-trade principles extend upon the Continent, and as commerce is gradually emancipated from the trammels imposed upon it, by the ignorance or folly of monarchs and statesmen, the condition of the wage-earning classes will improve *pari passu*. Better earnings will lead to a better diet, and the importation of food-supplies from abroad, will be necessarily accompanied by the exportation of manufactured articles to pay for them; by an increasing commerce, and by the augmentation of the general prosperity. And thus, in their case, as in that of the mother-country, there will be a reciprocity of benefits, and we may hope, that the multiplication of the ties arising out of mutual intercourse, and the influence of a common interest in prolonging such profitable relations, will diminish the liabilities to any interruption of those relations by war, and will constitute unanswerable arguments for the maintenance of peace.

Chapter X.

RAILWAYS AS FACTORS IN THE AUSTRALIAN EXPORT TRADE OF MEAT.

THE RAILWAYS OF VICTORIA, AND THE DISTRICTS TO WHICH THEY GIVE ACCESS—HER LIVE STOCK—SIMILAR INFORMATION WITH RESPECT TO NEW SOUTH WALES AND QUEENSLAND—PROJECTS FOR A TRANS-CONTINENTAL LINE, AND THE ROUTES IT IS PROPOSED THEY SHOULD ADOPT—DISTANCES FROM THE VARIOUS CAPITALS TO THE GULF OF CARPENTARIA—RAILWAYS AND LIVE STOCK IN SOUTH AUSTRALIA—ANOTHER TRANS-CONTINENTAL PROJECT—SPLENDID PASTORAL COUNTRY IN WESTERN AUSTRALIA—TASMANIA AND ITS RAILWAYS.

IN round numbers there are three thousand miles of railway open for traffic in Australia, the whole of which converge upon seaport towns or cities. The Victorian lines radiate from Melbourne in five directions. To the east, a railway crossing the Dividing Range descends into the rich pastures of Gippsland, where the soil and climate, under the combined influences of the heavily-timbered mountains, which separate this district from the rest of the colony, and of the ocean to the south, the winds from which blow inland, surcharged with vapour, are both favourable to the production of succulent natural grasses for fattening stock. A second line—the North-Eastern—extends to the River Murray, near Albury, and gives access to the extensive tract of country watered by the Upper Murray. A third—running nearly north—touches the same river at Echuca, where a branch line to Deniliquin penetrates almost to the very heart of the immense pastoral plains of Riverina. A fourth—tending in a north-westerly direction—terminates for the present at Horsham, on the confines of another large area of grazing country, known as the Wimmera; while a fifth, taking a south-westerly course, enters the fertile Western District, which may be called the garden of Victoria, much of it being of volcanic origin and rich in all the natural elements of productiveness. These trunk lines, together with such extensions of or feeders to them, as are in progress or contemplation, bring nearly the whole grazing area of the most southerly and compact of the Australian colonies on the mainland, into communication with its chief seaports. In addition to which, there is a railway from Portland, on the west coast, to Hamilton and Ararat, which likewise traverses a pastoral country. The live stock in Victoria on the 31st of December, 1878, we may add, was as follows:—

Horses.	Cattle.	Sheep.	Pigs.
210,105	1,184,843	9,379,276	177,373

From Sydney two great trunk lines diverge, the one in a southerly, and the other in a westerly direction. The former is already in operation as far as Wagga Wagga, a distance of 309 miles, and will be completed to Albury, on the Murray, by the end of the present year. Its extension to the westward from Cootamundra to Booligal, and thence to Pooneaira, in one direction, and from Wagga Wagga to Deniliquin and Hay in another, as merely a question of time; and this will give the occupants of the vast pastoral districts of the Lachlan, the Murrumbidgee, and the Darling, access to the port of Sydney on the one hand, and to that of Melbourne on the other; while the competition, which will be thus established for the traffic in live stock, or in frozen carcases, will have a natural tendency to lower the cost of transport. The Great Western line is finished as far as Orange, a distance of 192 miles; and it will be pushed on sooner or later to Bourke, on the Upper Darling, seventy or eighty miles from the northern boundaries of the colony. This will also traverse two extensive areas of grazing country, known as the Wellington and the Warrego pastoral districts respectively. From the important port of Newcastle, situated in the midst of the magnificent coal measures of New South Wales, a railway stretches to Tamworth, a distance of 182 miles; and extensions have been surveyed to Armidale in one direction, to Tenterfield, Casino, and Grafton in another, and to Walgett, on the Barwon, in a third. By these, the produce of the Liverpool Plains and the Gwyder, New England, and Clarence pastoral districts will be conveyed to the nearest port of shipment. We have given in another chapter the figures relating to the live stock of New South Wales, but, for purposes of comparison, we may repeat them here:—

Horses.	Cattle.	Sheep.	Pigs.
336,094	2,768,601	23,962,373	219,035

As little more than two decades have elapsed since Queensland was separated from New South Wales and erected into a distinct colony, the progress of railway construction there, has been relatively slow. There is a railway from Brisbane to Dalby, a distance of 152 miles, which is being carried on to Roma, about 330 miles from the capital. This will eventually be extended to the western boundary of Queensland, and will thus cross the highly productive table-lands of the interior. Another line runs from the port of Rockhampton to Blackwater, and will ultimately be carried to the westward; while a third line will connect the port of Townsville with the country lying at the back of it. But each of these, it is proposed, shall be articulated with a grand trunk line, which shall cross the continent from south to north, and have its terminus at Burke Town, in the Gulf of Carpentaria. By the liberality and enterprise of the proprietors of the

Queenslander, an admirable weekly paper published in Brisbane, an exploring expedition was fitted out to survey the country between the Diamantina, or Mueller Creek, at about the 141st meridian of east longitude, and Port Darwin, and successfully accomplished its task. That expedition demonstrated the practicability of a portion of the scheme referred to; and should it be carried into effect, the probabilities are, that another Singapore would spring up not far from where Burke and Wills caught sight of the sea at the end of their exciting race across the continent, and that momentous changes would take place in the chief channels of trade between Australia and Europe—changes, perhaps, hardly less important in their character and consequences than those which ensued, when, to old Venice,

> The unwelcome tidings came
> That in the Tagus had arrived a fleet
> From India, from the region of the sun,
> Fragrant with spices; that a way was found,
> A channel opened, and the golden stream
> Turned to enrich another.

The line thus projected would start from Deniliquin, in New South Wales—to which place a railway runs from Melbourne, at the southern extremity of the continent—and, proceeding due north, would have its central interchanging station at Bourke, upon which point the main lines from Sydney and Adelaide would converge. Still pursuing a northerly direction as far as Lansdown, on the 25th parallel of south latitude, and linking itself with the line from Brisbane at the intermediate station of Charleville, the trans-continental railway would then deflect its course to the north-west, and would be joined by a line from Rockhampton, at the head of the River Barcoo, and by one from Townsville at Cloncurry; from whence its course would again be almost northerly to its terminus at the Gulf, which would be distant by this route:—

From Rockhampton	...	875 miles.
,, Brisbane	...	1275 ,,
,, Sydney	...	1440 ,,
,, Adelaide	...	1600 ,,
,, Melbourne	...	1650 ,,

The number of miles to be constructed would be, in round numbers, 1500. An alternative line has been proposed for adoption as more economical in construction, commencing at the 30th parallel of south latitude, up to which a railway has been constructed from Port Augusta at the head of Spencer's Gulf, in South Australia, and following the 140th meridian of east longitude to the mouth of the Leichhardt, in the Gulf of Carpentaria. Both of these propositions emanate from the Government of Queensland but there is yet another project for a trans-continental line, to which we shall presently have occasion to refer.

With an area of 669,520 square miles, or more than double that of New South Wales, Queensland possesses pastoral capabilities of which it would be difficult to over-estimate the magnitude. At present her stock returns are these :—

Horses.	Cattle.	Sheep.	Pigs.
147,076	2,433,567	5,564,465	50,301

The railways of South Australia have all been constructed so as to bring the wheat-growing, mining and pastoral districts adjacent to the coast into communication with the nearest sea-port, while the River Murray, which has its embouchure in the South Australian territory, is also a valuable channel of commerce for the country through which it flows. Adelaide, the capital, is connected with the sea-board by two railways, one running to Glenelg in a south-westerly, and the other to Port Adelaide, in a north-westerly direction. From the metropolis, a main trunk line proceeds to Gawler, a few miles beyond which flourishing town it bifurcates, the right branch extending to Kapunda, while the left stretches northward to the celebrated Burra copper mines, a hundred miles distant from Adelaide. Another line connects Port Wakefield, at the head of Gulf St. Vincent, with Blyth's Plains, a distance of 42 miles; a third crosses Yorke's Peninsula, from Port Wakefield to Wallaroo Bay, in Spencer's Gulf, and thus avoids the detour of about 200 miles, which the traffic between the upper part of that Gulf and Adelaide would have to make, if it were sea-borne. Another railway proceeds from Port Augusta, at the head of that gulf, to Parina, following the line of telegraph, which crosses the continent. Another connects Port Pirie with Gladstone; another, Port Broughton with an agricultural area fourteen miles distant from the Gulf; another, Lacepede Bay with Narracoorte; another, Victor Harbour and Port Elliot with Strathalbyn, about 30 miles inland from Encounter Bay; and another, Rivoli Bay with Gambier.

There yet remains to speak of the grand trunk-line, which will span the continent at no distant date. The South Australians, who yield to none of their neighbours in a sagacious spirit of enterprise, and whose magnificent territory spreads from the Indian Ocean to the South Pacific, are naturally anxious, that such a railway should be constructed within their own boundaries, and at their own cost. The enormous area of land which they possess—903,690 square miles—would render this a task easy of accomplishment; because capitalists could be readily found, who would undertake the work, and accept payment in blocks of land lying contiguous to the proposed line, which has been surveyed from its starting point in the south to its terminus at Port Darwin in the north. The only consideration which restrains immediate action in the matter is, that of how best to prevent the creation of one of those gigantic land monopolies, which have been established under similar circumstances in the United States; although, perhaps, the word "monopoly" is scarcely applicable to the extensive ownership of land in a country, where the supply is virtually inexhaustible, and where the facilities for its acquisition are so great, that any sober and industrious working man can obtain possession of an eighty, one hundred and sixty, or three hundred-acre farm, by the exercise of frugality and self-denial.

From a South Australian point of view, the central railway scheme is the most desirable; and it would open up and promote the settlement of vast tracts of grazing land, much of which recent explorations have demonstrated to be of the finest character. It would also afford an outlet, and access to markets, for live stock to be raised hereafter in the northern districts of Western Australia, where there is some splendid country entirely unoccupied, because, until quite recently, altogether unknown. Some idea of it may be formed from the following passages in an account of its discovery contributed to the *Victorian Review* by Mr. Alexander Forrest, in December last :—" On the 8th of May (he says) we struck the Fitzroy, a magnificent river, four chains wide, running strongly, and with splendidly-grassed banks. This noble stream is the main artery and outlet of a most beautiful extent of territory, suitable in the highest degree for pastoral purposes. . . . . On the 1st June we re-crossed the Fitzroy, and next day left it, having followed the course of this magnificent river for 240 miles. It is the longest river in Western Australia, its banks being splendidly grassed for at least a breadth of 20 miles. I roughly calculate, that there are here four millions of acres of excellent pastoral land, capable of carrying at least a million and a-half of sheep, which is more than there are in Western Australia altogether. The country along its banks is seamed with creeks and gullies, all of which we found running. The water supply of this region appears to be both abundant and constant."

In conclusion, Mr. Forrest states that the Fitzroy and other large rivers flow through an available pastoral country of not less than 20,000,000 acres in extent, well-grassed and well watered, much of which would be suitable for the cultivation of sugar, coffee and rice.

Regarded from a purely Australian point of view, the transcontinental line, previously referred to as beginning at Deniliquin and having its terminus at Burketown, would appear to be the more desirable of the two; but before either project is carried into effect, it is probable, that an inter-colonial conference will be held on the subject; unless, indeed, the energetic people of South Australia should resolve in the meantime on carrying out their scheme single-handed and unaided. In any case, a railway bisecting the continent, and throwing out branches to the right and left, to meet the requirements of increasing settlement, cannot fail to communicate an immense and enduring stimulus to the breeding and fattening of sheep and cattle over vast areas of the interior, which are now virgin pastures, while at the same time providing facilities for their export not merely to Europe but to Asia, such as at present do not and can not exist.

The live stock of South Australia on the 31st of December, 1878, was as under :—

Horses.	Cattle.	Sheep.	Pigs.
121,553	251,802	6,377,812	103,422

In Western Australia, owing to its geographical isolation and sparse population, only three short lines of railway have been hitherto constructed, from as many of its sea-ports to places a few miles from the coast; but the enormous area of its territory, roughly estimated at a million square miles, and the nature of its soil and climate, justify the prediction, that its contributions to the food supplies of the world will one day assume gigantic proportions. At present it depastures the following stock :—

Horses.	Cattle.	Sheep.	Pigs.
32,801	56,158	869,325	16,762

Tasmania is traversed by a railway connecting its northern capital, Launceston, lying at the head of the estuary of the Tamar, with its southern capital, Hobart Town, seated on the shores of the Derwent. A second line unites the former city with Deloraine, from whence, following the valley of the Mersey, it extends to the port of Torquay, in Bass's Straits. The island is so abundantly watered, and its valleys are so well adapted for grazing purposes, that it ought to have a surplus of live stock available for exportation. Hitherto, however, the imports have exceeded the exports, and the official returns show the following to be the quantities in the island :—

Horses.	Cattle.	Sheep.	Pigs.
24,107	126,276	1,838,831	39,595

It only remains to give the totals of the various colonies, in order to enable our readers to gauge the future capabilities of Australia to supply the teeming millions of the old world with cheap and nutritious meat, fattened on natural grasses, under purely natural conditions, and therefore exempt from the diseases incidental to artificially fed and artificially housed cattle, in thickly-peopled countries, where the very air, at certain seasons of the year, and under certain states of the atmosphere, is impregnated with disease germs. These totals are as follows :—

Horses.	Cattle.	Sheep.	Pigs.
872,110	6,824,529	47,996,762	607,773

This represents but an insignificant fraction of the quantity of live-stock, which the Australian pastures will carry hereafter, as pastoral settlement spreads over the interior of the country, and the 2,000,000,000 acres embraced within its area are covered with flocks and herds, always excepting its desert patches, which artificial irrigation may, however, one day reclaim and transform, when all the good land has been profitably occupied. But this is a contingency too remote to concern us now. Enough to say, that, under the Southern Cross, England has planted the germs of future nations, on a continent capable of becoming the granary and the stock-yard, the vineyard and the dairy of the old world ; and that in the development of its incalculably vast and diversified resources there is ample room and verge for the employment of the idle capital and the surplus labour, not only of the mother-country, but of those continental states which resemble her most closely in the industry, ingenuity, enterprise and persevering energy of their populations.

Chapter XI.

AUSTRALIA, THE VINEYARD OF THE WORLD.

GREAT VARIETY OF WINES IT IS CAPABLE OF PRODUCING—THE VINEYARDS OF SOUTH AUSTRALIA—ONE OF THEM DESCRIBED—A FRENCHMAN'S VISIT TO ST. HUBERT'S, IN VICTORIA—THE VINE IN WESTERN AUSTRALIA—THE PIONEER OF THE INDUSTRY IN NEW SOUTH WALES—CHARACTER AND DIVERSITY OF THE WINES OF THAT COLONY—CULTIVATION OF THE VINE IN VICTORIA—QUEENSLAND—THE DYING-OUT OF THE FRENCH VINEYARDS SHOULD ACT AS A STIMULUS TO THE EXTENSION OF THE INDUSTRY IN AUSTRALIA—RAVAGES OF THE PHYLLOXERA IN FRANCE—THE VINEYARDS OF AUSTRALIA CONTAIN MINES OF UNDEVELOPED WEALTH—THE ANGLO-AUSTRALIANS BEING A WINE-PRODUCING PEOPLE WILL PROBABLY BE A SOBER POPULATION—SOME FRENCH STATISTICS BEARING ON THE SUBJECT.

By their geological formation, soil, and climate, large areas of this continent are marked out by the hand of nature as the future vineyard of the world. And practical experience has demonstrated, even at this early stage of viticulture in Australia, that it is capable of producing wines, which already closely approximate to, and will eventually rival, in quantity and quality, the choicest vintages of Spain, Portugal, Madeira, France, Germany, Hungary, and Italy. The colony of South Australia, which has taken the lead in this branch of husbandry, lies between the same isothermal lines as the Spanish Peninsula, Italy, Sicily, Greece, and the Levant. The climate is dry, the vintage season is usually rainless, and the character of the best wines produced there resembles that of the strong, generous, and full-bodied wines of Spain and Portugal. In the following list we have merely enumerated the principal varieties:—

WHITE WINES.

Verdeilho	Gouais	Sherry
Doradilla	Belas Blanco	Paolmina Blanco
White Tokay	Riesling	Frontignac
Madeira	Pedro Ximenes	

RED WINES.

Mataro	Malbec	Shiraz
Carbinet	Burgundy	Portugal
Grenâche	Espanoir	Hermitage
Muscat		

The Rev. Dr. Bleasdale, writing from an intimate knowledge of the subject acquired during his residence in Portugal, and after an extended visit to the vineyards of South Australia, says :—" The whole of the country about the capital seems formed to be the home of those vines which nature has destined to produce strong, generous, full-bodied wines. Several vineyards seem to want nothing but the experience and skill of the Portuguese *feitor* and Spanish *capitan* to turn out as good wines of the port and sherry character, as most of those now obtainable from Europe." And here we may remark, by way of parenthesis, that to a palate not vitiated by spirit-drinking, and not denaturalised by familiarity with the fortified and highly-artificial beverages, which now find their way to the tables of even professed connoisseurs under the name of port and sherry, the South Australian wines, which correspond in flavour and origin with these, will commend themselves as more delicate on the tongue, and as possessing a more exquisite bouquet than the brandied and doctored compounds over which many worthy persons smack their lips, under the impression that they are imbibing the pure juice of the grape. "In South Australia," continues Dr. Bleasdale, "nature herself is opposed to the production of those high-bouquet wines. Here she demands consideration for body, sweetness, and the other high qualities of generous wines. The Riesling and Verdeilho, when not tortured, yield wines second only to the Bucellas of Lisbon, and the sweeter kinds of Madeira ; while the Donzellinka, the Black Portugal, the Scyras, the Mataro, and Grenâche yield wines of the character of good Port, such as it is known in Portugal, and the strongest of Hermitage, and that peculiar produce known as Roussillon." In fact, South Australia may be described as a country beloved by the sun, who lavishes his fervour on the soil, which transmutes it, wherever the vine is grown, into the rich blood of the purple or of the golden grape.

With respect to the present condition of this branch of industry in the colony under notice, the statistics for 1878 furnish us with the following particulars :—

Total number of acres under vines ...	4,297
Quantity of wine made (gallons) ...	458,303

The more celebrated of the South Australian vignerons are :—Messrs. Patrick Auld, Joseph Gilbert, Thomas Hardy, Smith and Sons, Penfold and Co., and the South Australian United Vineyards Association.

The Auldana wines, produced in the vineyards of Mr. Auld, on the slopes of the Mount Lofty Range, about five miles distant from Adelaide, are not unknown in England, where the impending re-arrangement of the Customs tariff upon imported wines, is likely to facilitate the introduction and consumption of Australian vintages, which have hitherto been practically shut out from consumption in the mother-country, owing to the fact of their range in strength being above the 26 degrees of proof-spirit, which constitutes the line of demarcation between wine liable to the duty of one shilling per gallon, and that chargeable with the duty of half-a-crown per gallon.

As the Auldana vineyards are very good specimens of Australian vineyards generally, the following description of them by a South Australian may not be unacceptable to our readers :—" The vines are planted from five to six feet apart, and six or seven feet between the rows. In round numbers there are about 140,000 vines on the property. The yield of wine varies with the season, the lowest being only about 110 gallons per acre, and the highest nearly double as much. The vineyards are laid out with roads intersecting them, to facilitate the passage of carts during the vintage for conveying the grapes to the cellars. The cellars form two sides of a square, and one portion measures 100ft. by 70ft., the other at right angles with it, measuring 80ft. by 30ft. The other two sides of the square are appropriated to the workmen's quarters, cooperage, and workshops, stables, cartsheds, and bottle-washing department. The water supply at this elevated situation is derived from the rainfall collected from the roofs in underground tanks, holding about 40,000 gallons. A perennial creek or brook of excellent water, however, runs through the lower part of the property.

"The cellars are only partly underground, being excavated from the slope of the hill. The walls are fifteen feet in height, and over a portion of them the roof is double, the greatest depth below the surface of the ground being from ten to twelve feet. They afford ample accommodation for the storage of 100,000 gallons of wine. One of the larger vats has a capacity of 3000 gallons, and there are six or seven of 2000 each, fourteen slate tanks of from 500 to 800 gallons each, a number of casks of 500 and 300 gallons, and numerous pipes and hogsheads. The large press has two powerful iron screws worked by a fly-wheel; there are also smaller presses worked by hand.

"During a recent visit to Auldana, I found 45,000 gallons of excellent wine in the cellars, varying in age from eight months to eight years. At different times during a week I sampled the whole, and from a long experience with Australian wines, I can honestly say, that there was not a single hogshead of wine in the cellars but what was sound and good, and the great bulk of it of very superior quality. The wines of Auldana are now of almost world-wide fame, having gained prizes and honourable mention at every International and Intercolonial Exhibition for the past eighteen years. London, Vienna, Paris, Philadelphia, Sydney, Melbourne, and Adelaide have all given prize medals, cups, or certificates and honourable mention to these pure and delicious wines, and the numerous prizes and certificates form quite an art collection at Auldana."

As a companion picture to the above, we will do ourselves the pleasure of quoting an account given by M. de Charnay, a scientific French traveller, who recently visited Australia, of the impressions produced upon his mind by one of the principal vineyards in Victoria; that, namely, of Messrs. De Castella and Rowan, situated in the valley of the Upper Yarra, and in the immediate vicinity of a part of the colony, which has been appropriately called its Switzerland, by reason of the romantic beauty of its mountain scenery.

The news and opinions of a foreign visitor on such a subject will be necessarily free from the more or less unconscious bias, which might influence a Victorian, when speaking of one of the industries of his country, and describing scenes and persons in which and whom, it is more than probable, he feels the warmest interest. M. de Charnay, who was the guest of M. Hubert de Castella, a Swiss gentleman, whose *Sovenirs d'un Squatter Français en Australie* were published in Paris and very favourably received about twenty years ago, writes as follows:—" I visited, in company with my host, his fine property. It is the season of bloom *(floraison)*. Two hundred acres of vines in one compact block, spread their green and vigorous foliage, and the air is perfumed with the mignonnette scent of the vines in bloom. I doubt if there could be found in any part of France a more careful cultivation. There is not a weed between the vines, and the branches, all tied to sticks or trellised, disclose innumerable bunches. If the weather is propitious, the forthcoming vintage must be abundant, for I count up to sixty-two bunches on a single vine. Truly, it is a gladdening sight, especially for a Burgundian; it brings back to my memory the far away hill-sides of my own native land. Curious to say, here, in the same vineyard, a variety of kinds are cultivated, which all succeed. It is divided into large squares of these various kinds. Here the Sauvignon of Bordeaux, the Pineau of Burgundy, and there the Chasselas of Fontainebleau, which produces a delicious wine, and the Hermitage and the Riesling of the Rhine. At first I thought that the planting of all these varieties was in view of an extensive experiment, which would show the best kind to cultivate afterwards; but no! M. de Castella tells me, that he keeps each variety distinct, and that he makes Bordeaux wine, Burgundy wine, Hermitage and Rhine wine; and what will surprise our vignerons is, that all these wines have truly their distinctive bouquet, and that they have perfectly preserved the character of their origin. We shall pass in review the cellars. It is really Bordeaux, Burgundy, and Rhine wine which I taste. I cannot express my astonishment. This is contrary to the law of assimilation, it cannot remain so for ever. Every species of vegetation, as well as every race of living beings, is modified by outward influences of soil, climate, habits and food, and the transformation is the more rapid as the organisation of the individual is less perfect, and as it belongs to a lower order. It is evident, that this vineyard, producing to-day several wines, each of perfectly distinct character, will eventually produce only two types, one red and one white, which will bear uniform products, and will no longer be similar to European wines, but will be Australian St. Hubert's wines. Be this as it may, these wines are delicious. But it was not in a day that the grower obtained such results. At first, a virgin soil just freed from gum-trees, cold as all land long covered with forest is, and also a defective manipulation, had only given wines hard and retaining a strong earthy taste. To-day, careful cultivation, a soil well worked, and ten years of experience in the manufacture, have given these products which I found perfect, and which will sell at a premium in the markets of Europe from the day they become known there. The Australian wines have already gained prizes at several international exhibitions, notably at Vienna and Paris. Now, it behoves the Australians to show by their example the esteem they have for their products. They must use them themselves; they must leave off in part tea, which they abuse, and the alcohols, which pervert their taste; in a word, they must show by drinking them, that their own wines are good. Wealthy people in Australia, as much by ostentation as by taste, neglect the Australian wine. They would be ashamed of drinking cheap wine; it is expensive claret, burgundy, and champagne which they offer to their guests. Perhaps, also, they find their own too strong. For observe: I found at St. Hubert's an intelligent grower whose taste was formed in Europe, whose palate was accustomed to the wines of France; this man tried to give to Australian wines a body and a bouquet similar to ours, and he succeeded. So will others, for Australia is far from wanting in intelligent men; but at present the colonists, who have known, as wine, only foreign adulterated port and alcoholised sherries, have only one ambition—to grow deep-coloured and strong wines, which are, unfortunately, a natural production in a dry and hot climate. How often in my rambles about the Australian continent have I tasted these deplorable burning beverages! What wine! How intolerably strong! He used to tell me, the proud grower, that Europe produces nothing similar. Certainly it does not. *Mais malheureux*, that quality is a fault; your wine is not drinkable, and, moreover, it is unwholesome. If you intend to supply the world, you must alter your method. Do not make these extraordinary wines, which everybody will refuse; but produce light wines, of an easy digestion and fit for daily use. Leave off imitating Spanish wines, and take French wines as a model, and you will dispose of a hundred times more of your products than you now do!"

In Western Australia, which lies between warmer parallels than its neighbour South Australia, but has a cooler climate on the whole, because its temperature is modified by the sea-breezes, which sweep in upon its 2000 miles of coast-line facing the west, the vine flourishes luxuriantly, alike upon its arenaceous, marl, and limestone soils. Its wines exhibit most of the characteristics, which distinguish those of the South of Spain, and of the island of Madeira; but, at present, this form of industry is in a relatively backward condition, as the enterprise of a limited population finds abundance of scope in developing those resources of the colony which yield a larger and a more immediate return to capital and labour. But the growth of a large wine-making interest is merely a question of time.

New South Wales, the mother-colony of the Australian group, was the first to commence the cultivation of the vine; and to Mr. John Macarthur, of Camden, belongs the honour of having been the pioneer of an industry, which is destined, perhaps, to overshadow all others by the magnificent proportions which it will one day assume. That enlightened and far-seeing man, after having laid the foundation of our vast export of wool by the acclimatisation of a flock of pure-bred merino sheep in 1797, visited the continent of Europe in company with his two sons in 1815, and remained there for a twelvemonth, studying, among other subjects, the cultivation of the olive and the vine. They collected cuttings from some of the most celebrated vineyards in France, and, returning to Camden, planted a vineyard there. And in 1840, they sent an agent to Germany to make a second collection; which afterwards became the principal source of supply to the other colonies, although at a much later period, immigrants from Germany and Switzerland brought with them vine cuttings from both those countries, and established them in South Australia and Victoria.

The Messrs. Macarthur had many difficulties and prejudices to encounter, but they surmounted them all, and lived to witness Australian wool bearing away the palm from all competitors, and Australian wines extorting the eulogies of the best judges in Europe. Some day, perhaps, the magnitude of their benefaction to Australia and the world will receive its just, if tardy, recognition; but, in the meantime, any account of the wines of these colonies would be incomplete, if it omitted to make mention of the immense debt of gratitude due to the planters of the first vine in this portion of the globe.

An accurate classification of the wines of New South Wales by analogy with those of any particular country in Europe, would be extremely difficult and possibly misleading. It is scarcely too much to assert, that the choicest products of the most celebrated wine-growing districts in every part of that continent have, or will have, their counterparts, in the mother-colony. We say "or will have," because, in many instances, the colonial processes and appliances, as well as the means of storage, are inferior to those of older countries; and much yet remains to be learned with respect to the precise adaptation of varieties of the vine to soil, and also as to the modifications which certain species of grape undergo in an Australian climate. Certain it is, that these modifications do occur, and that they are not unfrequently in a highly beneficial direction; the wine expressed from a certain berry taking on new qualities, disclosing a finer aroma, and yielding a more delicate flavour.

Broadly speaking, it may be asserted that, within the limits of New South Wales, vineyards, or the sites of vineyards, are to be found, capable of producing the wines of Spain and Portugal, of Medoc and Bordeaux, of

Burgundy and Champagne, of Montepulciano, Orvieto, and Malvasia—some of the richness of a liqueur, others the dainty delicacy of Chateau Yquem, and others the seductive softness and subtle bouquet of Chateau Lafitte. The following are the principal varieties :—

WHITE WINES.

Verdeilho	Riesling	Aucarot	Blanquette
White Hermitage	Tokay	Madeira	Cawarra Hock
Muscatel	Pineau	Shiraz	Bebeah
Sherry	Cawarra	Kaludah	Pedro Ximenes
Tolle Blanc	Buculla	Dalwood	Champagne
Hock	Camden	Muscat	

RED WINES.

Pineau Noir	Albury Port	Riesling	Muscat
Virdot	Hermitage	Isabella	Dalwood
Black Spanish	Shiraz	Malbec	Buculla
Claret	Burgundy	Carbinet	Grenâche
Black Hamburg	Lambruscat	Camden	Lachryma Christi
Chateau Margaux	Verdeilho		

The official returns for 1880, supply the following statistics :—

Total number of acres under vines	4,266
Quantity of wine made	733,576 gallons
Grapes consumed for table use	1,017 tons

The principal vignerons in New South Wales are Messrs. J. and W. Macarthur, of Camden Park; J. T. Fallon, of Albury; J. Wyndham, of Dalwood; Arthur Danes and Co., of Mount Huntly; J. P. Doyle, of Kaludah; James Kelman, of Branxton; H. J. Lindeman, of Cawarra; Carl Brecht, of Denman; and A. Munro, of Singleton.

The cultivation of the vine in Victoria has made rapid progress of late years, owing, it may be believed, to the greater number and density of the population in that colony. It originated with some Swiss settlers near Geelong, about ten years after the foundation of the colony, and received a considerable stimulus from the enterprise of Messrs. Paul and Hubert de Castella, also Swiss gentlemen, who established vineyards about thirty years ago, at Yering, on the Upper Yarra. At the present time the wine-growing districts of Victoria are pretty numerous, and each has a distinctive character of its own. Those north of the Dividing Range assimilate in their products to the wines of Southern Europe; while those south of that line of demarcation approximate to the vineyards of Rhineland and northern and midland France. This generalisation, however, must not be accepted in too literal a sense; because the quality of the vintages will be certainly found to vary with the position of the vineyard—whether planted on a hill-side and at a certain elevation above the sea, as at Sunbury, or laid out in a valley as at Yering. Suffice it to say, however, that in the words of Dr. Bleasdale, "between the Barrabool Hills, and the valley of the Murray, Victoria possesses every variety of climate, exposure, and soil, that are to be met with between Neufchatel and Lisbon." And it is only right to add, that nearly every description of grape, that is popular among the vignerons of France, has been introduced into Victoria, and has proved to be capable of being cultivated with success south of the Dividing Range. Those kinds, which appear to find a peculiarly congenial habitation in this part of Australia, are Hermitage, Burgundy, Carbinet, Sauvignon and Malbec; but in the opinion of Dr. Bleasdale, if ever Victoria gains a name in the world's markets for any distinctive growths, Chasselas will take the first place, Aucarot the second, and Shepherd's Riesling, or some blend of it, the third.

The official returns for the year 1880 give the following particulars:—

Total number of acres under vines	4285
Quantity of wine made (gallons)	574,143
Grapes consumed for table use	16,275 cwt.

The principal vignerons in Victoria are Messrs. de Castella and Rowan, of St. Hubert's; Mr. J. S. Johnstone, of Sunbury; Mr. Carl Pohl, of Strathfieldsaye; Messrs. A. and R. Caughey, of the Murray; Mr. C. Braché, of Sandhurst; Mr. G. S. Smith, of Wahgunyah; Messrs. Trouette and Blampied, of Great Western; and Mr. J. Davies, of Moonee Ponds.

The wine-growing industry in Queensland is at present too young to enable us to speak with any degree of confidence and accuracy concerning it; but all the indications point to its becoming a large wine-producing colony in the future. At the International Exhibition in Sydney, 1879-80, six vignerons sent in samples of Espar, Verdeilho, Salvina, Mataro, Hermitage, Isabella, Black Spanish, Tokay-Riesling, and other unnamed varieties. The exhibitors were Mr. C. P. Chubb, of Ipswich; Messrs. D. J. Childs and Son, of Brisbane; Messrs. C. T. Gerler and Son, of Brisbane; Mr. Jacob Kitchen, of Warwick; Mr. J. J. Lade, of Brisbane; and Mr. Conrad Romer, of Warwick. These gentlemen had about 15,000 gallons in stock, the selling price ranging from 6s. 6d. to 10s. per gallon.

In view of the deplorable ravages of the phylloxera in France, this question of wine-growing in Australia is daily assuming greater importance; because not merely are the capabilities of production virtually unlimited, but the soil and climate are eminently favourable, as has been already stated, to the growth of every one of the varieties of the grape, which are so rapidly perishing in the country, from which the whole world has hitherto been accustomed to draw its supplies of the choicest wines. In the year 1869, when the production of the French vineyards had reached their maximum, it amounted—as we learn from the *Annuaire de l'Economie Politique*—to 70,000,000 hectolitres. In 1878 it had fallen to 48,720,553 hectolitres; and the particulars given with respect to the position of the vignobles in the year following, by *L'Année Scientifique*, show that the French diminution of the yield is continuing to assume alarming proportions. Thus, in the Département du Gard, where there were 99,000 hectares of vineyards ten years ago, there are now less than 9000 hectares. Out of 70,606 hectares in the arrondissement of Montpellier no less than 65,612 have been ravaged by the scourge. Out of 101,333 hectares in the arrondissement of Béziers only 57,376 remain intact. In that of Lodéve, 24,893 hectares out of 28,805 have been destroyed; and the full list of the arrondissements in which the dreaded pest is extending its ravages, comprehends no less than one hundred and twenty of these territorial divisions; so that, in the words of the publication just referred to, "nearly the whole of our wine-growing country is either invaded, or is about to be, by the phylloxera;" and it is now ascertained that at certain periods of the year—and notably in June and July—the young insects emigrate from localities in which the plant they feed upon has become scarce, and set out in search of "fresh fields and pastures new."

Under these circumstances, and taking into consideration the fact that maladies of this kind—as has been the case with respect to the potato disease—when they have once established themselves in a country, seem to take root there, and to become chronic, it does not require one to take a very sanguine view of the prospects of Australian viticulture in order to predict, that it has a great future before it. At present this industry is only in its infancy, and the product of 1879, which was, in round numbers, 1,600,000 gallons only, was very little more than that of the smallest of the French Departments, namely, that of Sarthe; but we are convinced that the day will come, when colossal fortunes will be made by syndicates of French wine-merchants and vinegrowers operating in Australia, and discovering in its vineyards mines of wealth far exceeding those, which were laid bare by adventurous miners in the early days of the gold-fields.

Nor can we quit the subject without referring to the moral aspects of the question. Reasoning from analogy, we may confidently expect to find the Anglo-Australians a sober, because a wine-growing people. The Spaniards are proverbially temperate, and it is a fact well established by experience, observes a French writer, that an habitual drinker of light wines rarely touches spirits, or is addicted to inebriety. Thus in the Haute-Garonne, Tarn, and Tarn-et-Garonne, that is to say, where the population is accustomed to the regular use of wine, the annual consumption of alcohol per head averages only 0·80, 0·83, and 0·64; while in the Nord, the Pas-de-Calais, the Somme, and the Seine-Inférieure Departments, in which the labouring classes do not drink wine, the average is 4·55, 6·47, 5·85, and 9·7·5. In 1873 the judicial statistics show, that in the first three departments, not more than two or three persons were convicted of drunkenness out of every thousand inhabitants, while in the last three the number of convictions for this offence was at the rate of 17·20, and even 60 per thousand.

CHAPTER XII.

IMMIGRATION TO AUSTRALIA.

APATHY ON THE SUBJECT IN ENGLAND—SYSTEMATIC COLONISATION WANTED—
A CAREER FOR ALL IN AUSTRALIA—ITS ATTRACTIONS AND ADVANTAGES—
A LAND OF PROMISE TO THE MANUAL LABOURER—THE DIVERSIFIED
RESOURCES OF THE COLONIES—THEIR HEALTHFULNESS—EACH OF THEM
REPRODUCES SOME OF THE BEST FEATURES OF THE MOTHER-COUNTRY—
SKETCHES OF VICTORIAN LIFE AND SCENERY—MELBOURNE ON THE EVE
OF THE CUP-DAY—ONE OF THE SUBURBS OF THE VICTORIAN METROPOLIS
—UP AMONG THE VINEYARDS AT YERING AND ST. HUBERT'S—THE FUTURE
BELONGS TO AUSTRALIA, AS THE PAST DOES TO THE OLD WORLD.

To an Anglo-Australian not devoid of human sympathies, few things appear more inexplicable, than the indifference, not to say apathy, which prevails in the minds of his fellow countrymen at home on the subject of emigration. It is one in which all classes of society, and men and women belonging to every grade in life, should feel a deep and vital interest. Nor can it be denied, that Great Britain is overcrowded, and that notwithstanding the enormous expansion, which every branch of industry has undergone since the country was emancipated from the galling and debasing manacles of protection, the struggle for existence continues to be an arduous one. Indeed, it may be said to be more arduous than ever, because one effect of free-trade has been to elevate, by the general prosperity it has diffused, every stratum of the social edifice. The labouring man of to-day is better off than the artisan of forty years ago; the artisan than the small shopkeeper of the same period; the large trader than the merchant; the merchant than the territorial magnate, and so on. But this remarkable change has not been accompanied or followed by greater thrift. On the contrary, the expenditure of all classes upon articles of food and clothing, of comfort and luxury, has increased even more than commensurately with the increase of their earnings or income; their artificial wants are greater and more numerous than ever they were, and the result is, that the battle of life has become increasingly severe, by reason of the higher standard of living which has been established, and the extravagance which has attended upon a lengthened period of unprecedented prosperity.

It is customary to speak of China as a densely-populated country, but the best estimates give it only 110 inhabitants to the square mile. In England and Wales, on the other hand, population is upwards of three times and a-half as dense, averaging 389 persons to the square mile. Surely this is not a satisfactory state of things, more especially when we take into consideration the fact, that the tendency of these masses of people is more and more towards aggregation in large towns and cities, under conditions necessarily unfavourable to health, physical vigour and morality. The popular idea, that the power and greatness of a state are to be measured by the number of its people, is proved by history to be an entirely erroneous one. It is the quality of a nation, and not its quantity, which determines its influence and potency, and secures its pre-eminence in the arts of war and peace. Better a handful of Athenians, than a horde of Persians; better the immortal three hundred, who fell under Leonidas, than a whole legion of the followers of Xerxes. Britain is more likely to be weakened than strengthened by the addition to her population of millions of manufacturing operatives, reared in the unwholesome atmosphere of a crowded city, and following occupations, which transform man into a piece of mechanism, and dwarf and enervate him by indoor confinement, while the very monotony of his employment tempts him to have recourse to artificial stimulants for excitement and for some exhilarating break in its dreary uniformity.

England is now so thickly peopled, and her population has now so completely outgrown the capacity of her soil to maintain it, that every child born beneath an English roof increases her dependence upon distant countries for her supply of food, and promises in after-life to become a competitor with his or her contemporaries for employment in an already crowded labour market. Every father of a family, from the estated nobleman or gentleman down to the farm labourer, must contemplate with anxiety the future of his children in a country, so thickly peopled as England is. In ancient Greece, under similar circumstances, some of the younger sons of the *aristoi* would have organised the elements of a miniature State, its husbandmen, its artisans, its artificers, its law-givers and its rulers, and would have gone forth in a body to found a colony on the shores of the Mediterranean, where this compact and well-balanced community would have reproduced a faithful copy of the society from which it had detached itself. And what might not be accomplished in the same way now, if some of the natural leaders of the people in the mother-country were to follow the example of a Raleigh or a Baltimore, and organise the materials for a complete settlement, composed of their old friends and neighbours, tenants and workmen; first of all personally selecting a suitable block of land in one of these colonies, then preparing for the temporary shelter and maintenance of the immigrants; and then chartering a vessel for the conveyance of themselves and families, their ministers of religion and the parish doctor, their household goods, farming implements, tools, stock-in-trade and the materials for their frame-houses and their places of worship. Such colonies, animated by the neighbourly feelings, which arise out of long and intimate association, could not fail to thrive, just as the Russian Mennonites have thriven in the United States; and they would also supply an element of unity and concord to our social and political life, which is sadly wanting in both. For as society in these colonies is literally "a fortuitous concourse of atoms" gathered together from all parts of Great Britain, as also of the continent of Europe, there is no homogeneity in the mass. Mutual repulsion is the rule, and not mutual attraction, and such cohesion as does exist is the result of merely class feelings, and too often takes the form of class antipathies, fomented by professional demagogues, and by the disreputable section of the cheap press.

This is one of the penalties, we are called upon to pay for unsystematic immigration in lieu of colonisation; but at the same time, the evil is a transitory one, for it will disappear with the growth of a generation born upon Australian soil, educated in our State schools, grammar schools and universities, habituated to mingle with each other in the playground and the cricket-field, and to participate afterwards in the recreations and enjoyments of social and domestic life.

Meanwhile, we would earnestly impress upon the minds of all classes of our fellow countrymen at home, that the Australian colonies offer a career alike to the able, the ambitious, the opulent and the needy. The capitalist, who invests his money in the English funds, in real estate, in railway debentures or on mortgage, at rates of interest ranging from three to five per cent., can obtain a return of from seven to ten per cent. by advancing it on undeniable securities in almost any part of Australia. The energetic agriculturist, with a few hundreds of pounds at his command, can easily obtain a farm of his own, and can look forward, with something like confidence, to its becoming more and more valuable year by year, as population increases, and as improved means of inter-communication facilitate his access to the largest local markets, or to the nearest sea-port for the sale or shipment of his produce. The artisan, who can earn ten shillings a day by eight hours' work, in a climate where the interruptions to out-door work are few and far between, and who can obtain board and lodging for fifteen shillings a week, has only to practise sobriety and thrift, in order to elevate himself into the position of a director of other men's labour in the course of a very few years. The necessaries of life are cheap and abundant, and although the cost of many articles of comfort and luxury, is artificially enhanced in the colony of Victoria by the protective tariff, this relic of barbarism is sure to be swept away sooner or later, by the advancing intelligence of the people.

In the present stage of their social development, the Australian colonies offer much that is attractive, even to those who have become wedded to the occupations and pleasures incidental to an older civilisation. We should be disposed to place their climatic advantages in the first rank. This is emphatically a land of sunshine and blue skies, of brightness and cheerfulness; a land in which the nervous system is stimulated to great activity, in which the incentives to effort, the motives for hope and the dissuasives from depression and despondency, are powerful and unintermittent. Something of the light of the world's morning, and the elasticity of its youth, seems to attach itself to the Australian landscape, and to make its subtle and vitalising influence felt in the Australian atmosphere. As there is no past for people's minds to dwell upon, no antiquities to ponder over, no ancient legends to decipher, and no archæological problems to vex their thoughts, they turn with all the greater ardour and earnestness to the present and the future. History is not a chequered record of wars and revolutions, of civil strife and foreign conflict, but a virgin page, upon which each community may inscribe its honourable record of the conquest of the wilderness, of the invasion of primeval solitudes by the ploughshare and the pick-axe, of cities founded without blooodshed, of institutions established without violence, and of the peaceful achievements of industry, the unsullied triumphs of science and the noble victories of agriculture and commerce.

The immigrant who quits old England for young Australia, soon discovers that the latter is reproducing all that is most admirable in the former. He leaves behind a State church, an hereditary peerage and an aristocratic republic with an hereditary president, it is true; but he makes the discovery, that in these colonies all the aspirations of the most advanced politicians in the mother-country have been already realised. Religion is free, the land is free, instruction is free; and the only trace of the spirit of feudalism is to be found in the fetters, which one province has foolishly imposed on commerce. Instead of the soil of Australia being monopolised by a particular class of the community, few in numbers, and carefully entrenched behind fortifications composed of venerable statutes and ancient parchments, its ownership is more widely distributed in proportion to the population, than it is in any part of Europe. Land can be transferred or encumbered almost as easily and inexpensively as chattel property. No working man, who is prudent, temperate and industrious, need occupy a house that is not his own. No farm-labourer need continue to be a wage-earner for more than a few years, for it is quite within his power to acquire a small farm for himself, by the practice of anything but severe economy.

To the operative classes, Australia is a veritable land of promise. Other countries have profited by the skill and labour of many preceding generations. In a new country, the work to be performed by willing hands is endless; and as the demand is almost incessant, the remuneration is necessarily liberal. Roads have to be made; forests to be cleared; bridges to be built; docks and harbours to be excavated; piers and jetties and lighthouses to be constructed; railways to be formed; public edifices and private residences to be erected; streets to be aligned, paved, and channelled; land to be fenced in, planted, stocked and cultivated; vineyards, orchards and gardens to be laid out; churches, chapels and schoolhouses to be reared; lines of electric telegraph to be run through the country; and reservoirs to be dug and embanked; and all these operations give rise to numbers of a correlative character—such as the quarrying of stone, the making of bricks, the preparation of timber, the cartage of materials and so forth. These furnish an immense variety of employments for handicraftsmen of every description; while there grow up simultaneously therewith, and by a process of natural development, numerous manufacturing industries, which, wherever the State has refrained from interfering with them, have acquired the utmost vigour and robustness.

No better proof of this could be supplied, than is furnished by the economic history of the colony of Victoria. From the year 1851, when it was separated from New South Wales, up to the year 1864, it enjoyed all the advantages of a free-trade tariff; and, in spite of the fact that the labour market was completely deranged by the gold discoveries, and that men were allured from settled employments, affording steady wages, by the chances of making a large fortune by a mere lucky stroke of the pick or shovel, numerous manufactories were successfully established by men of enterprise and spirit, and in the year 1863—the last of free trade—seventy-two distinct articles of Victorian manufacture* figured in the list of exports; and these manufactures have steadily increased in magnitude and importance ever since, in spite of the hostile and repressive influences of protection.

Thus, in the whole of the colonies, there prevails a wide diversity of industrial occupations, and labour of every description is sure of a liberal return; because, in the majority of cases, it is so productive, owing to the bountiful cooperation of nature in providing the *prima materia* of human wealth; and yet we are, at present, but superficially acquainted with the nature, or the extent of the treasures which lie buried in the Australian soil. Its mineral riches are literally incalculable. The area of the ascertained auriferous territory in Victoria alone is 25,000 square miles; in New South Wales, it is still more extensive; in Queensland it is probably far greater; and in the northern territory of South Australia the precious metal appears to be distributed over a great expanse of country, the limits of which are at present purely conjectural; while fresh discoveries of gold are announced from time to time in the island of Tasmania. It is unreasonable to conclude either, that the richest deposits were first discovered and have all been exhausted, or that gold-mining may

---

* These included apparel, agricultural implements, bags and sacks, biscuits, boots and shoes, carriages, candles, furniture, saddlery, soap, leather and leather-ware, iron and wooden houses, machinery, &c. &c.

not become as remunerative in the future, as it has been in the past. The colony of Victoria has been most celebrated for the magnificent yield of its gold-fields, out of which were taken, between 1851 and 1878, the enormous amount of *fifty million ounces, of the value of* £200,000,000 *sterling*. It is true, the yield has been steadily declining for some years past; but then it must be remembered, that it has been the policy of the Legislature to discourage that branch of industry by imposing heavy import duties upon everything the miner consumes or requires—his implements and machinery, his hauling tackle and candles, his food and clothing. The tariff of 1871 seems to have been framed for the special object of crushing mining enterprise, and the following official figures will serve to show how successful it has been in this respect:—

	Miners engaged.	Yield of gold.
1871	58,279	1,355,477 ounces.
1872	52,965	1,282,521 ,,
1873	50,595	1,241,205 ,,
1874	45,151	1,155,972 ,,
1875	41,717	1,095,787 ,,
1876	41,010	963,760 ,,
1877	38,005	809,653 ,,
1878	36,636	775,272 ,,

The yield of gold in Victoria is now just one-fourth of what it was twenty-five years ago; but there is a reasonable prospect, that the fiscal policy, which has contributed to bring about this deplorable decadence of one of the native industries of that colony, will be reversed ere long; and as the approximate area of auriferous ground over which mining operations have extended is only 1300 square miles out of 25,000 known to be auriferous, and as gold, in quartz, is now discovered at depths, where scientists formerly declared it was impossible it should be found, we may look forward to a revival of this branch of industry in that part of Australia, which is emphatically the land of nuggets.

But the eastern half of the continent, constituting, as it does, one segment of that great volcanic circle, which surrounds the Pacific with what M. Elisée Reclus calls "a ring of fire"—its course being marked in this part of the world by extinct craters, as it is elsewhere by active ones—teems with deposits of gold, silver, copper, lead, stream tin, iron, antimony, coal, kerosene shale, kaolin, cinnabar, lime-stone and fire-clays; besides quarries of marble, granite, slate, freestone and other minerals. In the soil itself, and underneath its surface, lie "the potentialities of becoming rich beyond the dreams of avarice." These await but the vivifying touch of capital and labour in order to bring them forth and make them ministers to the material prosperity of millions. Australia could absorb the entire population of Great Britain, and it would still be as thinly peopled as the United States. Its area is three fourths of that of the whole of Europe, and its entire population is only half that of Belgium. It embraces all climates within its geographical limits, from the tropical to the temperate; and, consequently, its products exhibit the same wide diversity, from the sugar, cotton and coffee of Northern Queensland to the British fruits, which flourish in Tasmania and in the southern parts of Victoria. In point of salubrity Australia may be confidently pronounced to enjoy an enviable pre-eminence. The mean death rate is only 17 in the thousand, as against 22·3 in Great Britain, 24·6 in France, 27·6 in Russia, 30·2 in Italy and 31·1 in Austria. Even in the colony of Queensland, we have the assurance of Mr. Carl A. Feilberg, the editor of the *Queenslander*, that European settlers can live and work as far north as Rockhampton, and he is of opinion, that, in the absence of a servile class in those regions, no degeneration need be feared in those regions; because, wherever this has occurred, he argues, that it has resulted from the dominant caste having isolated itself from, and become independent of, the active habits of those around them. "Race degeneracy," he observes, "has smitten every people that has maintained itself by the labour of an alien and inferior caste, from the republics of old Greece to the creole planters of Mauritius; they have withered, as plants wither, when their roots are cut away. The prevailing faults of Europeans domiciled in the tropics—want of perseverance and self-control, physical languor and lack of mental energy—can, I think, be traced entirely to the fact, that they have been completely relieved from the necessity of bodily exertion by a servile caste of workers, who have also encouraged them to throw off moral restraint by patient submission to their caprices."* These influences will not be experienced in Queensland, where the owners of the soil are exempt from the demoralisation, which accompanies the habitual control over a horde of coloured labourers; and Mr. Feilberg draws the following glowing picture of the future of the Queensland settlers:—" Conceive of them growing in numbers and taking possession of the material wealth lying around them—building cities, clearing fields and planting gardens—a people to whom cold and hunger would be unknown, and at whose hand would be almost every product of nature, that serves to secure the comfort or add beauty to the life of man. What palaces should be built under that blue sky! what marvels of art should emanate from the imagination of this happy people, living in a land beautiful now in its wilderness, and which would be made ten times more beautiful by the presence of civilised man! What bounds, indeed, can be set to the development of an offshoot of the most energetic of human races, placed in the very lap of the teeming mother, and nourished with the best of the good things, she dispenses to her human children."† Be this as it may, by far the larger half of the Australian continent—to say nothing of the beautiful island of Tasmania—lies outside the tropics, and even within their limits, there are extensive table-lands, which enjoy all the advantages of a temperate climate.

* *Victorian Review*, No. 5. † *Ibid.*

Nor must we omit to remind the intending emigrant to Australia, that his migration hither is not synonymous with exile. Instead of leaving England, Scotland, or Ireland behind him, he soon makes the discovery, that he has become a citizen of a country, which has reproduced or is reproducing the social, industrial and political life of the land he has left. He finds a popular form of government, under favour of which he himself may rise to be a Minister of the Crown, provided he possesses the requisite fluency of speech and "push." He finds local affairs managed by shire councils or municipalities elected by the ratepayers of the district. He finds churches and school-houses springing up in every little township, and police protection extending with the spread of settlement, while the post office, with its savings bank and electric telegraph station, is established in each small centre of population. He learns, with some degree of surprise, perhaps, that a population of less than two millions and a-half raise a revenue of nearly fifteen millions sterling, and transact a commerce of eighty millions sterling, that they have close upon 3000 miles of railway in operation and 20,000 miles of telegraph open; that they own upwards of 50,000,000 acres of land, nearly a million horses, about 7,000,000 head of cattle and upwards of 40,000,000 sheep; that the capital cities of the various colonies will compare favourably, in many respects, with the smaller capitals of Europe, and with the provincial cities of England, and that there is nothing to remind him, that he has quitted the old world, but the absence of antiquities, the newness of the public and domestic architecture, the purity, salubrity and brilliancy of the atmosphere, the different character of the vegetation, the absence of poverty and squalor, the abundance and cheapness of provisions, and the expression of alertness, vivacity, eager activity and hopefulness, which he will read on the countenances of the people he will meet with in the streets.

Let us suppose that our typical immigrant arrives in Melbourne, for example, a few days before the Cup is to be run for on the Flemington racecourse—an event which usually occurs on or about the 9th of November—and that during that time he has devoted himself to an exploration of the principal thoroughfares. If he writes home to his friends in England, his narrative to be truthful will be somewhat to the following effect:—" I have enjoyed a round of sight-seeing during the last few days. The jewellers' shops have been gleaming with gems, lustrous with gold, and lucent with silver. Diamonds have flashed and sparkled in every variety of form and setting, and the newest designs in necklaces, earrings, brooches, lockets and bracelets have attested the taste, skill and inventive fertility of local and foreign artificers. From the recesses of the largest furniture warehouses have been brought out suites of dining, drawing room, boudoir and library furniture, beautiful in material, elegant in form and choice in workmanship, with the loveliest of ornaments for the mantelpiece, the corner cupboard, the cabinet, the *étagère*, the china beaufet, and with such carpets and curtains, chandeliers and looking-glasses, as opulence might purchase and taste would approve. The dealers in glass and porcelain have collected, from all parts of Europe, the best ceramic fabrics of the best manufacturers, and you might spend an hour or two in the inspection of these with as much pleasure and profit as you would derive from a lengthened visit to a picture gallery or a collection of sculpture. As to the drapers and mercers, their windows have been blocked all day long for a week past by admiring crowds, composed—need it be added—of women, both young and old, who have looked with longing eyes upon those wonderful 'arrangements' and 'harmonies,' as Mr. Whistler might call them, in lilac, pale blue, dove-colour, creamy white and cardinal; those dainty Pompadour prints; those Watteau chintzes; and those mysteries of millinery prepared for the adornment of the female head, which possess such an irresistible fascination for that sex, of which each member has been defined by a wicked Frenchman to be *un être qui s'habille, babille, et se déshabille*. The shop windows of the print-sellers have undergone an eruption of sporting pictures, commemorative of famous contests at Epsom, Ascot and Goodwood, of renowned steeplechases and of celebrated exploits in the hunting-field. Fieldglasses have come to the front with a rush in the opticians' display of seasonable goods; and the outfitters have reminded the public, that, whether the Cup Day should prove to be one of storm or sunshine, dust or mud, they were prepared for any emergency. The large ironmongery establishments, which resemble oriental bazaars in the extent of ground they cover and in the multiplicity of the articles they exhibit for sale, have regarnished their windows and rearranged their stocks—out of which you might furnish forth a score or two of expeditions setting forth to colonise a newly discovered archipelago with everything they could possibly require—and have constituted not the least attractive of the gratuitous sights of Melbourne during the race-week, when the city is literally occupied by an invading army of the most acceptable kind, whose liberal requisitions are all paid for, and who, when they evacuate it, do so upon the best possible terms with its permanent garrison."

Let us picture another immigrant arriving in Victoria, in the spring of the year. We will assume that he has been brought up in the country at home, and that he possesses a keen appreciation of those natural beauties which confer such a charm upon the rural life of England. He is told that some of its picturesque features have been reproduced in the environs of Melbourne; and he visits some of its eastern suburbs; concerning one of which he finds occasion to write, as follows, to the members of his family at home: —" Half an hour's ride in an easterly direction from the city takes you quite into the country. You are among orchards white with blossom, as though it had been snowing flowers all night; and the gorse hedges are all ablaze with their gorgeous Persian yellow. Elm trees are tufted with pale-buff catkins, and the vines are putting forth their first leaves, which are of that 'glad light green' which Chaucer speaks of so affectionately. The air is full of freshness and perfume, brightness and breeziness, for

'A warm rain and gentle showers at night,
Have left a sparkling welcome for the light.'

and the crispness of the atmosphere and the brightness of the verdure remind you of an English spring. Reminiscent of England, too, are some of those cottage gardens, which glow with colour and are heavy with the fragrance of lilac, stocks and wallflowers. The flower-beds are bordered with double daisies, and the white and purple iris, the scarlet geranium, the bronzed leaves of the Sofranat rose and the tri-coloured loveliness of the choicer varieties of the fuchsia, combine to weave such a web of tapestry as art must despair of imitating. Whatever decorative work nature takes in hand, the result is invariably a masterpiece. She covers up the ugliness of human handicraft, hides its deformity, and never wearies of giving us lessons of grace and beauty. Here is a weatherboard cottage of the most primitive construction, with a wooden verandah and an unsightly chimney. Yellow banksias have been planted near the posts, and they not only envelop these with an intricacy of curved lines and spiral ornament, compared with which the apprentice's pillar at Melrose is poor in design and feeble in execution, but they festoon and garland the whole front of the building with a lavish ornamentation, every line of which is free and flowing, while every leaf and blossom would repay a separate study. As to the chimney, it has been transformed into a column of verdure, which will by-and-bye be resplendent in purple and crimson, when the scarlet passion-flower turns its ardent bosom to the sun, and the daily renewed loveliness of the ipomœa shall outvie the magnificence of a Tyrian mantle.

"Every house hereabouts is set in a framework of greenery, and you see how the beauty of the natural surroundings reacts upon the tastes, habits and feelings of the inhabitants. They are not a rich people. They are mostly wage-earners and market-gardeners and persons with salaries of from three to six pounds a week. But in almost every instance their dwellings have an air of neatness, comfort and brightness, in striking contrast with what has been described above. These are emphatically homes in which their owners take an honest pride and a legitimate delight. You see by the chairs and tables in it, that the verandah becomes an additional sittingroom in the summer evenings, and you may also infer, that garden husbandry is a favourite occupation with every member of the family."

Perhaps our imaginary immigrant travels into the country and obtains employment in one of the vineyards of the Upper Yarra—in that, let us say, which was planted by Hubert de Castella, whose *Souvenirs d'un Squatter Français en Australie*, contains so pleasant an account of bush life in Victoria. From this point, after a few months' residence in the neighbourhood of Yering, the new comer sends to his distant kindred the following pen-picture of the scenery of rural Victoria:—"I am settled about thirty miles from Melbourne. It is a part of the country, where cultivation has crept up to the feet of a labyrinth of mountains, and where an amphitheatre of softly-rounded hills girdles a broad valley, through which a lazy river, 'striking the ground with sinuous trace' winds more deviously, than I should have thought it possible for any river to wind, without losing its way or tying itself into an inextricable knot. And in the chain of peninsulas thus formed, Nature, in a frolic mood and with a kindly thought for the artists, who love her, has arranged groups of trees and patches of underwood with such grotesque diversities of form, with such fantastic disarray of branch and spray, with such an intermingling of straight and shapely silver shaft with ragged and distorted trunk, and with such admirable provision for the reduplication of gnarled bough and rugged stem, bare skeleton and leafy sapling in the languid water, that creeps about their snake-like roots, that at each bend of the river, there are to be found the materials for half-a-dozen cabinet pictures, in which nothing is left for the painter to vary, to improve upon or to recompose. But these peninsulas are only discoverable on a nearer survey. From the plateau upon which the house at St. Hubert's stands, you only take in the salient features of the landscape. In the foreground, a level lawn inlaid with beds of glowing portulac and many-coloured petunias. Beyond is a gentle slope, over which are deployed countless battalions of vines, purpling in the warm sun, while 'autumn lays a fiery finger on their leaves.' At the foot of the vineyard the wide valley spreads fanlike, and beyond are the encircling hills. These rise tier on tier, and are so mutable in colour, so rich in sober greys and russet greens and misty blues and solemn purples; so chequered with light and shade, with tint and demi-tint, with manifested form and veiled mystery, that every hour they wear a novel aspect and disclose an unexpected beauty; and the flush of morning has nothing in common with the refulgent lustre of the hot noon or the orange glow of the voluptuous evening; and wandering cloud-shadows stain them with Tyrian purple; and pencils of sunlight, dropping through rifts of feathery vapour and smiting on groves of withered trees, transform the white skeletons into silver fretwork. On a sudden there flashes across the landscape a flight of cockatoos, that look like snowflakes drifting before the wind, and the steadfastness of the mountains becomes all the more impressive by reason of the swift motion of these restless birds.

"Looking out upon these mountains, morning after morning, until they have become as familiar to you as the faces of old friends, until you have come to feel glad when they smile in the sunshine, and overcast when they seclude themselves behind a curtain of voluminous mist—you begin to imagine that you are hundreds of miles away from the dusty highways of thought and action, along which you have been travelling, and to understand the passion for mountains which Wordsworth felt, and Byron feigned—or felt also, perhaps. There grows upon you a sense of the insignificance and evanescence of even the greatest objects of concernment in the world of man, as you stand in the presence of these venerable mountains. The overthrow of a dynasty, or the foundation of an empire, appears a matter of trivial and transitory moment, when you reflect that Media and Persia, Babylon and Egypt, Greece and Rome, have risen and fallen during the lifetime of some of those many-centuried trees, that fringe the summits of the everlasting hills before you. To these giants of the forest the sullen yew tree of the finest series of elegiac poems in any language, with all its 'thousand years of gloom,' is 'but a thing of yesterday;' and 'the talking oak,' a mere latter-day sapling, a modern antique. But if you ponder persistently upon the duration of these huge relics of a pre-historic epoch, each a stately column crowned with a plume of foliage, you feel oppressed by the sentiment of solitude inspired by forests, which have stood for ages upon ages, and with which no incident of history, no consecrating association with human love and life, connects itself. You cannot people them with the graceful or grotesque beings with whom the active imagination of the Greeks filled the woods of Attica and Thessaly. You cannot hope

> 'To catch a glympse of Fauns and Dryades
> Coming with softest rustle through the trees;
> And garlands woven of flowers wild and sweet,
> Upheld on ivory wrists, or sporting feet.'

You cannot even imagine, that these lofty aisles and vaulted roofs have ever sheltered the beneficent elves and fairies of a later time, the sprightly creatures, which ministered to Bottom, and fulfilled the bidding of dainty Ariel, and spirited away bonny Kilmeny to

> 'The lowermost vales of the storied heaven;
> From whence they can view the world below,
> And heaven's blue gates with sapphires glow.'

Therefore from the past, upon which settles down such a depressing and oppressive weight of solitude, your thoughts make a sudden leap into the future, and you endeavour to picture to yourself, what these hills will be like a century hence, when their slopes will be inlaid with squares of brown fallow, green vineyard, and yellow cornfield; when the brightness of the hop-garden will be contrasted with the sombre sameness of the olive plantation; when avenues of walnut trees will lead to bartons populous with the spoils of autumn, and the wine-press, the oil-press, the cider-mill and the magnanerie will constitute the appurtenances of every farm; when the warmest recesses of the mountains will be filled with orange groves, and the fruits of chilly England will be gathered from orchards on the breezy plateaux; when the slopes will be scarped with roads, dotted with villages, and sprinkled with churches and schoolhouses, windmills and homesteads. By that time, perhaps, the vineyards of the Upper Yarra will be as celebrated as those of Barsac and Sauterne, and the names of the men, who planted the first vines in this once sequestered region, will be canonised in the recollections of a grateful and prosperous posterity; while some Redi of the twentieth century may indite a " Bacco in Victoria," and exclaim,

> 'Benedetto
> Quel Claretto
> Che si sprilla in Sant' Uberto,—
> Veramente di gran mer' to.
> La Vernaccia non si bella
> Come 'l vino di Castella.
> Manna dal ciel sulle tue trecce piove
> Vigna gentil, che questa ambrosia infondi;
> Ogni tua vite in ogni tempo muove
> Nuovi fior, nuovi frutti e nuove frondi.'"

Yes, the future belongs to Australia, as the past does to the four great continents of the globe. For the two Americas have witnessed the rise and fall of civilisations as ancient, and almost as remarkable, as those which were successively born, and severally passed away in Asia, Africa and Europe. But the great island in the South Seas has been waiting for centuries to be occupied, cultivated and developed by the Aryan race. It offers a home, a career and an unlimited enterprise to the industrious, the enterprising and the energetic, who feel themselves to be crowded out of the avenues to competence or wealth in the old world by the ever-increasing throng of competitors, and where

> "Every gate is throng'd with suitors, all the markets overflow."

CHAPTER XIII.

ADVANTAGES OF AUSTRALIA AS A PLACE OF RESIDENCE.

THE CLASSES OF PERSONS WHO SHOULD AND SHOULD NOT EMIGRATE—THE COLONIES AND THEIR PRODUCTS—ROOM AND ABUNDANCE FOR ALL—NATURAL ENDOWMENTS OF THE COUNTRY—ITS SOCIAL LIFE AS ATTRACTIVE AS THAT OF THE OLD WORLD—A SALUBRIOUS, BRIGHT, AND EXHILARATING CLIMATE—OPPORTUNITIES FOR HUSBANDMEN—CONDITION OF THE WAGE-EARNING CLASSES—TEMPTATIONS TO DISSIPATION AND DISCONTENT—THOSE WHO SUCCUMB TO THEM—ANGLO-AUSTRALIANS THE SPOILED CHILDREN OF THE FUTURE—PRODUCTIVE FORCES OF SOCIETY IN A NEW COUNTRY—WEALTH OF THE POPULATION—A SELF-MADE TERRITORIAL MAGNATE—THE STORY OF SOME FORTUNATE DIGGERS—CONCLUSION.

THE subject of this chapter, like the territory which falls within the designation of "the Australian colonies," is a very wide one. For the advantages, which a country presents to those who may contemplate taking up their residence in it, are not only various in themselves, but they are variously viewed by various persons belonging to the various classes of society. The minister of religion, the barrister, the physician, the surgeon, the solicitor, the mining speculator, the farmer, the small annuitant, the merchant, the shopkeeper, the skilled artisan, and the labourer would each regard the subject from a different standpoint, and would form his own particular estimate of the benefits, whether immediate or prospective, which might appear to be held out to him by embracing a career in Australia. And that estimate would be largely influenced, we may be sure, by individual temperament. The sanguine man would look upon everything through a rose-coloured medium, and would be pretty certain to form exaggerated expectations of success, and to shut his eyes to the difficulties and drawbacks inseparable from a new enterprise, which would be magnified, on the other hand, by the timid, the desponding, and the self-distrustful. The weak-willed and wavering man, again, would be liable to fluctuate in opinion from day to day, and from hour to hour, as to the advisability or otherwise of emigrating to Australia, while the cautious and reflective man would weigh well all the authentic information he could gather, would test its accuracy, as far as practicable, and, after careful deliberation, would arrive at a final decision, from which he would not recede.

It is related of a celebrated actor, that he was accustomed to fix his own attention upon some person in the stalls, whom he regarded as typifying the average intelligence and susceptibility to emotion of the spectators, and that he used to play at this person, and by the effect produced upon him, he was enabled to infer to what extent he had been successful in absorbing the interest and stirring the feelings of the audience. We should be glad if we could fix our imagination upon some typical reader, and address him, as encouragingly as might be in our power, with respect to the advantages which Australia holds out to the immigrant from the old world. But we fear this is impossible, on account of the diversity of minds and classes spoken of above. Nor must we omit to acknowledge that there are many persons to whom a residence in these colonies would be unattractive and undesirable in the extreme. To the "man about town," to the *flaneur*, to the Westend dandy, to the *habitué* of clubs, drawing-rooms, receptions, kettle-drums, picture galleries, English country mansions in the shooting season, garden parties in the summer, and of a hired palazzo on the shores of the Mediterranean in the winter, a new country must be altogether uninviting. They might pay it a flying visit in search of a new sensation, and in order to be able to say, that they had "done" Australia, and had found it "a doosed kweeaw place, inhabited by doosed kweeaw people," but they would be birds of passage only, and nobody would wish that they should be anything else.

But there are tens and even hundreds of thousands of people in Great Britain and Ireland, by whom no more judicious step could be taken, either for themselves or for their families, or for their future descendants, than to migrate to Australia. To them, it is a land of hope and promise, full of magnificent possibilities, and teeming with elements of wealth, so varied in character and so vast in extent, that to attempt to describe them with the utmost sobriety of language, would subject one to the imputation of dealing in hyperbole.

To speak, in the first place, of the area of Australia, and of the islands of New Zealand. It embraces upwards of 3,100,000 square miles of territory, which is only 700,000 less than the area of the whole of Europe; but while the population of the latter is estimated at nearly 300,000,000, that of the Australasian colonies does not reach one-tenth of that number. What an outlet does it present, therefore, for the surplus population of the old world! How many centuries must elapse before its waste places can be filled up, and before the natural increase of its inhabitants can overtake the productiveness of its soil! In the meantime, what a superabundance of the necessaries of life is being possessed and enjoyed by the handful of people, who are sparsely scattered over the enormous area of these highly favoured countries. These were their harvests, and the muster-roll of their live stock, in the year 1878 :—

Wheat	...	...	26,041,482	bushels
Oats...	...	...	11,950,800	,,
Barley	...	...	1,588,874	,,
Maize	...	...	6,001,140	,,
Other cereals...		...	446,386	,,
Potatoes	...	...	290,282	tons
Hay ...	...	...	734,731	,,
Wine	...	...	1,617,776	gallons
Horses	...	...	1,009,878	head
Cattle	...	...	7,402,659	,,
Sheep	...	...	61,066,100	,,
Pigs	...	...	815,110	,,

These figures are more eloquent than any words in the testimony they bear to the material welfare of the people of Australia and New Zealand, and if any further evidence were wanting, it would be supplied by the fact that the total trade of this portion of the British empire was of the value of £94,742,703 in that year. In other words, it is about two millions in excess of the total value of the imports and exports of Great Britain and Ireland in the year 1830, when the population of those islands was 24,000,000. At that time the revenue of the mother-country was £50,000,000, or £2 1s. 8d. per head of the population; and the pressure of taxation was greatly complained of in those days, materially aggravated, as it was, by the iniquitous system of taxation, which then prevailed. In the Australasian colonies the imposts average £2 8s. 3¾d. per head—they are much less in New South Wales, Victoria, and South Australia, and the burden is but lightly felt. As to that portion of the revenue which is applied in each country to meet the interest on the public debt, it is enough to remark, that that debt was contracted for the execution of public works, most of which are of a reproductive character, and 'that, at no distant date, the return from the works themselves—railways, reservoirs, &c.—may be expected to cover the interest on the capital expended, and perhaps prove a source of revenue in addition.

The prosperity of colonies like these, it cannot be too frequently repeated, or too strongly impressed upon the public mind, is attributable in an even greater degree to the beneficence of nature, than to human industry. The latter is only an auxiliary. The mines and quarries, the forests, the almost measureless expanse of pasturage, the fertility of a virgin soil, the marvellous influences upon vegetation of a warm and brilliant atmosphere, the natural increase of the flocks and herds, which graze on the succulent herbage of the country, and the enormous clips of wool yielded by the sixty millions of sheep, owned by the squatters and farmers of Australia and New Zealand, combine to enrich the population, to increase its accumulations of capital, and to communicate a perpetual impulse to the general prosperity and progress. The industrial activity of the people is stimulated by success, and new occupations are originated, new enterprises are engaged in, and new channels of employment are provided for the rising generation. The economic development of society proceeds according to the ancient order, but the stages of growth, which once covered centuries in the process of evolution, are now crowded into two or three decades. Succeeding the aborigines, who lived by fishing and the chase, came the pastoral lessees of the waste lands of the colonies; then agriculture arose, then mining was engaged in by tens of thousands of persons, allured to the country by the marvellous gold discoveries; then commerce assumed considerable proportions; then manufactories were established, and this led up to that division of labour, and that multiplicity of pursuits, which we find in older communities, and in more complex conditions of society. Hence a colonial population closely resembles, in its industrial and social aspects, the population of the nation out of which it originally went forth. It is not a graft from the old tree upon a new stock, but a lusty sapling which has been transplanted in a virgin soil, and rapidly grows up to maturity under more favourable conditions of light and air. Divest an Australian city of its freshness, rawness, and newness of appearance, soften the brilliancy of the sky, draw a veil of filmy moisture over the surrounding landscape, and lessen the activity of the people who fill the streets, and there is nothing to remind the new arrival that he has quitted the shores of England. There are the familiar churches, " pointing with silent finger unto heaven;" there is the stately town hall, the centre of municipal life; there are the commodious hotels, the banks, warehouses, auction marts, theatres, concert halls, arcades, markets, restaurants, and shops of every description, not forgetting the inevitable "loan and discount association," the pawnbroker's omnium-gatherum, the lock-up, the police-court, and the gaol. Omnibuses follow each other in quick succession, along the principal lines of thoroughfare; hansom cabs and waggonettes ply for hire at their appointed stands; and trunk lines of railway connect the city with its suburbs and with the chief centres of population in the interior. Morning newspapers record for the colonist the history of the previous day, and bring to his breakfast-table telegraphic messages from the capitals of the old world, descriptive of events which happened yesterday. To the man of business, the broker, and the speculator, the Hall of Commerce offers a rendezvous; to the student the Public Library opens its hospitable doors, without the necessity of an introduction or a certificate of character; and in the evening there is quite a varied list of amusements to choose from, including opera, the legitimate drama, organ recitals, concerts, lectures, and scientific meetings. There are philharmonic societies and Liedertafels for the musically inclined; chess and whist clubs and billiard rooms for others, and a succession of social entertainments for the enjoyment of the well-to-do classes of society. And it may be confidently asserted that it is in the power of every energetic, persevering, sober and prudent man, to become a member of these classes, by the exercise of industry and thrift during the early years of his manhood. Nowhere are the avenues to fortune or a competence so freely open to all comers as in Australia. Nowhere can a man rise in life so surely or so speedily as in these colonies, where it is confessedly so much easier to make money than to keep it after it has been made. For the comparative facility with which success is acquired is apt to engender a speculative spirit, while, on the other hand, wealth is occasionally amassed by men whose mental resources are unfortunately limited, so that when they have reached the goal of their ambition, and relinquish the occupation of money-making, which had previously served to engross their minds, they have no hobby or interesting pursuit to fall back upon, as a substitute for the former business of their lives, and they fly to the bottle, in order to procure for themselves the intellectual excitement, which they formerly found in the conduct of their successful avocation.

Considering how much human happiness depends upon climate, and that we are all consciously or unconsciously " servile to skiey influences," we must not omit to include this among the advantages which Australia holds out to the immigrant. The relations of climate to health of body clearness and vivacity of thought, nervous energy, cheerfulness of mind, and buoyancy of spirits, have not yet received the attention at the hands of men of science which they deserve. Mr. Buckle has declared, that the two primary causes of civilisation are fertility of soil and buoyancy of climate. Now, it may be claimed for a very large portion of the Australian continent, and for the whole of New Zealand and Tasmania, that the climate they enjoy, is essentially benignant, and, for the greater part of the year, extremely exhilarating. The air, as a general rule, is bright, dry, clear and pure. The latter quality is attributable in part to the remarkable character of the indigenous timber of the country, to which we have elsewhere alluded, and in part to the enormous expanse of ocean, by which this island continent is surrounded. In the northern hemisphere, land predominates; in the southern, water. And as Europe and Asia form virtually one continent, and the British Islands are severed from the mainland by a mere "silver streak of sea," it is easy to perceive how epidemics, having their birthplace in the far East, where countless millions upon millions of people have been committed to the earth, where the cities are contaminated by the accumulated filth of centuries, where the rivers have been poisoned by the sewage of incalculable generations of people living in open violation of the laws of health, where the balance of nature has been destroyed by the demolition of forests, the drying-up of rivers, and the formation of pestilential marshes; and where all the conditions are favourable to the genesis and propagation of deadly diseases, it is easy to perceive, we say, how these epidemics, thus engendered, would travel westward, as the cholera and plague have always done, and would come, in time, to ravage the mother-country, and to compel her to yield her contribution to the terrible harvest of premature death.

Australia is isolated from these dangers. It cannot be said of her, that the millions of living people, who walk on the surface of the soil, bear no proportion to the hundreds of millions who have been deposited a few feet below that surface. Its atmosphere is as virgin as its soil. Nature has specially prepared it for the healthful respiration of a vigorous and active race. Its geographical position would render it the sanatorium of the world, even if nature had not provided in its forests perennial distilleries of the purest oxygen. Upon the Australian continent, the neighbouring island of Tasmania, and the remoter cluster known as New Zealand, are to be found all the varieties of atmospheric temperature and of climate to be met with on the shores of the Mediterranean—that favoured region of the earth, which comprehends some of the finest portions of three continents, and has been the seat of the greatest empires, and the grandest civilisations, the world has ever seen. And, as a matter of course, while the climatic conditions of Southern Spain and France, of Italy and Sicily, of Dalmatia and Bulgaria, of Asia Minor, Greece, Egypt, Algeria and Morocco are reproduced in this part of the world, all the products of those countries are capable of, and numbers of them are, being cultivated in the Australasian colonies. Indeed, it would be impossible to enumerate a single plant growing between the 30th and 55th parallels of north latitude in the other hemisphere, which could not be grown with advantage in some part of Australia or New Zealand. And the importance of this fact, in an economic point of view, will readily commend itself to the minds of our readers in Europe, especially when taken in connection with the consideration that, in each of the colonies, land can be obtained upon terms not very far removed from a free gift. The opportunities for the introduction of *petites industries*, in connection with husbandry, are literally boundless, and remain almost intact. Here is the land, but where is the people? When we read that land, eligible for gardening purposes, is worth from £200 to £240 an acre, and lets at from £9 to £12 an acre, in some parts of France, and when we bear in mind that the winters are sufficiently cold in the northern departments of that country to render it necessary to go to a considerable expense in providing protection for many kinds of plants during that season of the year; when we remember the high price which small parcels of land suitable for culture by peasant proprietors will fetch in Belgium, the Netherlands, and in Guernsey and Jersey; and when we come to think that there is not one of the Australian colonies in which country land may not be obtained for a pound an acre, and suburban land in the immediate vicinity of excellent markets, at from £10 to £50 an acre, we are driven to the conclusion, that emigration from the thickly-populated countries of Europe to this part of the world, languishes, because so little is known of the advantages which are held out to the immigrant in Australia.

Take the case of a man who is content to settle down upon 80 acres of land, and who brings the whole of it by degrees into profitable cultivation. If he has a wife and family, so much the better. They can assist him in a variety of ways; and if he is moderately industrious, persevering, sober, and lucky, he will soon be in a position of independence. His farm will supply him with an abundance of food, and its surplus produce will be available for exchange with the storekeeper, from whom he obtains the flour, groceries, articles of clothing, and the miscellaneous commodities he requires. His milch cows, his pigs and poultry, his garden and his dairy will yield him the *causas vivendi* in liberal measure; and the value of his freehold will increase year by year, in proportion to the growth of population around him, and the improvements, which he effects by his own industry, and by the expenditure upon them of a portion of his annual profit. His children, growing up to man and womanhood, occasion him no anxiety, as they would be apt to do in older countries, where land is so dear, and the competition for employment is so eager. He knows that their assistance and co-operation will be increasingly valuable, as they advance towards maturity. He has no misgivings with respect to their future, because he is well assured that labour and skill of every description will be always greatly in demand, and always liberally remunerated in territories where the amount of work, which can be profitably performed, is so very much in excess of the number of hands available for its performance. Nor is this disproportion likely to cease for some generations to come, because a century or two must necessarily elapse before population begins to press on the means of subsistence in any one of the Australian colonies.

In no other part of the world, we believe, is the condition of the wage-earning classes so enviable as it is here. Nowhere else, we imagine, can the skilled artisan earn ten shillings a day by eight hours' labour, and get excellent board and lodging for one-fourth of the money. Nowhere are these fortunate classes so favourably situated and circumstanced as they are in Australia. They are lightly taxed, and it may be unhesitatingly declared, that the free education which they receive for their children is really equivalent in value to their contributions to the Treasury. Politically, they are all-powerful; inasmuch as, under a system of manhood suffrage, the numerical majority is absolutely supreme. There is nothing whatever to prevent workmen from entering the Legislature, as many of them have done; and, being there, the attainment of a seat in the Cabinet is comparatively easy. Indeed, there have been several Premiers in the various colonies who have risen to that post from the ranks of labour; and, if they have sometimes made an arbitrary use of that power, and have mistaken despotic authority for democratic freedom, considerable allowance must be made for the weaknesses of men whose minds were never disciplined in early life by the virtual republicanism of the great schools in

England, and who had no opportunity of having the conceit knocked out of them, by the salutary influences of a university career.

It must be frankly admitted that the advantages which the Australasian colonies hold out to the operative classes are greater than are presented to any other section of the community, because in new countries there is so much manual and mechanical labour to be accomplished, and so active a demand for this description of industry. But to the farmer with a moderate capital, and a family of sons and daughters approaching maturity, these colonies offer attractions which, we venture to think, are unequalled. Other parts of the Empire possess as fertile a territory, but as a set-off, there is in Canada a winter of almost arctic severity, and in South Africa, the insecurity arising from the neighbourhood of powerful tribes of indigenous races, hostile to British rule. In Australia the agriculturist has not to shelter his stock and to suspend all out-of-door work during four or five months of the year; nor is he liable in New South Wales, Victoria, South Australia, or Tasmania to defend his homestead against formidable marauders like those who massacred 366 men, women and children, and lifted 25,000 head of cattle in Natal, some years ago, as related by the Rev. W. C. Holden in *The Past and Future of the Kaffir Races*. On the contrary, he may, as good old Cranmer says—

> Eat in safety,
> Under his own vine, what he plants; and sing
> The merry songs of peace to all his neighbours.

He may enjoy the solid comforts so dear to Englishmen in a country which combines all the advantages of soil and climate which are ordinarily regarded as the precious privilege of the most beautiful regions of Southern Europe, and may well exclaim with the shepherd in the eclogue, *Deus nobis hæc otia fecit*. There are only two temptations he will have to contend against —drink and discontent. It may be asked, why should discontent arise in a country where labour is so liberally rewarded, and where living is so cheap? Paradoxical as it may appear, the answer is, that discontent is engendered by the very causes which ought to inspire satisfaction and gratitude. The very men and women, who were most familiar with pinching poverty and stern privation in the old world, are frequently those who are most demoralised by relative prosperity in the new. Like Jeshurun, they "wax fat and kick." Biddy O'Connor, who thought herself fortunate to obtain a situation in the County Kerry, where she could get meat three times a week for dinner, and a pound a quarter for wages, will turn up her "tip tilted" nose at the offer of thirty pounds a year, and every other Sunday out, in a respectable family ten or twenty miles from Melbourne, or Sydney, or Adelaide; and she will waste her time and spend her money in a lodging-house, until she can meet with an engagement at £36 per annum, in one of those cities, and dictate a number of minor conditions to the mistress of the household. Biddy will array herself on Sundays in a two guinea hat or bonnet, and an imitation seal-skin jacket, and she will lift up the skirts of her silk dress to show the dainty frilling in her petticoat, and the costly quality of her bronze-kid boots; and she will ruffle it bravely on Easter Sunday and Christmas Day, on Whit-Sunday, and St. Patrick's Day. But she is nevertheless the victim of a secret sorrow. She is sometimes obliged to sit down to cold meat, instead of grilled steak, fried sausages, or hot rissoles, for breakfast, and her hand has not been asked in marriage by a rich publican, or a richer squatter. The butcher, who calls for orders at the house in which she professes the art of cookery, and helps to waste her employers' substance, has made matrimonial overtures to her—for Biddy has the dark violet eye of some of her countrywomen—but she flouts his advances, and exclaims to the housemaid, "I do be shure I didn't come 16,000 miles to demane myself by takin' up with the likes of an omadhaun like him."

Job Hedgestake is also discontented with the colonies. Down in the Essex "Roothings" he was getting twelve shillings a week, and had a very hard time of it, in the winter months, when for weeks together he never earned a shilling. It is the dead season of the year in Victoria, and the times are dull besides. He is offered six shillings a day for pick and shovel work, the "day" consisting of eight hours. But Job resents the offer as an insult to his manhood. He is not going to work for "starvation wages" (N.B.—Bread is fourpence-halfpenny the four-pound loaf, and mutton can be bought for a penny a pound; while he can get either breakfast, dinner, or tea for sixpence in a working-man's restaurant); and, accordingly, he confers with several other down-trodden "sons of soil," and they get up a meeting of "the unemployed," and form themselves into a deputation, to wait upon the Minister of Public Works and obtain from him the promise of being set to work at "the Government stroke." In the evening, Job will be found refreshing himself with a pint of "two-ales" at his favourite public-house, and confidentially informing a number of loafers that, in his opinion, "this d——d country is almost played out," and that "he wishes he had never left England, or possessed the means of getting back to it." He is a grumbling malcontent; but if he should acquire the wherewithal for his passage to the mother-country, you may depend upon it, it is the very last place towards which he would turn his face.

Then there is the artisan, whose earnings averaged half-a-crown a day —a day of ten hours—at home, and who receives ten shillings for eight hours' work in Australia. He is discontented, because his pay is not double what it is; and he contends that, if no apprentices were allowed to be taken, and if all the Chinese were expelled from the colonies, and if a prohibitive tariff were adopted, wages would very soon go up to the maximum. And this kind of discontent prevails among all classes of society, not as a general rule, but in so many individual cases, as to force itself into prominence, when you are examining the social aspects of Australian communities. The simple truth of the matter appears to be, that, broadly speaking, we are all too well off; and that, like the fortunate husbandmen of Virgil, we are unaware of the true measure of the material prosperity we enjoy in a country where

> Procul discordibus armis,
> Fundit humo facilem victum justissima tellus.

For if we have no such palaces as those which the Mantuan describes in his sweet and stately verse; we have, nevertheless, the

> Secura quies, et nescia fallere vita,
> Dives opum variarum; at latis otia fundis,
> Speluncae, vivique lacus; at frigida Tempe,
> Mugitusque boum, mollesque sub arbore somni
> Non absunt.

Indeed, as we read the second Georgic, we seem to be brought into contact with rural life and scenery, with country occupations and pursuits, and with conditions of climate, resembling those of some parts of Australia, where tens of thousands of persons are thoroughly familiar with the "*sub arbore somni.*"

We are the spoiled children of nature. She comes to us, in our "*secura quies,*" with both hands full of lavish gifts, and she demoralises us by her opulent bounty. The wealth she has stored up in her cellarage—the ingots of gold and silver, compared with which the treasures of Aladdin's cave sink into insignificance, she suddenly laid bare; while at the same time disclosing pasturages, which were boundless, and magnificent areas of arable land, the rich elements of which she had elaborated hundreds of thousands of years ago, in the entrails of the volcanoes, which once belched forth their fountains of ashen dust and fiery vapour, and their glowing streams of red hot lava. During the lapse of countless centuries she had been robing the mountain ranges with their superb garments of forest, and massing and matting on the soil beneath successive layers of the richest humus, so that, when we felled the timber for constructive or domestic uses, the earth would be prepared to yield a succession of splendid harvests to the husbandman; and in one part of this great island-continent she had transformed the forests of a remote geological epoch into coal measures, which are virtually inexhaustible. Elsewhere she had hidden enormous deposits of copper, tin, and iron ore, of marble, granite, porphyry, and sand-stone, of kaolin clay, and of kerosene-shale; and when a few hundreds of thousands of people, numbers of whom were fugitives from poverty and hardship in the mother-country, came into possession of this magnificent property, it is not altogether to be wondered at, that it should have had the effect of upsetting their mental balance, in a great many instances, and that it should have stimulated the avidity of the acquisitive, encouraged the intemperance and thriftlessness of the thoughtless and the self-indulgent, weakened the force of old restraints, and strengthened the influence of new temptations!

The history of colonisation in early times offers nothing at all resembling or approaching the propitious circumstances under which the colonies of South Australia, Victoria, and Queensland were settled, because science has armed the modern pioneer with such mechanical and chemical appliances, that his power is that of a giant, as compared with that of the Greeks, for example, who founded new states and cities at various points on the shores of the Mediterranean, or with that of the Pilgrim Fathers, who landed on Plymouth Rock. The effectiveness of his labour has been increased a hundredfold by the agency of steam, and by the invention of labour-saving machinery, applicable to all the processes of human industry, and the useful arts of life. Dynamite is the Orphean lyre, with which he can move rocks and displace forests; with the diamond drill he can penetrate the secrets of the earth, and bore through mountains; and by the aid of fuel, water, and mechanism he can accomplish, in a few days, results which formerly would have tasked the efforts of a squad of men persistently labouring for as many months. Hence, the productive power of each individual, in a country where the "gratuitous utilities of nature" play so enormous and beneficent a *rôle* as auxiliaries to man, is necessarily very great indeed, and the accumulation of wealth proceeds very rapidly, although that accumulation is not so obvious as in older countries, because it does not take the shape of money lodged in banks and other institutions, but assumes that of fixed values. In other words, it is being continually transformed into real estate. It is represented by the reclamation, clearing, fencing, and cultivation of millions of acres of land; by the formation of roads and bridges, piers and harbours, tramways and railways; by the erection of dwelling-houses, churches, schools, warehouses, shops, manufactories, mills, hotels, and public buildings of every description. All these things, which have been the bequest of former generations of Englishmen in the mother-country to the generation which now is, require to be provided in a British colony, by the first and second generations of its settlers; and, accordingly, the ratable value of the property they possess represents approximately the accumulations of two, three, or four decades. At the present time, the total value of the ratable property in the colony of Victoria is £80,000,000, and as the valuation is generally about 20 per cent. below the real value of the property assessed, we may put the latter down at £100,000,000 in round numbers, and this does not include that of Government buildings, railways (all of which are Government property), bridges, reservoirs, churches, State schools, public libraries, public parks, markets, etc. The railways alone have cost £14,000,000; and their value is increasing year by year with the growth of population, and the consequent expansion of traffic.

It is estimated, that as regards agriculture alone, the value of the implements and machinery in use upon the various farms and stations in Victoria is upwards of £2,000,000, and that of the improvements £17,000,000, making a total of £19,000,000.

In such a colony—and what applies to one applies to all—men rise to affluence before they have reached the prime of life; and the number of those who have done so is larger perhaps, in proportion to the whole population, than in any of the older countries. One of two brothers, owning 80,000 acres of land in Victoria, at a dinner and ball given to 800 of his friends and neighbours, thus referred to his own career in returning thanks for his health having been drunk :—

"He could assure his guests, that he had been no loafer, but a hard-working man, in his early career in the colony. When he first came to Victoria, he had endured many hardships, and, in travelling with his sheep in search of a run, he slept out many a night with his saddle for a pillow, the widespreading branches of a gum tree for his covering, and the canopy of heaven for his roof. When he left home to go to Australia, he promised his father and mother, that he would be back to them again in five years, and he redeemed his promise so far, that he was back to them in the sixth year. He only stayed at home a short time, when he returned to Australia again, and coming to Victoria, which was then only a province of New South Wales, he took up a run at a place then known as the Deep Creek, but now called Clunes. He afterwards took up some country at Mount William, the farthest limit settlement had then reached, and he was happy to inform them that the gentleman, who was his overseer then, was one of the guests that night, and was also his equal in social station. To be a pioneer in those times was, he could assure them, no child's play ; and now that fortune had smiled upon him, and that his economy and determination to succeed in life had been crowned with success far beyond his expectations then, he was thankful for his success, inasmuch as it gave him the means of assisting to promote the interests of the country that had done so much for him, and which he loved so dearly."

Successful men of this stamp are to be met with in the whole of the Australian colonies; and many of their biographies, if written, would exemplify the romance of real life in a very striking manner, and would be found to be full of dramatic incident. This has been more particularly the case with respect to gold-mining, of which a couple of instances may suffice. In the early days of the Dunolly gold-fields, two working miners, named Oates and Deeson, after experiencing many vicissitudes of fortune, found themselves, in the *argot* of their class, "dead-broke." Their credit was exhausted at the neighbouring store, and one of them was actually in want of bread. In sheer desperation they began digging for gold in a very unpromising locality. "It seemed a very hopeless task, but the two men worked on steadily, standing close to one another. Deeson plied his pick in some hard bricklike clay, around the roots of an old tree, breaking up fresh earth and tearing away the grass from the surface of the ground. He aimed a blow at a clear space between two branches of the root; and the pick instead of sinking into the ground rebounded, as if it had struck upon quartz or granite. "Confound it!" he exclaimed; "I've broken my pick. I wish I had broken it, if it had only been over some nugget." A minute afterwards he called out to Oates, and told him to "come and see what this was." It was a mass of gold cropping several inches out of the ground, like a boulder on a hill. As each successive portion of the nugget was disclosed to view the men were lost in amazement at its enormous size. It was over a foot in length, and nearly the same in breadth. The weight was so great that it was difficult for the two men to move it. However, by dint of great exertion, they succeeded in carrying it down the hill to Deeson's cottage, where they commenced to inspect their wonderful treasure. It was so completely covered with black earth, and so tarnished in colour, that an inexperienced person might have supposed it to be merely a mass of auriferous earth or stone. But its weight at once dispelled all doubt on that point, for it was more than twice as heavy as a piece of iron of the same size.

Great was the rejoicing among Deeson's family. The wife piled up a huge fire, and Deeson placed the nugget on top, while the rest of the family stood around watching the operation of reducing the mass to the semblance of gold. All through the Friday night, Deeson sat up before the fire, burning the quartz, which adhered to the nugget, and picking off all the dirt and *débris*. This was so rich, that, on being washed in the puddling machine, it yielded ten pounds' weight of gold. Meanwhile Oates had procured a dray to convey the nugget to town, and on the Saturday morning the two men set off for Dunolly."* They carried their treasure to the London Chartered Bank, where it was weighed, and found to turn the scale at 2,268 ounces, or nearly two hundredweight, and the sum of ten thousand pounds was placed to their credit in that institution.

Among the pioneers of the once celebrated Woods Point gold-field, situated high up among the mountain ranges, about a hundred miles due east of Melbourne, were two brothers, named Colin and Duncan M'Dougal, who applied themselves, with singularly primitive crushing appliances, to the work of quartz-mining. With these they were enabled to satisfy themselves that some of the rich quartz of the district was capable of yielding as much as 44 ounces to the ton.

"The prospect of receiving £150 for every ton that they crushed, filled their minds with ideas of immense wealth to come, and they were determined not to lose it for want of energy.

"One of the M'Dougals was despatched to Melbourne, to order the necessary machinery, and to direct the making of it; for this crushing

* "Tales of the Gold-fields." By George Sutherland, M.A.

machine was to be unique of its kind. The battery was to have eight stampers, and yet, for convenience of carrying, no single piece was to exceed 200lbs. in weight. All the ironwork was therefore cast in very small portions, and new patterns had to be made for each piece.

"Meanwhile the other three men were working hard at alluvial digging, in order to gain enough of money to pay for the machine, as it was being constructed. They also cut a very long mill-race along the mountain sides to supply the water-wheel; for the motive power was to be obtained entirely from the mountain streams, and steam-engines were out of the question.

"When the machinery, in pieces, was brought to the town of Jamieson, about twenty miles to the north of Woods Point, an unexpected difficulty arose. No "packers" would undertake to convey it over the ranges. They said it would be absurd to expect, that horses, with a load of two hundredweight each, could keep their footing on the sides of these mountains. The four diggers were therefore obliged to procure horses and to convey the machinery themselves. This work alone occupied them over three months; it was fully a year, from the commencement, before they had the machine erected, and yet the whole weight did not exceed three tons.

"Having thus surmounted every obstacle, they gave to their reef the name of the "Morning Star;" and very soon it justified the name, for the brilliancy of its results for a year or two quite eclipsed all the other gold mines of the colony. The little clumsy machine, with wooden shanks to the stampers, with a wooden fly-wheel, and driven by an old-fashioned water-engine, turned out more gold than the large steam-driven batteries of Ballarat and Sandhurst.

"At first the M'Dougals kept these splendid results a great secret. A wild and lawless population had followed their footsteps up the mountains; and in such a place there could be no protection but in secrecy. The partners therefore concealed their good fortune from everyone, and hid all their gold in secluded places, among the thick scrub. At night time, they stole out from the settlement, and, taking the gold with them, they made their way by moonlight over the ranges, to a little hut, that was erected beyond the roughest country. Here a horse was kept in readiness to convey one of them, with his precious cargo on to Jamieson.

"Up to the end of 1866, the produce of the claim of M'Dougal and Company amounted to over £164,000, and several adjoining claims had also yielded extraordinary returns."*

It must be admitted, however, that the old adage of "light come, light go," has generally held good with most of the fortunes suddenly acquired by gold-mining; and that comparatively few, who have been exposed to a heavy shower of the precious metal, have escaped being demoralised by it;

* "Tales of the Goldfields." By George Sutherland, M.A.

for prosperity is so much harder to bear than adversity; and a man usually values his acquisitions, when they are the result of steady industry, of patient application and of persevering thrift, much more highly than when his wealth has fallen upon him in a copious cataract, by the caprice of fortune. But the incidents we have quoted, and the information we have laid before our readers in the foregoing chapter, will serve to exhibit the magnitude of the rewards which are held out to the labourers and frugal emigrant on the one hand, and the richness of the prizes which fall to the lot of a chosen few in that great lottery of fortune known as gold-mining.

QUANTITIES OF MAIZE OR INDIAN CORN IMPORTED INTO THE UNITED KINGDOM, 1861-1876.

From what Countries.	1861.	1862.	1863.	1864.	1865.	1866.	1867.	1868.	1869.	1870.	1871.	1872.	1873.	1874.	1875.	1876.
	cwts.	cwts.	cwts.	cwts.	cwts.	cwts.	cwts.	cwts.	cwts.	cwts.	cwts.	cwts.	cwts.	cwts.	cwts.	cwts.
Australian Territories	465,533	831,185	107,379	43,765	612,725	1,390,935	706,819	1,250,515	1,345,786	463,683	836,243	456,966	311,240	285,208	420,192	561,588
British North America	3,387,949	5,118,698	3,198,187	1,831,897	528,456	59,601	833,006	798,505	3,396,511	3,402,690	3,782,776	2,157,170	4,315,709	4,298,315	4,069,565	2,766,975
Chili	364,246	347,341	282,311	198,231	169,862	341,999	2,097,978	1,477,536	580,349	643,347	580,951	1,677,908	1,837,387	2,297,016	902,660	1,012,642
Denmark	674,325	419,148	334,894	776,175	687,763	563,007	564,963	817,173	779,884	580,243	293,432	611,283	475,354	455,394	831,850	832,030
Egypt	1,474,480	3,304,579	2,322,636	367,462	10,063	33,831	1,471,756	3,237,380	1,020,289	106,701	908,847	2,361,042	1,271,794	297,928	2,112,138	2,249,252
France	1,359,892	1,961,835	1,857,403	2,854,424	6,058,902	8,023,530	2,140,832	846,863	2,153,350	1,060,120	182,262	4,553,781	3,259,619	1,124,712	3,573,777	1,633,800
Germany	6,638,462	7,930,849	5,728,626	6,842,727	7,224,371	6,801,657	7,873,216	7,224,597	7,546,688	4,487,773	4,258,823	5,183,001	3,019,406	4,012,606	6,613,544	3,487,672
Holland	50,872	12,794	11,708	13,796	51,615	93,096	15,938	60,132	203,760	26,308	12,398	61,912	39,378	9,823	52,472	83,127
Russia	4,540,483	5,755,789	4,538,934	5,120,410	8,093,989	9,181,432	14,166,791	10,053,338	9,187,236	10,326,844	15,689,943	17,938,977	9,693,997	5,798,976	10,157,847	8,911,786
Spain	1,217,257	316,882	11,393	1,980	133,835	863,629	452,680	2,982	43,151	8,395	16,990	643,087	1,734,640	418,420	157,217	270,473
Sweden	66,352	19,280	26,810	80,479	26,808	30,009	18,244	24,509	62,955	37,322	20,538	44,382	34,038	24,077	100,052	58,420
Turkey & Dependencies	1,002,768	1,759,566	415,524	482,994	574,185	529,433	2,447,218	3,066,597	2,386,939	493,546	1,421,746	829,942	420,822	623,177	1,312,434	1,961,257
United States	15,610,472	21,765,087	11,860,179	10,077,431	1,498,579	986,229	5,091,733	6,753,389	15,320,257	15,057,236	15,625,331	9,634,349	21,775,110	27,306,052	26,372,151	22,223,403
Other Countrs.	693,574	499,361	132,908	131,448	172,379	474,391	1,253,603	890,529	418,617	211,907	722,947	1,458,296	3,442,483	2,561,529	2,870,722	6,502,006
Total	37,646,705	50,042,394	30,887,892	28,837,203	25,843,552	29,371,679	39,136,780	36,506,045	44,447,772	36,906,115	44,362,227	47,612,896	51,631,197	49,322,693	59,546,621	51,904,433

QUANTITIES OF MAIZE OR INDIAN CORN IMPORTED INTO THE UNITED KINGDOM, 1861-1876.

Countries.	1861.	1862.	1863.	1864.	1865.	1866.	1867.	1868.	1869.	1870.	1871.	1872.	1873.	1874.	1875.	1876.
	cwts.	cwts.	cwts.	cwts.	cwts.	cwts.	cwts.	cwts.	cwts.	cwts.	cwts.	cwts.	cwts.	cwts.	cwts.	cwts.
Australian Territories	188,490	...	206,876	79,538	26,617	45,863	526,263	1,079,564	2,927,056	1,225,056	156,049	155,656	134,328	96,767	1,188,707	65,749
British North America	506,249	1,425,892	391,440	9,641	302,173	859,578	338,032	339,831	33,847	12,400	1,346,069	3,537,896	1,761,175	1,320,229	873,776	1,878,415
Egypt	266,049	235,633	431,494	9,238	...	3,903	219,988	537,726	10,366	11,214	75,903	372,001	38,930	12,749	63,490	132,271
France	74,946	13,187	42,998	167,129	71,935	464,161	1,000,624	173,461	166,312	371,682	96,623	10,902	5,703	90,420	268,531	587
Russia	528,932	935,070	987,236	1,401,343	1,181,756	461,930	247,460	664,881	604,618	2,511,725	2,086,488	423,851	1,334,305	508,361	504,115	829,606
Turkey & Dependencies	3,734,751	2,211,368	5,390,430	4,311,795	3,697,848	5,372,873	1,030,968	4,027,131	11,008,607	1,321,280	5,548,271	2,558,028	4,033,561	1,529,765	4,418,555	9,290,280
United States	7,385,717	6,511,718	4,548,386	294,263	1,766,303	6,953,811	4,799,385	4,069,770	1,334,844	23,063	7,319,246	16,980,683	10,762,333	13,454,617	12,058,606	27,065,460
Other Countrs.	529,192	331,890	344,734	12,991	49,399	161,744	387,509	634,862	1,537,963	779,505	196,372	443,653	712,963	650,518	1,032,700	701,001

STATISTICAL SUMMARY OF POPULATION, AGRICULTURE, AN[D]

From 1874 t[o]

		Popula-tion.	Total Cultiva-tion.	Wheat.		Oats.		Barley.		Maize.		Other Cer[eals]	
				Acres.	Bushels.	Acres.	Bushels.	Acres.	Bushels.	Acres.	Bushels.	Acres.	Bu[shels]
1874.	Victoria	808,437	1,011,776	332,936	4,850,165	114,921	2,121,612	29,505	619,896	1,523	24,263	17,266	
	N. S. Wales	584,278	464,957	166,912	2,148,394	17,973	293,135	3,984	69,053	118,437	3,616,436	1,351	
	S. Australia	204,623	1,330,484	839,638	9,862,693	2,785	40,701	13,724	208,373	—	—	—	
	Queensland	163,517	70,331	3,592	No return	178	No return	361	No return	30,999	No return	387	No [return]
	W. Australia	26,209	45,292	23,427	281,124	1,067	17,072	4,702	75,232	88	1,320	1,022	
	New Zealand	341,860	549,844	105,674	2,974,330	157,545	5,548,729	16,236	477,162	—	—	—	
	Tasmania	104,176	326,486	57,633	1,666,861	32,704	877,243	5,129	125,469	—	—	5,714	1
		2,233,100	3,799,170	1,529,812	21,183,576	327,173	8,898,492	73,641	1,575,185	151,046	3,644,019	25,740	4
1875.	Victoria	823,272	1,120,831	321,401	4,978,914	124,100	2,719,795	31,568	700,665	2,346	37,177	20,146	4[?]
	N. S. Wales	606,652	451,139	133,610	1,958,640	18,856	352,966	4,817	98,576	117,582	3,410,517	1,091	
	S. Australia	210,442	1,444,586	898,820	10,739,834	3,640	60,749	13,969	197,315	—	—	4,854	
	Queensland	181,288	77,347	4,478	No return	114	No return	613	No return	38,711	No return	251	No [return]
	W. Australia	26,709	47,571	21,561	237,171	1,256	18,840	5,014	70,196	60	1,200	1,293	
	New Zealand	375,656	607,138	90,804	2,863,619	168,252	6,357,431	27,656	993,219	—	—	—	
	Tasmania	103,663	332,824	42,745	700,092	32,556	827,043	5,939	165,357	—	—	6,585	1[?]
		2,327,882	4,087,433	1,513,419	21,478,270	348,774	10,336,824	89,576	2,225,328	158,699	3,448,894	34,220	7[?]
1876.	Victoria	840,300	1,231,105	401,417	5,279,730	115,209	2,294,225	25,034	530,323	1,609	25,909	22,388	8[?]
	N. S. Wales	629,776	513,840	145,609	2,391,979	21,828	461,916	5,662	134,158	116,363	3,879,537	1,571	
	S. Australia	225,677	1,514,016	1,083,732	5,857,569	2,914	31,043	10,056	107,023	—	—	4,490	
	Queensland	187,100	85,569	5,700	No return	162	No return	688	No return	41,705	No return	270	No [return]
	W. Australia	27,321	45,933	18,769	225,168	1,461	21,915	6,245	93,675	70	1,470	1,378	
	New Zealand	399,075	787,824	141,614	4,054,377	150,717	4,707,836	22,679	801,379	—	—	—	
	Tasmania	105,484	332,558	38,977	752,070	23,609	571,485	6,258	147,537	—	—	7,263	1[?]
		2,414,733	4,511,745	1,835,818	18,560,893	315,900	8,089,420	76,622	1,814,095	159,749	3,906,916	37,360	9
1877.	Victoria	800,787	1,420,502	564,564	7,018,257	105,234	2,040,486	19,116	378,706	1,215	22,050	18,361	2
	N. S. Wales	662,212	546,556	176,587	2,445,507	18,581	358,853	5,055	99,485	105,510	3,551,806	1,465	
	S. Australia	236,864	1,828,115	1,163,646	9,034,692	3,515	42,039	11,991	143,586	—	—	3,832	
	Queensland	203,084	105,049	8,744	92,941	74	748	638	10,758	44,718	1,262,018	419	
	W. Australia	27,838	50,591	22,634	251,174	1,290	18,060	5,948	77,324	46	920	799	
	New Zealand	417,622	959,528	243,406	6,336,369	190,344	6,029,962	22,713	576,823	—	—	—	
	Tasmania	107,104	348,841	46,719	846,420	21,883	488,350	4,283	86,840	—	—	5,854	
		2,515,511	5,259,182	2,226,600	26,025,360	340,921	8,978,498	69,744	1,373,522	151,489	4,836,794	30,730	4
1878.	Victoria	879,442	1,609,278	691,622	6,060,737	134,428	2,366,026	22,871	417,157	1,939	40,754	16,932	2
	N. S. Wales	693,743	613,642	233,253	3,439,326	22,129	447,912	6,152	132,072	130,582	4,420,580	1,604	
	S. Australia	248,795	2,011,319	1,305,851	9,332,049	2,931	35,202	12,089	142,933	—	—	4,233	
	Queensland	210,510	117,489	9,618	130,452	132	1,274	1,065	16,904	53,799	1,539,510	348	No [return]
	W. Australia	28,166	51,065	23,008	229,342	1,568	28,249	5,927	72,498	40	296	817	
	New Zealand	432,519	1,134,185	264,577	6,070,599	277,547	8,357,150	28,646	709,465	—	—	—	
	Tasmania	109,947	355,403	48,392	778,977	28,802	714,987	4,040	97,845	—	—	5,003	
		2,603,122	5,892,381	2,576,321	26,041,482	467,537	11,050,800	80,790	1,588,874	186,360	6,001,140	29,233	4
Totals, 1874		2,233,100	3,799,170	1,529,812	21,183,576	327,173	8,898,492	73,641	1,575,185	151,046	3,644,019	25,740	4
,, 1875		2,327,882	4,087,430	1,513,419	21,478,270	348,774	10,336,824	89,576	2,225,328	158,699	3,448,894	34,220	7
,, 1876		2,414,733	4,511,745	1,835,818	18,560,893	315,900	8,088,420	76,622	1,814,095	159,749	3,906,916	37,360	8
,, 1877		2,515,511	5,259,182	2,226,600	26,025,360	340,921	8,978,498	69,744	1,373,522	151,489	4,836,794	30,730	4
,, 1878		2,603,122	5,892,381	2,576,321	26,041,482	467,537	11,950,800	80,790	1,588,874	186,360	6,001,140	29,233	4
					113,289,581		48,253,034		8,577,004		21,837,763		2[?]

POPULATION, AGRICULTURE, AND LIVE STOCK.   193

LIVE STOCK IN THE AUSTRALASIAN COLONIES.

1878 inclusive.

AGRICULTURE.								LIVE STOCK.			
Potatoes.		Hay.		Vines.		Green Forage.	Other Tillage.	Horses.	Cattle.	Sheep.	Pigs.
Acres.	Tons.	Acres.	Tons.	Acres.	Wine. Gallons.	Acres.	Acres.				
35,183	124,310	119,031	157,261	4,937	577,493	254,320	102,145	180,254	958,658	11,221,036	137,941
13,604	38,504	68,088	93,440	4,308	684,253	40,580	29,711	346,091	2,856,690	22,872,882	219,958
4,532	17,046	160,931	202,934	5,051	648,186	27,076	276,697	93,122	185,342	6,120,211	78,019
3,316	No return	5,354	No return	413	70,425	3,359	22,173	107,507	1,610,105	7,180,792	44,517
329	987	13,366	20,049	779	No return	—	512	26,636	46,748	777,861	13,290
12,154	63,635	62,216	52,202	—	—	196,019	—	99,859	494,917	11,704,853	123,921
6,978	26,169	30,486	41,144	—	—	94,234	93,608	23,208	110,450	1,724,053	51,468
76,146	270,761	459,672	567,030	15,488	1,980,362	419,587	720,865	877,277	6,262,919	61,602,588	669,114
36,901	124,377	155,274	206,613	5,081	755,000	308,405	121,609	196,184	1,054,598	11,749,532	140,765
13,806	41,203	77,125	88,008	4,459	831,749	50,634	29,159	357,696	3,134,036	24,382,536	199,950
5,941	26,833	161,429	194,794	4,972	727,979	37,261	313,700	107,164	219,240	6,170,395	100,562
3,056	No return	8,531	No return	376	77,404	2,963	18,354	121,497	1,812,576	7,227,774	46,447
393	1,179	17,319	17,319	675	No return	—	—	29,379	50,416	881,861	14,420
14,655	71,590	49,537	72,184	—	—	30,883	225,351	99,859	494,917	11,704,853	123,921
6,906	24,455	34,758	49,217	—	—	103,167	100,168	23,473	118,604	1,731,723	47,064
81,658	289,646	503,973	629,095	15,563	2,392,132	533,213	808,341	935,252	6,884,527	63,857,674	673,729
40,450	134,082	147,408	180,560	4,765	481,588	362,554	110,271	194,768	1,128,285	11,278,803	175,578
14,171	42,939	111,940	150,861	4,457	794,709	61,516	30,715	366,703	3,131,013	24,503,388	173,604
5,091	14,463	91,937	178,806	4,554	493,217	35,268	276,874	106,903	219,441	6,133,291	102,295
3,928	No return	9,423	No return	523	93,841	4,821	18,349	133,625	2,079,979	7,315,074	53,455
370	1,110	16,356	16,856	784	No return	—	—	33,502	54,058	890,494	18,108
16,204	86,922	49,760	65,060	—	—	32,459	369,391	99,859	494,917	11,704,853	123,921
7,954	27,290	29,664	35,007	—	—	114,978	103,855	23,022	124,459	1,768,785	60,681
88,168	306,806	456,094	636,910	15,083	1,868,355	611,596	909,455	958,982	7,232,132	63,603,778	707,642
37,107	115,419	176,951	208,151	4,419	457,535	390,330	103,205	203,150	1,169,576	10,117,867	163,391
13,862	34,958	125,778	154,076	4,184	708,431	65,073	30,360	329,150	2,746,385	20,962,244	191,677
5,367	13,452	223,905	253,374	4,164	339,277	36,265	375,430	110,684	230,679	6,098,358	104,527
4,603	8,778	9,914	12,919	655	87,051	10,771	24,513	140,174	2,299,582	6,272,766	52,074
354	708	18,013	18,013	713	No return	—	594	30,691	52,057	797,156	18,942
17,564	94,478	45,090	58,671	—	—	120,376	440,411	99,859	494,917	11,704,853	123,921
8,336	27,106	29,440	33,331	—	—	—	111,950	22,195	126,882	1,818,125	55,652
87,193	294,899	629,091	738,535	14,135	1,592,294	622,815	1,086,463	934,903	7,120,078	57,771,370	730,184
36,527	98,958	172,799	209,028	4,434	410,333	401,427	126,299	210,105	1,184,843	9,379,276	177,373
16,725	53,590	104,096	172,407	4,237	684,733	60,249	34,615	336,468	2,771,563	23,967,053	220,320
5,398	14,378	218,359	210,974	4,297	458,303	30,033	428,128	121,553	251,802	6,377,312	103,422
3,882	9,063	13,904	18,553	605	64,407	6,875	27,061	147,076	2,433,567	5,564,465	50,301
341	850	18,750	18,750	614	No return	—	—	32,801	56,158	869,325	16,762
17,299	86,186	53,022	64,520	—	—	49,187	443,007	137,768	578,430	13,069,338	207,337
8,079	27,257	33,933	40,499	—	—	118,478	105,580	24,107	126,276	1,838,831	39,595
88,251	290,282	614,863	734,731	14,187	1,617,776	666,249	1,165,590	1,009,878	7,402,659	61,066,100	815,110
76,146	270,761	459,672	567,030	15,488	1,980,362	419,587	720,865	877,277	6,262,919	61,602,588	669,114
81,658	289,646	503,973	629,095	15,563	2,392,132	533,213	808,341	935,252	6,884,527	63,857,674	673,729
88,168	306,806	456,994	636,910	15,083	1,868,355	611,596	909,455	958,982	7,232,132	63,603,778	707,642
87,193	294,899	629,091	738,535	14,135	1,592,294	622,815	1,086,463	934,903	7,120,078	57,771,370	730,184
88,251	290,282	614,863	734,731	14,167	1,617,776	666,249	1,165,590	1,009,878	7,402,659	61,066,100	815,110
	1,452,364		3,306,391		9,450,919						

O

STATISTICAL SUMMARY of the Principal Exports the Produce or Manufacture of each Colony.
From 1874 to 1878 Inclusive.

VICTORIA.

	Wool.		Flour.		Grain and Pulse.		Confectionery and Biscuits.	Refined Sugar.		Wine.		Horned Cattle, Horses, and Sheep.	Tallow.		Preserved Meats.	Leather.	Gold.	Other Minerals.	Bark and Timber.	Apparel and Slops.
	Quantity.	Value.	Qntity.	Value.	Qntity.	Value.	Value.	Qntity.	Value.	Qntity.	Value.	Value.	Qnty.	Value.	Value.	Value.	Value.	Value.	Value.	Value.
	Lbs.	£	Centals.	£	Centals.	£	£	Cwts.	£	Gallons.	£	£	Tns.	£	£	£	£	£	£	£
1874	67,092,092	4,906,745	59,687	39,022	6,329	3,611	25,378	91,772	150,366	8,219	2,681	106,421	6,067	199,564	175,774	190,199	4,972,012	25,177	17,864	107,581
1875	63,656,335	4,694,130	26,100	15,011	14,276	7,623	27,879	67,317	112,125	14,921	4,812	146,629	6,210	203,243	134,297	244,027	4,320,053	37,098	59,596	106,463
1876	77,270,033	4,852,233	17,507	11,457	22,048	10,615	29,793	34,663	53,856	14,249	4,705	152,939	5,100	174,507	166,570	194,033	3,613,557	53,440	80,845	125,460
1877	74,033,218	4,379,936	159,181	113,612	62,320	32,263	27,303	61,787	107,076	7,558	3,172	316,185	2,700	90,455	201,583	201,583	4,851,934	57,876	68,717	138,771
1878	73,330,839	4,330,622	318,159	196,515	197,310	96,613	48,110	77,352	130,566	12,354	3,192	431,736	3,298	103,879	74,337	215,717	3,783,510	76,059	100,817	204,525

NEW SOUTH WALES.

	Wool.		Refined Sugar.		Wine.		Live Stock—Horned Cattle, Horses, and Sheep	Tallow.		Preserved Meats.	Leather.	Tallow.	Gold.		Coal.		Tin and Tin Ore.		Timber.
	Quantity.	Value.	Quantity.	Value.	Qntity.	Value.	Value.	Qntity.	Value.	Value.	Value.	Qnty.	Value.	Quantity.	Value.	Quantity.	Value.	Value.
	Lb.	£	Cwts.	£	Ga lons.	£	£	Cwts.	£	£	£	Tns.	£	Tons.	£	Cwts.	£	£
1874	75,156,924	5,010,125	21,143	34,037	5,999	2,963	63,963	67,053	104,151	92,939	94,939	6,067	1,875,081	872,930	633,247	98,380	419,322	52,841
1875	87,634,290	5,651,643	49,761	80,181	5,903	3,971	90,740	69,553	112,072	56,473	108,347		2,097,740	927,007	671,433	111,126	430,920	67,341
1876	100,736,330	5,565,178	104,255	163,147	6,882	3,240	81,905	77,530	124,834	83,954	33,305		1,589,654	868,817	625,211	109,157	379,638	27,701
1877	102,150,846	6,356,038	80,124	137,234	10,591	4,502	892,122	90,169	147,790	126,382	91,466		1,824,188	915,727	643,977	161,079	508,510	29,337
1878	111,823,017	6,723,316	84,072	135,133	9,969	4,910	733,721	60,035	96,076	42,581	90,133		1,629,963	1,006,420	708,406	144,190	395,822	40,243

QUEENSLAND.

	Wool.		Raw Sugar.		Tallow.		Preserved Meats and Extracts.	Gold.	Coal.	Tin—Ore and Smelted.		Copper.		Timber.
	Quantity.	Value.	Quantity.	Value.	Quantity.	Value.	Value.	Value.	Value.	Quantity.	Value.	Quantity.	Value.	Value.
	Lbs.	£	Cwts.	£	Tons.	£	£	£	£	Cwts.	£	Cwts.	£	£
1874	20,359,344	1,420,381	84,576	100,982	1,140	43,045	58,459	1,356,071	1,049	114,052	353,550	35,320	146,038	26,616
1875	20,145,914	1,366,030	46,866	56,530	1,385	43,001	52,110	1,498,433	1,925	89,497	237,879	25,320	105,449	25,584
1876	22,018,560	1,499,576	8,380	11,881	1,940	67,311	94,974	1,427,929	1,290	87,702	187,201	42,040	172,332	35,670
1877	23,980,485	1,499,682	92,115	133,297	2,158	73,006	89,773	1,307,084	5,777	66,702	133,432	38,403	165,601	35,629
1878	21,608,122	1,186,659	67,616	89,420	749	23,853	6,265	1,052,490	3,686	61,114	87,711	9,814	32,825	56,233

STATISTICAL SUMMARY OF THE PRINCIPAL EXPORTS THE PRODUCE OR MANUFACTURE OF EACH COLONY. FROM 1874 TO 1878 INCLUSIVE.

SOUTH AUSTRALIA.

	Wool.		Breadstuffs.	Wine.		Tallow.		Minerals.
	Quantity.	Value.	Value.	Quantity.	Value.	Quantity.	Value.	Value.
	Lbs.	£	£	Gallons.	£	Tons.	£	£
1874	35,593,805	1,762,987	1,230,331	59,179	17,399	1,283½	38,511	700,323
1875	39,723,249	1,833,519	1,680,996	45,879	11,224	1,409	41,009	762,386
1876	30,435,346	1,836,299	1,988,716	36,299	9,357	591	20,593	602,386
1877	47,199,928	2,180,418	1,184,368	37,966	10,696	808	19,882	565,099
1878	56,710,851	2,417,397	1,672,623	49,691	25,256	1,668	48,056	400,749

WESTERN AUSTRALIA.

	Wool.		Live-stock.	Lead Ore.		Guano.		Pearls.	Sandal-wood and Timber.
	Quantity.	Value.	Value.	Quantity	Value.	Quantity.	Value.	Value.	Value.
	Lbs.	£	£	Tons.	£	Tons.	£	£	£
1874	2,874,992	215,624	6,123	2,143¾	25,725	—	—	12,000	94,764
1875	2,428,160	182,112	2,852	2,289	27,468	—	—	12,000	90,430
1876	2,831,174	165,151	11,272	2,191½	26,298	735	367	8,000	89,515
1877	3,092,487	199,624	9,168	3,955½	47,466	1,212	6,060	10,000	68,829
1878	3,019,051	150,952	12,089	3,617½	43,410	13,219	66,095	12,000	98,966

TASMANIA.

	Wool.		Grain, Flour, Bran, and Hay.	Fruit, Jams, and Vegetables.	Gold.	Tin—Ore and Smelted.		Timber.	Bark.
	Quantity.	Value.	Value.	Value.	Value.	Quantity.	Value.	Value.	Value.
	Lbs.	£	£	£	£	Tons.	£	£	£
1874	5,050,920	350,713	123,505	132,321	17,811	142	7,318	75,422	22,123
1875	6,190,248	433,550	130,044	144,546	13,771	366	31,325	88,645	40,542
1876	6,848,517	439,603	65,516	157,993	41,861	1,616	99,605	65,151	55,601
1877	8,016,396	522,885	93,729	176,286	26,904	5,747	296,941	72,909	33,349
1878	7,512,062	479,165	37,590	171,971	59,124	5,947	316,311	72,989	31,132

NEW ZEALAND.

	Wool.		Grain and Flour.	Pre-served Meats.	Tallow.		Flax.		Kauri Gum.		Gold.	Timber
	Quantity.	Value.	Value.	Value.	Value.	Qnty.	Value.	Qnty.	Value.	Value.	Value.
	Lbs.	£	£	£	£	Tons.	£	Tons.	£	£	£
1874	46,848,735	2,534,605	321,315	100,245	65,366	2,038	37,690	2,568	79,986	1,505,331	44,450
1875	54,401,540	3,398,155	243,938	7,180	55,865	639	11,742	3,230	138,523	1,407,770	40,046
1876	59,853,454	3,395,816	360,022	21,933	109,896	897	18,285	2,888	109,234	1,268,559	49,847
1877	64,481,324	3,658,938	309,635	53,401	156,551	1,053	18,826	3,632	118,348	1,496,080	50,901
1878	59,270,256	3,292,807	571,911	74,225	178,501	622	10,666	3,445	132,975	1,240,079	39,074

SOME OF THE LEADING MERCANTILE HOUSES IN AUSTRALIA.

In giving a commercial history of the great resources of Australia, the author has considered it judicious to introduce a few of the leading mercantile houses in Melbourne, Sydney, and Adelaide, in order to give Englishmen and Americans who may not have an opportunity of visiting Australia an idea of what the representative mercantile house is like there.

Some of the firms thus mentioned have taken a very prominent part in the development of the colonies of Victoria, New South Wales, and South Australia, and properly deserve notice in a commercial treatise of the country's specialties, having, by their indomitable enterprise and energy, assisted in bringing the colonies to the grand position they occupy to-day.

Judging the bulk of the mercantile interest of the whole country by the Melbourne examples, we think it will be freely admitted that the Australian average is a high one, and it is only right to add that, although the majority of the mercantile houses of Sydney and Adelaide are not so large as those of Melbourne, they are governed by the same energetic spirit, enterprise, and intelligence, which form the guiding policy, and constitute such prominent factors, of the world-wide reputation which the Melbourne firms enjoy.

R. GOLDSBROUGH AND CO.

It has been said, and doubtless with truth, that every firm engaged in the wool business—either in buying, selling, or manufacturing this staple article of commerce—all over the civilised world, has heard of and knows by repute R. Goldsbrough and Co. Not many of them, indeed, we venture to say very few of them, while realising that "R. Goldsbrough and Co." is a powerful name, and is synonymous with extensive transactions in wool, grain, hides, and tallow, have a full conception of the large operations of this firm. Nor do they know that this name is associated in the mind of every true Australian with a respect almost akin to that which attaches to the name of Mr. George Peabody in England and America. If the historian desires to be truthful, he cannot accord to the enterprise of Mr.

Richard Goldsbrough and his firm the entire credit due to them, nor a full measure of the appreciation felt by most Australians, without appearing to be lavish of compliment to a degree. But the facts cannot be concealed, they have become too manifest and too well known to be refuted. It is not too extravagant to say that what Sir Robert Peel and Mr. Cobden did for the advancement of British manufacturing industries, in the repeal of the corn law, Messrs. Goldsbrough and Co. have done, only in a less degree, for the advancement of the Australian wool trade, by advocating its steady development, until it has attained to an export of over £12,000,000 per annum. The persistent manner in which the head of this firm pushed the steady increment of the wool interest from his advent in the colonies in 1847, at which time only 30,029 bales were shipped from Melbourne, while now it is over 300,000 bales per annum, will live long after him in the minds of all who know him, and he will be recounted by the squatter to his son as the one man who may be justly designated the *Father of the Australian Wool Trade*. The history of the firm is briefly this:—In 1848, Mr. Richard Goldsbrough started a wool business, which grew so satisfactorily that he soon required larger premises for it. In 1851, he commenced his first bluestone warehouse, off Market-street, but could not get it completed until 1853, on account of the gold excitement producing an extraordinary exodus of all workmen to the auriferous fields. In this year, Mr. Goldsbrough joined Mr. Edward Row and Mr. George Kirk in the stock and station business. In 1854, he took Mr. Hugh Parker into business with him, who remained in the firm until his death, in 1878. In 1873, Mr. John S. Horsfall, who for many years previously had shown himself to be an almost indispensable adjunct to the business, became a partner; and on the 1st July, 1876, Messrs. David and Arthur Parker, who had served in the business for a very long period, were admitted into partnership, making the firm then five, but now four. The manner and the rate at which their business has grown will be most clearly indicated by a survey of their buildings. A glance at their enormous premises, in Bourke-street, would instantly convey to the intelligent mind that the nature of the operations conducted within their walls must be very large indeed, and compare favourably with the fine physical proportions of the head of the firm. But as everyone in whose hands this book will fall has neither had the advantage nor will have the opportunity of inspecting personally those huge piles of bluestone which rise so majestically at the corners of their different streets, it is our intention to give them a notice here, as we consider they have not only played an important part in the building up of Melbourne's commercial importance, but also not less so in that of Victoria—while indirectly affecting the whole of Australia. Many a cultivated and intelligent man will be surprised when he reads here that Melbourne can boast of a firm who have been enterprising enough to put £150,000 into stone and mortar for the sole purpose of accommodating the enormous transactions which come to their door in the shape of wool, grain, hides, tallow, &c., &c. I venture to assert there are not many firms in London whose premises occupy so large a superficial area as those of Messrs. Goldsbrough and Co.; few, if any, who are larger. The tonnage and storage capacity of Messrs. Goldsbrough's warehouses are so large that we give them as a matter of history and useful information to those who are anxious to form an idea of the colossal proportions which the wool business is acquiring in Melbourne, and the enormous wool depôt which Melbourne must ultimately become.

If we desired to produce an indisputable fact, as incontrovertible as is the quality of our wool, that Melbourne is not only steadily but rapidly extending her tentacles of commercial enterprise to the great cities of the old world, and gradually drawing the largest buyers of wool to Melbourne, we should not require to look further for a proof than the huge piles of bluestone warehouses owned by Messrs. Goldsbrough and Co. Year by year this enterprising and public-spirited firm find their warehouse accommodation too inadequate for the raw produce of their clients, and if this does not mean "steadily growing trade for Australia generally," we should like some one to give it a name. The fact that Messrs. Goldsbrough and Co. have, up to this time, found it necessary to provide a storage cubic measurement of over 2,000,000 feet, and a tonnage measurement of over 50,000 tons, is all we need say to put any intelligent mind upon a proper footing with this splendidly-managed firm. Nor do the transactions of this house lose by comparison, for the figures rush into millions. We find the gross cubic measurement of their storage capacity to be over two million feet; so, also, do we find that the gross returns of their sales for the year ending December, 1879, are over £2,000.000. The item of wool alone presumably makes up the larger portion of this amount. Out of 78,512 bales catalogued, they sold no less than 63,076 bales. It must be remembered that 78,512 bales of wool represents over one-eighth of the whole amount of wool produced in Australia last year, which was about 611,853 bales, and also represents an enormous sum of money, as well as many large operations; and argues that a singular mastery of commercial ethics must pervade the conduct and management of the business of a firm whose transactions are more of the character of a huge banking corporation than of a mercantile firm. Messrs. Goldsbrough and Co., after all, are, strictly speaking, a mercantile house, and absolutely commission-men. The singular facility, ease, and utter noiselessness with which these large financial transactions are consummated speaks well for the ability of each individual member of this firm who dovetails his special department into so harmonious a whole.

But it is in many more ways that we recognise that Messrs. Goldsbrough and Co. have been of permanent and substantial benefit to Melbourne, Victoria, and Australia. They have done and are doing that which every true historian must hand them down to posterity for, being not only foremost in helping forward the development of the wool and grain trade in the aggregate, but in developing its growth in Melbourne in particular, and with this growth the inevitable growth of Australia. Some little reflection is necessary to realise the extent that the enterprise of a firm like this may exercise over the steady and permanent growth of a country. In the first place, developing a large industry means the investment of a large amount of capital in buildings and places of convenience for the conduct of business. Next to this in importance, is the inducement held out to immigrants to come and settle in such a country where their labour, skill, and ability are so much more required than at home, and for all of which a premium is offered in the shape of higher wages. Thirdly, follows the influx of foreign capital to invest in real estate, and build places of domestic accommodation for the many thousands who have been attracted hither, and so by this enterprise is first a city, and finally a country, built, developed, and settled. But it must not be forgotten that to the enterprise of the pioneer firms is all this traceable, for they are the real fathers of the country.

So far as the creating of Melbourne as a large centre for the sale of Australian wools in the colonies, Messrs. Goldsbrough and Co. have had little less than all to do with. The advantages to the colonies of Melbourne speedily becoming, what it sooner or later must become, "the mart of the world for fine wools," are many, and easily recognised. Nothing more rapidly builds up a city or the surrounding country, than its becoming a market for any particular staple of importance. It was the fact of its being the grain centre and wheat market of the United States which made Chicago the rapidly-developed and beautiful city it is to-day. It came up almost like a mushroom, but no man who has seen the beautiful and substantial structures which adorn Chicago can call it a mushroom city. Of course, there were other natural resources, of a more ephemeral nature, which also helped its growth, such as its being a large timber and pork market. But the one great staple which made Chicago the attractive point of commerce towards which so many people now gravitate—those who come to buy, and those who come to sell—was the fact of her being the wheat market of the West. Cotton did the same for New York before wheat assumed the immense importance it now occupies in the exchange in New York; and wool will do the same thing for Melbourne. It is for this we recognise in these enterprising men who have been striving for so many years, and so successfully it now appears, to make Melbourne a great wool mart, such a philanthropical, as well as a commercial spirit. In making Melbourne the wool market of the world they are attracting people, capital, and commodity. They contribute to an increment of the country's wealth, first making it an attractive and profitable centre, towards which money will freely flow and remain ; also, by inducing buyers to become resident here for the acquisition of our staples. If Melbourne continues to grow in importance in the future as it has done in the past, it will be of paramount necessity to buyers of wool that they should compete against one another for our fine Riverina clips on the spot, and that will only be attainable in Melbourne, as it now appears there is a greater demand for fine Riverina clips than there are clips to satisfy this demand with. Again, wealthy men will be attracted to Melbourne as the place gets better known and talked about, and this means a trip to the principal cities in Australia. It is more than probable that many million acres of our present land will be thus disposed of to parties whose abundant capital is bringing them but 3 or 4 per cent. per annum.

The steady way in which Messrs. Goldsbrough and Co. have, by the most persistent effort, established Melbourne as one of the large wool marts of the world—ranking probably next to London—is clearly attested by the regular augmentation of wool sales at their own warehouses, and we shall give a table of these sales for the last five years, to establish this fact clearly. It is important, however, to notice before proceeding to give this table, that a very decided change is likely to overtake the Melbourne market hereafter, which may make its aggregate number of bales sold next year reach a more respectable figure than even the highly satisfactory one it reached this last year. We refer to the tendency in America to reduce, if not entirely repeal, the enormous duty with which wool is handicapped now, which means an increased outlet for Australian wool, although, in our own belief, it means in a year or two an almost greater inquiry for Australian wool than Australia will be able to supply. I am of opinion that within two or more years the demand for Australian wool will rapidly and steadily increase, instead of taking the fitful jumps it has in the last few years; and I will adduce good reasons for making this assertion. The tendency of the world is well known by political and social economists to be becoming more and more extravagant daily. People's tastes are most notoriously travelling at an inverse ratio with their incomes. Strange as it may appear, it is nevertheless a historical fact that the last quarter of the nineteenth century will record more improvidence on the part of the world's millions of inhabitants than any of the three quarters preceding it. It is, perhaps, the last part of the last quarter which will develop the greatest excess. It is only a little over two years ago, in passing through Providence, Rhode Island—the largest cotton piece goods manufacturing state in the United States—that I met two of the principal print manufacturers there. They complained sadly of the state of trade in cotton, and upon interrogating them as to the cause of the decline in this commodity, which had steadily lowered from 2s. per lb. in 1873, to 9d. per lb. in 1878, they quite united in one fact, that cotton goods were nothing like so much worn as formerly. Of course, an ephemeral cause was the general stagnation of trade. But the main facts in the menacing state of things that was confronting them seemed to weigh more upon their minds than did the transitory wave of depression then about to lift itself from them. The homely way in which one of these gentlemen put the condition of things amused me very much, and its apposite application has been more than corroborated by the turn wool has since taken in the United States. "The present dormant condition in cotton is to be accounted for," said he, "through the 'world growing prouder every day.' Girls and women, who in my time would consider themselves lucky to be clad in cotton, will not look at anything less costly than a mixture of silk and wool, of all wool or of all silk." However this feeling may be operating upon the minds of English people, it is a notorious fact that it has already metamorphosed the tastes of the American girl and woman. We see this very distinctly in the sharp inquiry for Australian wools on the part of American buyers at the close of last year, and Australian growers may be satisfied that this inquiry will be even more brisk in future years. To show what a striking change the wool trade with America has undergone this last year, we will quote some figures which are very suggestive. It appears that from October 1877 to October 1878, there were some 5277 bales shipped from Melbourne to all American ports, from October 1878 to October 1879 there were none, but from October 1879 up till this time, 17,451 bales have been disposed of in Melbourne alone for American account, not to say anything about that which may have been secured in Sydney, about 3000 bales more. It is very evident that Messrs. Goldsbrough and Co. incline to the opinion of the writer concerning the future of the Austral-American wool trade, for this is what they say in their circular, issued February 19th, 1880:—

" The American demand has been a prominent feature this season, not so much on account of the quantity purchased (17,451 bales) as for the general firmness imparted to the market through the spirited operations of the buyers. They have secured nearly all our best Riverine clips, and comparatively few of these will be offered in London this year. They have, in fact, almost monopolised the best unwashed wools that Australia can produce, and have undoubtedly displayed sound judgment in doing so, as they will probably thus command to a considerable extent the manufacture of the fine goods for which these clips are specially adapted. The French and German buyers competed against them with determination ; but being unwilling to give equal prices, they could secure only a small proportion of the best lots. All that is required in order to develop this important trade is a reduction or repeal of the present almost prohibitory duties ; and now that America is coming to the front as a manufacturing country, no doubt vigorous efforts will be made to free the raw material. The question is being thoroughly ventilated and strongly agitated in the United States, and a substantial reduction, if not a total repeal of the duties, so far as they refer to Australian wool, is expected. If these efforts are successful, a large proportion of the unrivalled combing descriptions grown here will undoubtedly be bought in this market for direct transmission to the American mills."

To come back, however, to the importance Melbourne is assuming, year by year, as a wool mart, we shall quote from Messrs. Goldsbrough's circulars for the last five years, the number of bales which have been offered for sale in Melbourne and Geelong, and the number of them which have been taken. The steady augmentation of each year's sales*, with the exception of any one particular bad year, through exceptional drought, stamp this trade as having received a positive installation in Melbourne, and as having taken permanent seed not to be again uprooted, to gather strength and recognition from the increasing number of buyers from year to year, who will find their interests so much better considered here than elsewhere. Of this fact, Messrs. Goldsbrough and Co., are fully seized. We quote from their circular once more to show the aspect of the coming changes. (Feb. 19, 1880.)

"In accordance with our usual custom at the close of the season, we now proceed to review the business which has been transacted during the year, and in doing so we have much pleasure in referring to the steadily increasing importance of this market. During the past twelve months, 121,663 bales have been catalogued at the auction sales in Melbourne, and 34,573 bales in Geelong; and 125,872 bales, representing an approximate value of probably £2,500,000, have been sold. It will thus be evident that the sales in this colony have acquired a first-class position, and from their rapidly-increasing popularity, both with sellers and buyers, we have good grounds for anticipating that they will annually assume greater importance. The grower can here realise the full value of his wool, and all further risk, so far as he is concerned, is avoided. His clip at once becomes the property of the manufacturer or merchant, and he can arrive at his exact returns without being dependent on the fluctuations of the London market. The manufacturer, on the other hand, can by buying here gain a first selection of our clips, and by taking advantage of the lines of steamers now available, viâ Suez, he can have the wool in his mills in seven weeks after he has purchased it here. Instead of waiting for the new clip to be offered at the February and March London sales, he can, by purchasing in Melbourne, place a good proportion of it in his factory by the end of December; thus gaining two clear months in the production of his new goods. The French, German, and American manufacturers and dealers have been quick to perceive the chances thus opened out, and they are present in this market each season in increasing numbers. The warehouses in Melbourne are probably unequalled in the world for storing and showing wool, and the natural advantages of its position as the seaport for the finest pastoral country in Australia, have firmly established this city as the chief wool mart of Australia. London has gradually monopolised the wool sales of Great Britain, until it has become recognised as being almost the only mart for the trade, and in like manner Melbourne is, we believe, destined to become the great depôt of Australia. The advantages of a recognised centre are obvious; the wool is concentrated in one place ready for the buyers, their undivided competition is thus secured, and their time is economised, instead of being lost in attending local sales in each colony. The great superiority, quantity, and variety of the clips offered in Melbourne, have combined to make it the leading wool depôt in Australia, and a large quantity has this season been diverted here from the adjoining colonies for disposal. The rates of freight per steamers are in some instances almost nominal, consequently the extra cost of forwarding wool here is comparatively trifling."

* Summary of Wool Sales in Melbourne and Geelong for the last five seasons :—

	Bales Catalogued.	Bales Sold.
1875	123,184	89,623
1876	132,409	103,827
1877	154,003	112,817
1878	140,312	104,236
1879	156,236	125,872

As a final illustration of Melbourne's growing importance as a wool mart, we must call the attention of our readers to a sale held at Messrs. Goldsbrough and Co., on Wednesday, 27th October, 1880, at which 11,439 bales of wool were catalogued, and out of which the extraordinary number of 9255 bales were sold. As far as we are aware, this is probably the largest number of bales that has ever been offered at one sale in the world, not excepting London, to which city, until of late years, the buying and selling of Australian wools was considered to belong almost exclusively. This is decidedly a red letter day in the history of wool selling in Australia, and larger sales may yet take place in Melbourne this season. But 9255 bales in one day is sufficient to establish Melbourne's name as now amongst the very largest wool marts in the world. Two important facts may be drawn from these figures: Firstly, that Sydney's increase of business in wool, is by no means diminishing that of Melbourne, and that the latter's inportance as the great Australian wool centre is steadily increasing.

NEW ZEALAND LOAN AND MERCANTILE AGENCY COMPANY, LIMITED.

There is little doubt but that Melbourne is destined to be the principal wool mart of Australia. The wool merchants of the Victorian capital are, both with regard to wealth and extent of business operations, far in advance of those engaged in the same branch of commerce in the other capitals of Australasia. This obtains not only with regard to individual wool merchants, but also with regard to those joint-stock companies which have been formed for the purpose, promoting by pecuniary support the extensive pastoral interests of the various colonies. Whatever may be the energy or enterprise of an individual, or whatever wealth he may command, it is unlikely that he can ever compete successfully with a company of gentlemen, each possessing these qualifications, and by their unity giving such strength, stability, and capital, as no single individual can possibly possess. Hence success, in all its ramifications, attends the efforts of joint-stock companies, but in few instances has it been so marked as in the case of the New Zealand Loan and Mercantile Agency Company, Limited. The company was incorporated on the 6th April, 1865, under the Companies Act of 1862, with the large capital of £3,000,000, in 120,000 shares of £25 each, of which there is £2 10s. paid up, and which are now quoted at £5. The company has a reserve fund of £160,000, and carried quite a handsome surplus to credit account after paying the last dividend. It was established about 1864, for the purpose of stimulating the growth of wool, through making advances to pastoral proprietors. The company is composed of gentlemen who have a keen insight into business, and whose commercial experience enables them to see the requirements of the times, and so keep pace with them, by taking advantage of whatever is calculated to develop the business satisfactorily to their clients and their shareholders, and which would not only sustain but increase the good reputation which they enjoy. With this view, the company operate with English capital, which they are enabled to borrow at very low rates of interest, and are consequently in a position to advance money to borrowers on much more advantageous terms than they otherwise could do. This important factor, together with the not less important one that the shareholders are satisfied with a very moderate rate of interest, secures to them a very large clientèle, and also as extensive business transactions in wool as are carried on by any other firm or company in Australia, with but one exception. Their business operations are co-extensive with Australasia, and are increasing year by year.

The following table, taken from the London wool market for 1878-9, of Australasian and Cape wool importers of over 10,000 bales, will give an adequate idea of the vast extent of their business and its importance over other export houses in the wool trade:—

	1878. Bales.	1879. Bales.
New Zealand Loan and Mercantile Agency Co., Limited...	65,223	83,972
Dalgety, Du Croz and Co.	51,753	65,368
Australasian Mortgage Land and Finance Co.	51,031	58,897
Sanderson, Murray and Co. ...	34,434	37,744
Young, Ehlers and Co.	20,145	33,809
A. L. Elder	29,185	29,994
F. Huth and Co.	16,784	20,919
Leishman, Inglis and Co.	17,556	19,816
R. Brooks and Co.	16,214	19,600
Commercial Bank of Sydney...	14,178	18,610
Redfern, Alexander and Co. ...	15,852	17,135
Bank of New South Wales ...	7,305	16,758
National Mortgage and Agency Co. of New Zealand	14,949	16,730
James Morrison and Co.	15,870	14,542
Australian Joint Stock Bank...	16,645	14,355
R. Jowitt and Co.	15,366	13,716
A. Barsdorf	6,545	11,088
Mills Brother and Co. ...	9,915	10,233
Blaine, Macdonald and Co. ...	9,177	10,019
Potter, Wilson and Co.	11,203	Nil
New Zealand and Australian Land Company	10,562	9,682

The head office of the company in London is situated in those magnificent premises, known as No. 1 Queen Victoria street. The board of directors in London is composed of gentlemen who are well known for their commercial integrity and the influential position which they hold in the financial world, as well as for their large business experience and distinguished social position. The following gentlemen form the home directorate: —The Right Hon. Sir James Fergusson, Bart., K.C.M.G., who was, until his recent appointment in India, chairman of the board of directors; the

Right Hon. A. J. Mundella, M.P.; Thos. Russell, Esq., C.M.G.; Emanuel Boutcher, Esq.; Falconer Larkworthy, Esq.; and Robert Porter, Esq. The colonial directors embrace the following gentlemen, whose names are familiar to all colonists for their business sagacity and financial reputation, viz.:—Hon. James Williamson, M.L.C.; Samuel Browning, Esq. John Logan Campbell, Esq.; Josiah Clifton Firth, Esq.; David Lomond Murdoch, Esq.; George Burgoyne Owen, Esq.; and C. J. Stone, Esq. The board of directors in London is well and ably conducted by F. Larkworthy, Esq., while that in the colonies is undertaken by D. L. Murdoch, Esq., whose large experience enables him to conduct the management to the benefit of all concerned. The duties of secretary, in London, are in the hands of Henry Moncrieff Paul, Esq., who spares neither time nor trouble, and brings a large amount of commercial knowledge and good business capacity to bear in the discharge of his important and onerous duties. We need scarcely say that the company has always occupied a prominent position as shippers of wool, and for some time carried on their business at No. 46 William-street, under the management of Mr. R. Murray Smith. With the view of largely extending their business, and offering growers every facility for the sale of wool, they have recently moved into their present extensive premises situated in Collins-street, and known as the Melbourne Wool and Grain Warehouses. Although the Melbourne market is rapidly rising into importance as a wool mart, it will be understood that it is a mere matter of choice on the part of the grower—so far as this company is concerned,—whether he ships his wool to London, or sells it in the Victorian capital. We understand that the company possesses very excellent facilities for the safe custody of, and dealing with, wool upon its arrival in London, as well as for its disposal; and that having secured the services of some of the best experts in the trade, the business there is conducted in such a way as to ensure to their clients every possible advantage. We must here notice that, a few months prior to their removal to their new premises, the mangement of the Melbourne business was placed under the charge of Mr. David Elder, a gentleman well and favourably known, in financial circles in Melbourne, for his business ability. In order to ensure the best possible execution of the business in all its branches, Mr. I. Younghusband was associated with Mr. Elder, and has undertaken the immediate supervision and charge of the wool, station and produce business. Mr. Younghusband has had many years' experience in wool, having been an extensive grower, and possessing a good knowledge of station property. The general manager for all the colonies is Mr. D. L. Murdoch, of Auckland, who has the appointment of all colonial officers; and much of the success which has attended the business operations of the company is due to that gentleman's ability and enterprise.

The company makes advances in the Australasian colonies on produce, on station property, stocks, and the growing clip of wool; and receives the consignment of wool, grain, tallow, &c., &c., for sale in London or Melbourne. It may be well, however, to state, that the company enters into no mercantile ventures on its own account, nor does it buy goods of any description on its own account; confining itself exclusively to the agency business. This is decidedly advantageous to their customers, who thus secure the undivided interest of the company. We may also mention that the company is prepared to execute indents in London, forwarded through its agencies in the colonies. From the number of their branches they are enabled to offer great facilities to growers or purchasers, on account of their exchanges being made with little or no difficulty.

The net profits of the company for the year 1879, after deduction of all expenses and interests, and making ample provision for bad and doubtful debts, shows a sum of £53,214 14s. 2d. In July last, an *ad interim* dividend was paid at the rate of ten per cent. per annum, amounting, with interest on calls paid in advance, to £14,358 12s. 10d.; so that there is now left for distribution the sum of £30,686 11s. 2d. Owing to the steady inflow of debenture money, the limit of the borrowing power of the company under the articles of association has been reached. There has been, we gather from their circular, a satisfactory increase of the amount of the guaranteed mortgage investments in New Zealand, which form an important branch of the agency business of the company. The consignments of wool and other produce have likewise during the past year been much augmented; and, notwithstanding the lower prices obtained for many colonial products, have proved the source of large additions to the revenue of the company. The information which we have been able to give, concerning the extent of business transactions done by the company, must be a matter of congratulation to the commercial world, not only of the home country, but of the colonies generally, seeing that such substantial aid is held out to those who have embarked in the business of wool growing.

THE AUSTRALASIAN MORTGAGE AND AGENCY COMPANY.

The development of the pastoral interests in Australia is so intimately allied to the future commercial prosperity of the colonies, that any financial project whose object is to foster and supplement this development cannot but be favourably regarded by all who have the real welfare of the colonies at heart. Capital is the nursing mother of commercial success, while in a new colony it is the bone and sinew of its prosperous commercial development. Whatever may be the resources of a new country, however unbounded may be its buried wealth, it is less than useless if not moved by the mighty lever of capital. The primitive origin of capital is older than that of labour. The one produces and germinates the other. The first human capital is that which nature itself has given. This capital is possessed by every normal individual of the human race. It is the human mechanism made up of the various machines of intelligence, will, and physical power. These are the constituents of what we may call natural capital, belonging as much to man at the creation of the world as to man in the nineteenth century. This natural human capital is the basis of that superstructed capital which we may denominate artificial, inasmuch as the one is the natural sequence of the other. The combination of the two is the point of universal material prosperity. It gives wealth to the individual, and its national fruit is, internally, prosperity in every branch of commerce, trade, and industry; externally, the respect, honour, and often fear of the other nations of the world. Thus in every man may be found the first principles of capital and labour. The first is represented by the mind, the second by the body. Time develops and adds to the reproductive powers of each. History has taught us that the greatness of a country depends upon its natural resources plus the wealth it possesses for their development, and the wealth which is amassed individually and collectively by this development. The important factors of enterprise, energy, and indomitable perseverance must be the characteristics of the people, if ultimate and permanent success be the object which is aimed at. Great Britain possesses all these factors; and what nation stands more pre-eminent among the nations of the world? But we doubt whether the natural resources of the mother-country are equal to those of Australia. We do not, in addition, hesitate to say that what we have called the natural capital of the individual belongs as much, if not more, to the population of this New Atlanta, as to the people of that country from which it has migrated. The Australians possess, in the very highest degree, the characteristics of energy, enterprise and perseverance. There are several examples of great individual wealth. There is, then, but the one thing wanting to make Australia one of, if not the greatest modern country in the world, and that is artificial capital, which is represented by money. This want has been recognised by keen-sighted men of business as the greatest desideratum, more particularly, if we may be permitted to say, with regard to the growth of the pastoral interests of this great country. They have realised to themselves the pecuniary advantages which will accrue to them individually, and in a greater degree have they realised the greater advantages which will accrue to their newly-adopted country. It is through the individual efforts of those enterprising colonists, that we may look with confidence to a prosperous future for our English colonies, but more particularly for Australia. The gentlemen who compose the directorate of the company which is the subject of our present chapter, have keenly recognised that if the pastoral productions of Australia have to compete successfully with those of other countries, they must be developed to their utmost extent, and means must be found to contribute successfully to the accomplishment of this, what we must be permitted to call, patriotic and praiseworthy object. They possess all the requirements of success, *i.e.*, financial ability, careful observation, commercial experience, individual reputation for commercial integrity, and, last but not least, the confidence of their fellow-colonists, more particularly the squatters, with whom their business operations are transacted. Alive to every exigency, and desirous of bringing the financial influence of the home money market to co-operate with the financial interests of the colony, in order that nothing may be wanting to ensure the most complete success, they have established their head office in Scotland, and secured a directorate whose names carry weight and confidence. The head office of the Australasian Mortgage and Agency Company, Limited, is situated at 10 Castle-street, Edinburgh, with a capital of £1,000,000 sterling, and with power to increase it if necessary. In order to inform our readers of the standing of the company in Edinburgh, we cannot do better than give the names of the gentlemen who compose the Edinburgh board, viz.:—James Cowan, Esq., M.P.; John Inglis, Esq.; H. Macduff Duncan, Esq.; Charles F. Mackinnon, Esq.; W. J. Menzies, Esq., and R. Erskine Scott, Esq. The gentlemen who compose the Melbourne board, are well known to Victorians; and their reputation for financial sagacity and commercial experience, is thoroughly established in the colony. The following gentlemen compose the directorate in Melbourne :—Sir James McCulloch (chairman); J. L. Currie, Esq.; Archibald Fisken, Esq.; Thomas Shaw, Esq.; Hastings Cuningham, Esq., and John K. Smyth, Esq., the last two gentlemen being the managing directors; while the duties of secretary are fulfilled by Mr. W. S. Mackenzie. The offices and warehouses are situated at Collins-street west, and are known as the "Australasian Wool Stores." In giving an epitomised history of the rise, progress, and present financial condition of the Australasian Mortgage and Agency Company, Limited, we will give a short account of the object of the operations.

In 1862, Mr. Hastings Cuningham, who is a well-known colonist, and whose long establishment as a squatter is familiar to the squatting interest of Victoria, originated the firm of Cuningham and Macredie, under which style the business was carried on until the year 1868. At this time, Mr. J. K. Smyth became associated with the firm, who with Mr. Cuningham made the sole partners, and those gentlemen carried on a large and successful business for a period of ten years, the firm being then known by the name of Hastings Cuningham and Co. About this time, the formation of joint stock companies became popular in the colony. These companies employed English capital, which they obtained at a lower rate of interest than it could be procured for in the colony, and in this way afforded greater facilities to woolgrowers who were desirous of enlarging their operations. Messrs.

Cuningham and Smyth, ever ready to keep pace, if not to be in advance of the times, took advantage of the popularity which joint stock companies enjoyed, to form their business into a limited company, in August, 1878, with a subscribed capital of £750,000, which was divided into 150,000 shares of £5 each, of which £1 was paid up. It will not be matter of surprise to our readers when they know that, in a few days following the announcement of the project, the whole number of shares reserved for allotment in the colony—viz., 100,000—was quickly taken up, the list of subscribers including the names of many well-known gentlemen engaged in the pastoral interests. In order, however, to secure loans of British capital on the debentures of the company, it was found necessary to establish a head office in Great Britain, for which purpose Mr. Cuningham visited England, in February, 1880. Within two months after his arrival there, a new company with the title as described at the head of this chapter was successfully founded, with which was incorporated on favourable terms the business and property of Hastings Cuningham and Co., Limited. The number of shares is 100,000 of £10 each, upon which £2 per share is paid, the colonial shareholders receiving, in exchange for their 100,000 shares in the late company, shares in the new company to the amount of 50,000 of the first issue. Of the 50,000 reserved for Great Britain, the number allotted was 35,000, beyond which it is not at present proposed to increase. The paid-up capital of the Australasian Mortgage and Agency Company, Limited, is therefore £170,000. We are told that the shareholders belong to that desirable class which has taken up the stock with a view to investment purposes solely. We understand that already a considerable sum has been subscribed to the company's debentures and remitted to Victoria. The financial position of the company has realised the expectations of those gentlemen to whom its inception is due; and it is now established on so substantial a basis as not only to become one of the permanent institutions of the colony, but to be able to compete with others of a similar nature. The active management in Melbourne, controlled by the local board of directors, is conducted by Messrs. Cuningham and Smyth, whose long experience has given them a practical knowledge of the business which is invaluable. One feature of the business transactions is worthy of notice, inasmuch as it secures to the clients the undivided interest of the company, and that is, that it is conducted on the commission principle solely, the company taking no other interest, direct or otherwise, in the produce which passes through its hands. The auction sales of the various articles coming under the head of station produce, are held four times a week, and the extent of business passing annually through the books of the company is second only to one wool-broking firm in the Australian colonies. The warehouses, which are freehold, are valued at upwards of £45,000, and cover an acre of ground, being contiguous to the railway stations and wharves, and capable of holding a very large quantity of wool, and are in every way adapted to the business for which they were specially erected. The show-rooms are well lighted for the display of sample bales, and the utmost care is taken for the valuation by experts of every lot offered for sale, be the clip large or small. The company receives consignments of wool, sheepskins, hides, tallow, and grain, and makes advances thereon for sale in the colonial market, or for shipment to London, as well as making advances on stock and station property, and in fact, except the sale of stock, transacts all business in connection with the pastoral interest. The quantity of hides, sheepskins, tallow, &c., sold during the year, is very large, the whole being disposed of by auction, a system which we understand was introduced by the company's predecessors, in 1869. Finally, we are glad to record that the business is growing to greater proportions, which is due to the able and energetic management.

WILLIAM SLOANE AND CO.

Although Melbourne can boast of having developed its banking business to a greater degree of strength and perfection than any other city of its size in the world, and a mere survey of the exterior of its financial institutions will establish this fact, while a glance at the huge columns of figures which go to make its daily clearances will confirm it; it appears that the banking business of Australia is not confined exclusively to the banking chambers of these institutions. One would imagine that, with such enormous facilities for accommodating financial transactions as Melbourne can boast, large loans on station property would be undertaken exclusively by the banks, on account of their being beyond the ability of private firms to grapple with. We find, however, that such financial operations as advancing on station property, and advancing on wool—both on the sheep's back, and in the bale—are done to a very large extent by private firms, calling themselves "financial agents and merchants." Of this class Messrs. Wm. Sloane and Co. take rank as one of the first, both in magnitude and standing. This firm offers every possible facility to wool-growers, firstly, if necessary, by advancing the funds with which to purchase station property—that is to say, the two-thirds of the original purchase, which is generally closed by long-dated bills, one-third only being demanded in cash. Secondly, they accept the consignment of their wool for foreign shipment. Thirdly, consign it to their London agents, who supervise its sale at the London Wool Sales. Fourthly, import, if necessary, any article of European produce in exchange for balance or part balance; and fifthly, they become bankers, commission agents, exchange agents, and importers at one and the same time, which saves the client not only various commissions, but a deal of trouble. In addition to advancing on **station** property, Messrs. Wm. Sloane and Co. advance largely on sugar properties in Queensland and are prepared to take an interest in stations with parties wishing to purchase. The advantage of this cannot be over estimated as far as English investors are concerned. The whole experience of Messrs. Wm. Sloane and Co., is thus placed at the service of those wishing to interest themselves and invest in station properties; and the fact of this firm retaining an interest in said property would be a sufficient guarantee of its efficient management. We cannot dwell too strongly upon this point, believing it to be an opportunity not generally afforded by the average run of houses in this line, and it should prove a strong inducement to English capital to find its way out here, for more profitable investments cannot be found anywhere than in Australia, if well superintended. Now, independent of this firm's acting in the capacity of financial agents for their clients, the advantages of being one of their constituents are very great to the inexperienced squatter. In the first place, this firm can offer the benefits of a large practical experience, from the fact that some of its members are practical squatters. They are thoroughly cognisant, one might say, of almost every mile of good country in Australia. The value they place upon a property may be said to be as near its actual value as men can accurately arrive at. Their advice as to whether property is desirable to acquire or not, is oftentimes worth as much as the property itself. It must be remembered that, amongst the huge blocks of property that are occasionally sold, it sometimes occurs that a large portion of the country is back country not easily attainable, and where it would take weeks and sometimes months of constant travel to reach them. Of course, if one were not buying such a property from a highly reliable firm it would be rather a hazardous transaction to lay out thousands of pounds upon the mere *ipse dixit* of the seller, and find when he had reached his newly-purchased home and country that its carrying capacity had receded from one sheep to the acre to four acres to the single sheep. This fact is mentioned, for the information of men in England or elsewhere, who may anticipate purchasing properties in Australia, to assure them that every possible information will be afforded, to put them upon an intelligent footing with the nature of the property they are buying. We recognise in the names of such firms as Messrs. Wm. Sloane and Co., Messrs. Dalgety, Blackwood and Co., and others, a certain guarantee against any deception being practised with regard to the nature of the property. Firstly, in the high respectability of such firms; secondly, in their personal knowledge of the country they are disposing of. Again, the opinions of such houses are often very valuable as to which way the market is likely to go—whether it would be more judicious to ship to London or sell in Melbourne. It can be easily understood that, with a long experience with figures and the necessary *data* at their command, it becomes a matter of simple calculation about the probability of the market being stronger or weaker in London than in

Melbourne. Allowing, of course, for contingencies which are bound to crop up in every business, the judgment of these houses in the main is very accurate. If we take this year as a precedent, we would invariably rely upon the advice administered by these financial houses as to the probability of the market; for in almost every shipment they have made they have had to hand over to the grower large cheques, being the difference between the amount they advanced upon the wool and its subsequent realisation. Firms of this class have certainly gained much knowledge in the many years they have been engaged in buying, selling, and advancing upon station property, and while much of this knowledge has been very costly to them, owing to critical seasons and disastrous depressions they have passed through, it is presented gratuitously to their constituents. The size of a transaction does not appal Messrs. Wm. Sloane and Co., for they are prepared to advance either £1000 or £250,000 on a property, provided the security is abundant; and proposals to a larger extent could be entertained if desired. Hence, the advantages offered by these firms are in every particular as great and as good as those offered by banks, with frequently this advantage in their favour, that "knowing the property personally," that is to say, knowing the character of its country, the carrying capacity, the available supply of water, and the probable waterfall during the year, they are in a position to appraise its value, if anything, more closely and accurately than the banks, and they frequently give growers the advantages of this knowledge by advancing to them right up to the marginal edge of the property. This may or may not be an advantage; it depends on the season. But in a season like the one now past, it is certainly an advantage. Messrs. Wm. Sloane and Co. have been established twenty-five years. The firm has its house in London, known under the name of John Young, Ehlers and Co., of Great St. Helens. The resident partners in Melbourne are Mr. R. J. Jeffray and Mr. Donald S. Wallace.

THE BRITISH AND AUSTRALASIAN TRUST AND LOAN COMPANY, LIMITED.

This company has come into existence to fulfil a want which has been long felt in the colony of Victoria, as well as in the whole of Australia. Such, however, is the nature of the enterprise of capitalists in Melbourne, that good security does not require to look long nor far for the circulating medium, which encompasses either its exchange or improvement, ere it find it. It is clear that in the van of progress, of which Melbourne is not only a beautiful but a striking illustration of its universality and popularity throughout the whole of Australia, monied institutions are as much to the fore as any of the indigenous products which are making such a world-wide reputation for the excellence of their quality—particularly wool. We find that capitalists, far from being slow to recognise the important part that cheap money plays in the rapid development of a country, almost indescribably rich with natural resources, anticipate the demand for it and formulate their institutions so that they may be ready when required. It is, perhaps, owing to this lofty enterprise, that we have so many first-class financial institutions in Melbourne to-day; yet their number, far from remaining *in statu quo*, is being augmented from time to time by the formation of additional companies. Conspicuous amongst these of recent growth, we may notice "The British and Australasian Trust and Loan Company Limited." The object of this company is to lend money on real and other property in Australia, New Zealand, Tasmania and elsewhere, and for such additional or extended objects as the company may from time to time, by special resolution, elect to engage in. But we must notice in passing, that much as this company may tend to promote speculation in real property, and enhance its value by advancing the funds with which it is to be improved, its operations are to be confined to those of a most cautious character, and the risk taken by them is to be of at least a minimum nature. This fact, while being an advantage to the shareholder in making losses rare in their occurrence, is not without utility to the borrower, for, the company which makes but few losses can surely afford to lend its money at a minimum rate, when the security is unexceptionable. This is evident from a clause in their articles of incorporation, from which it appears that "in all loans *freehold lands* must be the basis of the operations, and in the event of a larger advance being required than the value of the freehold alone would justify,' other security, such as stock, stations, &c., may be taken as collateral." This may appear *primâ facie* to be a rather discouraging outlook to the borrower, but it is certainly judicious in financial operations of a large scale that, where the "minimum of interest only, is demanded, the maximum of security should be a *sine qua non.*" Therefore, anyone applying for the money of the above company will do well to remember that "tangible security must be offered which has an ascertained value." The capital of the company is £2,000,000, with £100,000 already called up, being £2 10s. on the first issue of 40,000 shares of £25 each, and power to increase by issue of fresh shares from time to time, as they may deem it expedient. The capital stock is held both in London and the colonies. They borrow their money in the London market on terms of three and six years, at a very moderate interest, and are thus placed in a position to lend it on very reasonable terms in the colonies. The company came into existence in 1878, and has held one yearly meeting at which a dividend was declared of 5 per cent. At present it has the large sum of £860,000 invested and in process of investment in the colonies; but this must not be considered by any means as reaching the limit of its operations. It is in a position to obtain and supply any amount of money which may be required, at very reasonable rates, good security always governing such a loan. The company is governed by a board of directors in London, and also by a local board in Melbourne. We are pleased to note that none but responsible names compose the latter board, which of itself is a guarantee of the cautious management which will characterise its operations. The manager will be found at the office of the company, No. 55 Queen-street. It is fair to presume that he will not object to our terminating this notice of the company for which he acts, by inviting all gentlemen, who may be desirous of raising money on good real security, to give him a call at the above address.

FANNING, NANKIVELL AND CO.

It is certainly a highly commendable circumstance, and one of which Melbourne may be justly proud, that for a city as young as she is, a thoroughly conservative and dignified commercial tone pervades the management of many of her leading mercantile houses which is curiously antithetical to their age. The tone we speak of is, that unostentatious and unbustling exhibition in the conduct of business transactions, so foreign to new cities, but so characteristic of older ones, like London, Liverpool, and Manchester. There is no one feature of mercantile tone and etiquette, in which Melbourne can emulate London with more honour to herself, and also to her merchants, than in conducting her business in a manner not wholly calculated to impress lookers on, that business is done for the sole purpose of overawing them, to the exclusion of every other consideration. That there is something more substantial, more permanent and material, in the aim of the true merchant, than mere tall talk and display, to impress either his neighbours or others, is patent, from the aversion the old houses in Melbourne have for anything like notoriety. It is not our purpose in this work in noticing any merchant whose name may appear here, to attract attention to him simply as a merchant, nor to the volume of business he may be doing. We have, indeed, a much more important reason for collecting and describing some of the principal houses in Melbourne. It is principally to show that, as pioneer houses in the early days of the colony, they have figured conspicuously in the construction of a great commercial fabric, which has formed after comparatively few years—every minute of which has been improved by the introduction of a most indomitable toil, an untiring energy, and a keen sagacity—Melbourne's great commercial position in the scale of nations.

Small indeed is this position when compared with that of London, Paris, or New York. But its greatness, to be understood, must be viewed through the microscope of youth—indeed, one might say infancy; while its real greatness lies in the promising future it has before it, as the principal port of what must become a great producing country for the old world. It is difficult to discover in a community like Melbourne, whose business habits have such a strong smack of Yankee shrewdness about them, whence it inherited this quiet element of merchandising after the true old English fashion.

We are fully aware that the founders of some of these houses were men who came direct from the mother-country to establish branch houses in Melbourne. But once transplanted here, it is difficult to understand how they have retained the old traditional habits with surroundings of such pronounced heterogeneity. We know that the youth leaving his native soil, which may have been of the secondary formation, and transplanting himself to a country, the soil of which is of quaternary formation, after some years partakes of the habits that such a soil produces in its inhabitants, whether it be a nervous celerity of action characteristic of the inhabitants of the United States, or the enervated lethargy of those of Chili and Brazil. It is the preservation of this singularly conservative method of conducting transactions so pre-eminently British, upon a soil and amid surroundings so dissimilar, that strikes one as remarkable. Of the mercantile houses in Melbourne who partake of this character, may be mentioned Fanning, Nankivell and Co., general merchants, doing an import and export business with Mauritius, China, India, and London. About 1844, Griffiths, Gore and Co., of Sydney, which most New South Wales' people will remember as one of the best-known firms of that place, opened a branch in Melbourne, which in 1848, became Griffiths, Fanning and Co., under the management of Mr. T. J. Nankivell; the Sydney firm also taking the same name a little earlier. In 1858, the Melbourne firm changed the style of its name, and was thenceforth known as Fanning, Nankivell and Co. The resident partners of the firm are now Mr. T. J. Nankivell and Mr. Edward Fanning. About the time the South Australian trade developed such activity—now some ten years since—the above house recognised the desirability of having a branch there to meet the demands of their growing trade, which they subsequently opened and conducted under the name of Fanning and Co., of which Mr. T. J. Nankivell is the resident partner. This house has, from its earliest foundation in 1844, always been prominently associated with the importation of Eastern produce from India, China, and the Mauritius. They have invariably ranked amongst the largest—at times being the largest in certain lines—houses of the kind in Victoria. From present statistics, their importations of sugar excel by far those of any other house; while during their agency for the well-known house of Dent and Co., of China, the same was the case concerning their tea importation. In addition to their importing business, Fanning, Nankivell and Co., like many other leading merchants of Melbourne, are squatters, owning runs in Victoria, New South Wales, and Queensland. As such, they are large shippers of wool, which is consigned to the charge of their London house, Wm. Fanning and Co., and are consequently in a position to make as liberal advances in this staple as any house which makes it its special business to ship wool, and also to receive consignments, ship them, and superintend their sale in London. Since Victoria has taken up her position as a grain-producing country for England, they have largely interested themselves in the shipment of wheat, and were the first house to recognise the important position this cereal would ultimately occupy as an export from Victoria. They followed up this opinion in a very material and enterprising form by despatching the first whole cargo of Victorian-grown wheat to England, some two years ago. They are also agents for the Union Insurance Society, of Canton, and cover risks from Melbourne to any part of the world.

THE AUSTRALASIAN AGENCY AND BANKING CORPORATION (LIMITED).

The perseverance and energy which have been amongst the chief factors in developing one of the richest and most productive resources of Australia, have been in part recompensed by the confidence inspired in the minds of English capitalists. When we consider the careful and keen eye to business and its concomitant success which are characteristic of English financiers, we have just reason to be proud of the splendid and triumphant efforts of the Australian woolgrowers, who, through almost insuperable difficulties, have at last established themselves permanently as a branch of commerce in Australia, and at the same time introduced a confidence in their present and continued success into the hearts of the commercial and financial world of England. This result, though due in some measure to those who are immediately engaged in the growing of wool, could never have been attended with its present success, except through the enterprise and financial knowledge of gentlemen who discovered a branch of business necessarily growing out of that immediately connected with the production of wool, and at once adapted themselves to its exigencies. They saw that however great the supply, it was more than useless unless the demand for it was coextensive. They further discovered that the supply might almost be illimitable, certainly sufficient for the greatest demand that might by any possibility arise. They consequently concentrated their efforts in creating a demand. They found that the basis must be laid in bringing buyers and sellers into personal relation with each other. They found that capital must be supplied where it was wanting; and that if this could not be found in the money markets of Australia, they must go further afield, and, if necessary, seek it in the repleted markets of England. But to succeed in this new field required more than colonial eloquence, supported by mere figures or wild speculation. It required that the gentlemen who made themselves its representatives, should be known for their high commercial integrity and unimpeachable honour; and that their names should stand high in commerce and finance. No others, whatever might have been their reputation, if it did not include the conditions we have named, were likely to succeed. Their attempt would have ended in failure; their operations would have resulted in a miserable *fiasco*. But gentlemen having all the necessary qualifications for success, entered into the arena *con amore*. They plunged into the tide, which when taken advantage of in the affairs of men leads on to fortune. The success which has attended their efforts, has in every way been equal to, if it has not exceeded, their expectations. English capital has flowed through the channels which those gentlemen have created. They have succeeded in opening wide the purse-strings of the English money market, and the only necessary factor that remains for the perfect development of their scheme, is that of time. The commercial interests of Australasia owe them a debt of gratitude, which instead of diminishing with years, must ever and ever increase, with the increase of Australian wealth and Australian commerce. No effort has been wanting to make their undertaking an unparalleled success. Feeling that individually they might not have that weight which was necessary to inspire unlimited confidence, they saw the advisability of associating themselves together, and by thus incorporating themselves as a company, to leave no desideratum unprovided for, which seemed likely to be sought after by the English capitalists, before they could be induced to embark their money in a new and comparatively unknown country, and in a production which they must have supposed was in its infancy, especially when they considered that the country could only count its existence by a few decades of years. Though we have individual gentlemen in all the colonies of Australia who have embarked, and embarked successfully, in the business of wool brokers, yet it is scarcely likely that their operations can be carried on so extensively as those carried on by a corporation of gentlemen, each one of whom stands as high in finance and commerce, as the individual gentlemen to whom we have referred. Not only is unity strength, but the confidence it superinduces must be in exact proportion to the confidence superinduced by individual efforts. If the confidence inspired by the individuals be great, much greater must be the confidence inspired by their association. Their names, their influence, their position, when welded together, must be productive of all the necessary requirements for unqualified success. It cannot then be matter of surprise to our readers to know that the most sanguine expectations have been realised. That an undertaking, carried out under such conditions, has met with the recompense it deserves, and is worthy of being recorded amongst the successful undertakings of this new country, cannot be matter of question to those whose interests are so mixed up that they have become synonymous with the interests of the country which they have adopted as a new home. Its progress and prosperity must be their dearest wish. We refer especially to those who, having made their wealth, have invested it in their adopted country. We refer indirectly to those to whom is given the opportunity of investing their wealth in the development of the natural resources of a country, which is so bright a gem in the diadem of English exploring enterprise, and so practically convincing of that indomitable pluck that seeks out through almost impassable obstacles, other fields and pastures new for the exercise of that commercial and industrial talent which is one of the most marked idiosyncrasies of the Britisher.

The company whose name stands at the head of this chapter is a practical illustration of all we have said in our introductory remarks. It was established in Melbourne, in the early part of 1877, for the purpose of making advances on wool and accepting consignments, as well as for making advances on station property. Its existence consequently extends over a period of little more than three years. Its principal object is the introduction of English capital to assist in developing to maturity the pastoral resources of Australia. The first permanent board of directors consisted of Messrs. F. P. Hines (who was chairman), H. J. S. Cattanach, W. T. Moffat, and William Robertson. These gentlemen then laid the foundation of that which we are justified in now pronouncing a prosperous and flourishing company. Subsequently, the board was increased to six members, and is now composed of such names as the Hon. Sir W. H. F. Mitchell (chairman), the Hon. Sir Charles Sladen, the Hon. W. Campbell, Mr. J. S. Horsfall, and two of the first-named gentlemen who were associated with it on its first establishment, namely, Messrs. H. J. S. Cattanach and F. P. Hines. A stronger board than this we cannot well imagine. These gentlemen, possessing all the qualifications we have before enumerated, are a guarantee that the concern will be carried on in every way satisfactorily to those who, in the ordinary course of business, are led to have recourse to the Australasian Agency and Banking Corporation in all transactions which involve the buying and selling of wool. In recording the history of this corporation, it is gratifying to note that it was such as to necessitate the establishment, last year, of an office in London. This will be more completely understood when we mention that with the issue of shares there the present number allotted is 114,235, something quite large when we consider the youthful existence of the company. We understand that five-sixths of these shares are on the Melbourne register, and at the same time in the hands of a most influential proprietary, representing the whole of the Australian colonies, and holding, in pastoral stock alone, an aggregate of some four million sheep, and from a million and a-half to two millions of acres of freehold. We seldom have been privileged in recording such success which at the same time is represented by such substantial results. Nothing but that essential business capacity, which is quick to see and quick to seize opportunity, could have realised such a measure of success. Careful consideration, directed by gentlemen with practical minds, must be part of that firm basis upon which so successful a superstructure has been constructed. The operations of the company, we are told, were marked by success from the moment of the appointment of some two or three gentlemen who were very well known, and particularly of one, who is a tried and experienced man in all matters connected with wool; this we can fully understand by their continued success up to the present time. Another evidence of their condition can be gathered from one very important fact, and that is, that the reserve-fund already in hand amounts to more than one-fifth of the paid-up capital, while 10 per cent. dividends have been paid for the last three half-years. The company having secured, in connection with the London establishment, a directorate equally powerful in the financial circles of England, as is the Melbourne directorate in the financial circles of Australia, it may safely be prognosticated that ultimate and permanent success will attend the undertaking.

The London directorate, we are given to understand, is issuing debentures, which must, as a matter of foregone conclusion, result in a large increase of the colonial business. We are pleased to be able to record that very good judgment was shown in the selection of its present manager, Mr. Francis E. Stewart, late inspector of the National Bank of Australasia. Mr. Stewart comes to the company equipped with all the knowledge and experience of an old banker, and if it is at all possible to add further strength to this already very strong institution, this gentleman will accomplish it.

JAMES TURNER AND SON.

The generality of houses in Melbourne doing business with squatters, either in making them advances, receiving their wool, buying for them, or selling to them any sort of station property, call themselves financial agents. Messrs. James Turner and Son, however, choose rather to designate themselves "station and wool agents and commission merchants." That they do so, is because their business embraces some particular branches which the general run of financial agencies do not undertake, besides embracing all the different business operations, of whatever nature, that they do. This firm, now styled James Turner and Son (the present partners being George Napier Turner and John Moodie) is one of the oldest firms in Melbourne, having been originally founded, in 1841, by Mr. Andrew Russell, an alderman, and one of the first mayors of Melbourne, who arrived in the colony as far back as 1839. This gentleman, in conjunction with Mr. James Turner (father of one of the present proprietors), carried on the business of importers and commission merchants, under the name of Andrew Russell and Company, afterwards Rhind and Turner. The business then came into the hands of Mr. G. Napier Turner, who carried on the business at the old address for about two years. He, seeing the growing importance of the wool interest, determined to turn his attention solely to that branch of the business, and give up the importing. At that time, the business of wool growing was in a most embryonic condition, and formed the permanent occupation of but few sheep-farmers, compared with the number who are engaged in it to-day. It was mainly due to this fact, that Messrs. Russell and Co. paid more attention to their importing and consignment business, which was at that time a good paying one. With the appearance of *protection*, however, the volume of their imports so steadily declined, and consignments moved so slowly, that this firm quickly perceived, that it was only a question of time before the bulk of the importing trade would be gradually transferred to another colony, where such disadvantageous pressure did not exist. Simultaneously with their desire to cut loose from the fetters of protection and release their capital from the importing business, the wool trade began to assume proportions of importance, and received increased attention from all firms connected either directly or indirectly with wool, sheep and station property. Messrs. James Turner and Son, it would seem, were quick to perceive the new stimulus wool was henceforward destined to receive, and the important position it was bound to occupy as a future product of Australia. They clearly saw, in promoting the growth of this staple, an ever-increasing stream of profit to the grower, the commission agent and the country, which no vicious legislation like protection could strangle. Recognising the prominence wool would swiftly take as a staple in all sorts of manufactures in the mother-country, together with its likelihood of becoming the main article of export from Australia, they threw all their energies into the scale of fortune with it, and the result is that the firm now ranks amongst the first firms in Melbourne engaged in this line of business. Messrs. Turner and Son have now an agency in Sydney, from which port they make large shipments of wool, that may be consigned to their care from constituents near to that point, whose interests can be better served by shipments direct from Sydney than from Melbourne. In addition to the large experience that the wool and station commission business has equipped them with, they are armed with that more satisfactory weapon, now made more necessary by the sharp competition for business, "practical experience." Possessing, as they do, an intimate knowledge of most of the desirable districts in Australia, they are in a position to act as agents in negotiating sales or purchases of station property and produce, in a highly satisfactory manner, and can also give sound advice to parties desiring to purchase stations which are the best districts to embark in. Being largely interested in station property themselves, it is only natural that they should be in possession of accurate information as to the value and production of the different properties in the country, and this information, acquired only by a long experience, enables them to give to the capitalist from the home country, who may be disposed to invest his money in that profitable undertaking called squatting, many valuable points relative thereto.

The fact of such an investor being ignorant of practical squatting should not enter as a prejudicial factor against his purchasing squatting property, because the main point after all is to have a reliable and good manager; and having secured this, together with a good agent who knows the yield and almost exactly what the land can carry, a station owner might be in England, and still have his run as efficiently managed as if he were living on it. Too great a stress, therefore, cannot be attached to the importance of having a good agent; for it is he who secures the manager, and renders account to the owner. It is natural, too, that the agent should be fired with a desire to exercise great caution in advising the purchaser of a property, hoping to secure in the event of a purchase another constituent—an advantage not long enjoyed if the advice proves bad. It must be an infinite source of pleasure to a firm of this kind, to be able to state with truth that no property of which they have advised the purchase has turned out badly. An idea which is growing in favour is, for a number of persons of limited means, who may be engaged in other businesses, and who do not wish to withdraw their whole capital from such business, to club together, and with their spare capital buy a station property on joint account, secure, as previously indicated, a practical manager, either with an interest in the whole property or to be paid a salary, and work it on joint account. It will be seen that the opportunities thus offered to business men, who can each withdraw, say, a thousand or fifteen hundred pounds from their business, and invest it in a station property upon the plan suggested above, are well worthy the consideration of those in a position to take advantage of them, substantially, on account of the small amount of capital invested, the large returns incidental thereto, and the little risk involved; the financial management of such property being left in the hands of a reliable agent, who keeps a special set of books for the owners of such property, which books are always open to the inspection of the owners, and a statement furnished from time to time to each partner.

This branch Messrs. Turner and Son pay special attention to, and have now the management of several large station properties bought upon this plan. They also take charge of the management of the estates of deceased persons, or absentees; and from large experience in the conduct of such business, and an intimate knowledge of the value of town and country property, they are specially fitted to take charge of such, enabled to bring to bear the most efficient management wherever such trusts are confided to them; and the continued confidence they enjoy in the management of several important estates of old colonists is of itself a sufficient guarantee of the able manner in which this department is conducted. It may be here mentioned, that this branch of their business is treated as a special department, and a separate room is set apart for meetings of trustees, all records of which are carefully kept. Messrs. Turner and Son also execute indents, and receive consignments from Great Britain.

The firm is, in addition to the branches of business already pointed out, entrusted with the agency of one of the oldest fire and marine insurance companies in Australia. One, too, which has withstood many a shock in the shape of an insurance claim, and still stands on a solid, granite basis. This company, called the South Australian Insurance Company, was established in Adelaide in the year 1846, and has, under the able management of Mr. R. E. Tapley, and a no less able and influential board of directors, composed of such men as the Hon. Sir William Milne, the Hon. Alexander Hay, Hon. P. Santo, and others of similar standing, had a most successful career; having, in addition to paying large dividends to its shareholders, accumulated a very handsome reserve fund, every thousand pounds of which offers an extra security to the insurer against fire and marine risks in this company. Insurers cannot look too scrupulously into the security offered them by fire and marine companies, as it not unfrequently happens that a company's assets compared with its liabilities, are so immeasurably below what they should be as to afford the insurer very little, if any, guarantee against loss. The standing of the men connected with this company, and their fine business reputation, is a perfect surety against such alarms. But, if these facts were not as they are, the solid reserve fund would stand as a redeemer for the needy, when their wants were quickened by either the fire or water fiend.

JAMES BALFOUR AND CO.

The firm whose name stands at the head of this chapter is comparatively a new one in Melbourne, but it may be said to be more so nominally, than in reality.

Mr. Balfour, the head of the firm, was for nearly a quarter of a century an active partner in the well-known importing house of Messrs. James Henty and Co., during which period, he twice re-visited England, and passed through the leading cities of America. From *Victorian Men of the Time* we gather most of the following particulars:—

Mr. Balfour, who had acquired the greater part of his early mercantile training in London, arrived in Melbourne in 1852 as the representative of

Messrs. Matheson and Co., of London, who were desirous of extending their large eastern trade to the new gold colony of Victoria. In 1854, he opened a branch of James Henty and Co.'s business at the port of Geelong, which had a very considerable import trade before railway communication was opened up with Melbourne and Ballarat. The firm signalised its establishment in Geelong by loading the first large vessel for London at the Geelong wharf. Previous to December, 1854, ships of any considerable size were obliged to load and discharge their cargoes at Point Henry, five miles from the town.

During Mr. Balfour's residence in Geelong, he was actively engaged in the trade of the port, and filled several prominent positions, being at one time chairman of the Chamber of Commerce, a trustee of the Savings Bank, a director of the London Chartered Bank, and a member of the local board of the Liverpool and London Insurance Company. Mr. Balfour has also, since his return to the metropolis, been Chairman of the Board of Directors of the Australian Deposit and Mortgage Bank since its establishment, and one of the founders of the Trustees' and Executors' Company, of which he is also a director. We must not omit to mention his career as a politician, both in the Legislative Assembly and the Legislative Council. He is at present a representative for the Southern Province in the Upper House.

When Mr. Balfour returned to Melbourne, in 1863, he took an active part in the management of the business of his firm, and only retired in 1878, when the partnership of James Henty and Co. expired by effluxion of time. Early in 1879, Mr. Balfour established himself under the new style of James Balfour and Co., and continued to carry on business with his former correspondents in London. The firm imports English manufactures, tea and other Eastern produce, and executes indents for all description of goods. Special attention is given to commission and agency business. Wool also finds a place in the transactions of the firm, which, besides advancing on consignments to its London agents, ships regularly the well-known "Round Hill" clip from Mr. Balfour's property in Riverina. It also represents the following well-known insurance companies, viz.: — The Guardian Fire and Life Assurance Company of London, fire branch; the Triton Marine Insurance Company of Calcutta, and the City of Glasgow Life Assurance Company.

MONCKTON D. SYNNOT BROS.

The most imposing structures of the metropolis of the Southern Hemisphere are the banks and wool warehouses. The latter are the chief adornment of the west end of Melbourne. They are convincing proof that, amidst the money-making aims of life, the aesthetical taste of the Melbournians is far from being retrogressive. During our peregrinations through the Victorian capital, our attention was directed to warehouses recently erected at the west end of Bourke-street, which are occupied by Messrs. Monckton D. Synnot Bros., wool-brokers. Their business had previously been carried on in Flinders-lane, but their increasing requirements demanded more commodious premises. The front elevation of the building is in the Roman style of architecture. It is 70ft. high, and up to the level of the first floor is built entirely of Malmsbury bluestone, patent axed, and partly polished, with rusticated courses, and semicircular headed windows, giving a bold and striking appearance to the front. The upper portion is of brick and cement, having rusticated pilasters the full height of the upper stories, capped by a dentilled and modillioned entablature. The basement of the principal building comprises a spacious, well-lighted cellar, 48ft. by 120ft., with asphalte floor. The first and second flats are lofty, well lighted and ventilated, the floors being laid with narrow Kaurie pine boards. On the top flat is the showroom, in which the wool is exhibited by sample bales, prior to being submitted to public auction. The apartments on the ground floor are approached by a vestibule leading to a good-sized hall, which is environed by a suite of lofty offices, sample and waiting rooms, with grained oak and glass wainscot partitions having glass louvre ventilators, and all fitted with the latest improvements. In fact, the warehouses are fitted up in a way that combines space and light with usefulness, being in every possible manner suited to the display and sale of wool and other produce. We understand that they have the advantage of receiving and delivering goods under cover. At the rear, and quite distinct from the main buildings, are the hide, tallow and skin stores, with every accommodation for that branch of the business. The buildings are conveniently situated, and altogether fitted for the purposes of wool warehouses. Being near to Spencer-street and the Victorian railways, they are consequently convenient for those who are engaged in the buying branches of the trade. We doubt whether there is any commercial community in the world more ready to spend their capital in the building of imposing structures, which serve at once the purposes of their owners and the adornment of the city. They in this way become benefactors to the community. Their recompense is that they are contributors to the structural beauty of Melbourne, and aid in building up for it the well-earned reputation of the metropolis of Australia. The pastoral interest of Australia, which is already second to none, is year by year increasing in importance. We know that all land which is within the vicinity of any rainfall is capable of supporting sheep. Consequently, the pastoral resources of Australia are almost illimitable. It behoves then our wool-brokers to be in advance both for the more than probable increased demand, and, therefore, the necessary increase of supply. The Australian wool, and particularly that grown in the colonies of Victoria and New South Wales, finds a ready sale in the European markets. Its reputation has in no way diminished since its exportation abroad. In the colony itself there is no source of wealth more productive than wool-growing. No class of men do more for its ever-increasing development than the wool-brokers. Through them there need be no want of capital. Ever ready, where the security is sufficient, to aid the energetic and persevering squatter; his operations may be developed to an extent co-extensive with his ambition. Through him a market is found, and the very best prices are offered. We wish those gentlemen all success in the important position which they hold as media for the disposition of the wool which the country produces. Messrs. M. D. Synnot Bros. are not only wool-brokers, but also general station agents, and are at all times prepared to make liberal cash advances on wool of any ensuing clip, especially on clips for sale in Melbourne. They hold regular auction sales of wool every Thursday throughout the season, and of skins, hides, and tallow on three days in each week. This last is an important branch of their business. We are given to understand, from their circulars, that all account sales are rendered, with net proceeds, in cash, six days after the sales. On wool offered, but not sold, the charge is only one shilling per bale. Another branch of their business is the negotiation of loans. They also sell privately, as well as by auction, any station or other property which may be placed in their hands for disposal. The firm's agents in Sydney are Messrs. Allen and Co., Macquarie-place, who receive and forward wool to Melbourne, paying inland carriage, and all other charges thereon. We have pleasure in calling the special attention of farmers and others to the fact that Monckton D. Synnot Bros. have always on hand the very best samples of seed wheat, oats, barley, and other grain and grass seeds. They also give prompt attention to any orders for wool-packs, twine, wire, and other station requisites, and they undertake to furnish them at the lowest market rates. We notice, from their circular, the recommendation to woolgrowers and farmers that the former should adopt three letters, or some other distinguishing brand, and the latter two letters, or other brand, that might be easily recognised. This, it appears, would obviate endless trouble, confusion, and dispute, both with regard to the wool as well as the grain which is consigned to the firm. There is no doubt that the great practical experience of Monckton D. Synnot Bros. enables them to suggest practical and useful advice, which, if followed, would doubtless prove advantageous to the consigner and consignee, and materially tend to expedite the conduct of business—not the least important factor of commercial life in this go-ahead age.

M'MECKAN, BLACKWOOD AND CO.

Closely identified with shipping in Australia, especially with the colony of Victoria, must be mentioned the firm of Messrs. M'Meckan, Blackwood and Co. The rapid manner in which their line became extended from one ship to a large fleet speaks volumes for the growth of the colonial shipping trade. If we may judge by results, and there is nothing so successful as success, we cannot see how the operations of this firm, in their relation to the general development of shipping in the colonies, can be pronounced anything but a most unqualified success. It has taken them but few years to accomplish that which sometimes takes a lifetime in the mother-country. It is true they have enjoyed all the advantages which a new, rich, and rapidly-developing country offers to the enterprising and the industrious. But it is not so much as successful shipping merchants that we desire to notice the firm in this book, as it is to point out to our readers the rapid manner in which the shipping trade was developed in the colonies, and the prominent part that certain firms have played in helping forward this development, and with it no less the growth of the whole of Australia, by bringing the several colonies into closer communication, and facilitating an exchange of their produce, while also aiding the Post-office Department to carry out some of the most important reforms in the mail service. In no less a degree have they facilitated and relieved the over-crowded conditions of some colonies, where labour was too plethoric, and hence poorly remunerated, by taking the accretion of brawny sinew from a colony where it was a drug, to one where it was steadily in demand, and we recognise in this transmigration of capital's better-half—labour—a new motto. If *Quis separabit* is the challenge issued forth by the P. and O. Company, *Junximus* should be the answer expressed by the Union S. S. Company of New Zealand. It appears that Messrs. M'Meckan, Blackwood and Co. commenced their shipping business in 1853, with the simple agency of one steamer, called the *Havilah*, which was put into the Melbourne and Adelaide trade. Her accommodation answered so scantily for the requirements of this trade, that she was speedily supplemented by the *Marion*, *Queen*, *Burra Burra*, and the *White Swan*. Up to this time, the firm acted simply in the capacity of agents; but, in 1858 they had faith enough in the permanency of the trade to build, on their own account, the s. s. *Omeo*, which brought out from England the cable for the submarine telegraph from Cape Otway to Tasmania. After performing this service, she was placed by the owners upon the Melbourne and Adelaide trade. It appeared to them that a steadily-increasing trade was about to be established between the colony of Victoria and that of South Australia. Subsequent events proved that their judgment upon this point was sound, for the requirements of this trade developed into a demand for marine accommodation quite up to the ability of shipping companies to supply. Upon the development of the New Zealand trade, the business of this firm showed rather rapid extension, and they soon found that, to keep pace with it, they required more steamers. The *Oscar* and *Aldinga* were then added; and within a very short time of their addition, the *Gothenburg*, *Alhambra*, and *Coorong*. The line now comprised six ships, and at that time it was considered a substantial number for any one company to possess. But the continued increase of trade, through the rapid growth of New Zealand, made it necessary to still augment the carrying power of the line. A further addition was then made of six first-class steamers, namely, the *South Australian*, *Tararua*, *Rangitoto*, *Claud Hamilton*, *Albion*, and *Otago*. The line, now strengthened very considerably by the accession of these six steamers, profited at once by the great activity then displayed by the growing trade of New Zealand with Victoria. The rapid manner in which these two colonies unfolded their resources and manufactures to one another, and gladly exchanged both, is very vivid in the minds of many merchants and sea-faring men. In addition to the steamships already enumerated as plying between Victoria and New Zealand, the west coast of the little continent was served by the steam-tenders *Uno*, *Persevere*, and *Yarra*, built in Melbourne specially for that trade. In 1875, the fleet had assumed very respectable proportions, and was further augmented by the two splendid and equally comfortable steamers called the *Ringaroona* and *Arawata*. During the two years which followed this period, a most satisfactory traffic was worked up between Melbourne and Adelaide, and the south-east ports of South Australia, by the *Aldinga*, *Coorong*, and occasionally, when the trade required, one of the other steamers. Thus far, we have only spoken of the prosperity of this firm, during a career which cannot be pronounced anything but successful. We must not, however, fail to mention that its losses have not been of a very light character. For example, it lost in rather rapid succession the *Oscar*, the *South Australian*, the *Persevere*, the *Yarra*, the *Uno*, the *Rangitoto*, the *Gothenburg*, and the *Otago*. Except the *Gothenburg*, all of these were lost on the New Zealand coast. Upon the formation of the two companies—the Adelaide S. S. Company, and the Mount Gambier S. S. Company—overtures were made to Messrs. M'Meckan, Blackwood and Co., resulting in their disposal of the steamers *Aldinga* and *Coorong* to the above two companies respectively. The following year, the New Zealand business was transferred to the Union Steamship Company of that place, by their purchasing most of the large steamers running in that trade. The former owners now act as the Melbourne agents for the three companies. The Union Company, upon succeeding to the business, strengthened their service by the addition of the *Rotorua*, and subsequently added the two powerful screw-steamers *Rotomahana* and *Te Anau*, of about 1800 tons each. Besides the lines mentioned above, the firm of M'Meckan, Blackwood and Co. were engaged for many years in the Northern Territory service, and ran their ships from Melbourne and Adelaide to Port Darwin. In this trade, they employed the *Omeo, Claud Hamilton, Tararua,* and *Gothenburg.*

It is worth while mentioning that, in giving our readers a succinct history of the growth and progress of shipping in Australia, from its earliest infancy, we have illustrated it so far by the efforts of one firm only. Of others we shall speak later on. But it is quite worthy of notice how the ramifications of one firm have contributed, within the past thirty years, a very respectable quota to what is now a large shipping trade. As an illustration of this, we may mention that the Union Company of New Zealand, now working the Melbourne and New Zealand, and Sydney and New Zealand trades, has a capital of five hundred thousand pounds sterling, which would be a very respectable capital for an Atlantic or Pacific Ocean s. s. company, plying distances of 2500 or 3000 miles. Their present fleet consists of an aggregate tonnage of 14,000 tons, and a list of the ports to which their steamess run will be found in our advertising pages.

PENINSULAR AND ORIENTAL STEAM NAVIGATION COMPANY.

"*Quis separabit,*" the motto of the P. & O. Company, is a challenge to the powers of nature to prevent intercommunication between the inhabitants of the civilised world. The P. & O. S.N. Company has accepted this challenge, and up till now, we may say, successfully, if we judge of their future enterprise by that which they have shown in the past. One hundred years ago, the nations, whose manners and customs were then confined to the regions of the unknown, and in many cases the fabulous, are now brought into friendly, intimate, and even close connection with each other. Distance and time are being gradually relegated to the shades of the past. Out of this gradual, yet miraculous, annihilation of the two principal factors in the sum of immobility, surely though slowly grows the civilisation, which may not be improperly termed cosmopolitan. The effect of this must be humanising to every race, in whatever clime, or under whatever condition, they may live. It tends to establish peace, through the superinduction of feelings of friendliness. This peace must one day reign triumphant between *every nation* that has its seat between the cardinal points, because this peace is the great end of amalgamated nationalities. It will be permanent, and the discord of nationalities will cease to jar upon nature's nerve. Wars and rumours of wars will no longer be parts of national history. The northern is now joined to the southern hemisphere by links whose numbers are daily diminishing. The facilities for travelling are now so great, and comparatively so cheap, that nations and peoples are becoming as familiar with each other as they are with the nations to which these people severally owe their birth. Whether in one quarter of the globe or the other, the denizen of each nationality is to be found, whose most conspicuous feature is assimilation to the habits and language of the country in which he may temporarily or permanently sojourn. Neither ocean nor mountain, nor nature's most gigantic impediments, can stem the increasingly rapid tide that never ebbs, but continually flows towards the point in which nation, race, colour and creed, are becoming harmoniously, peaceably, and indissolubly blended into each other. The limits and landmarks of distinctions are being gradually forgotton and lost. Another hundred years, and who can say what will be the distinctions of country and race. The mere features of countries will be marked on the map, and the distinctions of nationalities, and the differences of religious culture, will be known no more. No commercial undertaking has been more instrumental in encompassing the results mentioned than the P. & O. S.N. Company. This company has, for upwards of twenty-five years, with slight intermission, supplied the connecting link between England and the Australian colonies, by regular mail communication. It has earned a reputation for efficiency and punctuality, which reflects alike credit upon the directors and officers of the company, as well as upon the various contracting governments. The latest agreement, which was signed in August, 1879, and which came into operation on 1st February, 1880, provides for a fortnightly communication between London and Melbourne in 39 days outwards, and 40 homewards. This contract has been entered into for a period of eight years, and the service is worked so as to facilitate and fit into similar contracts, entered into with the Imperial Government, for the conveyance of the India and China mails. We understand that the company's steamers, in carrying out the several mail contracts, have, for many years past, covered a distance of more than three miles in every minute of time, and this with comparative immunity from serious accident, during the forty years which have elapsed since it was first incorporated under Royal charter. Though the passenger traffic has not been, during this long period, far short of a million souls, not more than half-a-dozen casualties have been recorded. The company owes its origin to Messrs. Willcox and Anderson, shipbrokers of London, who first started it under the name of the Peninsular Company. They first entered into an agreement with the Government for the conveyance of mails from England to Gibraltar, calling at the intermediate ports of Vigo, Oporto, Lisbon and Cadiz. The magnitude of the company's present operations may be gathered from the fact that the subscribed share capital is £3,500,000 of which £2,900,000 are paid-up, while the authorised debenture capital is £800,000, none of which is at present availed of; and this enormous amount of money is represented by a fleet of steam-ships, fifty in number, measuring by customs register, 143,646 tons, and fitted with machinery of 24,940 horse-power, besides seventeen steam-tugs, &c., measuring 1217 tons, and 491 horse-power in all; also, property on shore consisting of freehold and leasehold houses, offices, docks, wharves, coaling depots, factories and repairing establishments in England and at Bombay, Hong Kong, Shanghai, Singapore, Calcutta, Point de Galle, Suez, Alexandria, Malta, and other places, and stocks of coal, and marine victualling and other stores in depot and in transit to these stations; the whole showing a value of £3,827,939 17s. 2d., as stated in the last annual report.

The question of steam communication with India, China and Australia was referred, in 1851, to a Parliamentary committee, and in pursuance of their report, a bi-monthly line between Singapore and Australia was established. This service formed a part of the P. & O. Company's contract, which they entered into two years after. The sudden outbreak of the Russian war, eventuated in the withdrawal of several steamers from the regular service for the transport-service of the Home Government, and the Australasian branch service was then temporarily discontinued. As many as eleven of their steamers were withdrawn for this purpose, and yet the company was able to work its other lines with regularity and success. After a short interval, during which a contract was entered into with the European and Australian Company, who failed in carrying it out, the mail service again reverted, in 1858, to the P. & O. Company, when, after the lapse of eight years, *i.e.*, in 1866, a new and modified contract was entered into by the company, after public tender. The new contract provided for a service of 12, 13, 24, or 26 departures in the year, from each end of the line, and was worked with very great success, until the commencement of 1874. The opening of the Suez Canal, in 1869, led to the establishment of an enormous fleet of cargo-carrying steamers, which quickly displaced the sailing-ship traffic *via* the Cape of Good Hope, and necessitated, in a great measure, the reconstruction of the company's large fleet. They were compelled, in order to keep pace with the times, to employ steamers that would carry cargoes at comparatively low rates of freight, instead of the light and valuable goods which had, up to this time, formed the staple commodities carried by the mail steamers. We may adduce, as an instance of the energy of purpose, and fertility of resource with which they performed that task, that, though in 1866 they had only six ships out of a fleet of fifty-two fitted with compound engines, in 1878 they had added to their fleet no less than twenty-two first-class steamers, of large tonnage, and had only one running vessel not fitted with the new compound engine.

Owing to the want of unanimity existing between the Australian colonies as to the best route for their respective mail communication with the mother-country, and to the difficulty experienced in meeting the views of so many conflicting interests, the Imperial Government suggested that on the termination of the P. & O. Company's Australian contract in 1873, the colonies in combination should undertake their own arrangements for the conveyance of their English correspondence. The Victorian Government entered, upon their own account, into a contract with the P. & O. Steam Company for the unbroken continuance of the existing mail service *via* Galle, on very favourable terms, one leading feature of the new contract being that Melbourne, instead of Sydney, was to be made the terminus of the line. The New South Wales Government, about the same time, contracted with another company for a service between Sydney and San Francisco, and the Queensland Government for a line *via* Torres Straits, to connect with the P. & O. steamers at Singapore. The P. & O. Company had, about the same time, arranged with the Imperial Government, again under competition, for a continuance of their India and China services, and their contracts were thoroughly conducted throughout. It was necessary, by the terms of the agreements, that two years' notice should be given of their discontinuance, and the requisite notice was served upon the company by both the Imperial and Victorian Governments. Very keen competition was the result for the India and China service, but eventually the company's tender for an eight years' contract was again successful, owing to its being the cheapest tender in point of price, while it was also superior in the quality of the service it offered to those sent in by other shipowners. It is worthy of note that, from the inception of the company, the competition, against which it has fought for the mail contracts, has been in nearly every instance very keen. The Victorian Government issued specifications for—1st, a direct service at a high rate of speed between Plymouth, or Southampton, and Melbourne, with Melbourne as the terminus; and 2nd, for a four-weekly, or bi-weekly, service, at a similar speed, between Aden, or Ceylon, and Melbourne, with no restrictions as to the terminal point. The P. & O. Company sent in a tender offering a fortnightly service between Ceylon and Melbourne, under the second set of conditions, and for a subsidy less by £5000 per annum than they had been receiving for a four-weekly service under the restrictions of the former contract. No tender whatever was sent in for the direct service, and theirs being the only one for the other service was accordingly accepted, and came into force on the 1st February last. It is worthy of notice that the contract will, from the estimates that have been made, be the first agreement for the carriage of ocean mails to offer an almost certain prospect of profit instead of loss to the contracting government. The last annual report of the company shows that the balance at credit of reserve account was £388,217, while the revenue for the year ending 30th September, 1879, was £1,893,496, but in some years it has been much higher, the dullness of trade and depression in freights throughout the world having led to a diminution of revenue in late years, which has necessitated rigid economy in working. The P. & O. Company is one of the wealthiest s.s. companies in the world. Its Australian business has been very ably conducted for many years past by Mr. Franklin R. Kendall.

This gentleman has recently been appointed to a position in the home office, and has been succeeded in Melbourne as general manager by Mr. George Withers, who is spoken of by those who know him as a very capable manager, an efficient officer, and a courteous gentleman.

Subjoined is a table showing the revenue and expenditure of the company for the years 1856 to 1879. Some idea of the complicated nature of the mail and other services which they are now performing may be gathered from a perusal of one of the time-tables published in the handbooks which they issue to passengers and shippers:—

RETURN SHOWING THE ANNUAL RECEIPTS AND EXPENDITURE OF THE COMPANY, FROM 1856 TO 1879.

Year.	Revenue.	Expenditure.	Balance.
1856	1,691,589	1,494,435	197,153
1857	1,877,420	1,645,748	231,772
1858	1,884,493	1,714,374	170,119
1859	2,176,590	2,006,363	170,227
1860	2,350,361	2,247,328	103,033
1861	2,288,289	2,131,432	156,857
1862	2,223,969	2,064,865	159,104
1863	2,296,305	2,060,849	235,454
1864	2,346,203	2,120,554	225,649
1865	2,136,076	1,976,999	159,077
1866	2,243,076	2,094,493	148,583
1867	2,084,393	2,261,440	177,047 deficiency.
1868	2,485,965	2,313,817	172,148
1869	2,559,627	2,390,518	169,109
1870	2,317,016	2,174.672	142,344
1871	2,092,656	1,923,881	168,775
1872	2,122,756	1,953,551	169,205
1873	2,173,371	2,007,761	165,610
1874	2,186,663	2,047,899	138,764
1875	2,099,334	2,021,159	78,175
1876	2,038,980	1,943,121	95,859
1877	2,134,627	2,003,485	131,142
1878	1,979,910	1,846,285	133,625
1879	1,893,396	1,758,588	134,808

WM. HOWARD SMITH AND SONS.

The shipping at the port of Melbourne, compared with that of Liverpool, is very insignificant indeed. Considering that Liverpool is the largest port in the world, it is natural that it should be so. But, to be able to make the comparison at all, notwithstanding the many hundred times removed that it is, is a great compliment to Melbourne. The rapid development which has attended the shipping interest in Melbourne, and the continued activity that it shows, promises well for its future as a port. At the same time, it must not be forgotten that the Victorian Government must be to the front, in aiding, as much as possible, masters of ships and s.s. navigation companies, in inducing them to continue to call at Melbourne, and not menace or harass them with conditions that cripple rather than second their exertions to increase Melbourne's importance as a port. There are rumours in the air that Sydney is diverting from Melbourne part of the shipping trade she formerly held; that the Government of that port is offering masters extra inducements to call there, to the exclusion of Melbourne. We have no reason, as yet, to believe that they have been influenced in any great degree to this end. At least, our shipping here has not fallen off to any appreciable extent. If it should, however, it will not be through any fault of our shipowners, who, for the most, are wealthy, energetic, and most enterprising men. Prominent among the leading wealthy corporations to the fore, who take time by the forelock, and invest their means wherever there is the slightest chance of getting a fair return, and developing any particular portion of new water-carrying trade, may be mentioned, with credit, Messrs. Wm. Howard Smith and Sons. In a very short space of time indeed, this firm has developed a shipping interest, which commenced with a single craft, of but 120 tons register, to one which now embraces ten steam-ships, of an aggregate tonnage of 7692 tons. Their business, which really commenced in 1854, virtually did not go into active operations until 1864, as the senior member of the firm, Captain W. H. Smith, passed a number of years in England. The first ventures of Captain Smith were, however, confined to the s.s. *Express*, of 120 tons, which he brought safely to Melbourne in July, 1854, and which he owned in conjunction with the engineer. The little steamer was employed in plying between Melbourne and Geelong, and evidently did her work well, for in 1861 the owner returned to England—having sold out his interest in the *Express*—to bring out something more useful. In May, 1864, he arrived with the steamship *You Yangs*, of 457 tons, which he determined to put in the Sydney trade (in opposition to the great A.S.N. Company). Finding this steamer too small for the requirements of his trade, he again visited England in 1867, and purchased the *Dandenong*, of 762 tons, which he brought out to Melbourne; and this appears to have been Captain Smith's last command. The owner of the *Dandenong* found that his time was absolutely required on shore, and hence his retirement from active marine service, in 1870. The *Macedon* was then built, and in 1873, Mr. W. H. Smith, jun., went to England, and built the *Barrabool*, of 1000 tons. Upon the arrival of this last ship, it was decided to extend their shipping interests to Queensland; in consequence of which the *Edina* was purchased and placed in the trade between Sydney, Brisbane and Maryborough. In 1876, the *Cheviot* was added to their line; in 1878, the *Derwent*, while the *Leura* arrived from England in October of the same year, having made the passage in 46 days. This vessel was followed by the *Keilawarra*, and subsequently, by the *Rodondo*. Before the accession of the three last-named steamers to the fleet, Captain Smith saw the rapidity with which Australian shipping was developing, and the necessity of having roomy and stout-built English vessels, for the purpose of accommodating the trade. It was on this account he went again to England in 1877, to personally superintend the building of these three fine steamers. Nor does it seem that his experience did not serve him well, for these last ships have been found eminently suited to the trade they are engaged upon. Upon his return to Melbourne, to make the business, if possible, more efficiently conducted, the head of this firm took into partnership his three sons; of whom, one has charge of the Melbourne office, and the other two Sydney and Brisbane respectively. The firm has already decided to reopen the Geelong trade. It is intimated that they will meet some opposition. But, with their indomitable energy and business sagacity, it is fair to assume that these agencies will not prejudice their operations very much. In addition to being large steamship owners, Messrs. Wm. Howard Smith and Sons are presumably the largest coal merchants in Melbourne. They are said to load and discharge from their steamers more cargoes per month than any other company, and this fact is gathered from the returns. They also own, besides the 7692 tons of steamers, a number of sailing vessels; and their ramifications, in the shape of offices, extend to Sydney, Newcastle, Brisbane, and Geelong, &c., and they employ about 700 men. They purpose building two more large steam colliers, of about 1500 tons each, and also a very powerful steel screw steamer, for the Sydney and Melbourne passenger trade. Travellers and shippers cannot go astray in patronising this very enterprising firm.

THE TRUSTEES, EXECUTORS AND AGENCY COMPANY, LIMITED.

There is nothing more characteristic of the age in which we live, than the conviction which is gradually, but surely, forcing itself upon the minds of enterprising men, that whatever the exigencies of life or death require to be done should be done well—

"*Ne tentes aut perfice.*"

Æsthetics, sciences, and commerce have been developed far beyond the most sanguine hopes or anticipations of our ancestors. Adornment is by degrees being sacrificed to utility; and what is most sought for in the nineteenth century is the greatest good, combined with the least inconvenience, and the greatest pleasure, combined with the least pain, either present or future, to the greatest number. The creative, or inventive, faculties of men were never more strained. New wants are daily growing and increasing; old ones are better supplied. So much is required of each individual who mixes himself with the affairs of men, that there are few who find the allotted space of life sufficient to crush into it all that nineteenth-century life exacts. There are still fewer who are able or willing to burden themselves with the affairs or concerns of others. If they do so, they seldom succeed in discharging their duties to the entire satisfaction of themselves, or of those for whom they act. One desideratum seems to be the decrease of manual labour, as a necessary factor for the fuller and better progression of other and higher aims of life. The concentrated sum of all energy seems to be that machinery should supply the substitute for everything that is likely to take away man from his legitimate destiny as a thinking being. Man's great work in active life is to invent, direct, and control. There is scarcely anything, with which man is brought into contact during life, that has not from its first birth been subject to, and obeyed the law of progress. This law has forced all living exigencies to adapt themselves to each successive generation. Their progression has been development and adaptability to the spirit of the age. But there is one domain which, for upwards of a thousand years, has been little troubled with any progressive necessity or adventitious aid. It has passed through three distinct ages—the *Fidei commissa* of the Romans, the Statute of Uses of the Eighth Henry, and the Statute of Trusts of the present reign. The salient and almost only differences of the three stages are their dates. The important question of what a man is to do with his worldly possessions after death, and the still more important, though subordinate, question of the fitness of the person, or persons, in whom a trust is reposed, to carry out a testator's last wishes, has hitherto not received that consideration, at the hands of the legislature, to which, on account of its pressing importance, it is entitled. Though it is, both by virtue and necessity, the last thing of which a man must think ere he quits this mortal coil, yet, notwithstanding all this, it has hitherto been relegated to the waste-paper basket of life. The importance of the proper arrangement, and the consideration of the fittest person to carry out that arrangement after death, has up till now been made subservient to the all-absorbing interest that mankind has ever shown in the affairs of life. We hesitate, either in business or professionally, to trust anyone, of whose absolute competency, honesty, and skill, we are not, in every possible way, assured. The only exception to this has generally been in the committal of the office of trustee, or executor, the most sacred, the most onerous, and one of the most important a man can undertake, to inexperienced men. The only qualification we seek is, that the person we may wish to appoint is friendly and willing. There is absolutely no guarantee to the heirs, nor any absolute assurance to the testator, that the person appointed is either capable of fulfilling the trust reposed, or if he be so, that his interest will not flag, that he will not become indifferent, or, in fact, will not seek in some way to shirk the responsibility. Or, if he be as much or all we can expect under the circumstances, what is the guarantee that the person appointed after his death will be the same. All these doubts and contingencies may now be avoided. The same guarantee of competency and ability, as is expected in a professional or a business man, is henceforth to be found in the trustee or executor. This proficiency of administration in deceased persons' estates is to be found in the Trustees, Executors and Agency Company, Limited. It supplies one of the greatest, and probably one of the most sacred, difficult, and onerous desiderata of the age. It is the development of the necessity and the provision for the exigencies of death. It is a corporate body, which never dies, empowered by Act of Parliament to take upon itself the offices either of executor, trustee, administrator with will annexed, receiver, committee (that is, manager) of an estate under the Lunacy Statute, and attorney under power. The Supreme Court is empowered to appoint this corporation a trustee. A further clause permits a trustee, desirous of being discharged from his trust, to delegate all his powers to the company, as he may, under the 73rd section of the Statute of Trusts, delegate them to a private person. The £10,000, which the Act requires to be deposited permanently with the Treasurer of Victoria, is considered, by the Supreme Court, amply sufficient for all purposes contemplated by the Statute of Trusts. Everything, so far as we can see, has been provided to ensure safety and security to all concerned. The Act passed last year to confer powers upon the Trustees, Executors and Agency Company, Limited (of which the short title is "The Executors' Company's Act") contained a proviso that it should not come into full operation until the paid-up capital was increased by £20,000. It will be seen from the subjoined extract from the *Argus*, of July 3rd,* that the provision has been more than complied with; and since that date the Act has been brought into full operation, and the company is now empowered to act in its corporate capacity as executors, &c.

* We are informed that the whole of the new issue of shares of the Trustees, Executors and Agency Company (Limited) have been taken up at a premium of 5s. each, or £25 per cent. on the amount called up on the shares. As the Executors' Company's Act only required the capital of the company to be increased by £20,000 before the Act could be brought into operation, the directors did not contemplate issuing more than 20,000 new shares (with £1 paid up) in the colony; but so many applications came in during the last month from influential persons, whom it was very desirable to have on the list of shareholders, that the directors determined to issue up to the full number mentioned in the prospectus, viz., 25,000, and applications largely in excess of even this number were received before the time fixed for closing. The directors will therefore be able to bring the Act into almost immediate operation, and the company will start with a paid-up capital of £30,000 (of which £10,000 will be invested in the name of the Treasurer of the colony in trust for the company), a subscribed capital of £75,000, and the shareholders will be liable, in case of liquidation, to a further sum of £75,000; and so the company will, in fact, be under a pecuniary bond of £150,000 for the due performance of its duties. The share-list now numbers, including original shareholders, 300, including representative names of all classes, and an unusually large number qualified to act as directors, and whom the public would at once recognise as eligible successors to the present board. The directors have just completed an arrangement with Mr. F. W. Prell, by which they will, on the 1st January next, secure permission, on a 14 years' lease, of the centre block of the new buildings which he is erecting near the Union Bank, in Queen-street; and an important part of the agreement is that Mr. Prell is to build, in the basement, a room 18ft. by 16ft., so strong as to be secure against everything but an earthquake. In this strong room, or muniment room as it might be better termed, the directors propose to lodge for safe keeping, any wills, deeds, policies of insurance, or other valuable documents or records which may be left with them. The want of such a place, where persons would, by paying a moderate charge, be entitled to deposit their records and other valuables, has long been felt, and will, no doubt, become more so as these records, etc., accumulate in private hands, and the directors may therefore reasonably expect that their enterprise will not only prove a lucrative one for the company, but will also confer a great benefit on the public.

MESSRS. JAMES M'EWAN AND CO.

Foremost amongst the many extensive mercantile firms in the city of Melbourne, stands that of Messrs. James M'Ewan and Co., wholesale and retail ironmongers, whose towering and substantial warehouses, situated at the intersection of Elizabeth-street and Little Collins-street west, present a very imposing appearance, and strike the visitor to Melbourne for the first time, as a real evidence of material prosperity. This, the first impression from an outside view, is substantially confirmed by a careful inspection of the vast and valuable stock displayed within the premises. Before, however, proceeding to details, it will be as well to give some slight sketch of the rise and progress of the firm in question, whose ramifications extend all over the civilised globe, and whose name has become almost a passport to the ironmongery trade of the world, not only for the magnitude of their operations, but also for the strict commercial integrity with which it is associated. This is one of the oldest houses extant in the hardware trade in the colony, and owes its origin to the late Mr. James M'Ewan, who established the business in 1852 (a year conspicuous in the history of Victoria, as the one which ushered in the golden era), and shortly afterwards associated with him, in partnership, Messrs. William Kerr Thomson and Samuel Renwick. Mr. M'Ewan died in 1868; and Messrs. Thomson and Renwick have, since that period, carried on the business under the well-known name of James M'Ewan and Co. In 1868, the spacious premises referred to, were erected at 81 and 83 Elizabeth-street, the firm having bought the property and stock of the late Mr. Thomas Jackson, and the old building being pulled down to make room for the new premises, of which we propose to give here a short description. The retail shop, counting-house, and private offices, are on the ground floor. Opposite the main entrance, a handsome staircase approaches capacious and elegantly fitted show-rooms, the immediate effect of which is to excite amazement and admiration at the costly display, which surrounds one on all sides.

Here, anything, from the simplest necessary of household utensils to the most superb adornments which embellish a gentleman's mansion, may be found. But, to enter into particulars would serve no purpose; "seeing is believing," and the best plan is to adopt that course, when hours may be pleasantly and instructively passed, with the knowledge of the fact before one that the latest improvements and inventions, in connection with their business, whether British, American, or Continental, are systematically arranged and placed within our reach. On the next floor, will be found all the articles requisite for dining-room, drawing-room, and bed-room furnishing, including a magnificent display of bedsteads in brass, iron, &c.; in fact, everything that comes within the ironmongery and furnishing catalogue. The firm strictly adhere to a judicious extension of every department of their business, by paying it the most scrupulous and undivided attention.

The entire premises in Elizabeth-street are devoted simply to the sale of goods in a retail manner, from articles of the smallest value to those representing hundreds of pounds each.

Next in order of inspection, we come to the wholesale warehouses, which almost adjoin the premises just described, and are situated at Nos. 4, 6, and 10, Little Collins-street West. They comprise five large three-storey buildings, containing items in the hardware trade which go out in large quantities to the country storekeepers, contractors, squatters, &c., both in this and the neighbouring colonies. The stock in this department is not surpassed in quantity, quality, or rarity by that of any other house engaged in this trade in the Australias. It consists principally of what may be denominated parcel goods, the more portable of manufacturing appliances, and the larger kinds of tools, &c., &c. But in this trade—which, from a reproductive point of view, is essentially the basis of most others—many articles are required whose size necessitates special facilities for display, and the firm have provided all the desiderata for this purpose, at 319 Elizabeth-street (north end), where they have a splendid freehold of about 3 acres, on which is erected a very large and substantial bluestone store, of handsome design, containing another retail shop, machinery show-rooms, building material show-rooms, and offices, with numerous buildings, conveniently situated on the land, for storage of heavy packages received direct from the ships. The stock kept on these premises is sufficiently large to meet any unforeseen demand, whether from an agricultural, squatting, building, or mining source. There is also here a very large and substantial iron rack, capable of holding 2000 tons of bar iron of all descriptions; whilst the yards are filled with steam engines for various purposes, ploughs, and all kinds of labour-saving appliances, whether of English, American, or Continental manufacture; and that, too, in the face of "protection to native industry," for really many things specified above cannot be manufactured locally, and yet must be kept in stock, in spite of fiscal restrictions. Here, too, is a marble-masons' workshop, where a number of men are constantly employed in the manufacture and fitting up of marble mantelpieces.

It might be thought that the distance (about half-a-mile) between this establishment and the central offices, would interfere with despatch of business, but this is not found to be the case, as the establishments are connected by "telephone," and therefore within easy speaking distance for any present inquiry, and there is regular communication carried on personally between the representatives.

Messrs. James M'Ewan and Co. have also a branch office at Nelson, New Zealand, equally distant from, and convenient for, the extremes of both islands; their representative there is the medium between New Zealand customers and their London and Melbourne houses, and thereby maintains a very important connection in that fair colony.

Within the last five years the firm have also established themselves in the Fiji Islands, where they do a very large business, through their extensive stores, situated at Suva, the capital, the stock held being of general description, meeting all the requirements of planters and settlers. Their establishment here has proved a very great boon to the producers, who find in the firm a ready and responsible medium for realising the varied produce of these magnificent islands, which, ere long, must become to these colonies what Mauritius, and other tropical regions, have hitherto been; and, in order to command this trade most effectually, the firm were the first to open up regular steam communication between Melbourne and the Fijis, the trade with the South Sea Islands, prior to their advent, having been almost entirely in the hands of Sydney merchants. Messrs. James M'Ewan and Co.'s own steamship, the *Suva*, is a regular and punctual trader, and has become noted for her speed and good sea-going qualities. The brig *Shannon* is also a regular trader, belonging to the firm. For the convenience of their own, and other steamers, they have here a large coal depôt; and they hold the contract for supplying Her Majesty's men-of-war.

Fiji, the youngest of the British colonies, makes a capital display at the Melbourne International Exhibition, and some of the exhibits are submitted with theé clat attaching to successful competition in Exhibitions of European note. Mr. W. K. Thomson (one of the members of the firm) is the Commissioner appointed by the Government of Fiji to represent that colony at the Great Melbourne Exhibition.

Having thus briefly, and inadequately, reviewed, in this epitome, the magnitude of the transactions of Messrs. J. M'Ewan and Co., it may not be out of place to state that the firm gives regular employment to about 150 hands, including, as may be imagined, a large and efficient counting-house staff, commercial travellers, salesmen, draymen, &c. Many of the *employés* have been over twenty years in their situations, a fact which speaks volumes on both sides, more especially in a young colony, where everything is so much subject to change. But, apart from those who may be termed the direct *employés* of the firm, there are many local manufacturers, such as brassfounders, whitesmiths, blacksmiths, ropespinners, saddlers, &c., who largely employ labour, and find in the enterprise of the firm a very tangible support to "native industry;" so that the benefits accruing to society through the operations of such a firm are materially important. But in order to best conserve these vast interests, the most important operations of the firm come direct from the great centre, London, where their offices, at 27 Lombard-street, are managed by the resident partner there, Mr. A. J. Malcolm, and an efficient clerical staff. The indent business transacted at this office is of an important and extensive nature, having connection with all the markets of the world. The facilities afforded by increased steam communication, tends to bring the antipodes into much closer relationship; whilst the electric telegraph is fully availed of to guide and guard the firm in their operations, as well as enabling orders to be executed when required, sometimes within forty-five days, from the other side of the world.

In conclusion, the great enterprise on which the colony of Victoria has entered by holding a world's fair, will, in whatever measure of success which may attend that undertaking, lack nothing from the individual efforts of the firm referred to, as they have undertaken to represent the interests of over one hundred manufacturers, whose exhibits aggregate many hundreds of tons, involving a large money expenditure, which it is to be trusted will eventuate in important and beneficial results to all concerned.

BRISCOE AND CO.

In a country where the interests embrace, at once, the pastoral, the agricultural, and the mining, the business of hardwaremen is one of no little consequence. This applies more particularly to a new country, where the greater part of those goods which are comprised in an ironmongery store requires to be imported. The careful and judicious selection of the various implements, tools, &c., which are peculiar to the successful carrying on of the interests named, requires a certain amount of discrimination, as also an intimate knowledge of the wants which are required to be supplied. Much interest is added to the business, when the supply of goods is extended to the want of the various paraphernalia, which contribute to the games and pastimes of those leisure hours, which, in the intervals of business, are indulged in by the majority of those who, during the day, are devoted to the serious pursuits of life. There is scarcely any calling in which men may be engaged, that does not require, in a greater or less degree, some or other of the articles sold by the hardwareman. He contributes to the comforts of home, the comforts also of those marts of business, where men spend the greater part of their lives, with the soul-absorbing aim of amassing wealth. Ironmongery is one of the most useful, as well as one of the most necessary wants of civilised life. Where this business is in a flourishing condition, it is the indication that trade, and every kind of industry, are fairly prosperous. There is no time, during the history of a colony, from the earliest settlement up to its maturest development, when the various articles which are to be found upon the business premises of an ironmonger are not great and important desiderata. There is no region, however remote from civilisation and the busy lives of the great emporiums of trade and commerce, where the wants which can only be supplied by the dealer in hardware goods, are not felt to a greater or lesser degree.

Probably the most complete stock of hardware goods in Australia is to be found on the premises of Messrs. Briscoe and Co. They first commenced business as general ironmongers, in 1854, at No. 68 Elizabeth-street. They moved from Elizabeth-street to Collins-street, about the year 1860. It may be somewhat interesting to know, that among the buildings at that time existing in Melbourne, the premises occupied by Briscoe and Co. towered above them all. In June, 1877, the building of the new establishment was started, and was not completed until 1878. The total cost, including the land and building, was somewhere about £55,000. From this we may form a very fair estimate of the size of the premises and the completeness, in every respect, of the buildings for the purposes for which they were required. The buildings extend from Collins-street to Little Collins-street, comprising a length of about 200 feet, and a frontage in Collins-street of 66 feet. Anxious to obtain a central position, they did not hesitate to pay the enormous price of £500 per foot, for a part of the land on which they have erected their splendid premises. The retail shop is 66 by 73 feet and has five floors of the same size. The basement contains such goods as woolpacks, oils, wooden ware, bellows, and bulk packages of stock. The ground floor contains what is generally understood as builders' and contractors' ironmongery, and tools of every description. Besides these, are fire-arms, cutlery, and plated ware. Above that, are large pieces of electroplate, and marble mantelpieces, grates of all styles and descriptions, bronzes, gas fittings and fixtures, and a large and varied stock of cricketing outfits, footballs, lawn-tennis, and croquet, and a thousand and one other things too innumerable to mention. The next floor is full of kitchen ranges, American stoves, gas stoves, mangles, and a cheaper description of marble mantels and register grates, together with all sorts and descriptions of culinary utensils. The top floor comprises a large stock of brass and iron bedsteads, in great variety, as well as bedding. This floor also contains a great variety of marble and encaustic tiles, as well as elegant china dessert services, and an assortment of table glass-ware, being of French, Venetian, Bohemian, and English manufacture, of the best quality.

Messrs. Briscoe and Co. cordially invite all who are connected with their line of business to inspect their large and varied stock. Those who visit their establishment for a specific purpose, as well as the public generally, will find that they can spend their time instructively and agreeably. We can assure all who visit their establishment, that they will meet with the utmost courtesy and attention, both from the head of the firm, and their employés; and no trouble will be spared in giving the fullest information, or in providing the exact article, which may be required. We strongly recommend our readers to pay a visit of inspection to the large and well-conducted establishment of Messrs. Briscoe and Co. The access to the upper stories is facilitated by a swift and powerful lift running to the top floor, from basement to roof. A double suite of offices between the two buildings, connect them together. The rear building is exclusively devoted to the wholesale department, and leads to a right-of-way in Little Collins-street. Its size is 120 feet by 54 feet, and it contains three floors. The stock comprises every possible thing that could be called for in the ironmongery line. From the rapid growth of the business, it was found that the premises, though large, were insufficient for the increased requirements. The consequence was that the firm was compelled to rent premises, which they specially devoted to general smiths' work. These premises are almost contiguous to the main establishment, being in the same right-of-way. At this place they fit up all their grates and ranges, and finish off their brass work, bronze, and lacquer-ware in brass, copper, tin, and iron. At the present time, the firm rents a large iron yard and premises, at 245 Elizabeth-street, as well as a large yard in Franklin-street, in addition to the premises already described. These premises are ostensibly required for the storage of bar and rod, plate, angle, tee, galvanized, plain and corrugated iron, as well as every description of steel used for the manufacture of tools, and also the particular kind of steel used for miners' drills. There is, too, a very large stock of fencing wire, both black and galvanized, tar and pitch, agricultural implements, engines, reaping machines, chaffcutters, &c., &c. The stock also includes axles for carts, mail phætons, and buggies, as well as springs, and every variety of American wooden ware, used in the manufacture of buggies.

Messrs. Briscoe and Co. are sole agents in Victoria for the following specialties, viz.:—Peacock and Buchan's non-corrossive paint, as well as the non-poisoning composition paint, which is perfectly innocuous. They are also agents for Noble and Co.'s genuine Hamburg dynamite, which is said to be the strongest explosive known. It may not be generally known that this establishment is a branch of the Wolverhampton firm of William Briscoe and Son, which was established as long back as 1750. Towards the end of the 18th century, Messrs. William Briscoe and Co. started branch busine   at Jamaica, and at the island of St. Thomas. We need scarcely say th   he business at Wolverhampton is still flourishing, and the two branch   which were established at the above-named place, are in every way prosperous and successful. The very fact of Messrs. Briscoe and Co.'s connection with such an old established firm as that at Wolverhampton, is a guarantee to the public that all goods which they supply will be of the very best quality, and remarkable for duration. It must be gratifying to the citizens of Melbourne, to know that they have in their midst, a firm of gentlemen of such long standing, both at home and in Australia, as those who are at the head of the establishment of Messrs. Briscoe and Co. This must be productive of implicit confidence in those who, being at a distance, are obliged to send their orders by post, and so trust themselves entirely to the probity of those with whom they deal.

In 1863, the New Zealand trade grew so rapidly that Messrs. Briscoe and Co. were compelled, in order to meet the growing requirements, to open a branch in that colony. This they accomplished by buying out the Carron Iron Warehouse, then conducted by Cairns, Wilson and Amos. Their buildings in New Zealand are very commodious, being three stories high, and about 120 in length by 66 feet in breadth. They have the same variety of stock there, as in their establishment at Melbourne; equally remarkable for its quality and the fact that it satisfies the usual requirements of their numerous customers. As the buildings of Messrs. Briscoe and Co. in Melbourne are creditable monuments to business enterprise, so their hardware store in New Zealand is one of the handsomest buildings that is to be found in the colony.

We are sure that the success which attends the careful attention to the wants of customers, will be a source of continued prosperity to the firm whose business is the subject of this chapter.

MESSRS. M'LEAN BROS. AND RIGG.

The visit which we paid to the firm of Messrs. M'Lean Bros. and Rigg, in the course of our peregrinations, supplied us with valuable information on a feature of Victorian trade in which they have taken a most important position. They are ironmongers and hardware merchants, on an extensive scale, and second to no other house in the colonies for enterprise ; and the energy and perseverance which they have introduced into their business may be counted amongst the chief factors of their success. Though the firm has not been established for more than eight years, we understand that the partners have individually been associated with the trade, in Melbourne, for upwards of a quarter of a century. This, we think, fully entitles them to be considered as possessing a thoroughly practical knowledge of the requirements in their particular branch of business, not only of Victoria, but of all the other colonies of Australia. The firm consists of Messrs. William Rigg, William M'Lean, Oliver M'Lean, and Joseph H.

Wood. The last-mentioned gentleman manages the London house, which the firm found necessary to open, not only for the purchase of goods for their own business, but also that their indent trade,—now an extensive and important department of their business,—might be attended to with greater advantage to their clients in all parts of Australasia and New Zealand. Many leading traders in New South Wales, Queensland, New Zealand, and Tasmania, import their goods through the flourishing firm of M'Lean Bros. and Rigg. The brand of the firm, familiar, no doubt, to those whose business carries them to the various wharves of the different colonies, is "the padlock," which, we assume, symbolises the care which is bestowed on all goods entrusted to their charge, or imported under their auspices. Their business already extends itself through the whole of Victoria, and through a considerable portion of the sister colonies. The name of the firm, and its high reputation, is equally familiar to the humble labourer and the wealthy squatter, whether in Victoria or the neighbouring colonies. Much of this reputation is due to the urbanity of the several partners, as well as to their thorough knowledge of the business, and the exact requirements of their numerous customers. The firm derives no inconsiderable κυδος from the fact that the oval Samson wire, for fencing, has been invented and patented by one of their number. Its utility over other wires, for like purposes, is enhanced by its cheapness; and where large tracts of country, as in Australia, require to be fenced in for many miles of area, it is likely to become a great desideratum.

The furnishing department is another specialty of this establishment, and is carried on with equal care and attendance to the wants and necessities of all whose ambition leads them to aspire to households of which they themselves may be lords and masters. We have particular pleasure in directing the special attention of all ladies who have any latent desire to become the heads of households—though we lament that the number in this intellectual age is so limited—to the great choice and cheapness of useful and elegant articles, which form, certainly, not the least important part of house furniture, from various designs of kettles to useful, and not-to-be-despised, nutmeg graters. If we judge from our own experience, we can assure both large and small purchasers that they will meet with equal civility and attention from the employés, as well as from the partners of the firm themselves. This assurance is to be appreciated by all those who have been disgusted at the *insouciance* and neglect that are sometimes met with amongst tradesmen who have no eye to the future.

The extensive business which is carried on by M'Lean Bros. and Rigg requires large and conveniently-situated premises. The retail business is conducted in premises situated at 69 Elizabeth-street. The counting-house comprises a portion of this building. It consists of three lofty stories running back to Collins Place, a distance of 130 feet. The building, in which a portion of the wholesale business is conducted, is connected with the first-mentioned building by a very handsome lattice bridge. It has a frontage of 66 feet, by a depth of 56, and is four stories in height. The premises in Fleming Place have a frontage of 66 feet; goods are received here, and hoisted at once to the respective flats by a hydraulic lift, working on the outside of the building. The firm was compelled, some four years ago, to provide further accommodation for the heavy portion of their trade, and they caused to be erected very extensive stores, in Bourke-street West, within a short distance of the Metropolitan Railway terminus, in Spencer-street. The frontage to Bourke-street is 116 feet, and runs back 313 feet, to Little Collins-street. The store occupies 58 feet frontage, and the other 58 feet is used as a yard, where are sheds for the storage of machinery, cast-iron pipes, and other heavy goods. There is access for drays to almost every part of the building, which necessarily effects a great saving in removing packages. In the centre, and equidistant from each street, is a travelling crane, for lifting heavy cases, &c., and which is so arranged that it can easily be managed by one man. The new premises have been evidently planned for convenience rather than for show, and they afford storage accommodation for 10,000 tons. They are in close proximity to the wharves, as well as to the principal railway station. The firm, consequently, saves annually a handsome sum in the matter of cartage and convenience. The number of hands employed by the company amounts to 70, which will give some idea of the size of their business. M'Lean Bros. and Rigg, for several successive years, have had the contracts to supply the Victorian Government with every description of ironmongery and hardware, which, in itself, speaks highly for the quality of their goods. About nine months ago, the firm purchased the old-established business of G. Phillips and Co., of Adelaide, thereby extending their already large connection to South Australia. The resident partners in Adelaide are Mr. C. E. Deeley, and Mr. M. Eyres, late of Eyres Bros., of Ballarat.

DALGETY, BLACKWOOD AND CO.

This is one of the oldest and most solidly established firms in Melbourne, dating as far back as the year 1846. Its title is "familiar in our mouths as household words," owing to the fact of its long standing and high character. Old colonists will remember it as having commenced operations at a time when even the most sanguine settlers never ventured to antici-pate that the commerce of the once obscure settlement of Port Phillip would assume, within a quarter of a century of its foundation, those large dimensions which it had attained between 1851 and 1860. With the development of that commerce, the house of Dalgety, Blackwood and Co.

has grown *pari passu*, and its transactions have increased in a proportionate scale. Indeed, when we come to look at the magnitude of the business carried on by the various mercantile houses in Melbourne, and at the fluctuations in values, which have occurred during the last thirty years, we cannot avoid being struck by the sound principles by which that business is regulated, and by the caution evinced at times and under circumstances calculated to stimulate a speculative excitement in some instances, and to inspire feelings of mistrust and apprehension of disaster in others. Yet there have been no "wild-cat banks" started, as in the United States, and remarkably few failures of any magnitude, such as have occurred in that country, for example, whenever there has been a temporary arrest of its progress and prosperity. We should not be very far wrong, perhaps, in attributing the circumspection with which business on a large scale is conducted in Melbourne, to the fact that the Scottish element has always been an influential one in financial and mercantile circles; and the Scottish character is proverbial for its wary caution. "In perseverance, in self command, in forethought, in all the virtues which conduce to success in life," writes Macaulay, "the Scots have never been surpassed." And this eulogy has been fully justified by the career of hundreds of prosperous Scotsmen in the Australian colonies. The firm under notice has exemplified in its rise and progress, the valuable qualities spoken of by the eminent historian, and has secured public confidence by its commercial ability and integrity. Combining the functions of a financial agency with those of an ordinary mercantile house, dealing in money as well as in merchandise, and extending its operations over a very wide area, it is probably one of the best known firms in the Australasian colonies. It makes advances upon stock and station property, as also on the produce entrusted to it for shipment to Europe. It does a large import business; and if some of our politicians and so-called statesmen had had the advantage of a year or two's training, as book-keepers, in such an office as that of Messrs. Dalgety, Blackwood and Co., they would have gained such an insight into the arcana of exchange, and the sources of national wealth, as might have prevented them from committing such egregious blunders as have been perpetrated by the adoption of a system of protection on the one hand, and a policy destructive of the pastoral interest on the other. They would have learned how our exports are paid for by imports, and would perceive that to check these, is to lessen those; that the production of wool is an industry which should be encouraged and not repressed; and that all classes are interested in turning the grazing land of the colony to the best advantage, while making every reasonable provision for the free growth and expansion of agriculture. Moreover, they would have discovered, by familiarity with the widely-ramified transactions of a large firm like this, that capital, instead of being the enemy of industry, as it is commonly represented to be by lazy and penniless demagogues, is a great creative and fertilising instrument, and that the more peaceful and secure the condition of society in any country, the cheaper and more abundant does it become. The firm under notice has its head office in London, while it is represented by branches and agencies throughout the whole of the Australasian colonies.

THE APOLLO STEARINE CANDLE COMPANY, LIMITED.

Amongst the many representative and flourishing industries of Victoria, the Apollo Stearine Candle Company is certainly entitled to take first rank. Its marked development, under difficulties which were at first apparently insuperable, reflects credit upon the enterprise and perseverance of the proprietors. Though we are staunch believers in freedom, both abstract and concrete, and specifically in the doctrine of free trade, we cannot, without being ungenerous, withhold our praise of the success, so marked, which has attended the practical exercise of opposite principles in the case of the Apollo Stearine Candle Company. We recognise, in the steady and progressive advancement of this company, an advantage considerably more than ordinary to the commercial interests of Australia. The first advantage is the permanent value which is given to a product which, from the length of time that it has been acclimatised, may now almost be said to have become indigenous. But a few short years ago, and tallow was an article for which there was, comparatively speaking, no local market. How to dispose of this commodity, except by export, was a question which any tallow-melter at one time would have found difficult to answer. This difficulty ceased to exist with the commencement of the Apollo Stearine Candle Company. The pastoral interests of Australia owe to this company a debt of gratitude that it is not easy to pay, for, through them, an article at one time comparatively difficult of disposal, has become a profitable production; and the consumers of candles, by the large operations of this company, are ensured an ample supply of a first-class article, free from the fluctuations in prices consequent upon lower stocks and speculation. There is no reason why we should not, in time, do a large export trade with England in the various products manufactured from tallow. The industry only requires efficient devglopment. The past history of the Apollo Company assures us that they will not let the grass grow under their feet, and to them we look to create this export trade with the mother-country, which, in time, must become a trade of great importance to the pastoral interests of Victoria and the sister colonies. Considering the factor that Australia is one of the great vantage grounds of tallow, the extent of pastoral resources being second to none in the world, we hope to see, through the instrumentality of the Apollo Company, a thriving and extensive export trade in candles carried on both with England and India.

The Apollo Company is of purely Victorian origin. The headquarters of the company are in Melbourne. The principal factory is at Footscray, on the Saltwater River, and it has branch factories at Pyrmont, Sydney; at Stanley-street, Brisbane; and an agency at Adelaide. The present consumption of tallow is upwards of 3500 tons annually, which is purchased in the markets of Queensland, New South Wales, Victoria, and South Australia.

Since the company commenced work, it has turned out about 8000 tons, equal to 720,000 boxes, of candles, and its present out-turn is over 176,000 boxes annually. Of course, this is susceptible of a large increase, and we are glad to say that the company is extending its plant, so as to be equal to the largest demand. The yearly payment in wages amounts to over £14,000. This does not include the extensive direct and incidental employment given to numerous other industries.

The utilisation of all by-products is not lost sight of by the company. Machinery has been purposely erected to refine chemically pure glycerine, one of the component parts of tallow. The Apollo glycerine has already an extensive sale throughout the colony. It is exclusively used by the Australian Lithofracteur Company for the manufacture of their explosive compounds. This by-product is also utilised by the Apollo Company themselves, in the manufacture of their various transparent glycerine soaps, in which a large and increasing trade is carried on. The company are the sole Australian makers of this excellent specialty, and may be called the pioneers of this industry in the southern hemisphere.

The oleate, or oleic acid, is by far the largest residue of the tallow after the extraction of stearine. The profitable disposal of this by-product was an important problem to the company. But it was long before it was solved. The great difficulty encountered in the disposal of oleic acid has now been partly overcome by the enterprise and energy of the proprietors. The company has introduced an entirely new Continental process for the manufacture of household and wool-scouring soaps from this oil, which has proved very successful. The soaps thus made are not only of superior quality, being strongly detergent, but are also sold at a lower price than the ordinary household soaps which are made from tallow. These latter they are rapidly superseding. The soft and hard soaps made specially for wool-scouring are stated to possess the valuable property of cleaning the wool without diminishing its weight, a feature which results from the soap being made exclusively from tallow oil, which possesses a natural affinity for the yolk of the wool.

The gradual growth of the soap business, and of other branch trades that may be created through the Australian consumption of tallow, may collaterally be developed into an importance only second to tallow itself.

The company does not confine itself to the manufacture of ordinary stearine candles. It is equally *au fait* in the making of every other description of candle used. If an altar candle be wanted, of any size, or any kind of fancy and coloured candles, made of the most varied material, such as paraffin, wax, spermaceti, &c., the Apollo Company can readily supply the want. Their stock ranges from the largest and most ornate altar candle to the small coloured taper that adorned the Christmas trees of our childhood, and which we now see adorning the Christmas trees of our children.

The distance of the head factory from the Melbourne office is about four miles. They are connected with each other by special telegraph wire, and by telephone. There is no cessation of work, day or night. The machinery never flags. At night the factory is lighted up with gas, manufactured on the premises. In addition to this gas there is the bright electric light produced by means of the Gramme machine, which, we believe, is the only one in the whole of Australia. This machine has been in use, night after night, for more than two years, and may be seen by visitors, with the permission of the manager.

We may mention that, in addition to colonial awards, the company obtained a bronze medal at Philadelphia, in 1876; a silver medal at Paris (the home of the stearine industry), two years afterwards; and has but recently been awarded the first prize, in Sydney, for soap and candles.

In taking leave of the Apollo Company, we heartily wish them every and all the success they so richly deserve, trusting that they will ever, as they have been, be in the van of Australian development, and that their practical motto will still be, "Advance Australia."

THE NATIONAL MUTUAL LIFE ASSOCIATION.

One of the most remarkable features of the nineteenth century is the gradual recognition that equal advantages are due to those who organise a beneficial institution as to those who are its supporters, and that no undue advantage should be exacted from either, but that as near an approach should be made as possible to strict and impartial justice to each. Those associations which are established by gentlemen on the basis named, no matter for what object, must commend themselves to all classes of society, if only on the abstract principle, that they offer to all concerned equal participation in their success. Such principles, when they affect us individually, cannot but be highly appreciated, but when they extend to those nearest and dearest to us in the event of our decease, their good efforts cannot be too highly prized or praised. Often amidst the business of life we are so bent upon the necessity of providing for present existence, as well as upon meeting ever-present liabilities, that we are altogether oblivious of those duties which belong to all men, and which, if not paramount, are certainly of as great importance, viz., to make provision after our death for those who during life have looked upon us as their sole support. All thinking men must have this brought before them almost daily, through the often times absolute destitution which some of their friends, who during the lifetime of the bread-winners have been in comparative affluence, have experienced after their death. It has often happened that, not through indifference, but through procrastination or thoughtlessness, some of these have been left in the very depths of poverty and helplessness. Intelligent and enterprising men recognised this great drawback to the perfect happiness of social and domestic life; and at once set their energies to work to provide means whereby it might be, if not wholly avoided, certainly materially modified. This they did through the medium of life assurance; and its history, since the idea was first started, has been one which, though slowly, has surely progressed year by year, both in the perfection of its principles and the extent of its ramifications through all grades of society. The principles which we have enumerated in the beginning of this chapter gradually obtained amongst the various associations for the assurance of life; but a very perfect development of them was first recognised, and has now been adopted, by the association which is the subject of our present remarks. We were going to say the old-fashioned policy, but as it still obtains in some assurance offices, we prefer to speak of it as present with us—viz., that a policy should be null and void if any premium remained unpaid for the space of thirty days after it was due,—was first recognised as an injustice by the Insurance Commissioners of the State of Massachusetts, who urged upon the legislature the advisability of placing upon their statute-book a law which would prevent the forfeiture of policies, for non-payment of premium, until the policy-holder had been insured for the term equivalent to the value of the premiums previously paid to the office. Mr. J. M. Templeton, who drafted the first prospectus of the National Mutual Life Association, and who had carefully studied the newest beneficial innovations in the system of life assurance, discovered that though the Massachusetts law was an improvement on the old system, yet that, by its operation, the forfeiture of the policy was not prevented, but merely postponed. To him is due the proposition of a principle which, when carried out, places those insured on a much more satisfactory basis than had hitherto prevailed. The idea was that a condition should be inserted in the policies of the National Mutual, which would provide that when default is made in the payment of a premium, the directors shall then pay the premium, and keep the policy in force for the benefit of the person assured, the premium so remaining as a debt against the policy, to be repaid with interest at the rate of 8 per cent. per annum, for the time during which it remains a debt. This proposition was adopted by the gentleman who originated this association, and thus a new and highly commendable era was opened out and adopted by the National Mutual Life Association. Thus was established the first office in the world which introduced into life policies a really effective non-forfeiture clause for the protection of those who may omit to pay their premiums. We need scarcely say, that up to the present time, it has met with the success which it so richly deserves, which is a signal proof of the soundness of its basis, and the equity of its principles. The sole credit for the introduction of this liberal principle into life assurance practice belongs to the gentleman whose name we have already mentioned, viz., Mr. J. M. Templeton, F.I.A., who is the able and enterprising actuary and secretary of the National Mutual Life Association. The following illustration, which we have taken from a neatly-bound, well-printed, and instructive little book, called the *Guide to Melbourne*, which has been printed and published by the National Mutual Life Association, is a striking example of the beneficence of the non-forfeiture principle :—" J. M. assured his life with the National Mutual Life Association, in 1869, and paid his premiums regularly until March, 1877, by which time he had contributed sixteen half-yearly payments, amounting to £97 13s. 4d. Owing, however, to the failure of his crops in three successive years, he was unable to pay any further premiums, and died on 27th April, 1880. Up to that date, six half-yearly premiums had become due, and remained unpaid, but the surrender value was sufficient to keep the policy in force, and at his death his widow received payment of £536 4s. 8d. as under :—

Sum assured		£500 0 0
Bonus additions		76 18 5
		£576 18 5
Less overdue premiums	£36 12 6	
Interest thereon	4 1 3	40 13 9
		£536 4 8

Thus, although no premiums had been paid to the office for three years, the whole of the amount originally assured, and £36 4s. 8d. besides, was paid to the widow."

A feature well worthy of notice, and which we must not omit to mention, is, that the National Mutual Life Association, which was the first mutual office in the colony of Victoria, is conducted on principles which are perfectly in accordance with the true idea of mutual assurance. The rule adopted by the National Mutual, and embodied in the articles of the association, is, that the profits should be divided among the members in proportion to their contribution thereto. The principles of mutual assurance have been strictly observed from and since the first inception of the association, no advantages being given to the first members, who were admitted on exactly the same terms as those upon which new members may now enter.

The National Mutual was established in 1869, and is conducted by the following directorate :—Matthew Lang, who is chairman ; G. D. Carter, Esq., M.P., who is vice-chairman ; and James Fergusson, Esq., J.P. ; the Hon. Edward Langton ; Thomas Moubray, Esq., J.P.; Andrew Newell, Esq.; and M. H. Davies, Esq. The head office is at No. 1 Market Buildings, Collins-street West, Melbourne. The business has now been extended to the following Australian colonies, viz. :—New South Wales, the following gentlemen being directors of this branch : Edward Chisholm, Esq. (Messrs. Brown and Co.), chairman ; D. G. E. Alsop, Esq., of the firm of Messrs. Harbottle, Biddulph, and Alsop ; and A. A. Smith, Esq., who is a well known merchant. The resident secretary is Mr. Henry F. Francis, and the office is at 77 Pitt-street, Sydney. The directors of the South Australian branch are :—The Hon. John Carr, chairman ; Alfred Ballantyne, Esq. ; John Gordon, Esq. ; Wm. Magarey, Esq., M.P. ; and H. C. E. Muecke, Esq., J.P. ; while the resident secretary is Mr. J. C. Minns. The office is in Waymouth-street, Adelaide. The New Zealand branch has the following gentlemen as a directorate, viz.: Edward Pearce, Esq., J.P., chairman ; Hon. P. A. Buckley, M.L.C. ; R. M. Greenfield, Esq. ; Wm. H. Levin, Esq., M.H.R. ; and James Smith, Esq. The office is at Temple Chambers, Featherston-street, Wellington, where Mr. Thomas Swain, the resident secretary, is to be found.

The following annual report of the directors will fully substantiate all we have said. It was presented at the eleventh annual general meeting of the members, which was held on Thursday, the 18th November, 1880 :—

DURING THE YEAR

3446 proposals for assurance have been received, amounting to	£876,102 0 0
1065 of these were declined or not completed, amounting to	301,065 0 0

LEAVING

2381 proposals for which policies were issued, amounting to	575,037 0 0
101 proposals for endowments were also received, all of which were accepted, and policies issued, amounting to	12,550 0 0

THERE WERE, THEREFORE,

2482 new policies issued during the year, amounting to	587,587 0 0

UPON WHICH

The new annual premiums amount to	18,989 18 6
Two annuities for the sum of £60 0s. 9d. have been granted during the year, the consideration for which amounted to £350	
36 deaths have occurred, involving claims to the amount of	9,650 15 2
After providing for all expenses and claims, the total funds at the close of the year amounted to	129,698 4 6
The annual income of the Association now amounts to	£67,295 12 10

An important special feature of the association is that of allowing all its members to pay their premiums at minimum rates. The following extract from the little book to which we have already referred may explain this principle succinctly and clearly: "Careful inquiry is made by the directors before accepting proposals for life assurance, and every case is decided on its merits." Should a proposal be accepted at a higher rate of premium than the ordinary rate for age, the proposer will have the option of paying the premium at the ordinary rate for age according to the tables; his policy will then be endorsed with a contingent debt equal to the present value of the extra premium sought to be charged. This debt will be deducted from the sum assured, if the member die under the average age, but if he attain the average age, the debt will be expunged, and he will then be precisely in the same position as if he had, in the first instance, been accepted without any addition. By the operation of this feature, no member is under the necessity of paying an extra premium throughout life, on account of some physical defect, which he may outgrow, or some circumstance of family history, which may never affect him. A no less important characteristic of the association is the liberality in settlement of claims. As there are no shareholders to share in its profits, interests adverse to policy-holders cannot possibly arise, the directors simply occupying the position of arbitrators between the members, with no inducement to take from one or give to another.

The progress of the National Mutual, since its establishment, is a good illustration of the old Scotch saying, "Creep before ye gang," and in this respect it forms a striking contrast to that of other offices. The National Mutual, at its inception, had no capital. It was established absolutely without funds, depending entirely upon the soundness of the grand principle of Mutual Life Assurance—viz., that if the premiums charged be sufficient to provide the sums assured under policies, then no capital is necessary. The expenditure, in the early years, was necessarily small, for the directors recognised the necessity of saving, and profitably investing, as large a proportion as possible of the premiums received. Their object was to make a good, substantial, foundation for the office, which nothing could shake; and, therefore, they would not spend more money, in seeking new business, than they had in hand available for the purpose. Thus proper reserves were made out of every year's receipts, and the interests of members were not endangered by the efforts made to introduce new members.

During the first five years, the business transacted, and the amount of funds accumulated, were as follow:—

Year.	No. of Policies Issued.	Amount Assured.	Funds Invested.
1869-70	202	£85,400	£781 3 5
1870-71	94	32,450	2,283 18 2
1871-72	161	60,670	3,873 4 11
1872-73	289	92,780	8,585 17 11
1873-74	395	108,200	15,464 16 6

At the end of this period, the first investigation was made, when it was found that a large surplus existed, and the sum of £3098 13s. 4d. was divided among the members, who thus reaped the advantage of a prudent and economical management. The members then had the right, if they chose, to take their bonuses in cash, and some of them did so, but the majority preferred to leave them to accumulate in the hands of the Association. The National Mutual is the only mutual office in the Australian colonies which paid cash bonuses so early as its sixth year. Owing partly to the profitable results of the first five years, and partly to the larger funds available for expenditure in extending the business, the increase in the next three years was most striking, especially in that immediately following the bonus year.

BUSINESS OF THE THREE YEARS FORMING THE SECOND PERIOD.

Year.	No. of Policies Issued.	Amount Assured.	Funds Invested.
1874-75	... 1023 ...	£270,722 ...	£22,768 8 10
1875-76	... 672 ...	161,000 ...	33,159 15 10
1876-77	... 818 ...	202,250 ...	53,470 8 10

As it had been arranged that, after the first five years, the investigations and divisions of profits should be triennial, the second investigation was now held, when the sum of £10,000 was divided among the members, and a further sum of £1900 was reserved for the cost of establishing branch offices in the other colonies, so as to carry out the intentions of the promoters that the association should be for the whole of Australasia.

During the next period, the extension of the business was prosecuted vigorously, and the office at once advanced to a front position, as regards the new business transacted.

BUSINESS OF THE THREE YEARS FORMING THE THIRD PERIOD.

Year.	No. of Policies Issued.	Amount Assured.	Funds Invested.
1877-78	... 1008 ...	£245,565 ...	£71,210 9 11
1878-79	... 2291 ...	488,420 ..	95,210 16 10
1879-80	... 2482 ...	587,587 ...	129,698 4 6

The new business of the last (the eleventh) year, was 60 per cent. greater than the average annual new business of offices doing business in the United Kingdom of Great Britain and Ireland, although most of them had been over forty years in existence, and transacted business over a much wider and more populous area.

The following table illustrates the progress of the association, during the three investigation periods :—

Term.	Total Premiums Received.			Claims and Surrenders.			Saved and Invested.			Profit Divided.		
	£	s.	d.	£	s.	d.	£	s.	d.	£	s.	d.
1st Period (5 years)	28,671	0	10	3,282	7	11	15,464	16	9	3,098	13	4
2nd ,, (3 years)	71,935	3	10	22,408	4	5	38,005	12	1	10,000	0	0
3rd ,, (3 years)	128,682	0	8	28,587	7	7	76,227	15	8	Not ascertained.		
Total	229,288	5	4	54,277	19	11	129,698	4	6	Not ascertained.		

The third investigation is now proceeding, and the members may fairly expect that it will result in further augmentation of the amounts of their policies.

In conclusion, we may add that the National Mutual Life Association is notable in the civic history of the colony, as having been the first mutual life office established in Victoria, as also the first in the world to introduce the principle of applying the surrender value of a policy in payment of the premiums when default is made by the holder of it, thus keeping the policy alive until the surrender value is exhausted.

HENRY P. WELCH AND COMPANY.

The facilities which the present age offers to purchasers of imported manufactures of Continental and English make, through the highly systematical and well organised condition of some of the leading commission houses in Melbourne, are indeed great. So complete is the representation of these, that merchant, squatter, and farmer has the opportunity presented, almost at his door, of viewing every conceivable line of goods manufactured for and used in the colonies, with almost the same despatch which introduces them to the world, from the showroom of the manufacturer. It is a most irrefutable sign of the progress which is fast belting our vast colony of Australia, that we, 12,000 miles away from the door of the manufacturer, offer his wares at almost an identical period at which they are offered at home. We clearly see the indefatigable energy of the Melbourne merchant at work in this, to promote the welfare of his country, and likewise, that of himself. So restless is this spirit of enterprise in him, that the merchant of to-day realises that he can only do the business of his constituents satisfactorily by keeping a resident partner at home. We need scarcely say that the business of this resident partner is to be ever watching the productions of the home market, and secure to the colonies the best of these productions—those most servicable to the geographical grandeur as well as the peculiarity of its construction—with the utmost despatch possible. The statement would have been subjected to ridicule some fifty years ago, if one had ventured to suggest that he could stand in the showroom, or office, of a Melbourne merchant, and without changing positions, could survey surroundings embracing anything from a *needle* to an *anchor*, which he could order and have in Melbourne within sixty days from time of order. Nevertheless, the telegraph on the one hand, swift steamer communication on the other, and colonial enterprise to cement the two, have placed all these advantages within the reach of every one of us. Of the firms who make special effort and have complete facilities for the accomplishment of this business, Messrs. Henry P. Welch and Co. rank as one of the foremost. So large and so varied is the nature of the agencies which culminate in their showrooms in Queen-street, that almost anything of whatever nature, may either be bought there or indented with the least possible delay. The ostensible business of this firm is that of commission merchants and importers. They indent largely every conceivable kind of merchandise, and especially do they give particular attention to all kinds of mining and agricultural machinery. The extensive accommodation which their warehouse in Queen-street supplies, enables them to keep a very large line of those bulky, but useful, appliances, so necessary to our agricultural and pastoral development, and as such, to the steady development of our wealth. These accommodations are further augmented by a yard for the erection and storage of machinery situated in Moray-street, on Yarra Bank. So numerous indeed are the agencies that this firm represent, that their business has come to be principally that of acting as agents for British, American, foreign, and colonial manufacturers, receiving consignments of their various productions and manufatures, and offering them to the colonial trade with a view to permanently establish relations between the Australasian colonies, and these foreign houses. The successful manner in which they have managed this business may be judged from the long list of names which are enumerated in their advertisements and for whom they act. In addition to this already large list, its length is becoming steadily augmented; and we could ask for no better proof of the manner in which they conduct their business, both to client and agent, than this. Through the residence of the senior member of the firm, Mr. Henry P. Welch, in London, at 78 Lombard-street, E.C., who, by the way, is thoroughly equipped with a knowledge of every Australian want, constant accessions of samples are being received by the Melbourne house, from which the trade is thoroughly canvassed for indent orders. But, notwithstanding this, their business is not confined exclusively to lines they represent; on the contrary, transactions are frequently consummated on lines quite outside their ordinary business. It would take far too much of our space to attempt to record all the different manufactures and wares that this firm are agents for, but we will state some of them for the benefit of our readers. They comprise:—ales, wines, spirits of various kinds, building materials, contractors' ironmongery, cement (Portland), china (both rich and common), earthenware, glassware, cutlery, chromos, oleographs, essences, perfumery, electroplated ware, fencing, fencing wire, floor cloths, galvanised iron, gates (iron) of handsome design for garden entrance and fields, hollowware, general Birmingham ware, hops and malt, iron and steel; pig, bar, rod, and other irons; printing and writing materials, and stationery, of all kinds; marble flooring, lamp ware of various kinds, leather belting for machinery; oils, paints and varnishes, and putty; oilmen's stores, plaster of Paris, pianofortes, steel shutters for dwellings, shops, &c.; scales, and weighing machines, from half ounce to ten tons; toys, fancy goods; window glass, sheet and plate of all descriptions; whiting, &c., &c., &c.

These goods are either represented by stock or sample, at the Queen-street establishment. The firm's relation with foreign houses also presents the advantage of constant receipt of novelties, and specialties, for offer to the colonial trade. They also act as agents for absentees for the purchase and disposal of property in the colonies. In addition to the very many articles we have enumerated for which they act as agents, their extensive connection among station owners and farmers has given them increased facilities for perfecting their relations with every class of machinery manufactured in the mother-country. For example, their line of farmers' and selectors' machinery is most comprehensive and complete, embracing everything from the clearing and ploughing of land, to the threshing of wheat, and for which they have received honourable mentions at the different agricultural shows. The same may be said of their line of machinery suitable to squatters, and finally their pumping and mining machinery. Regarding this last line, the item of *steel wire rope* seems to take prominent place. The signal success which has attended the application of this rope in mining in place of the old flaxen or hemp rope, has now established not only its economy in point of cost in the long run, but also its economy in the loss of life, which last fact should recommend it to universality in employment, and doubtless will, when its efficacy becomes known. In conclusion, we must not omit to mention that the firm issues a finely illustrated catalogue of all its principal wares, which contains some very valuable information for those who use machinery largely. This catalogue may be had upon application, and posted to any part of the colony.

MESSRS. PATERSON, LAING AND BRUCE.

The gigantic strides made by Melbourne, during its short existence, must be a matter for wonder to every man of practical experience. Extravagance of language, in speaking of commerce or trade, may appear, to the business man, as fulsome or unnecessary, because impracticable; but no other style is commensurate with a true descriptive narrative of the individual success of some of the merchants of Melbourne, as well as of the city itself. Plain Saxon may convey a superficial idea, which neither strikes nor arrests the attention; and where the history of a city has extended over centuries, and its present wealth has been amassed by gradual growth, and as a natural result of time, it may be perfectly appropriate; but we wish to deliver, to the old world, a true and faithful description of this new country, with its palatial cities of rapid growth, and we must not hesitate, in order that we may do justice, to use those words which will be the truest reflection of the results which have

S

been created by the almost boundless enterprise, and astonishing energy, of men whose history is the history of Melbourne, or the colony itself. There is no branch of commerce, or trade, which has not been pursued with success by most of those who have embarked therein their fortunes and their time during their sojourn in Australia. This is common to every colony, and to every principal town, and also, we might say, to every man of energy; it is not, as in the old country, peculiar to a certain class of individuals, or a certain class of large towns. The business man in England, who could never aspire beyond the line of mediocrity, no sooner sets his foot on the shores of the new country than he seems to be a changed man; so much so, that, instead of seeking that mediocrity of success which would have contented him at home, he makes that point itself the first start of his career, and his progress is so rapid that, in a few years, he is a wonder to those who have known him all his life, and more than all a wonder to himself. Is it that he has thrown off the trammels of English prejudice, or that here he sees virgin fields of enterprise and wealth, whose bounds stretch so far that they are more imagined than felt, and where he feels that unfettered freedom which is only limited by the fact that it is not unlicensed? or is it that the air, the climate, or the soil, unloose the chains which have hitherto fettered his latent powers, powers that only required new fields and pastures, that they might in developing themselves develop the country of their adopted home? The individual men who, in the old world, have made themselves a name by reaching the pinnacle of success through a sea of difficulty, may be almost counted on the fingers; but such a history seems common to every merchant or tradesman who, possessing energy and perseverance, makes Australia the field of their display. It has occurred to us that the flower of the commercial world of England may have migrated to these distant shores, and hence the universal history of success which belongs to so many of Melbourne's leading men. For we must remember that, with regard to the greater part, they have, unhelped except by their own talents, been the builders up of their own fortunes. They have had the luck or foresight to seize on every opportunity, to heed the smallest advantage and turn it to profit, and to see the actual and possible demand, and to provide the necessary supply of the demand as it existed and the demand which was likely to rise. Sharpened by trusting to their own resources, they have been enabled to cope with every possible and almost impossible difficulty, until at last they have made difficulties subservient to them, in the place of being subservient to difficulties. They have established their own fortunes, and the foundation of businesses that will be the pillars of the commercial future of Australia. They have found, unearthed, and utilised the wealth that is destined, at no distant future, to make Australia *facile princeps* amongst the nations of the world. The same features of success that are peculiar to those who engage in pastoral, agricultural, or money interest, are peculiar to those who engage in commerce or trade, no matter what branch of that commerce or trade it may be. The record of their success is the history of the wool merchant, the grain merchant, the hardware merchant, and the soft-goods merchant, and it is in this latter branch that Messrs. Paterson, Laing and Bruce have achieved such splendid success from such comparatively small beginnings. We ask our readers' attention while we exemplify all that we have said in our prefatory remarks, by a short history of the firm under notice.

In the year 1850, Mr. J. C. Young commenced business in Geelong, with a stock of £3000 and a staff of four all told. In 1851, just one year after this, circumstances arose which proved a check to the advance of their business. Gold having been discovered in New South Wales, Geelong was almost denuded of its population by the rush which was made to the newly discovered goldfields. Fortunately, this was destined to be in a great measure counterbalanced by a similar discovery in Ballarat. The depression gradually gave place to tenfold more prosperity in proportion, and Mr. J. C. Young was not slow to take advantage of the favourable crisis. In 1852, he engaged Mr. Paterson to take charge of a branch which, under his management, flourished successfully. But it was not until 1854 that the decisive increase of business required increased business accommodation; and with a man of Mr. Young's energy, the necessity had but to arise, to be at once met. He forthwith erected a new warehouse, and immediately after Mr. Palmer entered the concern as book-keeper. Another season of depression ensued, but it simply stimulated to further energy. Mr. Young, after his return from England, at once resolved to move his business to Melbourne, and no sooner saw the opportune moment, than he carried his intention into practice. Mr. Paterson was at this time taken into partnership, and the firm, as then constituted, started business at the corner of Flinders Lane and Russell-street, under the style of J. C. Young and Co. This was in the year 1856. The value of the stock at that time was estimated at £25,000, and the number of hands about sixteen. The business at once became successful, both as to amount and profit; and two years afterwards, the strength of the firm was increased by the admission of Mr. Palmer. On the retirement of Mr. Young, in 1860, the business was purchased by Messrs. Paterson and Palmer. These gentlemen having, at the same time, purchased the business of Ray, Glaister and Co., and taken in Mr. Briscoe Ray as partner, the two establishments were amalgamated under the style of Paterson, Ray, Palmer and Co. It was at this time that they removed from Russell-street to Flinders Lane West, opposite to Gibbs, Bright and Co. Mr. J. R. Bailey was about this time associated with the firm and subsequently entered as partner. It was at this period of the firm's existence, that the most decisive move was made to meet the growing requirements of the business. It was found that the rapid development had outgrown what had then become far from adequate premises for the business transactions of the firm. Thus, the necessity once more arising, the energy of the new firm was equal to the occasion, and the result was the erection of the present magnificent warehouses. We regret that the pride and pleasure with which the firm must have seen the gradual rise of their palatial premises was considerably modified by the premature, because unexpected, death of Mr. Bailey, who had taken a most active part in the construction. The history of the firm was one of advancement, and a dissolution took place in 1876, when Mr. Paterson purchased the interests of his partners. He was then joined by Mr. J. P. Laing, a gentleman who had retired, some years previously, from the well-known firm of Laing and Webster, and subsequently by Mr. John M. Bruce, who had previously been a partner of Mr. Laing's, and for many years the resident partner of Messrs. George Webster and Co., formerly Laing and Webster, and under whose management that business had been a grand success. The firm was then altered to Paterson, Laing and Bruce, under whose auspices the business increased so as to necessitate an extension of the premises, which was done by putting on an additional story, thus completing what is one of the largest and grandest warehouses in Australia. The trouble occasioned by this change was indeed great. Thus the basis has been laid of one of those great and increasing houses of commerce, which we have no doubt is destined to be, in the future, one of the pillars of strength of the reputation of Melbourne as a flourishing centre of commerce. At present, the firm carries on a trade as soft-goods merchants, which, if not more extensive, is certainly second to no other house in that branch in the whole of Australia.

On our visit to the premises, we were courteously conducted through the large warehouse of the firm, and during our stay we noted some of the leading features both of the building and the stock. The building itself would be an architectural ornament to any city, and in Melbourne, as a warehouse, it stands pre-eminent. Its stately proportions attract the eye of the visitor on his first visit to Melbourne. The basement of the building, which is 110 feet by 100 feet, is used as a receiving and despatching room for bulk packages. Adjoining this, is the entering room, which is divided into three compartments, viz., town, suburban and country, and intercolonial. The rest of the basement is occupied with Manchester goods, consisting of calicoes, blankets, flannels, &c., &c. Here wen oticed three hydraulic lifts which run right through the building. On the ground floor are woollens, clothing, hats, caps, and the finer classes of Manchester goods. It is worthy of remark that the whole of the clothing sold by them is manufactured by the firm in the city. The first floor comprises a large stock of white regatta shirts, ties, scarfs, belts, braces, hosiery, gloves, &c., of every style, make, and variety, the better class of white shirts being made by the firm's employés. On the same floor, are Bradford manufactured goods, also French merinoes, silks, and silk mixed goods of every description, as well as ribbons comprising all degrees of shade, colour and quality. In the ladies' department, we were struck with the admirable taste and elegance with which all the goods were arranged, as well as with the goods themselves, comprising mantles, shawls, underclothing, &c. On the second floor, were French and English millinery, gloves, feathers, plumes, straw hats, and bonnets, of the very latest fashion, as well as umbrellas, parasols, plain and fancy haberdashery, vases, pictures, &c. The third floor comprises a package floor for bulk and bonded goods for package trade. The advantage of this one floor is that it greatly facilitates the work of the firm in dealing with bonded goods for home consumption and the intercolonial trade, there being a Customs officer continually on the premises. The building runs through from Flinders Lane to within 100 feet of Collins-street, and covers an area of half-an-acre. There are eight commercial travellers constantly employed by the firm throughout the colonies, and they now employ about 100 hands. There are also, in addition, large yard accommodation for carts, stables, &c., an outbuilding of brick for additional bulk packages as they are delivered from the various steamers. We must not omit to draw attention to the splendidly-illustrated catalogue, which may be had from the firm on application, and which contains a large variety of information regarding the business and stock. The firm have also a branch in London, at 7 and 8 Australian Avenue, where all purchases are made, and from which all goods for the firm are shipped to Australia.

DE CASTELLA AND ROWAN.

The cultivation of the vine in Victoria is destined at no distant day to be second only to the pastoral resources of the colony. Victoria possesses all the requirements of a wine-growing country, which we doubt not each successive year will confirm. It has all the advantages which climate, cheapness of land, and great productiveness offer. There is no necessity for manure; the wood for the support of the vines is cheap, and there is a general absence of spring frosts. Even with manual labour so much more expensive here than in Europe, if we consider that food costs us a fourth of what it costs there, and also the reduced cost of land, the price of cultivation in Victoria, all operations being carefully performed, can be set down at £6 per acre in the cool, and £5 in the warm districts, where much less weeding is necessary. The possession of these desiderata make it a source of wealth that only requires the impetus of supply and demand. The cause of its present undevelopment is simply want of market. There are two conditions absolutely necessary to obviate this want. The first is large supplies; the second, wine merchants abroad, and increased consumption in the colonies, whereby those supplies may be exhausted. The first condition can only be met by an increase of our plantations, the attraction of skilled labour from the old wine countries, and a continued improvement of our vintages. There is at present a scarcity of wine in Europe, through the ravages of the phylloxera, and if large supplies be grown here, the second and important condition will be surely realised through the demand that this scarcity will insure.

Victoria, perhaps, better than all the Australian colonies, can grow all the varieties that the world produces. The liqueur wines, the strong wines of Spain and Portugal, on the Murray, and other warm regions; the hocks, sauternes, and clarets of France and Germany, in the many temperate localities south of the Dividing Ranges. It is these latter kind which daily gain ground in the markets of Europe, and which are, at the same time, most diminished by the phylloxera. Victoria, on account of its climate, can produce these wines better than either of the other colonies, the Cape, California, or even than the French colony of Algiers. The consumption of claret has increased in all countries. In England alone it has increased by nearly two million gallons during a decade of years. The demand for sherry has decreased proportionately. Many large vineyards have already been established in Victoria, amongst them that of St. Hubert's, the property of Messrs. de Castella and Rowan, is the largest in Australia, and an example of the enterprise of our colonists. In a compact block of 210 acres of vines are found the Sauvignon of Bordeaux, the Pineau of Burgundy, the Chasselas of Fontainebleau, which produces a delicious wine, and the Hermitage, and the Reisling of the Rhine. All these wines have the truly distinctive bouquet, and preserve, in every respect, the character of their origin. The vineyards, kept with all the care bestowed upon the most celebrated ones in Europe, are supplemented by extensive cellars in the centre of the city of Melbourne, where an excellent management bids fair to prove, by the success already attained by the St. Hubert's wines in the colony and abroad, the prosperous future which is in store for Victorian wines.

It was acknowledged in an article in the *Moniteur Vinicole*, during the Paris Exhibition, that the only possible wines which might rival those of France were the wines of Australia, which had all the character of French wines, and which were of good class and daily used. The St. Hubert's vineyard alone had sent 150 dozen, which was partly sold to the inquiring public, but for the most part offered as samples of Victorian wines. It is to the temperate climate of the vicinity of Melbourne, to the climate of the Upper Yarra especially, that this commendation of our light wines was due.

The Australian wines have already gained prizes at several exhibitions, especially at Vienna and Paris. One secret of their future success will be as we have said, the increased consumption by the Australians themselves. The difference in climate in the different colonies of Australia demands that there should be an interchange of the commodity to suit the different conditions of climate. For example, the heavy wines produced in South Australia could be beneficially drunk by Victorians, and the light wines which are produced to such perfection in Victoria would admirably suit those living in a climate like South Australia.

We may here ask—what would be the result if the vine were cultivated extensively in Victoria and other Australian colonies where, as a rule, every produce soon oversteps the demand? Would the wine remain an encumbrance in the hands of the grower? It is scarcely probable! We are daily brought nearer to the mother-country, and not only the markets of England can be ours, but those of all northern Europe. A limited production can never ensure an extensive reputation. Extensive commerce will only be attracted by extensive markets. The better the market is supplied the more widely it becomes known; special excellence in the goods offered, which shows diligent care, and scientific skill, will surely in time be remunerated by ever increasing demand.

MESSRS. W. H. ROCKE AND CO.

It is a matter of curious and interesting speculation to trace the improvements in the comforts of life from their first humble and crude beginning to the elegancies and requirements which characterise the comforts of the 19th century. To indulge in this speculation in any part of Europe, we must have recourse for assistance to the records of history. This, of course, has a great interest for those who, in tracing through the pages of history the gradual growth of the countries of the world, note how closely the comforts of life have followed in the rear of civilisation. The greater and more perfect in artistic taste are the various articles and designs which make up what we understand by the luxuries and comforts of life, the more developed is the refinement of the civilisation which a nation possesses. We could almost divine a nation's history, if the data which comprised the rise and progress of its existence consisted of nothing else than a detailed account of the first introduction of necessary conveniences, and the various stages of their gradual development into the refinements, real comforts and luxuries of life. But how much deeper is the interest, how much greater is the pleasure, when from our own personal experience, and within the span of our own lives, or even from the personal experience of others, we in the former case watch, and in the latter case listen to every detail of a young nation's history—we may say from the very beginning of a new country through the whole up to our own day. How the first settlers were satisfied with the rudest structures and the rudest furniture, as well as with the rudest embellishments. How, when their worldly wealth increased, these were removed for something better, and with the advance of years and increasing worldly circumstances, their comforts merely for their own sake were compatible with their increased riches; until after the lapse of years, the desire of comforts for their own sake was supplanted with the desire of comforts for the sake of appearance. How the progress was sometimes steady, sometimes spasmodic; and how, at last, it reached that stage which placed them on a level with those countries of the old world which first gave them birth. This has all happened in the various colonies of Australia within as many decades as have taken centuries in the countries on the other side of the line. It has all happened, and been personally experienced by many old colonists who are still living, and who narrate their early experiences with such graphic force and truth that you feel you are almost an eye-witness of all they themselves saw and experienced; and you are unwittingly carried away by their enthusiasm to feel the same deep personal interest as is felt by the various speaking historians of this New Atlantis. This peep behind the curtain of the past of Australia, enables you to imagine, very fairly, what will be ultimately realised as you look through the imaginary vista of the future. The population increased; no space of land without a native or European ownership; the federation of the colonies, followed in time by independence, with a thrilling future history of miraculous development in art, science, commerce, trade, and industry, and a universal brotherhood amongst men. This is no utopian view of Australia's future, it is all within the range not only of possibility, but even within the range of probability; and though we may not live to see its realisation, we will see signs of the times that will be convincing proofs that they can only be followed by, because they will be the sure precursors of, all that has been prognosticated. We have great faith in the innate powers of Australian colonists, and we have also great faith in the inexhaustible wealth that yet lies hid in the various interests which have already made a reputation for Australia throughout the world. One interesting feature, which in this chapter we propose to trace, in the comforts of life, is the beginning of the use of furniture by the earliest settlers, and to trace it up to our day when the houses of the colonists may, with respect to their furniture, be favourably compared both in artistic taste and design, as well as quality and durability, with the best furnished houses of the United Kingdom. We purpose quoting largely from the catalogue of Messrs. W. H. Rocke and Co., who have probably the most extensive and elegant stock of first-class furniture, as well as carpets and general furnishings, that are to be found in the whole of Australia. Their furniture comprises every variety of style and design, and the very latest novelties in drawing, dining, library, and bed-room furniture, as well as pier glasses and cabinets. Few changes have been experienced by the firm since the year

1845, when part of the present warehouse was erected and business was begun. Owing to the crude state of society in Melbourne at this early period of its history, the furniture used was of a very primitive and common kind, having no pretence whatever to grace or symmetry of form. In most residences in the bush furniture was almost unknown; in the place of chairs and tables rude stakes were driven into the earthen floor, and to form the seat or top a decorative slab of bark was nailed. Bedroom furniture, though somewhat after the same style, was, in a few respects, a little more refined; washstand and toilet being comprised of empty cases piled on top of one another, and to shed a lustre over the scene bottles took the place of candlesticks to hold the lights. But Melbourne was progressing; and in course of time the now well-known colonial sofa and cedar-bottom chair came into fashion. As people began to settle on the lands, a greater demand for furniture began to spring up; and Messrs. W. H. Rocke and Co. were equal to the occasion. A good brick building (which in those days was considered a magnificent structure) was erected, and their present business at this time found its first great impetus. Speculation as to the real wants of the people, convinced the firm that it was now time to import largely from the mother-country. They first began to import iron bedsteads, cane chairs, and other kinds of furnishing, suitable to the increased requirements of the people. Catering so ably for the wants of their customers, was the basis of their grand success in business. A new era now commences. Suddenly the country was thrown into a state of wild excitement; gold had been discovered, and the colony, which is now known as Victoria, became transformed from a quiet grazing country into a genuine Eldorado. Tens of thousands of the human race swarmed into the golden land, in pursuit of its treasure; and Hobson's Bay, from its hitherto quiet lake-like appearance and sleepy peace, became thronged with the shipping of the nations of the world. Though gold became a quick and prolific source of wealth, rapid fortunes were also made in the various businesses which were necessary to provide for this enormous influx of population; and it was then that Melbourne, as it is at present, first commenced to advance and take its position as the largest and most important town, not only of Victoria, but in the whole of Australia. The furnishing trade naturally became very prosperous; and when the fever of the gold excitement had somewhat abated, cabinet-makers, who had been drawn hither by the glitter, settled down to their usual occupation. Though at this time, all the principal furniture came direct from Europe, the medium and commoner kinds were largely made in Melbourne. The result was that this important industry gradually took its legitimate position among the other industries of the colony. Year after year, trade of all kinds increased, and grew into vast proportions; and it was in the year 1860 that Melbourne may be said to have been at the height of her prosperity. Ten years later still, things were progressing so rapidly that, to provide for the increasing wants of the colony, in the way of furnishing, the present warehouse of W. H. Rocke and Co., was completed. The principal member of the firm made a lengthened visit to Europe, in order to purchase furniture and furnishing of the greatest variety, taste, and design, which, upon arrival in Victoria, found immediate sale. In 1877, Mr. Rocke again visited Europe, there to purchase novelties in furniture, as well as to secure designs, and engage artists, and various skilled workmen. Mr. Rocke's object in doing this was to push forward and guide the naturally gifted and forward artisans engaged by the firm. Extensive strides were made in the manufacture of furniture, and the wealthy classes found it more to their advantage to purchase all their requirements in art, and other furnishings, in Victoria, than run the risk of the danger or damage and expense (and the heavy duty) attendant upon importing for themselves; hence, the present extensive warehouse (which was considerably added to in 1878) and its contents, representing the art of all nations, in the way of decoration and furnishing. As proving the position now held by W. H. Rocke and Co., we may state that recently they have had conferred upon them the appointment of first-class medallists, and holders of the diploma of the Grand Council of the Society of Arts, Letters, Science, and Industry, of Naples. The business, which is supervised strictly by the members of the firm, is managed on the principle of giving satisfaction to all, and the buyer whose orders are small, receives the same attention as the buyer whose orders are large. Every class of furnishing is undertaken, from the house of the wealthy citizen, to the cottage of the artisan. In the warehouse and factories, which are situated in Collins-street east, there are over 150 employés, and no less than £13,000 is annually paid in wages. The premises cover half an acre, and are valued at £40,000, in addition to which there is a stock of £70,000, from which the public can choose. We feel sure that a visit to this establishment will delight, as well as instruct, and that all who go will be received with the utmost urbanity, and all their wants in furniture fully and satisfactorily supplied. The stock comprises every description of furniture to fulfil the requirements of kitchen, sitting-rooms, and bedrooms, as well as every other additional room to be found in the richest or poorest residence. In addition to what we have already mentioned, they have brass and silver bedsteads, and parquet flooring, together with bronze statues, chandeliers, and other works of ornamental art. They also undertake interior art decorations, such as the painting of walls and ceilings, having a clever artist engaged specially for the purpose.

WILLIAM M‘CULLOCH AND CO. (LIMITED).

A very important factor in seconding the enterprises of squatters, and others engaged in the pastoral or agricultural interest, is the facility offered for the transport of their products to the large and important towns, as well as to the sea-boards of the colony. A matter of equal consideration is that of the conveyance of merchandise, including provisions, from the sea to the inland parts of Australia. This applies equally to those who are engaged on the inland gold-fields. None will understand this better than the earlier colonists of Australia, who experienced the almost insurmountable difficulties of transporting goods into the interior at a time when roads were comparatively unknown, and when the dangers of personal encounters with the aboriginal inhabitants were not infrequent. It often happened too, that the expense of carriage was more than the goods themselves were worth. Such impediments must have been discouraging, even to men of almost indomitable enterprise and energy, while they must have been disheartening to the last degree to men who were struggling, without extraneous aid, to rise into a position of independence or to obtain even the ordinary comforts of life. At this time, the business of carriers must have been second to none in importance. The colonists must have hailed with joy the first signs which showed that in time the difficulties of transport would be overcome, and it was only through men who were incited to greater efforts according to the greatness of the difficulties which they had to encounter, that the hopes of the first and later colonists could ever be realised. Such hopes as these gave the early colonists courage to push on further into the interior; the facilities of transport followed in their rear; and countries which, thirty years ago, were only known to the black man, are now explored and settled upon, and stocked with many millions of sheep and cattle. We refer to the country about the Murray, and to the vast territory to the north of that river, which, about twenty-five years ago were, to a great extent, unexplored, and necessarily unknown, except to the tribes who claimed the country as their own. The discovery of gold attracted to Australia many enterprising men, both from the mother-country and America, who, finding that greater wealth was to be obtained in providing for the comforts of others rather than in the search for gold itself, devoted their energies to the best and most expeditious means of transporting merchandise and wool. Foremost amongst these was Mr. William M'Culloch, who first established the system of contracting with squatters and others for the carriage of all goods to and from the various stations in the interior. Mr. M'Culloch quickly recognised that the inland rivers were the natural highways for the transport of pastoral and agricultural products. He consequently constructed steamboats and barges, which were at once patronised by the wool-growers and others who had settled in the district of the Murray River and its tributaries. In this way the expense of carriage was considerably reduced; and this opened out brighter prospects of future wealth to the squatters in those districts. Some three years ago, the business of Mr. M'Culloch and his partners became so extensive, that it was considered expedient to carry it on in future as a company, with the head-quarters in Collins-street, Melbourne. The premises which they caused to be erected, are in every way fitted for the very extensive business which is now undertaken by the Company. The rapid development of their transport business, aided by the opening out of the railways by the Government of Victoria in the direction of the Murray, has given such a ready and convenient mode for the conveyance of goods and every kind of supplies, that Bourke and the surrounding districts, which had been previously considered as almost inaccessible, are now brought within a distance of two to three weeks' journey from Melbourne. This has considerably facilitated the opening up the way for the settlement of millions of acres of country which would otherwise have remained unproductive. The business of William M'Culloch and Co. not only provides for the carriage of wool and every other description of goods, but embraces many other branches, separate in themselves, but all tending to form the most extensive carrying and forwarding business south of the line. They are at present the sole owners of a very large fleet of steamboats, trading on the inland rivers, carrying to and fro products of the colonies of New South Wales, South Australia, and Victoria. This enterprising and energetic firm has thus conferred inestimable advantage upon the commercial world of Victoria, in facilitating the means for opening out and extending settlement in remote districts of the colony. This more particularly applies to those engaged in pastoral and agricultural industries, which are one day destined to be the source of the greatest wealth that the colony holds out to men whose speculative enterprise may lead them to seek a home in the Southern Hemisphere. We doubt not that, as occasion requires, the carrying business of William M'Culloch and Co. will be developed to meet the emergency, and that their past efforts are faithful presages of their ability to cope with whatever may arise in the future, and which may require their active co-operation. We may mention that William M'Culloch and Co. do not wholly confine their operations to the carrying business, but that they also conduct an extensive insurance business, which is carried on as a separate concern, and which is known as the M'Culloch Insurance Company. The same energy and careful attention are noticeable in this specialty as in their larger operations as carriers. They are also agents for a well-known line of vessels trading between London, Liverpool, and Melbourne. This, as an adjunct to their business of general carriers, enables them to undertake the forwarding of goods from the far interior of Australia, not only to Melbourne, but, if need be, to the Northern Hemisphere. We must not omit to mention their business as shipping agents, which is carried on with the same efficiency which characterises their other branches. They are also the proprietors of an Express business, which has agencies in every part of the world. By this means, those who are anxious to forward presents to friends or consign goods to any part of the civilised world, will find prompt and ready means of accomplishing their object, through the Express business of William M'Culloch and Co. The Company's Express waggons for suburban deliveries are very largely patronised by the citizens of Melbourne and district. They are a source of great convenience, and are remarkable for their punctuality and dispatch. In taking leave of William M'Culloch and Co. we cannot but wish them every success, with the certainty that they will be found equal to the growing requirements of this great colony.

MESSRS. PERMEWAN, WRIGHT AND COMPANY, LIMITED.

Previously to the introduction of railways into the Australian colonies, the business of common carriers was not the least important branch of commercial enterprise. It must necessarily have been a very lucrative one, especially in a colony where the mode of transit of goods from town to town, as well as outlying districts, was performed wholly through the means of common carriers. At a time when roads were scarcely formed, and when they were almost impassable, the traffic, and other means of communication, must have been exceedingly limited. The exertions, and continued perseverance of enterprising men, gradually overcame the difficulties, and regular means of communication were, in course of time, opened out. Remote districts were supplied with the means of forwarding the results of their labour to distant markets, and also with the regular supply of commodities necessary for business purposes, as well as for the conveniences of life. As commerce increased, the necessity for more rapid means of conveyance was felt, as well as the necessity of greater facilities for transporting goods from one place to another; and though railway communication was gradually introduced, there still remains much need for the services of carriers, both in the towns as well as in those districts which steam has not reached. The large and substantial storehouses which are to be seen in Melbourne, are signs of the extent of trade which is done with other countries. The ship-lined wharves are ever stirring, and busy with traffic. The goods brought from other countries are transferred to the most distant parts of the colony as much by road, in the far interior, as by means of the railways near to and communicating with Melbourne. Nor is the business of common carriers of less importance now than it was a few years ago. True, as a more speedy mode of traffic is introduced, the carrier is driven further into the interior, but he is as necessary a factor there as railways are in the more thickly populated districts. Amongst the firms engaged in the business of carriers not the least enterprising and prominent is the firm of Permewan, Wright and Co., Limited. From small beginnings they advanced to considerable importance. The business was first begun in 1856, at Geelong, and their operations were, in the beginning, confined to the cartage of goods from the wharf to the town. In 1858, the storekeepers in the Western District found that the best method of transit for goods from Melbourne was by boat to Geelong, thence by horse and bullock teams to the respective districts. The firm at once put themselves into a position to supply this newly-discovered requirement. The rapid increase of the traffic to Ballarat obliged the firm, in 1860, to put on an express line of waggons, leaving Geelong at 12 a.m. and timed to reach Ballarat at 10 o'clock the next morning, a distance of 56 miles. These waggons carried seven tons of goods, and were drawn by eight horses. The punctuality of the deliveries, and the good condition in which the goods were found on arrival, compared favourably with the same factor in railway traffic. It was not long before the increasing trade and size of Ballarat made it necessary that railway accommodation should be extended to the town. The railway was consequently opened to Ballarat in 1862, but it did not wholly absorb the road traffic. The business of the firm, which had up to this time been carried on by Mr. Thomas Osborne, was now conducted under the firm of Browne, Osborne and Co., and its operations were considerably extended. It was carried on under this name for a period of ten years; when the junior partner purchased the whole concern, and continued to manage it as a private firm until 1878. In this year it was registered as a limited liability company, Mr. Wright taking an active part in its management. In spite of the numerous changes which the proprietary has undergone, the business has steadily and permanently increased. It has now absorbed other concerns of a limited character at Echuca, Sandhurst, and Wodonga, as well as many other important towns in the colony. This has all been accomplished within the last six years. No less than twenty branches have been opened in various parts of the colony. In all the large towns you will see well up-standing horses in lorries, &c., owned by the firm, taking delivery of goods from the railway stations, and delivering them to the various stores; and the company has not only a large connection in Victoria, but also throughout the Riverina district of New South Wales. They have a regular line of steamers trading on the Murray, Murrumbidgee, and Edwards rivers from Echuca, for carriage of stores and wool; each boat having carrying capacity of from 150 to 200 tons of stores, or from 1000 to 1500 bales of wool, each trip. During the wool season, the firm received from the various stations in Riverina from 30,000 to 35,000 bales of wool. In addition to a carrying trade, a good mercantile business is carried on, and this with considerable success. This will be understood when we state that the shareholders, at the last meeting, were paid 15 per cent. dividend out of $18\frac{1}{2}$ per cent. of net profits. The Hon. Henry Cuthbert, late Commissioner of Trade and Customs, with Mr. Charles W. Gibson, of Messrs. Fisken and Gibson, and the managing directors, constitute the board of management.

THE EXCHANGE.

Perhaps there is no one man in Melbourne whose commercial enterprise deserves more honourable mention than that of Mr. H. Byron Moore. The fact that it has furnished a long-felt want in commercial circles, and produced a medium which will cement closer the *entente cordiale* existing between our merchants, and put them *au courant* with the affairs of the world, is sufficient to recommend it to the notice of every intelligent man in itself. But we recognise, in the perfect manner in which the lessee of the Exchange has carried out his pledge to the owners of the property, and likewise to the public, in putting a building at their command which will facilitate all kinds of commerce, a much greater advantage than the most sanguine of us could have hoped for. It is true Mr. H. Byron Moore has had the advantages of the experience of all the merchants' exchanges throughout the colonies, as well as those throughout the United States, by which to gauge the requirements of the one in Melbourne, observe the points in which they were deficient, and improve them in the Melbourne plan. That he has done this in a highly satisfactory manner no one for a moment can doubt, who visits the establishment, and glances at the thousand and one perfect arrangements, each one of which, in a different way, facilitates the merchant's transacting his business. Not many of our readers may be aware of the numerous advantages this Merchants' and Commercial Exchange Club—for, in sooth, in comfort it is more like a club than a rendezvous for the consummation and exchange of mercantile ideas—of commerce accords to its members. They are so varied and useful, that we owe it to the public not to pass over them without minute mention. In the first place, we must state that the Exchange has been erected by the enterprise of Mr. R. J. Jeffray, of Wm. Sloane and Co., at a cost of over twenty thousand pounds sterling, upon the earnest suggestion of the lessee, and upon plans devised by him. Mr. H. Byron Moore conceived this idea some time ago, it having been experienced, from time to time, that the other buildings, previously devoted to and used for this purpose, were complete failures. Why they were failures does not exactly transpire, except that they were situated in inconvenient places, not easily accessible to merchants. The location of the present Exchange is simply perfect, so far as position is concerned, for it is situated right in the heart of commerce. It is, in fact, within speaking distance of every merchant's office, one might say. Concerning the advantages offered by this institution, they are really so numerous and so perfect that, while it may appear a little extravagant, it is nevertheless true that, provided a merchant did not want absolute cubic space for the depositing of his merchandise, during the period which intervenes between purchase and sale, he could to all intents and purposes conduct his business from the public room of the Exchange. So perfect indeed are all the details which lead up to, and govern the conduct of a first-class commercial house. It must not be forgotten that these immense advantages are offered at an immoderately low rent, in the shape of a subscription of two guineas per annum for town members, and one guinea only for country members. The lessee, of course, hopes, and deservedly so, that the Exchange will be liberally supported, and the subscription list amply subscribed to. Without an immense *clientèle*, it is utterly impossible to permanently secure to the public all the enjoyments, privileges, and conveniences which the subscriber to the Exchange now enjoys, unless this list be very liberally responded to, for the expense of obtaining the kind of different information which the management is now giving subscribers multiplies with alarming rapidity. Now, in order to keep pace with the large expenditure necessitated by the many different departments in the Exchange, Mr. H. Byron Moore has had to import into his scheme sufficient enterprise to make the investment reproductive; and considering that no expense has been spared which might contribute to the general convenience and comfort of subscribers, the prompt and reliable information obtained for their use, and the celerity with which telegraphic information is received from all parts of the world, and at once becomes the common property of those within the building, should commend it very highly. These manifold agencies, which, like a thousand little streams, flow into the main hall, and combine to make a perfect sea of information, are each one in itself expensive. It is this fact which we wish to point out particularly to the subscribers, and call their attention to a very important condition intimately associated with the continued prosperity of this undertaking. The expense of maintaining this Exchange, with its various functionaries, can only be defrayed by a large and continually augmenting subscription-list. Subscribers—especially those whose commercial undertakings are of such a nature as to receive more benefit from its ramifications than others—should exert themselves to get all their friends interested—substantially interested, we mean—in its welfare. They should remember that, if they are receiving a great benefit, by reason of its being particularly adapted to the peculiarities of their business, they owe it to their own interests, to work for its preservation.

Having thus reverted to the conditions which called this institution into existence, we will proceed to recount a few of the advantages which struck us as we made our peregrination through the large hall. We cannot promise our readers more than a limited description, as want of space prohibits the extended notice this undertaking deserves. Entering the main hall, one finds himself in a handsomely decorated chamber, well lighted, 80 feet by 32 feet, ornately paved with tessellated pavement—which, being colonial, at once marks the progress of æsthetical art in Victoria. Passing round the room from the left, we find the walls are divided off into arches, each one of which is devoted to a colony. Within the confines of each such archway are all the leading papers of the colony whose name it bears. Further on is a handsome mahogany table, devoted exclusively to the members of the press, and fitted up with every convenience for them. Facing this are rich mahogany desks, with lock and key drawers—which may be rented at a trifle extra expense—and used as a receptacle for letters, or valuable papers. A printed notice in these informs the writer that he may have the advantage of copying private letters for foreign or home circulation, and the necessary paper, furnished free of cost, upon application to the manager. Weather reports from all parts of the colonies, adorn the next pillar; and ships' manifests of their full cargo, which are posted immediately the vessels are telegraphed off Cape Otway, are suspended from the next.

Merchants will immediately see the advantage in the saving of time such a proceeding as this furnishes. They are able to discover, with no loss of time whatever, the number of packages any ship may have in her cargo consigned to their care. This arrangement is supplemented by partial manifests, despatched from the ship's landing, as each lot of her cargo is unloaded. The saving of clerks' time, and that of draymen, in this latter arrangement, is sufficient in a season to more than pay the member's subscription to the Exchange. Concerning railways, all goods received at the Spencer-street sheds through the night, up to 8.30 a.m., are posted in detail upon another pillar at 9 a.m.; a man being kept all night at the sheds in order to prepare the Exchange manifests. Travelling stock is reported by telegraph from the different crossing points, and is posted upon one of the large blackboards. Of these boards there are three, and the others are devoted to shipping telegrams, or any extraordinary despatch received from Reuter, or elsewhere. The number of sheep and cattle receivable during the week by rail is anticipated upon another pillar, by despatches, stating what trucks have been engaged. This gives dealers the opportunity of knowing the number of stock to be offered during the week. A number of tables here intercept the progress of the visitor and the eye. These are liberally, and literally, strewn with European, English, Indian, American, and Colonial papers, of all descriptions. Further on is a counter, containing the shipping registers. The same system which prevails at Lloyds' prevails here, namely, all ships spoken are entered when and where. A Law Court bulletin, upon which all important proceedings at the different courts are reported hourly, or more frequently if necessary, is conspicuous a little further on, and completes the main hall. Passing through the main hall, into one second in size to it, though perhaps not in importance, the visitor finds himself in a large and airy room, now rented by the Corn Exchange Committee, and used for conducting their operations in cereals. Opening off of this is a hairdresser's room, which appears to be largely patronized. The days of sales are Tuesdays and Thursdays. Taking the southern stairway, and passing upstairs, a very fine billiard-

T

room meets the eye, with every convenience and comfort for the scientific pursuit of the game. Light is made an important adjunct in this room, by a large skylight doing duty very effectively. Beyond this, are different suites of rooms, arranged for almost every conceivable business purpose that the necessities of a highly-developed mercantile community could demand, and furnished with the same excellent judgment. The lavatories and bath-rooms are equal to those in the most modern private residence, and will be largely appreciated during the heat of the summer. In some of the rooms on this floor, plans and specifications for all the large works in the adjoining colonies are exhibited. This feature will be found useful to Melbourne contractors. Another room worthy of notice is the shire and muncipal councils' room, well-fitted with every convenience, and at a saving of expense to such bodies, besides presenting them with the freedom of the Exchange. In the basement, a luncheon-room has been fitted up, which, it is said, is capable of satisfying the Epicurean taste which loiters in and about the Exchange; and beyond that, a handsome little fernery, with smoking lounge, etc., etc. Two more features, of not less importance than the Exchange itself, is the accessibility of communication with the whole world without going outside the building, Messrs. Reuter's offices occupying a portion of the main building, and also Thos. Cook & Son's tourists' office. Mr. Thomas Cook is the man who personally takes you round the world and introduces you to the more important cities, giving you his own experience at the same time.

In conclusion, we commend to the notice of all, this most useful addition to Melbourne's already progressive institutions. That she marches with the van of progress there can be no doubt, as in this case the Melbourne Exchange not only embraces all the advantages offered by similar insti-tutions, but a number of advantages which they do not. We suggest to those merchants and commercial men who are not subscribers, to speedily become such, for they cannot get similar advantages elsewhere for five times the cost of a year's subscription to this Exchange.

Mr. Lloyd Tayler is architect for the building.

A Telephone Exchange is also established in the building, on the upper gallery of the vestibule. Through this apartment—conducted by a staff of young ladies—any subscriber to the Telephone Exchange can converse with any other subscriber. A little ring from your telephone calls the attendant; you then say, "Connect me with Messrs. James Service and Co.," or anyone else you wish to speak with. In less time than it takes to write this, you hear the clear Scotch accent of our friend Mr. Service, who recognises your voice, and the business you desire is transacted. A little ring is then given, to indicate that your talk is over, and your wires are disconnected. The simplicity and usefulness of the whole arrangements are truly admirable. About sixty of the leading banks and firms are now connected, and the list is daily increasing.

A Telegraph office is established for the use of subscribers, and a pigeon express is kept on the roof (this is used for coursing and regattas, and such events as the wires cannot compass.)

DERHAM AND CO.

The agricultural resources of Australia are rapidly developing into importance. They are, without doubt, destined to form a part of the export trade of the colony. The part which they will form must of necessity be spasmodic in nature, until we ascertain the exact price at which other countries can afford to sell their wheat in England, and our relative position as competitors for this trade. Though the production is as yet comparatively limited, and consequently there is a limit in its volume as an export, yet the wheat which has found its way into the European markets, does not unsuccessfully compete with the wheat grown in England, or exported from other countries. If the same enterprise and energy be brought to bear upon the agricultural interests of the colonies, as have been hitherto concentrated upon the pastoral and mining interests, we are warranted in prognosticating that a future is in store in the near distance for the cereal productions of this new country. The soil in many parts, as well as the climate, are most favourable for the production of almost every description of corn. The vast area which is now opened, and the almost unlimited area which awaits settlement, are calculated, not only to supply all colonial consumption, but to leave a very large residue for exportation to the home markets. America and Russia are the only large grain-growing countries which export largely into the English markets; and it is very natural to conclude that, when the grain resources of Australia have been more fully developed, she will be in a better position to attract from England a greater part of the trade which is now done with the countries named than she is now. It is a natural conclusion that, all other things being equal, England will more willingly trade with this, one of her most important dependencies, than with countries where no other inducement exists for continued trading than the inducement which makes a virtue of necessity. Indeed, in time we do not see why some considerable portion of the import trade of England in cereals should not be chiefly carried on with her Australian colonies, for it must be an interest common to both to transact business with each other, on as large a scale as possible. The land laws of Victoria and the other colonies, are specially advantageous for encouraging the advancement of agricultural productions. With all those important factors which we have named, Australia is doubtless destined to become a great wheat-growing country, provided that the economic conditions are equal. The large population of the United Kingdom is sufficient to consume the home produce as well as, for some time to come, the greater part of the surplus of Australia. With such incentives as these, we trust that those of our colonists who are engaged in agricultural pursuits, as well as buyers who look hopefully for that successful future, which is really in their own hands, and only requires that perseverance and energy which are so largely imported into the other interests, such as the pastoral and the mining, and which are consequently in a condition at once flourishing and prosperous, will leave nothing undone to second an extension of the industry. The wheat trade, we are glad to say, has, within the last year or two, made rapid strides, and the quality has been such as to give great hopes that in time it may not be inferior to the very best wheat grown in other countries. During the past year, the export business in wheat has been carried on with considerable activity. A great part of this export trade has passed through the hands of the firm whose name will be found at the head of this chapter, Messrs. Derham and Co., whose business premises are situated at No. 4 Queen-street, in this city, and who have done much to develop the wheat trade of Victoria. The first vessel which left the shores of Australia for the United Kingdom, and laden with this season's growth of Australian wheat, was the *Loch Linnhe*, which left Victoria on 2nd February, this year, and carried something like 18,055 bags of wheat, the entire shipment being supplied by the firm of Derham and Co. This vessel was quickly followed by several other vessels carrying lesser quantities, and in this way, we may fairly say, that the export trade in wheat has been duly inaugurated, and it only requires to be more widely known that the export time has begun, in order to ensure its continuance and rapid increase. Thus, the initiative has begun in earnest, and in part through the firm whose business is under consideration; and we heartily wish them all the success which their enterprising efforts so richly deserve. The following statements of the various shipments of wheat and flour to the United Kingdom, and to the continent of Europe, are worthy of careful attention, and must possess considerable interest for those who have at heart the general welfare of the Australian colonies. From these statements will be shown the contributions of wheat to the various shipments which have been made by Messrs. Derham and Co. From these we may gather how important a part they take in this largely increasing new phase of Victorian commerce.

In the month of February, of this year, 16 ships sailed from Victorian, or neighbouring, ports, for England or the European continent. They carried a gross cargo of about 152,588 bags of wheat, and about 4802 bags of flour, and out of this something like 46,294 bags of wheat were contributed to the shipment by Messrs. Derham and Co., or a little less than a third part of the whole shipment. In March, of the same year, the gross export of wheat was 137,503 bags, together with 6316 bags of flour, and out of this number Messrs. Derham and Co. shipped about 46,053 bags of wheat, or a little more than a third part of the whole quantity. These cargoes were carried to England by the same number of ships as carried the entire cargoes in February. In the month of April, the whole export trade of wheat amounted to 91,619 bags, together with 2283 bags of flour, Messrs. Derham and Co. supplying 26,147 bags of wheat, or a little less than a third of the whole of the wheat exported during the month. Eleven ships were employed in carrying these cargoes to England or the continent. In the month of May, the following export trade in wheat and flour was done with the countries named, viz., 38,045 bags of wheat, and 16,376 bags of flour, out of which Messrs. Derham and Co. supplied 14,945 bags of wheat, while nine ships were chartered to carry the entire cargo. In the month of June, the number of ships employed in carrying cargoes of wheat and flour to England or the continent was seven, laden with 36,231 bags of wheat, and 17,111 bags of flour, of which 4901 bags of wheat were supplied by Messrs. Derham and Co. In the month of July, the export of wheat amounted to 14,375 bags of wheat, carried by three ships, the firm supplying 1804 bags. In the month of August, the good ship *Hydaspes* started for England, laden with 2749 bags of flour, none of which, as before, was supplied by the firm under review. The total exports to 7th August were 530,123 bags of wheat, and 154,896 bags of flour; out of which this firm shipped 140,144 bags of wheat, or more than a fourth of the whole number of bags of wheat exported. The total receipts of wheat from the country districts to 7th August, amount in gross to 797,398 bags of wheat, of which quantity Messrs. Derham and Co. have received, as consignments to their firm, 189,036 bags of wheat alone, besides large parcels of flour. In reviewing the extensive business conducted by Messrs. Derham and Co. in breadstuffs, during the present year, it must be borne in mind that their transactions are to a great extent on account of the various country constituents, for whom they act as Melbourne agents, in the disposal of their produce; and the large proportion the figures show them to have contributed to the gross export of breadstuffs indicates clearly the facilities possessed by this firm for the disposal of grain for export to Europe and elsewhere.

MESSRS. SWALLOW AND ARIELL.

Mr. Swallow, the founder of this firm, commenced business as a biscuit manufacturer, in Rouse-street, Sandridge, in March, 1854. In the same year, he exhibited, at the Exhibition held in Melbourne, the first biscuits manufactured by machinery in Victoria. In 1861, the firm, then Messrs. T. Swallow and Co., obtained the first-class certificate of merit for ship and cabin biscuits at the Exhibition of that year, and at the one held in 1866, they were awarded the medal for excellence of manufacture and quality of ship, fancy, and dessert biscuits. The following is an extract from the report then made:—" Biscuits.—The extensive variety of biscuits suitable for all purposes and climates, all stages of life and constitution, gave a pleasing proof of what Messrs. Swallow and Ariell, of Sandridge, have done, and continue to do, towards supplying the increasing demands of civilised life of the present day." It would be tedious to enumerate all the honours the firm has since obtained in colonial and intercolonial exhibitions, but we may mention, as a proof of their ability to compete with manufacturers in any part of the world, that they were awarded medals at the Philadelphia Exhibition of 1876, and the Paris Exhibition of 1878.

The factory as at present existing was commenced in 1858, and since then, wing after wing has been gradually added until it has attained its present extensive proportions. The principal buildings are in the form of a quadrangle, and inside the square are several accessory buildings, used for such purposes as butter cellars, raisin and currant rooms, packing-rooms, stables, etc., etc., the whole covering an area of about three acres. Situated as the factory is, within a hundred yards or so from the bay, a plentiful supply of water for condensing purposes, etc., can always be obtained, and after it has served its purpose be returned again to its source with little expense. The Sandridge railway-station is also within a stone's-throw, and thus, whether for inland traffic or its sea-board and shipping trade, the firm has advantages which are not easily superseded in such a combination.

The office entrance is in Rouse-street, and there we called on Mr. Swallow, with the object of inspecting the factory, and the various processes of manufacture. Our request was cordially granted, and Mr. Swallow courteously took the trouble to personally explain to us the respective missions of the several departments, which would otherwise have proved a bewildering labyrinth. His explanations, as we passed from room to room, and from wing to wing, reduced what might have appeared to us a conglomeration of machinery, to an arrangement so well adapted to the purposes of the business, and yet so simple, that the merest novice could not fail to understand its combinations. Before leaving Mr. Swallow's office, we noticed that it was fitted with telephonic apparatus, and were informed that they were thus in communication with their city depôt in Queen-street. In the first room we examined, Mr. Swallow pointed out to us a biscuit-machine, of which his firm had secured the sole use in Australia, and when we state that, for the same right in England, Messrs. Huntley and Palmer paid the sum of £10,000, it will be seen that Messrs. Swallow and Ariell spare no expense to obtain the newest and best mechanical appliances for the improvement of their manufactures. In this, and several adjoining rooms, we were shown the process of manufacturing the several varieties of biscuits, cakes and puddings, for which the firm have gained so well-known a reputation, and the automatic regularity with which everything went on, seemed very striking. Here was pointed out to us an elevator, which carried up the wheat to the higher stories; there a receiver, into which it was returned in the shape of flour, and close to this, apparatus by which it was mixed up, with all the necessary ingredients, into dough, rolled out into sheets, passed under stamp presses, and cut out into all imaginable shapes and sizes of biscuits. These are then transferred to revolving trays, and, when the latter have circumnavigated the centre of revolution, the biscuits are completed, baked, and, being met by a bar placed at an angle across the path of the tray, are swept off into receivers, and their place occupied by the next batch. The biscuits are now transferred to elevators, which discharge them into receivers in the rooms above, where another most interesting spectacle is presented to the view. Room after room is fitted up with tables, at which are seated boys and girls, busily engaged in imparting to the biscuits and comfits all those finishing touches which are requisite before they are presented in such tempting guise to the customer's view, in the windows of our confectioners. Here a score of girls, with deft fingers and acquired celerity, are decorating the biscuits with all manner of fanciful designs, pressed out from moulds, there a number of boys arranging and packing them into tins and boxes. From the packing-rooms, the loading and despatching is conducted with the least possible amount of trouble. We have seen, in our time, factories for the manufacture of all kinds of produce, both in the colonies and in the old country, but we do not remember having noticed lads of a more robust build, or girls of a more healthy appearance than we found here. Everywhere it seemed work, work, but nowhere any appearance of driving; and health, happiness and contentment, were reflected from every face. And, indeed, as regards health, it was not to be wondered at. There is very little of the conventional idea of a factory to be found about that of Messrs. Swallow and Ariell. Windows on both sides of the rooms, looking into the street on one side, and into the square on the other, afford a plentiful supply of light and air, the latter fresh and invigorating, owing to the contiguity of the Bay; while every requisite for the thorough ventilation of the premises is carefully supplied. It was, indeed, quite refreshing to note the good feeling which existed between employer and employed. Everywhere the first had a cheery word for the latter, especially for the boys and girls; and this was reciprocated by the respectful and unpresuming manner of their replies. Thus, we moved on from one department to another; in one room, they were busy mixing up all the ingredients—such as butter, eggs, fruit, &c.—necessary to give richness and taste to their cakes and puddings; in another, artists were skillfully designing pieces of decorative art for wedding cakes. And so on; every room having some new feature of interest, or in which some process hitherto a mystery to us was made clear. Throughout all our progress, one thing has most forcibly struck us, and that is the exquisite cleanliness which pervades the whole establishment; and to this is no doubt greatly due the fact that Messrs. Swallow and Ariell's manufactures have found their way into some of our first houses.

The enormous business here carried on gives employment to many other trades. The firm employ their own carpenters, their own coopers, and their own tinsmiths; and a sight of the rooms in which these trades are carried on would alone repay a visit. We were more particularly interested by the process of making the tin cases. Each worker seemed to have his particular part in the general division of labour. One cuts the sides to their exact size, another punches out the top and bottom, a third is employed in folding over the edge, when such is required to be done, and a fourth is employed in soldering the parts together; each one the director of a machine doing its work so perfectly that one would imagine improvement impossible, and yet, Mr. Swallow informed us that improvements were constantly being made and adopted. Our next stopping-point was at the egg-cellars. Enormous tanks built round the walls, barrels on barrels covering the space in the centre, all filled with eggs, and we are told that the stock is not so large as it sometimes is. These eggs are capable of being preserved for almost any period of time by being kept immersed in lime water, and we were informed that only a few weeks ago some eggs which had been thus packed twelve months before had been found as fresh as if only a day old. The butter cellars, of which we inspected two, are equally capacious and well-stored.

Messrs. Swallow and Ariell are also golden syrup and treacle refiners, but it would require almost a chapter to describe adequately all the processes through which the molasses, as received from the growers, has to pass before it attains the beautifully-golden appearance it possesses when sold by them. From notes taken in the various departments, we find the steam-power is created by three furnaces, consuming on an average 200 tons of coal per month, and is distributed through the factory and refinery by eight engines, aggregating 75 horse-power. Some idea of the amount of goods manufactured by the firm may be obtained from the fact that they use about 30 tons of flour, 5 tons of butter, 5 tons of sugar, 2000 dozen of eggs, and 3 tons of currants and sultanas every week, and give employment to over 300 hands, about 50 of whom are females.

Messrs. Swallow and Ariell have not, as yet, attempted to export their manufactures to the English markets, the colonial and ship-supplying trade providing them with quite as extensive a business as they care to cultivate; but Mr. Swallow is, at the same time, of opinion that should the attempt be made it could be done successfully. One of their biscuits would especially be a boon to many a thrifty housewife, with a small income, in the old country. We refer to the meat biscuit, a considerable percentage of which is composed of meat, and which can easily be made into most nutritive and tasty soup. Messrs. Swallow and Ariell's factory is one of the sights of Victoria—we should say of Australia—which no visitor should neglect to visit; and, judging from our own experience, we can promise a genial welcome from the firm.

ALSTON AND BROWN.

Our attention is now directed to what we are told is the first brick building in Collins-street. The age of the building, together with the long established respectability of the firm, makes it no unworthy compeer of the many stately edifices which adorn a street that has now justly become the pride of Melbourne. Our curiosity is naturally excited at the information which we receive, though, as a general rule, we must plead guilty to a stolid stoicism, the basis of which is to be astonished at nothing in this astonishing age. Our manifest indifference on entering the premises is suddenly and unexpectedly metamorphosed into surprise and admiration at the extensive and varied stock which meets our gaze as we are courteously and attentively conducted through the establishment. The respect superinduced by the perfect management of any concern whose ramifications are as numerous as must be those of the firm under review, impels us in the first outset to establish the sympathy of our numerous readers, by informing them that the house of Alston and Brown, general drapers, milliners, dressmakers, tailors, outfitters, upholsterers, house furnishers, &c., &c., has been in existence for nearly the fourth of a century, their predecessors being Messrs. Charles Williamson and Co., of which firm the present senior partner was for some years a member. In spite of the numerous branches of human requirements for which Alston and Brown are such successful caterers, the great Aristotelian dictum of the necessity of division of labour is not by any means unheeded. We found that separate rooms were devoted to the various departments, and that each branch had its sanctum and presiding spirit. There are special rooms for millinery, for dressmaking, mantlemaking, and for what is known by the mysterious and never-to-be-explained-to-man expression of ladies' work of all kinds. A trade which must be coeval with the introduction into the first language of the word deceiving, and is now, and has been for some time, specifically known as tailoring, is duly and efficiently provided for by Alston and Brown, by being placed under the superintendence of a responsible head. Cabinet-making, a more recent introduction into the economy of human convenience, is equally well provided for, and upholstery and other *et ceteras* are superintended with the same exclusive care.

More than half-an-acre is covered by the ground floor of the premises. The frontage to Collins-street is 33 feet, while that to Little Collins-street widens to 82 feet. The depth or distance from one street to the other, the premises extending right through, cannot be less than 314 feet. The show rooms for general drapery, &c., run back a considerable distance from Collins-street. The measurement of the millinery and mantle room is 92 by 25. We were somewhat struck with the very elegant appearance of the carpet room, more especially with the loftiness of its ceiling. It is well lighted, and of its kind, we venture to say, is unsurpassed in the colonies. It measures 80 feet by 35. The furniture rooms are on the ground and first floors, the entrance being from Little Collins-street. The tailoring and outfitting department is on the first floor entering from Collins-street.

One of the great wants of the present day is, that well ventilated and otherwise healthy rooms should be provided for those whose daily work keeps them in close confinement for so many consecutive hours. This has not been overlooked by Alston and Brown. Their work-rooms are on the first and second floors. They are large, well-lighted, and thoroughly well ventilated. The men, women, and girls who are at work seem to be contented and happy. They are engaged in making up the various kinds of goods required for stock and for special orders. We have no doubt that orders, however large or however small, would be executed with equal care and ability; and even those who are constitutionally dissatisfied with their tailors and drapers would in all probability find their first satisfaction in the result of their dealings with this firm.

There are also offices specially set apart for the clerks. The strong-room, the packing-room, as well as the room for unpacking received goods, seem admirably adapted to their several purposes. Near to these, but on the other side of Little Collins-street, are the stables, &c.

The London branch is at 27 Wallbrook, E.C. It is under the superintendence and management of Mr. Brown, who has been resident in England for some time. He, with the assistance of a local staff, attends to the execution of the orders sent from Melbourne.

We were told that the stock was always new and continually being replenished with the newest and latest styles.

The show-rooms offer fascinating temptation to the *homo* in its generic sense. We venture, with the utmost diffidence, to assert that the ladies of Melbourne are passionately fond of elegant dresses, pretty bonnets, and graceful mantles, and this must be our excuse to all husbands when we recommend to the said ladies continuous and lengthened visits to the establishment of Alston and Brown as an antidote for domestic ennui. With respect to gentlemen, we have much pleasure in recommending to their immediate and special notice, the fact that they can have within an incredibly short space of time any style of habiliment including the morning, evening, and afternoon promenade dress, at once well-fitting, becoming, and stylish, by visiting the establishment of Alston and Brown. In fact, there is very little in the way of comfort and elegance which this large firm with its extensive and varied stock, could not supply to satisfy the most fastidious taste.

THE "RED CROSS" PRESERVING COMPANY.

The progress of the colonial industries and the initiation of new ones have been marked features in the progress of the colony during the past decade. As a rule, the new industries which are introduced are not subjected to colonial competition; and so their prosperity and ultimate success are almost ensured. But an industry which is introduced for the first time into Victoria, and which has to compete with the supply which is provided by a colony which has already become so famous in the same production, and which has an established trade, requires to be undertaken by men of enterprise and ability, who see in difficulties but the necessity to overcome them, and whose perseverance is as untiring as their energy, before it can have any chance of success.

Tasmania has long been noted as the seat of the manufacture of preserved fruit jams, and it is only recently that there has been discovered a great decrease in the demand as compared with former years. At one time the Victorian market for preserved jams was supplied, if not wholly, certainly to a very great extent, by the Tasmanian manufacturers. Now, instead of going out of the colony for the article, it is supplied by an establishment in Victoria, which has already won a reputation for the quality of its jams in no way inferior to that formerly enjoyed by Tasmania. We refer to the "Red Cross" Preserving Company, which is situated in Chapel-street, South Yarra, and which has steadily grown into importance both with regard to the quantity as well as the quality of the article which it supplies; and from the large amount of labour which it employs, it has risen into an industry of considerable importance. The factors which have tended to this success, and to which we may say the success is really due, are unwearying energy, steady and continued perseverance, and an earnest desire to supply the best possible article, all of which have been and are the characteristics of the present courteous managing partner, Mr. Robotham.

The other partners in this large establishment are Messrs. Wright, Payne and Co., of Flinders Lane. These large manufacturing premises are the result of eight years' growth. Their history, like that of almost all colonial industries, had a small beginning, and grew in eight years into their present proportion. Mr. Marcus Robotham has been associated with that history from its beginning to the present time.

The company began eight years ago in a comparatively small way, in premises which they occupied in Fitzroy, and at that time their goods found a ready market. Subsequently, they purchased land in Chapel-street, South Yarra, not far from the Toorak road, and there erected premises which were considered very roomy and spacious and likely to afford all the accommodation for jam-making which seemed likely to be required. The site was well chosen for several reasons; and in time the brand of the Red Cross became so well known as to be associated with the very best jams which the colonial markets could supply. This resulted in a steadily-increasing business, until its proportions grew far in excess of the accommodation which they had at their disposal; and it was at last found necessary, in order to meet their growing requirements, to find other and larger premises. They were fortunate enough to secure a building known as the Brewery, which was immediately opposite the Jam Factory, and this they did at a cost of between £5000 and £6000. Such of the buildings as were suitable were enlarged and adapted to the necessary purposes, and additions were made, the whole of the alterations being from plans prepared by the manager, Mr. Robotham. The whole was carried out at a cost between £7000 and £8000, so that with the requisite plant for carrying on the business on a very large scale, there has been about £15,000 invested, independent of the old factory. We were struck with the cleanliness which, during our visit, we noticed throughout the factory, but we ceased to be astonished on being told how rigidly this cleanliness was daily enforced upon the work-people. The building is of bluestone, with a frontage of 190 feet by a depth of 300 feet. The store and packing-rooms, which are entered from the counting-house, where several clerks were at work, are 160 feet long by 30 feet wide. This store is full of goods ready to supply to orders as received, for pickles, jams, jellies, sauces, &c. The sugar-room is a large and spacious store capable of containing upwards of 400 tons of sugar. The tins for the jams are manufactured on the premises and here, as elsewhere, the most improved labour-saving machinery is employed. The next place we visited was the boiling-room, in which are 12 circular pans, each capable of holding fruit and sugar sufficient to turn out 400lbs. of jam. Leaving the boiling-room, we entered the engine-room, and after that a room where candied peel and tart fruits are manufactured. In a large store below the surface of the yard, the pickles, sauces, vinegar, &c., are manufactured; which branch of the business has been so successfully conducted as to have earned the company the right of being, in this southern hemisphere, what the famous Crosse and Blackwell are in the northern. As the company have entered somewhat largely into the manufacture of pickles, we may be excused for dwelling shortly on this branch of industry. A patent lift delivers the vegetables, after having been cleansed and stripped of all their waste leaves and other refuse, into the cellars, where there are long ranges of vats and casks, scrupulously clean, in which they are at once packed and covered with brine. In one part of the underground region, there are enamelled and other boilers for various uses and in which to scald the pickled vegetables for a brief period when taken out of the brine. They are next laid on the first series of tables, and are there cut into the sizes necessary for bottling, and then fall into the hands of the packers who fill the bottles. At the succeeding tables the bottles are drained, filled with vinegar, corked, waxed, capsuled, washed, labelled and papered, and are then conveyed to the packers to be placed in cases ready branded for delivery. Varying the processes, the manufacture of sauces is also carried on, in a like systematic manner and with equal care and attention to cleanliness. We cannot overestimate the importance of such an industry as the "Red Cross" Preserving Company, especially in Australia, where all varieties of fruits and culinary vegetables find a congenial soil, and grow to a size, and become prolific to a degree, unknown in the old country. There is now opening up to us a vast trade in meat, not only with the European markets, but also with the continent of India and its teeming millions, and it will be the result of our own apathy alone, if in addition to meat, wool, &c., we do not make a large addition to our exports in the way of horticultural produce. And, in fact, should the present operations of the Frozen Meat Company be successful, the "Red Cross" Preserving Company contemplate entering largely into the export of fresh fruits, butter, and other perishable articles of food, of which this country is capable of producing an almost inexhaustible supply. Their influence on the fruit and vegetable production of Victoria is already apparent to a very marked extent. Some years ago, with the view, primarily of ensuring for themselves a constant supply of vegetables suitable to their manufactures, the company imported seed of the most favorably known varieties of onions (silver-skins), chilies, capsicums, &c., and distributed them to Victorian market gardeners, who are now growing them in large quantities with considerable profit to themselves. The supply of currants and raspberries was also, until lately, drawn principally from Tasmania, the company having had always in use, employed in this traffic, a floating stock of 1000 barrels. But the large demand created by the company's operations, encouraged the growth of these fruits in the most favourable localities of Victoria, such as Macedon, Buninyong, Lilydale, Lal Lal, Fernshaw, Dandenong, and Gippsland, where a very large quantity is now grown; and in a year or so we may depend upon these districts, not only to satisfy our local demands, but also to have a large surplus available for export purposes.

The company use, as far as they can, all colonial-made articles, and this is another source of increased employment to bottle-makers and to printers —1,000,000 labels having been required during the last season. Their cases, their wrapping papers, and their corks and bungs, are all purchased in the colony. Their steam plant, too, is of colonial manufacture, and in their factory they give immediate employment to about 150 men. Certainly the company has entitled itself to the support of all Victorians, and we trust that its motto of "Ever foremost" may always, in the future, as in the present, describe its position in the ranks of our representative Victorian industries.

THE COLONIAL MUTUAL LIFE ASSURANCE SOCIETY (LIMITED.)

Up to the year 1835, no British or other Life Assurance Society had the temerity to effect a landing on the rugged shores of Australia, then supposed to be a somewhat deadly climate, and peopled by a sparse population of cannibal aborigines, and a few thousand nomadic criminals, some of whom were worse than the blacks in the atrocity of their crimes, and a small handful of officers and their families, and soldiers and police, all under the slow control of Downing-street. Slow it was in those days, when a despatch was rarely less than ten months in receiving its acknowledgment. At that time the Life Assurance offices at home confined their business within very narrow limits of voyage and residence, and charged any person on their books, desiring to go to Australia *(when they granted him the permit at all)* not less than £2 per cent. on the amount assured, for the voyage, and a continuous annual extra of about the like amount so long as residing within the then considered dangerous confines of Australia. Some of the settlers of that period, seeing that life and property were, in the settled districts, as safe as in any other part of the British Dominions, and finding, from their own experience, the salubrity of the climate, established, some 45 years ago, a Colonial Life Office. From its formation dates the history of Life Assurance in Australia; where, in the short period of an ordinary lifetime, it has taken firmer root than in England, or even in America.

On the development of the discovery of gold in Australia, in 1851, the companies then doing business in Australia refused any *permit* to their policyholders to go to the diggings; although some few instances remain on record, in which assured persons were permitted to go to the gold-fields, on paying an extra premium of about 3 per cent. Times are strangely altered now!

In 1854, there were not more than 600 lives assured in the whole of Australasia. In 1880, there is an army of provident persons not less than 80,000 in number doing battle (with proved health and stamina in their favour) against burthening the State with needless poverty. Day by day, hundreds of recruits of provident, healthy men, are joining the ranks, while those who are improvident enough not to do so, may die in harness, leaving no sort of provision for those they leave behind. There are a few deserters from the ranks, who are indiscreet enough to surrender their policies, or to allow them to lapse, but these few show a want of foresight for the future in such miscalculations.

Some idea of the principles of mutual confederation, by which individual loss became more bearable through the contributions of the many, may be found in the very earliest records, preserved in the invaluable library of the British Museum. Still earlier instances might even be traced to periods in the historical books of Holy Writ. But being concerned principally with the living, we may at once come to the beginning of the 18th century, when the science of probabilities began to attract the attention of the mathematicians of the period, helping alike to promote the failure of many bubbles, originated perhaps as often in fraud as in ignorance, and to uncover their gross trickery. The first legitimate Life Assurance office, was established in 1706, and called "The Amicable." This institution has continued to exist uninterruptedly, and without going through any severe crises, until now its affairs are administered by another office of more recent date; but it still maintains its proud supremacy of seniority. We learn that its rates were considered, by other assurance societies, as rather haphazard, and it possessed constitutional defects, which militated against its taking any active part in Life Assurance as it is carried on to-day.

Since the establishment of this pioneer company, the number of offices which have risen, and still maintain their honourable position, is very large, while many mushroom companies, started by ignorant and designing men, have disappeared.

As a representative Australian life assurance society, The Colonial Mutual Life Assurance Society, Limited, stands prominent. It was projected as recently as the latter part of 1873, and through the indomitable perseverance of its general manager, Mr. T. Jaques Martin, commenced active business towards the middle of 1874. In the short period since then, a business has been created exceeding £2,566,000 of assurances, while on foot at the date of the last annual meeting, the income, from premiums alone, exceeded £100,000 per annum. We understand that to this office and its energetic management, is due the practical abolition of all conditions of assurance other than payment of premium, and the absolute nonforfeiture of the policy, so long as a single day's surrender value remains unabsorbed. Thus, supposing the surrender value of a policy on the day of default in paying the premiums, was £50, and that sum were sufficient to maintain the risk for two years and 135 days, if death occurred on the last day, the society would pay the claims with equal alacrity as if the premiums had been regularly paid up, deducting only the unpaid premiums, with moderate interest. Besides these advantages, it has introduced the system of *absolute assurance*, by which the assured are protected against any loss whatever, no matter how adverse their personal circumstances may become hereafter. For instance, a person assuring for £1000, under the 10-premium scale, is assured for £1000 in the event of death within the first year of assurance, and if he fail to pay the second premium he remains assured for £100; if, however, he pays the second year's premium and die during that year, his representatives receive the £1000, while if he fail to pay the third premium his life continues to be assured for £200, and so on.

Space, however, does not permit us to dwell further on the special features of this great institution, beyond mentioning that its first quinquennial investigation recently completed, has borne the most crucial tests to which the affairs of any similar company have ever been submitted. In this investigation, the work was conducted by the society's actuary, Mr. Robert Thomson, F.I.A., and every figure of the results was submitted to two of the greatest living actuaries of the mother-country, Mr. T. B. Sprague and Mr. G. King, whose opinion corroborated in every respect his valuation, the result of which was that while providing for every possible liability, a very handsome percentage was carried forward to profit and loss.

In our future of Australia, no more cheering evidence of the high moral tone of our society can be found than in the progress of this, and kindred institutions, showing, as it does, the strong hold that providence and self-denial have obtained among all ranks.

Before closing this article, we must not omit to mention, that the Colonial Mutual Society is practically one of the pioneers of colonial federation, each colony possessing a board of co-ordinate powers, all controlled by a general committee of management, which committee we might style the Federal Council.

CRAIG, WILLIAMSON AND THOMAS.

The age we live in, being particularly one of advancement, it necessitates that our existing institutions should keep pace with it to maintain their position in the van of progress. So imperial a dictator is the law which governs progress, that all things, to hold their own, must bow to it. Some of the merchants of Melbourne are evidently alive to this, and also to the influence it exerts over commerce. Their recognition of it is seen from the adaptability they evince, in all the departments of commerce, to keep its path in sight, and then steadily follow in the track it leaves behind. Amongst those who have been foremost in recognising the radical changes which the progress of the times has demanded in the commerce of *soft goods*, may be mentioned Messrs. Craig, Williamson and Thomas. It appears that the depression of the last three years in Victoria, in commercial affairs, can not be said to have left no trace of good. On the contrary, it is distinctly asserted, and especially by the above firm, that this cycle of depression, so far as the general public is concerned, has been productive of good results. But the most palpable good wrought by these results is claimed to be more strongly arrayed on the side of the purchasing public, than on the side of the merchants. For example, some twelve months ago, when the depression in commercial affairs was, perhaps, at its height, the above firm were endeavouring to solve the best means by which they could recruit trade, primarily for the expansion of their own business, under a new system. So successful, however, were the means they adopted, that the new elasticity imparted to the business soon surpassed their own expectations. Before acting upon the determined new step, the firm realised that people had not the plethora of money for investment in *drapery*, and general *soft goods*, that they formerly had. Hence it was, they concluded that some means must be devised which would give the purchaser a larger purchasing power for his or her pound, than they formerly possessed. The only way in which this step could be accomplished was, to sink the retail profit entirely in the wholesale, and offer their whole stock—which is always extensive—in any quantities and lengths, at wholesale prices. They accordingly threw open their establishment, which was hitherto exclusively wholesale, to the smaller requirements and greater caprices of the retail trade. Whether this step will prove remunerative to them, the future alone can answer. Certain it is, however, that it must be an immense advantage to purchasers to be able to dictate their own quantities and lengths to the merchant, and enjoy his wholesale prices. The main object, it appears, is, to supply squatters, farmers, and others, in large or small quantities as they may elect. To mothers of families having only five pounds to spend where they formerly enjoyed ten, it is particularly suggestive of economy. It will readily be seen, that such a system as this firm have introduced would entail an immense amount of risk to the proprietors, if carried on in the ordinary credit system. In fact, it would be impossible to conduct it on any such basis; for the loss of an ordinary parcel sold on credit, would, perhaps, strip the profit from a whole day's transactions, so fine are the profits now cut in the wholesale drapery line. But Messrs. Craig, Williamson and Thomas shrewdly saw this, and anticipated the evils which might accrue from a credit business, by determining that their business should only be done for cash. They say "we are prepared to exchange our goods with the public for their money at the minimum of profit, but we must have the maximum of security for it." They have in consequence resolved upon a strictly cash business, and find it working extremely well. This factor in the undertaking—the cash system—seems to guarantee their ability to continue what they have begun; for, speaking for ourselves, we must confess that we could not perceive how one firm could sell goods cheaper than another and make the "game worth the candle," but if the percentage of risk is infinitely small, it becomes simply a problem of volume, and if the prices are what these gentlemen say they are, "unprecedentedly low," they will become most eloquent agents in attracting new trade in addition to their old. It may at first produce some prejudice against the firm who serves both wholesale and retail customers alike, without the conservation of the customary profit for the smaller retailer. But a little reflection will suggest the philosophy of the nineteenth century, of which this is the outcome, that "every man is trying to do the best he can for himself." The business of this firm (wholesale and family) is conducted in the one premises, one staff of salesmen performing the requisite attentions to customers. This firm is also a large importing house, having their own buyers in the English and Continental markets, which arms them with extra expedients for the attraction of new trade. They adhere to wholesale hours, namely, from 9 till 5 p.m., and on Saturday's until 1. Packages of any size are delivered with the utmost dispatch, and free, to any of the suburbs and on board steamers or at railway stations. The premises are also conveniently and centrally situated for buyers, either from town, suburbs, or country, being in Elizabeth-street, near the Hobson's Bay Railway Terminus.

The drawback received from the Government on all goods exported to the other colonies, and which have paid duty, is allowed to buyers, when the value reaches or exceeds the Customs limit of £5.

The firm have recently enlarged their premises by adding another story to the building, for the convenience of their female workers. A hydraulic lift, with patent safety gear attached, conveys visitors from the first to the second and third floor show-rooms, and the labour of ascending stairs is thus avoided.

The first floor is devoted to Manchester goods, such as blankets, flannels, sheetings, calico, &c.; also woollens and clothing, hats, shirts, gents' and boys' outfits, &c., &c. In the second floor, dresses, silks, mantles, costumes, haberdashery, hosiery, and lace and fancy goods, are displayed. The third floor accommodates the millinery show and sales-room, ladies' fitting-room, and the wholesale departments. The fourth floor is occupied by milliners, dressmakers, and mantle makers, placed in a comfortable, well lighted and ventilated room, measuring 60 ft. by 50 ft. The exterior appearance of the building, retaining as it does its original wholesale aspect, is likely to mislead those who have been accustomed to make their purchases at retail shops where a great display is made in the windows, and it is necessary to bear this in mind when looking for the establishment; but an inspection of the interior and its varied contents will soon convince the visitor of the many advantages to be obtained by making their retail purchases from this enterprising firm.

In conclusion, we have simply to say, that all visitors to Melbourne, as well as all metropolitan and suburban residents, should visit this unique establishment before making purchases elsewhere, in order to discover at what price goods are cheap, and where they are dear.

ROBERT HARPER AND CO.

An industry which will, in any way, contribute to make Melbourne a large manufacturing centre is well deserving of the greatest encouragement, and the highest meed of praise is due to those to whose inception the industry owes its rise and progress. An important and considerable factor in the development of the commercial importance of Melbourne, is the number and extent of the various industries which are to be found in its midst. According to the contributions of these industries to the growing necessities and requirements of the population, must we judge of the wealth and prosperity of the population itself. When the resources of a country are sufficient for its population, with the addition of a very large surplus existing for the supply of other markets, the progress and development of that country to a rank equal, and it may be superior, to the older countries of the world, are but matters of time and opportunity. The pastoral, agricultural, and mining wealth of Victoria must be apparent to every experienced eye, and we can scarcely wonder when we see so many enterprising men embarking their fortunes and their time in their development; but when we see industries created which can only be fairly or approximately judged with regard to their success, or the capabilities of the country to contribute to their success, we certainly are disposed to give a fair share of encouragement to those gentlemen whose keen insight into business is so remarkable, and whose attention is ever on the alert to seize and take advantage of the opportunities which are presented, and whose spirit of enterprise rises equal to every occasion which offers itself to their notice. The competition which they have to encounter in the importation of the several articles which they manufacture themselves, the prejudices they must overcome, in the natural disposition of the people to patronise what has long and successfully been before their notice, the almost insuperable difficulties which are continually and unexpectedly cropping up, can only be successfully mastered by men hopeful of the future, and resolved to be daunted by no amount of opposition in the accomplishment of their scheme. There is another and very important factor to be considered in the creation and successful career of a new industry, and that is, the amount of surplus labour which it swallows up. This factor cannot be overestimated. When we consider the large and growing population of Melbourne, with their equally large and growing requirements, we cannot do less than accord to those who initiate an industry that absorbs so much employment, and yields such great returns to so large a number of the population, the honour which is their due. They become public benefactors, and largely contribute to the welfare, not only of their adopted colony, but also to the other colonies of their adopted country. There is always a large percentage of the people who are, so to say, not suited to the general run of commerce and trade, and it is a source of difficulty to the political economist to what branch of productive labour such as these must be relegated. The question is at once practically answered by the continual introduction of new industries. Gratefully are such enterprises interviewed by those who have the prosperity of their adopted country at heart, and acceptable indeed must be the starting of a new and paying industry to those whose lives would otherwise be passed in the uncertainties that must ever be the natural concomitant of occasional and fugitive employment. We have every reason to hope, that with the rise of new branches in trade and commerce, not only will the city of Melbourne or the colony of Victoria be materially benefited, but that those benefits will extend to and be felt in the other colonies of this new country, as well as in the countries which are remote in name only.

Much of what we have said in this chapter can be applied to the business of Messrs. Robert Harper and Co., and a description will, we know, be not only interesting but instructive to our readers. We have taken some of the following particulars of the industry carried on by the firm from the exhibits of their productions made by them at the Melbourne International Exhibition, 1880. The exhibits of Messrs. Robert Harper and Co. are intended to show the development and progress necessary to the preparation for domestic use of the following articles:—Coffee and cocoa, chicory, pepper, spices, rice, oatmeal, &c. The manufacture of most of these goods are to a large extent separate trades, although carried on by one firm, and may be divided into two classes. 1st. Those which involve the manufacture and packing of foreign raw material. 2nd. Those which involve the manufacture and packing of raw material wholly or in part the produce of Victoria. Of the first class, coffee, cocoa, peppers, spices and rice are the chief; and of the second, oatmeal, mustard, and chicory are most prominent. Each class, being arranged in series, showed first the raw material and then the same at various stages of the process of manufacture, and finally, the finished goods packed in tins, bags, or other packages, ready for the grocer or storekeeper. Raw coffees were shown from all the chief producing countries, Ceylon, India, Java, &c.; then, the beans roasted, and finally, the same ground and packed in tins. Rice is shown in the husk or as it is technically termed, in the "paddy;" then as rough rice, and lastly as fine clean polished rice fit for the table. In oatmeal the raw and kiln-dried oats are shown, then the same hulled, then ground into oatmeal of various grades of fineness. So with mustard, pepper, spices, cocoa, chicory, &c. The preparation and packing of all these goods involves the employment of a very large amount of labour, skilled, and unskilled, and the industries are from that point of view of great importance, besides which the general use of these in nearly every household gives a special interest to their careful and genuine preparation. Special interest in a Victorian point of view attaches to the productions of Messrs. Robert Harper and Co., seeing that they utilise the raw material which is the produce of the colony, for instance :—Oatmeal, for the production of which Victoria has long been celebrated. Mustard, from seed grown in Victoria, equal if not superior to the well-known brands of Keene and Colman. Chicory, from root the produce of the Lancefield district, which is fully up to the best productions of Parry and Co., and Taylor Brothers of London.

The manufacture of the canisters for coffee, pepper, cocoas, mustard, &c., and the illuminated boxes for the same, is a large industry. All these are made in the factory and by the workmen of the firm, and they very fairly claim that their tin-canistered goods of every description, may in quality and general style of get-up compare favourably with any produce of Europe or America.

The firm was established in 1866 by Mr. Robert Harper, who was formerly in the same business as a member of another firm, and was subsequently joined by his brother. They are large importers of East Indian produce, which, as our readers are aware, consists of coffee, rice, and spices, &c., &c. In addition to importing and selling the raw material, they manufacture and prepare it for use, and also for local consumption.

The business is very extensive, and shows not only a large but increasing sale. It extends throughout the whole colony of Victoria, as well as throughout the other colonies. The firm have branches at Sydney and Adelaide, so that the supplies for New South Wales and South Australia may be drawn from convenient centres. We have already mentioned that the firm employs a large amount of labour, giving an instance of one new and successful industry, which may be augmented as the colonies grow, and of the occasion for employment offered to those skilled as well as those unskilled in the Victorian new industries. The premises first occupied by the firm were those in Flinders-lane East, which were erected by the first steam laundry company in Victoria; that business having been unsuccessful, the premises were vacant, and were adapted by Messrs. Harper and Co. to the requirements of their business. The extension of the operations of the firm led them to remove to more commodious premises in Flinders-street, erected originally by the well-known George F. Train, and at a later period occupied by the Oriental Rice Mill Company. Messrs. Harper and Co. having bought the machinery and business of this latter concern, removed the machinery to their newly-built rice mills in West Melbourne, and used the premises so vacated for their general coffee and spice business.

The mills built and occupied by Messrs. W. Degraves and Co. subsequently having come into the market, Messrs. Harper and Co. became the purchasers; and the premises being very extensive, they adapted them not only to the requirements of their general business, but made additions which enabled them to carry on their rice-cleaning mills in a separate compartment of the same building, thereby doing away with the inconvenience of separate establishments, and affording much greater effectiveness of supervision. These premises were well known, the machinery first-class, the engine and boiler by Fairbarn, of Manchester, being reckoned about the best in the colony.

DAVID MUNRO AND CO.

There is little doubt but that those persons who are capable of the practical application of discoveries to the ever-increasing exigencies of mankind are more important factors in the progressive civilisation of a country than the discoverers themselves. This may appear, at the first view, somewhat paradoxical, but it ceases to be so on reflection. A discovery properly so called may be the result of a particular search, or it may be accidental. In either case, when the discovery is once made, the work of the discoverer virtually ceases. True, he places in the hands of him who may be called the utiliser, the material for utilising. But it is to the so-called utiliser, rather than to the discoverer, that is due the application of the thing itself to the wants of man, either through the vehicles of necessity, or art, or science. The man who combines, for the purposes of utility, the productions of nature, or of man, so as to serve and satisfy each newly discovered want, with the greatest economy of time, money, and labour, is certainly of more importance in the social or national fabric than he who accidentally or designedly chances upon nature's arcana and then stops. No discovery is of any practical use until practical application has made it so. Of what use was the discovery of gold, silver, copper, tin, lead, iron, or coal, until they were found *desiderata* in the economy of human life. But it is to the two last named that the palm of real and absolute usefulness must be undoubtedly assigned. The possession of iron and coal to an almost unlimited extent has been the secret of England's greatness and her exalted position in the scale of nations. No nation of modern times can compete with the rapid advancement of art and science that is so striking a feature of the nineteenth century unless its mineral wealth embraces these two important factors. All other mineral productions sink into insignificance when compared with the surprising results that have evolved through the discovery of coal and iron. They are at once the sources of untold wealth, of a country's greatness, of the many comforts and conveniences of life, and have been made the vehicles or media of more remarkable discoveries, and have resulted in greater real benefits and usefulness to mankind than all the other minerals put together. The three landmarks or indications of successive stages of civilisation are those respectively called the stone, the bronze, and the iron ages. They were gradated developments, each one necessary to, and meeting the increasing wants which proceeded from, the ever-increasing knowledge of mankind. In the first two ages, the wants of man were few and comparatively unimportant, and the arcana which nature opened to human requirements were fully equal to all the necessities which existed. But immediately that man entered the vestibule of the iron age, new secrets were laid bare, wants generated new wants, until at last it has been forced upon the human mind that nature's great design was to yield resources that would in time almost obviate the necessity of all manual labour, and give leisure to human intellect to fulfil its mighty and sole end, the development and expansion of thought, until, in its lofty flight, it reached and made captive the sublime and eternal realms of truth. We have only to read the great practical benefits conferred upon our mother country by a Watt, a Stephenson, an Armstrong, and numerous others, in order to make the question at once arise in our minds as to what was the instrument, the medium, or the material through which these men laid an embargo of gratitude on all mankind. It was the unlimited supply of coal and iron, ready at hand, and works sufficiently large as to be capable of supplying wants co-extensive with the requirements of the civilised world. We find it the more remarkable then, in another hemisphere, 15,000 miles away from the large coal measures and iron deposits of the mother country, but equal to every exigency of a new country, that firms have risen in a little over two decades of years, to an importance in Australia comparatively for their requirements as great as the firms we have mentioned in preceding chapters, have attained to at home. Of these the firm of David Munro and Co., which has been associated with the various branches of the iron trade in Victoria for more than half the period which covers the history of the colony, takes rank as one. They are a fair illustration of what we have preliminarily stated. They have adapted the discoveries of the old world to the wants of their adopted country, and have given an impetus to the development of the mining and pastoral wealth of Australia, which has conferred benefits, and is likely to associate their names favourably with the future history of Victoria. Prior to 1870, the firm was chiefly occupied with Government contracts, and constructed a large number of railway bridges on the Geelong, Ballarat, and Sandhurst lines. Their name, too, is associated with the Moorabool Viaduct, which they constructed, as well as with many other equally large and skilful works of engineering. When the railway main lines were concluded, so far as the Government exchequer would permit, Messrs. Munro and Co. turned their attention to other fields and pastures new. They devoted special attention to the wants of the selector, and imported agricultural machinery, which they contrived to adapt to the peculiar character of husbandry that obtains in Australia. We may particularise the threshing machine of Ransomes, Sims and Head, which, through some adaptation on the part of Mr. Munro, satisfactorily fulfils each required function, and for particular purposes it now stands unique.

The adaptation of the portable engine, now generally used on farms and stations, is another instance of what can be done by one who, with the necessary practical knowledge, thoroughly studies the principles of supply and demand. Amongst their introduction of improvements, we may mention the colonial fire-box, the steam jacketted cylinder, the variable expansion gear, the sliding crank shaft bracket, the three way force-pumps, enlarged mud-holes, and extra-facilities for clearing out the boiler, rendered necessary by the muddy and brackish water, which it is sometimes unavoidably necessary to use. They supply portable engines of from 2 to 25 horse-power, as well as double cylinder engines. The latter are used principally for mining and sawing, and are frequently placed, minus their wheels and undergear, in steamboats. The single cylinder engines are used for threshing, pumping, chaffcutting, and a variety of itinerant occupations. Many kinds of engines are manufactured on the premises, and are not inferior to the best home productions. In the show rooms may be seen marine, semi-portable, straw-burning, vertical and horizontal engines, &c. An important department is the mining machinery for winding and pumping, for crushing the quartz, and for saving the least trace of gold from the tailings. This they send to all parts of Australia, wherever the ubiquitous gold-digger is to be found. The frequent drought with which the Australian farmers and squatters are familiar, only served as an occasion to develope still further the inventive faculties of colonial mechanicians. They successfully supplied the best steam-pumps, including the plunger and drawlift. They have also designed an effective gear for working deep well force-pumps in an economical manner with a small engine. Whims and whips, and similar contrivances, were largely supplied, so that through their instrumentality some of the evil effects of drought are reduced to a comparative minimum. They are also makers of centrifugal pumps, of a simpler and stronger construction than the common patterns, and capable of throwing a much greater body of water. Their stock also comprises hand-pumps, rotary-pumps and chain waterlifters. Mr. Munro is the patentee and manufacturer of an ingenious apparatus known at home and abroad as "the Victory Self-adjusting Windmill." The mill virtually looks after itself, it is comparatively inexpensive, and is a decided improvement on many of those now in use. There are five distinct sizes of windmills, ranging from one suitable to a cottage, to the larger machines with sail-wheel 20 feet in diameter, capable of raising large quantities of water to a height of 200 feet, and through many miles of piping. Each mill is provided with a metal column, or support, so that no extra expense is incurred in erection. The firm supplies ripping saw-benches, vertical frames, and firewood cutting apparatus. They have also patented a self-acting breaking down, travelling saw-bench, which combines the rapidity of the circular saw with the capacity of the vertical for taking large logs. It is self-acting, and, unlike the ordinary vertical frame, does not require the excavation of a pit, but may be set down on any level ground. It is also largely used by railway contractors for the preparation of sleepers, as well as by station owners, for cutting timber for fencing purposes. The firm has also introduced a post boring-machine, which turns out 130 posts per hour, completely bored for receiving wire. It may also be adapted to the preparation of the mortice for rails, or for a top-rail and wire. An important branch of this concern is that of contractors' plant for the removal of earth, as in railway excavation, &c., for which purpose the firm manufactures a patent automatic earth scoop, which is a decided improvement on some of those formerly in use. They also have imported and supply a brick-making machine, which is capable of making 10,000 bricks per day. Their stock also embraces derrick cranes of their own manufacture, travelling crane crab winches, pile driving machinery, stone breaking plants, Chilian mills, and most other appliances for public work. The millwright's art has also special attention, and many of the finest flour mills in the Australian colonies have been supplied by the firm. David Munro and Co. have introduced what they call the purchasing lease system, which accommodates itself to the means of all, enabling an enterprising energetic man to become in time the possessor of valuable plant. We commend this to the notice of beginners, as well as to those who are not overburdened with a large supply of capital. The head office and the No. 1 yard of the firm are situate at No. 154 Queen-street, and occupy a large area of ground. Their No. 3 yard is in a'Beckett-street, and has some fine storage buildings erected on it. The No. 4 yard, in Elizabeth-street, is of greater extent than the others. This yard has a fine two-story building, with a very complete duplicate workshop. The Queen-street premises are the head-quarters of the firm, and the counting-house, private offices, draughtsman's office, and workshops are all conveniently arranged. There are show-rooms containing the latest inventions and appliances. The manufactory contains several large screw-cutting lathes, one of the most effective planing machines in the colonies, drilling machines, punching and shearin gmachines, forges, and every necessary tool for executing the varied description of engineering work. A powerful steam engine supplies the motive power. The firm have in contemplation the concentration of their various depots on one or two central blocks of land, which will doubtless be found more convenient than present arrangements. Their illustrated catalogue, a very commendable production, will supply the most minute and comprehensive information to all who seek to be supplied at the hands of this energetic and very enterprising firm.

In conclusion, we would call attention to their fine line of machinery, the value of which is £3000, now being shown at the Melbourne International Exhibition. These comprise vertical engine, with winding and pumping gear, patent self-acting travelling circular saw bench, ripping bench and trucks, &c., &c.

ALLAN AND CO.

The people of Melbourne are essentially musical. This fact is evidenced by the number and excellent quality of the musical entertainments held in the city, and the enthusiastic reception they invariably accord to the artists, who, in the course of their peregrinations, sojourn in Melbourne. This just appreciation of music speaks well for the refinement and culture of the people. It is highly creditable that in a city of such recent growth as Melbourne there should be so large a portion of the population, at once ready and having time and wealth enough, to encourage this department of æsthetics, and to do so successfully.

In a colony, whose existence scarcely reaches the half of a century; but which, during that time, has increased to an importance which would astonish the wildest dreams of the early settlers, and which has, at the same time, extended its influence throughout the world, it is astonishing to find that in the midst of all this feverish excitement the people should not be too much engrossed with the practical cares of life to turn their attention towards the cultivation of musical taste. But in Victoria, and especially in Melbourne, music occupies no inconsiderable attention. We are glad that this is so, music is either the precursor of refinement and elegance, or its result. In either case it is an absolute essential of those qualities which are the sunbeams of social life.

The music of a country bears the impress of the main characteristics of its people. As the songs of a rude nation are barbaric and weird, so the melodies and music of a civilised people are smoothly harmonious and regular. The culture and civilisation of a nation may be judged as accurately by its national music as the leading points in the character and appearance of its people may be deduced from the physical features and scenery of the country by which that people is surrounded. In the early days of Melbourne, some 30 years ago, the theatres were poor and insignificant, and the audience often more enthusiastic than discerning. It is only within the last few years that theatres have risen, well built, comfortable, handsome, and commodious ; and though there are now three, each fairly large, yet they are fairly well patronised with appreciative and critical audiences. The Town Hall of Melbourne, a very handsome building, and covering a large piece of ground, is of recent date. On its platform many of the most celebrated singers and musicians of the present day have stood, and its walls have echoed with the applause of audiences that filled it in every part. This is the more remarkable when we know that the room itself is capable of holding, and accommodating comfortably, between two and three thousand people. There are few places in Europe where a true artist is better received than in Melbourne. He may be feted to his heart's content. No artistic sojourner in Melbourne can leave its city and its people without a certain amount of regret, and invariably, a great amount of gratitude, for the spontaneous and kind attention which they all receive. Our readers then will not be astonished to find that musical purveyors occupy a deservedly prominent position in the commercial life of Melbourne. The number of musical warehouses in Melbourne must be noticeable even to the most cursory observer. They are large and handsome, and occupy some of the most advantageous positions in the city.

One warehouse we must not omit to mention, and that is the musical warehouse of the firm of Allan and Co. (late Wilkie, Webster and Allan). This firm, we understand, is the oldest in Melbourne. It was established 30 years ago, by Mr. Joseph Wilkie. Its connection increased so considerably as to render the old premises utterly inadequate for the proper transaction of their largely additional business operations. The new premises occupy one of the finest business positions in Melbourne. The entrance to the ground floor is through glass doors, standing 12 feet back from the street and approached between handsome plate-glass windows. This part of the building, 90 feet by 27 feet and 17 feet high, is devoted to the music department, counting-house, and offices. Cases of music occupy an immense range of shelving, divided at intervals by electro pillars, from which spring gas brackets of gothic design. The first floor forms the grand salon, nearly 100 feet in length by 20 feet 6 inches high, for an imposing array of grand and cottage pianos. In the salon, the firm holds its matinees, the sitting accommodation being sufficient for upwards of 500 people. The second floor contains the organ room, 28 by 25 feet. On this floor are a number of sound-proof rooms, fitted up for teaching purposes, and on the door may be seen the names of the principal members of the Victorian musical profession. The back premises consist of stores, workshops, packing room, &c. A lift, worked by hydraulic power, conveys both customers and goods from one floor to another. The present proprietor, Mr. Geo. L. Allan, joined Mr. Wilkie in 1863. His knowledge of public taste, and his business capacity, account for the large increase in the firm's business, which has been quite extensive since his advent as sole proprietor. The firm was established in 1850, and is the leading house in the music trade throughout Australia. Mr. Joseph Wilkie commenced the business in 1850, Mr. Webster joined as a partner in 1862, and the year following Mr. Allan came into the firm. Messrs. Wilkie and Webster both died in the year 1875, and then Mr. Allan purchased the interest of both parties. The new premises were built exactly to Mr. Allan's design, and were opened in May, 1877. Since that date, the progress of the firm has been one of prosperity.

The firm were the originators, in 1860, of the time-payment system, by which pianos and organs can be bought by monthly payments, extending over a term of one or two years. Wilkies' has been the box-office and business centre for all the great artists who have visited Australia, viz. :—Catherine Hayes, Madame Anna Bishop, Arabella Goddard, Ristori, Ilma de Murska, all the Italian and English Opera companies, Carlotta Patti, Henry Ketten, &c. Mr. Allan visited England, Germany, and France 10 years ago, and laid the foundation of an extensive connection with Kapp, Rönisch, Lipp, Blüthner, Schmidt, Neumann, Schiedmayer, &c. About a year ago, Mr. Allan again visited Europe, and established business relations with Westermayer, Bosendorfen, Forster, Ecke, Ibach, Rösener, Rachal, Brinsmead, &c. The firm have for years represented the great houses of Broadwood, Collard, Erard (London and Paris), besides many other makers of great and known reputation. Mr. Allan is the representative of all the large London music publishing houses. The Smith organs were introduced by Mr. Allan five years ago. Allan and Co. now supply these organs throughout all the Australian colonies. These organs are conceded by many to be the most perfect imitation of the pipe organ, and the finest reed organs in the world. We understand that, at the Melbourne Exhibition, Allan and Co. represent some of the first houses in France, Germany, and America, viz. :—Erard, Schiedmayer, and the Smith American Organ Company, besides a number of other houses of great reputation. The firm have issued a handsome music catalogue, classified and arranged by Mr. Allan himself. It contains the publications of all the leading London houses. The firm's colonial publications include compositions by Ketten, Giorza, Pratt, Zelman, Emmett, Alfred Moul, G. B. Allan, Giammona, and a host of others. In the show-rooms are represented all the finest pianoforte-makers in England, Germany, and France, Messrs. Allan and Co. having been appointed sole agents in Victoria for many of the best houses. We are informed by the firm that their stock of pianos and cabinet organs kept, including those on hire, amounts to the large sum of £20,000 cost value, and the stock of musical instruments of other kinds, music, &c., brings it up to a grand total of about £27,000—a magnificent stock, and, in fact, inferior in point of variety and excellence to few even of the best establishments in the old country. Mr. Allan is ably assisted by a large staff of clerks, salesmen, tuners, repairers, &c. &c., many of whom have been in the firm's employ for a large number of years.

Mr. Allan certainly deserves credit for the efficient manner in which he caters for the musical taste of Melbourne.

NICHOLSON AND CO.

One of the noteworthy features of Melbourne in the shape of the development of culture is the establishment and business of Messrs. Nicholson and Co. We do not propose to notice either of these in the same spirit that has pervaded our remarks of preceding houses. The dissemination of the arts of the muses, and in particular Euterpe and her flute, cannot be held to lend any active part in the material development of a city or country. But the part they can be made to play, if not in the material, at least in the social and æsthetical development of a country, is none the less important in their department. They bring about that softening refinement so necessary to a keen appreciation of the weal that a successful commercial life has provided. They infuse into the homes, so bounteously provided with all that money can buy, an element which makes all these surroundings seem more beautiful. At least, they awaken the better nature—the soul—which may be latent in the merchant while he is driving his bargain with commercial life, and lead it into a temporary paradise it could not have occupied before. Mr. J. C. W. Nicholson, one of the present proprietors of this establishment, came to Melbourne in 1859, and commenced business on his own account in 1875. In 1876, he took in Mr. Ascherberg as partner, who retired from the firm in 1878. In 1876, they removed to the very handsome premises occupied by them now, in Collins-street East, where they presumably have one of the largest stocks of instruments and music of any house in Australia. The size of their premises is 32 feet front by 130 feet in depth, embracing a large gallery and numerous rooms for the instruction of music. There is also an extensive basement for packing, repairing, and tuning instruments, &c., &c. Their cottage piano room is capable of containing about 80 pianos, the organ room about 100 organs, and the grand piano gallery about 20 instruments. The fixtures in this establishment, for the accommodation of the immense stock of music that is kept, cost no less a sum than £2000. Adjacent to the counting-house is a theatre box-office, where seats may be booked in advance. It is a common thing for matinees to be given here, when the services of leading vocalists and instrumentalists are engaged. Some extent of the business that this firm do in instruments may be imagined when it is known that their stock in organs and pianos in the premises, reaches the high figure of £5000. They have also £3000 worth on hire, and about 1000 instruments of all kinds sold on the time-payment system. The stock of music on hand is very large. The amount of music sold yearly, at this and the Sydney establishment, is something quite extensive, and a conspicuous item in this amount is the music published here, composed by local men. Their enterprise in furthering the musical taste of the community has extended to literature, in publishing a musical magazine at intervals, price one shilling, larger and better finished than the one published in London. Of this they circulate between 20,000 and 30,000 each number. The magazine contains original copyrights, English compositions, &c. &c., purchased exclusively for it. Concerning the stock of pianos kept by this firm, the German makes are preferred, and of these the beautiful instruments made by Lipp, Schiedmayer, Rönisch, Westermayer, Beibstein, Grotrian, Heifferich and Schutz, and Steinway, of Germany. In addition to these they keep the well-known names of Erard, Collard, Broadwood, Pleyel, Kinkman, Aucher, and Bord. In organs, the Americans seem to have it all their own way, their instruments having almost entirely displaced the Alexandre. The names of Geo. Woods, Burdett, and others, seem to be most popularly known, especially the former, whose organs are said to have attained the acme of volume and melody. A very fine illustrated catalogue has been issued by this firm at a cost of £250, with every possible information in it. This can be had on written or personal application, and would greatly facilitate the purchaser's choice. Their Sydney house is conducted on precisely the same principle as governs the one in Melbourne. No expense is spared to make the stock new, novel, and complete. The variety on hand there is precisely as large and good as it is at the Melbourne house, and in this particular the enterprise of this concern must be applauded. They are in direct communication with all the leading pianoforte-makers and music-publishers, and are supposed to keep one of the largest stocks in Australia. Their present exhibit at the Melbourne Exhibition is regarded with interest, as the one they made at Sydney brought them much favourable notice. Either of their establishments are well worth a visit, everything being conveniently arranged for ladies, and for the facility of their purchases. We would strongly recommend all those who have not visited their two establishments, to do so at an early day, and all those who have visited them to be constant in their renewals, for they are receiving new music by every steamer.

KILPATRICK AND CO.

Among the idiosyncrasies of Australians, not the least important is the penchant for jewellery. It is noticeable to the most cursory outside observer. It not only exists among those whose lines have fallen in pleasant places, but it is even observable in the working digger, the agriculturist, the cabby, the working man, and last, though not least prominent, among the "larrikins" who infest the streets of the Australian towns and villages. Amongst precious metals, gold seems the weakness; while we often see rings, and other ornaments of jewellery, made of silver, chiefly among the rising generation. Diamonds, amongst the wealthy classes, seem to be the favourite in the order of precious stones. Rings are worn, as a rule, by every man, woman, and boy one meets. This characteristic is the sign-post, though a humble one, of a latent æsthetical taste, which must, sooner or later, be developed. As gold amongst metals, and diamonds amongst precious stones, seem to be the prevailing taste, it may not be uninteresting to our readers to give a few succinct particulars about the one and the other. If we estimate the yard of gold at £2,000,000, which it is in round numbers, all the gold in the world might, if melted into ingots, be contained in a cellar twenty-four feet square, and sixteen feet high. All the boasted wealth obtained from California and Australia, would go into an iron safe nine feet square, and nine feet high, so small is the cube of yellow metal that has carried the immigration of population, peopled a new country larger than the Continent of Europe, and roused the whole world to wonder. The late Keeper of the Mining Records states that for the uses of the arts, not less than 1000 ounces of fine gold are used in Birmingham alone every week, and that in the United Kingdom the weekly consumption of leaf-gold is as follows:—London, 400 oz.; Edinburgh, 35 oz.; Birmingham, 70 oz.; Manchester, 40 oz.; Dublin, 12 oz.; Liverpool, 15 oz.; Leeds, 6 oz.; Glasgow, 6 oz.; total, 584 oz. Of this, he states on the authority of an eminent gold-refiner, that not one-tenth part can be recovered, and he adds, that for gilding metals of the electrotype, and the water, or wash-gilding processes, not less than 10,000 ounces of gold are required annually. We are curious to know the consumption of gold in Victoria. It would be a matter of interest to compare it with the production. The superiority of the diamond, as an ornamental gem, depends, not only on its high reflective power, which alone separates the colours of white light to a very great degree, but also on its low dispersive power, which prevents them from being separated too much and detained, one might say, within the stone, or rather prevented from emerging from it after reflection. The word diamond is derived through the French *diamant*, from the Greek word ἀδάμας invincible, and this again from α and ςαμάω to crush or subdue, from its supposed property of resisting the action of fire, and the heaviest strokes of the hammer. The full-grown diamond exceeds in value more than a hundred thousand times its mass in gold; it is the most cherished possession, and the proudest ornament of emperors and kings; it is the most esteemed and the brightest gem in the chaplet of beauty, and yet it is but a lump of coal, which heat reduces to a cinder, and dissipates into that insalubrious gas which ascends from the most putrid marsh, and bubbles from the filthiest quagmire. Diamonds are cut by a horizontal iron plate, about ten inches in diameter, called a schyf, which revolves from 2000 to 3000 times per minute. The diamond is fixed in a ball of lead, which is fitted to an arm, one end of which rests upon the table, on which the plate revolves, and the other at which the ball containing the diamond is fixed, is pressed upon the plate by movable weights, varying according to the size of the facets to be cut, from two to thirty pounds. It is difficult to express in words, or in numbers, the commercial value of the diamond, but it has been said that a string of Koh-i-noors, a furlong in length, would purchase the fee-simple of the globe, while a ring, engirdling the Arctic zone, would buy up the whole of the planetary system. We have been disposed to these particulars through a notice, which we have before us, of the enterprising firm of Kilpatrick and Co., goldsmiths, &c. They have establishments both at London and at Melbourne, and their operations are on an extensive scale in both of these commercial centres, the one of the northern and the other of the southern hemisphere. It is upwards of a quarter of a century since they commenced business in Melbourne. In 1853, their first start was as wholesale dealers only, and this branch of their trade speedily developed into importance. Their importations were exclusively confined to London-made goods, thus insuring excellence and durability of workmanship combined with elegance of design, always in the newest style. These goods were naturally of a character and description superior to those which had been previously imported to the colony. The result was a steady and increasing demand for the goods imported by Kilpatrick and Co., and they were equal to the occasion. Two years later, that is in 1855, they opened their present establishment, in which they combined the wholesale with the retail business. They then not only continued to supply their former customers, but they were now able to cater for the tastes of Victorians generally and Melbournians specially. The growing demand for the best, the newest, and most artistic styles was readily and promptly met. By continuing to maintain their aim, of adding to their stock only high-class goods, of unquestionable taste, they have secured a *clientèle*, second we believe, to none in the colony. This principle of studying the growing tastes of the time, combined with the facilities which the firm have of procuring goods of such varied elegance, design, and at the same time durable, is, we apprehend, the great secret of the success which has attended the efforts of Messrs. Kilpatrick and Co. in supplying the growing demand for jewellery of gold, and other ornaments inlaid with the precious metal. A visit to their establishment would fully repay any time that might be spent in inspecting their well chosen stock.

THE VICTORIA ICE COMPANY, LIMITED.

Among the many industries which now flourish in Victoria, and which contribute to our comforts, our luxuries, and our ailments at one and the same time, none is more deserving of its meed of praise than the Victoria Ice Company, Limited. The difficulties which were experienced during the earlier settlement of the colony in importing ice, made it so expensive an article that few except the rich were able to have at hand a constant or even at times an occasional supply. It was originally imported from America at great risk, and often at great loss, so that the great expense which was incurred before it reached the colonial market, made it an article of luxury rather than one which could minister to comforts or alleviate ailments. This great desideratum in a hot climate, and the great expense of importing, naturally found its remedy, through men whose enterprise and aptitude enabled them to turn to account the resources which science had placed at their disposal. It was found that artificial ice could be manufactured at a less expense than the imported article, and would at the same time answer every purpose as well; and the result was that a company was formed for the manufacture of ice at a reasonable rate, under the style of the Victoria Ice Company, Limited. Their object was, by its cheapness, to bring it within the reach of all, at the same time ensuring a regular and almost unlimited supply. What was at one time a very expensive luxury, may now, through the instrumentality of the Victoria Ice Company, be found in almost every household where the existence of the company is known. The supply being increased to such an extent, has created a demand far exceeding, we may safely say, whatever the company expected at its inception would ever be realised. It may be interesting to our readers to be informed that the process of manufacture adopted by the company is that of forcing briny water through copper tanks of various sizes, until the water in these tanks is reduced to a freezing temperature. They have recently added powerful new machinery, by which they are now producing crystal and the white or berg ice. We cannot think that it is uninteresting to have inserted these remarks, especially for those of our readers who are living in the colonies or in those countries where the heat is so intense that any means of alleviating pleasantly the thirst which is so often felt, will be welcomed with, we might almost say, grateful pleasure. Our friends in England, even during the hottest summer, can never understand or fully appreciate how great a luxury ice is felt to be by those living in hot climates. The heat is often so great that water and other liquids, however exhilarating they may be themselves, are reduced to such a temperature as almost to be productive of that thirst which they are meant to allay. It is in such cases that ice is as necessary for health as it is for its cooling powers, producing, as it does, so refreshing and delicious a beverage. We are glad that the company, through its operations, has brought the supply as much within the means of the employed as the employer; and we cannot but feel grateful that, though a fair return is sought for the time and capital which are expended by the gentlemen forming the company, they are not unmindful of the necessity of contributing as largely as possible, and at a cheap rate, to the comforts, and oftentimes necessities, of every grade of our population. Another, and not less important factor, is the usefulness, as well as in many cases of sick ness, the absolute necessity, of ice as a cooling medicament, which, in this respect, is largely used in our hospitals, as well as among the sick who are to be found in our own houses. It often effectually allays or dissipates pain, and many times life has been saved where it has been ready to hand for use in cases of urgent necessity. The difficulties of limited supply, which prevailed under the system of imported ice, have now disappeared, and no one need be without a constant supply.

In addition to ministering to the comforts and luxuries of life, as well as to the alleviation of many of its ailments, this new industry of ice manufacturing gives additional employment to capital and labour, and provides the wherewithal for many families that might otherwise find it hard to obtain employment in the present condition of the labour market. Any augmentation to the field of labour must be welcomed by every true philanthropist; and in this respect, as well as those others to which we have referred, is the Victoria Ice Company deserving of the greatest encouragement. Wherever there is a new industry brought into operation, it adds to the wealth and importance of the colony, and finds employment for those who are already in this new country, as well as for any surplus of population through emigration from home. The works, which may be said to be on a fairly extensive scale, are in Franklin-street, and they give employment to a great number of workmen. The offices of the Company are situated at 77 Collins-street west. The management is in the hands of Mr. C. W. Umphelby, whose experience and knowledge of the business enable him to cater satisfactorily for the very numerous cliental which the Company now enjoys. The business is yearly increasing, and of course with this increase, the number of the workmen employed is increased at the same time.

MR. E. ROWLANDS.

Among the many industries which have sprung up in Australia, that for the manufacture of what we may designate temperance drinks, is one deserving of the very greatest encouragement. It is an important desideratum, not only in a social aspect, in such a climate as Victoria, where very often such extreme heat prevails, but also for sanitary considerations, seeing that the water supply of Melbourne is in every way so unsatisfactory. There is probably no city in the world where, in proportion to its numbers, more intoxicating drinks are consumed than in Melbourne. Hence, in the case of an industry, whose influence must tend to modify this great and lamentable evil, by the introduction of pleasant as well as invigorating beverages, we cannot but wish that it may be attended with unqualified success. Although the principle of temperance is advocated with persevering energy and ability, and powerful appeals are made to the masses to refrain from the excessive indulgence in spirituous and other stimulants, yet unless they are supplemented by some provision for the supply of drinks at once exhilarating and pleasant to the palate, the efforts of all philanthropists must be, to a very great extent, incomplete, and consequently unsuccessful. Those who, while seeking a fair return for their trouble and time, combine with this a real desire to contribute to the moral and social welfare of their fellow-men, by educating a demand, through the influence of the supply itself, are deserving of the highest praise from all those who have the true welfare of the colony at heart. We believe these last remarks are justly applicable to the gentleman whose industry, *i.e.*, the manufacture of soda-water, lemonade, and other equally pleasant drinks, is the subject of the present chapter. It is now, we understand, twenty-six years ago since Mr. Rowlands first started business for the manufacture of ærated waters, in conjunction with Mr. Robert Lewis, under the firm name of Rowland and Lewis. The firm first commenced operations at Ballarat, and erected a factory on a site situated on the edge of Youl's Swamp, now known as Lake Wendouree. The factory, like all buildings at that time, was of canvas, and was erected on a spot now known as View Point Esplanade. At this period, the firm had to contend against the competition of thirteen other ærated water factories, which we are glad to say rather stimulated than discouraged its efforts. During those primitive times, hand labour took the place of what is now done by the aid of machinery, and Messrs. Rowlands and Lewis, by the introduction of what are called Taylor's No. 1 machines, at once placed the other factories at a disadvantage. Their rolling-stock, at this time, was represented by one horse and a delivery-cart. Determined as the firm was to manufacture the very best article, it was soon found that success attended its efforts to accomplish this praiseworthy object, which being supplemented by steady energy and zeal, soon resulted in the abandonment of the primitive premises for more suitable and commodious ones, situated at the intersection of Sturt and Dawson-streets, Ballarat West. As business increased, it was found necessary to increase the appliances, and consequently the firm purchased an imported plant, which cost £1000 in England. The plant, which had been in use at what was then termed Spring Hill (now Redan), Ballarat, consisted of three of T. Boulton and Son's (of London) first-class machines, some of which we were told the firm retain to this day. As the plant was added to, the business increased proportionately. All kinds of mineral and other ærated waters, together with the cordials then in use, were manufactured in the factory. The firm still continued to produce drinks of the very best quality, and the result was the demand for a pure, palatable, and wholesome beverage increased to such an extent that it was found necessary to resort to steam power, which they did in 1858, or just four years after the factory was started. Probably the most important factor in the manufacturing of ærated waters is the abundant or sufficient supply of the purest water. The firm, recognising this, diligently sought for, and were rewarded by finding a spring at Warrenheip, the waters of which were proved to be rich in iron, lime, and other constituents peculiarly adapted to the manufacture of the higher classes of mineral waters. This naturally resulted in the supply of an article which met with approval on all sides, and which created, through its superior quality, a very large demand. The same history of continued prosperity, and increasing business, necessitated the construction of larger premises, and the firm at once secured a suitable site at the corner of Dana and Dofton-streets, and there erected, at considerable outlay, the factory which they built in 1870. The appliances and convenience for the carrying on of this important industry are probably superior to any other establishment of the kind south of the line. No expense was spared by the enterprising firm, in fitting up each department of the manufactory, so as to enable them to keep up an almost inexhaustible supply of the purest and best articles. As the business developed, and the reputation of the firm for the best quality of waters extended, it was deemed advisable to open a branch in Melbourne, and to carry on the same business of manufacturing waters in the metropolis of the colony. The factory at Melbourne is situated at 116 Collins-street west. From small beginnings, it has grown into an important metropolitan industry, and the firm finds at present full employment for fourteen horses and nine waggons, necessary for the efficient discharge of the present business requirements. The Ballarat factory still continued to supply the factory at Melbourne with soda, and all other mineral waters. The necessity of this arose from the fact that no water could be found superior, or even equal, to that obtained from the Spring at Warrenheip. Other ærated-waters which do not require any special constituents in the water of which they are made, were, and are now, manufactured for the use of the capital, at the Melbourne factory. The soda-water, which bears the well-known trade-mark of Mr. E. Rowlands, and which has earned so wide-spread a reputation for its superior quality, is still made at Ballarat. At the Dana-street factory, the principal plant comprises three double-action soda-water machines, worked by a powerful steam-engine. One machine is capable of turning out 1500 doz. of soda-water daily, and the capabilities of the other two in use are 1000 doz. per day each ; thus enabling the factory to produce 3500 doz. daily. The whole of the plant was made at Ballarat, by Mr. G. G. Norman, of Wills-street, under the personal supervision of Mr. Rowlands ; it contains all the latest improvements, and we question if, in adaptability to the requirements of the business and excellence in working, it is surpassed by that of any ærated manufactory in England, let alone in Victoria.

In the year 1876, Mr. Robert Lewis retired from the partnership, and Mr. Rowlands became the sole proprietor. Mr. Rowlands being continually alive to the necessity of improvement in every branch of the business, turned his attention to the soda-water bottles, and after careful study, invented and patented an improvement on Codd's patent, and succeeded in producing a bottle which for convenience and cleanliness (the latter always being considered a most important factor by Mr. Rowlands) stands, perhaps, unrivalled. We were informed that the present factory at Ballarat employs workmen who have been in the business of the firm for the last 24 years. The number of men employed by Mr. Rowlands is somewhere about 80, and he also finds employment for 30 horses, all the year round. A visit to the Dana-street factory would well repay in interest and instruction. The filtration of the water used is a most interesting and instructive sight. Each bottle of the soda-water passes through no less than four filtering processes, that purity, in all its completeness, may be ensured. The Melbourne trade has recently increased to a very great extent, but the tariff restrictions are severely felt by the industry; Mr. Rowlands estimates that the protective system which obtains in Victoria, costs him annually from £400 to £600. This, and the fact of Sydney having lately been made the depot of the P. & O., and the Orient fleet of steamers, tells heavily upon the outside and export business. A considerable portion of the sum referred to above is paid by Mr. Rowlands as duty on corks and bottles, and this, while it hampers his trade, is not of the slightest use in the object for which the duty is nominally imposed—the protection of native industry. Mr. Rowlands cannot obtain in this colony the quality of corks necessary for his business, and although he himself tried, at considerable outlay, the experiment of manufacturing the corks from the imported raw material, in the hope of being able to produce a more satisfactory article, he found it quite impracticable. Heavily handicapped as this business thus is, in competing in other colonial markets, it is the more flattering testimonial to the excellence of the specialties made by the firm under notice, that they have no inconsiderable number of customers outside the colony who prefer to pay an extra price in order to obtain the best article. In 1876, Mr. Rowlands introduced the now famous ginger-ale to Victoria, a great desideratum among the sons of temperance; and this and other drinks, have made his name a household word in the Australian colonies.

MR. JOHN STANWAY.

It would occasion a little surprise, on the part of the London or Paris crockery merchant, to be told that Melbourne can boast of a house in that line, whose necessities compel it to carry a stock of forty thousand pounds sterling. They might answer the statement by admitting that the amount in question was an enormous one to be invested in such ware, and spoke volumes for the extravagance and elegance of the stock that represented it, although as much could not be said for the financial ability which allowed a stock of crockery and glassware to eat into so much money. However this may be, the point that we wish to notice, as appealing more particularly to the critical observer, is this. If a house finds itself carrying an enormous stock of forty thousand pounds in a fragile and capricious ware like crockery and glassware, does this fact not produce an incontestable argument in favour of a refined and cultivated taste, which impels, if it does not compel, the merchant to place a very large sum in his business, in order that he may satisfy every demand that is made upon him, no matter how unfrequently it is made or how uncommon be the object sought for. If any proof were needed to establish the inherent refinement of many of the Melbourne people, we could not cite a clearer and a more irrefutable one than this. Nothing but a most critical taste could have called into requisition such an infinite variety, in every considerable shade, shape, and substance, as is on exhibition at the large establishment of Mr. John Stanway, situated at 175 Bourke-street east. To attempt to describe a stock so varied in its excellence and elegance, and so dense in its ramifications of pattern and purpose, would require much greater space than we have at command, hence we must confine ourselves to the briefest notice of it, recommending our readers to go and judge for themselves by a personal inspection of the goods. The founder of this house, Mr. John Stanway, went into business about the year 1852, and started in the premises he now occupies. His early career was beset with many trials and difficulties, as were many other merchants who went into commerce as early as '52. These difficulties no more enfeebled his ambition, than did the different crises incidental to them embarrass his ability to meet his engagements. Both were fought with zeal and determination, and both were mastered in that triumphant way which puts the youthful toiling merchant at comparative ease in his declining years. The result is that now this firm is said to have the largest and most desirable cliental of any house in Australia in their line. It is also said by those who claim to know, that for variety, quality and elegance, their stock will compare favourably with either Mortlock's or Phillips's, in London. In making our peregrinations, we inspected the premises, and found the size of them to be 64 feet front with a depth of 200 feet, every foot of which is closely packed with stock. The warehouse at the back contains three floors, each one being devoted to a special line of merchandise, with very little room left for the buyer to inspect stock from, so much of it is required for its accommodation. The entire capital invested in the business, including building, is nearly fifty thousand pounds. The firm do a large importing business and are weekly in receipt of consignments of the newest French, Dresden, Worcester, Minton, China, and other ware. In Copeland and Wedgwood ware, they are also continually receiving parcels of new goods. They have a resident buyer on the Continent, whose good taste in the selection of novel designs has become proverbial. For French and English vases, this house is no less remarkable, frequently importing very costly and beautifully worked out designs in every conceivable kind of ware. In English glassware they are looked upon as little less than an English house, so complete and large is their line. *Bric-à-brac* also claims a large share of their attention, and they are said to have the finest all-round line of these that find their way into Melbourne. In conclusion we have simply to say that, however graphic might be our description of their establishment, it could not thoroughly describe the completeness of its stock, which nothing short of a visit will enable one to understand, and we would suggest to those who are desirous of passing an instructive, as well as an interesting, hour to call at this establishment.

THOS. TOOHEY AND CO.

There is scarcely a single branch of industry which does not flourish in the Australian colonies. The industry may not be on so large a scale as in the old country, but this is generally made up by the enterprise and energy of the proprietors. Almost everything that is undertaken by the colonists prospers. It may be because so many things they do are done well. No time or trouble is spared, and all the requirements of their business are attended to with special care. Ever on the alert in watching the progress of the times, they quickly seize every opportunity for extending their business and replenishing their stock, as well as introducing the latest improvements. No sooner do they hear of a new article which is popular at home, than it is introduced, at the earliest moment possible, into their adopted country. They educate the tastes of their customers, and when this taste is educated they supply the demand which it has created. In this way they keep pace with the latest improvements in the mother-country. The new chum, as a fresh arrival is called, finds everything here in as great abundance and almost as cheap as he finds it in his own country. He is astonished that he sees comparatively little of what he has not been accustomed to in Europe; and it is only by the beautiful climate, which is varied, with little exception, with few extremes of heat or cold, that he recognises that he has been transplanted to another hemisphere. He finds the same stately buildings, the same style of streets (broader if anything), the same kind of shops, the same industries, the same commerce and the same trade, the same institutions (from a hospital for the body to a library for the mind), the same friendly societies for mutual help, and the same social intercourse; and oftentimes it is with difficulty that he realises, amongst those speaking his own vernacular, only with a little more purity, that he is not still in the country and in the town in which he was born. This, from mere book information, cannot be fully realised at home, and it is only to those who are familiarised with it through personal experience, that it is fully understood, and by whom the truth of our statements can be fully appreciated. If there be any qualification of what we have written, it is that the style and manner of business, as well as of social life, partakes somewhat of that which is peculiar to America. Though steadily progressive in its essential characteristics, it is occasionally spasmodic, and to use an American phrase, "go-ahead." Life seems to pass more quickly, the blood seems to circulate more freely, and there is a general sensation of freedom, which sometimes approaches to license, that certainly at moments reminds us that we are no longer in the country from which the major portion of the population of the Australian colonies has emigrated. Classes are so intermixed that there is scarcely any distinction between the wealthy merchant and the wealthy tradesman. The latter take a prominent position in the social ranks of Australian society, which is due in a great degree to their thrift and commercial integrity. To them also is due much of that prosperity which is so characteristic of Australian commerce and trade. Mindful, it is true, of their individul interests, they never forget the well-being and interests of their newly-adopted country. The gentlemen whose names head our present chapter are illustrations of what energy, perseverance, and enterprise can do for individuals, and how, both directly and indirectly, they contribute to the commercial development of the country.

The firm, which is composed of Messrs. Thos. Toohey, John Gleeson, and James Toohey, was established about 1855, or about a quarter of a century ago. The business embraces the selling of wines, spirits, groceries, and general provisions, in which they do an extensive business with the Australian colonies generally. One remarkable feature of the firm may here be noticed on account of its infrequency, and that is, that the business is in the same hands now as it was 25 years ago. They have experienced, during this long period, all the crises through which trade and commerce have passed since the settlement of Victoria, and this they have done without any or the slightest deterioration to the reputation of the firm, either commercially or with regard to the continued and increasing business which they do. They have always been able to rely upon the business capacity which they possess, and which has enabled them, in spite of difficulties, to weather triumphantly all the adverse times, which, in so many instances, have been fatal to others. This result must ever be the reward of industry and unflagging perseverance, combined with strict attention to all the requirements of their customers. Unsparing of time and trouble, they have devoted their whole energies to the industry in which they are engaged, and the outcome of these practical qualities is, that their establishment may now be considered one of the permanent businesses of Melbourne.

As the colonies have developed, so their business has kept pace; and in this particular branch, the extent of their transactions is equal to that of any other house. We have pleasure in recording this reward of steady attention to business.

THE SINGER SEWING MACHINE COMPANY.

Amongst the inventions of the 19th century, and their name is legion, none occupies a more deservedly prominent position than the invention of the sewing machine. Its end and purpose embrace at once the useful, expeditious, and the humanitarian in domestic economy. Whether the pathetic and thrilling truthfulness of that homely poem, "The song of the shirt," by Tom Hood, first gave an impetus to the philanthropic penchant of the first inventor we know not; but it is sufficient to know that the celebrated poem to which we have referred, was a valuable lever destined to stir up the minds of men of genius to serve at the same time the oppressed, and hard working, and uncomplaining sisters who through sewing found bread for themselves and for those near and dear to them, while it also served as the basis of well-earned and colossal fortunes. We are right, we think, in estimating the value of an invention according to the greatness of the number that it benefits. If we were to admit that sentiment is a factor of all human intelligence, we might also add that the usefulness of an invention is added to, when it enables the working artisans, be they seamstresses or tailors, to accomplish the greatest amount of labour, with the least trouble, and with the greatest profit to themselves, in the shortest time. If we take those two data as standards of the excellence of an invention, then we are justified in asserting that the sewing machine is almost *primus inter pares*. The invention of the sewing machine, like many others, has been claimed by various individuals; but we assume that it will not be controverted that the original idea is not more due to the itinerant Frenchman than to Walter Hunt, an American mechanic. Our cousins on the other side of the Pacific are fertile in inventions, and none does them greater credit than the invention of the sewing machine. We are here reminded of the injustice which runs through the law of patents in almost every nation where the law obtains. A poor man may be an inventor, but it is the rich man to whom he sells the invention, sometimes for a mere song, who becomes the patentee and ultimate millionaire. There is no provision made by the law whereby he can ever have his name enrolled as the first inventor, however conclusive the proof may be which entitles him to be considered as such. Could the law not make any provision which would remove the possibility of this, what every one must unhesitatingly call an injustice? Let the purchasing patentee have his full *quid pro quo*, but do not put off the inventor with the bonus of a stone. It is seldom that the man of genius, to whom the first conception of an invention may be due, has any selfish aim. Indeed, it is questionable whether he ever looks further than its accomplishment. Its necessity may, in the first instance, be to him a motive power; but once the idea is conceived, he simply devotes himself to materialise it, and leaves to his contemporaries or those who live after him the practical application. In this, we seldom, if ever, are enabled to give honour where honour is due. We are attracted to the man who carries the invention into practice; to him the honour is given, and he is generally quite content to rest satisfied, and bear willingly the weight of his borrowed plumage. We have, however, little doubt that for distinct, important, and really useful improvements of the sewing machine, the credit is due to Isaac Merrit Singer, a German by birth, and a man of enterprising energy and wonderful resource. It is a question worthy of consideration whether greater credit is due to the man who first applies an invention to practical ends, or to him who discovers other ends and other means which it is calculated to serve. We are inclined to yield the palm to the latter. In this case, Singer's invention has earned it deservedly. This machine is now a household word among housewives, as well as amongst those whose ambition leads them to hope that at no distant day they will be admitted within the magic circle, and we may also extend its adoption to those ladies who, through strong-mindedness, build to themselves an exclusive fortress which they dare any cavalier to storm successfully. One thing is pretty certain, that the Singer sewing machine has had, since its introduction, by far the largest sale and practical success of any sewing machine in the world. As we understand that the Singer copartnery is by far the largest company of existing sewing machine makers, a few particulars may not be uninteresting. They have works in America and in Scotland. The former are situated in James-street, Bridgeton, New York, while the latter are to be found in Glasgow. From the data which we have before us, we find that the company has very extensive works in both the countries named. The fast-increasing demand for the machine, decided the Singer Company to build a large factory in Glasgow in 1868. Though the Glasgow factory had a modest start, it speedily developed, under its energetic and able management, into a great success. The make-up of machines for 1868 was only 8037. In 1877 it approached 140,000, while in the following year it exceeded 160,000 machines, an enormous increase, which is all the more remarkable when it is remembered that for the first two years the machines were only "built," the shaped and milled parts having been shipped over from New York, while the machines with all their etceteras are now entirely manufactured in Glasgow. This factory gives constant employment to something like 1800 hands. The weekly make-up of machines in Glasgow alone is on an average about 3500. This output is, we understand, achieved by the Glasgow factory altogether independently of the company's gigantic works at Elizabeth Port, New Jersey, U.S.A., which have, we are told, an average weekly produce exceeding even these large figures.

The following extract from a letter, dated New York, Nov. 25th, 1879. from the vice-president of the Singer manufacturing company, to a friend in Melbourne, will give a very good idea of the rapid growth and enormous magnitude of the concern:—" We were fairly started on the course of prosperity, which has never yet been interrupted, when Mr. Singer returned from Europe. His partner insisted upon making it (the business) into a joint-stock company, and in 1863 it was organised, I remaining as manager for the first year, and then becoming vice-president, a position I have held ever since. Of the enormous growth and extension of the business you have doubtless some idea from general repute. In 1862, we sold a little over 12,000 machines, we are now turning out 11,000 every week, and will increase production soon as we are far behind our orders. The actual sales for this year will be about 430,000, and would have been more if we could have filled all orders. I can remember when only four (4) men besides myself were working in the factory, while now in manufacturing and distribution, directly and indirectly, we estimate about 40,000 are employed by us."

The sales of the company during the last ten years are as follows:—

Year	Machines	
1870	127,833	Singer machines
1871	181,260	,, ,,
1872	219,758	,, ,,
1873	232,444	,, ,,
1874	241,679	,, ,,
1875	249,852	,, ,,
1876	262,316	,, ,,
1877	282,812	,, ,,
1878	336,432	,, ,,
1879	431,167	,, ,,

These are not fictions, they are strong incontrovertible facts. They show an extraordinary increase, and are infallible signs that the increasing wants of the age, with respect to the age's improvement, are being met satisfactorily. We have some interesting facts before us as to the process of manufacture, which space only allows us to deal with briefly. In the needle department, one man cuts the steel to length, a second forges it to shape, a third dresses it, a fourth mills it, a fifth drills it, a sixth buffs it, a seventh fits it, an eighth inspects it, and so on. This is a division of labour that must make the shade of Adam Smith smile with unqualified pleasure. The workers of the machine needle are mostly females, and the present produce reaches 150,000 needles per week. A great deal of attention is paid to the manufacture of this important article, as unless it is perfect in temper, finish and fit, the whole machine suffers in efficiency. The Singer sewing machine is in itself a most ingenious and interesting piece of mechanism to look at, but its familiarity to the many by whom it is used, would render a description of it somewhat tedious to the reader, more particularly to those who work, or intend to work at it daily. The Singer company employ in the manufacture of their machines, steam hammers, drop hammers, and trip hammers. The trip hammer, we may mention, is a simply yet ingeniously constructed machine which strikes some 300 blows per minute. It is the introduction, from time to time, of the latest labour-saving aids and invention, which has enabled the company to put their machine into the market at a lower price than formerly, and with extended improvements and a higher style of finish, if possible, than they could previously accomplish. By these arrangements the public are the ultimate gainers. The Singer machine is exported to almost every civilised and, we were almost going to say, uncivilised portion of the habitable world ; and we believe it is the aim of the company to put this machine, so indispensable to the family economy, into every house, in which laudable object we earnestly wish them every success. The address of the Singer manufacturing company in London is 39 Foster Lane, E.C.

MR. S. MULLEN.

The advance of literature in Victoria has kept pace with the rapid advancement of commerce and trade. Progress in the latter is as a rule synonymous with the extension of the former. The introduction of high-class literary works tends to cultivate and elevate the taste of the population, and books which afford lighter and more digestible pabulum fill up the leisure hours of those, the greater part of whose time is taken up with the concerns of life. Such a result may be with confidence regarded as the outcome—the one of those books which are comprehended under the various heads of history, biography, and travels; the other of lighter reading, such as historical and other novels. To keep pace with the growing requirements of civilisation, necessitates so large an amount of reading, that it is important to choose judiciously the books of the most noted authors in order to avoid losing the time which would otherwise be taken up, and is in most cases disadvantageously, in going through an unnecessary amount of comparatively valueless literature. The vast number of books which are published at the present day, could never be even cursorily perused, much less carefully read, by the majority of men ; and even where time hangs heavily on the hands, it is impossible, whatever may be the amount of leisure, to read one-half of the books that daily come teeming from the press. It is an incalculable boon to have admission to the reading of the best authors, and this can only be fully appreciated by those who seek that advantage in vain. Even to the wealthier classes, the advantages of a library, public or private, are inestimable. Whatever may be the faults of those who affect culture in Victoria, a want of provision for the reading public is certainly not one of them, as witness the splendid Public Library in Melbourne. It is certainly a disadvantage that there is not in connection with this magnificent institution accorded the privilege of a lending-out library, combined with a reading library, and this may be one reason why greater numbers of the population do not take advantage of the privileges offered by a public library. However, one gentleman has come to the fore, and in addition to providing in part what is to be found at the Public Library, provides wholly for all that cannot be obtained there, except in some very special and favoured cases. The name of the gentleman to whom we refer stands at the head of the present chapter, and we would recommend all who are permanent or temporary sojourners in Melbourne to favour his large book and stationery warehouse, as well as his circulating library, with a visit. Established over 20 years, Mr. Mullen has succeeded in founding one of the largest bookselling and stationery warehouses in the colony. This can only be due to his diligence, his energy and enterprise, as well as careful consideration of the varied requirements of the reading public, and last though not least, the unwearying courtesy of himself and his assistants to all their customers, without regard to rank or position, or to a large or small demand. One thing we may be assured of, by the largeness and distinguished rank of their cliental, that they have maintained, and we doubt not, will continue to maintain, their deserved reputation for the supply of literature of the highest character. For from our own personal experience, we can assure our readers that at this establishment will be found, side by side with the latest fashionable travels, the classical productions of English literature in various choice editions. In fact, there the refined taste of the most cultivated mind can revel in the luxury of good editions of our most cherished and time-honoured authors. The circulating library, known as the Melbourne Mudie's, forms a special feature of the business. The library numbers several thousand volumes, and in the selection of books placed on the shelves, there is a comprehensiveness and variety which is not only unrivalled in the Australian colonies, but which may be most favourably compared with the most renowned circulating libraries that are to be found in the metropolis of Great Britain. We understand that about six weeks after publication in London, the newest book is to be found displayed for the perusal of all comers, on the table of this large library ; although novels of every kind and by every author abound, the selection of books embraces every branch of art, science, theology, voyages, travels, biography, &c., and every other instructive class of books. The periodicals and magazines of any European importance are also freely circulated in the library, and we only wonder that, with such allurements, the subscription is not larger than that which obtains in the leading circulating libraries of the world. However, the amount of subscribers is already large, and the increase has been conspicuously rapid during the period it has been in existence. It is patronised by all classes, and there, day by day, may be seen the *elite* of the literary and social world of Melbourne. We must heartily congratulate the public of this large and flourishing city on the possession of so great a desideratum, and we must also accord to Mr. Mullen himself the just meed of praise which is his due in providing so liberally and so completely for the reading penchant of Melbourne.

The premises present as handsome an appearance as would be expected from so large and important a business, and are situated in the best street in Melbourne. The shop, we ascertained, is 110 feet in length by 21 feet wide, and 15 feet high; at the back of the shop is a special apartment, 28 feet by 21 feet, and 13 feet high, which is wholly devoted to educational works, and in this branch we are given to understand that the firm does a very extensive and profitable business. Above this, is a store of similar size, to which is accorded its special branch. The bookshelves are faced with polished Kauri pine, crowned by a Grecian cornice of the same material, and these and other fittings contrasting with the generally dark covers of the books, give a bright and pleasing look to the whole. Over the library is a large skylight which gives an appearance of loftiness to the premises. The east wall is covered with well-filled shelves of books classified and so arranged as to invite the attention and interest of the book-hunter.

The stationery department is situated on the west side, adjoining the library, while the centre is fitted up with glass cases containing handsomely bound books and other articles *de luxe*. At the end of the shop a short staircase leads the visitor to the educational department, where college and school-books in endless variety are to be found, as well as a large and choice assortment of books written in the various continental languages of Europe. In this room also the counting-house is so arranged as to overlook the whole premises. Over the educational department is a store for reserve stock, which is conveyed thither by means of an American hoist, a simple machine now coming into general use in Melbourne. A cellar below runs under the whole length of the premises and affords ample room for opening consignments of goods and for storing the library duplicates. These are sent upstairs by ingeniously contrived lifts, which deposit their burdens under the counters above. A post-pillar box is erected near the entrance to the shop. This is cleared by the post-office pillar-men five times a day, which is a great convenience to the customers. We recommend those of our readers who have the opportunity and who seek to be instructed and amused to pay a visit to these interesting premises.

SOME OF THE LEADING BANKS IN MELBOURNE.

THE UNION BANK.

The handsomest buildings in Melbourne are its banks; and nothing is better calculated to impress a stranger, visiting the city for the first time, with the stability and solidity of its financial institutions, than the massive and impressive structures which have been erected by the various banking corporations and companies, to transact their business in. They bear the impress both of wealth and of permanence. There is an air of substantial respectability about them, which is at once imposing and free from pretentiousness. They have been built with a due regard to the magnitude of the operations now transacted inside their walls, and to the expansion which those operations must necessarily undergo as the colony grows in population and importance; and also with a view to their long duration. The institution itself is one of the oldest in the colony; and there was a time when the premises it occupied for so many years, at the corner of Queen-street and Collins-street west, were quite imposing by comparison with the neighbouring edifices. Now they look mean when contrasted with the large and spacious bank which occupies the site of the old Criterion Hotel—a famous place of resort in the early days of the goldfields, when it was thronged with visitors, and its "bridal chamber" was one of the sights of the city. How the place gradually declined, and how the tide of custom ebbed away from it and began to flow into a dozen new channels, it is unnecessary to relate. Suffice it to say, that it was bought by the directors of the Union Bank, pulled down, and replaced by the well-proportioned building which now graces its site, and has been reared at an outlay of £45,000, from the designs of Mr. M'Vicar Anderson, an eminent London architect, and Messrs. Smith and Johnson, of this city. The façade, which has a northerly aspect, is built in a style which combines some of the features of the Italian Renaissance with those of the Doric and Corinthian. A lower story of grey granite, with alternating courses of plain and rusticated bands, is pierced by three arches, giving access to a loggia, approached by a flight of steps, and opening into the vestibule, connecting the entrance with the interior of the bank. On either side is a bay, the massive walls of which mask and enclose a strong room, so situated as that, in the event of the building being gutted by fire, they would in all human probability remain intact, while their contents could be rescued with comparative ease. A niche has been hollowed out from the front of each, in which has been placed, on the one side a statue emblematic of the mother-country, and in the other a figure typifying the colony of Victoria; both of them relieving what might have otherwise been the sombre uniformity of the basement story. Above this, rises an arcade of New Zealand freestone with a balustraded base, flanked by pavilions with sunk panels. The upper loggia, corresponding in some of its dimensions with the lower one, but loftier and more ornate in character, has a vaulted ceiling, and the space enclosed resembles one of those deep balconies which lend such a charm to some of the Italian mansions erected from the designs of Vignola, Palladio, and Scamozzi. The columns which intervene between the arches of the arcade are of red granite, from Peterhead, highly polished, and thus introduce a pleasant bit of light colour into the greys and whites of the façade. Surmounting this portion of it is a balustraded parapet in three divisions; and on either side is one of those open turrets which the architects of the Renaissance period introduced with such happy effect into their palazzi; and of which some examples are to be found in the "stately homes of England" reared after the decline of the Tudor style of domestic architecture. Altogether, the elevation of the building is a striking one, and the general character of it may be regarded as suitable to a climate which has so much in common with that of the south of Europe. Entering the bank, through the vestibule previously spoken of, which is vaulted and panelled, we obtain admission to the bank chamber, a quadrangle of about 64 feet square, with a domed ceiling divided into glazed panels, and decorated with antique masks encircled by acanthus wreaths. Clustered columns of the Roman-Ionic order support this roof; above which is a second one, also partially glazed; and between the two is a considerable space, which, being filled with the non-conductive atmosphere, has the effect of moderating and equalising the temperature of the air in the banking chamber below, so as to render it free from extremes in both winter and summer. Independently of this, however, every precaution that modern science could suggest, has been adopted so as to secure the thorough ventilation of the whole premises. The domed ceiling, it may be added, terminates in a lantern, the sides of which are panelled, and fitted with ornamental gratings. Opposite the front entrance of the chamber, is the door by which ingress is obtained to another vestibule giving admission to the apartments occupied by the inspector, manager, and other officers connected with the establishment. Above these is a suite of rooms for the resident officers, in every respect complete; and in the rear of the bank, are the smelting house and assay office, which are the necessary adjuncts of such an institution in a country where large quantities of crude gold, the produce of its mines, are being constantly purchased by the managers of the numerous country branches, which are scattered all over the colony. Altogether, it will be seen, the new premises of the Union Bank are worthy of the wealthy corporation by which they have been erected, and of the great commercial city of which they constitute one of the chief architectural ornaments. The total capital of this institution, with reserve funds, is £5,316,500. Of this sum £1,500,000 is the paid-up capital, and the reserve fund runs into the large figures of £816,500. To this must be added a reserve liability of proprietors of £3,000,000 to complete the total capital. It is unnecessary to add any encomiums about the management of the bank, as the above figures speak eloquently enough. John F. M'Mullen, Esq., is the inspector and general manager; and Mr. John Curtayne, manager of the Melbourne branch.

THE BANK OF AUSTRALASIA.

We have said elsewhere in this book that Melbourne contains handsomer banking institutions than any other city of its size and age in the world. We cannot conscientiously except even the beautiful city of Chicago, in the United States, which, although twice the size of Melbourne, is much younger—if its age is considered to date from the re-building of the burnt district, 1871. It is true than Chicago contains some handsome banking establishments, but these are usually built of iron, and at an infinitely less cost than Melbourne's substantial banking quarters. If the internal solidity of these financial palaces compares with their outward solidity, then nothing remains to be said, for a mere survey of their exterior carries with it to the mind such abundant security, as to leave nothing unsatisfied there on the part of the most sceptical stockholder or depositor, concerning the careful management of the interior.

Of the many very handsome buildings which adorn Collins-street, that of the Bank of Australasia is, perhaps, one of the handsomest. It is situated in the north-west corner of Collins and Queen streets, and rises grandly to a height of 67 feet from the street. It is constructed of white freestone, and is very handsomely fitted up in the interior with every possible convenience to depositors and purchasers of foreign or domestic exchange. A broad stone stairway on the right, as one enters the bank, leads to a large suite of chambers up stairs, which are occupied by the superintendent and his staff. This bank was, it appears, the first bank established in Melbourne, being incorporated in 1835; but the capacious and elegant premises the bank now occupies were not completed until March, 1876. The bank was opened by Mr. D. C. M'Arthur, who came from Sydney to formally open the institution, and accept the position of superintendent, which he occupied for many years, finally retiring from any active participation, as an officer of the bank, to the position of local director, which post Mr. M'Arthur fills to this day.

The management of the bank has been carried out on the lines of that old English conservatism which has made banking so successful in England —London especially, and, following its example, we may now say Melbourne. But, with all this conservatism, there has been a vigorously enterprising system introduced by the colonial managers, quite foreign to the London manager, which, while it has assured extra accommodation to the clients of the bank, has done so to the profit of the shareholders, and without the incurrence of bad debts. This system is subject to a twofold advantage, of which one is the fine profit to the shareholder, and the other the substantial amount carried yearly to the reserve-fund, to provide for any unforeseen exigencies and bad debts. To eulogise the management of this bank would simply be accepted as our own opinion, notwithstanding the opinion is formed from the figures taken from the bank's own balance-sheet, made up 13th October, 1879. But to republish these figures will enable every one of the tens of thousands of readers who may read this book, to form his own estimate of this bank's management.

The forty-sixth annual report opens with the following remarks (stating also that the capital paid up is £1,200,000; guarantee and reserve-funds, £289,700; undivided profits, £151,624):—

The directors have the pleasure of congratulating the proprietors on the out-turn of the business of the bank for the year ending October, 1879, as exhibited in the annexed accounts, from which it will be seen that the net profit amounted to £174,624 19s, 1d., after making ample provision for bad and doubtful debts; and that, after appropriating £6000 in reduction of the cost of bank premises and £17,000 to the reserve fund, a sum of £151,624 19s. 1d. is available for distribution as dividend during the present year.

The accounts have been, as usual, carefully examined by the directors, and they beg to inform the proprietors that during the period under review the business of the bank was well maintained, and that in spite of the depression which prevailed, no serious losses were incurred.

The latest advices from the colonies are satisfactory, the harvest being one of unusual abundance, and the season very favourable to the stockholder. The improvement in the price of wool at the recent London sales will also exercise an important influence on the prosperity of the colonies during the current year.

At the close of the financial year, Mr. Samuel Tomkinson retired from the service of the bank, after having held the office of manager at the Adelaide Branch for 29 years, and the directors will submit to the proprietors a resolution for securing to him a suitable retiring allowance on the usual conditions.

Since the last meeting, a supplemental Royal Charter has been granted to the bank authorising the directors, with the consent of the proprietors, to increase the capital up to £2,000,000 sterling by the issue of new shares. When and to what extent this power should be exercised the directors are not yet prepared to give an opinion; but they consider that it will not be consistent with the interests of the bank to call up additional capital unless the new shares can be issued at a premium. The directors will, in due course, submit to a special meeting the expediency of altering the provision in the deed of settlement which prevents the issue of shares on such terms, and the necessary resolution will require, if carried, the confirmation of a second meeting.

The directors announce that they have declared a dividend for the half-year of £2 10s. per share, being at the rate of $12\frac{1}{2}$ per cent. per annum, which will be payable, free of income tax, in London on the 6th April next, and in the colonies on such date as the superintendent may arrange. This dividend will absorb £75,000, leaving £76,624 19s. 1d. available for future distribution.

PROFIT ACCOUNT,

From October 14, 1878, to October 13, 1879.

Undivided profit, October 14, 1878			£152,200 7 4	
Less dividends—				
In April, 1879	£75,000 0 0			
October ,, ...	75,000 0 0			
		150,000 0 0		
			£2,200 7 4	
Profit for the year to October 13, 1879, after making provision for bad and doubtful debts	£302,331 17 0			
Less Charges of Management—				
Colonial—				
Salaries and allowances to the Colonial Staff, including the Superintendent's Department, and 83 branches and agencies...	£81,297 10 4			
General expenses, including repairs, taxes, stationery, travelling, &c.	31,341 13 1			
London—				
Salaries	10,620 3 8			
General expenses	3,115 5 9			
	£126,374 12 10			
II. Income Tax	3,532 12 5			
		129,907 5 3		
			172,424 11 9	
Total amount of unappropriated profit ...		...	£174,624 19 1	
From which deduct—				
For reduction in cost of bank premises ...	£6,000 0 0			
For increase of Reserve Fund	17,000 0 0			
		23,000 0 0		
Leaving available for dividend ...		... ...	£151,624 19 1	

BALANCE-SHEET.

October 13, 1879.

LIABILITIES.

Circulation	£300,523 0 0	
Deposits	5,396,394 0 3	
Bills payable and other Liabilities	1,228,678 2 11	
		£6,925,595 3 2
Capital	£1,200,000 0 0	
Guarantee Fund	215,710 0 0	
Reserve Fund	74,000 0 0	
Profit Account—undivided balance	151,624 19 1	
		1,641,334 19 1
		£8,566,930 2 3

ASSETS.

Specie, Bullion and Cash Balances	£1,346,466 17	0
Bills receivable, Advances on Securities, and other Assets ...	6,782,099 14	6
Bank premises in Australia, New Zealand and London ...	222,653 10	9
Guarantee Fund Investments, as under	215,710 0	0
£166,850 Consols at 92 1/16 ... ... £153,820 0 0		
£70,000 Reduced 3 per cent. at 88⅜ 61,890 0 0		
£215,710 0 0		
	£8,566,930 2	3

THE ORIENTAL BANK CORPORATION.

The Oriental Bank Corporation was first established, in London, in 1848, as the Oriental Bank. In 1851, it was incorporated by Royal Charter, and at the same time took over the business of the two Eastern banks then existing there, viz., the then Western Bank of India and the Bank of Ceylon. From this date the connection of the Oriental Bank Corporation was rapidly extended throughout the East with most prosperous results.

Their head office is in Threadneedle-street, London; and they have branch establishments in Bombay, Calcutta, Madras, Colombo, Galle, Singapore, Hong Kong, Shanghai, Foo Chow, Yokohama and Hiogo.

The Melbourne branch was established in 1853, and their present offices, situated in Queen-street, were built in 1858, involving a very large outlay. They present a handsome and massive exterior, and the interior is commodious and ornamental; but, following the general movement to centralise business in Collins-street, the Oriental Bank Corporation have recently concluded arrangements which will, ere long, place them in occupation of the best and most commanding site in the city, in a building worthy both of the Corporation and of the site—the corner of Collins-street and Queen-street; thus evincing not only their satisfaction with their past experience of the colony, but their faith in its future, and their determination to keep pace with its progress.

Throughout all these years, the business of the Corporation in Australia has been of an unusually extensive character for a branch bank; and their connection throughout the goldfields and agricultural districts has been well maintained. They are represented by agencies at Beechworth, Bright, Stanley, Castlemaine, Chewton, Newstead, Stawell, Dimboola, Sandhurst, Eaglehawk and South Yarra.

They have also a branch at Sydney with inland agencies in New South Wales, at Araluen, Braidwood, Burrowa, Grenfell, Murrumburrah and Young.

Their paid-up capital is £1,500,000; and their share lists show a large and wealthy proprietary. The shares are £25 each, with liability limited to as much more. A local register is kept in Melbourne and Sydney, shares being held in both the colonies of Victoria and New South Wales.

The Melbourne branch and agencies in Victoria are under the management of Mr. George Hamilton Traill, who has held that appointment for about fifteen years. The Sydney branch and agencies in New South Wales are under the management of Mr. James Balfour.

THE NATIONAL BANK OF AUSTRALASIA.

The leading banks of Melbourne are all on such a firm basis that it is difficult to say anything of one which would not apply to the others. The impetus given to pastoral, agricultural and commercial industries within the past decade—1870 to 1880—by enterprising and energetic men engaged in these pursuits, has called upon and compelled all the leading financial institutions to increase their banking facilities to meet this almost unexampled elasticity in the development of natural resources. Especially has the pastoral industry contributed largely to this growth, inasmuch as the combined sheepfarmers of Australia have not only taken an average of about £12,000,000 sterling yearly off the sheep's backs, in the shape of wool, but have in addition, and almost to the same extent, in their unbroken continuity of extending the development of land, attracted new foreign capital, as year by year they placed so many million new acres at the back of the country in a productive condition, as collateral security, and gave it a marketable value. It is a question whether any other country in the world, with the same limited population as Australasia possesses, namely, 2,715,792, is armed with such splendid banking facilities as is this vast continent, which has a combined fiscal power of £64,535,477. That is to say that on the 30th September, 1879, the advances of the combined banks of the seven colonies amounted to this enormous sum. Their combined deposits, interest and non-interest bearing, on the 30th June, 1880, were no less a sum than £52,614,672. If this applies with force to Australia as a whole, it will apply more strongly to Melbourne in proportion to its population. Cincinnati is acknowledged to be the Queen city of the West in the United States, and is noted for its handsome and massive stone edifices; but even Cincinnati cannot boast of such solid, permanent and prosperous-looking banking edifices as Melbourne. Although there may be, and is, a very considerable difference in the capital of the leading banking institutions of Melbourne, the difference in the volume of their business is not so inversely great as the difference of capital by comparison with other banks would lead people to suppose. Hence it is that some banks, of which the National Bank of Australasia is one, with a capital of £800,000 and a reserve of £290,000, do not do so very much less business than the banks who have a capital of £1,500,000 to £2,500,000. This may be accounted for, perhaps, by some institutions, and not always those possessing the largest capital, having a much larger line of deposits than others. Whenever this is the case it is certainly a most cogent evidence of the thorough confidence reposed in its management by the public, and we are happy to find the National Bank of Australasia occupying this enviable position with the public of Australia. The building, which is very spacious and handsomely decorated, is situated at Nos. 14 and 16 Collins-street east, and could not be more centrally located. The banking chamber itself is a well-lighted room of about 65 feet square, with the administrative departments, such as receiving, paying, issuance of exchange, &c., running round the chamber except at the intersection of the entrance, and at the back of the bank, where access may be had to the manager and higher officers. The bank went into existence under its original deed of settlement, July 9, 1858, and was first opened on Monday, 4th October, 1858, with D. A. Hughes, Esq., as manager, who received his appointment August 31st of the same year. Its first board of directors consisted of Messrs. Andrew R. Cruikshank, Geo. W. Porter, John Houston, Alfred Cumberland, Thomas Brown, jun., and Thomas H. Lempriere. These gentlemen were subsequently replaced, either by retiring or from other causes, by Messrs. O. H. Gillies, E. M. Young, A. Cunningham, Fredk. Wright, and John Gulman. Their term of office varied from one year to six. The present chief manager is Mr. Francis Grey Smith, who took charge of the bank in 1872, and has shown fine business acumen in the management of its affairs. This gentleman has had probably as large an experience in bank matters as any manager in the Australias. He was at one time the manager of the Bank of Australasia, Melbourne, and afterwards general manager of the Bank of South Australia, whose head-quarters are in Adelaide. The board of directors now comprises Messrs. R. Murray Smith, Hon. W. Wilson, Thomas Smith, and W. H. Cropper. The London office was opened in 1863, with Mr. Fredk. Wright as manager.

THE BANK OF VICTORIA.

Conspicuous among the larger edifices which adorn the busy thoroughfare of Collins-street east, is one which visitors to Venice recognise as almost a *facsimile* of the façade of a palace overlooking the Grand Canal in that city; only the rusticated basement opens on a broad footpath, instead of upon the silent highway which flows through the Queen of the Adriatic. The Melbourne structure was erected on the site of the old Port Phillip Club; and to it was removed the business of the Bank of Victoria, which had long outgrown the limited accommodation available for it in the old premises in Swanston-street south. Founded in the year 1852, that is to say shortly after the gold discoveries in this colony, with a subscribed capital of one million sterling in 20,000 shares of £50 each, of which it was not found necessary to call up more than £28 per share, this institution now possesses a reserve fund of £115,000, landed property of the value of £844,455, and deposits to the amount of £3,250,000. It has sixty-six branches, besides six agencies in the colony; and ever since the date of its foundation, it has had the advantage of the personal direction and supervision of the shrewd and experienced financier who may appropriately be regarded as its founder, and who has been very fortunate, or perhaps it would be more accurate to say, characteristically sagacious in his choice of a manager, and of other responsible officials. Without derogating from the ability, energy, and experience of the board of directors, it may be fairly claimed for the Hon. Henry Miller, that the Bank of Victoria is his offspring, and that its present distinguished position and conspicuous success, as well as the magnitude of its transactions, are due, in part at least, to his sedulous devotion to its interests, and his untiring watchfulness over its development. With the exception of the Chemical Bank of New York, the shares of which rose in value, during a period of a quarter of a century, from 100 dollars to 1650 dollars each, and a few other exceptionally favoured institutions of a similar character, in other parts of the world, we know of scarcely any financial association which has enjoyed a larger measure of prosperity than the Commercial Bank in Sydney, and the Bank of Victoria in Melbourne. During the period the latter has been in existence, the colony of Victoria has not been exempt from vicissitudes, but these have had no effect whatever on the stability, and very little on the steady growth and progress of the bank. The large deposits lodged with it, which sometimes reach as high as £4,000,000, are a pretty good indication of the confidence reposed in it, and this has been certainly well deserved. When we come to investigate the causes of this confidence, we find them to be numerous, and to arise out of the respect entertained for the high character, long experience, and financial abilities of the chairman of the Board of Directors and the manager; out of the knowledge of the fact that for nearly three decades the business of the institution has been conducted with equal prudence, circumspection and success; and out of a well-founded assurance that a wise economy is habitually exercised in its management. We learn, for example, from the *Insurance and Banking Record*, that the expenses of managing the head office and its seventy-two branches and agencies were only £42,177 for the last year. When this is contrasted with the magnitude of the business done, and with the largeness of the amount turned over during that time, it must be admitted to denote unusually careful administration. The dividend declared by this bank, at its last half-yearly meeting, was at the rate of nine per cent., in spite of the unsatisfactory condition of trade and commerce in this country, the stagnation of enterprise brought about by political misrule, the accumulation of unemployed capital in all the banks, and the unwillingness of its owners to invest it either in the purchase or improvement of property, or in any reproductive undertakings, in view of its possible confiscation by taxes avowedly imposed with that object. The gross profits of the Bank of Victoria amounted to £66,347, of which £22,500 was appropriated to a dividend, while £8644 was carried to the reserve fund. The resources of the institution are now nine times as great as its original capital, and its board of directors is composed of the following gentlemen :—The Hon. H. Miller, chairman, and Messrs. W. Hoffman, J. K. Freyer, Germain Nicholson, E. Miller, and E. B. Wight. The general manager, Mr. John Matheson, is a gentleman well-known in financial circles, and the assistant manager is Mr. Richard Shann.

THE LONDON CHARTERED BANK OF AUSTRALIA.

Massive structures invariably give an appearance of strength, solidity, and prosperity, to the commercial enterprises they environ. They do so, because the generality of people judge the success of commercial undertakings by the substantiality of the buildings, or the elegance of the offices in which they are conducted. Either these or some other exterior forms of *primâ facie* prosperity will influence, rightly or wrongly, a large proportion of the public. It is true, however, that the massive and commanding appearance of an institution is often a very correct indication of its influence and power, because the ability to erect handsome edifices could only generally be accomplished through a thriftiness and caution in the conduct of its affairs, which have led up to a prosperity sufficiently assured to encourage the output of some of its profits in this form of investment. In Melbourne especially, does this form of investment find favour, and much to the credit of its projectors be it said, for in its prosecution employment is found for both capital and labour, while the majesty of the city's appearance is not less conserved. It must not, however, be supposed that unless a corporation put forth some of the accrued profits of its successful business coups in an elegant and imposing exterior, its prosperity or power is less potent than those who have gone into more showy apartments. There are, in Melbourne, some very solid concerns, whose influence and fiscal power are not one whit the less, in their unostentatious quarters, than those who transact their business in more pretentious and roomy ones, notwithstanding these few conduct their affairs within a very much smaller superficial area. Amongst these latter may be mentioned the London Chartered Bank of Australia, which may fairly take rank with the oldest established banks in Melbourne, it being now in the twenty-ninth year of its existence. This bank was projected in 1851, which will always be remembered as the year which ushered into the world the first of those useful promoters of social culture, industrial progression, and international goodfellowship—the Exhibition held in Hyde Park, London—and was launched upon the waters of active operation in the following year. Its founders were a number of influential colonists then residing in London, among whom may be mentioned the late Mr. Duncan Dunbar, of Limehouse, at that time the owner of a fine fleet of ships, engaged in the colonial trade, and Mr. Wm. Fane de Salis, who is still a director, and was, for many years, chairman of the Bank. In 1853, branches were established in Melbourne, Sydney, and Geelong, under the general management of the late Mr. Chas. Falconer, and the spot that this gentleman chose for the seat of his operations, in Melbourne, was adjoining the site upon which the Bank of Victoria now stands.

It was during the stirring times of the gold excitement, which followed shortly afterwards, that this bank made its influence felt, and accomplished the solidarity of its interests, extending its branches to Ballarat, Maryborough, Fiery Creek, Beechworth, Ararat, Dunolly, and elsewhere. Some of these branches are still in existence, while others have disappeared with the extinguishment of the towns which were called into existence by ephemeral alluvial leads, then so common. It may be thought, by some, that the policy of this bank has been somewhat inelastic, in not having extended its branches at the correlative pace of its contemporaries, but it appears to have been actuated more by a desire to establish for itself a reputation for stability, in the shape of sound and cautious banking, than any wish to append to its main branch some 60 or 70 minor ones, and thus court a great popularity. Its progress has, in consequence, been less rapid than that of some of its rivals; but has been less spasmodical and more permanent. Mr. Falconer's successor was Mr. John Bramwell, who was identified with the Bank for fourteen years, and subsequently retired in 1866, to take the London management of the Union Bank of Australia, which he held up to the time of his death. Mr. Bramwell was succeeded by Mr. Edwin Brett, who has recently retired from the service, after a tenure of office of about the same period. A very noticeable feature about this bank, which argues most potently for the harmony of its internal arrangements, is the unusually long tenure of office its leading officers have qualified for upon retirement; for example, the manager now about to leave, to take charge of the Australian Mortgage, Land and Finance Company, Mr. John Russell Ross, has been with this bank no less than twenty-seven years. For one officer to be in a bank over a quarter of a century, is an unheard-of thing, except in old English banking establishments, and speaks volumes for the great amount of experience this gentleman must carry with him to the company the charge of whose business he is about to assume. The same may be said with regard to the experience of the gentleman who is about to succeed

Mr. John Ross, namely, Mr. John Young, for many years manager of the City of Melbourne Bank. Mr. Young has evidenced his ability to manage such a corporation successfully in many ways, most notably in the manner in which he conducted the City of Melbourne Bank out of its threatened difficulty, during the run made upon it, incident to the crisis of 1879. The prompt manner in which this bank met all the demands made upon it in coin, showed conclusively its sound condition, and the good management which supervised this condition.

The capital of the bank is £1,000,000 paid up, and a reserve fund of £120,000. The soundness of the institution may be judged from the fact that, notwithstanding the hard hits it, in common with kindred institutions, experienced during the last two years, £42,000 were carried to the credit of profit and loss account for the last half-year, out of which a dividend of 7 per cent. was paid to the shareholders. The time deposits of this institution amount to nearly £2,000,000, and its capital, current accounts, time deposits, reserved funds, and note circulation, together make no less a sum than £4,000,000. Its principal offices are situated at No. 68 Collins-street West, while it has two other important branches in Melbourne, of which one is in Bourke-street, and the other in Carlton. These two branches are favoured with a very good share of business, and their popularity is continually bringing them into communication with fresh clients. The present Inspector-General who succeeds Mr. Edwin Brett, is Mr. Charles Guthrie, who brings with him the ability of a long experience in London. The directors at Melbourne are gentlemen of position and ability. They consist of Sir James M'Culloch, chairman, and the Hon. James Henty.

THE COLONIAL BANK OF AUSTRALASIA.

If the banking institutions of a country are in a flourishing state, we may safely judge that the country itself has a prosperous commerce and trade, and that all branches of industry are in a fairly prosperous condition. If we base our estimate of the commercial and industrial progress of the old countries on the premises upon which we have set out, how much more must it apply to a country which is as much remarkable for its youth as for its extraordinarily rapid development. But 40 years ago, and the city whose banks have now become permanent and flourishing factors in the van of Australian progress, and whose commercial relations extend to all the civilised countries of the world, was scarcely known by name to the great banking houses of Europe. Now, after the lapse of but four decades, their transactions have increased to such an extent, as to be a power, not only in the commercial world of Australia, but also in those countries which are celebrated for the extent of their wealth and commerce. The sojourner n Melbourne must have been struck with the palatial appearance which is presented by almost every bank in the city, and we know not whether the cursory observer or lover of architecture will be more pleased with our public buildings, or with the stately proportions of the Melbourne banks. Not only do the directorates seek to provide, in their buildings, all the requirements which are necessary for banking operations, but they, at the same time, seem to be inspired with a love for beautifying the city which has given such prosperity to their undertakings. We are proud to have amongst us men of such exemplary spirit, who do not aim solely at making money, but seek at the same time to improve the architectural appearance of the city. Prominent amongst our banking institutions, stands the Colonial Bank of Australasia. Those of our readers who are interested in architecture, as well as those who are interested in the welfare of the colony, and have, at the same time, a certain pride in the external beauty of the important buildings of Melbourne, will feel some curiosity to know the style and proportions of the new Colonial Bank of Australasia, which is about to be erected on the site of the old banking premises, at the corner of Elizabeth-street and Little Collins-street. The elevations to both streets are of three stories in height, the lower being of chiselled bluestone masonry, extending to the full height of the banking chamber, having a base rising to a height of about five feet above the footway, finishing with a bold string course, or capping, with massive piers above and deeply-recessed windows, the whole channelled into courses. The windows are square-headed and panelled under the sills, with perforated masks allowing the admission of fresh air between the double sashes. The cornice to this lowest stage of the structure, is carried through without interruption, except where broken at the angle of the two fronts. The story next above, as also the upper story, is decorated with attached columns of the Corinthian order spanning the full height, having the entablature broken over the columns. A balustrade crowns the whole with urns over the several columns. The windows of the first floor have balustraded pedestals and pediment heads. The top windows have projecting sills, breaking along a continuous string course. The angle of the building is rendered prominent by a boldly designed doorway, semi-headed with panelled architrave; the portion of the entablature before referred to, is broken above the doorway into a curved pediment carried by "Terms" in place of the ordinary cantilevers. Above the pediment, are two recumbent figures, representing respectively "Labour" and "Commerce," grouped with shields filled in with the seal of the company, &c. The window over the pediment is triple, and the composition is extended upwards and connected with a circlet containing inscriptions of the date of the institution of the bank, surmounted with festoons and other ornamental appendages, the whole combining together to mark this portion of the building, and to afford some contrast to the often-repeated features elsewhere throughout the façades. The upper portion of the building, above the bluestone lower story, is intended to be of brick, faced with cement. The height of the building will be about 70 feet above the footway. We understand that the design which we have just described was selected out of 26, which were recently submitted in competition; the designers being Messrs. Smith and Johnson, architects, of Melbourne. This bank was incorporated by Act of Council, assented to 9th March, 1856, giving it an existence of nearly a quarter of a century. It commenced business on the 14th April in the year cited, at the banking-house situated on the site on which the new premises are about to be erected. The nominal capital is £1,000,000 in 100,000 shares of £10 each, of which 62,500 have been issued. The paid-up capital, at present, is £406,250, and the reserve fund amounts to £86,000. During the years that the bank has been established, its history has been progressive, and success has attended its operations. Beginning in Melbourne, it gradually extended its business throughout the colony of Victoria, until now branches have been opened out in almost every place where business is carried on. At present, there are no less than 44 branches throughout the colony in connection with the Colonial Bank of Australasia. The first general manager of the bank, Mr. Thomas Elder Boyd, was a gentleman well-known to the commercial community of Melbourne; and the veteran statesman, Sir John O'Shanassy, M.L.A., was the first governor of the institution. To give our readers an idea of the rapid increase of business from its first commencement and its continued increase and importance at the present time, both at the head office and at the branches, we may mention that in 1858 it became one of the six contracting banks with the Government of Victoria. No better basis as an estimate of its importance, prosperity, and extensive business, could be offered to those experienced in banking affairs, than the facts which we have been privileged to place before our readers. We may further state that it has had, from its first starting, agencies in all the colonies of Australia, as well as in England, Scotland, Ireland, and other principal places connected with the business of the colony. The present governor, the Hon. W. J. Clarke, M.L.C., is a gentleman who is favourably known throughout Australia, and the general management of the bank is in the energetic and experienced hands of Mr. William Greenlaw.

SOME OF THE LEADING BANKS OF SYDNEY.

THE BANK OF NEW SOUTH WALES.

The year 1817, was a most important one in the history of Australian progress. Twenty-nine years had passed since Captain Arthur Phillip, in command of a little fleet of eleven sail, conveying somewhere about 1000 souls, had arrived in Port Jackson, and formed on the bank of the Tank

Stream, that settlement which was to form the nucleus of Australian colonisation. In that short time, however, enough had been effected, under difficulties and discouragements of no ordinary character, to prove that Anglo-Saxon pluck and energy, which had rescued the prairies and forests of America from their centuries of solitude, and turned them into fertile provinces, had lost none of their vitality. The earth huts and tents scattered in the forest brush surrounding Sydney Cove, and originally called the Camp, had been replaced by a town of considerable pretensions, with its streets regularly named, and with weekly markets fairly established; while the colonists were rapidly extending their farms and stations in every direction, and commerce had established its ramifications in every district. The one great difficulty, at this time, was the extreme scarcity of gold or silver coinage. The circulating medium consisted principally of the private notes of the various merchants, traders, and publicans; while the customary mode of payment for labour, was one-third in produce, and the remainder in money, and, in some cases, the small settlers paid entirely in kind. It was under circumstances of this nature, so depressing to commercial enterprise, that, in the year 1817, the Bank of New South Wales was established, under a charter for seven years, from the then Governor, Lachlan Macquarie, Esq., as a bank of loan, discount, deposit, and issue; the effect of which was to lessen to a marked extent the difficulties of exchange hitherto existing, the bank having from the first the confidence of the community, and its notes affording a convenient and reliable currency. The capital was limited to £20,000 in 200 shares of £100 each. At a general meeting held on the 7th February, 1817, the rules and regulations for the management of the bank, drawn up by a committee of fifteen, were approved, and the first directors, seven in number, were elected by ballot, as follows:—John Thomas Campbell, Esq., president; Darcy Wentworth, Esq.; John Harris, Esq.; Robert Jenkins, Esq.; Thomas Wylde, Esq.; Alexander Riley, Esq.; and William Redfern, Esq.

The original and, in many respects, quaint rules, bear evidence, not only of the wise caution animating the founders of the bank, but also of the scarcity of coinage as a circulating medium, already referred to as one of the characteristics of the time. They include the following:—

That notes should be issued of no other value than 2s. 6d., 5s., 10s., £1, or £5. That the advances on land or houses should not exceed one-fifth of the capital; and that no such loan should be for longer than twelve months.

That interest or discount should not exceed 10 per cent. per annum.

That not more than 8 per cent. should be paid on any deposit.

That no advance to any individual or company should exceed £500.

That no bill, note, or negotiable security should be discounted having more than three months to run, and that preference should be given to those having two months.

From the middle of 1823 till the 1st January, 1826, when the use of sterling was resumed, the accounts of the bank were kept, notes were issued, and payments made in Spanish dollars, at a valuation of 5s. per dollar.

In 1850, the bank was reconstructed on a new basis and under a new deed of settlement, made on the 23rd of August, the capital being fixed at £125,000 in shares of £20 each. An Act of the New South Wales Parliament, incorporating the company, was assented to on the 23rd November, 1850; and, under that Act, with some amendments, the bank now exists. The original power of issuing notes for 21 years was extended by an Act assented to on 27th April, 1870, for another 21 years. The progress of the institution, since its reconstruction, and the intimate relation of its affairs with the growth and vicissitudes of the colony, will be best illustrated by the following chronological view of its business:—

March	Paid-up Capital.	Reserve.	Dividend per cent.	Circulation.	Deposits.	Advances.
	£	£	£	£	£	£
1851	122,120	5,500	10	33,883	295,627	234,841
1852	150,000	12,507	10	143,332	624,693	401,197
1853	397,400	25,719	10*	376,110	1,558,161	543,841
1854	400,000	50,000	10	577,479	2,064,204	1,898,804
1855	500,000	80,317	10	640,313	1,859,547	2,207,720
1856	500,000	100,341	20	703,901	2,281,879	1,924,067
1857	500,000	126,946	20	682,414	2,492,255	2,866,636
1858	500,000	150,394	20	563,271	2,327,830	2,733,551
1859	500,000	178,321	20	535,828	2,350,741	2,999,914
1860	662,220	205,372	15	536,363	2,796,541	3,811,997
1861	750,000	210,482	15	483,814	2,757,489	3,900,035
1862	750,000	220,262	15	569,496	3,275,511	4,201,569
1863	750,000	250,000	15 & 2½	695,831	3,776,947	4,912,380
1864	750,000	250,000	15 & 2½	663,743	3,614,929	5,242,673
1865	976,080	325,360	15 & 3	598,574	3,815,444	5,330,733
1866	1,000,000	333,333	15 & 5	661,939	4,226,525	5,495,008
1867	1,000,000	333,333	15 & 5	622,803	4,643,799	5,855,215
1868	1,000,000	333,333	15	628,308	5,016,895	5,689,438
1869	1,000,000	333,333	15	630,364	5,083,826	6,212,532
1870	1,000,000	333,333	15	618,221	5,305,132	6,869,330
1871	1,000,000	300,000	10	588,340	5,037,036	5,609,576
1872	1,000,000	308,000	12½	537,787	5,822,947	5,922,961
1873	1,000,000	333,333	15	655,254	7,269,945	6,979,986
1874	1,000,000	333,333	15 & 2½	724,601	7,346,477	8,338,263
1875	1,000,000	363,333	15 & 2½	725,390	8,418,978	8,782,323
1876	1,000,000	400,000	15 & 2½	713,857	8,956,476	8,667,736
1877	1,000,000	420,000	15 & 2½	717,244	8,591,690	8,711,328
1878	1,000,000	440,000	15 & 2½	736,719	8,709,881	9,436,844
1879	1,000,000	460,000	15 & 2½	668,854	8,709,524	9,454,540
1880	1,000,000	480,000	15 & 2½	656,323	9,661,460	8,440,144

* And £6 13s. 4d. per Share added to Capital.

The business of the Bank was first carried on in a small building standing back from George-street, in its own garden, which reached to the Tank Stream, whence it was removed in 1823 to an adjoining house on the site of the present Bank auction rooms. Here it remained until the increase of business consequent on the gold discoveries, necessitated the erection of the present commodious and handsome building on the opposite side of George-street, at the corner of Wynyard-street. The new building was entered in October, 1852, and here the business is conducted, two extensive additions having been made by the purchase and alteration of the adjoining properties. The premises now occupy 73 feet in George-street, and 167 feet in Wynyard-street.

The first branch was established at Brisbane, in the Moreton Bay district, on the 14th November, 1850; followed by branches at Melbourne, in March 1851; Geelong, in December 1852; and London, in April 1853. Other branches were established as the wants of the various country districts appeared to require them; and in 1861, business was commenced in New Zealand by the opening of seven branches. The total number of branches at the present time is 149, spread all over the Australasian colonies, with the exception of Western Australia and Tasmania, in both of which the bank's business is conducted by agents. It has also agents in the United Kingdom, Hamburg, the United States, San Francisco, and throughout the East.

The number of officers in the service of the bank is at the present time 638. A fidelity guarantee and provident fund was established in January, 1863. It has received a grant of £10,000 from the shareholders, and is maintained by half-yearly subscriptions, according to salary, from every officer. Any defalcations satisfactorily established are charged to the fund, and the balance furnishes a retiring allowance, based upon salary and length of service, to officers resigning after the age of 55, and a payment to the widows and children of those who may die in the service after a certain period of membership.

The present directors of the bank are Thomas Walker, Esq., president; Thomas Cadell, Esq.; William Laidley, Esq.; Thomas Buckland, Esq.; James Milson, Esq., and Sir G. Wigram Allen, M.L.A. The board in London consists of Donald Larnach, Esq., chairman; Sir Daniel Cooper, Bart., and William Walker, Esq.; while that of Melbourne is formed by the Hon. J. G. Francis, David Moore, Esq., and the Hon. Sir James M'Culloch. The general manager of the bank is Shepherd Smith, Esq.

THE COMMERCIAL BANKING CO., OF SYDNEY.

The most successful bank in the Australasian colonies, is the Commercial Banking Company, of Sydney, and it is indeed a question whether its success has been exceeded, or equalled, in any part of the globe. The old Commercial Bank was established in 1834, and it was wound up in 1848, and reorganised and incorporated into the present bank, whose history commences accordingly in that year. We give some figures, from the balance-sheets presented from time to time, which will indicate the steady advancement in business and in prosperity made by the bank; but this advancement is particularly noticeable since the commencement of the third decade of the bank's existence.

First Half-yearly Report, to 30th December, 1848—

Capital paid up	£71,565
Notes in circulation	25,601
Deposits	148,470
Profit for half-year	6,542
Coin	79,724
Advances	168,382

Twentieth Half-yearly Report, to 30th June, 1858—

Capital paid up	£239,735
Reserve	44,000
Notes in circulation	164,937
Deposits	767,643
Profits for half-year	32,064
Coin	333,677
Advances	823,872

Fortieth Report, to 30th June, 1868—

Capital paid up	£400,000
Reserve Fund	110,000
Notes in circulation	195,091
Deposits	1,798,054
Profits for half-year	47,405
Coin	239,456
Advances	1,871,316

Sixtieth Report, to 30th June, 1878—

Capital paid up	£500,000
Reserve Fund	450,000
Notes in circulation	360,698
Deposits	4,570.294
Profit for half-year	103,023
Coin	654,637
Advances	4,983,855

Sixty-fourth Report, to 30th June, 1880—

Capital paid up	£600,000
Reserve Fund	570,000
Notes in circulation	324,813
Deposits	5,197,062
Profit for half-year	110,039
Coin	1,055,588
Advances	5,235,985

In 1868, the shares (£25 paid up) were worth £50, and the capital being £400,000, the total market value of the shares represented £800,000. The shares are now worth £105, which represents a total market value of £2,520,000 to the fortunate shareholders, the paid-up capital being £600,000. The reserve fund in 1868 was £110,000. It is now £570,000. It is worthy of note that the bank's dividend has never been reduced since 1862, when 15 per cent. was paid, and it has steadily increased up to 25 per cent., which it reached in 1876, and which has been maintained up to the present time.

If it be asked to what this extraordinary success is due, the answer will be that the bank is exceedingly fortunate in its directors and management, and it possesses a zealous and efficient staff, who work with a will to further the interests of an institution which treats them with liberality and consideration. The policy of the bank, also, has been of a nature calculated to inspire a spirit of confidence on the part of its customers, whose interests are recognised as identical with those of the bank; and when hard times have arrived, the bank has been found prepared, and has not had to withdraw its aid from those who have a right to expect it in time of need. This is an important matter, as it has been well said that it is of more consequence to carefully select the bank from whom you would borrow than one to deposit your money with.

To the excellent administration and organisation of the bank, must then fairly be attributed its great success, as it has had but the same opportunities, with the same trials, as its kindred institutions in the colonies.

Mr. T. A. Dibbs is the manager, and it is superfluous to make any comment on his financial ability further than to call the attention of our readers to the unprecedented growth of the bank's affairs since his advent, as evidenced by the figures above.

AUSTRALIAN JOINT STOCK BANK.

Amongst the banking institutions of Australia, the Australian Joint Stock Bank, whose head office is at Sydney, is deserving of special notice. The Act of Incorporation was assented to by the Parliament of New South Wales, on the 3rd of September, 1853, thus giving it an existence of more than a quarter of a century. During the whole of this period, its history has been marked by careful and steady development. Its capital, its shareholders, and its business operations, have since its commencement been steadily increasing, until it may now be looked upon as one of the permanent banking establishments of New South Wales. There is, probably, no better guarantee of the status, as well as of the past, present, and future success, of a banking company, than the social and commercial position of those gentlemen who form the directorate. It commands public confidence and the assurance of careful supervision of every banking operation, however extensive or minute, which in the usual course of business comes specifically within the province of private or public banks. The directors of the Australian Joint Stock Bank are gentlemen well-known in the commercial world of New South Wales, and their names are familiar to the whole banking community of the colony. The chairman is Edward Lord, Esq., while the other directors are Messrs. George A. Murray, Jeremiah R. Rundle, William B. Walford, William A. Long, and Moses Moss. The general manager of the Australian Joint Stock Bank is Mr. Vincent Wanostrocht Giblin, and Mr. Francis Adams is the assistant manager. The flourishing condition of the bank is due to the zeal, energy, and commercial enterprise of this efficient executive. Prudent and careful management is also an important factor in the increasing business of the bank. On the 5th of January, 1880, the Australian Joint Stock Bank had 67 branch banks, not including the head office in Sydney, viz., three suburban branches, and 45 branches throughout New South Wales, embracing the most important towns in the colony. They are also doing a very extensive business in the colony of Queensland. The branch inspector at Brisbane is Mr. H. P. Abbott, who is ably assisted by Mr. Alexander Kerr. In Queensland alone, there are 18 branches of the Australian Joint Stock Bank, including the office at Brisbane. The address of the London office is 18 King William-street, E.C. These figures are somewhat remarkable considering the time the bank has been in existence, and the great competition it has to contend against both in the premier colony and in the colony of Queensland. The paid-up capital of the company is £500,000, with power to increase to £1,000,000, while the reserve fund is £175,000. No better assurance of stability can be conveyed to shareholders and depositors than through the medium of a large reserve fund. The reserve fund is the bone and sinew of a prosperous banking institution, as well when the operations are on an extensive scale as when they are limited. Few banks in this respect are deserving of more congratulatory remarks than the Australian Joint Stock Bank. The nominal amount of each share is £10 and the amount per share paid-up is, we understand, £8, and the liability per share is the sum equalling the original amount of shares. The following figures will show the highest and lowest share prices quoted in the market during the years 1878, 1879, and the present year:—

	1878.	1879.	Present price.
Highest price	£14 2 6	£13 17 6	£16
Lowest do....	13 7 6	13 0 0	14 17 6

These figures are, to say the least, satisfactory, and a decided proof of public confidence.

We give below the dividend and bonus per cent. on capital during the last seven years:—

23rd Jan. 1873, 9¼ per cent.	30th June 1873, 9¼ per cent.	31st Dec. 1873, 10½ per cent.	30th June 1874, 10¼ per cent.
31st Dec. 1874, 10½ per cent.	30th June 1875, 10½ per cent.	31st Dec. 1875, 10¼ per cent.	30th June 1876, 10½ per cent.
31st Dec. 1876, 11¼ per cent.	30th June 1877, 11¼ per cent.	31st Dec. 1877, 12¼ per cent.	30th June 1878, 12¼ per cent.
30th Dec. 1878, 12¼ per cent.	30th June 1879, 12½ per cent.	31st Dec. 1879, 12½ per cent.	

This steadily progressive increase during the last seven years must be a source of great satisfaction to all concerned. It shows the growing confidence of the public in the business capacities of the Australian Joint Stock Bank, and we are justified in assuming that its continued prosperity, may now be said to stand on a firm and enduring basis.

We may state that the amount of note issue authorised is to the extent of amount of actual paid-up capital, and to any such further amount in excess of the capital, as the corporation itself shall hold coin for, apart from such as is reserved for ordinary operations. This, as a matter of solid information, must be satisfactory to the clientèle of the bank. It shows the adoption of precautions which insure safety alike to the bank, as well as to its numerous and ever increasing customers.

The means which are adopted for ascertaining by periodical inspection or otherwise that the issue is not in excess of the amount authorised, and that the bullion or securities (if any), held or required to be held specifically against such issue are really so held, are, that weekly statements are sent in by the branches, which are examined, and sworn statements are rendered to the Government at the end of every quarter. In this way, it is very improbable that any great mistake can ever be made.

The following figures will show the actual note circulation:—

		New South Wales.	Queensland.	Total.
1878	March 31	£196,441 10	£77,824 10	£274,266
,,	June 30	195,477	78,108 10	273,585 10
,,	Sept. 30	184,906 10	81,775	266,681 10
,,	Dec. 31	209,178 10	79,618 10	288,797
1879	March 31	180,180 10	74,360 10	254,541
,,	June 30	173,722 10	67,636 10	241,359
,,	Sept. 30	170,089 10	68,981	239,070 10
,,	Dec. 31	208,133	73,466	281,599

The limitation which is imposed on the holding of land by the bank or on the making of advances by the bank on merchandise, is that the bank can only purchase land and buildings necessary for the carrying on of its business, and is prohibited from making advances on landed property, &c., but can take promissory notes collaterally secured by deeds, &c. This is a further source of security to all concerned, and certainly not the least important. The qualification necessary to make a shareholder eligible for a directorship is *prima facie* that he should be the holder of 100 shares. Of course, it is understood, that this is only one test of fitness, and that each gentleman who is elected to the directorate, should have considerable experience in the commercial world, and at the same time, hold in a general way, a responsible and important position. His business capacity must be keen and observant, which must necessarily be important factors in the estimation of those, in whose hands the election of directors is vested.

The balance-sheet of the Australian Joint Stock Bank ending 30th June, 1880, shows that though the profits earned appear to have been about £12,000 less than those of the previous six months, yet the usual dividend at the rate of 12½ per cent., was declared and that, though no addition to the reserve fund was made out of accrued profits, yet that account was credited with £5000 recovered from debts previously written off as bad. We notice too that Mr. Moses Moss, who is at the head of a firm long established in Sydney, has been elected in the place of Mr. Walter Friend, who vacated by resignation his position at the board of directors.

Every description of banking business is done by the Australian Joint Stock Bank, such as the discounting of bills, making advances upon approved security, negotiating produce bills and documents, granting drafts and credits upon all its branches and agents, at current rates. Interest is also allowed upon fixed deposits. The bank negotiates or collects bills payable at any place where it has a branch or agent. It also collects dividends on local stocks for its customers free of commission, as well as the interest on debentures, and at the same undertakes their custody.

THE CITY BANK, SYDNEY.

Amongst the banking institutions of New South Wales, the City Bank, at Sydney, is not the least prominent; for the time that it has been in existence, it will not unfavourably compare with other banks, whose operations are consequently on a more extensive scale. It has been before the public little more than sixteen years, during which period, its history has been one of steady and progressive development. This, without doubt, is due to the able management of the bank, by the chairman, the directors, the manager, and the bank officers. The whole burden of success rests upon the zeal, energy, and business acumen of these gentlemen, who are not sparing of time and attention, in all that concerns the affairs of the bank. It must be gratifying to them to be recompensed for their steady attention to their respective duties, by the large amount of public confidence which they have succeeded in securing. To have been the means of enlarging the business of the bank to its present proportions, must be a source of satisfaction and self-gratulation to each and all of the gentlemen in whose hands rests the responsibility of success. We cannot be blind to the difficulties, which every undertaking must, at its outset, encounter, the most onerous of which, is the great competition, against which it has to fight its uphill battle. The conjectures of pessimists, who see nothing but barriers, which they feel sure will be insurmountable, have a certain quiet, and in many cases an unseen, influence, which only great commercial experience, business capacity, and a hopeful disposition, as well as indomitable and unflagging perseverance, can ever, by any possibility, overcome successfully. This remark applies, in a pronounced way, to those gentlemen who are, and have been, connected with the bank from its first commencement; and who have followed its successful career with the greatest watchfulness. The chairman of the directors is the Hon. James Watson, M.L.A., while the directorate is composed of the following gentlemen:—John Alger, Esq., Robert Gray, Esq., Hon. George Thornton, M.L.C., and Edmund Wrench, Esq., while the auditors are H. C. D'Ardier, Esq., and the Hon. John Blaxland, M.L.C. Mr. William Neill is the manager, Mr. Edward Rouse is the secretary, and the accountant is Mr. Thomas T. Orton. Such names as these must be a satisfactory guarantee, to the clientèle of the bank, that their interests will be scrupulously attended to, as well as that the varied business of the bank will receive the most careful management. We understand that the paid-up capital of the bank is £240,000, with power to increase to £500,000. This is a large sum, and is a fair standard from which we may judge of the extent of the transactions in which the bank engages. The amount to which the paid-up capital may be increased is also a fair prognostication of what the bank management anticipates, may be, in all likelihood, the amount of business done at no distant future. The head-office is situated in Pitt-street, Sydney, a central and commanding position, and wisely and well chosen, for its local advantages. The city branches compose what is known as the Eastern and Western branch, the former situated at 99 Oxford-street, under the management of Mr. E. B. Croft, while the latter is situated in King and Sussex streets. The bank has country branches at Young, Mr. A. G. H. Sandeman, manager; Bathurst, Mr. F. Strachan, manager; at Kiama, Mr. T. J. Fuller, manager; at Carcoar, Mr. G. M. Marsh, manager; and at Cootamundra, where the management is in the hands of Mr. G. R. M'Donald. All of these branches are flourishing institutions, doing a very fair share of the banking business carried on in the respective towns where they are situated. This extension of the business of the City Bank, is a sure indication of its growing prosperity. It is a result in every way satisfactory to all who are concerned. It is not of that character which is the characteristic of hasty and premature speculation; but of steady business capacity and careful foresight, and well-weighed judgment brought to bear upon offered opportunities. The bank has agents in the most important towns in the northern and southern hemispheres. This must be a great boon, and source of commercial convenience, to those clients whose business operations extend beyond the colony of New South Wales. Of course, the City Bank, like its more mature, and consequently successful rivals, extends its banking business, not only to all places within the colony, and to those towns abroad where it has agents; but to every other place to which the transactions of their customers extend. The following report of the board of directors of the City Bank, to the proprietors, at the thirty-third half-yearly general meeting, held at the banking-house of the company, Sydney, on Friday, 16th July, 1880, may not be uninteresting to those of our readers who have an interest in banking affairs.

The net profits, after deducting rebate on current bills, interest on fixed deposits, providing for bad and doubtful debts, and defraying all expenses of management, amount to £17,571 3s. 9d., to which is to be added the balance from last half-year, amounting to £2,893 19s. 3d., giving a total of £20,465 3s., available for distribution; which, by the recommendation of the directors, is appropriated as follows:—

	£	s.	d.
To dividend at rate of 10 per cent. per annum	12,000	0	0
,, Reserve Fund	5,000	0	0
,, Balance to next half-year	3,465	3	0
	20,465	3	0

The following figures show the liabilities and assets at 30th June, 1880:

Dr.

	£	s.	d.
To Capital paid up	240,000	0	0
,, Reserve Fund	70,000	0	0
,, Notes in circulation	33,172	10	0
,, Deposits and other liabilities	1,074,787	12	10
,, Profit and loss	23,106	15	1
	1,441,066	17	11

Cr.

	£	s.	d.
By coin and bullion on hand	192,464	7	8
,, Cash balance	121,487	17	1
,, Bills discounted and other debts due to the bank	1,107,114	13	2
,, Bank premises and furniture	20,000	0	0
	1,441,066	17	11

This report, which was so highly satisfactory, together with the statement of accounts, was ordered to be printed and circulated among the shareholders. It is a matter of congratulation to us to be able to speak so commendatorily of a comparatively young institution. We doubt not that, in the course of time, it will be able to show a balance-sheet which may not unfavourably compare with the other banks of the colony. So long as the same careful management is observed, and the same business capacity is available, the shareholders may be assured of a safe and steady progressive business, which will be a source of still further profit to themselves. The number of shareholders is 459, and amongst the names we notice many of those colonists who have established an enviable and enduring reputation. Several of the shareholders are inhabitants of the mother-country, an important factor in the confidence with which the City Bank is generally favoured. Many, too, are resident in the neighbouring colonies, which must contribute considerably to the wide-spread reputation, which is enjoyed by the bank in the colony of New South Wales.

SOME OF THE LEADING MERCANTILE HOUSES IN SYDNEY.

PRINCE, OGG AND CO.

The soft-goods business has contributed, perhaps, more substantial assistance to the rapid development of Australia and its resources than any other line of imports that we know of. To corroborate this assertion, we are able to exhibit pretty substantial data. It is well-known, at least to men who understand the force which equalises and controls exports and imports, that the more any nation *imports*, the greater impetus do they give their indigenous products and increase their value as *exports*. This is so, because bankers' exchanges can be more facilitated, and the price of foreign exchange made less feverish when the amount of merchandise vibrating between two countries—whether in raw or manufactured material—is nearly equal. There are, in consequence of this, secret forces invariably struggling to keep the export up with the import trade, and *vice versa*, in order to adjust the fiscal nerves of the market. If we wanted an example of this reasoning beyond our own borders, we need not look further than America. The United States was never the important commercial centre it is now until it commenced to import largely, which was about 1860. Following up its large volume of imports, bankers, of course, and other financial agencies began to look for something they could export largely in order to equalise exchanges, otherwise the withdrawal of such large amounts of bullion, as would be necessary to make settlings with, would so impoverish the banks as to make the atmosphere panicky and the position for the time dangerous. It is due, therefore, to those houses which have taken an important part in the *import* industries of this country, that credit should be given them in acknowledging the stimulus they have given our export trade, by helping it into substantial existence. The soft-goods men have naturally done more towards this accomplishment than any other trade that we know of, simply because their volume of imports is so much larger than any other branch of commerce. The sequence to this, following our own argument, is that they have, in consequence, made necessary a much larger line of exports to pay off our imports with. It is also in the nature of things that any country from whom we may take manufactured goods would cheerfully take in return raw material, especially if that material be of a nature to suit their manufacturing industries. There are many important soft-goods firms in Sydney, the largest and most important one perhaps being Messrs. Prince, Ogg and Company. The gentlemen who compose this firm are Messrs. Henry Prince, Wm. Anderson Ogg, and John Storey Jamieson. The firm came into existence in 1851, and their business comprises the importing of every possible kind of silk, woollen, and cotton goods, as well as drapery, millinery, and mercery. Their premises are situated in George-street, and run through to Pitt-street, covering about 2½ acres of land in their path. They do a business of between £500,000 and £600,000 per annum, and formerly kept up a stock of £260,000. Owing to communication with Europe being made so easily, through the use of the telegraph, they have been enabled to reduce their stock £100,000 and now require to keep up a stock varying from £160,000 to £180,000. This firm makes it a practice to order indents, and have them landed at two months from date of order; showing conclusively how well the internal workings of the firm are conducted. Comparisons are invited with other firms, in order to satisfy buyers of the advantages that this firm offers.

YOUNG AND LARK.

One of the characteristic features of Australian commerce is the amalgamation of the several branches of business, which is carried on by a single firm. The origin of this dates, no doubt, from the earliest settlement of the country, at a time when the exigencies of a sparse population were not equal to the support of distinct branches of business, carried on by separate establishments. The custom thus initiated by necessity has been carried on ever since, and some of the largest business houses of Australia are those who do not confine themselves to the buying and selling of articles belonging to a specific business, but whose commercial transactions extend over the widest imaginable range. We may lay it down as a safe guide, that wherever we find houses of commerce in any of the colonies who deal in a variety of articles, and whose business operations are not confined to any particular branch, that they are as a rule the oldest established businesses, not only in the particular colony in which they may be found, but in Australia generally. Their history is co-extensive with the history of the colony, and they stand as landmarks of what the country is capable of when energy, zeal, and perseverance are brought to bear upon its natural resources. Whatever interest may be felt by what we may call our outside readers in the staple products of Australia, they cannot but be favourably affected by the rapid and extensive growth of Australian commerce. It is an evidence of the business capabilities of our colonists, which are in no way inferior to those of the commercial men at home, as illustrated by the extensive transactions which are carried on by individual firms. Indomitable pluck, great enterprise, and capacity to discover beforehand the most pressing wants of the age, are the great characteristics of those merchants who settled in Australia. Another idiosyncrasy of our business men is the size, as well as the tasteful architecture, which distinguish the premises in which they carry on their commercial transactions. This is noticeable to the most cursory observer, and is a source of pleasure to all writers, but more particularly to those whose tastes are æsthetical. We were struck, during our peregrinations in Sydney, with the imposing, and often stately buildings which dot the city in every part. We forget the narrow streets in our admiration for the many fine business premises, which give an air of something of that which characterises the large cities of England, and for a time forget that we are not traversing the streets of some English town Sydney has many advantages which are not possessed by the sister cities of Australia. The harbour is, with, perhaps, one exception, *facile princeps* in the world; the city is, in a commercial point of view, favourably situated, and its central position in the Australian continent, may make it one day the chief port of Australian commerce.

It is our purpose, in this chapter, to refer specially to the firm of Young and Lark, of London, Sydney, and Launceston, as possessing, in a great degree, the salient features to which we have drawn attention in our previous remarks. The business premises of the firm are situated in Moore-street, in close proximity to the new post-office and neighbouring to the City Bank. They are somewhat plain, but at the same time, imposing in their appearance, a striking feature being the tower at the south-western corner. The firm whose offices and warehouses are comprised in this mass of buildings, is one of the oldest in Sydney. The house of Young and Lark, formerly known as Young, Lark, and Bennett, is the outcome of the amalgamation, in 1855, of the firms of Young and Co., and Lark, Bennett and Co., of Sydney, and Watson, Tyrrell and Lark, of London. One of these firms had already been in business for some years, and had established a very wide and influential connection. The firm of Young and Co. dates as far back as 1837. The business of the present firm has been carried on since 1868, under its present title. Messrs. Young and Lark carry on a very extensive and flourishing business as merchants, ship, and commission agents, and warehousemen. Their warehouse for soft-goods, in which they deal very largely, may be pronounced *primus inter pares* when compared with the other warehouses in the city. It consists of a basement and four floors, connected by handsome staircases and hydraulic lifts. There being no high-pressure water supply in Sydney, the hydraulic lifts have to be worked by steam-power, and to such a state of perfection has the system been carried, that four lifts, each capable of raising 15 cwt., can be put in motion at the same time. Some idea of the undertaking may be formed when it is stated that it was necessary to sink a shaft some 56 feet through some of the hardest rock which underlies the city of Sydney. Each flat of this stately building measures 100 feet by 84, and as there are no dividing walls or other obstacles, the effect is very striking. There is the very best and the most ample accommodation for the carrying on of a most extensive trade. This firm is an example of what we have said about the amalgamation into one of many branches of business. They not only import large quantities of soft goods, but they trade extensively in general merchandise.

Amongst their agencies may be numbered that of one of the largest exporters of Scotch ales to the colonies, we refer to Mr. Wm. McEwan, of Edinburgh. As exporters, a good deal of their attention is given to wool, tallow, copra, tin, and antimony. In the exportation of copra, a vessel is regularly employed in trading to the islands where that production is to be found. The London house accepted the agency of, and, at the same time, introduced the Pacific Insurance Company to the London market, and they succeeded in establishing so large a connection that it resulted in the formation of a branch in the English metropolis. Discharging inward, and loading or chartering outward-bound steamers and ships, and despatching them to all ports, is a large factor in the business. The firm is in treaty for the agency of a regular line of new steamers, which are being built for the Australian trade. It is expected that these steamers will be specially fitted up for the exportation of meat. Thus, it will be seen how varied is the business which the firm carries on, and how thoroughly representative it is of the trade of Australia. The branch at Launceston, in Tasmania, has been established about three years. The present partners are Messrs. J. R. Young, T. Lark, T. A. Strickland, F. B. Lark, and Fred. Lark. We are glad to say that these gentlemen take a great interest in all matters affecting the welfare of the colony. We were told that the adjoining block of buildings are the property of the firm, and truly they are evidence of the tasteful architecture which adorns the city.

FARMER AND COMPANY.

One of the great evidences of the commercial prosperity of a city is the number of stately buildings constructed at the instance of its citizens. Buildings of colossal proportions, and which would do honour to any city in Europe, have within the last few years made their appearance in Sydney. They have aided considerably in beautifying the city and rendering it a principal rival of Melbourne in architectural embellishment. It is a gratifying proof that the inhabitants of Sydney do not only look after their private interests, but have at the same time at heart the interests of the city, both aesthetically and commercially. We have the greatest pleasure in recording instances of private enterprise and public spirit on the part of the citizens of the colony. It is with this object that we feel called upon to devote a chapter to the splendid establishment of Messrs. Farmer and Company, general drapers, outfitters, and furnishers. No class of business men contribute more to our personal and home comforts than those who are engaged in the business of drapers. This remark applies in two ways, first in the substantial comfort we derive from the kind of goods in which they deal, and secondly in the domestic felicity which ensues from an unqualified permission on the part of paterfamilias to the lady members of their family, to visit and make all suitable and necessary purchases in the way of summer or winter clothing, or any other article which may be acceptable to, and desired by ladies generally. No greater variety, we are assured, could be found in any establishment in or out of Sydney. No greater courtesy and attention to the wants of customers are to be met with, however far the peregrinations of customers may extend. No greater convenience nor greater consideration for the various wants which are sought to be supplied can be found in the Australian colonies, or even in the shops in the West End of London, or in the fashionable quarters of Paris. The spacious dimensions of the business premises of Messrs. Farmer and Co., which are situated in Pitt-street, are architecturally one of the greatest ornaments of the city of Sydney, and in a business point of view, the largest establishment of the kind in New South Wales, if not in Australia. A general idea of the size and character of the edifice may be gathered from the following description. We must mention at the outset that this imposing building was first contemplated in 1869, though it was not begun until 1873. It is composed of, probably, the greatest variety of building stones that are to be found in any other structure, public or private, that adorns the streets of Sydney. There is granite, black and grey marble from near Goulburn, white marble from Bathurst, bluestone from Melbourne, white stone from Tasmania, and Sydney sandstone. We understand that special care and attention were given to the foundation work; strata of cement concrete, varying from 18 inches to 3 feet (known as "beton" by engineers), cover the whole area of the main trenches. Upon this, as foundation for front and back main walls, brick and cement inverts are built with hardest sandstone and Ballarat bluestone—upon which the columns and piers rest. The Pitt-street front has for the shop story an arcade carried by brick arches, having Melbourne bluestone pedestals, polished granite columns and bases, with polished black marble capitals, black piers having caps to match; the back main walls are carried on columns, with white marble shafts, grey marble caps and bases, all polished. The whole of the Pitt-street front is of brick and marble construction, enriched with bright coloured mural tiles from Worcester, England. The arcade is closed by revolving iron shutters, fixed at the back of the columns, to act, when required, as sun-blinds. The shop windows stand back from the main front, or building line of street, some eight feet, thus forming a colonnade, the whole length of the front, 140ft., and during business hours, giving a footpath 22 feet wide. There are three entrances from Pitt-street. The sashes of show windows returning into entrances are made of curved plate glass, bent to one-eighth part of a circle 12 feet in diameter. The whole of these sashes rest upon a base of white marble. Special care has evidently been bestowed upon each department so that it should be in every respect complete. A suite of rooms is provided on the first floor for the use of lady customers, having easy access from the ladies' department on the shop floor by a grand staircase. It is also a matter of general comfort and convenience to all lady customers in a climate where the heat is so intense as it sometimes is at Sydney. We do not remember to have heard of similar arrangements before in Australia, and we cannot but wish that the same innovation were common to all the business establishments of large cities, more particularly those establishments which are principally visited by ladies. This boon which has been conferred by Messrs. Farmer and Co. on those customers who visit their place of business is one which, we doubt not, is highly appreciated, and we feel sure must be productive of a great increase of business. This result seems natural, for it is always more than likely that people will be attracted most to those places where they find the greatest attention paid to their wants and the greatest consideration shown for their comforts. Every attention has also been paid to the gentlemen's department, and further extra care has been taken to provide commodious, well-ventilated, and well-lighted workrooms for the large staff of work-people employed on the premises. There is a ground floor area exceeding three-quarters of an acre, with an area of workroom flooring equal to half an acre, with ample provision for light, ventilation and drainage. To prevent damp arising from the foundation, the whole area of walling at the ground line has a layer of asphalt three-quarters of an inch thick. We understand that most valuable assistance was rendered to the architect by Mr. William Farmer in designing and planning out the building. The character and design are thoroughly different from anything else we have seen in Sydney. It would scarcely be appropriate to designate either the one or the other as novel, but nevertheless the difference when compared to other buildings in the city will strike the most cursory observer. We may here call attention to the fact that colonial-made bricks were used in the building of those premises, of a superior character, and which, we further understand, had never been used in the colony before. These bricks are the production of a firm established at Newtown.

The business of Farmer and Company was established in 1840 by Mr. Joseph Farmer, who retired from it in 1849. It was then carried on by Messrs. Price, Favence and Gwynn to 1854, who were reported to have amassed seventy-five thousand pounds during these five years. It must be remarked that this covered the period of the gold excitement in New South Wales and Victoria. The business was then taken up by Messrs. Farmer, Williams and Giles, (Mr. Farmer, the present senior partner), and carried on to 1860, when Mr. Richard Painter succeeded Messrs. Williams and Giles, whose term of partnership expired, and became partner with Mr. W. Farmer. No change took place until 1865, when the present senior resident partner in Sydney, Mr. John Pope, was admitted, and the business carried on under the style of Farmer, Painter and Pope, until Mr. Painter retired in 1869. At this time the last change in the name of the firm appeared to have taken place, when in deference to the wish of Mr. Joseph Farmer, it was mutually agreed that the names of all the members of the firm should be merged into Farmer and Company, under which name the firm are now universally known.

In 1874, on the occasion of Mr. W. Farmer's return to England, Messrs. William Seaward and George Parker Fitzgerald were admitted to the firm, and have since, in conjunction with Mr. Pope, managed the Sydney business.

Mr. William Farmer's connection with Victoria House, the name which has been given to the business premises of the firm, has extended over a period of nearly thirty years; he is now head of the firm of Farmer and Company. His arrival in the colony dates from 1849, when the business of the firm was of a comparatively limited character. At that time, the premises occupied a space of 24 feet by 75 feet; small, indeed, when compared with the space occupied by the present premises of the firm. Twenty hands were then employed in the various departments of the business, and this was found a sufficient number for the business as well as for the size of the premises. They have now accommodation for 400 work people, independent of those who are employed on the ground floor in disposing of goods; that is to say, that altogether they have ample accommodation at present for 550 hands. The steady but rapid progress which dates from the commencement of the business, is entirely due to the enterprising spirit of the members of the firm, as well as strict and conscientious attention to every want of their vast number of clients. This, when added to their general courtesy to all who visit their premises, combined with strict integrity and zealous attention to business, is the true basis of their remarkable success. Their employees, too, are assiduous in their attention to customers, and we can ensure a pleasant reception and profitable result to all those who may for business purposes, or any other reason, wish to visit the drapery establishment of Messrs. Farmer and Co. These gentlemen are illustrative of our preliminary remarks. While seeking their own personal advancement in life, they have not forgotten the consideration that is due to the progress of the city in architectural beauty, nor yet have they been oblivious to the fact that the people of Sydney are the builders up of their good fortune and success. It is a pleasing fact that the attention paid by the heads of the firm to the physical comfort as well as to the moral welfare of their employees is proverbial. There will be no prouder or more gratifying reminiscence on the eve of life than that their efforts were devoted, and devoted successfully, to the moral advancement and personal comfort of those whom they employed. May all fortune and success attend the efforts of gentlemen who consider the comfort and convenience of their workpeople an important factor, and who by their enterprise and energy have succeeded in erecting such splendid premises.

MAIDEN, HILL AND CLARK.

The staple product of Australia is wool, and so successfully has it been hitherto cultivated, that, with very few exceptions, whoever engages, directly or indirectly, in its commerce, seems to have but one history, which may be summed up in two words, success and prosperity. The public spirit which characterises those gentlemen who have embarked their fortunes in the wool trade, is so well known that it has now become proverbial. The most important factor in their success and prosperity is apparent at the first glance, and that is a thoroughly theoretical and practical study of the business in which they are engaged, and, at the same time, a complete knowledge of all its requirements. Such unqualified success could only have attended the efforts of gentlemen possessing these desiderata. The tact and knowledge, in the various departments of the wool trade, displayed, as a general rule, by the growers and sellers of wool, ought to be matter of congratulation to all who have an interest in the welfare and progress of the colonies of Australia. Those who in any way contribute to the material and commercial prosperity of a young country, are, without doubt, the country's benefactors. They must ever take a prominent social and public position, so intimately do they become connected with the country's weal. They must be, as they generally are, keen-witted and alive to all the exigences of the colony, as well as men of strict integrity and large business capacity and experience. Without such qualifications as these, the exportation of wool could never have been raised to the large figures with which it is now accredited. At some future day, when a Macaulay writes the history of Australia, the untiring and successful efforts of those colonists who have done so much towards the extension of this natural product of the country, and through whose endeavours the sure basis of its future progress has been established, will form a bright and enduring page in the annals of Australian history. The immense resources for wool-growing, which are possessed by this rich country, are, as yet, but imperfectly developed. Yet, we are enabled to say that, in spite of the youth of the colonies, the largeness of the figures which mark the amount of exportation, may not be unfavourably compared with the figures of exportation of those countries who reckon their age by more decades than Australia does by years. The only competition that has any chance to keep pace with Australia, is America's. This refers more particularly to the grain and dressed meat industries than to wool, for in this last product Australia has at present substantially no competitor. The breed of sheep has been so carefully and scientifically cultivated in Australia, that the wool-growers are enabled to bring into the market such superiority of fleece over other countries, that the trade must surely, in time, gravitate more and more to these colonies, until it culminates in their becoming the great centre of the wool trade, for the world at large. In addition to these advantages no other country offers such huge grazing facilities. As the earliest settlements took place in the colony of New South Wales, so to that colony belong the first small beginnings of the trade that is, no doubt, destined to make Sydney, although not as large as Melbourne, one of the great wool emporiums of Australia. In this branch of commerce, it may make its competition felt by its much larger neighbour Melbourne. Whatever may be the agricultural and mining resources of New South Wales, we certainly know that the pastoral resources are not superior in any part of the inhabited portion of this great continent. Besides, Sydney is so centrally situated, that it must be naturally the port for a great part of the produce of almost all districts lying inland. Its fine and commanding harbour, where ships of the largest tonnage may ride with safety, is not surpassed by any harbour in the world. For those who prefer to take in a mass of natural beauty, with all its surroundings, at one *coup d'œil*, the Bay of Naples may be preferred, but to those who prefer that beauties should unfold themselves gradually, the Bay of Sydney must have the preference. The development of the wool trade has given rise to a business which, in connection with the trade itself, is of the very greatest importance. Not only has it done this, but it has been the means of bringing forward gentlemen who, through natural qualifications, have been enabled to make it a successful and, financially, a very remunerative specialty. It has also resulted in the employment of a large number of workpeople, who, through constant engagement in the business, have become thoroughly adapted to, and perfectly *au fait* in, their several departments. Thus has been established a unanimity and *entente cordiale* between the growers, the auctioneers of wool, and the buyers, such as must materially advance the interests of the pastoral wealth of the various colonies. We are glad that it is in our power, so conscientiously to record such gratifying facts with regard to the staple commodity of New South Wales. The same may apply to other colonies of the Australian continent. These remarks we have considered necessary, as prefatory to the introduction to our readers of the firm of Maiden, Hill and Clark, who are the proprietors of very large wool stores, which are situated at Circular Quay. The offices are at 129 Pitt-street, Sydney. The history of this firm is an illustration of a great part of what we have said in our introductory remarks. From beginnings comparatively small when compared to the extensive business which they do at present, they have risen into an importance which may not unfavourably be compared with other large houses in the wool trade. The commencement of their business dates from 1874, thus giving them an existence of little more than six years. Though a young house, their business grew so rapidly that they were necessitated to take in an additional partner, whose practical knowledge and wide experience in business would enable the firm to attend to, and satisfy, the great increase in the number of their clients. The name of the gentleman who was introduced is a guarantee that nothing can be wanting in energy and skill, to meet every practical exigency which may arise. Mr. Clark, the name of the new partner, was at one time manager for Ettershank, Eaglestone and Co., which position he held for some years. There he gained an experience which must result advantageously to the business operations of the firm. Previously to Mr. Clark being associated with the firm of Ettershank, Eaglestone and Co., he was managing the office and finance of a large establishment in Sydney, which position he also held for many years. The experience gained by the senior partner, Mr. Maiden, as a store cattle buyer, which occupation he followed for several years, must, too, be an important desideratum in the successful conduct of the business of the firm. This, added to his experience in managing stations, which gave him an opportunity of knowing the wool-growing country from personal observation, must be a source of confidence to all those who have dealings with the firm of Maiden, Hill and Clark. Mr. Hill, we believe, can be credited with the same experience. The firm is also engaged as live stock salesmen, and sell annually in the fat stock market about 180,000 sheep, and from 12,000 to 15,000 live cattle. They further do a large business in selling station property and store stock. They sell and ship about 20,000 bales of wool yearly, and during the same period dispose of about 100,000 hides, and over 5000 casks of tallow, as well as doing a very heavy business in sheepskins. The selling and buying of the live stock is conducted by Mr. Geo. Maiden. The wool is supervised by Mr. W. C. Hill, and the finances of the concern are administered by Mr. Wm. Clark.

S. HOFFNUNG AND CO.

When the material wants of the population of a newly-settled country have been fairly supplied, it is but natural that they should seek after the gratification of those desires for comfort, convenience and ease, which are collateral and inalienable from the growing exigencies of the nineteenth century civilisation. To be confined to the pure necessities of existence, considerably modifies any pleasure or satisfaction that may be felt, even by pioneer settlers; but to have a continued prospect of the permanence of such an existence, must be pre-eminently distasteful. Such a mode of life as this is not uncommon where individual settlements are at a distance from each other; but it ceases to exist where settlers are congregated together, and naturally cultivate the amenities of social life. Beginning as unimportant villages, they gradually develop into important towns, vying in architectural beauty, opulence, and importance, with the larger towns of the United Kingdom. It is at this stage of progress that it becomes as much a necessity to satisfy the desire for comfort and elegance, and the refinements of life, as in the earlier period it was to have the merely material wants supplied. This necessity to which we have referred, is noticed by men who have a keen and practical insight into business, combined with energy of enterprise, and a desire to supply the growing and imperative wants of the public—and, of course, expecting a *quid pro quo* for their trouble. But what is particularly noticeable among the merchants of New South Wales is, that no expense or trouble is spared in erecting buildings of such stately proportions that they not only reflect credit upon the unusual success and desired prosperity of the colonists, but also prove the existence of a strong public spirit for the welfare, progress, and adornment of the towns or cities in which they have become located. In referring to the splendid premises of S. Hoffnung and Co., as an illustration of one feature of our remarks, and to the heads of the firm as an illustration of the other, we cannot do better than give a brief description of their establishment, and of the multifarious assortment of their stock.

The business was established in Sydney, in the year 1852, by Mr. Sigmond Hoffnung, now residing in London, in conjunction with Mr. Henry Nathan, of Birmingham, England, and was originally started in premises situated in Wynyard Lane. It was afterwards carried on for some few years in a more commodious building in George-street, which now forms portion of the Commercial Bank and of the Bank of New South Wales; and from thence was removed to Wynyard-street, where the firm carried on a large and successful business for a number of years, until the demands of their growing business necessitated the erection of their present palatial establishment in Pitt-street. This extensive warehouse, designed by Mr. T. Rowe, architect, which has replaced some of the oldest houses in the city, is one of the largest, and forms another architectural addition to the noble structures of Sydney. The site is sixty-two feet to Pitt-street, and terminates at the back by the Tank-stream, or main sewer, which, in the time of Governor Phillip, was a pleasant rivulet, overshadowed by a wood, and not more than a hundred yards from the then Government House. The disposition of plan shows an extensive warehouse with tram passage, or gateway, at the north side, to a back court, and large store-house in rear communicating on the upper floors with the front warehouse by means of enclosed bridges. The basement floor is devoted to the reception and forwarding of merchandise, or what is known as the packing and entry department. This is fitted with an excellent box-lift, made by Messrs. Burnett and Co., of London, on the most approved principle, for the purpose of carrying goods to and from the various departments. The basement and the ground-floor, on which the offices are situate, also contain the strong rooms. This treasury, so to speak, is built of brick and cement, with foundation on basement of solid stone; and gives two strong rooms, one on the basement and the other on the ground floor, with arched roofs and cemented floors. These are furnished with fireproof iron doors, manufactured by Messrs. Cotterell and Co., of

Birmingham. The doors are secured with the celebrated double acme locks, having keys of the most intricate construction—so singularly are they made that to take an impression of any of the keys has been found impossible. The strong room on the basement floor is devoted to the storage of the whole of the account-books, correspondence, and the many other documents which must be connected with the operations of such an extensive business. The upper strong room, on the ground-floor, is solely used for the custody of a large, diversified, and valuable stock of gold and silver jewellery and watches. The variety and value of these can only be estimated by dealers with the firm in this department, after having inspected the stock and examined the firm's printed catalogue, which, by the way, is one of the most useful works of the kind in Australia. It contains a hundred and eighty quarto pages, profusely and elegantly illustrated, and is supplied gratuitously on application. However, it may be stated, the watches and jewellery comprise a wonderful assortment—from the cheapest possible description up to those of the most costly material and workmanship. The ground-floor of the front warehouse is shelved, and specially fitted up with counters and show-cases for the display of their samples of stationery. Here will be found the usual variety of all descriptions of account-books, printed books, memorandum and pocket-books, writing paper, envelopes, wrapping paper, paper bags, and stationer's sundries. On this floor, the musical world will observe a large collection of pianofortes, by Bord, Aucher Frères, Neumeyer, Collard and Collard, Erard, Lipp, Ascherberg, Erhardt, and other celebrated makers; harmoniums, church organs, and musical boxes, can also be seen in many varieties, all the production of some of the best makers of the age. Ascending to the first floor, which is shelved throughout and fitted with extensive polished cedar glass cases, will be seen an elegant display of clocks of English, French and American make; optical instruments, papier-maché, bronze and marble occasional tables, and jardinieres; samples of fancy jewellery; tobaccoes, cigars, pipes, and other tobacconist's goods; fancy goods, perfumery, combs and brushware; patent and proprietary medicines, haberdashery, and Berlin wool goods, all in extraordinary variety.

The second floor, also elegantly fitted with polished cedar glass cases and shelved throughout, is devoted to the display of fourteen separate divisions of merchandise: American products; woodenware, chairs, &c.; hardware and ironmongery; holloware, tinware and galvanized ironware; cordage and twines, mats and matting; oils and colours, paperhangings; firearms, ammunition and sporting goods; fishing tackle; bedsteads and bedding; pier and looking glasses, mirrors; cutlery; electro-plated and metal goods; brushware; saddlery and saddlers' ironmongery, whips, &c.; and an extensive assortment of English, American, and Australian manufactured goods too numerous to mention, all of the most saleable description. On this floor are also displayed samples of their colonial-manufactured saddlery and harness. Messrs. Hoffnung and Co. have a large manufactory in the city, giving employment to over sixty hands in the execution of their extensive orders for saddlery and harness, which have carried highest honours at colonial, intercolonial and Philadelphia Exhibitions.

The third floor, or fifth story, is no exception to the others in point of variety and excellence of display. Here are exhibited specimens of engravings and oil-paintings, basket-ware, English and colonial billiard and bagatelle tables with fittings, cricketing goods and other indoor and outside games, toys, dolls, perambulators, walking-sticks, and thousands of other samples which must be overlooked by those who pass through the various compartments in this huge establishment, and which only represent the formidable bulk stock kept in the several stores of the firm.

The front of the main building, in Pitt-street, is built of Pyrmont stone, which abounds on the shores of Port Jackson and is of a yellow tint, in the Italian-Gothic style. The façade consists of a deeply recessed and moulded round arch, ornamented in the angles (as are all the piers of doors and windows, though different in detail) with the bullet-mould. The piers throughout have carved caps and moulded bases. The doorway, formed by richly-decorated folding doors with ornamental iron-work, is reached by a flight of six steps. At each side of the entrance there are two round-arched windows, richly moulded, supported on piers enriched as above, slated and surmounted by pointed gables on bosses. Beyond these, at each end of the front, is a larger semicircular arch, differing in detail from the others; the one on the south is fitted up with large plate glass panes in cedar sashes, with mullion in centre transom, and ornamental wrought-iron tympanum; the one on the north rests on columns and corbels carved, and fitted up with wrought-iron tympanum and folding gates, which are most elaborate in design and construction. The windows on this floor have moulded dadoes, carved, resting on a richly moulded base running unbroken along the front; below are the basement windows. At each side of the gateway and large windows, are piers projecting from the wall face and retiring, by means of water tables and goblets, at each story, around which the entablature is broken. Each story is marked by bold moulded strings, stopping against the piers, carved at the points of junction. The windows of the first, second, and third floors, preserve the same disposition, but differ considerably in detail. The first-floor openings are round arches, moulded, and surmounted by Gothic-arched labels with medallions, and rest on piers with cusped cups. The weatherings of the windows terminate in a string course. Over the large end window and archway are Gothic-arched couplets on central shafts carved. The second-floor windows differ in detail and height, and have round-arched tables with ornamental string course above. The third-floor windows have square heads, carved and moulded with square labels over, and supported by carved pier. The whole is crowned by a well-designed and moulded cornice with cusped medallion in frieze, and around piers a heavily moulded cornice, supported on ornamental corbels with mouldings between.

Over this there is a crowning feature consisting of a parapet broken by ornamental piers, and in centre a large gable rises with carved finial. In the gable is inscribed in a flowing band the words, "S. Hoffnung and Co., 1870."

These handsome and extensive premises are devoted solely to the display of samples and open stock; the bulk stock being kept in nine other stores situated in the immediate neighbourhood. The extensive store at the rear is occupied as a show-room for the display of a large and varied stock of earthenware, china, glass and lampware, which comprises a full assortment of all goods of this description in general use, giving every facility to the trade, storekeepers, and dealers in this line, to sort up their requirements either for open stock or bulk packages to suit their convenience.

The large and varied importations of this firm consist of all descriptions of British, Continental and American manufactures and products—the efforts of the firm being devoted towards supplying the wants of the retail traders, storekeepers, squatters, and dealers, with the numerous articles comprised in the fifty-two separate departments into which the business is divided. The following is a list of importations:—

I.

1. American Products.
2. Woodenware. Chairs, &c.
3. Hardware and Ironmongery.
4. Holloware, Tinware, and Galvanised Ironware.
5. Cordage and Twines, Mats, &c.
6. Oils and Colours, Paperhangings.
7. Firearms, Ammunition, and Sporting Goods.
8. Fishing Tackle.
9. Bedsteads, Bedding, &c.
10. Pier and Looking-glasses, Mirrors.
11. Cutlery.
12. Electroplated and metal goods.
13. Brushware.
14. Saddlery and Saddlers' Ironmongery, Whips.

II.

15. Account Books.
16. Memorandum and Pocket Books.
17. Stationers' sundries.
18. Writing Paper and Envelopes.
19. Wrapping Paper and Bags.
20. Printed Books.

III.

21. Earthenware, China, Granite and Stone-ware.
22. Glassware.
23. Ornaments and Vases.
24. Lampware.

IV.

25. Patent and Proprietary Medicines.
26. Perfumery, Combs, and Brushware.
27. Cabinet-ware and Fancy Wooden Goods.
28. Papier-maché Goods.
29. Fancy Leather Goods.
30. Portmanteaus and Travelling Bags.
31. Haberdashery and Berlin Wool Goods.
32. Albums and Fancy Goods.
33. Fancy Jewellery.
34. Vestas and Matches.
35. Tobacconists' Goods, Cigars, Tobacco, &c.
36. Clocks: English, French and American.
37. Optical Goods.
38. Musical Instruments.

V.

39. Engravings and Pictures.
40. Basket-ware.
41. Billiard and Bagatelle Tables.
42. Cricketing Goods, In and Out-door Games.
43. Toys and Dolls.
44. Perambulators.
45. Walking Sticks and Canes.
46. Stove Ornaments, Shell Goods, Fireworks, &c.

VI.
47. Sewing Machines and Fittings, Knitting Machines.

VII.
48. Watches : English, Geneva and American.
49. Gold Jewellery and Chains.
50. Silver Jewellery and Chains.
51. Silver Plate and Fancy Articles.
52. Jewellers' Cases and Sundries.

In the year 1871, Messrs. S. Sinauer and D. Marks were admitted as partners into this firm. In 1872, a branch establishment was opened in Brisbane, Queensland, and the firm have recently erected new and commodious premises in Charlotte-street, in that city, which rank in the first line amongst the great warehouses erected in the principal cities of Australia. In points of elegance, convenience, and accommodation, it surpasses any in Queensland, and has the distinction of being the first five-storied edifice built in that colony. The description of the building is almost a *fac simile* of that of the Sydney house, and the interior arrangements of stock similarly carried out. While the Brisbane house contains supplies of every article displayed in the firm's illustrated catalogue, the Sydney establishment is the most extensive of the kind in the southern hemisphere, and affords employment, both directly and indirectly, to the greatest number of hands. The freetrade policy of the people and Parliament of New South Wales must always render Sydney the headquarters of the manufacturing and importing industry, or in other words, make Port Jackson the emporium *par excellence* of Australia.

The vast area over which Messrs. Hoffnung and Co.'s mercantile transactions extend, is as diversified as their goods are multifarious—their business embracing the whole of the colonies from Port Darwin, in the north, to Albany in Western Australia, including Queensland, South Australia and New South Wales, and extending also to the neighbouring colonies of New Zealand, Tasmania and Fiji, and even as far as Honolulu and New Caledonia. To work up the trade over this extensive area, twelve commercial travellers are constantly employed by the firm, and it is necessary to retain ninety-nine hands in Sydney, and forty in Brisbane, for the receipt of merchandise and for despatching goods to the interior and for shipment. English merchandise is supplied by their London house, Messrs. H. Nathan and Co., who occupy extensive premises, 13 Basinghall-street, and whose duty it is to purchase and superintend the shipment of goods destined for the Australian market. Agents are specially employed at New York and San Francisco to operate with American manufacturers; and in Paris, Vienna, Berlin, Hamburg, and other manufacturing centres in Europe, the firm has representatives to watch over and guide their interests. The sale of Australian manufactured goods also forms a great feature in their business—a fact which is a credit to their discernment—and, indeed, they are themselves large manufacturers in New South Wales. The London house is under the personal supervision of an old and esteemed colonist, Mr. S. Hoffnung, assisted by the senior and junior resident partners, Messrs. H. Nathan and S. Sinauer, with an efficient staff of experienced clerks and packers, all of whom, from the principal down, have been more or less identified with the trade of the colonies and the special requirements of Australians. The business in the colonies and the whole operations of the firm, are controlled by the resident managing partner, Mr. D. Marks; the Brisbane branch is under the able management of Mr. B. F. Marks, who has been connected with the business of the firm for the past twelve years. The main establishment is situated at 117 Pitt-street, Sydney, and the branch establishment is at Charlotte-street, Brisbane. Messrs. Hoffnung and Co. style themselves general merchants, warehousemen, importers, and shipping agents.

HUDSON BROTHERS.

We have often wondered how, in practice, the individual prosperity of the few is absolutely adopted by the majority; while in theory, the general prosperity of the many, is adopted as self-evident by the whole human race. The doctrine of protection illustrates the former proposition, that of free trade the latter. What we mean may be adduced by what follows. Take half-a-dozen individuals, each engaged in the same branch of trade, and let us suppose that there is a protective duty of, say 20 per cent., on every article, in that branch of trade, which is introduced into the colony. Now, it is clear that the article can be bought in the home market for 20 per cent. less than that for which it can be bought here. Therefore, to compete successfully against importations subject to protective duty, the colonial article must be sold at something less than the imported article can be bought at. However much less the selling price may be, say 2 per cent., eighteen per cent. more than the real value must come out of the people's pockets. But it may be sold at exactly the same figure, and in this case the people pay exactly 20s. for that, the real value of which is about 16s. It is clear that the six individuals mentioned reap the benefit, while the loss is felt by every individual person who deals with them. The numbers may directly or indirectly be hundreds or thousands. But it may be said, that if protection be extended to every branch of trade, each branch is mutually benefited. Granted. But upon whom does the loss fall? Upon the large majority of the whole people. But it may again be said that they reap the benefit indirectly by increased wages. So far we admit this. But is the increase of wages equivalent to the increased price of every commodity that runs in the wake of protection? We will show, not only that it is not so, but that it cannot be so. Take a dozen articles which are used by the working man, and if there be a duty of 20 per cent. upon each article, he must absolutely pay, on buying the whole twelve articles, 48s. more than they are really worth, if they are sold, say at £1 each, *i.e.*, he pays £12 for what is only really worth £9 12s. Hence, when he receives a pound sterling in wages, that pound, under the system of protection, is only worth 16s. In this way the tinselled substance is dangled before him by the few, and it is only when he examines it that it is found to be but a shadow. This cannot happen in the case of free trade, for then every market is open to the buyer, instead of only the market represented by the six individuals. Competition is the natural sequence, the articles sink to their real value, and in buying them we get the exact *quid pro quo* for our money, minus the bogus that protection means increased wages, while the important factor of the spurious value laid upon the protected article entirely swamps, not only the apparent increase of wages but often much more. The first proposition in the opening part of our chapter is a symbol of Victorian policy, while the truth of the second part is not, and cannot be, denied by a single Victorian protectionist. Another source of wonder, during our sojourn in Australia, is the jealousy existing between the colonies, especially those of New South Wales and Victoria. We know that in nothing except their fiscal policy, do they differ from each other. They belong to the same race, they speak the same language, they have the same laws, they both claim a common fatherland, and yet on crossing from one border to the other your passage is arrested, as though you came, if not from the country of an enemy, certainly from the country of a foreigner. It is the protective policy of Victoria that has been provocative of this anomaly. The federation of the colonies will destroy it; the adoption of free trade in Victoria will be its death knell. One or the other will be welcomed by all those who have the true welfare of Australia at heart. There is no more remarkable instance in any colony of Australasia, of the most complete success attending indomitable energy, enterprise, and perseverance, opposed by all imaginable difficulties and obstacles, than is evidenced by the very successful career of Messrs. Hudson Brothers, of Sydney, New South Wales, who carry on the business of railway-carriage builders, together with extensive steam joinery and cabinet works, and saw-mills, under the flag of free trade. They are patronised largely by their own colony, and are contractors for the supply of all rolling-stock for the New South Wales Government for the next five years, and can successfully compete with any like article manufactured in the home trade. There is nothing like the same amount of work done in the same time in any other manufactory engaged in this branch of trade, in any part of Australia. Victoria is far behind. And yet Victoria, as well as South Australia, Queensland, and New Zealand, prefers to go to its home markets, though, in less time, with equal quality, it can have the same work done by its neighbours. This cannot last long, and we are sure the day is not far distant when the manufactures of Messrs. Hudson Brothers will meet with that appreciation in all the Australian colonies which they so richly and justly deserve. A short account of their earliest beginnings, and their steady, though rapid, progress to their present premier position, will, we feel sure, not only be a matter of interest, but of wonder to our readers. We may preface our remarks, by reminding our readers that a native industry of this kind, to a rising colony, is of the very greatest importance. Mr. W. H. Hudson, the father of the gentlemen who constitute the present firm, commenced business in a small shop, on the present site, about 25 years ago, built by his two apprentices—one of the apprentices being Mr. Robert Hudson, one of the firm of the present Hudson Brothers. His first undertaking of any magnitude, was the building of St. Paul's Church, in Cleveland-street, and he afterwards supplied the woodwork of Sydney University. Twelve years later, the present firm of gentlemen took over the business from their father. The premises, at that time, covered an area of something under 40 feet by 30 feet. At the end of three or four years, the increase in their business necessitated the introduction of steam power, for the purpose of reducing the larger pieces of timber into required sizes for buildings—Henry and Robert Hudson, at that time, being contractors for buildings under the architects of the city. A boiler and engine of 12-horse power, previously used by Pennell, and believed to be the first made in Sydney, was accordingly purchased. Not more than twelve months had elapsed when they were further obliged to purchase a 25-horse power engine, boiler, and shafting, as well as a planing-machine. We need scarcely say that, as the business grew, the premises were enlarged. Within two years from this, to meet the still growing requirements of their business, they ordered two engines of an aggregate power of between 70 and 100 horses, to be manufactured by Mort's Dock Company. Their business still rapidly increasing, it required the utmost energy and enterprise of the firm to keep pace with the increase. Machine followed machine in endless variety, till, at the present time, there is scarcely room to thread your way through them, although they are so arranged that each machine has its own clear space for working economically, with the aid of a sufficient staff of men constantly supplying and removing the timber to and from the many machines; and the sight is quite interesting, when looking at the mass of belts moving in all directions, and the various lines of shafting carrying the motion to the various and very useful labour-saving machines. The first contract entered into by Messrs. Hudson with the Government, for rolling stock, was at the beginning of 1876, when 200 D waggons were required; so that, at the present time, this particular industry is not five years old. Ten waggons per month for the first hundred, and 15 waggons per month for the second hundred, were stipulated for in the conditions. At that time, there was not a blacksmith's forge on the premises, nor one bar of iron, and the site of the present smith's shop was occupied with stacks of timber, all of which had not only to be cleared away, but a shop had to be built in which to carry on the work. The smith's work was started about March, and soon after an engineer's shop was erected and fitted with lathes, drills, &c. The first 14 waggons were delivered during May, and the whole of the 200 were completed by the end of the year, which was 11 months under contract time. During their last engagement with the Government for supplying rolling stock, the firm turned out no less than 90 D waggons in one month; and this wonderful feat was accomplished to meet the demand for the carriage of wool by railway; in fact, from the commencement to the finish of the contract, 300 waggons were supplied in less than four months. It may be better understood by those who do not practically understand this branch of industry, when we explain that 726,000lb. weight of iron and about 300,000ft. of timber were used in building these waggons, the gross weight of manufactured materials passing through the hands of workmen amounted to about 1,800 tons. From 1876 to March 1879, there have been built in the establishment 700 waggons, 12 carriages (saloon, first and second class, and composite), 100 cattle, four sheep, 26 coal waggons, and 100 coal skips, altogether amounting in value to something like £76,000. The premises have now been so enlarged, the machinery increased to such an extent, that the firm is fully able to supply all the rolling stock for the railways of New South Wales, and, we might almost say, the railways of the rest of Australia. Since March 1879, to the present time, October 1880, more than twice the value of rolling stock has been delivered, than was done in the first three years. Certainly if such a demand were made we feel that the enterprising firm of Messrs. Hudson Brothers would be equal to the occasion. All that we have mentioned has been accomplished in the incredibly short space of four years. During the past year, over 6,000,000 feet of timber has been worked up or passed through the establishment in one shape or another; when the works are in full operation, employment is given to about 550 men, so that it will probably be within the mark to assert that at least 1500 persons are dependent for their living upon this establishment. Wages to the amount of about £44,000 were paid during the past year. A branch establishment also exists at the Myall Lakes, where locomotive tramways, horses, punts, and sailing vessels, are brought into requisition for the carriage of timber. The site of the carriage works embraces an area of 380 feet by 292 feet. The buildings, which are built of brick, timber, and galvanised iron, vary from one to three stories in height. A railway siding runs alongside the mill, where trucks bring immense logs from the interior. These are hauled up by the travellers and carried to the gang frames, where they undergo the first process of preparation. Independent of the carriage and waggon shops, is the spacious joinery department from whence so many builders draw their supplies, rendering contracting for buildings a very easy matter ; as contractors merely consult the price lists for the price of all wood-work, prepared ready for fixing, and by consulting the pattern book in connection with the monthly price list, they know what each article will cost, and merely have to add the cost of fixing. We understand that Messrs. Hudson Bros. are about to remove their workshops to Granville, late Parramatta Junction, having purchased in that neighbourhood, 100 acres of land, upon which they are about to build forthwith. Mr. Henry Hudson is about to proceed to England, through America, for the purpose of seeing the newest designs in railway cars, in order to suggest any alterations tending to the comfort and convenience of railway travellers. Mr. Hudson will also patent in England a new automatic safety coupler which will preclude the possibility of accident to men who are engaged in making up the trains.

Messrs. Hudson Bros. are always pleased to show visitors through their works; and they are ever ready to accept any suggestions which may be offered. There is invariably one of the firm to be found on the premises, and he is very frequently in the workshop. From the fact of all of them being practically acquainted with their business, they are usually to be found working amongst their operatives, endeavouring to carry out their motto, "to persevere is to succeed."

MR. E. VICKERY.

There is probably no country in the world where self-made men are more numerous in proportion to the population than they are in Australia. This may be ascertained from a study of the history of a few of the leading men in the Australian colonies. Not only have these men been the pioneers of a new country; but by the force of character which they have introduced into all their undertakings, they have been the founders of an entirely new order of things, which is singularly peculiar to the colonists of their adopted country. Though wealth is a great factor in our general estimate of men, and such estimation is common to every country of the world, yet here perseverance and energy are regarded as no less valuable factors in the estimate which we form of our leading citizens. Such a basis as this must be invaluable in our judgment of men's characters. It is the foundation of that reputation for commercial integrity which seems to follow Englishmen in whatever country they may settle. It establishes a confidence amongst those with whom they daily come in contact, and it extends its signal influence even outside of the world of commerce. It is the foundation of those mutual amenities and pleasant intercourses which characterise a flourishing and prosperous community. Its influence is felt not only within the community where it is practised, but also amongst the distant nations with which the co¹ y has transactions. It produces a healthy emulation, and is more than likely to leaven, to a greater or lesser degree, the whole population. It contributes, in a very large degree, to the moral, the social, and the national welfare of a people, and it is the most lasting basis of true progressive development in every part of public and private life. Fortunate, indeed, is that country which, amongst its inhabitants, possesses men whose zeal, energy, perseverance and commercial integrity extend their influence through all the ramifications of society. Their character for careful speculation and business talents becomes so firmly and so quickly established, that their success is a foregone conclusion. Such men are the truest benefactors of humanity at large. Their whole lives are devoted, with a remarkable singleness of aim, to the accomplishment of their great purposes. Such concentration of energies must precede and be followed by success and general advancement. We cannot but admire the lives which are passed in such laudable efforts, and our admiration, though natives of another country, can never be accompanied even with the shadow of envy. Cosmopolitan as we are in our judgment of men and manners, we become signally one-sided when recording the lives of such men as those who have become creditors in the account-book of the colony's prosperity. They take captive our sympathies, and superinduce the conviction that no truer aphorism was ever introduced into our language than the one which tells us that honesty is the best policy. If this be used in a specific sense, then we must add to honesty, integrity of purpose and singleness of aim. Mr. Vickery, whose business is the subject of this chapter, is a true representative of the class of men which we have singled out. He arrived in the colony of New South Wales at a comparatively early age. He then began to wrestle with the battle of life, and he has succeeded in fighting that battle manfully and successfully. He has also repeatedly identified himself with the social, industrial, and commercial progress of his adopted country. We believe that we are justified in stating that it is to Mr. Vickery that Sydney owes the initiative of the great series of buildings remarkable for their architectural beauty, which now adorn the streets of Sydney. These improvements bid fair, at no distant date, to make the capital of New South Wales one of the finest cities in the world, and in every respect worthy of the magnificent site which it occupies. Mr. Vickery does not dabble much in public matters ; but like most real public benefactors, he is contented to discharge his duties as a citizen, leaving to others the struggle for popular applause and honours, which, though they may be well deserved, are after all but of little value when compared with the satisfaction experienced in having done one's duty to one's fellow-man. None of the colonists of New South Wales is more deserving than Mr. Vickery, who does, as a matter of fact, enjoy the respect and esteem of all who value true manliness and public spirit.

The buildings in which Mr. Vickery carries on the business of general merchant, commission agent, and importer of boots, shoes, and leather, are palatial in their appearance, and form one of the chief ornaments of Pitt-street, which is remarkable for its stately and spacious edifices. We may here mention that this gentleman is the proprietor of the Greta Coal Mine, which is situated at Newcastle, in New South Wales. Mr. Vickery, in 1851, succeeded to the business of his father as a boot and leather merchant, since which time, his career, in that branch, has been one of continued and marked success. Like all men of speculative proclivities, he did not confine himself to this business; but, in course of time, extended his efforts to other branches of commerce. In the year 1866, he visited the mother-country, and was induced to spend part of his capital in the building of the well-known ship *Parramatta*, and subsequently became part owner in the *Sobraon*, the *Hawkesbury*, and the *La Hogue*. As pioneer in the improved architecture of Sydney, he started, in 1864, the building of the magnificent pile in Pitt-street, known as Vickery's buildings. During the year 1866, Mr. Vickery, in conjunction with other gentlemen, started the manufactory of iron from the rich hematite iron ores of the Fitzroy mines. The company imported skilled labour and plant at great cost, and produced over 3000 tons of the best of iron; but not having perfected their plant, and being obliged to have recourse to men who required training in the business of manufacturing from iron ore, they were not able to turn out iron at a remunerative profit, such as to warrant them in continuing the business. Yet they manfully struggled on against the competition of European prices, until the shareholders were unwilling, or unable, to contribute further, and the venture came to an untimely end. This we extremely regret, not only for the colony itself, but also for the sake of Mr. Vickery; for we doubt not that had he been ably seconded, both financially and in the supply of skilled workmen, he might have developed another industry, which might have been of great commercial importance to New South Wales, and which was calculated to raise her above the rest of the colonies, both in wealth and commercial reputation. We mention this, inasmuch as there is abundance of the raw material in New South Wales, favourably situated, and which only requires energy and zeal, supplemented by capital, to work successfully. Mr. Vickery is one of the largest squatters in the colony. He has not only made his money in the colony, but there has he also invested all his savings, thus associating himself more closely with its present and future.

HARDIE AND GORMAN.

A very accurate estimate of the commercial prosperity of any community can be formed from the success which attends the sale of real property. According to the number of those who are owners of freehold estate, are we able to form a fair estimate of the individual success of the citizens of a small or large city. From individual affluence it necessarily follows that we can realise the approximate wealth of the collective population. But the basis of all our calculations must rest upon the extent of business operations carried on by those in whose hands the selling of real estate is vested. If those whose calling in life is the auctioneering of houses and land, have a large and ever-increasing custom, we may be sure that the portent is commercial prosperity and general solvency. For it is scarcely possible that their business can be confined exclusively, or even in great part, to the sale of large landed estates, particularly when we know that in and about Sydney, the number of large landed estates is rapidly becoming limited. This is further confirmed by the fact that whatever large estates there may be in the suburbs of Sydney, they are, for the most part, day after day being brought into the market, for the purpose of being sold in small building allotments. This is specially applicable to land on the shore of Port Jackson, along the railway line, in the direction of Botany Bay, and in suburbs which stretch towards the coast, betwixt the South and Botany Heads. The increase of population, which necessarily results in the increase of commerce, creates a want for additional buildings, the outcome of which is that a special line of business grows into existence, at once important and prognosticative of accumulating wealth. The business we refer to is that of auctioneers of real estate, &c.; and amongst the few leading firms, whose transactions in the sale of real estate in Sydney and its suburbs are on an extensive scale, none is deserving of a more prominent notice than the firm of Messrs. Hardie and Gorman. This firm has been established about eight years, but the property branch has been carried on for not more than five years, during which time their zeal and energy, as well as careful attention to the details of their business, have steadily developed the concern to its present extensive transactions and flourishing condition. The business of selling property successfully in order that purchasers may not regret their investments, requires large experience as well as native acumen, a nice sense of honesty and honour, a clear discrimination of value, together with high personal qualifications. The buyer is comparatively at the mercy of the salesman, for while one is a professional expert the other is a mere novice, and hence the possession of the qualifications we have enumerated is a *sine qua non*, if the wish be to superinduce unlimited confidence and to establish a large and increasing business. What we have just said, is, we believe, the secret of the success which has attended the increasing efforts of Messrs. Hardie and Gorman to establish a permanent and successful business as auctioneers of real property. Sydney, as the commercial centre of Australia, must sooner or later take a position, not even second to its prosperous and splendid rival, Melbourne. Increasing population, followed by increase in the number of buildings, and so resulting in the extension of the city and suburbs, have necessarily caused a large amount of both improved and unimproved property to change hands by the subdivision and otherwise of suburban estates, and in this way fulfilling the desire of those, an ever increasing number of the population, whose ambition it is to become the owners of freehold estates. The number of freeholders in and around Sydney may not be unfavourably compared with the number of freeholders in any other city in the world having the same population and age. Hitherto the business transactions of the firm have succeeded in securing a very large proportion of the public confidence, and we have no hesitation in saying that the future of the concern may fairly be judged by its business operations in the past. We understand that Messrs. Hardie and Gorman have laid down as a basis of all their operations, the important principle of confining themselves entirely to a commission and agency business; and they propose steadily to set their faces against all dabbling or speculations in properties, which we regret to say is done so often in the case of those whose business it is to sell land, &c. No better or more satisfactory principles could have been adopted by Messrs. Hardie and Gorman to secure the confidence of their clients. In this way they are enabled to give themselves entirely up to the interests of their customers. Success must attend those whose whole study is to give satisfaction to the persons whose business they transact, and whose principle is to devote the whole of their time and attention to all the transactions with which they are entrusted.

Five years ago, Messrs. Hardie and Gorman removed to the premises which they at present occupy, on the ground floor of Bell's Chambers, opposite the City Bank. During this time, the steady increase of business has clearly proved that the premises which they originally occupied were in every way insufficient for their increasing requirements. Negotiations were opened for the purchase of other and larger premises, but eventually arrangements were made with the proprietor of Bell's Chambers, whereby Messrs. Hardie and Gorman leased, for a long term of years, the whole of the buildings known as Nos. 129, 131, and 133, Pitt-street. They were thus enabled to make such alterations in their rooms as the growing exigencies of their business required. This was accomplished by the pulling down of party-walls, and the building of additional office accommodation at the rear. Their auction-rooms and offices were thus enlarged, and the best lighted and ventilated sale-rooms in the city was the result. The position occupied by these premises is very central. It is close to the banks, as well as to the Government and mercantile centres. Each member of the firm has his separate office, and there is ample and convenient accommodation for the accountant and clerks. The whole is well and compactly arranged on the ground floor. Weekly auction sales of houses and land are held on Wednesdays, at the rooms. From Messrs. Hardie and Gorman's "Property Circular," which we have before us, we notice that properties of high value are entrusted to them. No better instance of the confidence placed in the firm could be adduced than the fact, that estates comprising valuable interests, should be placed in their hands. We must not omit to mention, that sales of property are also held on other days, if there is a special arrangement. The out-door sales of subdivided estates are conducted on Saturday afternoons. We understand that particulars of properties for sale are inserted in their "Property Circular" free of charge. Of course, if any property, so inserted, be sold, the ordinary commission becomes payable. Such an advantage as this merely requires to be known, for it must be the interest of all to advertise as largely as possible any intended sale. They also undertake the collection of rents, as well as the entire management of estates, at a commission on the weekly, monthly, quarterly, or yearly rents, while for the management of large estates, special terms may be arranged.

As a striking illustration of the condition, of not only this firm's business, but of the activity in real property transactions in Sydney, at this moment, we must not omit to give our readers a few figures, which are so significant in their importance, that we need not comment upon them. It will be admitted by all that no truer thermometer of the state of commerce, finance, and prosperity, could exist, than the real estate market. The *bona fide* sales which take place from Monday to Saturday in each week, mean, if anything at all, that, from the banker down to his messenger, from the merchant down to his porter, from the manufacturer down to his packer, each one is, according to his means and requirements, securing land, either for permanent investment on the one part, or a local habitation on the other. The consequence is, that the ever augmenting increment of profits and labour is being continually re-invested in the city of Sydney and its suburbs. This course has a twofold advantage to the state or city in which it occurs. Firstly, by keeping the money in the country in which it is made, and preventing its enforced emigration to more disadvantageous centres of investment; and secondly, by creating a healthy increment in the value of real property by renewed inquiry for it, and thereby contributing to a permanent advance of every kind of property which is directly or indirectly affected. Concomitant with these advantages, may be mentioned the salubrious effect it exerts over the wage-earning mind, in steadily, if slowly, transforming it into a more conservative type. This influence is shown in the most practical manner by the following remarks, which we gather from the November circular issued by this firm :—

We have again to report a very heavy business in real estate—indeed, a far larger amount of attention has been paid to the property market by capitalists, investors, and speculators, during the past month than for any similar period for a long time. The amount of accumulated money in all hands, seeking safe as well as profitable investment, no doubt is the chief cause of this ; but a sounder reason may be found in the fact that the investing public have a great faith in the future of Sydney, increasing, as it most undoubtedly is, in every quarter, and extending its suburbs north, south, east, and west.

City properties are promptly placed as they come into the market, at advancing rates ; the favour in which such investments are held being very marked.

Suburban residences and villas have found ready buyers, and many purchasers are unsupplied.

Terrace properties and dwellings on the railway line and tramway routes are much inquired for, and those offering, if of good value, are soon disposed of.

Several large properties in the immediate suburbs have changed hands during the month, and we are now negotiating the sale of three or four extensive estates.

Small dwellings and mechanics' houses are much sought after, caused probably, by the increase of population from the United Kingdom, as well as from most of the neighbouring colonies.

We have many inquiries for good country properties, but few are offering.

The tramway to the eastern suburbs has been commenced, and within a few months the suburbs of Paddington, Woollahra, Waverley, Coogee, and Bondi, will have the advantage of rapid communication with the city.

We have sold the "Warren property" at Marrickville, well-known as the residence and extensive estate of Hon. Thomas Holt, M.L.C., for the sum of £50,000.

The same circular reports the almost astounding fact that their total sales during the month of October, were £139,200.

GOODLET AND SMITH.

The indigenous timber which is to be found in Australia, is so varied and, at the same time, growing in such considerable quantity, that there is no branch of trade in which wood is required, that it is not, and will not be, able to supply *ad nauseam*. Not only is there sufficient for native industry for years to come, but it is fully equal to the supply of a large export trade. Some of the wood, such as the ironbark and others of this species, possesses all the durability and strength of the English oak, and serves the same purposes in this new country, as the oak is used for in the countries of Europe. Hence, the timber trade is coeval in age with the other industries of the the colonies, and is gradually developing into an important and useful and paying industry. Since the introduction of brick and stone buildings, there is not so much timber used in that branch of the business as formerly, but still the demand is considerable. The rapid increase of population, requires a proportionately rapid increase in the construction of buildings; and where the demand for the building of wooden houses has decreased, it has been fully made up by the amount of wood material required for the increased number of dwellings, shops, warehouses, and other structures, that are daily rearing their heads in the city and its suburbs, as well as in the towns of minor importance in the interior, and those situated near the coast. Thus, though one specific branch of the trade is not so flourishing, the new branch which has been the natural outcome, that is the supply of timber for the new species of building, has more than made up for the decrease in the number of wooden houses that are at present constructed. Among the largest and most complete establishments of the kind in the colony, are the Victoria Saw Mills, belonging to the gentlemen whose names stand at the head of this chapter. The works are admirably situated, having a large extent of water frontage, which gives great facility for the shipping trade of this firm, and allows their log timber from the coast districts, to be landed at the mills with the greatest ease. Vessels being moored alongside the wharf, the logs are lifted out of the hold by means of steam travelling-cranes, and are carried direct to the sawing machines without any trouble, there being roller tramways laid down, leading to the saws, and with these accessories, logs of two or three tons' weight are handled easily by a couple of men. There are here two large saw frames, one a breaking-down frame, by which the first slices are taken off the outside of the rough logs, the other is a boarding frame, in which any number of saws can be placed to work simultaneously, so as to reduce the whole of the log, at one operation, into as many planks as may be desired, and of any thickness. Their frames, as well as all the other machinery in the place, are worked by steam power. The engines used are on the horizontal principle, and are of 60-horse power. They have an enormous fly-wheel, 16 feet in diameter. The steam is supplied by three large boilers, set in brick-work, and furnished with all the modern appliances for economising heat. No coal is used for generating the steam, the only fuel employed being saw-dust, shavings, chips, and other refuse from the works, of which more than sufficient is produced for that purpose, and indeed, large quantities have to be carted away during the course of the year. There is an ingenious automatic contrivance, for conveying the saw-dust to the stoke-hole. Next to the frame saws, is one of Fay's large re-sawing machines, consisting of an endless band saw, by means of which timber can be cut of any thickness, from the 16th of an inch by 30 inches wide, and the action being continuous, this machine turns out the work with astonishing rapidity and unerring accuracy, between cylindrical rollers, which can be set to any gauge, and all the workman has to do is to keep on passing up the pieces of timber to be sawn, and the machine does all the rest, turning out the planks without further trouble. Among the other labour-saving contrivances on this floor, there is a number of sawing and planing machines, including eight circular saws, for ripping and cross-cutting, and two machines for grooving and tongueing. There is also an engineer's shop, with forge, lathes, and other apparatus, where all repairs required for the machinery are effected. There are two machines for sharpening the many saws used in the establishment. The carpenters' shop is on the floor above, a magnificent room 100 feet square, without a partition, and, therefore, open to the view to the fullest extent, except where the industry of the workmen has raised piles of doors, sashes, or other manufactured articles. Here, as below, every contrivance that modern science and skill can devise, is put into practice in order to save labour, and produce superiority of workmanship. Very naturally, there always remains a large amount of finishing and putting together to be done by hand, after the parts have been constructed by machinery, and a number of skilful joiners are kept constantly at work. Of course, the carpenters and joiners use their own special tools in the process of their finishing operations, and we find they can sharpen these tools, when necessary, on a series of emery wheels, turned by steam power, and which grind them as effectually, and much more rapidly, than the old-fashioned and laborious grindstone could do. Before leaving this floor, we find that there are patent lifts of novel and ingenious construction, which enable the timber to be carried up, and the manufactured article to be lowered down, with the smallest possible amount of trouble or labour to the men. There is yet another story to the building, which is chiefly devoted to the sash department, and the finishing of the work done below. Here, in fact, the various articles receive the final touches which are to render them fit for immediate use, and we see piles of sashes, doors, and other manufactured goods, in astonishing variety, both as to size and form. There are four turning lathes on this upper floor, and three sand-papering machines, the latter being a new idea, and only just added to the collection. We find here the glazing department, where the wooden sashes are glazed, and we notice large quantities of this material cut up into squares or panes ready for use, as well as cases upon cases of glass as yet unopened. Messrs. Goodlet and Smith have erected a new drying shed, which is 43 feet long and 22 feet 6 inches wide, with a height, from floor to ceiling, of 10 feet. There are over 150 men employed by the firm at the Victoria Saw Mills. The firm has a powerful steam launch which is used in connection with the works, for the purpose of conveying timber or manufactured goods about the harbour, whenever required. The trade of the firm extends all over the colony, and large quantities of their goods are shipped coastwise, as well as sent by train. The wages paid at this establishment vary, according to the kind of labour, from about £2 weekly for rough and unskilled labour, to 1s. 6d. per hour for skilled hands. The eight-hours' system prevails among the carpenters, but most of the other trades work nine hours a day. The mechanical resources of these mills enable them to cut up over 100,000 feet of timber per week, a good proportion of which is made up into articles requiring a considerable amount of taste and skill, and involving a good deal of labour. Such results can only be realised, even in so large an establishment, by means of a thorough and well-organised system of working. Every man must know his work, and must be able to do it. This is carried out in these mills under the superintendence of Mr. Spalding, to whom Messrs. Goodlet and Smith have confided the management of the works.

The firm has six establishments altogether: the head-office, Brickfield Hill; a branch yard in Parramatta-street, Victoria Saw Mills at Pyrmont, and a bush saw-mill near Ulladulla; the other two are for the manufacture of bricks and sewerage drain-pipes, in which branch they also do a large trade. The above works, with the exception of the bush saw-mill, are connected by a telegraph wire; they also have the Bell-Edison telephone in use.

WRIGHT, HEATON AND COMPANY, LIMITED.

The business of general carriers is one that contributes as much as, if not more than any other, to the opening out and development of a new country. However rich the resources of a country may be, unless provision is made for their carriage to and fro, those resources are of little avail. One incentive to the pioneer squatter is that he should be followed up by ways and means of transportation of the results of his industry and enterprise. The certainty that means of carriage will ever follow in his rear, gives him courage in opening out new country, however far it may be removed from the haunts of men. The enterprising squatter, supplemented by the assistance of the general carrier, are the two factors which, in the commencement of Australian history, gave an impetus to its general advancement, of which the beneficial effects are evidenced by the present general prosperity of the colonies.

At a time when the various carriage appliances of modern civilisation were unknown in Australia, the inestimable advantages of carriers who were reliable and trustworthy, can only be appreciated by those early settlers in the colony, who remember the great and almost insurmountable difficulties presented by impassable roads and other attendant dangers, which at this early period were associated with the carriage of goods to and from those stations which were far distant from the emporiums of commerce and trade, or even from the small villages which have now developed into large towns. Our knowledge of the great pastoral, agricultural and mining wealth of Australia, would have been limited indeed, but for the valuable services of those persevering and energetic carriers who surmounted every obstacle which presented itself, in the conveyance of merchandise, and vigorously followed in the wake of the Australian squatter, as well as the wake of the agriculturist and gold-digger. No matter how distant or how remote from civilisation these embodiments of Australian wealth might go, the carrier soon found his way into their neighbourhood, introducing many of the comforts of civilised life, and making that bearable which, through deprivation, was enervating their minds and weakening their bodies; and after supplying them with the necessaries, and in many cases the luxuries, of existence, were ready to convey their produce to markets where it found a ready sale. Thus, in encouraging the opening out of new runs, the selection of new farms, and the development of new goldfields, the general carrier was materially aiding the progress and increasing the wealth of this new country. As population increased, unattended, as it was in some cases, by the introduction of steam power, the business of general carrier assumed wide importance as well as greater proportions, and it necessitated increasing energy and earnestness to meet the exigencies of the growing requirements. Men were readily found possessing the necessary capabilities, but none more so than the company which stands at the head of our present chapter. The date of their establishment goes far back in the history of New South Wales, the business having been first started in 1862, under the name of Wright, Barber and Co., at 485 George-street, Sydney. The business having increased to such vast proportion, and requiring so great an amount of capital, the proprietary was merged into a Joint Stock Company (Limited), of which the present managing directors are Mr. F. A. Wright and Mr. Edward Heaton, gentlemen who are ever on the alert to satisfy the growing requirements of a rapidly-growing business, and whose qualifications as directors are in every way equal to their position. In the commencement of the firm's career they confined themselves to the carrying business entirely; the limit of their transactions being Penrith, which was then the terminus of the Western Railway, and about 32 miles from Sydney. On the Southern line, their ramifications extended as far as Picton only, about 52 miles from Sydney. The increase of their business has been simultaneous with the extension of railways, until now they have reached proportions which are commmensurate with the great increase of population. They have no less than 25 branches of their own, as well as agencies in the principal towns. The great progress in their business of general carriers is an important chapter in the history of the colony. Following it from its commencement to the present time, is to follow and know the history of the colony with which it has been so closely associated. We perceive in its gradual development, the causes which have contributed to this result, and the groundwork of the colony's present prosperity. On inquiry, we found that the first year's business in wool was limited to the carriage of 10,000 bales; while this year it is no less than 120,000 bales. Thus, in little more than a decade and a half, the increase in the carrying branch of the business was exactly 12 times the amount of bales carried in the first year. We understand that the bulk of the wool carrying is done by contract, and the arrangements for this purpose are entered into beforehand. This firm contracts to take the wool from the shed of the grower, and convey it to any part of Australia, principally to Melbourne or Sydney, or at the option of the grower, direct, at a through rate, to docks in London. All the incidental expenses are defrayed by the company, including insurance. Their dealings in grain are not confined to the mere carrying, but they also carry on at the same time, a large trade as buyers of that staple article. The carriage of minerals is also an important branch of their business as general carriers. All the copper which is transported from the *Cobar* mines—about 3000 tons annually—is conveyed through their agency. This is undertaken by contract, which seems to extend over a period of five years, two years of which we are informed have expired. The distance traversed in carrying the copper is something like 330 miles, all being done by what is understood as land carriage. The importance of this particular branch of carrying will be more perfectly understood by our readers, when we mention that no less than 140 teams are employed constantly in this particular work. The company owns about 800 horses, which are constantly employed in the large teaming business which they do throughout the colony of New South Wales. Another, and no less important branch of their business, is what is technically known as the Intercolonial parcel trade. Having facilities at their command for the conveyance of the smallest packages, they are largely patronised by the general public throughout Australia, and, consequently, do an extensive trade in this department. They guarantee the prompt despatch of all parcels entrusted to their care, not only to all parts of Australia, but Europe and America. Their agencies are almost co-extensive with civilisation, and besides the work they do on their own account, they, through these means, bring the rest of the world into direct communication with Australia.

The Advance of Literature in New South Wales.

WILLIAM MADDOCK.

The natural and inordinate desire for information which characterises the nineteenth century, is not confined nor is it peculiar to the old world. It is a plant which is nourished and watered by education, and which has spread its roots to the furthermost bounds of civilisation. The spirit of inquiry has penetrated into all classes of the human race; and there is no subject to which it does not extend. Information is the natural sequence of inquiry, and education is its nursing mother. Whatever opinion may be held as to the bases upon which the mind should be superstructed, there can be no doubt that the materials of mind building should be the best possible within our reach. Hence the desideratum of a healthy class of literature; and the equally necessary desideratum of the facilities which are supplied in order to ensure its propagation amongst all classes of the population. The public taste for reading deserves all the encouragement which can be offered; but the no less important factor of educating that taste to as high a standard as possible, should not be lost sight of. The majority of the reading public may be said to be devoted, in a great measure, to that class of literature which is known as sensational, and which forms the chief plot and incident of the popular novels of our day. This demand has resulted in a supply of a spurious, and ofttimes meretricious and prurient class of books, which administer pabulum to the baser passions of our nature, and give a superficial impetus to the practical development of what was before a mere latent, undefined existence. We must look forward to the introduction of books equally interesting, if not so sensational, which rouse the dormant faculties and feelings of our higher nature, and which supply the safeguard, and modify, and we hope in time will supplant, the baser literature which is now so increasingly prevalent. The higher class of literature such as biography, history, travels, and knowledge-giving essays, when introduced prominently before the reading public, educates the taste, and acts as a corrective in the proper choice of the books which should be read. To educate the public taste up to this degree, is a work of some considerable difficulty, and ought only to be undertaken by wise, judicious, and well-informed men who see in difficulties but the incentives to perseverance. Such a work as this is of the very greatest importance, second to no other walk in life, and is well worthy of a life's devotion. He who undertakes it is the schoolmaster of the maturer life of humanity or of the world's school. This sphere is one which, when carried out on a high moral basis, is as noble and good producing to a nation, as the incipent instruction and education are to those who are the fathers and mothers of the future generation. To those of our readers who are dwelling in the other hemisphere, the notion of a high literature, a high education, and the possession of every publication of note in the old or new world, being a strong feature of the Australian colonies, may seem too romantic and ideal to be accepted as a fact. We trust that these ideas may be dispelled in great part, through the information we have striven to give of Australia and its adjuncts, in the present publication. The colonists possess the advantages of a free education, and that up to a very fair standard, which are not surpassed in any country in the world; they are not only great readers but deep thinkers, and, though the indigenous literature is somewhat limited, it is supplemented by the demand and supply of every class of literature which obtains in older countries.

We have daily and weekly papers, conducted by men of talent and experience, and there are monthly reviews, which reflect the opinions of the people on every possible question. We have large public libraries, open to every class of the population without money and without price, and we have large circulating libraries, conducted by enterprising and intelligent men. Amongst those of the latter which are deserving of note, is that conducted by Mr. Wm. Maddock, at 381 George-street, Sydney, and known to Sydneyites as "Maddock's Select Library." The strong impression that is so prevalent in the minds of a large majority of the population of Great Britain, more especially among the working classes, that Australia has undergone comparatively little change since the rushes that followed the discovery of gold some thirty years ago, will we trust be completely dispelled after a careful perusal of this work. Though there is yet a certain amount of "roughing" to be undergone by those who find themselves in the goldfields, or who engage in agricultural pursuits in the more isolated parts of the colony, the life in the cities and towns of this new country is in no respect different, with regard to physical comforts and even luxuries, as well as all the amenities of civilisation, to what it is in the oldest established and most civilised portions of the old world. How erroneous are the impressions of Australia will, we trust, be discovered far and wide, and wherever this book may find circulation. Our great object is to throw a correct light through which as yet undiscovered advantages may be widely known, and to supply accurate information with regard to this, the fifth section of the globe, its customs, and its peoples. What must first strike the "new chums," or, in other words, the fresh arrivals, must be the resemblance, in almost every respect, between the towns and cities they have left behind, and the towns and cities of their newly adopted home. They note the same extensive warehouses, the same magnificent shops, the same public buildings, and the graceful and ofttimes ornate dwellings of our citizens, and see at a *coup d'œil* that civilisation has made such rapid strides in this New Atlantis, as to be abreast of the civilisation that has taken as many centuries to develop as its existence here may be counted by decades. In addition to this, what must strike them as really wonderful, is that in most districts there are schools of art, mechanics' institutes, and public and circulating libraries, which are patronised certainly as largely as they are in the mother-country. As an instance of the rapid development of the love of literature amongst the colonists of New South Wales, the proportions reached by Maddock's Select Library are such that it may with justice be called the Mudie's of Sydney. It is probably the most notable institution of its kind in the colonies. It has been established for about eighteen (18) years; and in addition to the extensive patronage which it enjoys, of the *élite* of Sydney, and of very many of the wealthy landed proprietors throughout the country, it has also been patronised by the various representatives of Royalty who in succession have found themselves the occupiers of Government House. We understand that, some little time ago, the proprietor, Mr. Maddock, interested himself with the Commissioner of Railways, to obtain a reduction in the rates of carriage per rail on library exchanges, and the commissioner, after duly considering the application, was pleased to reduce the charge to one-fourth of ordinary parcels' rate. This must be a great boon to country residents living within rail communication of the city; and we hope, in no very long time, to see a similar process every morning from Maddock's, as there is from Mudie's, when boxes of new books are sent off by rail all over England. We do not see that such a result may not be realised, and that shortly, for our reading-loving population is increasing in the ratio of the supply of new publications. By means of this library, which has supplied a long-felt want, the best and most readable books, in all departments of literature, are selected by an agent at home, and despatched by the overland mails directly they are published. Thus books are often in circulation from this institution long before they can be purchased in the shops. Besides the current literature of the day, the library contains many hundred volumes of standard works. English and American periodicals are also issued to the subscribers. Visitors, who intend to remain in Sydney for a limited time, may have the advantage of this library, by joining for as short a period as one month, the terms being in every respect extremely reasonable. The front part of Mr. Maddock's establishment is employed as a book and stationery warehouse, in which a large trade is carried on, the premises being well stocked with every article that may be required in this branch of the business. At the rear of the shop is a large room which forms the library, and which, on our visit, we found filled with what we should consider *la crème de la crème* of the reading society of Sydney. The ladies were there in greater numbers than the sterner sex; and we were glad to note their selection of high-class novels and other branches of light literature. Nothing certainly is more conducive to the pleasure of life—nothing seems to be so much linked to every form of the most advanced civilisation, especially for those who are buried in the dull, retired, and isolated stations of the interior—than a constant change of new books and magazines, and in this way inter-communicating with the advanced thought of the rest of the world. We certainly must congratulate the city on the possession of this great desideratum of life, a large select library, which, at the same time that it educates the desire for reading, supplies the educated taste with the required pabulum.

SOME OF THE LEADING MERCANTILE HOUSES IN ADELAIDE.

ELDER, SMITH AND CO.

It is an interesting question, which of the colonies in Australia is likely, in the future, to take the foremost position in the production of wool, both in regard to quantity as well as quality. This, to us, seems to depend mainly upon three conditions; firstly, the amount of land which may be available in every way for grazing purposes; secondly, the breed of sheep which may be introduced and cultivated; and lastly, a plethora of capital in the hands of enterprising and energetic pastoral tenants. The last condition, if limited in its volume of supply, might be supplemented through the hands of Australian or European capitalists. The colony where these conditions are to be found in the most complete stage, will undoubtedly hold the sway in the extent of the development of pastoral interests. Each of the factors mentioned would be doubtlessly incomplete if they stood alone; but with regard to the first of these, nature, in this new country, has made ample provision. The second depends, in a great degree, upon individual efforts, which must be combined with great discrimination and thorough knowledge of ovine qualities. The supply of the third depends wholly upon the two preceding. However, we may say that whatever may be the extent of grazing country in a colony, it is comparatively valueless unless it is supplemented by a good breed of sheep and unlimited capital for its development. In the early history of the colonies, the great desiderata of breed and capital were wants but ill supplied. But as time progressed these wants were gradually minimised, until now the breed of sheep cultivated in the Australian colonies is not exceeded by any country in the world. The fine and silky texture of the wool has made it so famous in the home market, that there is no scarcity for its demand, nor want of capital for its development. Whatever may be the unknown resources of this great country, which in time may be brought to light, we know not, but we do know that in no branch of commerce is she likely to become more famous in the eyes of the world, than in the important one of wool productions. The resources in this respect are almost unlimited, and those which have already been made available are capable of supplying a very considerable part of the demand of the markets of the world. Though gold is always associated with Australia in the minds of the οἱ πολλα, the country is as well known, for its wool-producing power, to the men of commerce and trade, as it is known for its splendid gold discoveries to the rest of the world. Gold, except in some few instances, has been what may be denominated a spasmodic product, rushes being made from one district to another, which is no sooner worked out than another exodus is made, seldom leaving behind it a permanent population, or even a permanent settlement. One feature of that part of the population whose wealth has been derived through the discovery of gold is, that they seldom, if ever, remain in the country; and if they do, they certainly, with only some exceptions, never take up their abodes on the spot from which their riches have been drawn. We are not depreciating the gold-mining interest, but rather pointing out what we would term its drawbacks to the general progress, moral as well as social, of those districts where it has been found in small quantities, as well in some instances of those districts where the yield has been larger. Now, with regard to the pastoral interests, those drawbacks are considerably modified. In order to develop them to that degree of perfection which is likely to result in profitable return, it is necessary to settle for several years on the runs taken up, to give time for the perfection of breed, and to acquire that reputation for quality which alone can secure a permanent and large demand. Once a station is entered upon, we must conclude that judgment, perfected by experience, has been brought to bear in its selection, and hence there is neither necessity nor desire to remove. In this way we consider that the pastoral interest, if not superior to all others, is certainly second to none. There is another and not unimportant factor, which we must be permitted to mention, and that is that the class of men who engage in it is, as a rule, far superior in intellectual and social qualifications to those who are engaged in mining. This is another and important reason why this interest should be as widely encouraged as possible. We mean that a colony where the population is supplemented by enterprising men whose social position gives them an interest in the true welfare of the colony, is infinitely more likely to be prosperous and to have a higher commercial reputation than where the colonists are men of little culture or experience, and where wealth is not, as a rule, acquired by length of time, but spasmodically and accidentally, which is invariably the case with those who engage in gold-mining operations. Second, if not equal, in importance to those who are immediately engaged in wool-growing, are those who are engaged in wool-selling, and one of the most important firms in this branch of business in South Australia, is that of Elder, Smith and Co. Through difficulties which are generally the concomitants of those who have engaged in the development of the wool-selling business, the firm of Elder, Smith and Co. have successfully laboured until now that their standing in Adelaide is somewhat similar to the standing of the great firm of Goldsbrough and Co. in Melbourne. Sir Thomas Elder, who is the head of the firm, is a director in the Wallaroo Mine, and chairman of the Moonta Directorate. The business was begun, in 1840, by Mr. A. L. Elder, now a merchant in London, and has been continued by various members of the family up to the present time. We may mention that the present senior partner has, what is perhaps, the most complete establishment for the breeding and training of thoroughbred horses which is to be found in Australia. The number of foals, yearlings, horses, and mares, which comprise the breeding stock, &c., cannnot be less than 100. The training stables are at Glenelg, about six miles from Adelaide. Sir Thomas purposes to forward to the old country, as an experiment, two of his best-bred yearlings, with a view to being trained and entered for the Derby and Oaks. This fact we have great satisfaction in recording as a conclusive proof of the interest and taste which are so universally cultivated, both in field sports and in the breed of stock; and it is through gentlemen like Sir Thomas Elder, that the capabilities of Australian horses will become known at large.

The introduction of camels has also been carried out by this gentleman, a ship-load having been imported from India, in 1863, which have now increased to upwards of 600. These animals are found extremely useful as beasts of burden on sheep stations, and are also occasionally employed in exploring the interior.

JOSEPH STILLING AND CO.

The commercial progress of Adelaide is a feature in the development of the colony of South Australia which is deserving of more than passing notice. The trade and industry of the colony have already been adverted to in our pages. We will now direct our attention more particularly to the intercommunication between Adelaide and other parts of the world to which her commerce has already extended. Whatever may be the internal wealth of a colony, it remains invariable until a market has been created for its demand. This can only be done successfully by men of enterprise and energy, as well as large business capabilities, who are ever on the alert to seize and take advantage of every opportunity which is presented to their notice. They must, as a matter of course, have a pretty extensive connection in the commercial circles of other countries, and they must, at the same time, possess the confidence of those with whom they have business transactions. It is the possession of such important factors as we have named that, as a rule, commands success in commercial undertakings. They are enabled to place those who possess the supply in communication with those who have the means of indicating the channels of demand, and thus commercial relations are originated, and the first seeds of progressive development are sown. The gentlemen who have taken up this branch of commerce occupy a very important position in a young colony, more important, perhaps, than those who are immediately engaged in pastoral, agricultural, or mining pursuits.

It is in one or other, or all of these, that South Australia, and particularly Adelaide, where most of the exports are shipped for London and other parts of Europe, will, at no distant date, occupy an important position in the commercial world. The business we refer to is that of commission agents, which is carried on by the gentlemen who comprise the firm whose name heads the present chapter. They have been successful in their efforts, and have succeeded in acquiring that confidence which has resulted in a large and increasing business. They have contributed materially to the development of the various branches of colonial products, and done much towards increasing the export trade of South Australia. Another and very important branch in which they are engaged, is that of ship agents, and the extent of business and connection which they have secured enables us to gauge, at least approximately, the extent of the commercial transactions which are carried on between South Australia and Europe. We understand that the business has been established during the long period of thirty-five years; and that during the whole of that time it has been steadily advancing to its present proportions. Its first commencement is due to Mr. Joseph Stilling, who was ably seconded for some years by his partner, Mr. H. Noltenius. In 1849, Mr. H. Charnock joined the firm as a junior partner, and after the death of Messrs. Stilling it was considered advisable to carry on the business under the style of Joseph Stilling and Co., as previously, and so it has remained until the present day. Mr. W. H. Charnock has had considerable mercantile experience, both at home and in the colonies, and this is evidently appreciated from the fact that the previous large connection and confidence which the firm enjoyed, has not only been retained but considerably added to since Mr. Charnock has undertaken the active management of the business. The firm act as agents for Anderson, Anderson and Co.'s line of sailing packets between South Australia and London. They are also agents for the direct line of steamers calling at the Semaphore, off Port Adelaide. Their business as ship agents comprising, as it does, the two lines which we have named, also embraces the other ships carrying exports or passengers from the colonies, as well as the various articles of import with which those ships are laden on their arrival at Adelaide. The great respect in which Mr. W. H. Charnock is held, is evidenced by the important positions which he has filled, one of which was the chairmanship of the Chamber of Commerce and of the Adelaide Underwriters' Association. When our citizens' success in their own business has been deemed so adequate that they are justly considered to be entitled to fill those public positions, where not only business capabilities but also the strictest integrity are necessary qualifications, we are certainly justified in assuming that the success of the commercial progress of the colony has been, in a great measure, due to their exertions. Not confining themselves to the business which is immediately connected with their own success in life, they place their talents and experience at the disposal of their fellow townsmen, and in this way secure the regard and respect of those amongst whom they live. It is to the philanthropic disposition of such gentlemen that the support and, we may say, continued existence of our eleemosynary institutions are due. Mr. Charnock is president of the Prince Alfred Sailors' Home, an institution which is a credit to Adelaide, and which all our colonies would do well to emulate. He is also connected with several companies, being chairman of the Spencer's Gulf Steamship Company, as well as chairman of the Commercial Union Assurance Company. In addition to those important offices, he also holds the position of a director of the Bushmen's Club, and a trustee for the Savings Bank at Adelaide.

No better guarantee of the success with which Mr. Charnock has carried on his business as general commission merchant and ship agent, could be offered than the fact of his fulfilling so many and such important public positions. It is a further guarantee to those commercial circles at home that all business conducted through the firm of Stilling and Co., of which Mr. Charnock is the principal representative, will be transacted on a firm and satisfactory basis. It is on grounds such as these that a great commercial future may be built up by the various Australian colonies. The unlimited resources which Australia possesses can only be made current through her merchants, and the more energy and perseverance which merchants possess, the more certain are those resources to be developed, and that at no very distant period. It is matter of astonishment the prominence which, through their efforts, has been given to Australian products in the markets of Europe. We need not here refer to the Australian wool, which now takes so decided a stand amongst the other wool-growing countries of the world; but we would refer more particularly to the grain, which is daily increasing both in the amount grown and the amount exported. Much has been done in the colony of South Australia to develop this important commerce, and we cannot conceal from ourselves that much still remains to be done. The same remark may apply to the trades and industries of the colonies, as well as to the cultivation of the vine, which is destined to take a foremost position. The firm of Joseph Stilling and Co. negotiates between the sellers and the buyer in almost every branch of Australian production, and their widespread connection enables them to bring together the very best sellers and buyers who are to be found either in the colonial or English markets. They are further able to secure the safe and speedy carriage of all goods through their business as ship agents.

D. AND J. FOWLER.

The number, size, and architectural beauty of the buildings of any large city, must be the first attraction to the ordinary visitor, while to a man of business it is the principal basis on which he calculates the extent of its commercial prosperity. To one who has visited the colony for the first time, it presents a further, and not less interesting index of the prosperity and advancement of the colony at large in the various branches of industry and commerce. The business premises and the dwelling-houses of a city are visible data to the passing traveller or temporary sojourner. They afford him the fairest and most reliable premises from which he can deduce conclusions, which, on the whole, must be fairly accurate, as to the condition of its present and past, for trade, commerce, and industry. The number of business buildings gives him an idea approximately near of the general condition of the population, their size furnishes him with data as to the individual prosperity of the citizens, at the same time characterising their enterprise and energy, while the architectural beauty of the structures enables him to judge of the æsthetical taste of their owners, which, when indulged in to any extent, shows the large and more praiseworthy element of practical interest and pride in the appearance as well as in the continued welfare and prosperity of the city itself. Such observations as these are not only interesting to the last degree, but instructive in whatever light they may be regarded. They add considerably to our knowledge, not only of men's minds, but also to the more practical element of men's works, and increase our respect both for the one and the other. Men who aim not only at the building of their own fortunes, but at the same time extend their aim to the improvement of their native or adopted city, are amongst the most valuable elements which contribute to its internal advancement, and to the external estimate which is formed, not only by visitors, but by the world at large. They are deservedly looked upon as benefactors to the city directly, while indirectly they contribute in no small degree to the general welfare of the colony or country in which the city may be situated. If the branch of industry, trade, or commerce in which they are engaged be in a flourishing condition, it is due to their energy, perseverance, and business capacity. This must be judged of relatively according to the success which attends their efforts individually or in co-operation, in the particular branch in which they are engaged. The greater the difficulties which they have encountered, the greater the meed of their success; but when they have succeeded in developing any special branch to such an extent as to make it an important factor in the progressive history of the city or colony in which the business is carried on, they at once establish themselves as important instruments in the present and future development of the commercial interests of the whole population. Much of what we have said must occur to a reflective mind on its first visit to Adelaide, the capital of South Australia. But one important item of interest, which is wanting to the old-established cities and towns of the mother-country, is the incredibly short space of time that it has taken to place Adelaide, with respect to the number and size of its buildings, the flourishing condition of its trade, its commerce, and its industry, and the general wealth of its citizens, upon an equality with any city having the same population in any part of the world. The gentlemen whose names stand at the head of this chapter have succeeded in developing, to a large extent, a branch of business which, through their efforts, has risen into signal importance. The firm of Messrs. D. and J. Fowler, who carry on the business of importing and indenting merchants and wholesale grocers, has succeeded in making the extent of its business operations second to no other which is carried on in Adelaide. So great has the business progressed since its commencement, that premises which when first occupied were ample for their requirements, have more than once been found wholly inadequate to meet the rapidly-increasing trade which their energy and perseverance has created.

Figures in relation to commerce are frequently the most accurate thermometrical indication of its condition; we wish to give a few in relation to the business of this firm, prefacing them with one or two remarks.

The firm of Messrs. D. and J. Fowler was established in 1854, as wholesale and retail grocers. The retail branch was disposed of in 1865, when the firm moved into large and, for the time, commodious premises, at 18 King

William-street, Adelaide, and the senior partner, Mr. D. Fowler, established a London office in the same year. After this date, their business grew at a very rapid rate, necessitating the erection of buildings over all the unoccupied ground at the rear of their stores. Being still cramped for room, they, in 1873, decided to establish stores at Port Adelaide; and entered into possession of a building on M'Laren Wharf, affording 7500 square feet of floor area, which it was considered would afford ample room for the storage of the quantity of both bonded and free goods necessary to their business at that time. In 1874 they were enabled to secure additional land at the rear of their stores in town, and immediately proceeded to erect new buildings, affording about 12,000 feet floor space; and the convenience of storage at Port Adelaide being found increasingly useful, they, towards the end of 1875, added 6000 feet to their stores on M'Laren Wharf. The growing requirements of the business urging still further expansion, they, in 1877, acquired two other buildings in St. Vincent-street, Port Adelaide, giving 13,000 feet of additional floor area. The bond was removed to one of these buildings, the other being used for free goods. The inconveniences attendant upon their having their merchandise scattered in several warehouses, now began to be felt, and called for a remedy; and the opening of the New Port Dock in 1880, affording an opportunity of acquiring land in a convenient position, they again decided to build, and are now erecting stores upon such an extended scale that, when finished, they will be unequalled for size in the colony of South Australia, and will probably afford more storage space than any other building, erected for private storage only, in any of the Australian colonies. The enterprise and business capacity that alone could develop a business of the kind to such proportions, are among the secrets to which Adelaide is indebted for its wonderfully rapid rise and progress, in the short space of less than half-a-century. Our attention was directed to these stores, and the size of the building which is being erected excited our interest. We at once saw the important position which the owners of such large premises must occupy in the ranks of commerce, and we further felt that they were to be added to the long list of names with which history will associate the future greatness of Australia. An account of a building on such a large scale, and significant of such enterprise and energy, may not be uninteresting to our readers in Australia, nor to those who, in other parts of the world, feel an interest in this new country. The following particulars will give a fair idea of the appearance which will be presented by the building when completed. It has a frontage of 150 feet to South Parade (the southern frontage to the dock), by a depth of 244 feet; at the other end it has a frontage of 150 feet to St. Vincent-street. In this street are situated the railway station, and very many, if indeed not the greater part, of the principal buildings of Port Adelaide. It is intended to use about one-fourth of the building as a bonded store, the remaining three-fourths being available for free goods. It may be technically described as a bulk store, only whole packages, as received from the various import vessels, being dealt with on these premises. To facilitate the handling of the immense quantity of goods that will annually pass through these stores, they are arranged so that a line of railway communicating with the Government lines from the wharves and connected with the main lines of the colony, is laid down through the centre of the store. This admirable convenience is largely added to by five hydraulic lifts, placed at suitable intervals along the branch line, and by which very considerable facility is given for the rapid and safe transit of goods to and from the railway trucks. These hydraulic lifts are arranged to deliver at a considerable height above the platform, if required for stacking goods or for lifting bales or cases to the second tier of a partially loaded truck or waggon, or will deliver at the platform level, or in the cellars at any level required. The cellarage is of great capacity, extending under three-fourths of the building—the remaining fourth being solidly built up to the level of the rail and road-ways—and is used for the storage of rough or very heavy goods. A roadway enters at the middle of this side, and as the railway is planked flush, there is thus every facility given for the passage of horse waggons as well as railway trucks. The cellars have a height of $7\frac{1}{2}$ feet in the clear, and are provided with sub-ways under the railway line, to facilitate transfer of goods from side to side. The main floors are very strong, heavy rolled girders being used to carry the joists, which fit into them nearly flush on the underside, and thus space is economised. The girders are supported by 120 cast-iron columns, which give an appearance of substantial endurance, without the bulk and heaviness of the timber supports generally seen in this class of building. The floor is raised four feet above the roadways, so as to be level with the floor of the railway trucks. The height from the ground floor to the beams of the roof, is 18 feet, and the total area of flooring, including the cellars, is about an acre and one-third, giving a storage capacity of some 21,000 tons, although at present built only one story above the cellars. No convenience or requisite is wanting, to facilitate and fulfil every possible requirement which the exigencies of the business demand. This, amongst other and more varied appliances, is evidenced by the provision of a travelling crane of 25-feet span, which is used to facilitate the handling of heavy goods. This crane, which travels from one side of the store to the other, is easily and conveniently worked from the floor. In addition to this, there is a hydraulic hoist for lifting in various parts of the floor. The offices face the dock and occupy the greater part of one side of the frontage. The provision made for lighting is abundant, and in every possible way adequate to the requirements. In addition to the windows provided in the two fronts, lights have been inserted the entire length of the roof, so that nothing in the important desideratum of light should be wanting. The walls, which are most substantially built, aiming at durability as well as architectural taste, are of a hard stone from Dry Creek quarries, and, with the columns in the basement, are constructed to carry a second floor when the exigencies of the business warrant the increase. The dressings, which are Italian in character, are in imitation of freestone. A more approximate idea of the attention which has been paid, not only to the general conveniences and requirements of such an extensive store, but also to more minute and less important points, which are, nevertheless, as necessary as all those which at once meet the eye on entering the store, may be formed from the fact that, when completed, their cost will be somewhere about £14,000, exclusive of the cost of the land on which the stores are built. The contract for the builders' work alone, which has been undertaken by Mr. Honey, is £9663. The designing and carrying out of the building is under the able and careful supervision of Mr. Cumming, the well-known architect, who has left nothing undone that could tend to insure a substantial structure, fitted in every respect for rapid and convenient handling of goods. The possession of such premises indicates a proportionally large and flourishing business; some idea of the extent of which may be gathered, when it is stated that this firm have, for the past year or two, paid more than one-tenth of the whole of the custom duties collected in South Australia, being the fee simple of duties on imports for their own trade. Even this large proportion does not cover the whole of their imports, a large quantity of goods being shipped under bond to the neighbouring colonies, on which duty is not paid. They have recently added a shipping department to their business; and during the past season, negotiated charters, on behalf of owners, for fully one-fourth of the large grain export of South Australia.

The limited space of the premises in Adelaide, render them impracticable for other use than as offices and sale and sample rooms, further than serving as a store-house for a small stock for town and suburban trade, and for sales where less than a bulk package is required. This, however, is not a disadvantage; the bulk stores being at Port Adelaide, in immediate proximity to the wharves for coastwise trade, and from whence railway charges are as low as they are from Adelaide city, they can unload goods immediately from the import vessels, and run them right through into the interior—as far as the railways penetrate—or ship them to the numerous ports with which the coast-line of South Australia is indented, without extra labour or cost to themselves—which simply means, without extra charge to their clients. The partners of the firm are Messrs. David Fowler, George Swan Fowler, and Edwin Vaughan Joyner; the former having charge of the business in London, the two latter of its extensive ramifications in South Australia.

D. AND W. MURRAY.

Adelaide, since its first establishment as the capital of the large tract of country which is comprehended in South Australia, has made astonishingly rapid progress, industrially as well as commercially. Though its backward date does not extend to more than half a century, its forward advancement may be not unfavourably compared to any town or city in Europe whose age covers twice the period during which Adelaide, as a city, has been in existence. Adelaide, like the other capitals in the colonies of Australia, has been fortunate in drawing to it men of vast energy, enterprise, and perseverance. It is to such men that this city, as well as other cities of this new country, owe their remarkable prosperity and their steady, though rapid, advancement. Establishing themselves in the various branches of business which were necessary to meet the growing requirements of the population, they have, as a rule, succeeded beyond what could have been their most sanguine expectations. As commerce and trade and industry were developed, they were followed in their wake by wealth, with its natural outcome—the demand for the concomitants of civilised life. The result is that in Adelaide at the present day there is ample provision for every comfort which characterises the nineteenth century; and one striking feature of this provision is the well and fashionably dressed men and women that one meets with in a day's peregrination. This feature, as much as any other of the population, generally carries a certain amount of connection to the mind that civilisation is not only behind, but has followed closely in the steps of the material welfare of the colony. We were struck with its prominence on our visit to Adelaide, and were pleased to see that it was accompanied by a refined taste. It naturally occurred to our minds, that the branch of trade which so fully contributed to this important feature, must be in the hands of men who were in every way equal to the requirement, and who were doing a flourishing business. On inquiry we were directed to the establishment of Messrs. D. and W. Murray, the general idea evidently being that they were the principal representatives of the soft goods trade, and we were certainly not disappointed with our visit. There we found every description of soft goods that could be imported, with a combination of quantity and quality that to no little degree excited our astonishment. There were goods to satisfy the largest demand, and suitable to every taste and every requirement of youth, middle, and old age of both sexes. The catering of this branch of the people's wants, requires experience, judgment, taste, and a just appreciation of what will exactly suit the people who are living under the influence of a new climate, and so require, in some cases, patterns and materials that may be somewhat different to those required in such a country as England. There is no doubt that Messrs. D. and W. Murray owe their success in great part, if not wholly, to the possession of these desiderata which we have just enumerated. There is another important fact which we must not omit to mention, and that is their courtesy and attention to the several wants of their customers. When we think that not only within the Australian city of Adelaide, but also in the far bush, the people are in possession of most, if not all, the requirements, and in the city itself of the luxuries of the most advanced civilised life which are to be found in the most civilised countries of the world, we cannot but express our astonishment and, at the same time, feel what an important factor in this feature is the soft goods which are supplied by the firms engaged in that branch of business. Our attention at this moment being taken up with the establishment of Messrs. D. and W. Murray, we will give a description of the premises and a history of the concern, and at the same time enumerate the other branches of business in which they are engaged.

The premises occupied by the firm stand in a central position in King William-street. It is a plain but handsome building of two stories, with a capacious cellar floor on which are stored heavy linen and cotton goods. The frontage of the building is 60 feet, and the extreme length 210 feet. The whole building is admirably suited to the soft goods trade, a large amount of money having been spent from time to time in extending, improving, and rebuilding the premises. The interior arrangements are very compact and convenient, having a broad central flight of stairs, from which radiate, through open archways, the eleven departments into which the warehouse is divided.

The existence of the firm dates from October, 1853. At that time, David and William Murray commenced business as retail drapers, in a shop at the corner of Gilbert Place, in King William-street. These gentlemen had been thoroughly well trained in their business, and as a consequence their energetic efforts, combined with this training, resulted in a prosperous and well-established business. The father, Mr. Wm. Murray, senior, has been identified with the business from the first, being for many years the buyer, financier, and general agent at home. The firm has adopted as a trade mark the arms of their native town—a triangle on a shield, on the three sides of which are severally a fishing boat, an anchor, and three fish—Anstruther, in Scotland. At the end of two years the business was removed to Grenfell-street. A wholesale department was now added to the retail trade, and this department was carried on at the rear of the shop. In course of time the business so increased that they were obliged to secure additional premises, neighbouring to their own. It was at this juncture, in the year 1862, that the retail portion of the business was given up, and the firm gave their undivided attention to the trade of wholesale warehousemen, sending out their representatives to the various country districts, and increasing their English agency as the business enlarged. From this time the progress of the business was very rapid, so that in 1866, their premises were again exchanged for larger and more suitable ones. The present warehouse was then secured and occupied in its original form, and has since been largely extended and improved. We have to record one drawback in the progress of this extensive business. In February, 1868, a most disastrous fire occurred, by which nearly the whole of the stock (over £70,000 worth) was destroyed by fire or badly damaged by water. This entailed a heavy loss, and for a time brought business to a standstill. There was, however, a counteracting advantage in the entire clearance of the old stock and the necessary repurchasing of new goods, which fortunately resulted in an increase of business. Two years after this the firm was strengthened by the introduction of Mr. John Gordon and Mr. Richard Searle, as partners. The amount of trade done at this time showed an annual return of £150,000, but so rapid was the advance of the colony, so prosperous were the following six years, that in 1877 the trade of the house had more than trebled. The first clothing factory in South Australia was started by Mr. David Murray in 1867. This industry was in itself so successful a venture, that shortly afterwards a shirt factory and boot factory were established in the same premises, Waymouth-street. This department is still carried on, and in it some 200 hands find constant employment. There is one feature in this business that we record with very much pleasure. We refer to the provision which the firm has made for the comfort of their employees. There is a lavatory, and there are also library and reading rooms, and the ventilation and lighting are all that could be desired. In 1874 another branch was added to the business, viz., an indenting and general merchandise department. A separate entrance is provided to this part of the building. Orders are taken on commission for any and every kind of merchandise. In this way a very extensive bulk business has been secured. The homeward business consists, mainly, of colonial produce, such as gum, wax, bark, wheat, and wool. These shipments are sometimes made on account of the firm; but as a general rule they are made for clients, who gladly take advantage of this channel of commerce. The extensive premises in London at 12, 13, and 14 Barbican, provide all necessary facilities for carrying on so large an import and export trade. The latest change in the history of the firm, is the admission of two new partners, viz., Mr. James Martin, the head of the London buying staff, and Mr. Robert Knowles, one of the leading department managers in Adelaide. May the future of this firm be as prosperous as the past, is our heartiest wish.

JOHN DARLING AND SON.

South Australia is essentially a wheat-producing colony. This cereal is grown there to such an extent already as during the last season to have given an available surplus for export of about 300,000 tons. When we consider the youth of the colony, the comparatively small population, and the limited extent of land taken up for wheat-growing purposes, we mean when compared to the land area of the whole colony, we cannot but be astonished at such great results in so short a time. When markets have, from almost time immemorial, been supplied from regular and unfailing sources, there is always an amount of prejudice to contend against in the introduction and acceptance of any new source of supply, which nothing but indomitable perseverance, combined with equal or superior quality in the article offered, can ever successfully and permanently overcome. The difficulties are certainly not decreased by the greater distance of the new source of supply. When we remember that such have been the impediments which the South Australian wheat-growers have had to encounter, we cannot but think that there is some resource which is now only opened out, and which, when fully developed, will make the colony equal in time to any wheat-growing country of equal area in the world. We naturally ask ourselves what this resource, or these resources, can be which have accomplished such beneficial results in so short a time. This question can only be answered from personal experience arising from attentive observation. Our object in the publication of this book being to afford our readers all available information, we have in each production of the colony carefully studied the cause of their present success and its most probable ultimate results. We have discovered the following factors in the case of South Australian wheat-growing, which are not confined to those who are there, but which are open to every new colonist whose occupation is agricultural. The first is the appropriateness of the soil, and its extraordinary productive powers; the second is the cheapness of land and the great facilities which are afforded for its acquirement; the third is the wonderful energy and agricultural skill of the wheat-growers, who leave nothing undone to ensure both quantity and quality in their crops; and the last, and a very important factor, is the enterprise and zeal of the export grain merchants of the colony. Under the last comes the firm whose business of exporting wheat merchants we are now discussing.

The average yield of wheat per acre has been this last season exactly 9·47 bushels, giving an export surplus, as we said, of over 300,000 tons, the greater part of which has been shipped to Europe. Though the new season's prospects are in defect, when compared with the last yield, yet there is no reason to be discouraged, seeing that the surplus for export, in spite of the unusually bad season, is likely to be somewhere about 150,000 tons, which will be equal to an average yield of six bushels per acre (not at all bad when compared to some of the wheat-growing farms in the north of England, where every improvement has been introduced, and where the newest inventions for enriching land have been availed of). The following return of the export of wheat and flour will show the quantity which has been shipped to England and the Continent by this extensive firm during the season of 1880. The shipments are from the following ports, namely, Port Adelaide, Port Broughton, Port Victoria, Wallaroo, Port Pirie, and Port Wakefield. The number of ships which were loaded by the firm at Port Adelaide was in round numbers 16, which carried 3,772 bags of flour, and the large quantity of 557,099 bushels of wheat. There were six ships loaded by the firm at Port Broughton, which carried away exactly 294,455 bushels. From Port Victoria they loaded four ships with 143,911 bushels of wheat. From Wallaroo two ships left with 86,611 bushels of wheat, which had been loaded by the firm. From Port Pirie there was the largest shipment by the firm, viz., 24 ships carrying 9530 bags of flour, and 1,203,288 bushels of wheat; while from Port Wakefield the firm shipped 149,311 bushels of the cereal in three ships. With regard to the ensuing harvest, the critical period, as we are writing, is now at hand, and a great deal depends upon the weather within the next month, as to the result of the harvest; we sincerely trust that it may be propitious. The price at the opening of the past season was very remunerative to the growers, opening about 5s. 4d. per bushel, at which many of the farmers were wise enough to sell; but early in the year the price gradually declined, in sympathy with the English markets, until sales were made at 4s. 1d. per bushel, and which those who held were very reluctant to accept. After a season of depression a slight improvement has been experienced in the English markets, which has had the desired effect here; and with the advanced price there is some disposition to sell, and some large parcels have been placed at 4s. 6d. to 4s. 8d. per bushel; the latter price is not now obtainable, a reaction having taken place. With an average yield of eight bushels per acre, the South Australian farmers can secure a fair return for their labour if 4s. 6d. per bushel can be obtained. At least this calculation will be found approximate. We understand that all the grain is reaped, cleaned, and bagged in the field, and taken from thence to the shipping ports or railway stations. It is estimated that to bag a crop of about 250,000 tons, 9000 bales cornsacks are required, which are imported from Calcutta at a cost of about 7s. 6d. per dozen. The wheat harvest in the early districts commences about the first week in November, and towards the end of the month becomes general. The shipping season commences about the middle to end of December, and continues until the end of March, after which time shipments are only made on a moderate scale and freights generally recede somewhat from opening rates. The freights to the United Kingdom opened at 50s. per ton, but rapidly advanced to 60s. and 62s. 6d., at which a large quantity of tonnage was secured; as the season advanced a gradual decline took place, until 40s. and 42s. 6d. was the highest obtainable, which is, we believe, at present the ruling rate. If the coming season give a surplus of 150,000 tons, it is quite probable that freights may advance to 50s., in any case there is little prospect of last season's rates being repeated.

The principal shipping ports in South Australia are those named, in addition to the following, viz., Ardrossan, Port Parham, Edithburgh, Stansbury, M'Leod Bay, Noarlunga, Point Turton, Port Augusta, Franklin Harbour, Beachport, Kingston, Port Vincent and Port Victor.

Port Adelaide, which at one time was the only direct shipping port to the United Kingdom, has been deprived of much of the wheat trade, in consequence of the rapid development of the country and the opening up of many other ports on the coast. From being the principal port of shipment, Adelaide now only holds second rank, its place having been taken by Port Pirie. This last-named port of shipment, is now the largest in South Australia, and this is mainly due to the large back country which gives the supply, and there is little doubt but that it will maintain its premier position for some years to come. It is situated a short distance up a river (an inlet from the Gulf), which is perfectly safe for large vessels, when drawing 12 to 13 feet, to which draught they generally load and proceed to the anchorage to receive balance of their cargo. We are glad to say that the dredger is now at work, and in about 12 months it is expected that vessels will be able to go in and out, at a draught of 16 feet. It is at this port that early deliveries are made, new wheat having been shipped here by 5th November; but the coming season will, in all probability, be later, and it is not anticipated that any wheat will come to hand until the middle of November. The exports of wheat and flour from this port, amount to about 95,000 tons. The shipments from Port Broughton are generally made direct to the United Kingdom, which this season amounted to about 11,000 tons. Port Victoria, which is situated at the north end of Hardwick Bay, is a new port for shipment of wheat, and being the outlet of a large tract of country, the shipments are likely to increase. The exports this season were about 10,000 tons. Wallaroo has during the last season come to the fore, this year being the first in which large shipments of wheat and flour can be recorded, and we have no doubt that with fair seasons the shipments will continue to increase. We are justified in prognosticating a considerable development in the export trade of this new port, considering that about 16,000 tons have been shipped from here during the season of 1880. Port Wakefield, in St. Vincent's Gulf, is situated to the north of Port Adelaide, and one great desideratum for ships is to be found here, viz., a safe anchorage. We might add that most of the ports, as mentioned herein, have been thus favoured by nature. The export of wheat and flour per season is averaged at about 25,000 tons. Kingston exports 2500 tons, but will probably increase considerably within a few years. The other ports named have also their fair share.

In order that our readers may see at a glance the extensive character of this firm's shipments of wheat, we append the following:—

LIST OF VESSELS LOADED BY MESSRS. JOHN DARLING & SON FOR UNITED KINGDOM AND CONTINENT DURING SEASON 1880.

Port of Loading.	Vessel.	Bags of Flour.	Bushels of Wheat.	Destination.	Date of Sailing.
Port Adelaide	Excelsior		20211	U.K. orders	Nov. 5, 1879.
,,	Mary Stenhouse		53282	,,	Jan. 15, 1880.
,,	Ellerbank		59966	,,	Feb. 5 ,,
,,	Alice Platt		6C659	Havre	March 15 ,,
,,	City of Paris		49793	U.K. orders	April 15 ,,
,,	Nordenskjold		37008	,,	June 1 ,,
,,	Castle Holme	2222	47933	London	July 21 ,,
,,	Brier Holme	1550	41198	Liverpool	Sept. 2 ,,
,,	Glanpadarn		60318	U.K. orders	Oct. 11 ,,
,,	Aconcagua, s.s.		6772	London	Oct. 25 ,,
,,	Dunkeld		23717	,,	Oct. 29 ,,
,,	Oaklands		22230	,,	Nov. 7 ,,
,,	Astracan		11000	,,	
,,	Lindores Abbey		46952	U.K. orders	
,,	Hesperus		11340	London	
,,	South Australian		4620	,,	
,,	Argus		25000	,,	
Port Pirie	Derbyshire		4094	U.K. orders	Oct. 25, 1879.
,,	Cedric the Saxon		84790	,,	Dec. 17, 1879.
,,	Saron		18161	,,	Jan. 5, 1880.
,,	Lady Kinnaird		35568	,,	Jan. 16 ,,
,,	Delphine Melanie		21122	Bordeaux	Jan. 22 ,,
,,	Dunedin		61880	Belfast	Feb. 20 ,,
,,	Rokeby Hall		56744	U.K. orders	Feb. 28 ,,
,,	Kilmeny		44710	,,	March 10 ,,
,,	Seiriol Wyn		60868	,,	April 2 ,,
,,	Loweswater		31113	,,	April 14 ,,
,,	China		39324	,,	April 20 ,,
,,	Callixene	2800	63440	Liverpool	May 16 ,,
,,	Excelsior		36914	U.K. orders	May 16 ,,
,,	Argyleshire		41190	,,	May 27 ,,
,,	Rydalmere	1767	60771	Hull	June 10 ,,
,,	Woodville		39413	Dublin	July 5 ,,
,,	Mirzapore		66354	U.K. orders	July 11 ,,
,,	Iron Duke		77776	,,	Aug. 8 ,,
,,	City of Athens		63186	,,	Aug. 21 ,,
,,	Firth of Dornoch		54459	,,	Aug. 31 ,,
,,	Melanesia		71582	Dublin	Sept. 23 ,,
,,	Shakespeare		44282	Hull	Nov. 2 ,,
,,	The Frederick	4963	28050	,,	Nov. 16 ,,
,,	Jane Sproth		37500	U.K. orders	
Port Broughton	Taranaki		58934	,,	March 16 ,,
,,	Mountain Laurel		38638	,,	April 6 ,,
,,	Japan		34006	,,	April 16 ,,
,,	India		46000	,,	May 20 ,,
,,	Kepler		66279	,,	June 25 ,,
,,	Renfrewshire		50598	,,	Aug. 15 ,,
Port Victoria	Fusilier		20519	,,	March 1 ,,
,,	Sarah Bell		45872	,,	April 30 ,,
,,	Bengal		37892	Calais	June 4 ,,
,,	Selim		39628	U.K. orders	Aug. 3 ,,
Wallaroo	Bankfields		47700	,,	Sept. 30 ,,
,,	Spirit of the Dawn		38911	,,	Oct. 6 ,,
Port Wakefield	Talisman		63259	,,	Jan. 30 ,,
,,	Gainsborough		45115	Havre	March 6 ,,
,,	Wigton		40937	U.K. orders	Oct. 13

JOHN DUNN AND CO.

Russia has, for some years past, carried on a large, if not the largest, export trade with Great Britain of any other country in the world. The natural resources of America in the way of extensive grain-growing, brought that country largely into competition, in the exportation of grain, with the country before named. Up to forty years ago, England was to a great extent entirely dependent upon Russia and America, for the grain she required in excess of that grown on her own soil. But, at this time, a new era in the supply of grain was opened out, which has been developed already to a great extent, and which in the future is likely to supplant the almost gigantic demand of English capitalists for grain in the foreign markets. The emigration to Australia of men inured to agricultural pursuits, the energy with which they applied themselves to the growth of grain, the perseverance which they brought to bear in preparing the virgin soil so rich in grain-growing power, and the success which has crowned their efforts, have opened up for England a market which may be illimitable in its power of supplying all the grain that may be required by the mother-country. South Australia, with natural resources unsurpassed by any other country in the world, possesses at the same time an army of settlers which is determined that the grass shall not be allowed to grow under its feet, and which has set to work with a sternness of will, that means that those natural resources shall not languish through any want of effort on its part. That this colony, in the comparative infancy of its existence, should yet be able to supply the demand of its own population, and at the same time have a surplus such as to make its production an important factor in the markets of Europe, is a phase in the rapid and wonderful growth of her agriculture that should be a source of justifiable pride, not only to the colonists, but to that country which has sent them forth from its shores. It must be more gratifying to Great Britain to have commercial relations with a country whose inhabitants are allied to it by ties of kindred, a common government, and the common life of a common fatherland, than to depend for their importations upon a country which on the one hand has separated itself from England and generated distinct interests, and with a country which, on the other hand, is alien in race and diverse in interest. It must, too, be a matter of self-gratulation and honest pride to the colonists of this new country, that in so short a time they have been enabled by their enterprise to accomplish all that was foreseen by the representative men in England when they advocated the colonisation of Australia. The proportions to which the pastoral, agricultural, and mining interest of this country may one day be developed, will, we prognosticate, far exceed the wildest dreams of the most enthusiastic lover of this New Atlantis. The encouragement held out to the South Australian farmers through the ready demand for all the grain they may be able to grow, will act as a powerful incentive towards that concentration of energy of purpose which seeks to combine *quality* with *quantity*. Already the superiority of South Australian wheat is evidently appreciated, as evinced by its commanding the highest price in the great wheat markets of the world, and its reputation for quality exceeds that enjoyed by the oldest grain-growing countries. Besides, the advantages which are possessed by the farmers of this colony are far in excess of those enjoyed by the farmers of older countries. First there is the climate, which is obtained in almost every variety; next the soil, the natural qualities of which are suitable in the highest degree to the cultivation of every species of grain, more especially wheat; then the great and incalculable benefit of, in many cases, no rent, and in many more of rent that is merely nominal; the comparative immunity from taxation; and last, though not least, the small expense, in some cases none at all, to which they are put for the manuring of the soil. With important factors such as these, why should they not successfully compete in the exportation of grain to Europe, and ultimately succeed in supplying much of the demand of the grain markets of the old world? Since the introduction of steam, the length of the voyage between England and Australia has been considerably diminished, and the opening of the Suez Canal has tended to decrease it still more, so that now instead of months it takes but weeks to load cargo in Australia, carry it over, and deliver it in the mother-country. Facilities, then, for the exportation of grain or any other produce to the Northern hemisphere, are daily becoming greater and greater. But not only in the exportation of raw produce is the trade increasing, but there is also a daily increasing export trade doing in flour. This is a branch of industry which, from its great importance, not only deserves every and the greatest encouragement, but which, by its very nature, must force itself in a short time into the vanguard of exported merchandise. For it is natural to suppose that there must be a greater demand in the markets for an article that is already prepared for use, than for that same article in its raw state, and which on arrival must go through a process of grinding before it is really ready for consumption, or with regard to the major quantity before it is really ready for use. This, then, has created an industry of importance to the national wealth, as well as of importance to the future of Australian agricultural interests. It has combined itself with the export of the raw material, and has already grown into some importance. This result, it is only just to say, is in a great measure due to those gentlemen whose names stand at the head of this chapter. Their history has been one of unflagging perseverance attended with almost unexampled success in this branch of industry, namely, flour and grain merchants. Until now they stand at the head of that branch of commerce in Australia. They have been established for about forty years, thus making their existence almost coeval with the existence of the colony of South

Australia, or at least of Adelaide, its capital. The flour mills which they have established, are the most complete of their kind in Australia.

In 1841, the senior member of the firm commenced as a miller near Adelaide. He carried on the business on his own responsibility for something like eleven years, until, in 1852, his son was admitted as partner. The number of partners during the ensuing thirteen years, was increased by the admission of others. At the present time, the following gentlemen constitute the firm, viz.:—John Dunn, Esq., senior (who was the founder of the firm); the Hon. John Dunn, jun.; W. Hill, Esq.; and George Shorney, Esq. We need not say that with the exigencies of increasing business, the mill power was increased also. The last mill, we understand, which was built by the firm was at Port Augusta, and was completed in February of the present year. We are indebted for several particulars which are contained in this chapter to the *South Australian Register* for that month, and here we will give an extract from a speech delivered by the Mayor of Port Augusta, on the occasion of the mills first opening. This extract will furnish our readers with particulars that will be found at once interesting and instructive. He said: "Mr. John Dunn, senior, was one of their oldest colonists, and had by his industry and integrity succeeded in establishing one of the greatest enterprises in South Australia. The firm of which Mr. J. Dunn, senr., was the head, is not only the largest milling firm of the colony, but they are also very large exporters of grain, and the largest exporters of grain and flour combined in South Australia. It was a matter of extreme satisfaction that through the enterprise of the firm of John Dunn and Co. they now had in their town the most complete flour mill in all the Australian colonies. It was a great contrast to look back through the past years, and note the small beginning made by the firm of Dunn and Co., and then compare it with the extensive proportions their commercial operations had attained that day. About forty years ago, Mr. Dunn, senr., started business near Mount Barker with a windmill. Cautious and industrious, he had risen step by step, until he became the proprietor of the Mount Barker Mill, then the Bridgewater Mill, worked by steam and water, and of the Nairne Mill, and now they had mills at the three most important ports of the colony, in addition to those at Quorn and Wilmington. The mill in which they were then assembled was the best of its kind in all Australia. However much they might respect Mr. Dunn, senr., he was sure that his worthy son, Mr. John Dunn, jun., who was that day present with them, was no less respected. To testify to that gentleman's ingenuity, they were there that day. He had planned the whole of the mill. The engines had been selected in England by him, and of their quality and utility there could be little doubt." We may supplement this by saying that the largest mills of the firm are at Port Adelaide, Port Pirie, and Port Augusta. The grinding machinery in connection with these mills is driven by 10 steam engines besides the water power, and when all are at full work is capable of converting upwards of eighteen hundred tons of wheat into flour every week. Their international prize medal flour is now well-known in all parts of the world. They employ agents in all the grain-producing districts of the colony, who purchase the wheat direct from the farmers, and send it forward to the mills, or wharves for shipment as required. The facilities for carrying on their business as exporters of grain, are very complete, their wharves and jetties being all connected by branch lines with the main lines of railway of the colony, so that no time is lost, and the utmost despatch is given to the large number of vessels which they have in their service.

WM. PEACOCK AND SON.

The development of the wool trade, the staple product of Australia, must ever be matter of the deepest interest to those who are concerned with the welfare of the country. Second only to this in importance, are the appliances which enterprising men have succeeded in introducing into the colony, whereby the value of the wool has been increased to such an extent as to create a greater demand, and so augment materially what would have been the natural output, into an ever-increasing supply. Amongst the appliances to which we refer are those which have been introduced in the art of wool-scouring, accompanied by a great saving of time and labour, and resulting in the utilisation of thousands of skins, which could not have been so profitably employed without this process. In fact, improvements in this branch of the wool industry are continually coming to the fore, by whose aid the business of wool-scouring is not only growing in importance as an industry, but in its efficacy as a channel of supply to a consuming manufacturing world of no mean insignificance.

Important as is the business of wool-growing, hardly less important is the business of properly preparing that wool for the various markets of the world. An idea may be formed of the large amount of wool the fellmongering and wool-scouring establishments contribute to the main supply, when it is stated that this one firm, during the season of 1879-80, scoured nearly 4000 bales. This shows how important an adjunct the business of fellmongers and wool-scourers is to the general wool trade of Australia. They have, in fact, been the minor channels which have helped forward the present world-wide reputation of the clean condition in which Australian wool reaches the London market. The pastoral interests of Australasia have been developed from the smallest beginnings, to their present extraordinary proportion, in some measure, by the enterprising spirit of men who have introduced, at considerable expense, the very newest inventions for the scouring of the raw material, as well as by those who have taken up large tracts of country exclusively for the purpose of wool-growing. The efforts of the wool-grower, however energetic they might have been, would have been of less avail had they not been ably seconded by those who have devoted their capital and energies to the important branch of wool-scouring and wool-cleansing, whereby it is introduced into the European markets under the most favourable conditions. Through the efforts of Messrs. Peacock and Son, we may say that, with regard to the improvements which they have introduced, regardless of expense, in the art of wool scouring and cleansing, advantages have been secured for the increased development of wool-growing in the colony of South Australia, that are not possessed to a greater degree by Victoria, New South Wales, or Queensland. The colony, generally, is indebted to them for their enterprise, which has surmounted the greatest difficulties, and overcome every imaginable obstacle in the accomplishment of their praiseworthy and commendable object. We did not know whether the ordinary rules of the establishment were transgressed in admitting us to the factory while it was in operation, but we were speedily assured of the contrary by the courtesy of our reception, and the evident pleasure of the proprietor and others, in showing and explaining to us the whole operation, in its minutest detail, of wool-scouring and wool-cleansing; while we found that time and trouble, important factors with most men of business, were lavishly distributed during the whole of our most instructive, most interesting, and most pleasurable visit. We would certainly recommend all travellers to Adelaide, however important a factor time may be in their sojourn, to visit this, we understand, the largest wool-scouring establishment in South Australia. The interest which will be excited, the instruction which will be reaped, and the utter disregard to trouble shown by the proprietors or their employees, whose obliging and courteous demeanour takes one by storm, will well repay even a lengthy visit to their extensive premises, in which is carried on this very interesting branch of industry. We have much pleasure in reproducing, for the benefit of our readers, some of the details which we gathered during our visit to the establishment.

The present firm was established by the late Mr. William Peacock, on the present site of the tannery, in Grenfell-street, in the year 1839. The original wooden house, with brick foundation, all brought from England, is still standing. The business premises stand on portions of three acres, a large yard being required for the reception of wattle bark during the season. At the time of our visit, we understood that 200 ox-hides were put in to work weekly, with calf, kangaroo, wallaby, &c., and over 100 dozen sheepskins. The sole tanning material is Mimosa-bark, which is produced in large quantities in South Australia, and forms a staple of export, both to Great Britain and New Zealand. Messrs. Peacock and Son, alone, have exported as much as 1038 tons during one year. The best of the leather manufactured is sold for local consumption, and the lighter qualities are sent to Europe, as also are the basils, or tanned sheepskins, and the brand of the firm is favourably known in the London markets. It is a noticeable fact in this old-established business, that a large proportion of the employees have been with the firm for a great number of years, and eight or ten (some of them now middle-aged men) entered the employ as lads, and have never left it. Very shortly after settling at Grenfell-street, the founder of this firm turned his attention to wool-washing; but for many years the extremely limited number of sheep in the colony made the industry a very small one. The W.P. brand was originally sent *via* Sydney, as no direct vessels were laid on from the infantine colony of South Australia, and the shipments were very small. The wool was washed on the river Torrens, on the skins, from which it was afterwards removed by the old process of sweating. As years advanced, premises were secured at Hindmarsh, a suburb to the westward of the city, in the direction of the port, and here the wool-scouring and fellmongering portion of the business of the firm has been carried on for the past twenty-seven years. Until 1874, all the washing and cleansing of wool was done in the bed of the river Torrens, men washing in crates in a somewhat similar method to that pursued on the Yarra at the present day. During the latter part of 1873, in consequence of a lawsuit by the riparian proprietors, a perpetual injunction was granted by the Supreme Court against any pollution of the stream, and forbidding during the summer months any water to be taken from the stream for wool-washing purposes. This simply incited the firm to perseverance in their efforts. They sent to England for the newest and most complete wool-washing machines that could be procured. They then erected suitable buildings for the machinery, and sank a large well at the bottom of which they bored for water, with such success, that after striking the gravel at about 140 feet, water, of excellent quality, rose to within 40 feet of the surface, and this well now gives a supply of 60,000 gallons daily, when it is required. At the time of our visit the wool season of 1880 had not opened, but the fellmongery operations were in full force. Sheepskins are procured from produce sales four or five times a week. On their arrival at the yard, if fresh they are at once painted over on the flesh side with a composition which has the effect of so loosening the wool that it readily slips off at the expiration of an hour or so, the skins being placed over a beam in the usual way, and the wool classed and sorted as it is removed. If skins are dry, from stations or country butchers, they are soaked for two or three days in large concrete tanks provided for the purpose, and then painted with the composition as in case of fresh ones. This process is an immense advantage over the old system, in which wool was removed by sweating the skins in close rooms, till the wool detached itself by decay of the outer cuticle. In addition to great saving of time, all the skins so treated are fit for tanning, and none except the very cut or weevil eaten ones are thrown away or sent to the glue factory. When wool has been thus removed, it is taken to the scouring room, which is the ground floor of a fine two-storied building and contains the machinery, and engine power, which are kept in the best order. The wool is first placed in a hot lye composed of water, soap, soda, and other necessary ingredients, where it is allowed to remain about two minutes, and is then fed on to a moving apron or brat, which conducts it between two indiarubber-covered rollers, which squeeze out the lye, returning it to the tank, whilst the wool falls into the first washing trough, where it is immersed by an ingenious revolving brass drum, and is then taken on by forks, which work with remarkable precision, one picking up the wool at the moment the other one leaves it, to another pair of rollers similarily covered to the first. Passing through these, under a douche of clear water, the wool, now nearly clean, falls into a trough, No. 2, where it is similarly hauled, and then passed through another pair of rubber-covered rollers, from which it is thrown off by a rapidly revolving fan, ready for drying. The wool is now spread on sheets, on a prepared floor, opening off machine room, and partially dried. From here it goes to the drying room, the floors of which are heated by flues, passing under the lower one which is of iron. A short time here finishes the drying operation, and the wool is then conveyed to the upper floor of the packing shed, through a pneumatic tube, the air for which is supplied from a Boston blower, which runs at the rate of 2160 revolutions per minute, and causes such a rush of air that the wool is most easily conveyed up the tube, and by a clever arrangement of the intelligent foreman of the works, Mr. Burnell, it is distributed to any one of the ten bins, which is destined to receive it. From these bins the wool is put into the press, which is on the rack and pinion principle, and of great power, four men exerting a pressure of over 21 tons vertically with second purchase. The bales are taken out of the press in restrainers, which fasten to a false top and bottom of iron. Thus, a saving of time is effected by bales being sewn outside the press, and the bales are uniform at the ends, and vary slightly, besides being treated as dumped by ships. The W.P. and S. brand of wool is now well-known in the London market, and the prices realised during several of the past years have equalled, where not exceeding, any prices obtained for similar sorts at same sales. During the season 1879-80, nearly 4000 bales were turned out of this establishment, and the appliances are capable of a much larger number. During the summer months the premises are most busily occupied, the winter operations being, as we understand, almost entirely, if not wholly, confined to sheepskins.

The present proprietor of the business, Mr. Caleb Peacock, is a gentleman very widely and favourably known, not only in South Australia, but also in Victoria. He is the managing partner of the firm, which consists of himself and the widow of his eldest brother. Mr. Peacock was born on the site of the present tannery, during the early history of the colony, was Mayor of his native city in 1876-7, and now represents a most important constituency in Parliament, namely, the northern district in the heart of Adelaide.

F. H. FAULDING AND CO.

The firm which we have at present under notice is the largest of its kind in South Australia. Its existence extends over a period of thirty-five years, a very considerable part of half a century. Prosperity and success have attended its history during the whole of that long period. It has succeeded in inspiring an amount of public confidence, which has resulted in continued extended operations, and which necessitated improvements in the premises to meet the growing demands of the increasing business. The history which we have recorded of the various establishments that have come under our notice in the other colonies of Australia, attended as they have been with such marked and signal success, is in reality the history of the firm whose name stands at the head of this chapter, but they, from the very business which they follow, have had opportunities which do not belong to others who have had to meet created or at least growing wants, while the articles supplied by Messrs. F. H. Faulding and Co., are synchronous with the greatest desideratum of human life, namely, the necessity of health. Such wants are coeval with the birth of mankind, as with the birth of a colony. Whatever may be the climate of a new country, and however robust the health of the new settler, yet the advisableness of having at hand those medicaments which minister to health or alleviate disease or sickness is apparent even to the most absent minded, and if it be not, no length of time, as a rule, elapses before it forces itself into notice as an absolute necessity of a continued healthy existence. Next to food and drink and clothing, medicine is the most important factor in a household. The other necessaries of life may, under certain conditions, be dispensed with, certainly the luxuries; but the necessity of preserving health creates the necessity of having within reach the medicine adapted to that end. In view of all this, it is evident that Messrs. F. H. Faulding and Co., have not had the same difficulties to contend with as are common to, and inalienable from other branches of business. The necessary factors are ordinary skill, intimate knowledge of drugs, together with strict integrity, close attention to business, and a recognition of the wants which require to be supplied. This business was founded in 1845 by the late Mr. F. H. Faulding, who originally came from Yorkshire, and who died in 1869. The present senior partner, Mr. L. Scammell, was admitted into the concern in 1861, and was shortly afterwards joined by Mr. R. Foale, and Mr. Phillip Dakers. The latter gentleman took up his residence in London, and took charge of the London office, which is situated at Gresham Buildings, Basinghall-street. The business was begun at No. 5 Rundle-street, where the present retail branch is still carried on. Mr. Scammell was in business at Port Adelaide when he first joined the firm. Here the largest business in the port is still carried on, and all the shipping business is also transacted here. Since 1861, the business has been under the charge of Mr. Hustler. Unlike many other firms in the colonies, each member has been brought up to the business, which must be advantageous alike to themselves and their customers. The advantage to themselves consists in the skill and knowledge which they are enabled to import into their business; that to their customers is the confidence it must, as a matter of course, inspire. When the retail transactions became extensive, it was thought advisable to enter into more extended operations, and the wholesale branch was entered into, and was carried on in a warehouse in Clarence Place, off King William-street, but the increasing requirements of trade requiring larger premises, those at present occupied by the firm were erected by them in 1875. The old warehouse, however, is still in the occupation of the firm. We noticed a gas-engine which is always at work in the various processes required in the trade. The present buildings of the firm present a frontage to the best part of King William-street, opposite the Bank of South Australia. The style in which the premises are built is such as to harmonise with the large edifice occupied by the bank. The new building used by the firm covers an area of 90 feet by 38 feet, and consists of three floors and basement. The appearance is enhanced by the material of which it is built, being chiefly freestone, which gives an air of solidity and endurance to the structure. There is noticeable an hydraulic lift for transferring heavy goods to the various floors. The appliances at the disposal of the firm enable them to manufacture many specialties which are in daily use, and a large number of chemicals and pharmaceutical preparations are manufactured on the premises. Messrs. F. H. Faulding and Co. undertake assays of all descriptions of organic or inorganic substances. The business premises at the Port were also rebuilt in 1877, and are now about the best and most commodious which are to be found in Port Adelaide. The wholesale business consists in supplying retail dealers throughout the colony, and the reputation which the drugs imported and manufactured by the firm have acquired is alike remarkable for quality as for variety. The conveniences which they possess for manufacturing purposes enable them to ensure to their customers regular supplies, an important desideratum in the selling of drugs and other chemicals.

Another and important branch of business which has been started by Messrs. Faulding and Co., and carried on in a separate warehouse and cellar in Morphet-street, Adelaide, is the manufacture of sparkling wines, which they began eighteen months ago. We will quote the exact words of Monsieur Bourband, whose reputation as a wine-grower may be gathered from the following extract from the report of the Adelaide Chamber of Manufactures, 1876. After mentioning that through the co-operation of the Agent-General, several French families have been introduced into the colony, it goes on to say, " They congratulate the Government upon having in this way secured for the province the services of so talented a gentleman as M. Bourband, whose practical experience has been largely availed of by our vignerons, and whose useful contributions on subjects of much interest have been disseminated by the press throughout the country." M. Bourband states "that the manufacture of sparkling wines started eighteen months ago in Adelaide, by Messrs. F. H. Faulding and Co., has been attended with the greatest success that could be expected, and fully confirms the statements made by him before the Vignerons' Club of South Australia on the 23rd February, 1871, that all classes of wines, from the strong and sweet to the lighter ones, can be produced in this colony." Indeed, the best kind of grapes required for champagne — with which specialty Messrs. F. H. Faulding and Co. particularly occupy themselves—are cultivated on a large scale in South Australia, which possesses in many parts of the vast tract of its territory land suitable for vine-growing. The nature of the soils is very similar to that which is to be found in some of the most renowned wine districts of Champagne, Rhine, and Mosel, and offers to any practical vine-grower, either in the hills or in the plains, places the most suitable as to situation and exposure, and which cannot in any country be surpassed. These wines, which have met with the greatest esteem and favour of the South Australian connoisseurs, and which may bear a very favourable comparison with many European brands, have been made under the supervision of Mons. Ed. Bourband, who has devoted his time for a period of over twenty-two years to the study and progress of viti-culture and wine trade development in France, Spain, and latterly in South Australia, where his practical experience has been largely availed of by our vignerons; and who, as manager for an important firm in France, has had opportunities of making large quantities of wine as specially required, and for the use of the champagne district manufacturers. The South Australian champagne, which is principally manufactured by F. H. Faulding and Co., is a blend of selected wines, amongst which are the best types that are made in the colony. This blend has been treated with the same care and in a similar manner to that in use in the French champagne district, and bottled according to the system recommended by the eminent chemist, Monsieur Maumere, of Reims, whose excellent method has been approved and adopted by several respectable firms in Champagne and other countries where well-known sparkling wines are manufactured and exported. The firm obtained a medal and certificate at the Sydney Exhibition for their champagne; and they are now exhibiting at Melbourne. They also hope shortly to supply the public with sparkling hock, moselle, and burgundy, for each of which very desirable blends have been obtained from the vineyards of the colony. In 1864, they, in connection with Messrs. Sinnett and Tocchi, established the manufacture of olive oil, making about 400 gallons the first year, the production of which has since considerably increased.

THE KENT TOWN BREWERY.

The subject of our present chapter, namely, the Kent Town Brewery, owes its, we may say, entire success to the enterprise and energy of the present proprietor, E. T. Smith, Esq., M.P. This industry, into which Mr. Smith has thrown so much of his time and capital, has attained such large proportions that the Kent Town Brewery may fairly be considered the largest and most complete in the Australian colonies. A measure of its success is also owing to the celebrated quality of the ales which are brewed, and which may be said to compete successfully with those imported from the mother country. We are glad to notice this feature in the South Australian Brewery, for we do not see why ale equally as good as that brewed in England should not be produced in the colonies. This industry deserves encouragement, and we fail to see why English ale should be so much sought after, when the beer which is sent out by the Kent Town Brewery is of such superior quality. The Kent Town Brewery beer is well known throughout South Australia, and its fame is gradually extending further. Its consumption, as compared with the imported article, is greatly on the increase, and its introduction into so many households speaks well of its repute as a drinking beverage. The prejudice which exists against colonial beer in Australia is a strange feature of the English character, exhibiting as it does that national vanity which even long residence in another country is not sufficient to abate. However, we are glad to note that amongst the Australians proper, that is, those born in Australia, the spirit of nationalities is gradually growing up together with an appreciation of ale which their native country produces, in preference to anything that may be imported. It is amongst those that the consumption of colonial beer is the largest, while its qualities are being gradually recognised even by those who have not yet forgotten English hearts and English homes. A description of the buildings in which so large a business is carried on may be a matter of interest to our readers, especially when it is remembered that they have risen to their present fine proportions in spite of the powerful competition which colonial beer has up till now been obliged to encounter. The brewery buildings measure 216 feet by 210 feet. The front elevation is to De Quettville Terrace, the centre of which is the principal gateway, 14 feet wide and 15 feet high, with bold pilasters, cornice, and pediments in the Grecian order of architecture, finished with Portland cement dressings. Passing through the principal gateway, the quadrangle, 150 feet by 92 feet, is reached. The brewery proper is situated at the south-eastern angle, and is 34 by 34 feet clear of walls, and 72 feet high to the floor of the look-out, consisting of five stories. On the north side of the quadrangle is the barley store, beneath which is the malt floor, each 160 feet by 34 feet. The kiln is situated in the north-eastern corner, between the malt and malt stores, is 35 feet by 34 feet clear of walls, and covered with cast-iron perforated tiles. It is 58 feet high to the cowl. The buildings are from one to five stories, according to the requirements of the different departments, and contain, in addition to the above, English and Colonial malt stores, 104 feet by 33 feet each, sugar and hop stores, fermenting rooms, cooling floors, commodious offices, &c. In the yard, at the rear of the main buildings, are large roomy sheds, outhouses, stables, &c.; stables and loose boxes are provided for sixteen horses. The cellarage, which is 213 feet by 34 feet, will contain about 600 hogsheads, and is covered with 2-inch Mintaro slate. The walls of the whole are of Glen Osmond stone, 2 feet and 2 feet 6 inches thick. The plant and machinery are of the latest and most approved principle, and complete in every respect. The workmen's buildings are built on land at the rear of the brewery, and are large, lofty, and replete with every comfort. We understand that the Hon. Thomas English was the architect, and the works under his able superintendence were completed in a most satisfactory manner by Messrs. Brown and Thomson, contractors, at a total cost of from £17,000 to £18,000. A short sketch of the career of a gentleman who has raised this new industry into such a prominent position, against such great odds, is, we feel, well worthy of a place in our book. Mr. E. T. Smith, the proprietor of the Kent Town Brewery, was born at Walsall, in Staffordshire, nearly fifty years ago, and is descended from an old and respectable family. We are induced to go back thus early in Mr. Smith's career, as it was destined to be associated somewhat intimately with the politics and politicians of the time. The various branches of Mr. Smith's family had long taken a deep interest in political questions, especially when the agitation for the repeal of the Corn Laws caused such excitement, which was, doubtless, the origin of Mr. Smith's love for political life. At twenty years of age he was appointed chairman of the non-electors' committee when Sir Charles Foster, Bart., was first elected in the liberal interest for South Staffordshire, and delivered his maiden speech in the presence of Cobden, Bright, Villiers and others, in response to the toast of "The Non-Electors' Committee," at the banquet given to celebrate the great liberal victory. Two years later, in 1853, he arrived in South Australia and commenced business in Blyth-street as an importer in the South Staffordshire general ironmongery line. Shortly after, questions of a highly important and momentous character were agitating the public mind, viz., manhood suffrage, the ballot, abolition of state aid to religion, etc. Mr. Smith threw his whole heart and soul into these matters, especially during the years 1853-4 and 5. In 1860 he joined the late Mr. E. Logue at the Old Kent Brewery, and on that gentleman's decease, two years afterwards, the whole business fell into Mr. Smith's hands. In 1875 he built the extensive and commodious premises which we have, in a preceding part of the chapter, described. He was elected Mayor of Kensington and Norwood without opposition during the several municipal years of 1867-8-9, and largely contributed to the progress of those rising suburbs. In 1870 he paid a visit to England, and on his return was again elected to the office of mayor. In the same year he entered Parliament as member for East Torrens, and has since continued to represent that constituency. Mr. Smith has refused many offices and appointments which have been offered him during his parliamentary career, the most notable being that of Chairmanship of Committees under the Blyth Administration. As a mark of respect both Houses of the Legislature united in giving him a banquet on his leaving the colony for Europe in 1877. Many local institutions owe their existence to his instrumentality, and he may be truly designated "the father of Australian tramways." He is connected either as patron, president, or vice-president, with twelve associations and clubs in and round the city. He has been connected with the Hospital, Savings Bank, Deaf, Dumb and Blind Asylum, and other Boards, and has ever shown his readiness to assist in religious and charitable works.

The Advance of Literature in South Australia.

E. S. WIGG AND SON.

A desire for knowledge and information must ever follow in the train of civilisation. Even in a young colony, among a people in a state of almost semi-civilisation, the want of books is felt; though, perhaps, of a very inferior kind. There is always a certain number among the population, who require some relaxation, different from what the very primitive amusements of the place can supply, from the daily routine of work. This they must find in reading; and hence, the necessity for books. A taste for literature will be found in all lands and among all nations; among the lower classes of society, though naturally to a lesser degree, as well as among the educated. With increased education, the demand for books becomes necessarily greater. In great cities and among a wealthy population, the number of books yearly published and sold is enormous. Literature of every description is required suitable to the various tastes, understandings and purses of the numerous classes resident in a populous city. To this Southern land, so lately discovered, the literature of the old world has found its way. The gold mines were its earliest sources of wealth. Magnificent gold discoveries, and fortunes drawn suddenly from, what then seemed, never-failing sources of riches, raised large cities as if by magic and summoned luxuries from the four quarters of the globe. Some few of the libraries and the picture galleries of England were soon to be found in miniature in the cities of Australia. The children of the old world quickly gathered round them the comforts and the luxuries that their native land possessed. It was not long before books ceased to be a luxury and became a necessity. Booksellers' shops were established, and circulating libraries soon instituted. Amongst those which were established in the early existence of the colony, that of Messrs. E. S. Wigg and Son may be considered to stand in the front rank. Begun in 1849, by Mr. E. S. Wigg, the business has during the intervening years steadily increased. The first premises occupied were at No. 4 Rundle-street, Adelaide. The early beginnings were small, and the business comprised that of bookseller, stationer, and acccount-book manufacturer. Mr. Wigg, however, speedily made a good connection in commercial stationery, besides opening up a branch, new to the colony, in Sunday-school books and requirements; having received the support of the London School Union and Religious Tract Society. At this time, communication with Europe was exceedingly tedious, steam not being then in the ascendant, and supplies of stock were largely drawn from the auction mart. The paper duty at this time existed in England, and for every hundredweight of paper, whether in the form of books or stationery, the exporter experienced a considerable drawback. In 1858, increase of business necessitated the removal of the firm to larger premises. The old auction mart then existing at No. 12 Rundle-street was demolished, and a new building erected, which, from time to time, has been extended. Very shortly afterwards, Mr. Wigg had his attention attracted to Homeopathy, and, becoming a convert to its principles, was gradually drawn into the sale of medicines. The new system of medicine gained such a hold upon the colonists that Mr. Wigg found it necessary to transfer the new business to 34 King William-street, and since this time he has there carried on the business of Homeopathic chemist and medical bookseller. We may mention that this business is entirely carried on by Mr. Wigg himself, and is in no way connected with the original book and stationery trade. In 1871, Mr. Wigg took his eldest son, Mr. C. N. Wigg, who had been absent for two years in Europe, into partnership. Through the purchase of the stock and business of Mr. Platt, the oldest established bookseller in Adelaide, the firm obtained a large increase in their magazine and retail trade. This business is now the oldest bookselling house in Adelaide. The new departments of fancy goods and cricketware were soon opened, and these immediately supplemented by the addition of pictures and picture-frame mouldings, which, of course, necessitated the services of picture-framers on the premises, and this department has developed into one of the most important branches of the business. Growing requirements demanding more warehouseroom, temporary arrangements were made in Peel-street and other places, followed by the erection of a large and substantial store immediately in the rear of 12 Rundle-street, and in Apollo Place. In 1877, a circulating library of a high class was added to the business, and has been steadily and increasingly supported by the public of Adelaide and suburbs. About this time, as the outcome of the fine art department, frequent representations were made to the firm that the Society of Arts being entirely dormant, and the Government inert, art was languishing and amateurs helpless to obtain assistance. As a preliminary step and tangible aid to a better state of things, as well as an advertisement for their large stock of pictures, the firm decided upon a large and popular display of imported pictures, engaging the Town Hall for a fortnight, and introducing the attractive feature of promenade organ recitals, by the eminent Signor Giorza, both the organ and artist being new to the public. A part of the establishment was reserved for colonial amateurs, and though the pictures were, as might be expected, crude attempts, the scheme was very successful, both as a pecuniary venture—the outlay being considerable—and as a means of attracting public attention to the necessity for establishing public picture galleries and schools of art. In 1878, a similar exhibition was held, and it is noticeable that since that time the formation of a public collection has been kept prominently before the public, and the first steps have been taken by the purchase of £2000 worth of pictures at the Melbourne Exhibition. In 1878, the firm undertook the collection and publication, as far as practicable, of the best and most reliable records and works on the South Australian aborigines. Many of the tribes had entirely passed away, others were fast going, and death was speedily thinning the ranks of those who had been most intimately connected with them. Consequently, much valuable information was being irretrievably lost to men of science. This work was contributed to by Dr. Wyatt and others, and was published as a handsome volume. No profit was expected, but, though not a remunerative work, good service has been done by its publication; the records, traditions, habits, and customs of these races having been thus secured and written by those who were alone able to do it. The rapid and increasing growth of education has caused a considerable increase in the business of Messrs. E. S. Wigg and Son. The school trade has been speedily developed into a large and important branch. Owing to the special requirements of this new and improved state of things, the firm has issued two maps of the colony, a large one, for which a second edition was speedily called, a smaller and more convenient one for travellers and small offices; outline maps of Australia and South Australia for public school teaching; and various educational works and helps. The firm has attained to and maintains the leading position in this important branch. They are also contractors and booksellers to the South Australian Sunday School Union, and Church of England Sunday School Union. Their connection as legal, commercial, and professional stationers, and artists' colourmen, is very considerable. They represent many of the best London and foreign manufacturers. Their premises are commodious, and extend to a depth of over 200 feet, divided into the various departments referred to in this chapter. A further change in the firm is immediately contemplated, by the retirement of the senior partner, after a career of something over thirty years. Mr. W. L. Davidson, brother-in-law of the junior partner, and who has, for some years, been connected with the business, will then join the firm.

Thus, we see, that from the very smallest beginnings, the firm has not only reached its present business proportions, but has added many important and interesting branches, which they have succeeded equally well in developing and bringing before the Adelaide public. None does them greater credit than that branch which has given an impetus to the taste for fine arts.

W. GORDON AND CO.

One of the great necessities for the development of the wool trade has grown naturally out of the requirements that supply and demand have exacted. The intervention of a third distinct business between wool-growing and wool-buying, viz., that of wool broker, has done more for the development of the wool trade in Australia than is commonly imagined. Not only are producers of wool and wool merchants brought together, but the pastoral tenants are enabled through the wool brokers to obtain all reasonable pecuniary aid in cases where such aid is absolutely necessary. This necessity is often felt by those who are struggling into a business, and who have to contend against the frequent droughts, which are peculiar to the Australian climate. It is also felt by those who, though in comparatively affluent circumstances, are desirous of extending their business to greater dimensions. The wool broker not only has a store for the wool which is consigned to his care for sale in the colonial or home markets, but he is prepared at all times to advance money on the consignment, which is found in many cases to be a very great convenience. The firm which is the subject of our present chapter is one that has long existed in Adelaide, and that has deservedly acquired a distinguished reputation in the branch of business referred to. It was established in 1868, and was, on the 6th June, 1878, assigned to and carried on by the Hon. J. Crozier, and we understand that it is one of the few firms in Adelaide which have succeeded well in that particular branch of business.

In addition to being stock and station commission agents, the firm also undertakes the sale of sheep and cattle. This also is a very important branch of trade in Australia, more particularly since the country has commenced to export frozen meat. The number of sheep and cattle grazing on the extensive plains of Australia, would be a matter of wonder and astonishment to those who have only seen, at the most, droves of one hundred or a thousand. Ample for the supply of the whole population, there is, in addition, a very considerable surplus available for export; but until means were discovered to export the meat in a fresh state to the home markets, the value of stock in Australia was considerably below what it ought to have been. Though many thousands of sheep and cattle were slaughtered for meat preserving purposes, for the purpose of exportation, yet preserved Australian meat has never become very popular amongst the working classes of the home country. A great prejudice prevailed against it from its first beginning, but we are glad to say that this prejudice is gradually giving way before the superior quality which is now being sent abroad. However, what with the stock changing hands for pastoral or slaughtering purposes, the firm does a very extensive business as salesmen of sheep and cattle. Their place of business is situated at Cowra Buildings, Grenfell-street, Adelaide. We understand that their auction sales for live stock are held every Monday and Wednesday in each week. Another branch of business, in which the firm deals largely, is the sale of hides, skins, and tallow. The sales for these commodities, including wool, are every Tuesday, Thursday, and Saturday, in each week. The development of these industries has, of late years, made great and rapid strides in South Australia, as well as in other colonies of this new country. The resources which are presented through the immense flocks of sheep, and herds of cattle, are calculated, at no distant time, to make the hide, skin, and tallow industries of great importance, not only for colonial requirements, but also for exportation abroad. There is abundant material, and any amount of demand, which only requires the energy and business capacities of enterprising men, to develop to an almost unlimited extent in the way of abundant supply. The importation of these articles, in the raw state or manufactured, is gradually diminishing, a good sign that Australia is gradually supplying from its own resources, these great desiderata of civilised life. And we believe that Australian leather is quickly rising in the estimation of the buyers, not only in Australia, but also at home. This estimation of Australian-manufactured leather may be increased; and to accomplish such a result, only rests with those who give their whole time and attention to its manufacture, and who take advantage of the newest appliances in its production. Tallow, too, may become, and is to a certain extent already, an industry of great importance. The almost inexhaustible resources which Australia offers for the successful development of this branch of trade, are unsurpassed by any country in the world. The firm of Gordon and Co. has contributed greatly in Adelaide to the creation of an export trade in wool, hides, skins, and tallow, themselves shipping these articles direct to London. One other important fact we must mention, and that is, the firm is always prompt in its cash settlements.

M'ARTHUR AND CO.,
SYDNEY, AUCKLAND AND LONDON.

M'ARTHUR, MORROW AND BRIND,
MELBOURNE.

Whatever credit may be due to the energy and ability of men who have risen from the position of insignificance in the commercial world to opulence and power in the dictates of business transactions in their particular sphere, it would be difficult to find an illustration more cordially deserving such praise than Mr. Alexander M'Arthur of the above firm. Nothing short of sincere admiration will be produced in the minds of our readers who peruse the history of M'Arthur and Co., since its first initiation in Sydney up to the present time, together with its extensive ramifications throughout the Australian group. "Virtue has its own reward" is not a mere abstract sentence, framed for the purpose of materialising what many practical men place under the category of Utopianisms; but it is a reality of a practicable and tangible nature, illustrated in all truth by the history of the gentlemen whose names constitute the firm which is the subject of the present chapter. Australia is a country whose history is a combination of more facts and fictions, within the domain of individual lives, than most of the newly-discovered lands that have now taken their places amongst the civilised nations of the world. The stern realities of life develop latent powers and produce effects that shape the existence and fortune of enterprising and talented men, which results, in the majority of instances, in ample competency for themselves, oftentimes combined with the realisation of fair competency for those who are associated with them, additional progress and development of their adopted country, and, in the instance of some, of honour and wealth and position in their native land. Whatever might have been the chances of success in life, had their talents found no other field for action than that offered in the country of their birth, we are justfied in advancing the opinion that, in all probability, they would never have reached so high a step on the ladder of specific and general success had they not sought "other fields and pastures new."

About 40 years ago, when Melbourne was comparatively unknown, when cities whose commercial reputation now reaches every part of the habitable globe, were scarcely known out of Australia, when Sydney, then *facile princeps* when compared with any other city in Australia, was just emerging into intermundane commercial communication, a gentleman landed in New South Wales who was destined, from small beginnings, to be the founder of a business on a basis of high commercial integrity, which was not only to take if not the first position, certainly one not inferior to any other business undertaking amongst the establishments of the New South Wales metropolis, but at the same time to extend its ramifications throughout the adjacent colonies, as well as to the more distant one of New Zealand. We refer to the gentleman who, at present, in the old country, represents the town of Leicester in the British House of Commons, and who is the brother of the gentleman who at present occupies the civic chair of London, the metropolis of the world, and at the same time represents in the House of Commons the important borough of Lambeth, not second to any other of the great metropolitan constituencies.

Mr. Alexander M'Arthur, who is the founder of the firm of M'Arthur and Co., served his apprenticeship with his brother, the present Lord Mayor of London, who was then in business in the town of Londonderry immortalised in history through the bravery, in circumstances of great national danger, of its apprentices; and being naturally ambitious, found that the scope that was there offered to his enterprise, his energy, and ability, was too limited. He embarked for New South Wales, and on arrival, with an intuitive capacity for the inception of great undertakings, at once initiated a business which the necessities and exigencies of a new colony disclosed to him as calculated not only, at no short time, to recompense him individually with wealth, but to serve the wants of the settlers, and in this way to give an impetus to the development of the colony, which is felt at the present day. This first undertaking was not on a large scale, but by the exercise of that industry and strict integrity for which his name is now proverbial, he succeeded in extending the sphere of his operations, until with the assistance of Messrs. Little and Atkinson, he was enabled to remove to more extensive premises in Pitt-street, Sydney, where under the style of M'Arthur, Little and Atkinson, a business was established on so firm a basis, that there was no possible anxiety with regard to its permanent and ultimate success. In 1854, after a well-earned competency, Mr. Little retired from the business and returned to England, and thenceforth the firm was carried on and known as the firm of M'Arthur and Atkinson. The firm now extended its business to the wholesale department, which was really the beginning of its present large local and intercolonial trade. A succession of branch establishments was founded firstly at Adelaide under the style of M'Arthur, Kingsborough and Co., then at Melbourne, which still exists under the style of M'Arthur, Morrow and Brind, and which is one of the handsomest and most capacious soft-goods warehouses in Melbourne —the resident partners of this branch being Messrs. John James Morrow and George Frederick Brind. The establishment at Adelaide was ultimately wound up and the premises disposed of. The last effort of Mr. M'Arthur, before finally leaving the colonies, was to establish another branch at Auckland, which, after various changes, is now doing a large business, in newly-built premises, under the style of Wm. M'Arthur and Co. Up to within two years ago, the business in Sydney, since Mr. M'Arthur's withdrawal to London, was managed by Mr. A. H. C. Macasie, to whose business talent, enterprise, and high sense of commercial honour, the firm owes the extraordinary progress which of late years has attended its history, no less than its reputation for fair and straightforward dealing. The lamentable death of Mr. Macasie necessitated new arrangements, and the duties of managing partners now devolve upon Messrs. M'Millan and Munro, who were previously employés of the firm, but are now partners.

The head office of W. and A. M'Arthur, situated in Silk-street, Cripplegate, London, represents all the colonial houses in the English and European markets. This firm was the first to initiate the building of those palatial warehouses suitable to the trade of the colonies, which now form one of the chief embellishments of Sydney. Their example was soon followed by others, but to them belongs the first inception, to them belongs the establishment of a business second in importance and extent of operations to no other in the colonies, and which has been the great means of familiarising the rest of the world with the great natural resources of Australia.

ALDERSON AND SONS,
Sydney and Brisbane.

"Architect of his own fortune" has come into a proverb when spoken of the great mass of successful men in Australia. The general success which has attended those of the early settlers of Australia who possessed enterprise, energy and integrity, must be matter of astonishment to our readers in the old world, when compared with the slow and uniform mode and manner of success which characterises the various industries and trades which are carried on at home. There is scarcely a single settler in this new country, who, starting with the factors mentioned above, in whatever trade or industry he has embarked, has not succeeded beyond what could have been his most sanguine hopes. But the most successful industrialist or tradesman, as a rule, has been the man who possessed sufficient foresight and discrimination to notice the absence of, and at once to supply not only the most necessary wants of the colonists, but to discover and at once to set to work to develop the rich resources of the country, whether through the initiation of new industries, or the manufacture of the indigenous and raw article, not only for the supply of the colonial market, but for exportation to the markets of Europe and the rest of the world. An industry in Australia must be estimated according to the impetus, the progress, and the increased demand it creates for the staple products of the country, and according to its success in this respect must it stand pre-eminent. Pastoral pursuits, probably more than any other, are those which are destined to be developed to the great and almost unlimited extent of which in this country they are capable, and any industry which supplements the pastoral interest, is of the very greatest importance in the commercial world of the colony. The industry of the firm which stands at the head of this chapter may rank as second to none in importance, and this will at once be recognised when we state that their business embraces that of tanners, curriers; patent enamel, fancy coloured, dyed, and levant leather-dressers; boot, shoe and upper manufacturers; and also manufacturers of saddlery, harness, and bridles, as well as mill belt, fire and suction hose; and last, though not least in personal usefulness, portemanteaus, trunks, satchels, and bags. The estimated value of the plant and works of the firm is somewhere about £10,000, and the following summary of hides, skins, &c. used by Alderson and Sons, whose business is carried on in the neighbourhood of Sydney, may give some idea of the large and extensive operations of the firm. It extends over a period of seven years, from 1873 to 1879, inclusive :—

	BULLOCK HIDES.			HORSE HIDES.			CALF HIDES.		
	No.	Value.		No.	Value.		No.	Value.	
		£ s. d.			£ s. d.			£ s. d.	
1873	17,288	£21,513 18 8		2,459	£1,175 16 0		4,113	£891 3 0	
1874	17,886	20,121 15 0		5,012	2,081 5 4		5,072	636 16 0	
1875	17,776	19,339 19 4		3,528	1,374 9 0		8,340	1,893 17 10	
1876	16,860	14,331 0 0		2,338	818 16 0		8,338	1,493 17 10	
1877	17,529	16,068 5 0		2,255	770 8 10		2,987	373 7 6	
1878	16,244	12,386 1 0		996	352 15 0		2,069	189 13 2	
1879	10,580	7,670 10 0		731	255 17 0		1,994	174 9 6	
	114,103	£111,431 9 0		17,319	£6,829 7 2		32,913	£5,653 4 10	

The number of yearlings' hides used during the seven years was 3899, valued at £1302 1s. 11d., while that of goats for the same period amounted to 15,061, valued at £621 7s. 11d. The value of sheep hides during the seven years is estimated at £40,914 0s. 6d., averaging £5845 yearly. We also give a summary of the produce purchased within the same period of time:—

	1873 to 1879.					YEARLY AVERAGE.			
	WEIGHT.	VALUE.				WEIGHT.	VALUE.		
	tns. cwt. qrs. lbs.	£ s. d.				tns. cwt. qrs. lbs.	£ s. d.		
Bark ...	4,845 6 2 20	...28,340 6 0			Bark ...	692 3 3 0	... 4,048 12 6		
Tallow	104 2 1 10	... 2,842 0 4			Tallow	14 17 1 25 ...	406 0 0		
Kangaroo	... 10,580¼ doz.	... 8,723 14 4			Kangaroo	... 1,511½ doz.	... 1,246 5 0		
Pelts	... 35,816 ,,	... 5,337 4 6			Pelts	... 5116 ,,	... 762 9 0		
Oil ...	... 30,694 gals.	... 4,369 19 11			Oil ...	... 4,385 gals.	... 624 5 0		
Lime	... 30,720 bshls	... 1,456 13 8			Lime	... 4,390 bshls	... 208 2 0		
	tns. cwt. qrs.					tns. cwt. qrs.			
Shumac ...	758 2 10...	898 12 0			Shumac ...	108 6 0...	128 7 6		
Dyes, Blues, }					Dyes, Blues, }				
Lampblack }	...	... 2,961 1 5			Lampblack }	...	... 423 0 0		
Coal	... ...	... 4,106 0 0			Coal	... ...	... 586 11 6		

The average number of weekly employés is 365, and the average yearly wages for the last seven years have been £28,848. From these figures it will be seen how large and important the industry is in New South Wales; it is, in fact, the very largest of its kind in the Australian colonies. The firm has a large connection in Queensland, and, in order to consolidate and enlarge it, they purchased the establishment of the late firm of J. and G. Harris and Co., of Brisbane, where, having considerably enlarged and improved the premises, they carry on the business of tanning, currying, woolwashing, and fellmongering.

The following is the yearly average of the number of hides and other products purchased by their Queensland branch, together with their respective values:—5800 hides, valued at £5755; 50 horse hides, value £25; 172 yearlings, value £42 16s.; and 500 calfskins, value £27 12s. Under the head of products purchased we find 250 tons of bark, valued at £1750; 1860 bushels lime, value £93; tallow, £59 8s. 8d.; 2650 dozen pelts, valued at £397 10s. The yearly wages in Brisbane amount to £3113 10s. 6d.; and there are about thirty workmen employed weekly. The business extends to every established colony in the Southern Hemisphere. The firm has been the first to introduce into the colony a new branch of the business, viz., coloured morocco enamel hides, which has been largely patronised by the Government for railway carriages. The firm has been carrying on for many years the business of wool-washing and fellmongering in Waterloo, a suburb of Sydney, which has been supplementary to their general business.

The various vicissitudes and ultimate success of the senior partner of the firm, Mr. William Maddison Alderson, extending from his apprenticeship, which he served in Newcastle-on-Tyne, up to and including his embarkation and voyage to Australia, where he landed nearly 40 years ago, is as strange and eventful as the fictions which, by their variety, succeed in establishing the reputation of writers. We have not space in the present chapter to follow his varied fortunes, which may rank amongst the most remarkable of the very remarkable examples of final success from small beginnings, which Australia affords in such great abundance. Difficulties and obstacles were but incentives to his perseverance and energy, and no opportunity offered which was not at once seized and there and then taken advantage of. Mr. Alderson was the first to properly dress in Australia, the first colonial calf-skin, *black grain kips*, and harness leathers. He has the same claim with regard to the first enamel hide which was dressed in Australia. His first partner was Mr. T. B. Hall, to whom he proposed and who accepted a joint business on the terms that Mr. Hall should find the capital and Mr. Alderson the general knowledge and working of the business. In 1857, the firm of Hall and Alderson exhibited their leathers and saddlery at the Horticultural Society Show held in the Botanical Gardens, Sydney, where they were awarded a gold medal. Henceforth the history of the firm was one continued success, as evidenced by the prizes which they have taken at the various exhibitions which have been held, both in and outside of the colonies, notably at the late Sydney International Exhibition, where they were awarded a special first-class prize. The factory, which was carried on at Surry Hills, ultimately passed, together with other parts of the business, into the hands of Mr. Alderson and his sons, Mr. Hall having retired from the business and left for England, and from this time the style of the firm has been Alderson and Sons. The large business experience possessed by Mr. Alderson, and his technical knowledge of the industry, all of which he has ably communicated to his sons, are fair guarantees that the operations of the firm are likely to increase with the increasing wants of the colonial and export trade. The firm is constituted at present of William Maddison Alderson, Thomas Alderson, and Lancelot Alderson.

PASTORAL

AND

AGRICULTURAL

DIRECTORY

OF

VICTORIA,

NEW SOUTH WALES,

SOUTH AUSTRALIA,

QUEENSLAND,

AND

WESTERN AUSTRALIA.

PASTORAL AND AGRICULTURAL DIRECTORY
OF AUSTRALIA.

VICTORIA.

Aberline Bros., Wangoorn, Warrnambool.
Absolon, William, Mortlake.
Acock, Mrs. C. E, Wangaratta.
Adam, John, Stoney Creek, Talbot.
Adam Bros., Mountain Creek, Moonambel.
Adams, Captain T., Sunday Creek, Seymour.
Adams, W., Mountain Creek, Moonambel.
Adams and M'Kinnon Bros., Allansford.
Adamson, John, Hill Plains, via Benalla.
Adcock, Wm., Terang.
Addnesell, J. D, Murphy's Creek, Hamilton.
Ahearn Bros., Kanabaal.
Airey and Kerr, Killingworth, Yea.
Aitchison, J., Chesterdale, Sutherland's Creek.
Aitken, David Breakfast Creek, Macarthur.
Aitken, D., Stanhope, Rushworth.
Aitken, James, Banyenong Station, Donald.
Aitken, James, Tooan.
Alexander, James, Woodhouse, Penshurst.
Alexander, W., Lake Bolac.
Allan, Richard, Pannoobamawn.
Allan, W. B., Ashmore, Winslow.
Allanson, R. K., Strathbogie.
Allen, A. E. M., Lara Boort.
Allen, Charles, Colac.
Allen, James, Wail, via Horsham.
Allen, Richard, Commeredghip, Rokewood.
Allen, William, Colautet, Tunderook P. O.
Allen, William, Violet Town.
Allen, W. T., and C., Warrior's Hill, Colac.
Allen, William, Cowwarr Station, Cowwarr.
Allfleck, C. S., Nerranda, Allansford.
Allfrey, E. H., Fernihurst, Inglewood.
Allfrey, Robert, Edgar's Plains, Durham Ox.
Allingham, J., Rees, Stawell.
Ambler, Thomas, Toolleen.
Amos, J. C., The Nook, Terrick.
Amos, A. A. Gunnewarre, Kerang.
Anderson, A. E., Woodleigh Farm, Rupanyup North.
Anderson, A. T., Runnymede Station, Digby.
Anderson, A. and Co., Mokepillie Station, Stawell.
Anderson, Charles, Montajup.
Anderson, C. J., a'Beckett Plains, Loddon.
Anderson, D. K., Springvale, Lockwood.
Anderson, Dr. H., Netherwood, Bass.
Anderson, J., Ghin Ghin, Doogalook.
Anderson, James, Ta man Cottage, Ceres.
Anderson, James, Tarranginnie.
Anderson, James, Pimpinio.
Anderson, James, Bullock Creek.
Anderson, M., Durham Ox.
Anderson, R., Cape Schanck, Dromana.
Anderson, Thomas, Griffith's Point.
Anderson, William, Ghin Ghin, Doogalook.
Anderson Brothers, Smeaton.
Anderson and Cox, Kennypaniel.
Anderson, James, and Stewart, Dimboola.
Andrew, —, Finnis, Mount Williams, Pyalong Junction.
Andrew, John, Kingoner, via Inglewood.
Andrew, Joseph, High Plains, Pyalong.
Andrews, J., Ballan.
Andrews, Joseph, Pentland Hills, Bacchus Marsh.
Angus, J. A., Pyramid Hill.
Angus, Jos., Mount Pyramid.
Angus, T., Mount Hope, Terrick.
Anthony, James, Colac.
Anthony, William, Sandford, Casterton.
Anthony, S., Currapook, near Casterton.
Anthony and Co., Fernihurst, near Wedderburn.

Archibald, J. H., Moolort.
Archer, J. R., Mannima, Queenscliff-road.
Archer, M. A., Casterton.
Archer, W., Maryborough.
Arden, Alfred, Claude Lorraine, Tahara.
Arelett, John, Birregurra.
Armitage, Mrs. S. E., Wimmera Park, Eversley.
Armstrong, Alexander, Warrenheim Station, Half-way House, near Shelford.
Armstrong, A., Kewell.
Armstrong, James, Keilambite.
Armstrong, R. G., Salt Creek, Woorndoo.
Armstrong, Thomas, Mount Gellibrand.
Arnolds, Joseph, Ashens.
Atcheson, B., Dennington.
Atkinson and Co., Reedy Creek Station, Kerang.
Atkinson, Messrs., Ballan.
Attenborough, —, Lake Boya Station, Kerang.
Attenborough, Thomas, Tooan.
Attenborough, W. and Co., Murrabil Station, Kerang.
Austin, A., Eilyer, Lake Bolac.
Austin, J. E., Yeo, Colac.
Austin, Josiah, Leighwood, Toorak.
Austin, S. and A. A., Barwon Park, Winchelsea.
Austin, Sydney, Brisbane Hill, Hamilton.
Austin, W. J., Greenvale, Wickcliffe.
Austen and Bullivant, Longerenong, Horsham.
Ayrey, Charles, Warranooke, Glenorchy.
Backholy, Lewis, Deep Creek, Macarthur.
Backie, James, Sandy Creek, Maldon.
Baglin, Samuel, Montajup.
Bailie, John, Mount Taurus, Koroit.
Bailie, Nicholas, Pitfield.
Bailey, Benj., Corop.
Bailey, James, White-street, Coleraine.
Baillie, T. C., Milloo, Runnymede.
Baird, H. M., Linton.
Baird, James, Macorna, via Mount Pyramid.
Baird, S. and M., Kangatong, Hawkesdale.
Bakey, —, Joyce's Creek.
Baker Brothers, Kolora, Terang.
Baker Brothers, Taararak, Camperdown.
Baker, John, Cavendish.
Baker, John, Kanawalla, Hamilton.
Baker, R. C., Lillymur, Dimboola.
Baker, Thomas, Noorat.
Baker, Thomas, Campaspe Inn, Mount Pleasant Creek, via Runnymede.
Balderson, Thomas, Terrick Terrick.
Balding. N. S., Wharparilla.
Baldwin, Henry, Gunbower P. O.
Baldwin, James, Gre Gre.
Ballantyne, —, Benalla.
Ballenger, Arthur, Narrabiel.
Ballier, William, Dereel.
Ballment and Aitken, Ararat.
Bamford, —, Benalla.
Bandy, W., Mount Jeffcott.
Bankin, Ellis, Long Acre, Avon Plains.
Banks, Jos., Eaglehawk, North Gipps Land.
Banks, Robert, Bungeeltap, Ballan.
Barber, C. H., Gundouriry, Yackandandah.
Barber, G. P., Staywood, Wangoom, Warrnambool.
Barber, R., Warranooke, Glenorchy.
Barber, R., Wickliffe.
Barber, Thomas, Dimboola.
Barber, William, Laanecoorie.
Barker, D., Landsborough.
Barker, James, Mount Camel, Redcastle.
Barker and Son, Cape Schanck, Dromana.

VICTORIA.

Barge and Scamble, Joyce's Creek.
Barnes, E. and J., Donald.
Barnes, J. C., Laen, by McDonald.
Barnes, M., Boort, P. O.
Barnett, George, Emu Creek.
Barr, Robert, Hill Plains, via Benalla.
Barrington, P., Maud P. O., Steiglitz.
Bartrop, John James, Wharparilla.
Barrow, M., Boort P.O.
Barr, John, Ondit.
Barclay, Isaac, Boort.
Basley, W. M., Rushworth.
Batey, Isaac, Sunbury.
Bates, Mrs. E., Cannum.
Bath, John, Hesse.
Bath, Thomas, Ceres, Learmonth.
Batson, E., Lake Town.
Bautch, J., Macarthur.
Bayles and Melville, Weerangourt, Byaduk.
Bayly, Alexander, Kerang.
Bazeley, W., Mona, by Elmore.
Beal, Charles, Bleak House, Birregurra.
Beard and Little, Lancefield.
Beasley, John, Kirkstall.
Beattie, Henry, Mount Aitken, Diggers' Rest.
Beatty, J., Tarwin Station, Stockyard Creek.
Beggs, C., Violet Town.
Beggs, G., Mount Cole, Beaufort.
Begg, James, Bamgamie P. O., via Meredith.
Beggs, H. L. M., Brushy Creek, Wickliffe.
Beggs, Jno., Mt. Camel Station, Redcastle.
Beggs, Thomas, Mogolimby, Violet Town.
Beggs, Thomas, Condah.
Behrens, D. Barjarg, Mansfield.
Belcher, Joseph, Smeaton.
Bell Brothers, Werrigai, Werracknabeal.
Bell, Edward S., Werracknabeal.
Bell, H. E., Werracknabeal.
Bell, J., Dunolly.
Bell, J., Barunah Plains, Hesse.
Bell, James, Cherry Mount, Wickliffe.
Bell, Joseph, Burmewang, Elmore.
Bell, R. L., Mount Mercer.
Bell, R. N., Wonwondah, South Horsham.
Bell, William, Morago
Bell, W., Mitiamo.
Bell, William, Pannobarnawn.
Bemworth, Denis, Macarthur.
Benjamin, E., Wail, via Horsham.
Bennet, H. G., Linton.
Bennet, Mrs. L., Kyneton.
Bennet, T., Kewell, via Horsham.
Benton, B., Schnapper Point.
Berndt, Charles, Devenish.
Berndt, C. and W., Major Plain.
Bergin, William, Pimpinio, near Horsham.
Berret, P., Green Hill, via Horsham.
Berthou, Major, Inverleigh.
Betts, T. and G., Torrumbarry.
Beveridge Brothers, Clunes.
Beveridge, G. S., Woodbourne, Kilmore.
Bice, L., Bridgewater.
Bickot, Hugh, Benalla.
Bickley, J., South Tylden.
Bielby, James, Bangerong, Tarkedia.
Biggin, H., Horsham.
Biggs, W. G., Glenmore, Buchan P. O
Bingham, B., Coorington.
Bingham, B., Yambuck.
Binney, George, Bacchus Marsh.
Bird, J., Ballan.
Birmington, Eaglehawk, North Gippsland.
Birney, Robert, Romsey.
Birrel, R., Baynton.
Bishop, W., Terrick Terrick East
Bisset, W., New Hope Park, Serpentine.
Black, James, Benalla.
Black, Hon. Niel, Mount Noorat P. O.
Black, William, Traralgon.
Black, W. J., Durham Ox.
Blackham, —, c/o R. Dixon and Co., William street, Melbourne.
Blackley, William, Munyip.
Blackwood, T., Morrisons.
Blain, J., Clunic, Harrow.
Blake and Co., E., French Island, Hastings.
Blake, T., Mount Camel.
Bland, James, Ceres.
Bland, James H., Kewel East.
Bland, T. and H., Minyip P. O.
Blaney, Thomas, Nagambie.

Blayney. John. Avenel.
Bligh, W., Woodford, Warrnambool.
Bliss, W., Torrumbarry.
Block, N.M.. Ararat.
Bloomfield, R., Hamilton.
Blosset, J., Preston Vale.
Blume, C. A., Karabeal P. O., Dunkeld.
Blunden Bros., Eurella, Durham Ox.
Boag, J. C., Boort.
Boden, E. H., Strathfieldsaye.
Bolden, W., Bacchus Marsh.
Bolger, A., Mortlake.
Bolger, Martin, Terrick Terrick.
Bolliston, John, Piper's Creek.
Bond, John, Horsham.
Bond, W., jun., Eddington.
Bond, T. and H., c/o John Bond, Horsham.
Bone, David, Kiata, Dimboola.
Bon, Mrs. J., Wappan Station, Doon.
Bonning, W., Ballan.
Booley, Edward, Lake Bolac.
Booley, George, Gheringhap.
Booth, Abraham, Coburg.
Booth, S., and Co., Mount Hope, Bald Rock.
Borgett, A., Kiata, Dimboola.
Boucher, James, Condair.
Bourke, James, Comandai.
Bourke, Mrs., Wooronooke P. O.
Bourke, Mrs. M. A., East Charlton.
Bourke, Patrick, Mitiamo.
Bowe, J. M., Lexington, via Stawell.
Bowe, M., Watgania, Ararat.
Bower, D. D., Comandai.
Bowie, J., Yea.
Bowman, J. W. and C., Ridge Estate, Rosedale, Gippsland.
Bowman, M., Ballan.
Bowyer, E., Carlsruhe.
Box, B., Dean's Marsh.
Boyd, — Benalla.
Boyd, A., Newtown Hill, Geelong.
Boyd and Henderson, Commeralghip.
Boyd, Hugh, Skene-street, Colac.
Boyd, H. E., Gooramadda, Wahgunyah.
Boyd and M'Naught, Cargarie P. O., via Elaine.
Boyd, W., Mickleham.
Boyes, J. and H. A., P. O., Rushworth.
Boyle, E., Mitiamo.
Boys, R., Inglewood.
Bradshaw, J., Glenlyon.
Brady Bros., Gisborne.
Brady, F., Dunkeld.
Brady, J. H., Minyip.
Braid, Charles, Byaduk.
Braim, A. W., Hawkesdale.
Braim, —, Kilmory, Woolsthorpe.
Braine, Isaac, Kolora.
Bramley, W. H., Pyramid.
Brandt, C., Kiata, Dimboola.
Branston, W., Kinneypaniel.
Branstone, H., Half-way House, Powlett Plains.
Brayshay, D. W., Hamilton.
Breen, Jeremiah, Dargalong.
Breed, H., Traralgon.
Broe, Dickens and Co., Hamilton.
Breaden, William, Traralgon.
Bremmer, Thomas, Mepunga. Allansford.
Brennan, John M., Langli Logan, Ararat.
Brennan, M., Emu Creek.
Brennan, P., Winton.
Brennan, T., Emu Station, near Benalla.
Bretag, F., Dimboola.
Bretag and Kruse, Natimuk.
Briggs, Thos., Woodstock on Loddon.
Brien, Henry, Macorna.
Brien, H., Freshwater Creek.
Brien, Sproul, Freshwater Creek.
Brien, W., Tahara P. O.
Brian, Jno., Wangaratta.
Brilliant, —, Mochpilly Hotel, Kewell.
Brimacombe, Jno., Yuppekiar, Glenthompson.
Brimston, James, jun., Glenorchy.
Bristow, E., Allansford, Warrnambool.
Brit, John, Terang.
Britnell, J., Violet Town.
Britt, Dennis, Murtoa.
Brock, R., Kinloch.
Brommell, Thos., Hensley Park, Hamilton.
Brooks, G. W., Tarkedia.
Brooks, Jas., Eaglehawk, N. Gippsland.
Broomfield, A., Newlyn.

VICTORIA. iii

Broomfield, —, Green Hills, Camperdown.
Broughton, J. B., Lemon Spring, Apsley.
Broughton and Son, Kout Narin, Harrow.
Broughton, R. B., Mount Kerim, Harrow.
Broughton, W. E., Bunyip, Dimboola.
Brown, Andrew, c/o W. Bailie, Parkfoot, Dennington.
Brown Bros., Boort.
Brown, D., Hamilton.
Brown, Edward, Winchelsea.
Brown, E., Nattie Yallock.
Brown, G., Berwick.
Brown, J., Ledcourt.
Brown, J., Curyo South, Morton Plains.
Brown, Jas., Bacchus Marsh.
Brown and Hunt, Melool, Swan Hill.
Brown, J., Natimuk.
Brown, J. M., Anakie Park, Anakie.
Brown, John, Framlingham.
Brown, Joseph, Hamilton.
Brown and Roy, Catto's Run, Bridgewater on Loddon.
Brown, Robert, Natimuk.
Brown, William, Framlingham.
Browne, A. J., Navarre Station, Navarre.
Browning, A., Wangaratta.
Browning, W., Doctor's Creek.
Bruce, E. H., Yea.
Bruder, T., Lawloit.
Bruhn, A., Emu Creek.
Brumley, William, Mount Shadwell, Mortlake.
Bruntin, Robert, Toongabbie.
Bryant and Co., M., Baringhup.
Bryant, James, Kensington.
Bryant, R., Victoria Lagoon, Cavendish.
Bryant, W. S., Ararat.
Bryce, James, Newham.
Bryden, —, Arndo West, via Lindsay.
Bryden, J., Arndo West, Strathdownie E., via Casterton.
Buchan Brothers, Woorndoo, near Mortlake.
Buchanan, Alexander, Titanga, Lismore.
Buchanan, —, Benalla.
Buchanan, Norman, Ninyeunook.
Buckholy, S., Hamilton.
Buckingham, Thomas, Mount Cole, Warrack, via Ararat.
Buckland, C. W., Shelbourne West.
Buckland, E. H., Shelbourne.
Buckley, James, Mount Pyramid.
Buckley, M., Mount Pyramid via Mount Pyramid.
Buckley and Nunn, Melville Forest, Coleraine.
Bucknall, A., Rodborough Vale, Majorca.
Bucknall, F., Cotswood, Majorca.
Bucknall, H., Kilgobbin, Majorca.
Bucknill, Chas., and Co., Narraport, Morton Plains.
Bulger, M., Terrick Terrick.
Bull, —, near Saltwater Lake.
Bull, George, Ballan.
Bull, H. T., Darlington.
Bull, Samuel, Campaspe P. O., Runnymede.
Bullivant, W. H., Avalon, Lara.
Bullock, John, Corindhup.
Bulmer, John, Mission Station, Lake Tyers, Gippsland.
Bunting, J., Pompapeil, Serpentine.
Bunworth, Peter, Oxford.
Bunyan, John, Smeaton.
Bunyan, John, Moorookyle.
Buler, Thomas, Deighton, Fernbank.
Burckner, C. W., Yan Yan Gart, Wurdie, Bolac.
Burdett, R. A., Kyneton.
Burgoyne, Thomas, Rochester.
Burley, Johnson, Toongabbie.
Burnham and Arthur, Nicholson River, Bullumwaal P. O.
Burnie, J. D., Nirranda.
Burns, —, Huntley.
Burns, G. T., Durham Ox.
Burris, J. H., Laen, by M'Donald.
Burrows, J., Hughes' Creek, near Avenel.
Buscombe, J. H. K., Kyneton.
Butcher, E., Wickliffe.
Butler, J., St. Arnaud.
Butler, M., Kellalac.
Butler, William, Rokewood.
Byrne, Edward, Avon Plains P. O.
Byrne, J., Glen Thompson.
Byrne, P., Wangaratta.
Caddy, —, Berrybank, near Lismore.
Caffray, M., Casterton.

Cahill, —, near Foxhow.
Cain, Thomas, jun., Bacchus Marsh.
Calvert, J., Truwara, Colac P. O.
Callaghan, Mrs. Dennis, Pleasant Banks, via Horsham.
Callaghan, Robert. Yan Yan Gart, Birregurra.
Calder, Robert. Polkemet, Horsham.
Callinan, —, dairy and farm, Sheepwash.
Cameron, A., Balleston.
Cameron, A., Springfield, Towaninnie.
Cameron, A., Wanayure, near Hamilton.
Cameron, A., Craubourne.
Cameron, Alexander, Bald Hill.
Cameron, Alexander C., Casterton.
Cameron, Allan, Avoca Forest, Burke's Flat.
Cameron, Archibald, Byaduk.
Cameron Bros., Wattle Dale, Werracknabeal.
Cameron and Co., Mortlake.
Cameron, D., Mortlake.
Cameron, D., Kewell West.
Cameron, D., Kerang.
Cameron, D., Oakbank, Heywood.
Cameron, Donald, Kilgray, Coleraine.
Cameron, Donald, Oakbank, Heywood.
Cameron, Donald, South Branxholme.
Cameron, Donald, Lake Mundi.
Cameron, Donald, Lake Meran, Kerang.
Cameron, Dugald, Bald Hill, Dunkeld.
Cameron, Ewen, Dalymong, Stuart Mill.
Cameron, John, Strathfillan, Peter's Diggings.
Cameron, J., Fort Cameron P. O.
Cameron, J. H., Lake Goldsmith, Beaufort.
Cameron, Lewis, Mount Wycheproof.
Cameron, Mrs. E., Rokewood.
Cameron, Mrs. Donald, Barcaldine Farm, Rokewood.
Cameron, Mrs. Christina, Arradoorong, Hamilton.
Cameron, S. Macarthur, Natte Yallock.
Cameron, —, Natte Yallock.
Campbell, A., Glenorchy.
Campbell, A. M., Ellingerrin, Inverleigh.
Campbell Bros., Oakfields, Gisborne.
Campbell, Colin, Glen Bucky, Cargarie P.O., via Elaine.
Campbell, Dugall, Traralgon Park, Grangies.
Campbell, Finlay, Archmore, Kamarooka.
Campbell, Hugh, Cobram, via Benalla.
Campbell, H. and J., Cobram, via Benalla.
Campbell, H., Woolshed Farm, Mia Mia.
Campbell, John, jun., Glenorchy.
Campbell, John, Meredith.
Campbell, John, Woolshed Farm, Mia Mia.
Campbell, John, Trio Farm, Kyneton.
Campbell, John, Roseneath, Coleraine.
Campbell, John and H., Ensay, Ensay.
Campbell, J. S., Oaklee, Rupanyup.
Campbell, James, Kinloch.
Campbell, James, Farmer, Eaglehawk, North Gippsland.
Campbell, James, Woolshed Farm, Mia Mia.
Campbell, L., Romsey.
Campbell, Nichol, Traralgon Park, Grangies.
Campbell, Robert, Farmer, Eaglehawk, North Gippsland.
Campbell, Ronald, Longerenong.
Campbell, Ronald, Reefs, Pleasant Creek.
Campbell, W., Woolshed Farm, Mia Mia.
Camen, John E., Corindhap.
Camp, W. J. Wateheim, Morton Plains.
Cantwell, P., Hunter's Town, Ballan.
Cantwell, P. and M., farmers, Corop.
Cantwell, Patrick, Mount Egerton.
Cantwell, Richard, Bullingrook, near Bacchus Marsh.
Cantwell, T., Ballan.
Carne, A., Riddell's Creek.
Carta Brothers, Glenisla, Cavendish.
Carrol, Francis, Ballark, Egerton.
Carmichael, George, Retreat. Casterton.
Carmichael, G. J., Burnbank, Macarthur.
Carmichael, —. Terang.
Carter, J., Ross's Bridge.
Carter, J., Bower Creek, Talbot.
Carter and Sons, Rosebrook, Cavendish.
Carter, William, North Brighton, Horsham.
Carr, John, Frankston.
Carr, William, jun., Corindhap, Rokewood.
Carr, Walter, Swan Hill.
Carey, Martin, grazier, Torrumbarry.
Carey, M., Ganoo Ganoo, Casterton.
Carey, M., Torrumbarry.

Carnie, J., Tallarook.
Carrolan, John, Tatyoon.
Carry, W., farmer, Eaglehawk, North Gippsland.
Carruthers, W., Durham Ox.
Cathcart, James, Donald.
Cay, R., Elmsford, Newbridge.
Cay, Robert, Woodstock-on-Loddon.
Chalmers Brothers Wychetella.
Charsley, E. W., Beaconsfield, Buln Buln.
Chasey, Frederick, Linton.
Chapman, G., and Co., Clunes.
Charlesworth, J., farmer, Bullock Creek.
Charlesworth, J., farmer, Upper Sheepwash.
Chappell, J., Treeve, Rochester.
Chappell, John J., Bardsey, Yarawalla, Durham Ox.
Chambers. John, Rokewood.
Charlton, Mrs. R. squatter, Sebastian.
Chaffey, R.. Little River.
Chapman, R., Swan Hill.
Chatterton, —, Coco Dain, Dimboola.
Cheetham, R., French Island.
Chirnside, F. and A., Werribee Park, Wyndham.
Chirnside, Robert, Monyong, Little River.
Chirnside and Watson, West Charlton, Yowen Hill.
Childe, John, Reefs, Pleasant Creek.
Chivers, J., Benalla.
Chisholm, Mrs., Kariah, Camperdown.
Christensen, C., Eaglehawk, North Gippsland.
Christensen, Yne. Eaglehawk, North Gippsland.
Chrystal, J. H., Droopsmor, Seymour.
Churchill, Henry, Emu Park, Warragul Park.
Church, —, Sutton Grange.
Clarke, A., Pine Grove, via Rochester.
Clarke, Adolphus Leura, Camperdown.
Clarke, G. H., Cowwarra.
Clarke, John, Terrick Terrick.
Clarke, —, Ingleston, Ballan.
Clarke, —, Emu Hill, Happy Valley.
Clarke, P., Terrick Terrick.
Clarke, R., sen., J.P., Horsham.
Clarke, R., Maree, Casterton.
Clarke, T., vineyard proprietor, and market gardener, Axe Creek.
Clarke, Thomas, Toongabbie.
Clarke, W. J., Numeralla, Sunbury.
Clarke, W. J., Tildersly, Sunbury.
Clarke, William, Minyip.
Clarke, W., Maffra.
Clarke, —, Mount Sturgeon, Dunkeld.
Clapperton, C. J., Amphitheatre.
Clapham, H., Coleraine.
Cay, M., Bagshot.
Clancy, —, Tooan.
Cleary, Jas., Wycheproof.
Cleary, Michael, Mount Wycheproof.
Clements, Jno., Woodford, Warrnambool.
Clements, Thos., Sutherlands, Gunbower.
Clough, Jno., Moyston.
Clyne, Geo., Lake Rowan.
Clyde, J., Howlong.
Coates, S., St. Arnaud.
Coates, W., Bamganie P. O., via Meredith.
Coates, E. C., Casterton.
Cocks Bros., Wild Duck.
Cocks, R. and J., Langwooner.
Cochran, Chas., Dargalong.
Cochrane, J. C., Highton.
Cochrane, J., Hazelwood, Bourke-road, South Camberwell.
Coftey, M., Kewell.
Coffee, P., Riversdale P. O., Avoca.
Coghill, J. L., Dookie South.
Cole, A., Kiata, Dimboola.
Cole, Mrs. Eliz., Darlington.
Cole, Mrs. Nicholas, Cloven Hills, Darlington.
Collins, Francis, Pyke's Flat, M. Ballan.
Collins, Henry, Ballyrogan, Tatyoon.
Collins, Patrick, Minyip.
Collins, Samuel, Devon Farm, Bridgewater.
Collins, Samuel, Bridgewater.
Collins, Thos., Colac.
Colins, W. P., Colac.
Coldham, John, Grassdale, Tahara.
Collier, R. H., Powlett Plains.
Colclough, Thos., Deep Creek, Talbot.
Colledick, —, farmer, Traralgon.
Compston, Arthur, Pleasant, via Horsham.
Conielly, John, Leigh Road.
Combridge, John, Shelford.
Conign Brothers, Murtoa.

Connor, George, Kewell.
Connor, Henry, Lake Bolac.
Connor, J. H., Ryrie-street East, Geelong.
Connor, J., Eldorado, Clear Creek.
Connor, Morris, Tarrawingee.
Conway, Thomas, Upper Emu Creek.
Conway. J., Kilmore.
Conisber. James, Bonegulla via Wodonga.
Condon, W. Jindwick, Buln Buln.
Cooper, A., Bridgewater.
Cook, Archibald. Colac.
Cook. G. W., Horsham.
Cooke, Cecil Pybus, Green Hills, Branxholme.
Coombs. G. E., Mangalore.
Cook, J., Emu Creek.
Cook, P., White Hart Hotel, Pyalong.
Cooper, O., Bridgewater.
Cooper, P., Tooborac Station, P. O.
Cooper, Robert, Laen.
Cooper, W., Lake Rowan.
Cope, A., Macarthur.
Copeland, James, Buln Buln.
Corker, James, Meredith.
Cornish, Thomas, Powlett Plains.
Costello Brothers, Timor.
Cotter, E., Murtoa.
Cotter, J., Werracknabeal.
Cottish. Mrs., Roxby, Gnarwarre.
Coutts Brothers. Powlett, Inglewood.
Coutts, James, squatter, Mitiamo.
Coutts, James, Mitiamo.
Coutts, Peter, Mitiamo.
Courick, P., Koroit.
Cowell, A. A., Brippick, Apsley.
Cowan, James, Myrniong.
Cowper, John, Westgarth.
Cox, James, Terrick Terrick.
Cox, John, Karabeal, Dunkeld.
Cox, John, Casterton.
Cox and Son, Hamilton.
Cox, Thomas, Barrapoort, via Boort.
Cox, Uriah, Lake Rowan.
Cox, W. J., Lucknow, Bullunwad.
Cozens, Ebenezer B., Mount Cairn, Little River.
Crawford, John, Murchison.
Crawford, John, Pine Grove, via Rochester.
Crawford, John, jun., Victoria Valley, Dunkeld.
Crawford, John, Karabeal, Dunkeld.
Crawford, James, Benalla.
Crawford, Robert, Roseneath, Casterton.
Crawford, R., Warrock, Coleraine.
Crawford, William, Victoria Valley, Dunkeld.
Crawford and Dyring, Wagra, Tallangatta.
Craig, Mathew, Ondit.
Craig, S. E., Corack, Donald.
Cranwell, W., Dookie South.
Cranage, W. H., Edenhope.
Creed, James, Cargarie P.O., via Elaine.
Creed, Stephen, Barmonside, Gnarwarre.
Crossley, Edward, Kenilworth, Hamilton.
Crossley, Edward and Eli, Tatyoon, Streatham.
Crossley, James, Kilmore.
Croslie, P., Balmattum.
Crockett, A. T. P., Mansfield.
Crofts, C., Murchison.
Croad, George, Moyston, via Ararat.
Crouch, G. G., Lower Crawford, Heywood.
Crook, J. R., Bacchus Marsh.
Crooke, James E., Bacchus Marsh.
Crowe, John J., Jingellic, Upper Murray, via Wodonga.
Crow, John, Powlett Plains, P.O.
Crouch, John, Westgarth, via Ararat.
Crouin, Mrs., Westgarth, via Ararat.
Crow. W., Ballan.
Crook and Sons, Bacchus Marsh.
Crocker, W. D., Honeysuckle, Violet Town.
Cross, W. A., Chatsworth.
Crossthwaite and M'Caul, Buffalo Station, Myrtleford.
Cruickshank, G., Macarthur.
Cullinane, C., Montajup.
Culnane, E., Mowen.
Cumming Bros., Avon Plains.
Cumming, T. C., Stoney Point, Darlington.
Cumming, William, Toorak.
Cummings, Thomas F., Toorak.
Cummings, —, Mount Fyans, Darlington.
Cunningham, F., Mitiamo.
Cunningham, P., Heathcote.
Cunningham, T., Ganoo Ganoo, Casterton.

VICTORIA.

Cunningham and Hardy, Ranges, Redbank.
Currie, D., c/o. A. Wilson. Esq., Creswick.
Currie, G., Strathmerton, West Shepparton.
Currie, J. L., Lara, Derinallum.
Curdie, Doctor, Tanderook, Camperdown.
Curtain, Thomas, Riversdale P.O., Avoca.
Cusack, J., jun., Euroa.
Cust, W., Rupanyup.
Cussen, W., Merino.
Dahson, H., Burrumbeet.
Daffray, L., farmer, Mitiamo.
Dahlenberg and Sons, Dimboola.
Dalgleish, A. J., Woorndoo.
Dalgleish Bros., Lake Bolac.
Dalgleish, Peter, Woorndoo.
Daly, Anthony, Kewell.
Daly, P., Springbank, Natimuk.
Daley, Jno., Karabeal.
Daley, Jno., Terrick Terrick.
Dalgety, Ibbotson and Co., Geelong.
Daniel and Co., Acheron.
Daniel, Joseph, Inverleigh.
Dandus, Jas., Mansfield.
Dalton, Pat., Hopkins, Warrnambool.
Darragh, J., Ballan.
Dardel, J. H., Batesford.
Darcy, A. V., Sandhurst P. O.
Darcy, Jno., Ondit.
Davon, P., Euroa.
Davidson, A. B., Fanwick.
Davidson Bros., Quintelle Kinloch, near Glenlochy.
Davidson, J. L., Hurd'e Creek, Whorowly.
Davidson, J., Serpentine.
Davidson, W., Hurdle Creek, Wangaratta.
Davies, Captain W., Echuca.
Davies, Thos., Rochester.
Davies, W. E., Echuca.
Davey, Joseph, Stawell.
Day, Fredk., Tarrangine, Dimboola.
Day, James, Pimpinio.
Day, James, Ondit.
Day, Mrs. Ann, Murchison.
Day, Wm., Traralgon.
Day, Wm., Boort.
Dawson, J., Basin Banks, Camperdown.
Dawson, Thos., Condair.
Dawson, Thos., Corop.
Dean, Thos., Goornong.
Dean, W., Phil'ip Island.
Dean, W., Kiata, Dimboola.
De Beare, Warrack P. O.
De Boos, J. and C. L., Ellerslee Estate, Euroa.
De Boltt, —, Bacchus Marsh.
Doe, M. and T., Mount Pyramid.
Deefey, D., Tarrawingee.
Delahay, H., Bacchus Marsh.
Delahunty, Jas., Murtoa.
Delahunty, R., Murtoa.
Dempsey, Edward, Mount Wycheproof.
Dennis, Alexander, jun., Enjulse. Mortlake.
Dennis, R. V., Tarndwarnecourt, Birregurra.
Densley, —, East Ballan.
Doradin, J. F., farmer, Upper Sheepwash.
Devine, A., Curlewis.
Desailly, J. T. { Deighton East.
  Emu Vale.
  Sandy's Creek, Fernbank P.O.
  Faberbera.
Dickison, Joshua, P. O., Donald.
Dickson, P., Bacchus Marsh.
Dickson, T., Indigo Creek, Yackandandah.
Dillon, John, Terrick Terrick.
Dinan, John, Warrnambool.
Dittenich, J., Warragul.
Dixon, H. R., Gisborne.
Dixon, J. E., Chiltern.
Dixon, Jno., Kiata, Dimboola.
Doake. T., Axe Creek.
Dobson, H., Burrumbeet.
Docker, F. G. and B., Wangaratta.
Dodds, Thomas, Pol goleet, Darlington.
Dodd, William, Wangaratta.
Doherty, A., Seymour, Mangalore.
Doig, J. G., Bobinawarrah.
Donald, George, Bungeeltop, via Morrisons.
Donald, James, Bungeeltop, via Morrisons.
Donaldson, J., Harrow.
Donaldson, John. Natimuk.
Donaldson, W., Hughes' Creek, near Avenel.
Donoghue, P., farmer, Mount Cotterell.

Donoghue, Patrick, Morton Plains, via Donald.
Donelan, Robert, Karabeal, Dunkeld.
Donahue, T., Maude.
Doogan, Hugh, Pyalong.
Dooly, J., Bear's Lagoon, Serpentine.
Dorward, Captain George, Echuca.
Doroderain, M., Bridgewater.
Douglas and Co., A., Geelong.
Douglas, H., and Co., Wallan Wallan, Germantown.
Douglas, J., Laanecoorie.
Douglas, William, Boort.
Douse, J., Callawadda.
Dowie, A. F., Lake Side, Moolort.
Dowling, F., Sale.
Dowling, H., Caramut.
Doyle, John, Grassy Gully, Rokewood.
Doyle, John, Dereel.
Doyle, James. Carapook, Casterton.
Drane, Alexander, farmer. Traralgon.
Drane, John, farmer, Traralgon.
Drane, Thomas, farmer, Traralgon.
Draffin, J. W., Dimboola.
Drayton. Jos., Panmure.
Drake. P., Axedale. near Sandhurst.
Draper, T., farmer. Raywood.
Drabsch, —, Dimboola.
Drapeby, —, farmer, Upper Emu.
Dreyer, August, South Branxholme.
Drewry, J., Winchelsea.
Drewitt, Thomas, Heathcote.
Drummond, James, Merino.
Drummond, Mrs., Hookham.
Drury, J., Myrniong P. O.
Duell, Henry, Merton P. O.
Duff, John, Baringhup.
Duff, R. E. C., Malmlample.
Duffus, William, Turkeith.
Dugdale, L., Myrniong.
Duke, John, farmer, Eaglehawk, North Gippsland.
Duke, Lewis, Callawadda, Glenorchy.
Dundas, F. A., Mansfield.
Dundas, James, Buffalo River, Myrtleford.
Dunne, M. J., Koroit.
Dunne, Michael, Winslow.
Dunne, Thomas, Mortlake.
Dunne, William, Wooroonooke, East Charlton.
Dunn, Edmund, Boweya.
Dunn, E., Springs.
Duncan Gordon, Benalla.
Duncan, John. Yuppeekiar Glen, Thompson.
Duncan. William, Sandhurst Road, Heathcote.
Dunbar, William, Pentland Hills.
Dunster, James, Joyce's Creek.
Dwyer, E. J. and J., Dwyer-tead, Buln Buln.
Dwyer, J. J., Bahgallah, near Casterton.
Dwyer, John, Mochamboro, Dwyer's Creek.
Dwyer, Michael, Emu Flat, Lancefield.
Dwyer, Michael, Tahara P.O., near Branxholme.
Dyer, L., Glenlyon.
Eadie and Phillips, Boort.
Eagan, M., Woorndoo, Mortlake.
Eager, F., Carisbrook.
Eagle, C., Newlyn, via Creswick.
Earls, John, Penshurst.
East, G. S., Penhurst.
East, W., Penshurst.
Eastman, Alexander, Goornong.
Eddington, A. C., Ballangeich.
Edelston, S. J., Carapoore.
Edgar, D., Pine Hills. Harrow.
Edgar, J., Koolomert, Casterton.
Edgar, J., Kadnook, Harrow.
Edgar, J. and D., Cannum, Horsham.
Edgar, Samuel, c/o J. Bond, Horsham.
Edgar, W., Koolomert, Casterton.
Edkins, H., Lochiel, via Horsham.
Edmondson, William, Mortat, via Horsham.
Edmundson, William, Elliminook, Birregurra.
Edols, Thomas, Morongoo. Geelong.
Edols and Francis, Tatonga, via Wodonga.
Edrick, O., Serpentine P. O.
Edwards, Edgar H., Kewell.
Edwards, Robert, Mortlake.
Edwards, Benjamin, Hamilton, P.O.
Egan, Anthony, Ondit.
Egan, M., Merton P.O.
Egan Bros., Greendale.
Elder, R. M., Fort Cameron P.O., via East Charlton.
Elliot, E., sheep farmer, Eddington.
Elliot, R., Mount Elliot, Wickliffe Road.

Elliot, R., Watgania, Kiora.
Ellwood, Thomas, Bungeeltop, Ballan.
Emerson, James, Armstrong's.
Enders, J. B., Corop.
Enders, J. B., Union Saw Mills. Trentham.
Ennis, Thomas, Pentland Hills.
Enright, Michael, Carrie. Traralgon.
Eriven, William, Wirchilleba, via Glenorchy.
Ettershank and Eagleston, East Loddon, Serpentine.
Evans, B., Whitefield, West Moyhu.
Evans, Isaac, farmer, Pentland Hills.
Evans, J. R., Warrnambool.
Evans, James, Benalla.
Everett, R. J., Euroa.
Ewance, James, Clover Hill, Warrnambool.
Fabrian, David, Terrick Terrick.
Fallon. M., Condah.
Fanning. Joseph, North Crack, St. Arnaud.
Faueco, F. R., Myrtle Grove. Tatyoon, via Ararat.
Farie, Dr., Dunmore, Oxford.
Faris, W. J., Fern Hills Estate, Balmattum.
Farmers, —, Tarranginie, Dimboola.
Farquar, A. and Son, farmers, Sheepwash.
Farrell, William, New Gisborne.
Fawcett, Joseph, Farmer, Smeaton.
Fay, James. Shirley.
Featherly, H. Montajup, Dunkeld.
Fechner, Ernest, Dimboola.
Feehan, Richard, Powlett South. Wedderburn.
Feighey, James. Kewell West, Horsham.
Fell, John, Reserve Hotel, Conangalt.
Ferguson. Donald, Flowerdale, Broadford.
Ferguson, G. C., Natmiuk.
Ferguson, T. L., Runnymede.
Ferrier, John. Carapook. Casterton.
Ferry, —, Kewell West, Horsham.
Fick, H. M., Goornong.
Field, John, Violet Town.
Field, John, Ballan.
Field, William, Wordiebolne, near Winchelsea.
Fielding, Samuel, Morton Plains.
Findlay, James, Towong, Tintaldra P. O., via Yackandandah.
Finlay Brothers, Tarcombe, Longwood.
Finlay, C. and A., Bethanga.
Finlay, C. and A., Glenormiston, Camperdown.
Finlay, James, Glenmore, Bacchus Marsh.
Finlayson, M., Gunbowar P. O.
Finlayson, P., farmer, Smeaton.
Finn, D., Pleasant Banks, via Natimuk.
Finn, P., Pleasant Banks, via Natimuk.
Finn, Patrick, Torrumbarry.
Finn, Patrick, Mortlake.
Finn, Michael. Mortlake.
Firmin, George, Hazelwood, Gippsland.
Fischer, —, Emu Creek.
Fisher, C. B., Maribyrnong.
Fisher, M., farmer, Emu Point. Raywood.
Fisher, William, Walla Walla.
Fisken, G. B., Buangor.
Fitzgerald, Bryan, Carapook, Casterton.
Fitzgerald, G. S., Mortlake.
Fitzgerald, J., Lake Mowanla, Streatham.
Fitzgerald, —, sheep farmer, Wareek.
Fizelle, T., White Hills.
Flack and Son, Ballan.
Flaming, E. Deep Creek.
Flat, George. and Sons, Parkside, Ballan.
Flattely, Thomas, Cathcart.
Fleming A., Creswick.
Fleming, J., Terrick P. O.
Fleming, James, Echuca.
Fleming, James, Macorne, via Mount Pyramid.
Flett, D., Pentland Hills.
Fletcher, Robert, Ravenswood, Duneed.
Fletcher, William, Gnarwarre.
Flinn, Barbara, Germantown.
Flood. M., Mount Gellibrand.
Flottman, —. Dimboola.
Flynn, J., and Co., Kilmore.
Flynn, James, farmer, Traralgon.
Fogarty, Cornelius, Drysdale.
Foley, Herbert, Hollymount, Pyalong.
Forbes and Co., Burnumbeep, Ararat.
Ford, William, Echuca.
Forest, F., Belfast.
Forrest, John, Mansfield.
Forster, James, Rangeworth, Piper's Creek.
Forsyth, Archibald, Twin Hill, Rochford.
Forsyth, J., Belfast.

Forsyth, Messrs., Kerabeel.
Forsyth, R., and Sons, Mamtoongoon, Mansfield.
Foster, Mrs. Margaret, Wabdallah.
Fowler, —, Glenlyon.
Fox, A. W., Emu Creeck.
Frampton, Jacob, Kewell East.
Francis, Charles, Tatonga, Tallangatta.
Franklin, F., Joyce's Creek.
Fraser, A., Toolong, Belfast.
Fraser, C., and Co., Benalla Station, Benalla.
Fraser, C. F., Pemberley, Malmsbury.
Fraser, Charles, Nalinga.
Fraser, Donald, Moyston, P.O.,
Fraser, P. P., Dimboola.
Fraser, Peter, Evansford.
Fraser, Peter, Dunach Forest.
Fraser, Robert, Lovat Dale, Strathmore.
Fraser, T. C., Lausberg House, Pentland Hills.
Fraser, William, Tallagaroopna, Shepparton.
French, A. E., Bawowgill, Skipton.
Freeman, Michael, Ararat.
Fry, James. Bullarook Estate, Newlyn.
Fry, James, Minnieboro, Glenorchy.
Fry, James, Ballarat.
Fuge, Frederick, Eaglehawk.
Furphy, Isaac. Rushworth.
Gadd, W. B., Avenel.
Gall, J.. Balmattum.
Gallagher, J., Warrigal.
Galletty, R., Half-way House, Glenorchy.
Gamble, Frederick, Mitiamo P.O.
Gardener, William, Durham Ox.
Gardiner, A. M., Baangal. Skipton.
Garratty, Patrick, Tarranginnie, Mount Elgin
Gash, William, jun., Glaumire. Harrow
Gavan. E., Tatooke, Broadford.
Gay, James, Kiata, Dimboola.
Gearing, Bung Bong.
Geddes, James, Woorndoo, Mortlake.
Gee Wah. Dimboola.
Gemmell, J. J., Taripta, via Mooroopna.
Gemson, G., Noorilliue.
Georani, —. Upper Emu Creek.
George, G., Yackandandah.
Gerrand, J. F., Rushworth.
Gibb, M. G., Bridgewater.
Gibb, Septinus, Majorca.
Gibbins, W., Macarthur.
Gibbons, Stephen, Inglewood.
Gibbs, J.. Berwick.
Gibby, W. B., Carabost, Kiamba.
Gibson. H. R.. Malara, by Wentworth.
Gibson, John, Euroa.
Gibson and M'Arthur, Glenample, via Camperdown.
Giddings, J. E., Newbridge.
Gillahan, John. Rochford.
Gillespie, A., The Meadows Rokewood.
Gillespie, A. and J., Stockyard Hill, Beaufort.
Gillespie, John, Shelford.
Gillespie, John. Four Post.
Gillespie, John, Ellerslie, Jarklin.
Gillespie, J., Rokewood.
Gillespie, Peter and D. C., Shelford.
Gillies, John, Jackson's Creek, Ararat.
Gilligan, John, Rochford.
Gillott, Charles, Warrambone, Shelford.
Glancey, James, Bahgallah, Casterton.
Glassford, H. G., Mewburn Park, Maffra, Gippsland.
Gleeson, Martin, Kiora.
Glen, A., Kariah, Camperdown.
Glenny, Thomas, Ballan.
Gloster, A., Barnedown.
Glover, —, Marong.
Glover, —, Bung Bong.
Glover and Edwards. Kerrisdale, via Talla rook.
Glover. W., and Co., Woodend.
Goddard, Arthur, Corop.
Godfrey, William, Gnarwarre.
Golding, —, Benalla.
Golding Bros., Branxholme.
Gooch, John, Piper's Creek.
Good, Edward, Torrumbary.
Good, John, Ingumera, Winsow.
Goodall, Alexander, Corindhap.
Goodall, W., sen.. Warrnambool.
Goode, Joseph, farmer, East Ballan.
Gordon, David, Victoria Valley P.O.
Gordon, Henry, Warragul.
Gordon, Hugh, Ballyrogan.

VICTORIA. vii

Gordon, James, Beckwith P. O.
Gordon, Messrs., Bung Bong.
Gorrie, Alexander, Avon Plains.
Gottard, Jacob, Corindhap.
Gould, E. Maria, Cannum, Werracknabeal.
Goullett, Charles, Dunolly.
Graham Bros., Mount Mercer.
Graham Bros., Lalvaluk, Mount Mercer.
Graham, John, Kialla West.
Graham, Joseph, Mooralla P. O., via Cavendish.
Graham, Mary Ann, Sandy Creek, Jungellie, via Germantown.
Graham, R. H., Euroa.
Graham, —, Greendale.
Grano, G. W. H., Ararat.
Grant, Alexander, Ingliston, Ballan.
Grant, Donald, Moolort.
Grant, George, Pentland Hills.
Grant, George, Metung.
Grant, J., Pentland Hills.
Grant, J. S., Bahgallah, Casterton.
Grant, James, Myrniong.
Grant, James, Raglan.
Grant, John, Hesse.
Grant, John, Myrniong.
Grant, Joseph, Pentland Hills.
Grant, L. A., Mount Cameron.
Grant, Lachlan, Ballyrogan, via Buangor.
Grant, Neil, Rupanyup.
Grant, Peter, Pentland Hills.
Grant, Peter, Egerton.
Grant, R., Tooan.
Grant and Co., Portland.
Grant and Co., Belfast.
Grant, Childe and Co., Corack, St. Arnaud.
Grattan, Humphrey, Gowangardie, Nalinga.
Graves, J. H., M.P., Vaucluse, Richmond.
Graves and Murchison, Chintern Grange, Darraweit.
Gray, Andrew, Terrick Terrick.
Gray, Charles, Nareeb Nareep, Wickliffe.
Gray, P., Coco Dam, Dimboola.
Greaves, Edward, Booryallock, Skipton.
Green, R. and Sons, Springfarm, Baynton.
Green, Geo., Upper Sheepwash.
Green, G. R., Colonial Bank, Branxholme.
Green, H., Black Swamp, Mansfield.
Green, Jas., Upper Sheepwash.
Greene, M. R., Greystanes, Bacchus Marsh.
Greenwell, Geo., Corindhap.
Greenwood, —, Coco Dam, Dimboola.
Greeves, E. G., Borryallock, Skipton.
Gregerson, J., Benalla.
Grieffenhagan, T., Upper Axe Creek.
Grieve, John, Mortlake.
Griffin, P., Arcadia P. O.
Griffiths, G., Werracknabeal.
Griffiths, George, Mangalore.
Griffiths, John, Strathmore.
Griffiths, John J., Mangalore.
Griffiths, Richard, Cannum, Werracknabeal
Griffiths, Thomas, Boort, Wedderburn.
Griffiths, Thomas, Mangalore.
Grimes, Henry, North Barnawartha
Grinter, C., Moolap.
Grist, J., Skipton.
Grylls, Thos., and Son, Laanecoorie
Guilfoyle, Jno., Powlett Plains.
Gundry, Edward, Willow Grove, Wharparilla, Echuca.
Gunivan, W., Benalla.
Gunn, —, Benalla.
Gunn, Donald, Burrumbeet.
Gunn, W., Raywood.
Gunyon, —, Myrniong, Pentland Hills.
Guppy, W., Yonurrang, via Benalla,
Guthridge, R., Sale.
Guthrie, H. M., Wallan Wallan.
Guthrie, Thos., Brim, via Horsham.
Guthrie and Co., Ballarat.
Habel, Carl, Murtoa.
Hackerman, William, Walbundrie.
Hadden, C., Cavendish.
Haddock, John, Tamanick.
Hadland, Charles, Ararat.
Haidhaugh, — Belfast.
Haines, Robert, Rochester.
Hair, Thomas, Warrambean, Shelford.
Haitwick, August, Freshwater Creek.
Haley, W. H., Strathbogie.
Halligan, farmer, near Goornong.

Hall, B. L., Yass.
Hall, David, Rokewood.
Hall, J. M., Anakics.
Hall, Joseph, Park Hill, Kyneton.
Hall, Michael, Break O' Day, Rokewood.
Hall, T. A., Crossy.
Hall, W. and A., Anakies.
Hall and Whiteman, Geelong.
Hallam, F. J., care of Mr. Wilks, Albion Hotel, Stawell.
Hambrock, B., farmer, Eaglehawk, North Gippsland.
Hambrock, Stephen, farmer, Eaglehawk, North Gippsland.
Hamilton, David, Inverleigh.
Hamilton, F. M., Wangoon, Warrnambool.
Hamilton, J. B., Doogalook, Tallarook.
Hamilton, M., Clarendon.
Hamilton, R., Terrick Terrick.
Hamilton, Thomas, Sandon.
Hamilton, Thomas, Greenvale.
Hamilton, Hon. T. F., Riddell's Creek.
Hamilton, W., Durham Ox.
Hamilton, W. D., Tullich, Casterton.
Hamilton, William, Mooroduc, Mornington.
Hamilton and Humphrey, Mount Taylor, Bairnsdale.
Hamling, Thomas, Oak Hill Farm, Bridgewater.
Hammond, George, Winchelsea.
Hannah, A., Boort.
Hannah, Samuel, Lal Lal, Rupanyup.
Hannan, Daniel, Natimuk.
Hansen, H., farmer, Heathcote.
Harbison, W., Phillip Island.
Harborn, —, Doncaster.
Hardiman, James, Mitiamo.
Hardiman, John, Mitiamo.
Hardus, Heinrich, Dimboola.
Hardy, G., farmer, Emu Creek.
Hardy, W. F., Bridgewater.
Hare, Thomas, Half way House, near Shelford.
Harmer, H., Flora Hill, Connella.
Harper, Joseph, Snugborough Park, Woodend.
Harris, D., Concongilla Creek, Great Western.
Harris, F., Buangor P. O.
Harris, J., Casterton.
Harris, James, Lothbridge.
Harrison, H. R., Melton, Elmore.
Harvey, Frederick, Morrison's Diggings P. O.
Harvey, James, St. Arnaud.
Harvey, R. and J., Poplar Flat, Murgheboluc.
Hassett, John, Minyip.
Hassett, Martin, Minyip.
Hastie, John, Ballan.
Hasty, John H., Ballan.
Hawlock, Benjamin, Condah.
Hay Brothers, Kamarooka.
Haycroft, —, Tarranginnie.
Hayes, Edmund, Strathmore.
Hayes, Sarjeant, Echuca.
Hayes, W., Dunolly.
Hazel, James, farmer, Toongabbie.
Heaney, Robert, Condah.
Heard, J. T., Ceres.
Heard, J. T. C., Lake Banks, Tooan.
Heard, G., Natimuk.
Heard, S., and Sons, St. Mary's Lake, Horsham.
Hearn, Eli, Rokewood Junction.
Hearn, Humphrey, Colac.
Hearne, Edward, Lake Wallace, Apsley.
Heath, —, Cobran Station, Hill Plain.
Heaton, William, Rokewood Junction.
Hedley, —, Oxford.
Heffernan, W., Axedale.
Helmes, Joseph, and Sons, Terrick Terrick.
Helyar, George, Kewell.
Henderson Bros., Egerton.
Henderson, C. V., Rosedale.
Henderson, H. C., Mount Pyramid.
Henderson, J., farmer, Bung Bong.
Henderson, John, Tongala, Echuca.
Henderson, John, Benalla.
Henderson, John, South Branxholme.
Henderson, John, Tooan.
Henley, —, Clear Creek, Wangaratta.
Henne, William, Divong.
Hensley, J., Mount Moriac.
Hensley, John, Geelong.
Henty, Edward, Casterton.
Hepple, W., Gunbower P. O.
Herbertson, A., Chapman's, Moyston.

PASTORAL AND AGRICULTURAL DIRECTORY.

Herbertson, W., Chapman's, Moyston.
Herrick, P. M., Pyramid.
Hetherill, —, Yambuck.
Hetherington, S., Balmoral.
Hetherington, W. S., Elizabeth-street, Melbourne.
Hewatson, James Watchill.
Hewitt, W., Dookie South.
Hewitt, W., and Son, Rupanyup North.
Heyward, T., Hearman's Forest.
Hibbett, —, farmer, Emu Creek.
Hick, John, Ardonachie, Macarthur.
Hickey, John Killawara.
Higgins, James, Winchelsea.
Highett, J. M., Mitiamo.
Highett, Hon. William, Maindample.
Hill, A. G., Stratford Lodge, Medcalf.
Hill, E., Warock.
Hill, G. H., Noradjuha.
Hill, H. Murchison.
Hill, John, Tarnagulla.
Hill, Theo., Crossover Junction.
Hill, Thomas, Maude.
Hill, W., Kewell.
Hindhough, J. R., Boojorie, Moe.
Hine, W., Bacchus Marsh.
Hines, F. P., Newarpurr, Apsley.
Hinley, J., Milawa, Oxley.
Hinsh, H. T., Baringhup.
Hinton, Captain, Clear Creek, Eldorado.
Hirth Brothers, Dimboola.
Hoar, M., Kiata, Dimboola.
Hobart, William, Nagambie.
Hobbs, John, Waurn Ponds.
Hobbs, John. Belmont.
Hobbs, William, Green Hills. Horsham.
Hobby, W., Campi ell's Creek.
Hobson, E., Tooleybuc.
Hocking, R., Gordon.
Hoddinot, James. grazier, Toongabbie.
Hoddinot, W., Castle Hill.
Hodgett Bros., Landsborough.
Hogan, F., Wallan Wallan.
Hogan, Thomas, Kellalac.
Hogan, —, Kewell.
Hogg, W., Strathbogie.
Hole, Thomas, Winchelsea.
Holland. B., Kewell West, Horsham.
Holloway, Edward, Tragonell.
Holloway, George, and Co., Duck Swamp Station, Durham Ox.
Holloway, George, and Co., Boort Station, Boort.
Holloway, Seward, Tyntyndyer, Swan.
Holmes, Andrew. Casterton.
Holmes, E. R., Sutherland. Gunbower P. O.
Holmes, John, farmer. Strathfieldsaye.
Holmes, Robert, Lake Rowan.
Holmes, S. B., Winchelsea.
Holmes, William, East Charlton.
Holten, Thomas, Greenfell.
Home, J., Claremont. Cambrian Hill, Ballarat.
Hona, Martin, Portland.
Honeychurch, J., farmer, Goornong.
Hood, Robert, Morriang. Hexham.
Hood, W. W., Barton, near Ararat.
Hope, George Darriwil. Moorabool.
Hope, R. A., Fernside Apsley.
Hope. Dr. T. C. Inverleigh.
Hopkins. Arthur, Murdeduke, Winchelsea.
Hopkins, J. R., Wormbeti, Winchelsea.
Hopwood, Robert, Macorna, via Pyramid.
Horne, John, Myrniong.
Horne, W., Mitiamo.
Horne, William, farmer, Traralgon, South Gippsland.
Horwood, J., Sandhurst.
Horwood, Joel. Bridgewater Park, Bridgewater.
Hoskins, Thos., Violet Town.
Houlahan, —, Ballyrogan, Buangor.
Houleston John, Derby.
Hourigan, Jas. Crossley near Koroit.
Houston. J., Newbridge-on-Loddon.
How, Michael, Ondit.
Howe, J. G., Daylesford.
Howe, Martin. Macarthur.
Howe Wm., Pig Hill, Mount Cole.
Howell Thomas, Greenhills, Penshurst.
Howell. W. T., Strathbogie.
Howell and Purch Amphitheatre, Avoca.
Hudson, W., Bowman's Forest.
Hughes, Thomas. Durham Ox.
Hume, Thomas. Dallarburn, Buln Buln.

Hume, D., Moyston.
Hume and Goodwin, Rupanyup.
Humphries, Fred., Toongabbie.
Humphries, P., Toongabbie.
Hunt, Hugh, South Brighton.
Hunter, James, Wordiebolne, Winchelsea.
Hunter, Thos., Windieboluk, Winchelsea.
Huntley, J. L., Glen Huntly, Macarthur.
Huon, Wm., De Kerrillian, Wodonga.
Hurnall, John, Garden Gully, Armstrongs.
Hurst, E., Eumerella East, Macarthur.
Hurst, Henry, Carisbrook.
Hurst, John, Romsey.
Hurst, Jno., Lancefield Road.
Hurstfield, Randal, Ararat.
Husband, A., Lake Rowan.
Hutchins Bros., Glywillen. Stawell.
Hutchinson, Archd., Goornong.
Hutchinson, H.. c/o J. Bond. Horsham.
Hutchinson. J., farmer. Mitiamo.
Hutchinson, John, Murchison.
Hutton Bros., Belfast.
Hutton Bros., Clear Creek. Eldorado.
Hutton, D. and J.. Rhymney Reef. Ararat P. O.
Hutton, J. A. and T., Cheviot Hills, Mount Rouse.
Hutton, R., Bruk Bruk, Coleraine.
Hyatt, John M., Mitiamo.
Hyem, W., Beechworth.
Hymers, Thos., Yamirp.
Iliffe, John, Dixon's Swamp.
Ingham, M., Quarry Hotel Axedale.
Ingham, N., farmer. Axedale.
Inglis, J., Tangambalanga. Kiewa.
Inglis, J. O., Ingliston Ballan.
Inglis and M'Donald, Buchan, Buchan.
Ingram, E., Book Book. Tarcutta.
Irving, Charles, Bald Hill. Dunkeld.
Jacob, Joseph, Kialla West.
Jackson, F. B., Sandford, Casterton.
Jackson, John, Sandford, Casterton.
Jackson, J. H., Sandford.
Jackson, W., Argoon.
James and Brooks, Drysdale.
James, John, Panoobamawn.
James, W., Runnymede.
James, Rich., Crowlands.
James, W. Colles. Spring Hill, Moe.
Janetsky and Sons, Dimboola.
Jarret, J. and H., Kyneton.
Jarret, Job, Mangalore.
Jasper, Thomas. Hyanimi P. O.
Jasper, Thomas, Mitiamo P. O.
Jasperson, J. H., Lake Rowan.
Jeffrey, John, Lowsdale P. O.
Jeffrey, William, Coimadai P. O.
Jenkins, Allan, Cooramook, Woodford.
Jenkins, David. Sheephill.
Jenkins, Dougal, Cooramook, Woodford.
Jenkins, Duncan, Cooramook, Woodford.
Jenkins, Jenkin, Woodford, Warrnambool.
Jenkins, John, Winterevali, Buckland.
Jennings, George, Woodside, Casterton.
Jewell, Edwin, Clovelly Farm, Bridgewater.
Jobson, R. and A., Kyneton.
John, John, Bridgewater.
Johns, Edward, Condair.
Johnson, A., The Gums, Carapook, Casterton.
Johnson, Alfred, Woodford, Warrnambool.
Johnson, Archibald, Tahara.
Johnson, B., Quira (grazing right), Bairnsdale
Johnson, D., Boolahpool.
Johnson, David, Strangways.
Johnson, Henry, Condair.
Johnson, James. Shelbourne.
Johnson, John, Fernihurst.
Johnson, Joseph, Bradford Creek. Laanecoorie.
Johnson, R., Nog Nog, W. A., Myrtle Creek.
Johnson, R., Myrniong.
Johnson, R. H., Alexandra.
Johnson, G. W., Ellison, Lauriston.
Johnstone, E., Easton, Colac.
Johnstone, John, Tower Hill. Illowa.
Johnstone, Thomas, Pyramid Creek, Kerang.
Johnstone, W., Neoyong, Ensay.
Johnstone, W. W., Purnim, Woodford.
Jones, Arthur, Camperdown.
Jones, Wononga Creek.
Jones, E. A., Ellangowan, Heywood.
Jones, Edward, farmer, Cowwarr.
Jones, G., Upper Macedon.
Jones, J., Kiata, Dimboola.

VICTORIA.

Jones. John, Goornong.
Jones, John, Cooramuck, Warrnambool.
Jones Joseph, Kerang.
Jones, Lloyd Avenel.
Jones. Thomas Sandy Creek North, Stratford.
Jones William, Sheepwash.
Jones. William, Cooramuck, Warrnambool.
Junoe, D., Gisborne.
Joyce, Alfred. Norwood, Maryborough.
Kane, W. C., Warrabiel.
Kaufmann, L., Dunkeld.
Kaye, J., Maryborough.
Keady, Pat.. Nagambie.
Kearney, Michael, Noorilim.
Kearney, William, Glenthompson.
Keath, D., St. Arnaud.
Keefe, A. O , farmer, Axedale.
Keefte, H., Horsham.
Keenan, Patrick, Coromby, near Murtoa.
Kelly, Henry, Eddington P. O.
Kelly, James, Minyip.
Kelly and Mortimer, Bridgewater.
Kelly, Phillip, Mangalore, via Seymour.
Kelly, P. J., Burrowije, Upper Murray, via Wodonga.
Kelly, R., sheepfarmer, Powlett Plains.
Kelly, Thomas, Warrambine, Hesse.
Kelly, Thomas, Nekeya Moyston.
Kelly, T. J. D., Langley Vale, Langley.
Kelsall, J., Buninyong.
Kelsall, J., Werracknabeal.
Kemp. James, Costerfield.
Kemp, R., Durham Ox.
Kennedy, —, Kiata, Dimboola.
Kennedy, —, jun., Kiata, Dimboola.
Kennedy, David, Union, Woolsthorpe.
Kennedy, J., Glenorchy.
Kennedy, Messrs., sheep-farmers, Bungeeltop, Ballan.
Kennet, John, Dookie South.
Kerby, H., Tarkedia.
Ker, W. L., Killingworth, Yea.
Kerr, James, farmer, Bacchus Marsh.
Kerr, James, Rockbank Farm, Gisborne.
Kerr, John, Kerang.
Kerr, Michael, Ondit.
Kerr, Robt., Parwan, Bacchus Marsh.
Kettyle, Geo., Corindhap.
Keyte, —, Nathnuk.
Keyte, H. R., Kiata, Dimboola.
Kiernan, Robert, Longwood.
Kilby, D., Branxholme.
Kilby, James, Elderslie, Apsley.
Kilgarriff, M., Kellalac.
Kilpatrick, A. and A., Macorna, via Mt. Pyramid.
Kilpatrick, John, Green Hills, Winche'sea.
Kimpton, Thos. W., Watgania, near Ararat.
Kimpton, W. T., Kalymna, Moyston.
King, Charles A., Casterton.
King, E., Minyip.
King, George, Kingston.
King, Hugh, Minyip.
King, Michael, Mount Shadwell, Mortlake.
King, Robert, Tatook (Grazing-right), Bruthen.
King, T., farmer, Eaglehawk, North Gippsland.
King, W., farmer, Eaglehawk, North Gippsland.
King, William, Gorunni, Ararat.
Kinghorn, F., Byaduk.
Kinimonth, James, Barunah Plains, Hesse.
Kinsella, P. J., Muroon.
Kipping, Thomas, Merton.
Kipping, W., Merton.
Kirby, James, Sheephills, Minyip.
Kirby, W., Blakeville, near Ballan.
Kirchner, Heinrich, Tarkedia.
Klows. John, Dimboola.
Knaggs, James, Bernchah, Hamilton.
Knight, John, Tooan.
Knight, John, Westbrook, Lake Bolac.
Knight, Thomas, Goornong.
Knight and Lydiard, Kooroongah, Belfast.
Knott, Joseph, farmer, Lockwood.
Krieg, Charles, Dimboola.
Kyne, Owen, Major Plains, Benalla.
Lacey, J., Buln Buln.
Laidlaw, W., Mundara, Edenhope.
Laidlaw, W. G., Ozenkadnook.
Laidlaw, W., and Co., Newlands, Apsley.
Laing, J., sen., Echuca.
Lalor, W., St. Hubert's.
Lamb, W., Camperdown.

Lambell, W., Strathbogie.
Lambrick, J., Major Road, Benalla.
Lamont, J., Darlington.
Lane, Alfred, Gone Station, near Kerang.
Lane, F., Maryvale, Harrow.
Lane, John, Warranooke Lake, East Charlton.
Lane, Joseph, Marnoo.
Lane, Martin, Woorndoo.
Lane, Richard, Warrnambool.
Lanyon, H. S., Lake Boort.
Lanyon, R., Boort.
Lanyon, T., Tarnagulla.
Larkie, Michael, a'Beckett Plains, Inglewood.
Larkins. —, sheep-farmer, Bridgewater.
Laurie, J. P. D., Moulamein, via Swan Hill.
Lavender, Thomas, Woolville, Mia Mia.
Lawlaw, William, Allansford.
Lawler, Thomas, Turkeith.
Lawson, A., Kewell.
Lay, John, East Ballan.
Lay, W., Ballan.
Leahy, Alfred, Shepparton Park, Shepparton.
Leak, John, Winchelsea.
Leake, John, Merino.
Learmonth, A. and R., Tarkedia (Aregrea loose bag).
Leason, James, Lillymar Cove. Dimboola.
Ledden, John, Yambuck.
Ledwell, George, Hawthorne Hill, Bamganie Flat, via Meredith.
Ledwell, James, Rokewood.
Lee, John, sen., St. Mary's, Warrnambool.
Leech, H. A., Bridgewater.
Leech, H. F., Lake Boort.
Lees, James, Runnymede.
Legg, Thomas T., Kyneton.
Lehman, — , Dimboola.
Leich, H. T., The Grange, Woolobee, Lake Boort.
Leijo, Peter, Rokewood.
Leishman, John, Kingston.
Le Louef, A., Gembrook.
Lellicoe, Andrew, Worndoo, Mortlake.
Lemont, Farquhar, Mount Fyans, Darlington.
Lennon, James, Rokewood.
Lennox, Marshall, Moyston.
Leslie, — , Swan Hill.
Leslie, Alexander, Pimpinio, Horsham.
Lethbridge, R. C., Toongabbie.
Lett, W., Williamsvale, Merriman's Creek, Stratford.
Leverett, William, Point Henry.
Lewers, S., Bank N.S.W., Linton.
Lewington, J., Bundalong.
Lewis, George, farmer, Emu Creek.
Lewis, Hugh, Merino.
Lewis, J., Yambuk.
Lewis, J., Moyhu.
Lewis, Lewis, Boort.
Lewis, Owen, Mount Duneed.
Lewis, Thomas, Jackson's Creek, Ararat.
Lewis, W., Moyhu.
Lewis, W., Stoneleigh, Beaufort.
Lewis, W. H., Pine Lodge, Benalla.
Liddy, P., farmer, near Goornong.
Light, Thomas, Tooan.
Limbley, Thomas, farmer, Traralgon, South Gippsland.
Lindsay, —, Nattie Yallock.
Lindsay, P., Macarthur.
Lindsey, James Quamby, Woolsthorpe.
Lintott, E., Buln Buln.
Liston, Thomas, Shirley P. O.
Little, J., Eversley.
Livingstone, D., Argyle Park, Kellalac.
Lloyd. T., Stratford.
Lloyd, W. H., Dimboola.
Lloyd and Atkinson, Wimeani, via Dimboola.
Locke, J., Oakleigh.
Loeman, W., Bulla.
Loffell, J. P., Dimboola.
Logan, John, and Co., Mount Elephant, Lismore.
Logan, J. M., and Co., Black Logan P. O., St. Germain.
Logie, Thomas, Kilmore.
Logie, W., Kilmore.
Loney, James, Darragon
Loney, J., Kewell.
Long, John, St. Arnaud.
Lord, W., Karabeal.
Loughran, Mrs. B., Wordiebolne, Winchelsea.

PASTORAL AND AGRICULTURAL DIRECTORY.

Lovell, James, farmer, Toongabbie, North Gippsland.
Low, William, Mornington.
Lowe, Joseph, Mortlake P. O.
Lowe, Thomas, farmer. Upper Sheepwash.
Lowe, W. and T., Nurriong, Ensay.
Lueff, H. A. W., Terrick Terrick East.
Luff, E., Kewell.
Lumsden, Alexander, sen., Mepunga, Warrnambool.
Lush, Robert, Woolegal Road, Tarnagulla.
Luxton, Thomas, Kangaroo Flat.
Luxton, W., Mount Eccles, Macarthur.
Lyall, James, Heywood.
Lyell, John, Bacchus Marsh.
Lynch Brothers, Kewell.
Lynch, Matthew, Mitiamo.
Lynch, Thomas, Watgania P. O., near Moyston.
Lyon, C. H., Ballan Ballan.
Lyon, P., Laanecoorie.
Mack, Austin, The Prairie, Rochester.
Mack, Joseph, Berry Bank, Cressy.
Mackintosh, A., and Son, Carr's Plains, Glenorchy.
Mackintosh, C., Condah.
Mackintosh, M., South Branxholme.
Mackintosh, Murdoch, Culqmundie, Stratford.
Macrae, Alex., Horse Shoe Bend, Noorat.
Macrae, Farquhar, Glenormiston, Terang.
Mackay, Jno., Gunbower P. O.
Mackay, J., Baringhup.
Mackay, J., Terrick Terrick.
Mackay, I., Torrumbarry.
Mackay, Wm., Greenville.
Mackie, Jno., Baringhup.
Mackie, Jno., Powlett Plains, Inglewood.
Macbean, Alex., Howlong, via Chiltern.
Mackredie Bros., Piangie, Swan Hill.
Maconochie, Jas., Westbank, Camperdown.
Mackin, Josh., grazier, Powlett Plains.
Macarthur, John, Croxton.
Macabe, Mrs., Moyston.
MacDonald, Horseshoe Bend, Noorat.
Madden, S., Kewell.
Magill, Wm., Rokewood.
Mahoney, Geo., Ann Vale, Dunkeld.
Maher, M., Minyip.
Malcolm, Alex., Sheepfields, Kinloch.
Malone Bros., Jane Vale, Laanecoorie.
Malcolm, James, Mount Ridley P. O., Craigieburn.
Malone, Jas., Moorooky.
Malone, James, Smeaton.
Maloney, Pat., Terang.
Maltby, T. K., Barnedown.
Malone, Wm., Doble's Bridge.
Manti, A. farmer, Upper Sheepwash.
Mandeville, A. and Co., Lake Coorong, via Horsham.
Mann Bros., Mount Pyramid.
Mann, Ephraim, Sheep Hills.
Manning, G., Merrigum P.O.
Manifold, J. and P., Camperdown.
Managhan, John, Torrumbarry.
Managhan, Maurice, Torrumbarry.
Mankey, Tobias, Cargarie P.O., via Elaine.
Martin, A., Minthill, Bairnsdale.
Martin, Charles, Chiltern.
Martin, F. and M., Kerang.
Martin, James F., Brown's Plains.
Martin, J. F., Chiltern.
Martin, James, sheep-farmer, Yea.
Martin, Michael, Smeaton.
Martin, Norman, near Shelford.
Martin, Sam., farmer, Strathfieldsaye.
Martin, William, Milloo, Runnymede.
Martin, William, farmer, Strathfieldsaye.
Marshall, D., Baringhup.
Marshall, George, Violet-street, Sandhurst.
Marshall, Robert, Wild Duck P.O.
Marshall, R. F., Ballan.
Marfleet, J., Lincoln Grange, Durham Ox.
Manabel, J. C., Brandy Creek.
Marebant, John J., Werracknabeal.
Marong, P., Hughes Creek, near Avenel.
Marchant, Samuel, Cannum, Werracknabeal.
Mason Bros. Clifton, Hamilton.
Mason, F. Watgania.
Mason, R., Moyston.
Mason, W., farmer, Traralgon.
Mathieson, Alexander. Coleraine P.O.
Mathieson, E., Mia Mia.

Mathieson, E., Mia Mia.
Mathieson, Murdoch, Dwyer's Creek, near Casterton.
Mathieson, John, Quambatook.
Matheson Bros., Ullswater, Apsley.
Matheson, Donald, Lal Lal, Rupanyup.
Matheson, George, Winchelsea.
Mathews, J. H., Point Henry.
Mathews, P., Mortat.
Mathews, W., Jalukar, Moyston.
Mathews, William, Noorat.
Mathews, William, Myrtle Grove, Terang.
Mathews, W. J., Point Henry.
Matchett, J., Sandhurst.
May, Andrew, Mayfield Park, Fernihurst.
May, John, sheep farmer, Joyce's Creek.
Mayberry, D., Tooan.
Mayberry, William, Natimuk.
Meallin, G. R., Swan Hill.
Meery, John, Kilmore, Bruthen.
Meery, John, Deighton, West Bruthen.
Meedham, P., Yea.
Meldrum, T., Heywood.
Menzies, William, Haugh, Skipton.
Meredith, Gilbert, Inverleigh.
Merriman, George, Yass.
Messer, W. C., Yarrock.
Messer, W. C., Bonginni, Hamilton.
Michael, Hans, Goornong.
Michael, James, Hughes Creek, via Avenel.
Michael, J., farmer, Newbridge.
Midglu, A. and E., Durham Ox.
Midgby, R., Durham Ox.
Middleton, J., Mount Pyramid.
Milner, C. H., Freshwater Creek.
Mill, David, sheep-farmer, Yea.
Mills, George, Glenmona Park, Bung Bong.
Milwain, H., Doulach Park, Malmsbury.
Miller, F. G., Dimboola.
Miller, James, Nooriline, Murchison.
Miller, John, Morton Plains.
Miller, John, Jallukar, Moyston.
Miller, Mrs. H. Ellen, Beaufort.
Miller, Will, Koolamart, Casterton.
Miller, William, farmer, Merri, Warrnambool.
Mills, S. F., Goornong.
Millear, Thomas, Edgarly, Maroona.
Ming, S., Pyalong.
Missen, John, sen., Warrion, Cundare.
Missen, John, Warrion.
Mitchell, A. and D., Natimuk.
Mitchell, Josiah, Skilemergh Hall, Kyneton.
Mitchell, J., farmer, Newbridge.
Mitchell and Kennedy, Glenorchy.
Mitchell, P., Milloo, Elmore.
Mitchell, Robert, Macorme, via Mount Pyramid.
Mitchell, Sir W. H. F., Darfold, Kyneton.
Mitchell, Thomas, Rupanyup.
Mitchell, T., Bungeeluke.
Mitchell, Thomas, Bringembrong, Upper Murray.
Moffat, Robert, Ravenswood.
Moffat, William, Bunyang, Rochester.
Mogg, V. N., Swan Water, St. Arnaud.
Moller, P., Dimboola.
Moncrief, A., Avenel.
Monk, J., Grandville.
Monckton, J. R., Redesdale, Benalla.
Monohan, P., Lake Town.
Moore, Alexander, Bald Hill, Dunkeld.
Moore Brothers, Lawloit, Dimboola.
Moore, James, sheep-farmer, Joyce's Creek.
Moore, S., Mount Mercer.
Moore, W., Buffalo River, Egerton.
Moore, W., Myrtle.
Mooney, J. and L., Mooney's Gap, Ararat.
Mooney, John, Torrumbarry.
Mooney, John, Torrumbarry.
Mooney, W. and J., Wando Vale, Casterton.
Morris, Alex., Minyip, Horsham.
Morrison, D., Glen'elth, by East Charlton.
Morrison, G., Craigie, Avenel.
Morrison, G. H., Meloul, Swan Hill.
Morrison, H. C., Myrniong.
Morrison, Jno., Towanmire, East Charlton.
Morrison, Jas. D., Mangalore.
Morrison, J., Oxley Plains.
Moran, Edw., Mount Tournes, Koroit.
Morgan, Edward, Inverleigh.
Morgan, F. J., Mitiamo.
Morgan, J. P., Hughes Creek, via Avenel.
Morrisy, D., Terrick Terrick.

VICTORIA.

Morey, E., c/o T. Young, Danagon.
Morton, G., Labona, Ballarat.
Morrissy, J. P., Nagambie.
Morris, S., Bealiba.
Mortray, S., Yambuk.
Moreton, Saml., Lake Bolac.
Motherwell, A., Woodfield, via Longwood.
Motherwell, A., Woodfield, Doon.
Motherwell, C., Woodford. Doon.
Mote, Joseph, sheep-farmer, Hamilton.
Mountjoy Bros., Wharparilla.
Mountjoy, Caleb, Wharparilla.
Moylan, John, Mount Koroit.
Muir, J., Myrniong.
Mullins, J., Echuca.
Mullins, J., and Sons, Eddington.
Mumford, Coles. Rushworth.
Mummery, C., Bowman's Forest.
Munro Brothers, Fair View, Burrereo.
Munro, D. McG., Woorndoo.
Munro, E. and P., Sandhurst.
Murray, A. S., Dunnolun, Casterton.
Murray, A. and M., Colac.
Murray, A., Campbell-street, Ararat.
Murray, D., Toolamba.
Murray, J. S., Casterton.
Murray, James, farmer, Moorookyle.
Murray, Robert, Freshwater Creek.
Murray, T. C , Warrions, Larpent.
Murray, William, Dunrobin, Casterton.
Murphy, Arthur, Murtoa P. O.
Murphy, D., Oxley.
Murphy, H., Hawkesdale.
Murphy, James, Casterton.
Murphy, Martin, Kewell.
Murphy, Mrs., Mount Egerton Hotel, Egerton.
Murphy, Patrick, Terrick Terrick East.
Murrell, E., Pyramid Hill P. O.
Murrowood, G., Wilduck P. O.
Musgrave, William, Yarrarara, via Germantown.
Myers, J. and J., Myrniong.
McAdam, George, Lethbridge.
McAdam, R., East Charlton.
McAllister and Sons, Callawadda.
McAndrew, J., Greendale.
McAndrew, J., Kangaroo Grounds.
McAndrew, W., Kangaroo Ground, Tallangatta.
McArthur, Dugald, Watgania.
McArthur, Duncan, Wychetella.
McArthur, P., Menningworth, Camperdown.
McArthur, Peter, Merringorret, Camperdown.
McArthur and Sons, Victoria Valley, Dunkeld.
McBride, —, St. Arnaud.
McCabe, Edward, Moyston.
McCall, Allen, Molesworth Park. Darlington.
McCallum, D., Ardgarten, Branxholme.
McCallum, Mrs., Dean's Marsh.
McCallum, Neil, Wychetella.
McCann, C. A., Casterton.
McCard, William, Little River.
McCarthy, D., farmer, Waterhole, Murphy Creek, Laanecoorie.
McCarthy, John, Lake View, Corop.
McCarthy, Michael, grazier, Green Hills, Winslow.
McCarthy, Richard, Condah.
McCarthy, W., Mount Jeffcott, Donald.
McClure, James, c/o J. Fry and Co., Horsham.
McClure, John, Natimuk.
McClusky, P., Myrniong.
McColl, James, Yat Nat. Balmoral.
McConachie, G., Burrum View, Glenorchy.
McConachie, J., Lismore.
McConachie, John, Burrum, Glenorchy.
McConachy, R., Mirnie, Winchelsea.
McConnel, —, Mysia.
McCormack, J., Beveridge.
McCormack, J., Mount Mistake, Buangor.
McCormack O., Terrick Terrick P. O.
McCormack, T., Dooan.
McCormack, Francis, Lake Rowan.
McCrae, Kenneth, Tooan, via Horsham.
McCredie, H. A., Piangil, Swan Hill.
McCuish, C., Natimuk.
McCulloch, W. G., Maryborough.
McCullough, A., sheep-dealer, Kangaroo Flat.
McCullough, F., Clunes.
McDonald, A., Werracknabeal.
McDonald, A., Condah.
McDonald, —, May Bank, Goornong.
McDona'd, Angus, G'edewood, Rupanyup.
McDonald Bros., Rocky Point, Ararat.

McDonald Bros., Oak Hills, Werracknabeal.
McDonald, Chas., Mooroopna.
McDonald, D., Carapooee, Coleraine.
McDonald, D. M., and Co., Murtoa.
McDonald, Donald, Carrarie.
McDonald, D. and M., Toorak, Mortlake.
McDonald, D. W., Narrabiel.
McDonald, Ewen, Warrion.
McDonald, Ewen, Terang.
McDonald, G. R., farmer, Heathcote.
McDonald, G., Carapooee. Coleraine.
McDonald, G., Deurang, Coleraine.
McDonald, Geo., Carapook.
McDonald and Greenwell, Corindhap.
McDonald, Hugh, Cannum School, via Horsham.
McDona'd, Hugh, Mount Ararat, Cathcart.
McDonald, Jno., grazing right, Glenaladale North, Coongulmerang.
McDonald, Jno., Fern Bank, Panmure.
McDonald, Jno., Bahgallah, Coleraine.
McDonald, J. and K., Banyena, via Glenorchy.
McDonald, J., Deurang, Coleraine.
McDonald, J., Panmure.
McDonald, J., Kerang.
McDonald, John, Garooc, Panmure.
McDonald, Murdoch, Noorat.
McDonald, M. and T., Mount Fyans, Darlington.
McDonald, M., Wallalo, Glenorchy.
McDonald, Neil, Echuca.
McDonald, P., Mount Egerton.
McDonald, R., Dowding, Coleraine.
McDonald, S., Noorat, Terang.
McDona'd and Sons, Toorak, Mortlake.
McDonald, Wm., Dimboola.
McDonald, W. H., Corindhap.
McDonald, Wm., Parwan.
McDougall, A., Lcruefield, Tahara.
McDougall, A. C., Spring Bank, Hedi, Moyhu.
McDougall, Allan, Parupa Park, Lake Bolac.
McDougall, Arch., Corack, St. Arnaud.
McDougall, Archd., Spring Bank, Glen Rowan.
McDougall, J., Bundalong, near Wangaratta.
McDougall, Jno., Kinneypaniel.
McEachran, Wm., Wilkin, Casterton.
McElvie, W., Mount Wycheproof.
McEvoy, Thos., Carrapooee. Coleraine.
McEvoy, Thos., Baygallah. near Casterton.
McEwan, James, Arapiles, Horsham.
McFarland, J., Glenaladale, South Coongulmerang.
McFarlane, D., Maldon.
McFarlane, Malcolm. Minyup, via Horsham.
McFarlane, Walter, Long Lake, Kerang.
McFarland, Wm. and Hy., Bacchus Marsh.
McFeters, Wm., Corop.
McFighe, —, Jackson's Creek, Westgarth, Mount Ararat.
McGann, Wm., Kiora.
McGeoch, —, Mount Jeffcott, Donald.
McGeorge, Bros., Gisborne.
McGhie, Matthew, Dry Lake, Warrnambool.
McGillivray, A., Terrick Terrick.
McGliph, A., Rupanyup North.
McGliph, D., Rupanyup North.
McGliph, N., Rupanyup North.
McGinnis, Jas., Werracknabeal.
McGinniskin, —, Tarkedin P. O.
McGonigal, S., St. Arnaud.
McGrane, R., Bacchus Marsh.
McGregor, D., Milawa.
McGrigor, D., Branxholme.
McGrigor and Malcolm. Callawadda.
McGuffie, —, Kinneypaniel.
McGuinness, Jas., Purnim, Warrnambool.
McGuiness, Jas., Dookie North.
McGuinness, —, Mount Cole.
McHalley, D. Kinneypaniel.
McIltree, H., Biggera, Upper Murray.
McIncrow, —, farmer, Upper Emu.
McIlvena, Robt., Horsham.
McInnes, D. and Co., Wychetella.
McInnes, J., Mount Elgin, Dimboola.
McInnes, S., Bukrabanyule.
McIntosh, Angus, Tragwell.
McIntosh, Evan, Bungeeltop, Morrison's.
McIntosh, Jno., Kewell West.
McIntosh, N., Beaufort.
McIntosh and Sons, Callawadda, Glenorchy.
McIntyre, A., Koolamart, Casterton.
McIntyre, A., Mount Moriac.
McIntyre, John, Kilnaborris, North Hamilton.
McIntyre, J. J., Green Hills.

McIntyre, John, Meadow, via Bowna.
McIntyre, J. P., Macorna, via Mount Pyramid.
McIntyre, J. S., Jallukar, Rhymney Reef.
McIntyre, Mrs., Glenroe, Penshurst.
McIntyre, Matthew, Victoria Valley, Dunkeld.
McIntyre, Mrs. Janet, Kerabeal, Dunkeld.
McIntyre, Peter, Kewell West.
McIntyre, P., Mawallock, Beaufort.
McIntyre and Scott, Victoria Valley.
Mackay, A. B., Warrnambool.
Mackay, W. S., The Grange, Everton.
McKay, Alexander, Glendonald, Creswick.
McKay, Andrew, Joyce's Creek.
McKay, Charles, Wirchilliba.
McKay, Hugh, Woodford, Warrnambool.
McKay, James, Gunbower.
McKay, John, Terrick Terrick.
McKay, Miss, Larpent.
McKay and Sons, Clarendon.
McKee Bros., Mount Wallace, Ballan.
McKellar, N. P., Elmore.
McKellar, Archibald, Hesse.
McKellar Bros., Tarrone, Koroit.
McKellar, D., Kirkella, Stawell.
McKellar, Thomas, Strathkellar, Hamilton.
McKelar, T. John, Tarrone, Kirkstall.
McKenna, Laurence, Montajup P. O.
McKenney, W. G., Euroa.
McKenzie, A., Connewarran, Mortlake.
McKenzie, Alexander, Moy Park, Kellalac.
McKenzie, C. A., Worrough, Tallarook.
McKenzie, D., Kolora, Terang.
McKenzie, Donald, Wallaloo.
McKenzie, D. and T., Burnt Creek, Horsham.
McKenzie, Donald, Lismore.
McKenzie, Donald, Chepstowe.
McKenzie, Duncan, Allendale, Durham Ox.
McKenzie, F. and J., Dimboola.
McKenzie, G., Yea.
McKenzie, G. and R., Dimboola.
McKenzie, J., Wyuna.
McKenzie, J., Bundalong.
McKenzie, James, Wallaloo, Glenorchy.
McKenzie, John, Thalia, Mount Wycheproof.
McKenzie, John, Rupanyup North.
McKenzie, John, Flodden Field, Cressy.
McKenzie, Kenneth, Dunmunkle, Minyip.
McKenzie, Kenneth, Clonbumane Station, Wandong.
McKenzie, Roderick, Dimboola.
McKenzie, William, Honeysuckle Swamp, Winchelsea.
McKewer, James, farmer, Terrick Terrick.
McKillop, P., Melrose, Lara.
McKin, John, Kinucypaniel.
McKinnon, Daniel, Maridayallock, Terang.
McKinnon, J. and M., Mount Shadwell, Mortlake.
McKinnon, L., Werracknabeal.
McKinnon, M., Moorabbee, Heathcote.
McKinnon, N. and J., Mortlake.
McKinnon and Sons, Wallaloo, Glenorchy.
McKnight, P., Glenmore, Bacchus Marsh.
McLachlan Bros., Kellalac.
McLachlan, Dugald, Kellalac, via Horsham.
McLachlan, Hugh, Branxholme.
McLachlan Jas., farmer, Terrick Terrick.
McLachlan, Peter. Rokewood.
McLaren, D., Russell's Station, Mount Mercer.
McLaren, John, Purnim, Woodford.
McLaren, Wm., Kialla West.
McLarkin, —, a'Beckett Plains.
McLay, James, Moolort.
McLay, John, Moolort.
McLean, A., Coleraine.
McLean Bros., Boort.
McLean, Cowen Pimpinio.
McLean, Donald, Werracknabeal.
McLean, Hector, Pigeon Ponds, Harrow.
McLean, Jno., Kewell.
McLean, Jno., Branxholme P. O.
McLean, L., Burnside, Kialla West.
McLeish, D. and D., Glenmore, Muddy Creek, Yea.
McLellan, C., Glenloth, Wedderburn.
McLellan, D., Manor House, Hamilton.
McLellan, D. and N., Cooe, Lockhart, via Dimboola.
McLellan, N. and D., Cooe, via Horsham.
McLelland, W., Yea.
McLennan, J., Glenthompson.

McLennan, J. W., Avon Plains.
McLennan, J. W., Marnoo, via Glenorchy.
McLennan, K., Kellalac.
McLennan, L., Clunes.
McLennan, Murdock, Rokewood.
McLennan, R., Warrambine.
McLennan, Roderick, Half-way House, near Shelford.
McLennon, F., Carapooe, Coleraine.
McLennen, J. R., Carapooe, Coleraine.
McLeod, A., Marnoo.
McLeod, Archibald, Wallaloo, Glenorchy.
McLeod, Chas., Marnoo.
McLeod, Ewan, Buangor.
McLeod, H. L., Benayer, Apsley.
McLeod, Malcolm, Minyip, via Horsham.
McLeod, Martin, Dunmunkle, Minyip.
McLeod, R and N., Condah.
McLeod, Roderick, Bald Hills, Dunkeld.
McLeod and Son, Dunmunkle, Minyip.
McLoughlin, Owen, Colivel, via Terang.
McMahon, Jas., Camperdown.
McMahon, Martin, Pirron Yaloak.
McMahon, Michael, Ondit.
McMahon, Pat., Camperdown.
McMahon, Patrick, Stoneyford, near Colac.
McMartin, Archd., Pine Lodge.
McMaster Bros., Kiata, Dimboola.
McMillan, Alex., Rhymney Reef.
McMillan, Alex., Lake Leagheur, near Boort.
McMillan, D., Hexham.
McMillan, F., Ararat.
McMillan, Godfrey, Sheep Hills, Horsham.
McMillan and McDonn, Kerang.
McMurtrie, —, c/o J. Chadwick, Stawell.
McMurtrie, Jno., Moyston.
McNair, D., Fir Grove, Moutajup.
McNaught and Boyd, Nambool, Clarendon.
McNaughten, Geo., Cargarie P. O., via Elaine.
McNaughton, A., Lake Gower, Durham Ox.
McNaughton, P., Strangways.
McNeal, Angus, Argyle Park, Meredith P. O.
McNeal, Dugald, Ondit.
McNeil, Hector, farmer, Traralgon, South Gippsland.
McNeil and Purcell, Yea.
McNeill, A., c/o A. and D. Mitchell, Natimuk.
McNeill Bros., Victoria Valley, Dunkeld.
McNeill and Carr, Avon Plains.
McNeill, D., c/o A. and D. Mitchell, Natimuk.
McNeill, J., c/o J. Costin, Esq., Lydiard-street, Ballarat.
McNeill, James, Avon Plains.
McNicholl, Donald, Ben Borrey, Camperdown.
McNutt, B., Wild Duck Creek P. O.
McPhail, A., St. Arnaud.
McPhee, Donald, Corea, Penshurst.
McPhee, J., Vieteo.
McPherson, Angus, Waterloo Inn, Tahara.
McPherson, A., Durham Ox.
McPherson, A W., Wangeeta, Casterton.
McPherson, A. W., Woodlands near Casterton.
McPherson, A. L., Rochester.
McPherson Bros., Nerrim Nerrim, Streatham.
McPherson, D., Bungeeltap, Ballan.
McPherson, John, Tahara.
McPherson, L., and Co., Sandhurst.
McQuilkin, Isaac, Sylvannia, Sale, Gippsland.
McRae, Alexander, Noorat.
McRae, F., Wallup.
McRae, Farquhar, Noorat.
McRae, John, Buangor.
McRea and Sons, Katryll.
McRorie, D., c/o J. Westcott, Boort.
McRorie, P., c/o J. Westcott, Smeaton.
McRorie, William, c/o J. Westcott, Boort.
McTavish, John, North Wonnondah.
McTurish, —, Horsham.
McVean, —, Strathvean, Cressy.
McVean, John, Kerang P. O.
McWilliam, D., and Son, Fair View, Terang.
Najorka, C., Hamilton.
Nalder, Geo., Tottington, Navarre.
Nalone Bros., Jane Vale, Laanecoorie.
Nangle, George, Cargarie, Meredith.
Napier, C., Carisbrook.
Napier, Wm., Majorca.
Naples, Charles, Dooan.
Nash and Buchanan. Ballangeich.
Nash, J. B., Woodburn. Yea.
Nason, G. S., Armstrongs

VICTORIA.

National Bank, Cudgewa.
Nattrass, J. and W., 12 Mile Kalkee.
Naylor and Co., Warrnambool.
Newcomen, —, Taminick Station, via Benalla.
Neod, H., Nirranda, Allansford.
Nelson, John, near Cressy.
Nelson, Peter, near Cressy.
Newham, W., Seymour.
Newman, Sam., farmer, Traralgon.
Newton and Robinson, Bauyena P. O., via Glenorchy.
Nice, J., Benalla.
Nichol and Sons, Bukwith Court, Clunes.
Nichol, Robt., Yowen Hill.
Nichol and Telford, Yarrawonga, Wangaratta.
Nichol, T., Conover, Charlton East.
Nichol, Thos., Spring Bank, Yowen Hill.
Nicholas, J., Barnedown.
Nicholas, Robt., Torbeck Station, Darlingford.
Nicholls, S., Tarnagulla.
Nicholls, W. E., Ararat.
Nicholson, J. A., McCallum's Creek, Talbot.
Nicholson, Wm., Newbridge.
Nickells, S., Moe.
Nickols, —, Ararat.
Nicol, Gideon, Panmure.
Nitschke, Mary, Tarkedia.
Noble, J., sheep farmer, Connewarre.
Noble, J. C., Mount Maria Station, Modewarre.
Nolan, B., Merton.
Nolan, James, Ganoo Ganoo, Casterton.
Norman, J., Terrick Terrick.
Norrie, David, Cudgewa.
Northfield, H., Natimuk.
Noske, T., Dimboola.
Noyster, P., Berwick.
Nugent, J., Kilmore.
Nurke, W., Macarthur.
Nurns, P., Burnt Creek.
Nutchell, F., Spring Bank, Creswick.
Oakes, C., Belfast.
Oakley, A., Milloo, via Elmore.
O'Brien, C., Dookie.
O'Brien, Denis, grazier, Cowwarra.
O'Brien, John E., Swan Reach, Swan Reach
O'Brien, K., Crowlands.
O'Brien, M., Crowlands.
O'Brien, Michael, Stonyford.
O'Brien, P., Mount Eccles, Macarthur.
O'Brien, Patrick, grazier, Cowwarra.
O'Brien, Terence, Springfield, near Hamilton.
O'Brien, Terence, Penshurst.
O'Callaghan, T., Minyip.
O'Callaghan, T., Werracknabeal.
O'Connor Bros., Morton Plains.
O'Connor, J., Pimpinio, Horsham.
O'Connor, J., Yea.
O'Connor, J., Waurn Ponds.
O'Connor, J., grazier, Berwick.
O'Connor, J., Patrick's Vale, Ballan.
O'Connor, John, Muddy Creek.
O'Connor, M., Belfast.
O'Connor, P., Mangalore.
O'Connor, Thomas, farmer, Torrumbarry.
O'Connor, —, Mount Pyramid.
Oddie and Rodgers, Freehold Land Bank, Ballarat.
Oddie, T. R., Pretty Tower, Carngham.
O'Donnell, M., Dederang East, Yackandandah.
O'Donnell, P., Bamgamie.
O'Donnell, Patrick, Goornong.
O'Dwyer, John, Mangalore.
O'Dwyer, M., Mangalore.
Officer, C., Toorak.
Officer, C. S., Mount Talbot, Balmoral.
Officer, John J. P., Koroit.
Officer, S. H., Murray Downs, via Swan Hill.
O'Gorman, John, Terrick Terrick East.
Ogram, George, Burrereo P. O.
O'Halloran, —, Dunkeld.
O'Halloran, E., Warrabkoop, Byaduk.
O'Keefe, A., Barnedown P. O.
O'Keefe, D., Bacchus Marsh.
Oliver, Andrew, Diggora.
Oliver, W., Yea.
Olney, John, Lal Lal.
Oman, Mrs. J., Streatham.
Oman, William, Lismore.
O'Meara, D., Eaglehawk, North Gippsland.
O'Meara, Edward, farmer, Eaglehawk, North Gippsland.
O'Meara, James, sen., Eaglehawk, North Gippsland.

O'Meara, James, jun., Eaglehawk, North Gippsland.
O'Meara, William, farmer, Eaglehawk, North Gippsland.
O'Meara, William, sen., Eaglehawk, North Gippsland.
O'Neil, B., Avenel.
O'Neil, Joseph, Buln Buln.
O'Neill, Bernard, Nagambie.
Opie, James, farmer, Eaglehawk, North Gippsland.
Oram, John, Rupanyup North.
Orchard, Thomas, Winchelsea.
Orme, William W., Seymour.
Orr, C. B., Rochester.
Orr, Edward, Woodpark, Heathcote.
Orr, F., farmer, Axe Creek.
Orr, Jackson, Eaglehawk, North Gippsland.
Orr, John, Mia Mia.
O'Reilly, —, Woodburn, near Casterton.
O'Reilly, Bernard, Altdoy. Freeburgh.
O'Reilly, O., Wando, Casterton.
O'Reilly, Owen, Steep Bank, Casterton.
O'Rourke, C., Ingeegobie, Buchan.
O'Rourke, E., Guggan Buggan, Buchan.
O'Rourke, Edward. Tarkedia.
O'Rourke, Edwin, Black Mountain, Buchan.
O'Rourke, Edwin, Little River, Buchan.
O'Rourke, Thomas, Wingilgoodbin.
Osborne, H., farmer, Emu Creek.
Osborne, J., Yackandandah.
Osborne, John, Ballarat.
O'Shanassy, Sir John, Tara, Hawthorn.
O'Shannessy, Jno., Banyena.
O'Shanessy, Thos., Lake Rowan.
O'Shea, John, Doctor's Creek, Greendale.
O'Shea, John, Greendale.
Owen, David, Kin och, via Glenorchy.
Padgett, Geo., Mount Cole, Buangor.
Page, J. H., Framlingham.
Pagles, Louis, Wickliffe.
Palmer, E. J., Goulburn's Downs, Echuca.
Palmer, H., farmer, Marong.
Palmer, Mrs. M. A., Rokewood.
Palmer, T. M., Sand Creek South, Fernbank.
Parfrey, Jas., Cannum.
Parish, James, Wensleydale, Winchelsea.
Parker, —, Quiamong, Conargo.
Parker, F. G., Rokewood.
Parker, H. S., Oak Farm, Rokewood.
Parker, T. P., Rokewood.
Parkinson, E., Roseneath, Coleraine.
Parkinson, J. G., Deep Creek, Macarthur.
Parry, R. H., Lismore Park, Conargo.
Pascoe, J. H., Mitiamo.
Paterson, A., Wallup.
Paterson, D., Macorna.
Patience and Lee, Marnoo, Glenorchy.
Paton, Andrew, & Sons { Noorongong W., Benalla. Noorongong, Mitta Mitta. Tallandoon, Mitta Mitta.
Paton, Wm., Woodford.
Paton, James, Sailor's Water Hole, Lancefield.
Patson, J., grazier, Pyalong.
Patterson, Alex., Nangeeta, Casterton.
Patterson, D., Bowman's Forest.
Patterson, J., Wedderburn.
Patterson, Robt., Murchison.
Patterson, R. C., Tallarook.
Patterson, W., Cape Schanck.
Patterson, W., Fernhurst.
Patton, J., Yarrawonga, via Wangaratta.
Paul, R., Green's Creek, via Stawell.
Payne, F., Echuca.
Payne, H. M., Rokewood.
Peachey, J. S. W., Casterton.
Peachey, E., Casterton.
Peacock, M., Kerang.
Pearce, T., Gisborne.
Pearce, James, Cressy.
Pearson, Joseph, Tara, Strentham.
Pearson, John, Muntham, Coleraine.
Pearson, J. G., Mount Ridley, Craigieburn.
Pearson, J. S., Wonga Lake, via Horsham.
Peck, R., French Island.
Peiper, —, Axe Creek.
Penrose, W. T., Brunlool.
Pentreath, N. F., Mitiamo P. O., via Rochester
Petering, C. and W., Minyip.
Peters, E., St. Arnaud.
Peters, James, Gart Station, Newham.

Peters, Mrs., Broadmeadows.
Peterson, G., Martha Vale, Bairnsdale.
Petschlcil, August, Dimboola.
Pettes, W. H. and G. E., Streatham.
Phillips, C., Queenscliffe.
Phillips, E., Springs.
Phillips, Henry, Bryan O'Lynn, via Warrnambool.
Phillips and Hill, Mooroopna.
Phillips, J., St. Mary's Lake, Horsham.
Phillip, John, Harrow.
Phipps, C., farmer, Heathcote.
Phipps, Charles, Costerfield.
Pickens, T. and J., Wharparilla.
Pike, Sarah, Ballan.
Piltz, Adolph, Walian Walan.
Pilver, C., Hamilton.
Pimblet, Richard, Noorat.
Pimblet, Richard, Clover Hills, Darlington.
Pink, Mrs. Rebecca, Ondit.
Pittock, — , Hamilton.
Plant, Mrs. R., Laketown.
Player and Kitchen, Mansfield.
Playford, W., Heathcote.
Pliers, Lewis, sheep farmer, Marong.
Pocklington, Thos., Bungil, Upper Murray.
Podger, Charles, Noorat.
Podger, Charles, Terang.
Podmore, R., Woomargoona.
Pollock and Ellis, Inglewood.
Polly, Isaac, Toorak, Mortlake.
Poole, F., Cranbourne.
Pope, William, Woodside.
Porter, J., Natimuk.
Porter, William, Natimuk.
Powell, Cornelius, Glenthompson, via Hamilton.
Powell, Cornelius, Woodlands, Kewell.
Powell, H., Wangoon, Warrnambool.
Powell, John, Kellalac.
Powell, Mrs. Margaret, Kellalac.
Powell, Thomas, Corop.
Powell, T. S., Saniana, via Benalla.
Powell, William, Baringhup.
Powell, W., Newry Lands, Glenthompson.
Power Brothers, Rupanyup P. O.
Power, W. E., Power's Court, Maffra.
Poynton, E., Macarthur.
Pratt, Thos., farmer, Eaglehawk, North Gippsland.
Prendergast, P., Maude.
Prentice, J., farmer, Romsey.
Prewett, J., Bald Rock, via Durham Ox.
Price, J., Terrick Terrick P. O.
Prideaux, —, Dookie South.
Pring, W. and C., Bailan.
Proctor, Charles, Creen's Creek, near Pleasant Creek.
Prosser, David, Colac.
Prosser, N., Terrick Terrick.
Prowse, S. R., Corop.
Pugh, W. T., Brumbool.
Pullen, R. W., Woodlands, Piper's Creek.
Purcell and Pearce, Myrniong.
Pyers, Geo., Lawler, Donald.
Pyle, J. and P., Elmore.
Pyle, James, Murroon.
Quarrell, Jno., Break o' Day.
Quarrell, Jno., Corindhap.
Quild, Jno., Seymour.
Quinlan, Wm., Mount Pyramid.
Radley, S., Grey-street, Hamilton.
Raliegh, John, Tandura, Raywood.
Ramage, A., Crowlands.
Ramey, Jno., Woodford, Warrnambool.
Ramey, James, Mepunga.
Ramsay, J. B. F., Boort.
Rankin Bros., Condair.
Rankin Bros., Boinbowlee, Tumut.
Rankin, J., Victoria Valley, Dunkeld.
Rankin, J. D., Jerilderie.
Raper, Chas., Pannoon Milloo, via Rochester.
Rasmussen, G. E., Horsham.
Rathgen, H., Colbinabbin.
Rattray, W., Buel Buel, Kerang.
Read, W., farmer, Goornong.
Read, W., Weatherboard, Burrumbeet, via Ballarat.
Reddie, Duncan, Beear.
Reddie, Danl., Ondit.
Redwood, Richard, Barton Farm, Bridgewater.
Redwood, R., Inglewood.
Redford, T., and Co., Warrnambool.

Reeves, Edwd., Western Grove, Boort.
Reeves, John, Boort.
Reeves, Mrs. E., Wordiebolue.
Reeves, Mrs., Winchelsea.
Reeves, T. T., Milloo, Runnymede.
Reeves, T. T., Milloo, via Elmore.
Rees, J. E., Noradjuha.
Reedy, Thos., Wodonga.
Reegan, —, farmer, near Goornong.
Regan Bros., Benalla.
Reily, Bernard, Banyena.
Reily and Colac, Pheasant Park, Dargo.
Reily, F. and A., Banyena.
Reily, —, near Saltwater Lake, Corop.
Reid, D., Philip Island.
Reid, J., Fryerstown.
Reid, Stuart, Eldington, Camperdown.
Reid, W., Hazelton.
Reynolds, Mrs., Winchelsea.
Reynolds, R., Rokewood.
Reynolds, Thomas, Chipman, by Moyston.
Rhodes, W., Carapooee, Coleraine.
Rhodes, Wm., Dwyer's Creek, near Casterton.
Richards, Alf., Rochester.
Richardson, Andrew, Torrumbarry.
Richardson, Hy., Barnawartha, Wodonga West.
Richardson, John, farmer, Newlyn.
Richardson, J., Creswick.
Richardson, James, Gorrinu, Dobie's Bridge.
Richardson, Joseph, Cowes, Phillip Island.
Richardson, Thos., North Corack, St. Arnaud.
Richertson, Henry, Gelantipy, Buchan.
Rice, James, grazier, Cowwar.
Rice, W., Gunnewarre, Kerang.
Richey, W., Pleasant Hill, Kyneton.
Rich, —, Allanvale, Great Western.
Ridge Bros., Inglewood.
Riddle, Chas., Murgheboluc.
Riddell, James, Gillangall, Buchan.
Rigby, M'Kellar and Co., Elmore.
Riggal, Edw., Joyce's Creek.
Riy, Albert, Monax Vale, Hamilton.
Rippon, Wm., Irrewillipe.
Ritchie Bros., Gororie Park, Tullamarine.
Ritchie, Geo., Warrambine, Shelford.
Ritchie, John, Blackwood, Penshurst.
Robinson, Alex., North Mount Fyans, Darlington.
Robinson, Angus, Mount Enuu, Skipton.
Robertson, A. W., Tallarook, Seymour.
Robertson Bros., Colac.
Robertson, Charles, Minyip.
Robertson, David, Bacchus Marsh.
Robertson, D. Engefield, Balmoral.
Robertson, D., Myrniong.
Robertson, Ewan, Whittlesea.
Robertson, E., Halfway House, Glenorchy.
Robertson, F., Myrtle Creek, near Goornong.
Robertson, F. O., Mount Moriac.
Robertson, George, Warrock, Apsley.
Robertson, G., Hilton, Bacchus Marsh.
Robertson, G., Barnooleat, Casterton.
Robertson, G., Warrock, Coleraine.
Robertson, G. P., Colac.
Robertson, Henry, Dry Creek, Broadford.
Robertson, Henry F., Essendon.
Robertson, James, Aberfeldy.
Robertson, James, Colac.
Robertson, John, Elderslie, near Edenhope.
Robertson, John, Victoria Valley, Duukeld.
Robertson, John, Carlsruhe.
Robertson, J., Carlsruhe.
Robertson, J., Kangaroo Ground.
Robertson, J., Barwon, Echuca.
Robertson, J., Baun, Shepparton.
Robertson, Neil and Duncan, Wallaloo.
Robertson and Sons, Gargette, Penshurst.
Robertson and Sons, Yarram Yarram, Dunkeld.
Robertson, Thomas, Clare Inn, Goornong.
Robertson and Tossel', Thornton.
Robertson, William, Woollen Farm, New Gisborne.
Robertson, William, Corangamorah, Colac.
Robertson, —, Mayor's Line Station, Graytown.
Robertson, —, Lochart, Dimboola.
Robins, J., Oak Hill, Pimpinio.
Robins, Richard, Hill Plains, via Benalla.
Robinson, James, Purnim, Warrnambool.
Roberts, John, Dookie South.
Roberts, Mrs., Gunnewarre, Kerang.
Robinson, R. N., Oxley.
Robbie, William, Woorndoo.
Roche, Edward, Garvoc.

VICTORIA.

Rochfort, J. A., Yellerwoode, Kerang.
Rochfort, J., Gunnewarre, Kerang.
Rodgers, Baillie, Kellalac.
Rodgers, James, jun., farmer, Eaglehawk, North Gippsland.
Rodgers, James, sen., farmer, Eaglehawk, North Gippsland.
Rodgers, Mrs., Pimpinio, Horsham.
Rodger, James, Kellalac.
Roe, R., Roe's Park, Benalla.
Rogers, Joseph, Kyneton.
Rogers, John, Glenwood, Buln Buln.
Rogers and Sons, Morella, via Cavendish.
Rogers, W., Camellia Creek.
Rogers, —, farmer, near Goornong.
Rolla, Alexander, Mangoon, Warrnambool.
Roman, August, Mt. Egerton.
Roper, Frederick, Mt. York, Beechworth.
Ross, C. and F., Natte Yallock.
Ross, Charles, Bridgewater.
Ross, Donald, Meadow Valley, Wilduck.
Ross, H. W., Benalla.
Ross, William, The Gums, Caramut.
Ross, John George, Woodlea, Kyneton.
Rose, D., Buln Buln.
Rose, H., Ballan.
Rose, H., Ballan.
Rosendale, J., Barwon, Echuca.
Rossal, T., Kingston.
Rourke, Hugh, Oak Park, Rochester.
Rowe, Charles, Wilderness, Coleraine.
Rowe and Stodart, Miller's Ponds, Alexandra.
Rowe, Thomas, Leigh Road P. O.
Rowe, W., Naringie, via Ballarat.
Rowe, William Thomas, Glenfine, Cape Clear.
Rowlett, J., Ballan.
Roware, John, Casterton.
Rowitt, James, Ballan.
Ruddle, George, Kyneton.
Rundle, J., farmer, Upper Emu Creek.
Rundell, M., farmer, Sheepwash.
Rundell, Thomas, farmer, Upper Emu Creek.
Russell, C. and J., Lancefield Road.
Russell, George, Golf Hill, Shelford.
Russell, Hon. P., Carngham.
Russell, John, Winslow.
Russell, Thomas, and Co., Baroona Plains, Hesse.
Russell's Station, Yarrima, Cressy.
Ruthledge Brothers, Farnham Park, Warrnambool.
Ruthledge, —, farmer, Corop.
Rutherford and Guthrie, Mambatook, Towaninnie.
Rutherford, James, Eurobin, Bright.
Rutherford, James, Mapara, via Echuca.
Rutherford, William, Goornong.
Ryan, D., Benalla.
Ryan, Innetty, farmer, Corop.
Ryan, James, Morton Plains.
Ryan, John, Green Hills, Camperdown.
Ryan, J., Bacchus Marsh.
Ryan, J., Kerish, Camperdown.
Ryan, J., Horsham.
Ryan, W., Ganoo Ganoo, Casterton.
Ryan, P., Goomalibee, Benalla.
Ryan, P., Koolomart, Casterton.
Ryan, Thomas, Goldie, Kilmore.
Ryan, Thomas, Bahgallah, near Casterton.
Ryan, William, Green Hills, Horsham.
Ryan, W., Dookie South.
Ryley, G. F., Wangaratta.
Ryley, Michael, Mitiamo.
Salinan, Matthias, Dimboola.
Salisbury, R. J., Spottiswoode, Springsure.
Sampey, C. J., Chetwynd.
Sanger, J. M., Wanamong, Corowa.
Sanderson, John, Lake Clear, via Horsham.
Sanderson, James, Boort.
Sanderson, Thomas, Archdale, Bealiba.
Sanford, W., Minyip, Dunmunkle.
Sargeant, C. W., Glenrowan.
Saunders, J. M., Inglewood.
Savill, William, Macarthur.
Scale, W., Alexandra.
Schuter, Q., Bacchus Marsh.
Schmidt, F. W., Kiata, Dimboola.
Schultz, —, Kiata Dimboola.
Soliger, Ernest, Dimboola.
Scott, Andrew, jun., Woolbrook, Teesdale.
Scott, Andrew, Edenhope.
Scott, Andrew, Carrica, Hawthorn.
Scott, D., and Son, Torrumbarry.

Scott, Daniel, Deloin, Fernbank.
Scott, Henry, Natimuk.
Scott, Robert, Tarkedia House, East Melbourne.
Scott, R. D., Camperdown.
Scott. Spence and Co., Tullynea, Dimboola.
Scoullan, —, Rose Hill, Stawell.
Secombe, John, West Charlton.
Seward, S., Ringwood. Rochester.
Seymour, Sydney, Romsey, Burton Romsey
Shaw, Angus, Coleraine.
Shaw, F. C., Port Albert.
Shaw, Thomas, Edgecombe. Ceres.
Shaw, J. R., Quamby. Dobie's Bridge.
Shaw, J. and T. J., Table Top, Wangaratta.
Shaw, —, farmer, Goornong.
Shannon, D., Wilkin, Casterton.
Shanneahan, M., Molka, Euroa.
Shalders, Henry, Moyston.
Shawhorn, Andrew, Rushworth.
Shawhorn, A., Black Hill, Kyneton.
Sherwood, C., Natimuk.
Sherwood, R. W. and F., Natimuk.
Shelton, E., Avenel.
Shea, John, Doctor's Creek, Greendale.
Shea, John, Purnim.
Sheppard, J., Sussex, St. Linton's.
Shephenson, J., Bass River, Bass.
Shepherd, Selina, Swan Bay, Queenscliff.
Sherogg. Robert, c/o J. Shodt, Minyennook.
Sheffields, Samuel, Glenthompson.
Sherrin, William, Birregurra.
Shearer, W., Donald P. O.
Sheehan, W., Nagambie.
Sheridan, —, St. Arnaud.
Shangles, E., farmer, Sebastian.
Shiel and Helier, Scrubby Forest, Traralgon.
Shiels, Patrick, Murchison.
Short, J., Strathbogie.
Shuter, C., Greendale.
Siamering, W., Kiata, Dimboola.
Sides, John, Mount Mercer.
Silk, Henry, Murphy's Creek, Tarnagulla.
Simpson Bros., Wangoon, Warrnambool.
Simpson, J., Dergholm.
Simpson, W. and T., Terrick Terrick East.
Simpson, —, Dry Lake, Warrnambool.
Simmie and Craig, Cornelia Creek, Rochester.
Sims, D. D., Charlotte Plains, near Maryborough
Sims, D., Heathcote.
Sims, J. S., Ganoo Ganoo, Casterton.
Simson, Hon. Robert, Melbourne.
Simson, James, Geelong.
Simmonds, W., Noradjuha.
Simmonds, —, Waurn Ponds Junction, Colac.
Simmons, —, Stawell.
Singleton Bros., Annandale, Upper Murray, via Kiewa.
Sinnott. Michael, Armstrong's, Mount Ararat.
Sinnott, J., Armstrong's.
Sinclair, P. A., Arcadia, Murchison.
Skene, Thomas, Bassett, Branxholme.
Skene, William and D., Skene, Hamilton.
Skeggs, George, Tarranginnie.
Skilbeck, R., Koroit.
Skinner, —, farmer, near Waldon.
Slaperty, J. and P., farmers, near Goornong.
Slater, James, publican and farmer, Toongabbie.
Slater, James, farmer, Eaglehawk, North Gippsland.
Slee, Charles, sheep farmer, Strangways.
Slee, Edgar, Newstead.
Sloan, Thomas, grazier, Bridgewater.
Smart, J. J., Morton Plains.
Smallman, R. C., Millot, Bairnsdale.
Smale, Thomas, Edgecombe, Ceres.
Smith, Alexander, Marloo, Coongulmerang.
Smith, Alexander, Dahna.
Smith, A., Kiata, Dimboola.
Smith, Charles, Russell's Creek, Warrnambool.
Smith, C. G., Kiata, Dimboola.
Smith, Duncan, Branxholme.
Smith, David, near Corop.
Smith, D., Bundalong.
Smith, Francis, Dimboola.
Smith, F., Swan Hill, Murray Downs.
Smith, F., Swan Hill.
Smith, George, Port Albert.
Smith, Henry, farmer, Gunbower.
Smith, H. P., farmer, Sheepwash.
Smith, John, fellmonger, Werracknabeal.
Smith, Joseph, Benalla.

Smith, J. D., Lindenow, Bairnsdale.
Smith, J., Dimboola.
Smith, Mrs. Alice, Lagoon Farm, Burrumbeet.
Smith. Thomas, Tweedside, Essendon.
Smith, William, Green's Creek, Stawell.
Smith, W., Burramine.
Smith, —, farmer, Eaglehawk, North Gippsland.
Smyth, R. J., Ryan's Peak, Bullumwaal.
Snell, E., Avoca.
Someville and Sons, Strathfieldsaye.
Sorrigan, Owen, Seymour.
Spoedie, A., Woodside Farm, Panoobamawn.
Spelling, Honora. Glenorchy.
Spedding, James, Laanecoorie.
Spears, Matthew, Moystou.
Spears, R., Watgania.
Spe rs, W., Watgania.
Speed, William, Derrinal, Heathcote.
Spier, James, Mysia.
Splatt, Mrs. S. A., Hesse.
Spowart, Thomas, Macorna.
Stan ey, Alexander, Wild Duck P. O.
Stanley, G. H , farmer, Axedale.
Stanley, R., Moyhu.
Staugton Bros., Eynsbury, Melton.
Staugton, H. W., Erford, Melton.
Staugton. S. F., Brisbane Ranges, Anakies.
Staugton, S. F., Little River.
Stanhope, Stephen, Niranda, Warrnambool.
Stanbrook, G. H., Quambatook.
Starbruck, J. W., Hamilton.
Stapleton, John, West Charlton.
Stafford, William, Jackson's Creek, via Ararat.
Stewart, Andrew, Devenish, Major Plains.
Stewart, A., Nanapumelah, Wyckliffe,
Stewart, Alexander, Tholocolong, Wodonga.
Stewart Bros., Warrong, via Hawkesdale.
Stewart Brothers, Carapooee.
Stewart, Charles, Carisbrook.
Stewart, D., Tregothuan.
Stewart, D., Ballan.
Stewart, Ewen, Wychetella.
Stewart, G., Ganoo Ganoo, Casterton.
Stewart, James, Mount Fyans, Darlington
Stewart, John, Rochester.
Stewart, J. S., Talbot.
Stewart, Robert, Burramine.
Stewart, Robert, farmer, Dookie South.
Stewart, Robert, Burramine.
Stewart, R., and Co., Corop.
Stewart, T., Devenish P. O., Stewarton.
Stewart, William Lyne, Branxholme.
Stephen, G., Dimboola.
Stephen, —, Rushes' Bridge, Eddington.
Stephens, James, Kangaroo Flat, Koroit.
Steane, J., farmer, Emu Creek.
Steen, J., farmer, Axe Creek.
Steel and Sons, Wedderburn.
Stevenson, Thomas C., Laanecoorie.
Stevens, Thomas, Bolinda, Riddell's Creek.
Stevens, William, Ross's Bridge.
Sterton, W., Dookie South.
Stohn, W., Natimuk.
Sterling, T. T. { Lake Tyers, Snowy River.
                { Tambo, Nowa Nowa.
Stoneham Brothers, Wangoon, Warrnambool.
Storie, Edward, Laanecoorie.
Stock, John, Carapork.
Stock, William, Concongella, Armstrong's.
Storer, Joseph. Branxholme.
Stokes, J., Waurn Ponds.
Stoop, W., Tullagaroopna.
Stratford Brothers, Avon Plains.
Stratford, John, Roseneath, Casterton.
Strickland, C., Wensleydale, Winchelsea.
Strachan, J. F., Ripple Vale, Birregurra.
Street, W., Barandudah, via Wodonga.
Stuart, Archibald, Wongan, Streatham.
Sturton, William, Major Plains.
Stuckey, W. H., Bungoona, via Wodonga.
Sweet and Sweeting, Shelbourne.
Sugden, A., Kilmore.
Sullivan, F., Major Plains.
Sullivan, —, Benalla.
Sullivan, —, sheep farmer, Allansford.
Sullivan, F. P., Kewell East.
Sutherland, Benjamin, Stawell.
Sutherland, C. F., Tatyoon.
Sutherland, D., farmer, Gunbower.
Sutherland, D., near Cressy.
Sutherland, G., Ballan.

Sutherland, James, Bamganie P. O.
Sutterley, Thomas, Moolap.
Swann, David, Tarnagulla.
Swanson. D., Ross's Bridge, Kiora.
Swallow and Sons, Shepparton.
Swanston, Willi, and Stephen, Geelong.
Sweet, —, farmer, Bradford Creek, Laanecoorie.
Sylvester, T. W., Thenio.
Symmons, Herman, Noradjuha.
Symmons, William, Noradjuha.
Symington, John, Craigton, Piper's Creek.
Symes, W., Lake Rowan.
Tacka, John, Rokewood.
Tait, James, East Charlton.
Talbett, H., Wakool.
Talbot, S., Birregurra.
Tanner, R. W., Mount Egerton.
Tunsey, T., Ganoo Ganoo, Casterton.
Tapps, Peter, Mortlake.
Tarran, A. S., Dimboola.
Tarrant, William, Werracknabeal.
Taylor, A., Fairlie Farm, South Grenville.
Taylor, Adam, Kiata, Dimboola.
Taylor, A. J., Azwarby, Yea.
Taylor, A., Morabee, Heathcote.
Taylor, George, Montajup.
Taylor, George, Nowley, Piper's Creek.
Taylor, John, Woodford, Warrnambool.
Taylor, Samuel, Macarthur.
Taylor, Walter, Larpent.
Taylor, William, near Saltwater Lake, Corop.
Taylor, W. D., Timmering, Rochester.
Telford, John, Lawloit.
Tellett, George, Half-way House, near Shelford.
Templeton, J., Terrick Terrick.
Templeton, M., Bogalaro, Coleraine.
Thacker, George, Glenthompson.
Thistlewaite, W., Smeaton.
Thom, J., and Sons, Burramine, Wangaratta.
Thomas, J., Ballan.
Thomas, Mrs., Sutton Grange P. O.
Thomas, R., Dimboola.
Thomas, W., Penrose Farm, Grenville.
Thomber, James, Minyip.
Thomson, B., Kyneton.
Thomson, Geo. W., Challicum, Buangor.
Thomson, J. B., Boynton.
Thomson, Patrick, Lal Lal, Yendon.
Thomson, W., Prospect, Kyneton.
Thomson, W., Dolical, Werracknabeal.
Thomson, W., Edenhope.
Thomson, —, Pierre Point, Hamilton.
Thompson, —, Powlett Plains.
Thompson, G., Green Hills, Kyneton.
Thompson, James, Pieraeli, via Hamilton.
Thompson, J., Pyke's Flat.
Thompson, J., Momair, Hamilton.
Thompson, P., Spreyden, Ballan.
Thompson, P., Broadmeadows.
Thompson, R. and J., Cove, Dimboola.
Thompson, T., and Co., Alexandra.
Thompson, W., Myrniong.
Thompson, William, Green Creek, via Stawell.
Thorn, A., Alexandra.
Thorne, Henry, Murchison.
Thorne, James, Burramine.
Thorne, Robert, Burramine.
Thornley, George, Kiata, Dimboola.
Thornton, John, Mount Myrtoon, Camperdown.
Threlfall, —, Ellerslie, Warrnambool.
Thrupp, W., Sutton Grange.
Thurgood, H. J., Montajup, near Dunkeld.
Thwaites, E., Winslow.
Thwaites, J., Allansford, Warrnambool.
Thwaites, Simon, Koroit.
Thyers, E., Wychetella.
Tidboald, Thomas, Dargalong.
Timms Brothers, Mount Hesse, Winchelsea.
Tindale, Thomas, Beaufort.
Tinker and Davey, Dora Dora.
Titley, George Thomas, Glenthompson.
Tlett, William, Warrion Park, via Ondit.
Tobin, A., Panmure.
Tobin. P., Upper Emu.
Todd, Colin, Bacchus Marsh.
Todd, James. Caramut.
Toleman, —, Mortlake.
Toll, George, Gunbower.
Tolmie, E , Denvean, Mansfield,
Tomlinson, Cargarie P. O.
Toohey, M., Breakwater, Geelong.

VICTORIA. xvii

Toose, Frederick, c/o F. Westcott, Ullina, P. O. Smeaton.
Toose, L. E., Boort.
Toose, W. J., Smeaton.
Towart, Robert, Casterton.
Towell, George, Torrumbarry.
Townsend, A., Mitiamo.
Townsend, W., Heathcote.
Tozer, T., Wangoon Park, Warrnambool.
Tracy, W., Tatyoon.
Travers, George, Terrick Terrick.
Treacy, M. M., Terricks.
Trerarchus, T. S. and Co., Castlemaine.
Tremayne, J., Yea.
Trethowan, E., Drysdale.
Trethowan, N. and Co., Dunn's Town.
Trevaskis, J., Heathcote.
Trewin, John, Newlyn.
Trigger, S., Macarthur.
Trimble, James, Rochester P. O.
Troy, Michael. Ondit.
Tucker Bros., Linton.
Tucker, C. and J. L., Woodstock, Bungeeluke, via East Charlton.
Tucker, George, Noradjuha, Natimuk.
Tucker, S. W., Bungeeluke, via East Charlton.
Tucker, T., and Son, Bald Rock, via Durham Ox.
Tuckett, R., Bushes Bridge, Eddington.
Tuckett, R. G., Burnt Creek.
Tuffnell, Robert, Nangeeta, Casterton.
Tulley, Stephen, Kiora, near Ararat.
Tullogh, H., Tallarook.
Tupper, William, Eddington.
Turnbull Bros., Emu Plains, Benalla.
Turnbull, James D., Kotupna, Shepparton.
Turnbull, Mark, Kilcunda, Bass.
Turner, A., Dergholm.
Turner, R., Corindhap.
Turner, Thomas. Serpentine.
Tweedie, William, Rupanyup.
Twigg, G., Wingfield Park, Derby.
Twomey, E., Langulac, Penshurst.
Twomey, T., Mount Rouse, Penshurst.
Twycross, S.. Mooroopna.
Uebergang, C., Allansford, Warrnambool.
Uncles, R. E., Yambuk.
Underwood, H.. Glenthompson.
Underwood, Thomas, Muddy Creek, Yea.
Upham, William, Jackson's Creek, Ararat.
Urquhart, A. and R., Yangery, Warrnambool.
Vandenburg, Charles, Framlingham.
Vancy, Alfred, Eaglehawk, North Gippsland.
Vanrennan, Mrs., Yarra-street, Geelong.
Vanrennan, H. P., Lethbridge.
Vanston, William, Moyston.
Varcoe, C., Tomarro, Echuca.
Vaughan, Josh, sheep farmer, Byaduk.
Vaughan, Samuel, Larpent.
Vaughan, S., and Co., Ballarat.
Vaughan, S., and Co., St. Arnaud.
Vaughan, Thomas, Mark Tree Line, Elmore.
Vaughan, W. and C., Warrenbayne, Violet Town.
Vearing, T., Hughes' Creek, near Avenel.
Veale Brothers, Lake Bolac.
Veitch, Walter, Pine Grove, Rochester.
Vernon, Joseph, Mount Mercer.
Verrey, F. P., Camperdown.
Vian, John, Kensington.
Vicker Brothers, Hill Plain, Benalla.
Vickers, Robert, Panmure.
Vigar, J. D., Yeo, Colac.
Virtue, G., Woodford, Warrnambool.
Vogh, E., farmer, Sebastian.
Waddell, William, North Hamilton.
Wakeman, R. G., c/o Mr. Langford, Durham Ox.
Walker, Charles, Montajup, Dunkeld.
Walker, E. K., Melool, Swan Hill.
Walker, George, Kiata, Dimboola.
Walker, George, sen., Lake Baker, Swan Hill.
Walker, John, Darlington Station, Baynton.
Walker, P. W., Mansfield.
Walker, W., Serpentine.
Walker, W. O., Glen Pedder, Grundale.
Walker, W. M., Powlett P. O.
Wall, John, Teesdale P. O.
Wall, M., Teesdale.
Wall, T., Ballan.
Wallace, — Bung Bong.
Wallace, D, S., Bullane, Morrisons.
Wallace, J., Bullane, Morrisons.
Wallace, J., Mount Hope, Pyramid.

Wallis, A. R., Studley Park, Kew.
Wallis, J., St. James.
Wallsgot, G., Dimboola.
Walsh, J., Glenthompson, Wickliffe.
Walsh, James, Stawell East.
Walsh, M., Ararat.
Walsh, T., Duck Ponds.
Walsh and O'Brien, Mount Ararat Creek, Pakenham.
Walter, Joseph, Yuppecklar, Glenthompson.
Walters, A. W., Noradjuha.
Walters, E. and C., Noradjuha.
Walters, J. H., Tarranginie, Dimboola.
Walters, W., North Hamilton.
Walton, A. L., Deringal, Wild Duck Creek.
Walton, Thomas, Tarween, Crossover.
Ward Bros., Taranginle, Dimboola.
Ward, M., Bungeeltap, Ballan.
Ward, Martin, Inglewood.
Wardlaw. W., Grassmere, Warrnambool.
Wardle, Thomas, Watgania.
Wardrop, —, Benalla.
Ware, B., Joyce's Creek.
Ware, J., Yalla-y-poora, Streatham.
Ware, J. G., Koort Koort Nong, Camperdown P.O.
Warne, Elias, Wycheproof.
Warner Bros., Warrion Hill, Colac.
Warner, Charles, Winchelsea.
Warrington, Michael, Boosey branch.
Watt, David, Murchison.
Watt, G. A., Buln Buln.
Watt, Messrs., Dookie South.
Watt and Barratt, Major Plains.
Watt and Bennett, Benalla.
Watts, W., Dimboola.
Watts and M'Bean, Benalla.
Watson, A., Ballarat.
Watson, A., Lindsay.
Watson, A. M., Wychetella.
Watson, C. M., Lydiard-street, Ballarat.
Watson and Fell, Toolern.
Watson, H., Ardno East, Macarthur.
Watson, Joseph, Panoobamawn.
Watson, Sydney G., Tintaldra.
Watson, Thomas, Green Valley P. O., Conangalt.
Watson, W. W., Kirkstall.
Waugh, John, Conover P. O., near St. Arnaud.
Weaver, E., c o Thomas Westcott, Lake Boort.
Webster, D., Katandra.
Webster, E. G., Yea.
Webster, John, Cobram, via Benalla.
Webster, William, Bidura, Alma-road, St. Kilda.
Wehl, Carl, Stawell West.
Weight, —, Joyce's Creek.
Weight, Thomas, Moolort.
Weiss, Edward, Tatyoon. via Ararat.
Weldon, Geo., Tourangabby, Boundary, Echuca.
Weldon, J., Daylesford.
Wells, James, Baynton.
Wennyss, Charles, Murchison.
Weppnex, Henry, Colbinabbin.
West, William, Barrudge, near Beechworth.
West, W., Myrtleford.
Westblade, G., and Co., Mia Mia.
Westcott and Son. Isaac, Moorabool Creek.
Westcott. Thomas and H. S., Lanyon, Maynard Park, Boort.
Weston Bros., Ballan.
Westrop, W. W., Upper Morwell, Traralgon.
Weymess, Wm., Laanecoorie.
Whale, George, Ballan.
Whaley and Bedford, Stratford-on-Avon, North Gippsland.
Whaley, T., and Son, Traralgon.
Whaley and Williams. Bairnsdale.
Wheeler, J., Colac Colac, Upper Murray.
Whelan, J., Drysdale.
Whicher, T., Cape Clear.
White, Andrew, Hillside, Mount Duneed.
White, C., Yambuk.
White, E., Winnicott, Carapook, via Coleraine.
White, E., Cavendish.
White, E. R., Springvale, Coleraine.
White, E. T., Traralgon.
White, James, Springbank, Casterton.
White, James, Montajup, Dunkeld.
White, John, Joyce's Creek.
White, Thomas, Bacchus Marsh.
White, William, Bacchus Marsh.
White, W., Bushy Park, Mooroopna.
White, W., Mortlake P. O.

Whitehead, F., Kialla West.
Whitehead, J. R., Burrabunnia.
Whitehead, Robert, Goodwood, Caramut.
Whitehead, Thomas, Wabba, Camperdown.
Whitehead, W. R., Belfast.
Whittaker, James, Fern Hill, Traralgon.
Whittaker, W., Fern Hill, Traralgon.
Whitson, William, Mortlake.
Whyte, J., Gisborne.
Widerman, H., Dimboola.
Widger, F. C., Kellalac, Horsham.
Wight, E. B., Kensington.
Wight, Ernest, Meltham, near Geelong.
Williams, David, Woodford.
Williams, Edward, Wingall, Shelford P. O.
Williams, E., and Co., Avenel.
Williams, George, Mount Duneed.
Williams, J., St. Arnaud.
Williams, J. H., Donnybrook.
Williams, J., Morone Park, Maffra.
Williams, J., Morone Park, Maffra.
Williams and Mills, c o J. Bond, Horsham.
Williams, S., Yangery, Woodford.
Williams, T. S., Kilmore Estate, Heathcote.
Williams, W., Kalinga.
Williamson, Charles, Decameron, St. Arnaud.
Williamson, D., Alberton.
Williamson, Dr., Decameron, Elmshurst.
Williamson, E. D., Wychetella.
Williamson, John, Glenthompson.
Williamson, James, Yea.
Williamson, R., Ballan.
William, P. C., Gunbower.
Willis, D., Koolomert, Casterton.
Willis, Edward, Moree, Harrow.
Willis, H. S., Shadwell Park, Mortlake.
Willis, Richard, Meredith.
Willis, Richard, Borhoneyghurk North, Morrison's Diggings.
Willis, William, Commercial Hotel, Colac.
Wilkinson, Thomas, Trangway, Traralgon.
Wilkinson, T., Bacchus Marsh.
Wilkinson, T., Kialla West.
Wilmore, J. B., Meering, Cressy.
Wilson, Alexander, Mount Emu, Skipton.
Wilson, Alexander, Mokepillie, Stawell.
Wilson, A. C., Tarraberb, Sebastian.
Wilson, A., Creswick.
Wilson, A. L., Derinall, Heathcote.
Wilson, C. A., Wareek.
Wilson, Donald, Milool, Swan Hill.
Wilson, David, Mount Egerton.
Wilson, D., Swan Hill.
Wilson, Geo., Marmion, Cavendish.
Wilson, Henry, Wildwood Farm, Conaiogalt.
Wilson, John, Wharparilla.
Wilson, John, Wychetella.
Wilson, John, Woodlands, Ararat.
Wilson, John, Gala, Lismore.
Wilson, Mrs., Murchison.
Wilson, S., and Co., Luna, Benalla.
Wilson, Sir Samuel, Corangamite, Pirron Yaloak P. O.
Wilson, Thomas, Oxley.
Wilson, T. and R., Warrnambool.
Wilson, William, Glenthompson.
Wilson, W. H., Braemore.
Wilson, —, Craigieburn.
Wilson, —, Tarranginnie, Dimboola.
Wills, Thomas, Sailors' Home, Kewell West.
Wiltenhall, H. H., Carro Plains, Glenorchy.
Wiltshire, Geo., Winchelsea.
Wiltshire, G., Winchelsea.
Wimmera Fellmongery Co., Horsham.
Wingfield and Sons, Bridgewater.
Winterbottom, W. H., Kyan Goom Station, Kerang.
Winter, W. J., Noorilim, Dargalong.
Wiseman, L., sen., Newham.
Wood Bros. and Co., Lalbert, Towaninnie, East Charlton.
Wood, James, Myan farm, Mitiamo.
Wood, Mrs., Baringhup.
Wood and Sons, C., Woodlands, Durham Ox.
Woods, John, Woodlands, Moe.
Woods, John, Terrick Terrick.
Woods, J. R., and Co., Portland.
Woodburn, John, Dunkeld.
Woodhead, J., Dunkeld.
Woodley and O'Brien, Uro. Bairnsdale.
Woodside, James, Happy Valley, Myrtleford.
Woodside, Job, Kiewa, Yackandandah.
Woolcott, R. R., View Hill Station, Yarra Flats.
Woolwood, Samuel, Tullygampna.
Wolstenholme, J., Mitiamo.
Worth, Geo., J.P., Shepparton.
Wotherspoon Bros., Beaufort.
Wright, A. J., Waterloo, Gippsland.
Wright, Geo., Majorca.
Wright, James, Majorca.
Wright, S., Pimpinio, Horsham.
Wyatt, Charles, Fyansford.
Yates, David, Kornong, Streatham.
Young, A., Kewell.
Young, Andrew, Pettavel.
Young, Andrew, Willartook, Warrnambool.
Young Bros., Kewell.
Young, David, Woodlands. Echuca.
Young, J., farmer, Upper Emu.
Young, James, Bournont, Tatyoon.
Young, T., Prestonvale.
Young, Thomas, Horsham.
Young, W., Barnerside, near Gordons.
Young, W., Malmsbury.
Younger, Richard, Hamilton.
Younghusband, J., Kileen, Longwood.
Younghusband, J. C., Terrick Terrick, Raywood, via Sandhurst.
Yuille, Geo., Lake Bolac.
Zeppell, William, Bungallaby, via Horsham.
Ziebell, C., Craigieburn.

NEW SOUTH WALES.

Aarons, Jos., Nanima, Wellington.
Abbott, B., Cuerindi North, Liverpool Plains District.
Abbott, James, Coonyal, Mudgee.
Abbott, W. E., Abbotsford, Wingen.
Abbot Brothers, American Yards, Tarcutta, via Albury.
Abercrombie, J., Bombala.
Acres, H., Buckamble, Darling.
Adams, F., Tillilu, Millie.
Adams, H. J., Bogindina, Walgett. via Sydney.
Adams, T. A., General, Gwydir District.
Affleck, William, Gundaroo, via Sydney.
Agnew, Adam, Warner's Corner, Cooma.
Agnew, Edward, Middle Flat, Cooma.
Agnew, Henry, Warren's Corner, Monaro District.
Alderton, William, Leybourne, Liverpool Plains District.
Alexander and Co., Cumberoona, by Bowna.
Alexander, Samuel, and Isaac, Molong Myrong, Wellington District.
Allan, James, Clerwa, Monaro District.
Allen, Benjamin. Kirkelong. Bombala.
Allen, Geo. W., Tharamboue, Liverpool Plains District.
Allen, Mrs. J., Carrol.
Allen, J., Stoney Creek, Little Burringong, Young.
Allen, John, Illunie, Lachlan District.
Allen, W. and Co., Thule, Lachlan.
Alley, A. W., Underwood Farm, Springside.
Allison, J. M., Oakley Creek, Coolah, via Sydney.
Ambery, Geo., Seymour.
Ambrose, R. C., Kangarooby, Lachlan District.
Amos, A. and R., Mount Mitchell, Glen Innes.
Anderson, C., Morago Hotel, Deniliquin.
Anderson and Co., Trida, via Hay.
Anderson, James, Argoon, Jerilderie.
Anderson, J. A., Goona'goa, Albert District.
Anderson and Leigh, North Gyra, Armidale.
Anderson, Mary, Newstead, New England District.
Anderson, T., Stoney Park, Albury.
Andrew, John. Berembed, via Wagga Wagga.
Andrews, —, Harbourne, Daraba, Deniliquin.
Annand and Co., Burtundy, River Darling.
Anson, T., Pretty Pine Hotel, Morago, Deniliquin.
Anstey, Geo., Mohonga, near Urana.
Anstey and Barton, Kajulljah, Booligal, via Hay.
Armstrong, T. and W., Yarrara, Ten-mile Creek, Albury.
Armstrong, W. H., Urana.
Armstrong, —, Noorong, via Deniliquin.
Armitage, F. W., Nocoleche, via Wilcannia.
Armour, John, Cocopara, Lachlan District.
Armour, Matthew, Bogalong, Lachlan District.
Armstrong, A., and Co., Alma, Booligal, via Hay.
Armstrong, Thomas, Wangaradgerie or Neimur, Murrumbidgee District.
Arnold, William, Deniliquin.
Arnold, William, Bellfield, Argoon, Jerilderie.
Arudell, J. A. G.. Glen Diru, near Murrumundi.
Ashcroft, E., Tootal, via Wagga Wagga.
Ashcroft, G., Water View, North Jerilderie.
Ashcroft, James, Canonbar East, via Dubbo.
Ashcroft, W., Corobira, Tumberumba, via Albury.
Astill, Jane, Yullundry, via Sydney and Orange
Atkin, James, Bukelong, Bombala.
Atkin, William, Maharatta, Bombala.
Atkinson, James, Mudgee.
Atkinson, W., Goberagandera, Murrumbidgee District.
Australian Agency and Banking Corporation, Limited, Burrangong, Murrumbidgee District.
Australian Joint Stock Bank, Wilcannia.
Australian Joint Stock Bank, Centre Block No. 3, Liverpool Plains District.
Australian Joint Stock Bank, Wagga Wagga.
Australian Joint Stock Bank, Pedoe Creek. Macleay District.
Australian Joint Stock Bank, Albury.
Austin and Millear, Wanganella, Deniliquin.

Avery, Geo., Jerilderie.
Ayling, C.. Rock Flat, Cooma.
Ayre and Martin, Murtee, via Wilcannia.
Badgery and Badgery, Burrow, Monaro District.
Badham, J. D., Wilton Park, Appin.
Bagot, E. M., Tarrawonda, Albert District.
Bailey, C. W., Ashwell Park, Goondiwindi.
Bailey, —, Havilla, Wellington.
Baily J., Albury road, near Deniliquin.
Baillie, Thomas, Berambah, via Hay.
Baird, —, Obley.
Baird, D. and D., Springs, Wellington District.
Baird, T., Dundallwal, Dubbo.
Baird, W. D., The Springs, Dubbo.
Baker. John, West Jandra, Young.
Baldwin, Charles, Durham Court, Manilla.
Baldwin, Otto, Dinawarindi, Liverpool Plains District.
Balfour, James, Round Hill, via Albury.
Ballantyne, W., Pine Lodge, Tuppal road, via Deniliquin.
Banfather Bros., graziers. Wanganella.
Bank of New South Wales, Wabbra, Liverpool Plains District.
Barber, G. W., Currangorambla South, Monaro District.
Barber, R. A., Humewood, near Yass.
Barber and Burcher, Boniga, via Forbes.
Barber and Dale, Bongalaro, Lachlan District.
Barber, Samuel, Couradigley South, Monaro District.
Barbour, R., Mathoura, near Deniliquin.
Barden, James, Coonabalong, Coonamble.
Barden. Alfred, Mount King East, Albert District.
Bardwell, C. D., Oberne, Tarcutta, via Albury.
Barker, John, Mount Mitchell, New England District.
Barker, R. A., Humewood, Yass.
Barkley, Patrick, Brothers Creek, Cooma.
Barnes and Barnes, Yarringarry, Lachlan District.
Barnes, Richard. Buckley's Crossing, Cooma.
Barnes, Smith and Smith, Ettrick Forest, Clarence District.
Barr, J., Eulumbie, Walgett.
Barrett, J., Morara, Darling River, via Wentworth.
Barrett, George, Bolaro, Cooma.
Barrett, Alexander, Bolaro, Cooma.
Barritt and Wrexford, Morara Station, Wentworth.
Barry, John, Moonbar, Cooma.
Bartholemew and Tressilan, Adelong.
Bartley, Richard, Brothers Creek, Cooma.
Bartley, Thomas, Cooma Creek, Cooma.
Barton, F. G., Miparo North, Lachlan District
Barton, R., Mooculta, via Bourke, Darling River.
Barton, —, Hajulligah.
Barton, Richard, Milgourie, Coonamble.
Basche, Carl, Congarina, Liverpool Plains District.
Bates and Son, Corrly, Darling River, via Wilcannia.
Battye, Captain, Cooma.
Bayliss, Henry, Albert District.
Bear, T., Grong Grong, Wagga Wagga.
Bear, T. H., Pinbeyan Scuth, Monaro District.
Beaumont, J. T., Narengo, near Young.
Beaumont, William, West Bend, Warrego District
Beeby, Geo., Corowa.
Beggs, Thomas, Jindibyne. Cooma.
Beggs and Norman, Blowering, Tumut, via Albury.
Begling, W., Adelong.
Behl, —, Pandula, Eden.
Bell, Benjamin, Munderoo, via Tumberumba.
Bell, David, Spring Flat, Monaro District.
Bell, Henry. Culmier Station, Walgett.
Bell and Hay. Munderoo, Murrumbidgee District.
Bell, James, and Co., Merrungle, via Hay.
Bell, W. W., Morago, near Deniliquin.
Bennett, W., Yandabah, Booligal, via Hay.
Best, J., Back Coronga Peak East. Warrego District.
Bettington, J. B., Brindley Park, Merrima.
Betts, —, sheepowner, Molong.

Bevan, James, Hillston.
Bevan, Matthew, Hillston.
Bevan, P., Hay.
Beveridge, James, Tenandra Peak, Gundagai, N.S.W.
Bigg, Henry E., Thalgarah, New England District.
Biggs and Norman, Blowering, Tumut.
Binnie, R., Mooki, Quirindi.
Black, —, Blue Loby, Inverell.
Blackett, George, Bimble, Coonamble.
Blackman, John, Bigga, via Albury, N.S.W.
Blackwood, James, Gungahman East, Bligh District.
Blackwood, R., Arlington Plains, Darling District.
Blackwood and Moore, Grawin South, Warrego District.
Blair, R., Bungil, Albury.
Blair, James, Jerilderie.
Blair and Caldow, Jerilderie.
Blake, H. P., and Co., Coonimbia, Quambone.
Blake, Matthew, Spring View, Cooma.
Blake, M., Brothers Creek, Cooma.
Blake, Thomas, Golden Spring, Cooma.
Blake, William, Allen's Flat, Cooma.
Blaxland, C., Fordwick, Singleton.
Blaxland and Hayes, Stoney Batter, Armidale, via Sydney.
Blckemore, Isaac and George J., Boomley, Bligh District.
Blomfield, A., Murkadool, Walgett.
Blomfield, A. G., Mongulla West, Warrego District.
Bloomfield, Dr. J., The Willows, Molong, via Sydney.
Bloxham, E. J., North Darling, Warrego District.
Bloxsome, Oswald, Gournama, Gwydir District.
Blyth, John, Ungaree, Lachlan District.
Blyton, Charles, Bobundra, Cooma.
Blyton, J., Jennybrother, Cooma.
Blyton, J., Buckley's Crossing, Cooma.
Bobbin, Geoffrey. Turn Hills, Cooma.
Bobbin, James. Jenny Brothers Creek, Cooma.
Bobbin, John E., Cooma.
Bolger and Cormie, Cumble, Wee Waa.
Bomholdt, Nicholas, Cuddle Creek. Narrandera.
Bonarius, John Charles, Wombromurra, Liverpool Plains District.
Bond, E., Mountain Creek, Billabong, via Albury.
Bond, E. M., Benambra, Germanton. via Albury.
Bonnley, C. S. and Co., Mount Murchison.
Bootes, Wm., Bangus, Murrumbidgee District.
Booth, Abraham, Gobagomlin, Lachlan District.
Booth, Oakden and Co., Wirlong, Hillston, via Hay.
Booth, John, Gobbagomba, Wagga Wagga.
Boots, W., Mundarloo, via Tarcutta.
Botterill, William, Coree, via Deniliquin.
Boucher and Balgetty, Carcour.
Boucher, John, Bukelong, Bombala.
Boulton, E. D., Bergen op Zoon, New England District.
Bowland, Mrs., Back Creek, Cookardinia, via Albury.
Bowland, P., Bald Hill. Greenfell.
Bowman, Alexander, Black Swamp, New England District.
Bowman, E. and A., Skellatar, Muswellbrook, via Sydney.
Boyd, —, Corowa.
Bradley, William, Executors of the late, Bulgar Creek, Monaro District.
Brand, J., Sixteen-mile Hotel, Wangone'la.
Brandon, R. J., Gumanaldry, Warrego District.
Brassil, Patrick, Waroo, Yass.
Brayshaw, E., Bolaro, Cooma.
Breed, J., Mittagong, Wagga Wagga.
Brennan, Edward, Eurobin, Tumut.
Breslan, —, Fuckinginga, Cookardinia, via Albury.
Brewer, John, Merri Merrigal, Lachlan, via Hay.
Brewer and Hines, Naradhun, Lachlan District.
Briesse, —, near Moorwatha, via Albury.
Briscoe, H. H., Kayrunna, Wilcannia.
Britton Bros., Bogenong Station, Coonamble, via Sydney.
Broadhead, F., Kilkite, Cooma.
Brodie, David, Waugra, Cooma.
Brodie, William, Little Plain.
Brodribb and Heal, Tarrawonga, via Hay.
Brodribb, W. A., Duckhurst, Double Bay, Sydney.
Brodribb and Bennett, Moolah, via Hay.
Brooke, H. G., Conaparia, Narrandera.

Brooke, T. C., Taplon, Wentworth, via Swan Hill.
Brooks, A. Weston. Jezederick, Cooma.
Brooks, Henry, Bobundrab.
Brosnan, Patrick, Gum Flat, Cooma.
Broughton and Co., Nubba, via Young.
Broughton, Robert, Gadara, Murrumbidgee District.
Broughton and Sinclair, Nubba Station, Wallendbeen.
Broughton, Thomas, Muttama. Lachlan District.
Brown, Andrew, Brookong, Urana.
Brown, E. G., and Harris, H. L., Tumut Plains, Murrumbidgee District.
Brown, C. W., Branston, Deniliquin.
Brown, C. W. T., Four Bob Camp, Woolangough, via Wagga Wagga.
Brown, D., Kallara, Wilcannia.
Brown, Henry, Boona West, Wellington District.
Brown, Henry, Bendinine, Tangiuan, Garoo.
Brown, Jacob, Narengo, New England District.
Brown, James, Googongs, Queanbeyan.
Brown, James, Norongo, Monaro District.
Brown, John, Guy Fawkes, New England District.
Brown, J. L. and W. F., Yarriman, Liverpool Plains District.
Brown, Joseph, Coaldale, Clarence District.
Brown, R., Dight's Forest, via Albury.
Brown, Thomas, Colombo, Urana, via Deniliquin.
Brown, Thomas, Half-moon Bay, Wellington District.
Brown, Thomas, and Co., Tuppal, via Deniliquin.
Brown, Wallace, Brookong, via Urana.
Brown, —, Hanlons, Conargo Road, Deniliquin.
Brown and Hunt, Melool. via Swan Hill.
Browne, John, Pullaming, Liverpool Plains District.
Bruce, R., Loombah, Molong.
Brunker, Cook and Button, Burran, Liverpool Plains District.
Bruxner, C. A., Sandilands, Clarence District.
Bryan, James, Tendery Vale, Cooma.
Bryant, M., Coolmalong, Monaro, via Sydney.
Bryant Brothers, Hillston and Lachlan River, via Hay.
Bryne, Bros., Rock Road, Wagga Wagga.
Buchan, S., Nyinbodie, Clarence District.
Buchanan, W. F., Kellot House, Sydney.
Buchanan, —. Warana, Coonamble.
Buchanan and Mort, Coolah, Liverpool Plains District.
Buckley, A., Oakville, Jerilderie.
Bucknall, A. and W. W., West Gingham, Gwydir District.
Bucknell Brothers, Yarawa, Narrabri, via Sydney.
Budd, H. F. H., Lalatte, Tocumwal, via Deniliquin.
Budd, Rodd and Co., storekeepers, Adelong.
Bulgary, J., Ando, Bombala.
Bull, Charles, Big River Station, Gwydir District.
Bull, E. B., Ballimore, Dubbo.
Bull, F. W., Prairie Park, Jerilderie.
Bull and Carrol, Yanko Creek, Urana, via Deniliquin.
Bundock, W. E., Waingarie, Casino, via Sydney.
Burcher, W. J. and A. G., Tarranwindie, Coonabarabran.
Burgess, W., Moulamein.
Burke, Edward, Dairiginans Plain, Cooma.
Burke, John, Nunitabeile, Cooma.
Burke, Mrs., Daisy Hill, Mittagong.
Burns, John, Jerrea Jerrea, Albury.
Burns, John, J.P., Cookardinia, via Albury.
Burns and M'Kenzie. Geary, Wellington, N.S.W.
Burritt, Thomas, Rossi Creek, Lower End, Eureka, Lachlan District.
Burrows Brothers, Latay, via Albury.
Burt, R. L., Medway Station, Cobbaro Road, via Dubbo.
Burton, H., Mathoura.
Butler Brothers, Berrima, Goulburn.
Butler, —, Adelong.
Butler, Andrew, Brick Hill Creek, Cooma.
Butter, H., Bathurst.
Butter, John, Butler's Valley, Cooma.
Byrne, Dennis, Back Creek, via Albury.
Byrne, W. A., Cootamundra.
Byrne, David, Billabong, Germantown.
Byrne, G., Tara Hall, Bundara, via Sydney.
Byrne, John, Seymour, Cooma.
Byrnes, M. and V., Winaralla, Cooma.

NEW SOUTH WALES. xxi

Cadell, James John, Dungowan, Liverpool Plains District.
Caddell, A. C., Mudgee.
Caddell, W. T., Deepwater, Dundee.
Caldow, William, Willow Bank, Jerilderie.
Caldwell, John, Mapa, Bombala.
Caldwell, Robert, M'Laughlin River, Bombala.
Callaghan, M. N., Bologamy, Gulliman, Lachlan District.
Cameron, A., Urana.
Cameron, A., Chowar, or Neimur, Murrumbidgee District.
Cameron, D., Jerilderie.
Cameron, D., Tamborough, near Scone.
Cameron, D., Marra Creek, via Willeroon.
Cameron, D., New Babinda, Condobalin, Lachlan, via Hay.
Cameron, D., Noonbar, Warren.
Cameron, Ewen, Broome, Jerilderie.
Cameron, John, Bombala.
Cameron, John, Millie, Moree.
Cameron, K., Water Hole, Queanbeyan.
Cameron, Robert, Burra Creek, Queanbeyan.
Cameron and Co., Pine Grove, Moulamein.
Cameron and Stewart, Bombala.
Campbell, —, Tognemain.
Campbell, Allan, New England District.
Campbell, Anne, Burnima, Monaro District.
Campbell, A. B., Urawilkie, Coonamble.
Campbell Bros., Inverell.
Campbell and Campbell, Toggolo, New England District.
Campbell, D., Tomlong, Bombala.
Campbell, D., Thistlebrook, Cooma.
Campbell, D., Gobondry Station, Forbes.
Campbell, Finlay, Coonargo, Murrumbidgee District.
Campbell, George, M'Laughlin River, Bombala.
Campbell, George, Duntroon. via Queanbeyan.
Campbell, J. S., Glantezlland, Baroorange, via Wilcannia.
Campbell, James. Jerilderie.
Campbell, John, Trigamon, Gwydir District.
Campbell, M., Bungal, Jambie, Dubbo.
Campbell, Ronald, Bombala Station, Bombala.
Campbell, Sophia Jane, Delegat, Monaro District.
Campbell, W. D., Beverly, Burrowa.
Capel, D., Piedmont Gwydir District.
Capp and Loder, Weetalabar, Liverpool Plains District.
Capron, —, Hartwood, via Conargo.
Capron, John, Jindera, via Albury.
Carana, Patrick, Queanbeyan.
Carey, W. Boswell. Cooma.
Carey, Mrs., Bungowannah. via Albury.
Carroll, Edward, Chedowld, Lachlan District.
Carter, Robert, Teviot Bank, Seymour. Cooma.
Cartwright, James, Woodbury. Queanbeyan.
Cartwright, Wm., Cook's Vale, Peelwood, via Goulburn.
Cassidy, P., Noyea, Cowra.
Castle, J. F., Cavan, Murrumbidgee District.
Caton, Mrs. Martha. Wingenbar, Bligh District.
Causley, Thomas, Cowbed. Cooma.
Chalker, Henry, Gangoandra, Cooma.
Chalker, Joseph. Seymour. Cooma.
Chambers, —, Pevensey, Hay.
Chambers, Splatt and Co., Carwell, Gilgandra.
Chapman, —, Delto, near Deniliquin.
Chapman, Mr., Daisy Vale, Deniliquin.
Chapman, W. R., Mullah, Macquarie River, via Dubbo.
Charters, Robert, Woodlands, Queanbeyan.
Cheers, A. B., New Klybucca. Macleay District.
Chenery Brothers, Owinie. Upper Murray.
Cheney, H., Murraguldra P. O.
Cheney, Robert, American Yards, Tarcutta, via Albury.
Chenton, R. H., Holloways, Hay Road, near Deniliquin.
Cheriton, H., Wanganella road, Deniliquin.
Cherry, H., Caraboost, Little Billabong.
Chew, representative of the late John, Danambilla, Lachlan District.
Chippendale, Thomas, Bolero, Monaro District.
Chirnside and Co., Billilla, Darling River, via Wilcannia.
Chirnside, Robert, Honuna, Moon Moon, Lachlan District.
Chisholm, Hon. James, Kippi'aw, Goulburn, via Albury.

Chisholm and Stackey, Wollograng, Goulburn, via Albury.
Chrystal. —, Mulurula, Balranald.
City Bank, Mount Mitchell, New England District.
Clancy, D., Brookong, Urana.
Clancy. J., Brookong, Urana.
Clark Bros., Cullendulvly, Bozgabie, via Sydney.
Clark and Clark, Cullatin, Macleay District.
Clark, John, Kerebury, Hay.
Clark and Macleay, Uratta, Murrumbidgee District.
Clarke, Thomas, Dog Kennel. Cooma.
Clarke. Thomas, Callaghan Swamp, New England District.
Clements, H., Engoura, via Sydney.
Clements, Joseph, Bigga, Goulburn.
Clements, W. H., Lower Cagildry, Obley, via Sydney.
Clifford. James, Bredbow Station, Cooma.
Clifford, P. J., Rose Valley, Cooma.
Clift Bros., Breeza, Tamworth, via Sydney.
Clifton, J., Corowa.
Clive, C. F., Collaroy, Merriwa, via Sydney.
Clive and Hamilton, Colligblu, Liverpool Plains District.
Close, Sydney, Curra, Forbes.
Clough, J. H. and C., Bent's Hills, Lachlan District.
Cobb and Co., Bathurst.
Cobcroft, J., Mathegar No. 2, Gwydir District.
Cobcroft, J., jun., Mathegar No. 2, Gwydir District.
Cochran, James, Widgiewa, Urana.
Cochrane, Lachlan, Yasuk, Monaro District.
Cochrane, Mary Anne, Long Flat, New England District.
Codie, S., Jingerra, Monaro District.
Codrington, C. and J., Warialda, via Sydney.
Codrington, C., Coolatai, Inverell.
Coffey, Michael, Bobundrah, Cooma.
Cogan, David, Boloca Creek, Cooma.
Cohen, A., Lindsay, Gwydir District.
Cohen and Levy, Gyra, New England District.
Cohen, Levy, Cohen and Cohen, Bangalore, Bligh District.
Cohen, George, Cooma.
Coleman, John, Big Range, Bowna.
Coleman, Henry, Big Range. Bowna.
Coleman, Thomas, Back Creek, Gundaroo.
Coleman, W. J., Brigalow Scrub, Liverpool Plains.
Colles, Arthur, Come-by-Chance, Pilliga.
Colles, Arthur and William, Jim-a-long-josey, Liverpool Plains District.
Collins, G. R. W., Mohonga, via Urana.
Colliss and Co., Errombinka Station, Cooper's Creek, via Bourke.
Colman, John, Wicklow, Block A., Wellington.
Colman, Thomas, William, Charles, John. Edward, Robert, and A., Belleroy, Bligh District.
Colman, William, Gunyillah, Bligh District.
Comans, M., Conibaning, Cootamundra, via Wagga Wagga.
Comans and Heffernan, Houlahan's Creek, North Lachlan District.
Comford, James, Tyagong Creek, via Young.
Commercial Bank, Albury.
Commercial Bank, Bourke.
Condor, Francis, Mickey, Gunegal, Bligh District.
Connall, J., and Mrs. A. D., Ingleba. New England District.
Connell, —, Dixon's Swamp, via Albury.
Connell, James, Jerilderie.
Connell, William M., Merri Merri Station, Gilgandra, via Sydney.
Connelly, Peter, sen., Briobo Station, Cooma.
Conroy, John, Stony Creek, Lachlan District.
Constance, James, Coolahalantra, Cooma.
Conway, Matthew, Baugalai B, Lachlan District.
Cook, John, Bolaro, Cooma.
Cook, J. R., Colombo, via Jerilderie.
Cook, R., Bonangra Station, Goondiwindi.
Cook, Thomas, Turanville, Scone.
Cookes, J. W., Bibbenlake, Bombala.
Cooper and Buckland. Thoco, Monaro District.
Cooper, M. E., Wanganella.
Cooper, Theophilus, Beverley, New England District.
Cooper, V., Lake George.
Cooper, W., Wanganella.
Copeland, Henry, Narybaba, Monaro District.
Copeland, James, Conbanning, near Wagga Wagga.
Corcoran, Jos., Bombala.
Correlli, R. Victor, Little Forest Lodge, Cooma.

Corrigan, H., Bowna.
Cormack, A., Yanga, Balranald.
Cornish, T., Mundadoo, Cannoulan.
Corso, John, Numeralla, Monaro District.
Cosgrove, J., jun., Engeldry, Wellington District.
Cosgrove, J., sen., Billilingera, Cooma.
Cosgrove, William, Riversdale.
Cotter, Garrett, Michaelago, Cooma.
Cotter, James, Naas Creek, Queanbeyan.
Cousins, R. J., Wardry, Lachlan District.
Coventry, William, Kangaroo Hills, New England District.
Coward, Dr. H., Germantown, via Albury.
Cowled, C. W., Junee.
Cox, A., Willunga, Mudgee.
Cox and Callaghan, Upper Wyalong, Lachlan District.
Cox, Charles, Broomby, Mudgee.
Cox, E. K., Rawdon, Mudgee.
Cox and Hore, Cookaburragong, Lachlan District.
Cox, Mrs. John, Mangoplah, via Albury.
Cox, J. D., Cullenbone, near Mudgee.
Cox, O., Grubbon, via Wagga Wagga.
Cox, P. J., Merringreen, Wagga Wagga.
Cox, R., Marrar, via Wagga Wagga.
Cox, R. W., Bengman Station, near Rylstone, via Sydney.
Cox, R. and P., Kildary, Wagga Wagga.
Crane, O'Connor and Co., Balranald.
Cramsie, Bowden and Co., Balranald.
Craven and M'Auliffe, Glenroy, Murrumbidgee District.
Crawford, Archd., Brookong, via Urana.
Crawford and Brayshaw, Baboyan, Monaro District.
Crawford, —, Urangeline Creek, via Albury.
Crawford, Eliza, Enmore, New England District.
Crawford, John, Springfield, Cooma.
Crawford, Patrick, Boloca, Cooma.
Crane, Andrew, Garryowen P. O., via Albury.
Creed, J., Wangamong Plains, Murrumbidgee District.
Creswick, H., Liewah, via Deniliquin.
Crisp, A., Buckley's Crossing.
Crisp and Lintatt, Torrens Creek, Albert District.
Crisp, H. M., Mathoura, near Deniliquin.
Croaker, A., Piallaway, Breeza.
Croaker, J. W., Burrumundra, Young.
Croft, H. A., Cookardinia.
Cross, George, Filbuster, Armidale.
Crosse and Featherstonhaugh, Corella, Brewarrna.
Crossing and Cox, Mudgee.
Crossley, Eli, Whoey, Euabalong, Lachlan.
Crowe, B., Hamsley, Cooma, via Sydney.
Crowe, J. B., Germantown.
Crowe and Carberry, Goburrabong, Lachlan District.
Crowe, J. J., Jingellac.
Crowley, W., Cobbidah, Gwydir District.
Crozier, John, Kulnine, Lower Murray, via Swan Hill.
Crozier, W., Ana Branch, Wentworth.
Cruge, Henry, Gilgunnia, via Hillston.
Cudmore, D. and D. H., Avoca, Wentworth, via Swan Hill.
Culigan, J., The Wells, West Blowering, Tumut.
Culkane, Edward, Morilu, via Wagga Road.
Cullen, John, Bunyan, Cooma.
Cummings, M., sen., Waterhole, Queanbeyan.
Cummings, W. and C., Gunbar, via Hay.
Cunningham, A. J., Lanyon, Queanbeyan.
Cunningham, Hastings, Berembed, North Lachlan District.
Curtin, M., Jerilderie.
Curtis, A. J., The Denison Reserve, Macleay District.
Curtis, James, Mount Adrah, Adelong.
Curtis, Peter, Cooma.
Cust, John, Deniliquin.
Cust, Thomas, Pretty Pine Hotel, Hay Road, Deniliquin.
Dale, John, Bogalero, Bookham, via Albury.
Daley, Patrick, Wanganella, Deniliquin.
Daley, Owen, Mullingandra, via Albury.
Dalgleish, A., Willow Vale, Hanlon, Deniliquin.
Dallas, J. A., Berembed, via Narandera.
Dalton, James and Thomas, Geweroo, Wellington District.
Dangar Brothers, Uralla, via Sydney.
Dangar and M'Donald, Wantabadgery, Lachlan River.

Dangar, A. A., Baroona, Singleton.
Dangar, T. G., Bullerawa, Wee Waa.
Dangar, W. J., Neatsfield, Singleton.
Daniel, Giles, Jerilderie.
Darby, S. H., Tiengah, New England District.
Darby and Everett, Winscombe, Inverell.
Darchy, William, Tarcoola, Darling River, via Wentworth.
Darchy, T., Oxley, via Balranald.
Darlot and Co., Gelam, Maude, via Hay.
Darlot, H., Bundyulumblah, via Deniliquin.
Darmody, James, Majura, Queanbeyan.
Davey and Linker, Wallangandra, via Albury.
Davidson, A. and H. T., Mandamah, via Wagga Wagga.
Davidson Brothers and Co., Geraldra, Young.
Davison, Thomas, Extended Curraweena, Warrego District.
Davidson, W., Billebong, via Wagga Wagga.
Davis, F., Cathcart, Bombala.
Davis, Samuel, Yeumburra, Queanbeyan.
Davis, William, Gongohleen, Ginninderra, via Sydney.
Davis, W. W., Forbes.
Davy, J., Dora Dora, Upper Murray.
Dawson, Henry, Cooma.
Day, Geo., Albury.
Day, Hayes and M'Lennan, Moama Block T, Albert District.
Day, James, Daysdale, via Albury.
Day, James and William, Mohonga, near Urana.
Deakin, J., Tocumwal.
Deegan, James, Little Plain, Cooma.
Deegan, M., Little Plain, Cooma.
Delaney, Fenton, Euacumbyne, Cooma.
Delaney, James, Buckenderry, Cooma.
Delbouse, T. L., Eight-mile Hotel, Couargo Road, Deniliquin.
Dolves, Daniel, Numitabelle.
Denne, R. H., Tia River, New England District.
Dennis, John, Tara, Eubalong, via Hay.
Dent, John, Oma Creek, Greenfell.
Desailly, Alfred, Netallic, via Wilcannia.
Devereux, Edward, Spring Flat, Cooma.
Devereux, J. J., The Springs, Dangelong, near Cooma.
Devlin, A. A., Newfoundland, Clarence District.
Dickson and Dickson, Frochester, Clarence District.
Dickson, G. L., Nabba, Lachlan River.
Dickson, John, Murryang, Monaro District.
Dickson, J. and J., Caroonboon, via Deniliquin.
Dickson, W. and T. C., Yarrawin, Marra Creek, via Wellcroon.
Diggs and Cameron, Mandoran, Bligh District.
Dight Brothers, Bungowannah.
Dight, G. W., Yetman, Narrabri.
Dight and Mackay, Bulgandramine, Obley.
Dight, S. B., Clifford, Singleton.
Dillon, John, Dolto, near Deniliquin.
Dines, G. and R., Merrewah, Warialda.
Dingwell, Mrs., Wanganella.
Ditchfield, W., Springfield, Cookardinia, via Albury.
Donaldson, Richard, Cookardinia, Back Creek, near Wagga Wagga.
Donnelly, John, Toolong, Murrumbidgee District.
Donnelly, J. J., Borambula, Tarcutta, via Albury.
Donnelly, P. J. J., Bywong, Gundaroo.
Donohue Brothers, Bourbah, Gilgandra.
Doods, E., Eumerella, Cooma.
Douch, William, Bombala.
Doubledeay, G. and R., Albury.
Dougharty, J. G., Ilyandra East, Lachlan District.
Douglas, H., and Co., Walla Walla, Ten-mile Creek, via Albury.
Dowe, Joshua, Woolomal, Liverpool Plains District.
Dowling and Co., Ganangie, via Parkes.
Dowling and Martin, Snow Vale, Monaro District.
Dowling, Reginald, Geanigle, Bulgandramine, via Orange.
Downey, Robert, Manus Creek, Reedy Flat, Murrumbidgee District.
Downing, Robert, Tumut.
Doyle, B. W., Wanganella.
Doyle, L. P., Box, near Quipolly, via Sydney.
Doyle, —, Muckorama, Darling River, via Bourke.
Doyle, M., sen., Yamma, via Albury.

Doyle, R. R., Dumble, Goodooga.
Drake, F. G. and C., Albury.
Draper, James, Weiragandria, Wellington District.
Draper, M. and H., Redbank, near Molong, via Sydney.
Driscoll, James, Summer Hill, Numitabelle, Cooma.
Druitt, Rev. T., Cooma.
Druitt, W. T., Bolaca, Buckley's Crossing, Cooma.
Drummond, W., Bogalong, Bookham, via Albury.
Duff, James William, Pingobla, Warrego District.
Dugan, William, Minore, Wellington District.
Dunn, Job, Hillis Creek, via Tarcutta.
Dunn, John, sen., Quidong, Bombala.
Dunn, P., Mulwala, via Deniliquin.
Dunn, Thomas, Buckley's Crossing, Cooma.
Dunne, John, Netley, Darling River, via Swan Hill.
Dunne, W., Mathoura, near Deniliquin.
Durham, E., Deniliquin.
Durham, W., and Co., Wombat, Singleton.
Dyball, Henry, Arable, Cooma
Dwyer, Thomas, Molonglo, Queanbeyan.
Earls, —, Wangonella, via Deniliquin.
Easons, Geo., Gigullalong, Burrowa.
Ecclestone, David, Rock Forest, Cooma.
Ecclestone, Henry John, Snowy River, Monaro District.
Eckford, John, Burren Burren, Warrego District.
Edgar Brothers, Erebendery, Enbalong, Lachlan via Hay.
Edgehill, Charles, Mundawaddera, via Wagga Wagga.
Edols, Mrs., Burryjaa, via Corowa.
Edols, Thomas and Co., Burrawong, Lachlan, via Forbes.
Edwards, E. S., Bastobrick, Clarence District.
Edwards, H. T., Bombala.
Edwards, J. P., Adelong.
Egan Brothers, Mount Harris.
Egan, W., Spring Vale, Toojong, via Sydney.
Elliott, G. A., Thagoara, Albert District.
Elliott, T. N., Dutjon or Bellapalah, Murrumbidgee District.
Elliott, W. R., Turio Colah, via Sydney.
Ellis, J. W., South Darling, via Hillston or Cobar.
Elmslie, A. and A. D., Strachan, Glen Ken, Murrumbidgee District.
Emanuel and Real, Green Hills, Murrumbidgee District.
Englebert, —, Felton Waterhole, near Deniliquin.
English, E., Jerilderie.
Erles, John, Wangonella.
Evans and Welsh, Gilgunina, Lachlan, via Hay.
Evans, David, Kyra Lake, Bombala.
Evans, Evan, Roto, via Booligal, Lachlan River.
Evans. R., Kiah Lake, Gejedezeriek. via Sydney.
Everett, Isaac, Monago, near Deniliquin.
Everett, R. J., Tchelory, via Deniliquin.
Faed, —, Bukewah, Urana.
Fahey, F., Ketchenary and Brogo, Murrumbidgee District.
Faithful, W. P., Brewarrina, Murrumbidgee District.
Faithful, —, Springfield, Goulburn, via Albury.
Falconer, Mrs. C., Woolloomoolenby, Bligh District.
Falconer, F. F., Murwillimba, Clarence District.
Falconer, J. L., Cobranragy, Bligh District.
Falkner, F. S., and Co., Boonooke, Conargo, via Deniliquin.
Fallon, L., Bullina, near Deniliquin.
Fanning, W. and F., Mungogery or Busby's Flat, Clarence District.
Farley, John, River Tree East, Clarence District.
Farley, M., Albury.
Farquharson, G., Inverey, Namoi River, via Sydney.
Father, H. C. and E., Norfolk, Liverpool Plains District.
Fennell, Stephen, Eringoara, via Wagga Wagga.
Fergers, John, Bombala.
Fergusson Brothers, Neurea, near Molong and Wellington.
Ferrier, James, Hillston.
Field, Joseph, Deniliquin.
Field, P., Carowobitty, near Forbes.
Fink and Levien, Jumble Plains, block H, Wellington District.
Finlay, A. G., Mulga, No. 2, Warrego District.

Finlay and Gibson, Kenilworth Station, Goulburn.
Finlay and Moore, Darlington Point, via Hay.
Finn, W., Colombo, via Deniliquin.
Finnessy, John, Mathoura, near Deniliquin.
Firth, P. J., Tubbo Station, Lower Murrumbidgee.
Fisher and Beaumont, Keelandi, Pilliga.
Fisher, C. B., Moon Moon, Curra, Lachlan District.
Fisher and Hoskins, Cooma.
Fisher, Hill, Bullamon, Mungindi.
Fisher, J., Gulgo, via Forbes.
Fisher, R., Willow Station, Bokhara Creek, via Brewarrina.
Fitzgerald and Co., Tinapage, Paroo River, via Wilcannia.
Fitzpatrick, Thomas, Carcoar.
Flavelle, John, Berembed, Lachlan District.
Fletcher, James, Wee Waa, Liverpool Plains District.
Fletcher, Jane, Ballagalar, Bligh District.
Fletcher, J. A., Jandra River, Darling.
Flood, E., jun., New Bellemore, Bligh District.
Flood, Hon. E., Berada, Sydney.
Flood, J. J., Bolero, Wagga Wagga.
Flynn Bros., Mountain Creek, Germantown, via Albury.
Flynn, J., Countigany, Monaro District.
Flynn, M., Kalki, Jerilderie.
Foord, J. C., Terawinda Plains, No. 2, Albert District.
Forlong, W., Murrumbidgeriee, Wellington.
Forrester, W. J., Yarramon, Liverpool Plains District.
Forsyth, George, c/o C. E. Brown, Esq., Tumut.
Foster, John S., West Bogan, No. 6, Wellington District.
Fowler, — Upper Coolagong, via Young.
Fox, —, Towal, Forbes.
Framfielder, Brookong, Urana.
Framfielder, C. F., Colombo Creek P.O.
Francis, Henry, Bungowannah.
Francis, Owen, Killawarra.
Franklin, G. T. and J. M., Erindebilla, Monaro District.
Franklin, Thomas, Bramina, Monaro District.
Fraser, A., Vine Lodge Farm, Albury Road, via Deniliquin.
Fraser, Colin C., Milroy, Brewarrina.
Frazer, D., Darlington Point, via Hay.
Freebody, James, Woolway, Cooma.
Freebody, John, jun., Middling Bank, Cooma.
Freebody, John, sen., Woolway, Cooma.
Freebody, Simon, sen., Woolway, Cooma.
Freeman, W., Greenwich, Clarence District.
Frew, George, Euabalong, Lachlan River, via Hillston.
Gagie, W., Corowa.
Gain, Mrs. Johanna, Bowna.
Gallagher, J., Warraberry Station, near Parkes, via Sydney.
Gallagher, Michael and Martin, Moodong, Monaro District.
Galvin Brothers, Oberne, via Adelong.
Galvin, George, Glenburn, Tarcutta, via Albury.
Galvin, Thomas, Oberne, Tarcutta, via Albury.
Gang, John, Mybrea, Bookham, via Albury.
Gardiner, —, Chesterley, Wanganella.
Gardiner, A., Yanko Creek, Jerilderie.
Gardiner, Andrew, Upper Weeli East, Wellington District.
Gardiner, John, Willa Marra Creek, Wellington District.
Gardiner, J. A., Gobolion, Wellington.
Gardiner, J. C., Barah West, Coonabarabran.
Garland, J., Wilcannia.
Garland, R., Wilcannia.
Garnock, Charles, Mount Pleasant, Bombala.
Garnock, George, Mount Pleasant, Bombala.
Garry, L., Garryowen P.O., via Albury.
Garry, J. J., Mylora Station, near Binalong, via Albury.
Gatenby, U. and E., Burra Burra, Forbes.
Gayer and Hamilton, Modern Station, Wilcannia.
Geldmacher, J., Numitabel, Cooma.
Gell and Walker, Burrangong, Urana.
George, Joseph, Bendeddra, Monaro District.
Geraghty, Michael, Cathcart.
Geraghty, Thomas, Avon Lake, Cooma.
Gibbs, A., Yarralumla, Queanbeyan.
Gibson, Braime and Co., Deniliquin.

Gibbs, G., Carabost, Kyamba.
Gibbs and Sons, James, Berthong, Young.
Gibbs, Robert, Walbundrie.
Gibbs, W. and B., Carabost, Tarcutta, via Albury.
Gibson, A., Terina, Goulburn.
Gibson, A. N., Warwillah, Wanzonella.
Gibson, G. L., Longford, New England District.
Gibson, J., Naringa, Hay.
Gibson, J. and R., Mallara, Darling River, via Wentworth.
Gibson, L., Bombala Station, Bombala.
Gibson, T. J., Burrumbuttock, near Albury.
Gibson, T. J. T. and A. F., Tantangara, or Gulph, Monaro District.
Gilbert, Alex., Dry Plain, Cooma.
Giles, Edgar, Morna Station, near Wentworth.
Gill, G. R., Emu Plains, Walcha.
Gill, John, Moonbi Moonbi.
Gillard, W., Binda, via Goulburn.
Gillies, A. C., Molonga Station, Nerandera.
Gillingham, M., Wangonella.
Gilman, R. J., Millagong, via Wagga Wagga.
Gilmour, John N., Bulgandamine, Bogan River, via Sydney.
Glanville, William, Myack, Cooma.
Glass and Corrigan, Eurie Eurie, Wa'gett, via Sydney.
Glasscock, R., Upper Miroo, Mudgee.
Glasson Brothers, Blayney.
Gleeson, —, Crangeline Creek, via Albury.
Gleeson, John, Brookong, Urana.
Glennan, Jos., Cooma Creek, Cooma.
Godfrey, F. R., Pevensey, Hay.
Golby, Thomas, Numbla, Buckley's Crossing, Cooma.
Goldsbrough and Maiden. Telleraga, Moree.
Goldsbrough and Parker, Muralebale, Lachlan District.
Goodison, R. G., Robertson, Warrego District.
Goodwin, G., Goodwin Brook, Cooma.
Goodwin, Robert, Middle Flat, Cooma.
Goodwin, W., Cranky Dan's Flat, Cooma.
Goorning, Patrick, Nerandera.
Gordon, H., Bundy, Coonamble.
Gordon, Samuel D., Bundy, Bligh District.
Gordon and Waugh, Drungalear, Walgett.
Gordon, W., Millie.
Gormley, James, Coronga Peak, Burke.
Gorton, Geo., and Son, Coneac, New England District.
Gowland, F. W., Wagga Wagga.
Gowing, Daniel, Murrah, Monaro District.
Goyder and Walsh, Sussex Station, Cobar P. O., via Hay and Hillston.
Grant, Henry, Yaelama, Monaro District.
Grant, John, jun., Merriganowy, Lachlan District.
Graves and Maher, Bolygamygulman, via Rankin Springs, Nerandera.
Graves, W. H., Oberwells, Darling District.
Gray and Niell, Sandy Ridges, Corowa.
Gray, Basil, Welareguang, Upper Murray.
Gray, Geo., Sandy Ridges, Corowa.
Gray, John D., Gombargona, Corowa.
Greaves and Mack, Rock and Tinora, Wagga Wagga.
Greaves, W. A. B., Bald Hills, Clarence District.
Greenfield, C. S., Gudgenbie, Monaro District.
Gregson, J., Albury.
Griffiths, —, Conargo, near Deniliquin.
Griffiths, J. A., Hillas Creek, via Tarcutta.
Groves, Jessie, Bobundrah, Cooma.
Gruggen, C. P., North Quirindi, Liverpool Plains, via Sydney.
Guest, Richard, Yaven Creek, Adelong.
Guest, Robert, Jindera, via Albury.
Gunning, A., Gejezerick West, Monaro.
Gwyden, —, Mathoura P. O., near Deniliquin.
Hagens and Kirkpatrick, Wensley Chase, Deniliquin.
Hain, James, Cooma.
Hall, Charles, Teviot Dale, Moonwatha.
Hall, D., Cooma.
Hall, Reuben, Pially, Liverpool Plains District.
Halliday, Wm., Brookong, Urana.
Ham, George, Cooma.
Hamilton, Matthew, Bankside, Clarendon, via Wagga Wagga.
Hamilton, R. and C., Baullan, Nerandera.
Hamlet, Fletcher and Co., Boolcarral, or Tooladumia, Wee Waa.

Hammett, John, Peak Creek, Cooma.
Hanley, Thomas, Numitabelle, Cooma.
Hanlon, John, Lauriston Farm, Deniliquin.
Hansen, Thomas, Wensley Chase, Deniliquin.
Hannah Bros., Cowabee Station, Wagga Wagga.
Hannah, L. H., Reedy Creek, Jugiong.
Hannan, J., Cave Flat, Lachlan District.
Hanniford, James, Rock Flat Creek, Cooma.
Harden, T., Manilla, Manilla..
Hardie and Miller, Goangra, Walgett, via Sydney.
Hardiman, J., Pudman's Creek, Barrowa.
Harding, W., Mathoura, Deniliquin.
Hargrave, E., Hermani, New England District.
Hargrave, R., Hillgrove.
Harkness, Wm., Jennybrother, Cooma.
Harmon, George, Quandary, Lachlan District.
Harnett, Mrs. Mary, Eucumbene, Monaro District.
Harnett, Maurice, Rosebrook, Cooma.
Harper, —, Numitabelle, Cooma.
Harper, —, Charles, A., Crankie's Plain, Bomba'a.
Harris, George, Wheeo, near Goulburn.
Harrison, H. W., Wangunella.
Hart, Richard, Hartwood Grove, Corec.
Hart and Horn, Umberumberka, Albert District.
Harvey, George, Umarella, Cooma.
Haslingdon, E. J., Big Badger, Cooma.
Hassell, J. M., Wainbrook Lake, Cooma.
Hastings, M., Nora, Tooleybuc, Deniliquin.
Hatson, William, Jandra, Fort Bourke, Darling River.
Hawkins and M'Kenzie, Geary, Bligh District.
Hawson, Scott and Co., Wilcannia.
Hay, Thomas, sen., Rock Flat, Cooma.
Hay, William, Collindia, Murrumbidgee.
Hay, Hon. William, Boomanoomana, via Deniliquin.
Haydon, H., Delegate Station, near Cooma.
Haylock, Cornelius, Cooma.
Heath, —, Cobram, near Deniliquin.
Hebden, —, Cooma.
Hebden, G. H., Chaa., S. B. and Wm. W., Geolgdrie, Lachlan District.
Hedgers, George, Munbla, Buckley's Crossing, Cooma.
Hefferman and M'Kenzie, New Bombaldry, Forbes.
Hellman, J., Beanba, Coonamble.
Hempenstall, G., Barham, near Deniliquin.
Henderson, —, Tooleybuc,Balranald.
Henderson, —, The Rock, Junee, Wagga Wagga.
Henderson Bros., Tathong, Hillston.
Hennessy, Bros., Tocumwal.
Hensleigh, J. A., Tinbilica.
Hepburn and Leonard, Bynya, Nerandera, via Wagga Wagga.
Hepburn, Robert, Collamatong, Monaro District.
Hepburn, Wm., Collamatong, Cooma.
Herbert, W. C., Bolaro, Cooma.
Heriot, E., Carabobala, Germantown, via Albury.
Hervey, D., Wanganella.
Hession, Patrick, Albury.
Hetherington, Paul, Wangonella.
Hey, E., Water-hole, Forbes.
Higgins, A., Albury.
Higgins, R. G., Kickerbill, Liverpool Plains.
Higgins and Smith, Burrell, Liverpool Plains.
Higgins, Wm., Merrimerriwa, Lachlan District.
Hill, D., Warbreecan, near Deniliquin.
Hill, Hector, Grawley, Mount Harris.
Hill, R., and Sons, Butterbone, Mount Harris.
Hillier, Henry, Bowna.
Hillson, E., Tocumwal, via Deniliquin.
Hinchcliffe, Andrew, Oura Oma, Lachlan District.
Hinds. E., Newington, Gundaroo.
Hogan, Patrick, Dry Plain, Cooma.
Holloway and Sons, Moonbooldool, via Wagga Wagga.
Holmes, D., Warbreccan, Deniliquin.
Holmes, R., Brassie Farm, via Deniliquin.
Holmes, William, Delto, Deniliquin.
Holscheer, — Moama P. O.
Homan. E., Moama.
Home, J. H. L., Bibbenluke, Bombala.
Hope, A., Bumbaldry, Lachlan District.
Hope, J., Para Station, Darling.
Hope and Scott, Bombery, Brewarrina, Darling River.
Hopkins, W. H., Bombala.
Hore, Andrew, Mugmugwong, Murrumbidgee District.
Hore, J., Cumberoona, via Albury.
Hore, Thomas, Albury.

Horsley, E. J., Yabtree, Wagga Wagga.
Horsley, R. F., Yabtree, Gundagai, via Albury.
Horton, J. S., Moulamein.
Hoskisson, Thomas, Barraba Creek, Liverpool Plains District.
Hough, H. A., Mulwala P. O.
Houston, —, Coobang, Forbes.
Howard Brothers, Goombargona, Corowa.
Howatson and Strachan, Boondara, via Hay.
Howe, Mrs. Leah, Gunongjugerawah, Murrumbidgee District.
Howell, F. W., Hawthorne.
Howell, Theodore, Yeumburra, Queanbeyan.
Hudson, C., Coonarong, Cooma.
Hudson, J., Moolpar, Moulamein, via Deniliquin.
Huggins, Thomas, Louth, River Darling.
Hughes and Maher, Nairamine, via Dubbo.
Hughes, H. B., Kinchega, Wentworth.
Hume, A. H., Rye Park, Everton, Pudmore Creek, Burrowa.
Hume, F. R., jun., Frankfield, Gunning.
Hume, F. W., Castlestead, Burrowa.
Hungerford, T., Baeninie, Denman.
Hunt, G. T., Obbela Park, Obley.
Hunt, M., Tuppal, near Deniliquin.
Hunt and Leslie, Ungaree, Woolangong.
Hunter, J., Haddon Rig, Dubbo.
Huon and Collins, North Bolaro, Lachlan District.
Hyde, E., Bombala.
Ibbotson and Blackwood, Darling, block D, Darling District.
Icely, T. R., Coombing Park, Carcoar
Hould, W., Echerboon East, Albert District.
Inglis, Russell A., Moothumbil, via Forbes.
Ingram and Co., Book Book, Tarcutta, via Albury.
Ingram, Henry, Burmind, Bombala.
Ingram, John, Bombala.
Inlary, A., Comongin, Thorgomindah.
Innes, W., near Jerilderie.
Irby, E., Bolivia Station, near Tenterfield, via Sydney.
Iredale, L. F., Goolhi Gunnedah, via Sydney.
Irvine, W. and J., Terraminganic, Dubbo.
Irving and Irving, West Moonul, Bligh District
Irving, Thomas, Deniliquin Run, near Deniliquin.
Ives, Joseph, Bombala.
Jackson, —, Wangra River, Monaro, via Sydney.
Jackson, James, Moulamein.
Jackson, John, Borce Creek, Urana.
Jackson, R., Bobrah or Morbi, Bligh District.
Jackson, W., Jerilderie.
Jaffrey, —, Burryjaa, Corowa.
James, G. W., Bungowannah.
Jamieson, T. C., Pindhoe Grange, Tuppal River, Deniliquin.
Jardine, C., Jindabyne, Cooma.
Jardine, William, Curry Flat, Cooma.
Jeffrey, Robert J., Medoway, Bligh District.
Jeffreys, H. C., Murrumbidgee, Wellington District.
Jell, —, near Howlong.
Jenkins, Francis, Buckingbong, Norandera.
Jenkins, John, Gundagai, via Albury.
Jenkins, J. T., Burthong North, Lachlan District.
Jenkins, R. L., Carbuckery, Gwydir District.
Jillett, Thomas, Buddingower, via Wagga Wagga.
Johns, —, Hay.
Johnson, Charles, Coohalamba, Cooma.
Johnson, J., Murrumbidgee, Cooma.
Johnson, J. H., Hartfell. Gunnedah, via Sydney.
Johnson, W., Redbank, Cooma.
Jones, A. G., Wheogo, Bland, via Wagga Wagga.
Jones, —, Wilson, Yanko Creek.
Jones, A., Jerilderie.
Jones, Evan, Coree, near Deniliquin.
Jones, F., Walgiers, near Booligal, via Hay.
Jones, Geo., Murray Hut, Tocumwal.
Jones, Green and Sullivan, Chowchowbroo, Albert District.
Jones, H., Chasing, Deniliquin.
Jones, Jessie, Tooleybuc, Balranald.
Jones, John, Delegate, Bombala.
Jones, J. R., Derra Derra, Gwydir District.
Jones, Rees, Yass.
Jones, Richard, Back Creek, Germanton, via Albury.
Jones, William, Ten-mile Selection, Albury Road, near Albury.
Josephs, H. M., Mahratta, Bombala.

Joss, A., Mathoura.
Joss. A. S., Mathoura.
Julian. Richard. Bogalong, Lachlan District.
Jurd, John, Orraba. New England District.
Kain, J., Pullitop, Germantou.
Kahns, G., Walla Walla.
Kahns, J. G., Jindera.
Kane, Frank, Clifton, Little Billabong, Ten-mile Creek.
Keane, E. J., Moony Moony, Lachlan District.
Keane, J., Burke's Creek, Wagga Wagga.
Keane, J. J., Narraburrah, Greenfell, Bland.
Kearns and Curtis, Rock Forest, Monaro District.
Keating, M., Seymour, Cooma.
Keefe, Garrett, Michaelago.
Keop, Day and Ronald, Pretty Plains, block B, Liverpool Plains District.
Keighran, Thomas, Dudal, Cooma, via Albury.
Keim, Patrick, Cookardinia, Albury.
Kelly, —, Calabash, Young.
Kelly and Gillett, Glen Iligh West, Clarence District.
Kelly, C., Stoney Creek, Bundaria, via Sydney.
Kelly, D., Rosebrook, Cooma.
Kelly, J. E., Rankin's Hill, No. 3 C, Warrego District.
Kelly and Martin, Stoney Creek, New England District.
Kelly and Parkman, Calabash. Lachlan District.
Kelly, R., Mara Creek, Cannonbar.
Kennedy and Clarence, Narrawah, near Gunning, via Albury.
Kennedy and Hume, Currangorambla West, Monaro District.
Kennedy, J., Bugegang, Yanko Creek, Colombo, via Jerilderie.
Kennedy, R., Collingwood, Gunning.
Kennedy, R. H., Kayrunnera, via Wilcannia.
Kentish, S. P., Kiandra.
Keog, —, Wagra, Bowan.
Keogh and Bennett, Cuthowarra, Albert District.
Keon, Ferdinand, Kara, Cooma.
Kearns, Walter, Rock Forest, Cooma.
Kerr, J., Werribong, Dandoolah.
Kerrison, G. P., Candelo.
Kesby and Kesby, Currungula, Mac'eay District.
Keys and White, Egerton, New England District.
Kiddle, L., and Co., Steam Plains, Conargo, via Deniliquin.
Killeen, E., Yanko, Jerilderie.
Kimber, Geo., Bombala.
Kindham, —, Yanko, near Deniliquin.
King, Geo., jun., Eumarella, Cooma.
King, Geo., sen., Eumarella, Cooma.
King, John, Bolaro.
King and King, Kingston, New England District.
King, John, Hanging Rock, Mangoplah, via Albury.
King, P. G., Gonoo Gonoo, Tamworth, via Sydney.
King, P., Halfway House, Ballangeich.
King, R. N. and F., Boolooroo, Moree.
King, W. E., Calpaulln, River Darling.
Kinnear, R. S., Overflow Station, Eubalong, via Hay.
Kirby, J., Candelo.
Kirby, F. J., Brookong, via Urana.
Kirk, Geo., Gulnanbar, St. George.
Kirkpatrick, Hagens and Co., woolscourers, Wilcannia.
Kirkpatrick, Luke and Co., Wilcannia.
Kirwin, Thomas, Bobindrah, Cooma.
Kiss, William, Bobindrah, Cooma.
Kite, W., Bathurst.
Klemble, G., Albury.
Klemke, Geo., Walla Walla.
Krelner, —, Slack Plain, Cooma.
Kook, H., Darlington, via Hay.
Kyle, John, Gallagher's Plains, Bombala.
Kyle, J. and D., Bombala.
Lalor, William, Beelec, Gwydir District.
Lambenfelde, H. G. von, Younzara, Wollongough.
Lamb, Kiddle and Co., Willurah, via Deniliquin
Lamb, Kiddle and Dale, Yanko, block A, Murrumbidgee District
Lamb, O., Ashton, Bombala.
Lampe, Mrs. Sarah, Talbingo, North Murrumbidgee District.
Landale and Patterson, Tankie, Darling District.

Landall Brothers, Deniliquin.
Lane, E. H., Dubbo.
Lane, G. D., Youie, Coonamble.
Lang and Cope, Wirkenbergal, B, Murrumbidgee District.
Lang, William, Wirkenbergal, A, Murrumbidgee District.
Lang, W., Wargam, near Deniliquin.
Langmore and Tullock, Charlton, Gongolgon.
Lassetter, Frederic, Bullumbulla, Liverpool Plains District.
Latham, Thos., Illll Plain, Deniliquin.
Lauder, John, Darlington Point, near Hay.
Laurie, Robert, Kangaroo Flat, New England District.
Laurie, Thomas, Newindock, New England District.
Lawler, R. J., Cowang, near Gundagai, via Albury.
Lawrence, B., Conargo Road, near Deniliquin.
Lawrence, G., and Co., Canally, Balranald.
Lawrence, James, and Son, Puon Buon, via Swan Hill.
Lawson, C., sen., Craigie, Bombala.
Lawson, J. J., Craigie, Bombala.
Lazarus, D. E., Cooma.
Leahy, R., Howlong.
Learmonth, T. and S., Grongal, via Hay.
Leatham, W., Hill Plains, near Deniliquin.
Lecount, John, Riversdale, Cooma.
Ledger, John, Mallion Forest, Murrumbidgee District.
Ledger and Walker, Mullion, Monaro District.
Lee, James, Larras, Lake Molong, via Sydney.
Leeds, A., Buckyingguy, Mount Harris.
Leigh, Christopher, Blair Hill, New England District.
Leitch, John, Berry Jerry, via Wagga Wagga.
Leslie and Dixon, Gora, Coonanbarabran.
Leslie, James, Bungaldi, Liverpool Plains District.
Leslie, J., Binyia Downs, Coolah, via Sydney.
Lett, J. M., Kiandra, Cooma.
Lewis, J. A., Nariah, Rankin Springs, via Corowa and Nerandera.
Lewis, Thomas, Kingsdale, Goulburn, via Albury.
Lightbody, Thomas, Bombala.
Lintott, —, Quat Quatta, Howlong.
Litchfield, A., near Cooma.
Litchfield, J., Springwell, Cooma.
Little and Comas, Greenfell.
Lloyd, C. M., Yamma, Urana.
Lloyd, G. A., Terembone, near Coonamble, via Sydney.
Locker, Henry, Bolaro, Cooma.
Lockyer, E. C., Evelyn Creek, Albert District.
Loder, Andrew, Doughboy Hollow, Liverpool Plains District.
Loder, George, Abbey Green, Singleton.
Loeman, J., Jindera, Jindera.
Logan, Robert, Mongola, New England District.
Lomax and Severn, Molloy, Narribri.
Lomax, J. R., Wirrah, Moree.
London Chartered Bank of Australia, Mandoe, Gwydir District.
Long, Benjamin, Gegullalong, Lachlan District.
Loomes, James and John, jun., Sheep Station Creek, Lachlan District.
Lord, E., Warry, Lachlan District.
Lord, The Hon. Francis, Wellington, Lachlan District.
Loughnan Bros., Hunthawong Station, Lachlan River, via Hay.
Love, William, Egan Creek, Mangoplah, via Albury.
Lowe, William, Bolaro, Bligh District.
Lowe and Co., Ariah, via Wagga.
Lucas, Samuel, Countigany, Cooma.
Lucy, Michael, Umarella.
Lunt, Thomas, Little Billabong.
Lyell and Simpson, Nowrarie.
Lynch, John, Mogermul, Bligh District.
Lynch, Owen, Bulgundra, Buckley's Crossing, Cooma.
Lyne, Bishop, Garryowen, Germanton.
Lyne, W. J., Bowna, via Albury.
Mack Bros., Murgah, via Deniliquin.
Mack and Greeves, Timora, via Wagga.
Mackay, John, Curricabundi, New England District.
Mackay, A., Wallanbean, Young.

Mackay, S., Range View, Cooma.
Mackay, W., Wallardibby Station, Delegate, Bombala.
Mackie, J., Jerilderie.
Macleay, Taylor and Co., Bogira, East, Warrego District.
Macleod, John, Beilsdowne Creek, Clarence District.
Madden, —, Upper Billabong.
Madden, George, Billabong Creek, via Ten-mile Creek.
Madden, —, Wallan Wallan, Walbundrie.
Maguire, E., Tugland, Bligh District.
Maguire, John, Gilbican, Liverpool Plains District.
Maguire, J. F., and Co., Goonanawah, Mundooran, via Sydney.
Maher, M. E., Narramine, Dubbo.
Maher, P., Walbundrie, Billabong.
Mahoney, T., Boggy Plains, Monaro District.
Main, D., Murrumbueka, Cooma.
Maley, A., Executors of, Nimmo, Monaro District.
Malleson and Inglis, Moothumbool, Lachlan District.
Mallon, J., Merecombene, Monaro District.
Maloney, Patrick, Burrowa, Goulburn District.
Maloney, Patrick, jun., Goba Creek, Lachlan District.
Maloney, Thomas, Toole's Creek, Murrumbidgee District.
Malton, James, Jerilderie.
Manchie, J. C., Phillips' Creek, Murrum.
Manning, F., Hillside, Tarcutta.
Manning, F. G., Hillside, Little Billabong, via Albury.
Manning, John, Yellow Water-hole, near Deniliquin.
Manning and Stiles, Bibbenluke, Monaro District.
March Brothers, North Wakool, near Deniliquin.
March, Thomas, Bombala.
Marino, Carlo, Moppity, Young.
Marooney, John, Lower Collagong, Lachlan District.
Marsden, Samuel, North Moonul, Bligh District.
Marshall, Mrs. M., New Gerilgambone, Bligh District.
Marshall, Thomas, Jerilderie, Coree, Deniliquin.
Martin, F., Murtee, Wilcannia.
Martin, James, Crankies Plains, Bombala.
Martin, J., Gobo Creek, near Burrowa.
Martin, Thomas, Delegate, Bombala.
Martin, W. F., Corowa.
Martin, W. J., Corowa.
Mason, E. R., Corowa.
Matchett, G., Merven, via Albury.
Matchett, John, Jerilderie.
Mate, H., and Co., Albury.
Mate, T. N., Tarcutta, Tarcutta.
Mathieson, Sir J., Aston, Monaro District.
Mawson, J. J., Dairyman's Plains, Cooma.
Maxwell, D., Goombargona.
Medcalf, A. T., Cookardinia.
Medlicott, C. H., Harp of Erin Hotel, Tatarino, Lower Darling, Wentworth.
Mein, G. A. and P., Moolpar, Moulamein.
Mellow, —, Green Swamp, Jerilderie.
Melville, Geo., Bolaro, Cooma.
Mercantile Bank, Enocks, Lachlan District.
Merinthal, —, Bombala.
Merritt, —, Coonhoughbula, Buckley's Crossing, Cooma.
Merritt, Thomas, Cardies River, Nerandera.
Metcalfe, Joshua, Winsleydale, Deniliquin.
Mitchell, J. B., Hay.
Middleton, G., Burrowana.
Middleton and Rodgers, Kalangan, Cunningham.
Miller Brothers, Moulamein.
Miller, E. A., Buckelong, Bombala.
Miller, Geo., Redan, Albert District.
Miller, Joseph, Bogandillon, Lachlan District.
Millis, William, West Gwyra, New England District.
Mills, Nelson and Smith, Nardry, Hay.
Milne, James, The Rock, Junee, Wagga Wagga.
Minchan, Daniel, Bowning, Lachlan District.
Mitchell, G., Urangeline Creek, Urana.
Mitchell, J., Tabletop, Bowna, via Albury.
Mitchell, J., Dunmore, New England District.
Mitchell, J., Yanko, Thurowa, near Deniliquin.

Mitchell, Thomas, Womargama, via Albury.
Mitchellhill, P., The Grange, Mathoura.
Moffat, A., Maranda, Urana.
Moffat, W. T., Wanaaring, Paroo River, via Wilcannia.
Molesworth, P. H. and C., Cowl Cowl, Lachlan, via Hay.
Monohan, James, Jerilderie.
Montague, Alexander, Green Hills, Cooma.
Montefiore, Graham and Co., Bungaria, Gwydir District.
Montgomerie, D., Little Plain, Cooma.
Moodie, Donaldson and Co., Crawie Creek, Euabalong, Lachlan, via Hay.
Moore, E. L., Bungebar, Bligh District.
Moore, J. J. O., Towarra, Tuppal, near Deniliquin.
Moore, Richard, sen., Burra, Queanbeyan.
Morehead and Young, Texas, New England District.
Moreland, William, Jerilderie.
Morgan, D. T. J. and B. J., Kenn, Lachlan District.
Morgan, Henry, Grong Grong, Nerandera.
Morgan, J. H., Commercial Hotel, Bombala.
Morgan, P., Pier Pier, Coonamble.
Morris, —, Womargama, via Albury.
Morris, Grant, Pier Pier, Bligh District.
Morris, J. O., Mountain Creek, via Albury.
Morris, Thomas, Bogobegat, Forbes.
Morris, W., Culimer, Coonamble.
Morrison, James, The Pond, Gwydir District.
Morse Bros., Abington, New England District.
Morse and Towle, Balala, New England District.
Mortimer, B., Boabula, Wonganella.
Morton, C., Jindera.
Morton, M'Donald and Wright, Crowl Creek, Lachlan District.
Mould, J. F., Boconok, Cooma.
Mudy, Alex., Bebbenluke, Bombala.
Mudy, John, Bebbenluke, Bombala.
Mugridge, Hugh, Buckley's Crossing, Cooma.
Mulheron, John, Dangelong, Cooma.
Mulholland, G. J., Wallace Town, via Wagga Wagga.
Muller Bros., Walla Walla.
Muncey, Phillip, Bungowannah.
Munro, D., Broome, Jerilderie.
Munro, D., Keera, Gwydir District.
Munro, W. and A., Weeboolaballah, Moree.
Murphy, —, Bullgrade, via Albury.
Murphy, J., Bibbenluke, Bombala.
Murphy, J. W., Calangan, Murrambah.
Murray, Mrs. Anne, Auburn Vale, New England District.
Murray, John, Darlington Point, via Hay.
Murray, Robert, Hannin, New England District.
Murray, Strachan and Shannon, North Whoey, Lachlan District.
Murray, Thomas, Newfoundland, via Wilcannia.
Mylechrane, W. P., Waterview, Young.
Myres, David, One Tree Hill, Cooma.
Myers, Samuel. Rock Brook, Cooma.
McAlice, G., Calombo, via Jerilderie.
McAuley, Samuel, Deniliquin.
McAuliffe, M., Glenroy, via Tumberumba.
McBean, L., Woorooma, via Deniliquin.
McBean Bros., Yass.
McBean, William J. and Alex. H., Black Range, Lachlan District.
McBride, D., Stuart's Depot Glen, via Wilcannia, Darling River.
McCahman, J. and D., Darlington Point, via Hay.
McCallum Bros., Brymedura, Molong, via Sydney.
McCallum and Walker, Upper Lette, Darling District.
McCarthy, Kingscote, Bective, Tamworth.
McCarthy, John, Cootalantia, Cooma.
McCarthy, M., Springwell, Cooma.
McCartney and Co., Tooma, Tumberumba, Albury.
McCaughey, S., Coonong, Urana, via Deniliquin.
McClure, D., West Jindabyne, Cooma.
McComas, —, Combanning, Wagga Wagga.
McCrae, James, Turundgerie, via Albury.
McCrae, John, Moulamein.
McCulloch, A. H., Stephen Court, Elizabeth-street, Sydney.
McCulloch and Cunningham, Jingellic, Murrumbidgee District.
McCulloch, J., Colombo Plains, Urana.
McDonald, A., Tara, Bombala.

McDonald, Alex., Myalla, Cooma.
McDonald, Alex., Glen Finion, Cooma.
McDonald, Alex., Curry Flat, Cooma.
McDonald, Angus, Burrgundra, Cooma.
McDonald, Angus, Mowhawk, Bombala.
McDonald and Campbell, Burrangandra, Monaro District.
McDonald, Donald, Glen Finion, Cooma.
McDonald, George, Bullambalong, Cooma.
McDonald, George, Merulan, Junee, Wagga Wagga.
McDonald, Hugh, Glenarra, Queanbeyan.
McDonald, J., Kilfera, via Balranald.
McDonald, J., Deniliquin.
McDuald and Johnstone, Alberbaldie, New England District.
McDonald, J., and Co., Mungi Bundi, Warialdo, via Sydney.
McDonald, James, Jerilderie.
McDonald, John, Uriaria, Queanbeyan.
McDonald, John W. J., Burrandown, Warrego District.
McDonald, Peter, Yullakool, Deniliquin.
McDonald, Rawdon, Ulourie, Gwydir District.
McDonald, Samuel, Nunnitabelle, Cooma.
McDonald, Smith and Co., Rocky Plain, Monaro District.
McDougall, John, Bundalong.
McEdward, Alex., Mildura, via Swan Hill.
McElhone, J., Weira Warra, Warrego District.
McEvoy Brothers, Tarrabandra, Gundagai.
McEvoy, James, Crackenback, Jindabyne, Cooma.
McEwan, R., Deniliquin.
McFadden, H., Wallaugandri.
McFadden, Robert and Patrick, Murray Run, Murrumbidgee District.
McFarland, Thomas, Nap Nap, near Hay.
McFarland and Co., Barooga, Tocumwal.
McFarlane and McFarlane, East Paringi, Darling District.
McFarlane, H., Paika, near Deniliquin.
McFarlane, M. and R., Malle Cliffs, Euston, via Swan Hill.
McFarlane and McDonald, Malle Cliffs, Darling District.
McGaffick, William, Early, Cooma.
McGaw and Co., Burrabogie, via Hay.
McGeoch Bros., Kilnyarra, Mulwala.
McGregor, Charles, Jindabyne, Cooma.
McGregor, D., and Co., Morangarel, Bland, via Young.
McGregor, J., Balandang, Nerandera.
McGrwyer, T., Walbundrie P.O., Billabong.
McGufficke and Hale, Old Bull, Monaro District.
McGufficke and Thompson, Mowenbah, Monaro District.
McGufficke, W. J., Jacob's River, Monaro District.
McGuire and Cafe, Booradah, Bligh District.
McIlree, Henry, Agintoothbong, Murrumbidgee District.
McInnes, Finlay, Marowan, New England District.
McInnes, J. and D., Darlington Point, via Hay.
McIntosh, Alex., Bingara, Gwydir District.
McIntyre, J. P., Grong Grong.
McIntyre, Rev. D. K., Waterloo, New England District.
McIntyre, Edward, Pine Flat, Cooma.
McIntyre and McLean, Boona West, via Condobolin, Lachlan, via Hay.
McKay, Charles and John, Wilkie Plains, Warrego District.
McKay, D. F., Dulcalmah, Whittingham.
McKay, George, Bukelong, Bombala.
McKay, George E., Stoney Park, Albury.
McKay, J. K. and C. B., Willoree, Wellington District.
McKay, Samuel, Frying Pan Creek, Monaro District.
McKeachie, A. A., Mount Cooper, Bombala.
McKeachino, A., Orraral, Monaro District.
McKeachine, Charles, Booromba, Monaro District.
McKee, Joseph, Nunitabelle.
McKees, —, Cornargo, near Deniliquin.
McKees, J., Urana.
McKellar and Burnett, Hawksview, via Albury.
McKellar, A., Kyogle, formerly Fairy Mount, Clarence District.
McKenzie, C., Wengen Back, Liverpool Plains District.
McKenzie, Kenneth, Arramagong, Lachlan District.

McKenzie, —, Woodlands, Wagga Wagga.
McKenzie, Joseph, Upper Bundaballa East, New England District.
McKersie, Alex., Yanko, Jerilderie P.O.
McKinnon, G. B., North Goonamble, Urana.
McKinnon, J. A., Memagonog, Young.
McKinnon, W., Betts, Urana.
McKoy, Patrick, Archer's Flat, Bombala.
McLachlan, D., Mimosa, Cootamundra, *via* Wagga Wagga.
McLachlan, G., Jerilderie.
McLaggan, D., Toogimbee, Hay.
McLaurin, —, Morocco.
McLaurin, James, Yarra Yarra.
McLean and Cowan, Cemblebong, Clarence District.
McLean and Co., Queensborough, Coolah.
McLean, John, Back Carabear, Bligh District.
McLean, L., and Co., Boona West, Condobiin.
McLeay, —, Goondarrin, Hay.
McLennan, John, Cowar. New England District.
McLeod, J. C., Mount Pleasant, *via* Deniliquin.
McLeod, John. Bunborneth, Edwards River.
McLure, Donald, Jindabyne West, Monaro District.
McMahon, Thomas, Bungundrah Creek, Cooma.
McMahon, Mrs., Eurime, Coonamble.
McManus and Colwell, Birrible, Liverpool Plains District.
McMaster, John, Weetalabah, Coolah.
McMaster, D. and J., Bundulla, Liverpool Plains District.
McMaugh, Andrew, W. Elsineur, Macleay District.
McMeckan, Paton and Co.. Marsfield, Wilcannia.
McMicking, —, Manus, Tumberumba, *via* Albury.
McMillan, Mrs. Ann, Oregon, Gwydir District.
McMillan, John, Deniliquin.
McMillan, J. F., Mole River, New England District.
McNamara, J., sen., London Bridge, Queanbeyan.
McNamara, T. and T. H., Carinili, Bligh District.
McNee, Hugh, Archer's Flat, Bombala.
McNicol, William, Boorthumble, Euabalong, Lachlan.
McPhail and Turner, Toogimble, Hay.
McPhee, Malcolm, Numino, Cooma.
McPhee, Angus, Wilson.
McPherson and Co., Paddington, *via* Hay.
McPherson, D., Lake Victoria, by Wentworth.
McPherson, E., Benduck, Hay.
McPherson, P., and Co., Paika, *via* Swan Hill.
McPherson, William, Bullambalong, Jindabyne, Cooma.
McPherson, William, Bombala.
McPhillamy, Charles and John, Engowra, Wellington District.
McPhillamy, Robert, Neurrea, Wellington District.
McQueen and McPherson, Nap Nap, *via* Hay.
McQuade Bros., Quambone, Quambone.
McRae, Duncan, Turidgerie North, Liverpool Plains.
McVean, Alex., Howlong.
McVean, J. H., Euston, *via* Swan Hill.
McVicar, Dougald, Naran, Bligh District.
McWilliam, Urangeline Creek, *via* Albury.
Nash, —, Conargo, near Deniliquin.
Nash and Smith, Waibundrie, *via* Albury.
Needham, G. A., Koreelah, Clarence District.
Neely, Thomas, Mount Thorley, near Singleton.
Neilson, Mills and Co., Wardry, Hay.
Nelson, R., Gunn Creek, Hay.
Nesbitt, W., Tholobin, Deniliquin.
Newby, R., and Sons, Paddysland, New England District.
Newell, A., Barandon, Forbes.
Newell, James, Bandan, Lachlan District.
Nowell, J. J., jun., D. T. and B., Back Daroubalgie, Wellington District.
Newsome and M'Coy, Archer's Flat, Monaro District.
New Zealand Loan and Mercantile Agency Company (Limited), Woolabra, Liverpool Plains District.
Nicholls, E. W., Ferryhill, Taroutta, *via* Albury.
Nicholson, A. J., Greenwall, Booligal.
Nicholson, E. J., Woolingumrah, Monaro District.
Nicholson, John, Little Plains, Bombala.
Nicholson, Thomas, Little Plains, Bombala.
Nixon, C., Gregadoo.
Nixon and Ellis, Harbourne, Deniliquin.

Nixon, J., Gregadoo.
Nixon, J. H.. Deniliquin.
Nixon, W., Gregadoo.
Nixon, W. M., Wonganella.
Northam, H. D., Jeff's Creek, Cooma.
Newlan, John, Eelah, West Maitland.
Norrie, George, Sevenstrath, Clarence.
Norrie, —, Cudgewa, Upper Murray, *via* Kewa.
Norton, Edward, Tiara, New England District.
Nowlan, John, Wentworth Gully, or Long Flat, Lachlan District.
Nunn, George, Dunnykymine, Bligh District.
Nyhan Bros., Mountain Creek, Germanton, *via* Albury.
Oakes and Oakes, Walla Walla and Caringatel, Lachlan District.
O'Brien, C., Gunning East, *via* Forbes.
O'Brien, Edward, Rev., Cooma.
O'Brien, James, Tullunga North, Salamo, near Deniliquin.
O'Brien, John, Coree.
O'Brien, John, Corowa Hotel, Deniliquin.
O'Brien, J. and J., Jindabyne, Cooma.
O'Brien, Thomas, Cowabee, *via* Wagga Wagga.
O'Brion, W., Gundibendal, Cootamundra, *via* Albury.
O'Brien, W., jun., Grogan Creek, Lachlan District.
O'Connell, M., Mountain Creek, *via* Albury.
O'Connell, M., Dickson's Swamp.
O'Connor, J., jun., Ironbong, Cootamundra, *via* Albury.
O'Donnell and Ryan Bros., Willara, Karoo River, *via* Wilcannia.
O'Donnell, Patrick and James, Mingey, Lachlan District.
O'Donoghue, J. F., Glencoe, Mullamana, Inverell.
O'Donohue, Ann, Bourbah, Bligh District.
Officer Bros., Murray Downs, *via* Swan Hill.
Officer, W., Zara, *via* Deniliquin.
Ogilvie, W. and E. D., Cattle Station, Clarence District.
O'Hara, James, Corrowong, Bombala.
O'Keefe, D., Temora, Cootamundra, *via* Wagga Wagga.
O'Leary Brothers, Cocomington, *via* Young.
Oliver, W., Berridale, Cooma.
Oliver, W., and Co., Melrose, Condobolin, Lachlan, *via* Hay.
O'Mara, Denis, Numitabelle, Cooma.
O'Mara, J., Buckenderrah, Cooma.
O'Meara, Timothy, Bobindra, Monaro District.
O'Mullane, J., Baldwin's Springs, Manilla, *via* Sydney.
O'Neill, D. J., Osaca, No. 2, Albert District.
O'Neill, Patrick, Buckenderry, Monaro District.
Onions, W. B., Direngabal, Lachlan District.
Onus and Heather, Willow Station, Nambria, *via* Sydney.
Orchard, Charles E., Bombala.
O'Reilly, Patrick, Narana, Deniliquin.
Oriental Bank Corporation, Glenariff, Mia Run, Warrego District.
O'Rourke, D., Royal Hotel, Cooma.
O'Rourke, Patrick, Isolaro, Cooma.
O'Rourke, Thomas, Numitabelle, Cooma.
Orr, Robert, Warbreccan, near Deniliquin.
Orr, Wm., Ellerslie, Cooma.
Osborne, B. M., Redbank, Jugong, *via* Albury.
Osborne, H., Foxlough, Bungendore.
Osborne, H., Bungaroo, Carcoar, *via* Sydney.
Osborne, J. and H., Colombo Creek, Murrumbidgee District.
Osborne, Moss, Yalgogrin, Warrandera.
Osborne, P., Currandooley, Bungendore.
Osborne, W., Wanganella.
O'Shanassy, Sir John, Moira, Murrumbidgee District.
O'Shanassy, John, Tappal Farm, Deniliquin.
O'Shea, D., Thorowa, Jerilderie.
O'Sullivan, P. J., Mount Harris.
O'Sullivan, S., Carrott, Monaro District.
O'Sullivan, S. and J. P., Mount Forster, Dubbo.
Owen, R., Darbalara.
Palmer, G., Pinpampa, *via* Hay.
Palmer, M., Canoon, *via* Hay.
Panter and Turner, Breakfast Creek Station, Frogwoor, Burrowa.
Panton, F. G., Bellbrook, Macleay District.
Panton, W. W., Toocooke, Macleay District.
Park, E., Guy Fawkes, Clarence District.

NEW SOUTH WALES.   xxix

Parkinson, Mrs. Ann, Monument.
Parry, R. H., Yarrap, Deniliquin.
Patey, T. Wanganella.
Patrick, James, Warree, Bligh District.
Patrick, J. J., West Demson, Cooma.
Patterson, G. O., Bowna. via Albury.
Patterson, H., and Co., Wallaby, via Hay.
Patterson, J., and Co., Monga, Deniliquin.
Patterson, W., Rock Plain, Cooma.
Peacock, Jas., Warrigan, Coonamble, via Mudgee.
Peacock, W., No. 7, West Bogan, Cannonbar.
Pearce, A., Conargo.
Pearce, John, Jerilderie.
Pearce, J. E., Hay.
Pearson, —, Wangajong, via Forbes.
Pearson, E. C., Sandy Creek, Mangoplah, via Albury.
Peberdy, Thomas, Bookookoorara, Clarence District.
Pedan, N. J., Bega.
Peebles, David, Coormore South, Liverpool Plains District.
Pegrin, John, Billibingra, Cooma.
Penhallorick and Son, Deniliquin.
Penny, Robert, Upper Bugaldie, Liverpool Plains District.
Peppin, G. H. and G. and F., Wanganella, South Murrumbidgee District.
Peppin, Lamond and Gibson, Long Plain, Monaro.
Perks, Charles, Lower Tabratong, Wellington District.
Perrin, J., Howlong Station, via Hay.
Perrot, J., Terringham, Clarence District.
Perry, John, Marebone, Bligh District.
Perry, T. A.. Bendemeer, via Sydney.
Peters, J., Walgiers, via Hay.
Peters, John, Tom Grogan's Creek, Cooma.
Peters, Tobias, Tom Grogan's Creek, Cooma.
Peterson and Sargood, Jerilderie.
Phelps, J. and J., Albemarle, Darling River, via Wentworth.
Phillips, G. A., Wren Glen, near Casalis, near Sydney.
Phillips, J., Arthur's Lee, Jerilderie.
Pierce, John, Gri Grick, Upper Murray.
Pike, James, Carmody Hotel, Urana.
Pile, James, Darling River, via Wentworth.
Pile, John, Cathero Station, Wentworth.
Pile, W., Polia Station, Wentworth.
Pinning, G., Warrawah. Gunning, via Sydney.
Plunkett, T. G., Little Billabong.
Plunkett, James, Bowna, via Albury.
Podmore, R., Woomargoma, Dickson's Swamp, via Albury.
Pollock, M., Jindera, via Albury.
Post, E. and J., Cookardinia.
Post, J. J., Billabong.
Potter, C., Cooma.
Power, M., Broga Creek, Buckley's Crossing, via Cooma.
Power, Wm., Boloco, Cooma.
Prendergast, C., Middling Bank, Cooma.
Prendergast, W., Woolway, Cooma.
Prendergast and Barry, Moonbar, Monaro District.
Prentice, H. L., Upper Indi, Murrumbidgee District.
Preston, W., Moama.
Pring, John, Crowther, Merango, via Albury.
Pryde, J., Jerilderie.
Purcell, —, Adelong.
Purcell, J., Gundaroo, via Sydney.
Purday, Wm., Gorah Back, Liverpool Plains District.
Purtell, Wm., Ten-mile Creek, Germanton, via Albury.
Ramsay, David, Excelsior, Monaro District.
Ramsay, —, Namana, via Yass.
Ramsay, J., Findagrey, Cobar, via Hillston.
Ramsay, R. and J., Narrow Plains, via Corowa.
Rand, E. S., Mountain Creek, Billabong.
Rand, John, Oura, near Wagga Wagga.
Rand, Robert, Urangeline, Urana.
Rand, R., Mohonga, Urana, via Deniliquin.
Rankin, Angus, Numitabelle, Cooma.
Rankin, Angus, Native Dog Flat, Monaro District.
Rankin Bros., Bumbowlee, Tumut, via Albury.
Rankin, D., Delegate, Bombala.
Rankin, Jno., South Merecumbene, Monaro District.
Rankin, John, Mount Cooper, Bombala.
Rankin, J. A. G. and R., Merool Creek, Lachlan.

Rankin, Samuel, Glen Finnan, Cooma.
Rawson, C., Jerilderie.
Rawlings, W., S. Yathong Station, Jerilderie.
Rawsthorne, James, Gungaliwan West, Bligh District.
Read, E., Cambelong Creek, or Cooma, via Sydney.
Redman, George, Moama.
Reed, Charles, Waterloo Station, Bombala.
Reed, George, Back Creek, Gundaroo.
Reid, Andrew, Deniliquin.
Reid, John, Tatrabong, Bogan River, Obley.
Reid, W. J., Yencannia Station, Wilcannia, via Booligal.
Reid, W. L. and R. T., Tolarno, Darling River, via Wentworth.
Reid and Shaw, Yencannia Station, Wilcannia.
Reynolds, F., Tocal, Patterson.
Reynolds, G., Three Brothers, Bathurst.
Reynolds, A., Kyloe, Cooma.
Rhodes, W., Carldural. Clarence District.
Riall Bros., Four-mile Creek, Little Billabong, Albury.
Richards, Mary, Opossum Point, Murrumbidgee District.
Richards, W., Condobolin.
Richards, W., jun., North Cabbalong, Lachlan District.
Richardson, George, Armytree, Gilgandra.
Richardson, James, Billapalap, Adelong.
Richardson, Mark, Jeff's Creek, Cooma.
Richardson, T. L., Berawinia Downs, No. 2, Albert District.
Richardson, W. and J., Murrawombe, Cannonbar via Sydney.
Richarwson, W. and T., Duck Creek, Cannonbar.
Ricketson, H., Baratta, via Deniliquin.
Ricketson, H., Noumerrimang, via Tumberumba.
Ricketson and Ghium, Lake Cowal, Marsden.
Riddle, John, Walbundrie.
Ridge Bros., Willie, Mount Harris.
Ridge, Richard, Hermaden, Warrego District.
Ridley, E., Roseberg, Bathurst.
Riddock, George, Weinteriga, Darling, via Bourke.
Riley, James, Wagra, Bowna.
Risley, George, Moulamein.
Ritchie, W., jun., Fullarton, via Goulburn.
Roache, A. K., Curven, Yass.
Roache, D., Rock Vale, Myalla, near Monaro, via Sydney.
Roberts, R. H., Currawang, Lachlan District.
Robertson, A., Eight-mile Hotel, Conargo Road, Deniliquin.
Robertson, Alex., Poppong, Cooma.
Robertson, August, Bros., Yarrabee, Urana.
Robertson Bros., Benalbo, Tabulam.
Robertson Bros., Mimosa, via Wagga Wagga.
Robertson, D., Rockview, Junee, Wagga Wagga.
Robertson, F., Buckley's Crossing, Cooma.
Robertson, James and John, Bygro, Lachlan District.
Robertson, J. J., Blind Creek, Murrumburrah.
Robertson, L. P. and J., Barnedown, Lachlan District.
Robertson, Peter, Yanko, Jerilderie.
Robertson, P. and J., Shaking Bog, Murrumbidgee District.
Robertson, Thomas, Tognemain, via Hay.
Robertson, Thomas, Woolgarlo, Lachlan District.
Robertson, T. and C., North Deniliquin.
Robertson, W. and J., Wargam, via Deniliquin.
Robertson, Wm., Jerilderie.
Robertson, Wagner and Co., Perricouta, Moama.
Robinson, B., Forbes.
Robinson, Charles E., Hayundra, Cooma.
Robinson, James, Kimo, Gundagai, via Albury.
Robinson, Septimus, Brewarinna, Darling River.
Robinson, T., Copabella, via Tumberumba.
Robinson, Thomas L., and Son, Hugandra, Monaro District.
Robson, Adam, Glen Barnett, New England District.
Robson and Robson, Coan Downs, Condobolin, Lachlan.
Roche, David, Rockdale, Cooma.
Rocke, John, Meadows, Wellington District.
Rodgers, Alex., Attunga. Attunga.
Rodgers, James, Curraidurah, Grafton.
Rolfe, E., Tea Gardens, Queanbeyan.
Rolfe, George, Queanbeyan.
Ronald and Day, Nebea, Coonamble via Sydney.

Ronald and McBain, Eunonyareenya, Lachlan District.
Rorke Bros., The Meadows, Obley.
Rose, F., Rosewater, Deniliquin.
Rosenfeld Bros., Deniliquin.
Roset, E., Booligal, via Hay.
Ross, —, Moulamein.
Ross, —, Tara Plains, near Deniliquin.
Ross, A., Argoon, Jerilderie, via Deniliquin.
Ross, E. O., Burrawang, via Sydney.
Ross, J., Billabong, Germanton.
Ross, John, Balaclava, Glen Innes, via Sydney.
Ross, M. F., Tuppal, near Deniliquin.
Rossie, F. R. L., Rosseville, Goulburn.
Rourke and Delaney, Addicumbene, Monaro District.
Rouse and Knight, Tunnabar, Bligh District.
Rouse, George, Guntawang, Mudgee, via Sydney.
Rouse, R. and E. S., Spicer's Creek, Bligh District.
Rowe, J. P., and Co., Borambil. via Forbes.
Rowe, Thomas, McLaughlan, Bombala.
Rudd and Buckley, Borah, Coonabarabian, via Sydney.
Rudd, J. and J., Colombo, Urana, via Deniliquin.
Rudd, James, Wigamboramby, Murrumbidgee District.
Rudd, Thomas, Howlong Station, via Hay.
Rudd, W., jun., T. Y. S. and J. and B., Carrejo, Lachlan District.
Rundle, —, Deniliquin.
Rusden, T. G., Shannon Park, Glen Innes, via Sydney.
Rush, Arthur, Maryville, Cooma.
Russ, Thomas, Yanko, Jerilderie.
Russell, George, and Co., South Thononga, via Hay.
Russell and Black, Wallangra, Warialdra, Sydney.
Russell and Shaw, Eli, Elwah, Hay.
Russell, Wm., Cabanurra, Monaro District.
Rutherford, John, Trumby, Morangarel.
Rutherford, James, and Co., via Hay.
Rutherford, Wm., Bibbenluke, Bombala.
Rutledge, F., Godleigh Station, Bungendore.
Rutledge, Thomas, Molonglo, Queanbeyan, Albury.
Ryall, Alfred, Spring Plain, Cooma.
Ryan, Annie, Yarra. Monaro District.
Ryan, Edward, Galong West, Lachlan District.
Ryan, J., Pine Hills, Jerilderie, via Deniliquin.
Ryan, James, Spring Mount, New England District.
Ryan, Jeremiah, Glenroy, Bombala.
Ryan, John, Jerilderie.
Ryan, M., South Fall, Quinfolly, via Sydney.
Ryan, Michael. Ryansville. Goulburn.
Ryan, Mrs. Mary, Reedy Creek, Lachlan District.
Ryan, L., Wallandool, Walbundrie, via Albury.
Ryan, P., West Agintoothbong, Murrumbidgee District.
Ryan, R., Deniliquin.
Ryan, R., Tocumwal.
Rygate, Robert, Tarrangan East, Wellington District.
Ryrie, Alex., Michaelago, Cooma.
Ryrie, David, Coobington, Cooma.
Ryrie, Donald, Kalkite, Cooma.
Ryrie, G., sen., Coodravah, Caven, Yass.
Ryrie, John, Weeomabah, via Dubbo.
Sadlier, —, Albemarle, Darling.
Salting, L. K., Cumbamarra, Lachlan District.
Samuel, J. R., and Co., Wilcannia.
Saner, Henry, Nullah Nullah Creek, Macleay District.
Scanlon, Thomas, Sawyers' Creek, Lachlan District.
Schaefer, E. C., Seymour, Cooma.
Schardt, Frederick, Queanbeyan Flat, Molonglo.
Scholes, Robert, Tara, New England District.
Scott, J., Garra, Currabubla, via Sydney.
Scott, James, Surveyors' Creek, New England District.
Scott, Robert, Womargama.
Scott, W., Cochrane Creek, Deniliquin.
Scott, W., Belalie, Bourke.
Scott, W. D., Toorambee, Macleay District.
Scott, W. R., and Co., Bogamildi, Warialda, via Sydney.
Sears, Alex., Seymour, Cooma.
Sears, Wm., Seymour, Cooma.
Sears, John, Bibbenluke, Bombala.

Seary, John, Black Heath, Molonglo.
Secombe, E., Calatine, Macleay District.
Sellar, Robert, Yungnulgar Plains, Albert District.
Severne, A. E. C. and E. W., Benduck, Lachlan District.
Shanahan and Jennings, Warbreccan, Deniliquin.
Shanahan, Thomas, The Briars, Molonglo.
Shandley, M., Cooma.
Sharp, Henry, Green Hills, Adelong.
Sharp, M., Bombala.
Shaw, W. G., Kerribree, Culgoa, via Bourke.
Shawhorn Bros., Wando Waudong, Abley.
Sheehan, D., Oak Creek, near Jugong, via Albury.
Sheehan, M., Blackheath, Molonglo.
Shelby, R. M., Tumut Plains, Tumut.
Shelly, —, Adelong.
Sherwood, Thomas H., Head of the Richmond, Unumgar, Clarence District.
Shields, John, Bobundra, Cooma.
Shiels, E. and J., Ingregoodby, Monaro District.
Silk, E. O., Numitabelle, Cooma.
Silk, J., Cooma.
Silk, J. W., Square Range, or Numitabelle, Monaro District.
Silk, Mrs. Maria. Boca Creek, Monaro District.
Silk, O., Boca Creek, Bombala.
Silverman, Godfrey, Cooma.
Simmonds, H., Deniliquin.
Simmons, T., Moulamein.
Simpson, G. F., Kouraine, near Deniliquin.
Simpson and Readett, Tenterfield.
Simpson, C. W., Mungadal, via Hay.
Sinclair, D., Mathoura, near Deniliquin.
Sinclair, W., Nubbo, Wallanbeen, via Albury.
Sindall, R., sen., Seymour, Cooma.
Single, G. A., Summer Hill, Liverpool Plains.
Single, J. D., Tallaraga, Gwydir District.
Singleton, E. G., Walla Walla Station, near Albury.
Skelling, T., Beregawana, Upper Murray, Deniliquin.
Skelly, Wm., Moama, near Deniliquin.
Skinner, Alfred, Bouramitty, or Yaminginbah North, Liverpool Plains District.
Slattery, F., Forest Creek, near Deniliquin.
Sloman, John, Annandale, New England District.
Sloane, A., Mulwala, via Deniliquin.
Small, Thomas, Weelgoola, Clarence District.
Smart Bros., Combardelo, Narrabri.
Smith, A., Kyemba, via Albury.
Smith, Charles, Gurley and Bumble, Gwydir District.
Smith, C., Bogongo Station, Tumut.
Smith, E. A., Warragul, Ironbark, via Albury.
Smith, F. J., Toogong. Wellington District.
Smith, John, Rock Flat, Cooma.
Smith, John, Kyamba, Tarcutta, via Albury.
Smith, John, Gamboola, Molong.
Smith, J., Yelta, River Murray.
Smith, John, East Gwyra, New England District.
Smith, J. S., Eurimbla, Molong, via Sydney.
Smith, Lance, Boreo Station, Orange.
Smith, Merton, Cheviot Hills, South Clarence District.
Smith, R., and Co., Erimeran, Condobolin, Lachlan via Hay.
Smith, R. and T., Urambee, No. 5, Lachlan District.
Smith, G., Warrigal, via Forbes.
Smith, Thomas, Coconingla, Lachlan District.
Smith, W., Carlean, Mudgee.
Smith, W. K., Moquilamba, Lachlan River.
Smith and Brown, Eatonswill, Clarence District.
Smith and Cairns. Corowa.
Smith and Nash, Walbundrie.
Smith and Ware, Fairfield, Clarence District.
Smithwick, Wm., Talmalma, Upper Murray.
Smyth, P., Papuecu, Deniliquin.
Somerville, G., Hillside, near Corowa.
Sowden, Samuel, Meayula, Bligh District.
Spencer, James, Waste Point, Cooma.
Spencer, Wm. Lamprell, Ironbark Creek, Liverpool Plains District.
Spicer and Co., Gnalta, via Wilcannia.
Spottiswood, D., Mathoura.
Spragg, M., Tooleybuc, Lower Murray.
Spring, W. G., Cooma.
Stafford, J. D., Archer's Fiat, Bombala.
Stanbridge and McGaw, The Gulf, Monaro District.
Star, T., Buckwaroon, Warrego.

NEW SOUTH WALES.   xxxi

Staughton Bros., Tintynallegy, Darling.
St. Baker and Harwood, Forbes.
Steadman, Henry, Back Wardry, Lachlan.
Steer, H., Coreen, Corowa.
Stephenson, R., Aston, Bombala.
Stevens, A., Bredbo Station, Cooma.
Stevens, J. H., Nerandera, via Wagga Wagga.
Stewart, A., Cathcart, Bombala.
Stewart, A., Bowna.
Stewart, A., Millera, Clarence District.
Stewart, A., Woodhill, Branxholme.
Stewart, Henry, Tarvine, Bombala.
Stewart, Hugh, Pine Valley, Cooma.
Stewart, James, Wangonella.
Stewart, John, Tarvine, Bombala.
Stewart, J., Bygro, Wagga Wagga.
Stewart, Margaret, Taylor's Flat, Monaro District.
Stiles, C. F., and Co., Kanoona, Bega.
Stinson, John, Keandra Creek, via Wagga Wagga.
Stinson, Samuel, Berrigerry, Lachlan District.
Still, Mrs., Piney Range. Billabong, Walbundrie.
Stitt, Dr., Weral, via Deniliquin.
Stokes, Alfred, Wooingeragong, Lachlan District.
Storey, Samuel, Junee, Wagga Wagga.
Strachan, James, Daisy Hill, Tarcutta.
Strachan, A. D., Yarrara, Murrumbidgee District.
Strachan, John. Maracket, Upper Murray.
Strahan, Isabella, Bowna, via Albury.
Strahorn, A. C. and A., Graddell, Wellington District.
Strahorn Bros., Bullock Creek, Wellington District.
Strahorn, John, Wando, Wandong, Wellington District.
Strahorn, Robert, Corses, Courle, Wellington District.
Strickland, Josiah, Forbes.
Strickland, Philip, Lachlan River, Forbes.
Sturgeon, Andrew, Moonbar, Cooma.
Sugden, G. F., Tocumwal.
Sugden, J., Booligal.
Sugden and Wright, Hillston.
Sullivan, Henry, Wentworth.
Sullivan, J., Rock Forest, Bathurst
Sumner and Faed, Butherwah, Murrumbidgee District.
Sunderland and Kisby, Yarrowell, Macleay District.
Sutherland, C., Belimbaring, Macleay District.
Sutherland, Jos., Berawina Downs, No. 3, Albert District.
Sutton and Co., Walla Walla, via Forbes.
Sutton, G. and F., Cultowa, Wilcannia.
Sutton, Hilton, Tamanbell, Forbes.
Suttor, G. and F., Donald's Plains, Albert District.
Swain, S. and G., Rangers' Valley, Liverpool Plains District.
Swift, S. M., Manosa West, Cootamundra, via Wagga Wagga.
Swift and Halm, Head of Gilmore Creek, Murrumbidgee District.
Swinton, E. G., Cope's Creek, New England District.
Talbert, —, near Deniliquin.
Talbot, George, Davis Plains, Wellington District.
Tange and Cousins, Pallal, Gwydir District.
Taylor, Charles, Burmina. Bombala.
Taylor, E., Rose Mount, near Young.
Taylor, H. T., Colombo, via Jerilderie.
Taylor, J., Dobilkin, Narrabri, via Sydney.
Taylor, Josiah, Laggan, Goulburn.
Taylor, S. and W. G., Polly Brenan, Walgett.
Taylor, William, North Abbotsford, Lachlan District.
Taylor, W. T., Terrible Vale, New England District.
Telford, J. C., Cobran, Deniliquin.
Telford and Rutherford, Milong, near Young.
Temple, G., Tattong, near Albury.
Tenney and Clifton, Burryjaa, Corowa.
Tenney, T., Corowa.
Terry, Thomas, Rudd's Point, Hay.
Terry, P. B., Mellilah, Wagga Wagga.
Thatcher, —, near Forbes.
Thatcher, Wm., Yanko Station, Jerilderie.
Thom, Thomas, Bartley's Creek, Parkes.
Thomas Bros., Whooey, Lachlan River, Hillston.
Thomas, H. A., Rampsbeck, New England District.

Thomas, James, Collinruley, Nerandera.
Thomas, Joseph, Crewah, Bombala.
Thomas, Whitmill and Morris, Bogabogil, Wellington District.
Thompson, —, Fernbank, Walcona, Jerilderie.
Thompson, Charles, Long Corner, Bombala.
Thompson, James, Cobbon, Cooma.
Thompson, James, Avon Lake, Bombala.
Thompson, Jos., Cudgell Creek, Young.
Thorburn and Brodie, Wangarah Creek, Monaro District.
Thorburn, Richard, Good Good, Cooma.
Thornton, J. and P., Square Range Station, Monaro, via Sydney.
Thornton, Morgan, sen., Square Range Station, Monaro, via Sydney.
Thrupp, W., Jerilderie.
Tibeando, O. T., Waginheagle, by Wagga Wagga.
Tindale, E. and A., Byalong, via Mudgee.
Tindall, O., Numitabelle Station, Cooma.
Tinker, Davy and Co., Dora Dora, via Albury.
Tivey, Alfred, Moles, Monaro District.
Tobin, Andrew, Wingadee, Coonamble.
Todd, John, Brewarrina Station, Brewarrina.
Todd, R., Adelong.
Tolan, —, Deniliquin.
Tomkins, H. B., Retreat, Bendemeer, via Sydney.
Tomkins, James, Merrunerrewa, Hillston.
Tomkins, J. V. S., Conargo.
Tomkins, W., South Merrowie, Hillston.
Tonkins, John, Prairie Park, Deniliquin.
Toper, Slader, Moulamein.
Tout, T. and J., Melrose Plains, via Forbes.
Town, Andrew, Midkin, Moree.
Town, John, sen., Warren South. Gwydir District.
Town, Onus and Benson, Boonoona, Gwydir District.
Townsend, John, Billabong, Wellington District.
Townsend. Thomas, Townsville, Coonawindra, near Bathurst.
Tozer, Thomas, sen., Arable, Cooma.
Tracey, Phillip, Hanlons, Conargo Road, via Deniliquin.
Tracey and Stokes, Kydra, Monaro District.
Tragnair and Co., G. E., Guabothero, Merri Merri, Coonamble.
Trøll, R. J., Morodevil, Liverpool Plains District.
Traine, G., Tierrill Creek, near Cassilis, via Sydney.
Trapputts, W. T., Yullundry, via Orange.
Tressilian, —, Eden.
Trewick Bros., Blow Clear, Parkes.
Tripp, A., Albury Road, near Deniliquin.
Trollope, Frederick, Booroondara East, Warrego District.
Tulley, H., Illitwah, near Hay.
Tupholme, R., Moama.
Tures, Wm., Cauraawyalpa Station, Bourke, Darling River.
Turner, C., Springvale, Monaro, via Sydney.
Turner, G. F. and Mrs. Emma J., Junction, Monaro District.
Turner, G. J., Angora, Booligal.
Turner, G. N., Eribindery, Lachlan District.
Turner, Jones and Co., Myang, Edwards River, via Deniliquin.
Turner, Mrs., Barigagama, Tocumwal.
Turner, W., Wyang, near Deniliquin.
Turnbu'l and Co., Hay.
Turnbull, S., Gunngrah, Bombala.
Tyson, James, Tupra, near Balranald.
Tyson, P. and J., Corrong, via Hay.
Tyson, Wm., Gerneny, Lachlan District.
Umphelby and Umphelby, Ticehurst, Lachlan District.
Uphill, Charles, Deniliquin.
Vagg Brothers, Deniliquin.
Vagg. Thomas, Fergusson, Eight-mile Hotel, Conargo Road, Deniliquin.
Van der Maal, C., Deniliquin.
Varcoe, B., Wanganella.
Varcoe, R., Holloways, near Deniliquin.
Varcoe, R. H., Moama.
Vaughan, —, Young.
Venables, G., Bolero, Cooma, via Sydney.
Verge, Christian and Christian, Elybucca, Macleay District.
Vickery, E., Mungyer, Millie.
Vickery, E. B., Edgerton, Narribri, via Sydney.
Ville, J., Moorwatha, via Albury.

Vincent, B., Bowna.
Vincent and Chance, Yamma, *via* Jerilderie.
Vincent, Jonathan Wm., Daradilea, Warrego District.
Vivers, E. O., Tittalia, near Moama.
Vivers, W. and T., Trinkey, Somertou.
Von Laubenfelde, H. G., Youngara Creek, Lachlan District.
Waite, Wm., jun., Bowna.
Wakely, J. J., Yanko Creek, *via* Jerilderie.
Waldron, Wm., Argoon, Jerilderie.
Walker Bros. and Porter, Wangeribone, Orange.
Walker, Francis, Ravenswood, Germanton, *via* Albury.
Walker, James, Woodside, Jerilderie.
Walker, J., Roadstone, King's Plains, near Inverell, *via* Sydney.
Walker, J., Silver Pines, Jerilderie.
Walker, J. C., Priory, Ifillston, Lachlan, *via* Hay.
Walker, Messrs., Cornargo, near Deniliquin.
Walker and Alcock, Greenland, Monaro District.
Walker, Robert, Mogul Mogil, Warrego District.
Wall, J., Branxton, Walcha.
Wallace, Henry, Dandelong, Cooma.
Wallace, J. C., and Co., The Priory Station, *via* Hillston.
Wallace, J. H., Tumbleton, Young.
Wallace, Hon. John Alston, Quat Quatta, Murrumbidgee District.
Wallace, Wm., Sandy Creek, Young.
Wallace, Wm., Kalkite, Cooma.
Wallace, Wm., Wrens' Nests, Cooma.
Walsh, M., Huaba, Lachlan District.
Walsh, P., Kikeamah, Lachlan District.
Wanchope, Andrew, Moredun, New England District.
Wanim, —, Boabula, near Deniliquin.
Warby, J. E., Billenbah, Nerandera, *via* Hay.
Warby, C., Cunningham Creek, Lachlan District.
Warby, M., Deniliquin.
Ward, W. D., Windy Creek, Monaro District.
Ware, Alex., Collinton, Cooma.
Warren, M., Moulamein.
Warren, Richard, Wanganella.
Watkins, J., Lake Plains, Monaro, *via* Sydney.
Watson, —, Barham, near Deniliquin.
Watson Bros., Matong, Buckley's Crossing.
Watson, M., Narrawa, Wheeo, Goulburn.
Watson, S., Gerogery, *via* Albury.
Watson, T., Woolendool, *via* Hay.
Watson, W. J., Bald Hills Station, Grenfell.
Watt Brothers, Derra, Moree.
Watt and Gilchrist, Clifton, New England District.
Watt, D. J., Pine Ridge, Coolah.
Watt, Gilchrist and Gilchrist, Coonabarabran, Bligh District.
Watt, T. R., Back Creek, Young.
Watt and M'Master, The Fancy Ground, Bligh District.
Watt, W. R., Bumbaldry, Grenfell.
Waugh Brothers, Spring Creek, near Walcha, *via* Sydney.
Webb, A. and C., Ellerslie, Adelong, *via* Albury.
Webb, J. W., Middle Cotter, Monaro District.
Webb, R. C., Woomargama, *via* Albury.
Webber, J., Boonoke, Deniliquin.
Webber, J. R., Guise's Creek, Queanbeyan.
Weir, J. W., Corowa.
Welman, J. H., Barwang, Young.
Wellman and Co., H., Navena, Brewarrina.
Wells, Edward, Bigga, Goulburn.
Welsh, John, Jillamlong, Cooma.
West and Allan, Goolagong, Lachlan District.
West, Henry, Galmmatta, Monaro District.
West, J., Goolagong, Young.
West, J., Binda, Forbes.
West, Major, Nanima, Forbes.
Westby, E. and A., Pullitop, Wagga Wagga.
Westerndoff, C., Jindera, *via* Albury.
Weston, J., Boloca, Cooma.
Wheeler Brothers, Deniliquin.
Whetten, Richard, Bombala.
White, F. R., Bando, Gunnedah, *via* Sydney.
White, James, Burrangong, Lachlan River.
White, Hon. James, Martindale, Denman, *via* Hay.
White, J. T. H., Belltrees, near Scone, *via* Sydney.
White, Matthew, Jindabyne, Cooma.
White, Stephen, Merrybandinah, near Gundagai.

Whitehead, O., Teriwinda Plains, No. 1, Albert District.
Whitehead and Sutherland, Yourie, Monaro District.
Whiteman, P., New Kirban, Bligh District.
Whittaker, R., Jellingro, Murrumbidgee District.
Whitton, H., Springfield, Ganoo Ganoo, Tamworth.
Whittley, J. C., Tiruna, Cornea.
Whitty and Whitty, Turmia, Murrumbidgee District.
Whyte, Henry, Bombala, Cooma.
Whyte, John, Bombala, Cooma.
Wild, Mrs. Jane, Trialgara, Wellington District.
Wilding, Thomas, Spring Creek, Lachlan District.
Wilds, T., Grathery, Queenbone.
Wilds and Wood, Gerajusee or Weelah, Bligh District.
Wilkinson and Co., Tom's Lake, Booligal, Lachlan, *via* Hay.
Wilkinson, J. and J., Yellowin, Murrumbidgee District.
Willan, R., Bombala.
Williams and Hole, Woolomon, Liverpool Plains District.
Williams, G. E. and William, Bald Hills, Monaro District.
Williams, J., Kuthie, New England District.
Williams, William, Adelong Crossing-place, *via* Tarcutta.
Williams, W. H., Little Billabong, Little Billabong.
Wills, Allan T. P., Gunnedah.
Wilson, A., Nelly Springs Station, *via* Bourke, Darling River.
Wilson, A., Coree, *via* Deniliquin.
Wilson, A. C., Lela Springs, *via* Bourke.
Wilson, D. R., Bongate, Walgett.
Wilson, G., O'Brien's Creek, Wagga Wagga.
Wilson, H. C. and T. D., Booningil, Macleay District.
Wilson, J., Cariali Farm, Jerilderie.
Wilson, J., Dunlop, *via* Bourke.
Wilson and M'Callum, Pomingalarma, *via* Wagga Wagga.
Wilson, Samuel, Carrah Farm, Jerilderie.
Wilson, Thomas, Gilmore, *via* Adelong.
Wilson, W., North Yathong, Murrumbidgee District.
Windeyer and Macansh, Deepwater, New England District.
Winter, A. G., Carroll P.O., *via* Tamworth.
Winter, Irving, Tulcumbah, Carroll P.O., Tamworth.
Winter, John, Dungaroon, Queanbeyan.
Wilton, S. H., Mudgee.
Witcombe Bros., Hay.
Witcombe, J. and Co., Hillston.
Withers, Henry, Coolamatong, Cooma.
Wittenhall, W. E., Werichibba, *via* Hay.
Witts, A. E., Cooma.
Wittycombe, James, Lower Wilgie, Warrego District.
Wolseley, F. Y., Euroka, Walgett.
Wood, George, New Gradgery, Bligh District.
Wood, H. G., Delegate, Bombala.
Wood, James, South Bulladoran.
Wool. J., Dubbo.
Woodcroft, Joseph, Bunyan, Cooma.
Woodhouse, Mrs. E., Inchbyra, Monaro District.
Woodhouse, W., Jugebira, Cooma.
Woods, G., Ballaree, Wellington District.
Woods, J., Wanganella.
Woods, J. G., Gorman's Hill Station, Rankin Spring P.O., *via* Nerandera.
Woods, T., Bumbaldry, near Greenfell.
Woolcott and Creswick, Upper Wyalong, Hiawa.
Woolett, G., Bombala.
Woolfe Bros., Moulamein.
Worland, James, Allen's Flat, Cooma.
Wotton, W. J. E., Broughtonsworth, *via* Burrowa.
Wragge, Thomas, Beromaged, Murrumbidgee District.
Wragge, W. R., and Co., Howlong.
Wragge and Hearn, Cultowa, Darling River, *via* Wilcannia.
Wreford, —, Marra Station, Darling.
Wren, Henry, Kamaroka, Candulo.
Wren, W. L., Eastwood, Deniliquin.

Wright, A. H., Burmina, Bombala.
Wright, Charles, Jennybrother, Cooma.
Wright, J. J. M., Mila Station, Bombala.
Wright, Wm., Bobundrah, Cooma.
Wright, W. T., Fourfold Station, Euabalong, viâ Hay.
Wrightman, J. P., Merigula, near Tamber Springs, via Sydney.
Wrightley, Thomas, Carlginda, Bligh District.

Wroe, John, Burmina, Bombala.
Wyndham, F., Winton, Goondi Windi.
Young, C. J., and Co., Caidmurra, Mogil Mogil, Barwon River, viâ Millie.
Younghusband, J., Yathong, via Hay.
Zuill, J. and W., jun., Blake's Creek, Clarence District.
Zuile, J., Southgate, Clarence District.

SOUTH AUSTRALIA.

Acraman, H., station overseer, Yardea.
Acraman, Mann and Co., Adelaide.
Addison, A., Point Sturt.
Affleck, John, overseer, Kyrbybolite.
Affleck, James, Kyrbybolite.
Agars, Geo., J.P., Talia. Venus Bay.
Allen, William, Cape Jervis.
Alston, G., jun., Blakiston.
Alston, W. H., overseer, Comaun, Penola.
Anderson, James, Roleo.
Anderson, P., overseer, Maryvale, Streaky Bay.
Angas, J. H., J.P., Collingrove, near Angaston.
Angas, J. H., Angaston.
Angus, John, overseer, Paratoo.
Armstrong, John, Booborowie.
Attiwell, A., station manager, Narracoorte.
Atkin, Thomas, Torrence Vale, Mount Gambier.
Axford, Thomas, overseer, Hill River Station, near Clare.
Ayers, Sir Henry, Adelaide.
Badenock, J., Port M'Donnell.
Bagot, E. M., stock and station agent, Gresham-street, Adelaide.
Bagot, F. M., jun., Dalhousie Springs.
Bagot, J. and C. M., Mount Robe Station.
Baird, A., Okelaibie, Talia.
Baker, E. H., Emu Flat, Mount Monster.
Baker, H., Terlinga.
Baker, Henry, Terlinga.
Baker, Hon. R. C., Morialta.
Baker, P. B., Emu Flat Station, Mount Monster.
Baker, R. H. H., Emu Flat, Mount Monster.
Baker, T. B., Emu Flat, Mount Monster.
Baker, William, Stone Hut.
Baker, E., Mount Monster.
Barrand, J. P., Tod River, Port Lincoln.
Barret Brothers, Mount Gambier.
Barker, W. P., Baldina.
Barrman, W. M., near Robe.
Baron, C. J., overseer, Coonatto.
Bartlett, G. A. and H., stock and station agents, Adelaide.
Baseby, Mrs. E., Mannum.
Bateson, R. H., East Wellington.
Bateson, W., manager, Kanyaka.
Batton, R., overseer, Tilley's Swamp, Coolatoo.
Beard, A., Okiltabie, Venus Bay.
Beare, W. L., J.P., Clare.
Beck, F. J., and Co., Medindie.
Beck, D., overseer, Fowler's Bay.
Beck, L., station manager, Fowler's Bay.
Bell, Allan, jun., near Wellington.
Bell, Andrew, Apoinga.
Bellingham, Mrs., Bletchley.
Bennett, G., Rapid Bay.
Berchmore, A., Kangaroo Island.
Berry, E. W., overseer, M'Coy's Well.
Berryman, R., Yongala.
Blackmore, J., Penola.
Blight, J., sen., Mount Barker Springs.
Blinne, Carl, Green Point, Hundred of Caroline, Mount Gambier.
Bolte, C. A. F., Mount Gambier.
Boneham, William, Kalangadoo.
Bonnin, Josiah, overseer, Nalpa, Wellington.
Bonnin, James, overseer, Wood's Point.
Borthwick, A., overseer, Lockleys.

Bosworth, C. R., manager, Wintabatinyina.
Bosworth, J., M.P., Efigo Hill, near Reverton.
Bosworth, John, Edgehill.
Botham and Winters, Kanmantoo.
Boothby, E., Two Wells.
Boothby, J. H., J.P., Weinteriga, Darling.
Boothby, Jos., stock and station agent, Adelaide.
Bowman Brothers, Campbell House, Poltalloch.
Bowman Brothers, Poltalloch.
Bowman Brothers, Manoora.
Bowman Brothers, Campbell House, Meningie.
Bowman, E., Black Springs.
Bowman, G., Delamere.
Bowman, J., Stockyards, Rapid Bay.
Bowman, James, manager, Cookitabie and Carra-willia, Port Augusta.
Bowman, John, Poltalloch.
Bowman, Parker, Parara.
Bowman, T. R., near Meningie.
Bowman and Young, Euro Bluff.
Brady, Daniel, Lochiel.
Braley, W. J., Ulooloo, Hallett.
Broad, T. H., Sod Hut, Kooringa.
Brodie, Alexander, J.P., Point Sturt.
Brodribt, K. E., Poolamacca.
Brook, Benjamin, Burkside, Goot Well.
Brooks, Benjamin, Goot Well.
Brooks, H. J., East Robe.
Brown, A., sen., near Harrogate.
Brown Brothers, Nettalie.
Brown, F., station overseer, Betaloo.
Brown, James, Harrogate.
Brown, John, Mount James.
Brown, L. G., Buckland's Park.
Brown, R., overseer, New Brainfield.
Brown, T. S., overseer, Olnina.
Brown, W. J., Moorak.
Brown, W. J., Woodlands.
Browne, J. H., Talia.
Browne, J. H., Mikkira.
Browne, J. H., Koppio.
Browne, W. J., Port Gawler.
Bruce, J. D., overseer, Poonindie, Port Lincoln.
Bruce, J. E., manager, Gum Flat, West District.
Bruce, K. J., Walelberdina North.
Bryant, J., Yardea, Gawler Ranges.
Bryce, W., overseer, Mount Bryan.
Buchanan, W., overseer, Port Lincoln.
Budge, William, Wallerberdina.
Buick, William, Hog Bay River, Kangaroo Island.
Burkitt, W. C., Tingatingana.
Burn, T., Tintinarra.
Burt, W., Kercoonda.
Butcher, James, Lacepede Bay.
Butcher, J. S., sheep overseer, Westons Flat.
Butler and Sells, Moralina.
Butler and Sells, Yattalunga.
Cadby, John, overseer, Booborowie.
Cain, M., Kingscote, Kangaroo Island.
Cameron, Alexander, station manager, Poudina, Yardea.
Cameron, Alexander, station manager, Cootanoor-mira.
Cameron, Ann, Mount Burr, S.E.
Cameron, J., Wattle Range.
Cameron, J., Mount Burr, S.E.
Campbell, Robert, Kingston.

Carroll and Fullerton, Narracoorte.
Castles, Wm., Long Valley.
Chambers, John, Richmond.
Chandler, A., overseer, Watervale.
Chapman, A. A., overseer, Mundoudna.
Chapman, Edgar, Adelaide.
Chapman, R., River Eleanor, Kangaroo Island.
Chapman, William, manager, Tolka, Port Lincoln.
Chapman, W., North Cape, Kangaroo Island.
Chappel, C., overseer, Wilpena.
Chapple, Geo., overseer, Wilpena.
Chartier, Geo., station overseer, Mount Nor'-West.
Checker, Edward, Maidstone.
Cheriton, John J. B., stock and station agent, Strathalbyn.
Chewings, George, Moopina.
Cheyne, M., Three Lakes.
Chisholm, James, East Wellington.
Clarke, Charles, Mount Gambier.
Clarke, Charles, Myponga.
Clarke, George, Myponga.
Clarke, John, Myponga.
Clarke, Peter, Myponga.
Clarke, Thomas, Myponga.
Clark and Sons, F., Adelaide.
Clark, T. F., Port Macdonnell.
Cleary, John, overseer, Rhynie.
Cleland, G. F., Beaumont.
Cockram, G., Catarpoo.
Cock, John, Mount Gambier.
Colbey, A. H., overseer, Coonatto.
Coleman, J. E., Uraparinga, Weinstown.
Coleman, Mrs. A., Saddleworth.
Colley, E. J., Lillymuir, via Penola.
Coles and Goodchild, Kapunda.
Collins, G. G., Fairfield Farm, Mount Gambier.
Colton, Hon. John, Adelaide.
Conner, C., near Mannum.
Cooke, A., Naringa. Wellington.
Cook, Archibald, Kingston.
Coombe, W., Georgetown.
Cutter, H. R., overseer, Nepowie, Nort North.
Cotton, James, overseer, Lake Hamilton.
Cotton, T., Pantalpie, Western District.
Couch, Richard, sheep farmer, Couch Run.
Couch and Mills, sheep farmers, Streaky Bay.
Crabble, stockholder, Roonka Roonka.
Crawford, John, sheep farmer, Karcultaby, Streaky Bay.
Crawford, W. B., sheep farmer, Karcultaby, Streaky Bay.
Crossman, John, sheep farmer, Inman Valley.
Crouch, E. F., station manager, Tarpeena.
Crouch, W. A., sheep farmer, Tarpeena, Penola.
Crowe, Richard, sheep farmer, Mingbool, Mount Gambier.
Crozier, H. J., Oaklands.
Cudmore, J. F., sheep farmer, Paringa, River Murray.
Curner, A., sheep farmer, Lochiel.
Dallison, W. J., stationholder, Hell House,Coorong.
Dament, James, stationholder, Mount Monster.
Dare, W., sheep farmer, Piltimitteappa N.E.
Dashwood Bros., stationholders, Thurloo, Mannum.
Davenport, S., stationholder, Beaumont.
Davies, C. W., sheep farmer, Mattawanangala.
Davies, Edward, sheep farmer, Spalding.
Davison, James, stationholder, Little Hampton.
Daw, J. N., sheep farmer, Cyguet River, Kangaroo Island.
Dawson, sheep farmer, Aberdeen.
Day, W., and Co., George-street, Millicent.
Dean, W., stock and station agent, Campbelltown.
Debney, G. L., stationholder, Lake Eyre and Crystal Brook.
Denford, R. J., sheep farmer, East Wellington.
Denning, W. J. D., sheep farmer, Daubury Station, Munkoora.
Dennis, Richard, stationholder, Inman Valley.
Depledge, W., sheep farmer, Encounter Bay.
Dodd, Thomas, Adelaide.
Dodd, T., Mundoo Island.
Doudy, —, stationholder, Lower Light.
Douglas, W., Mount Gambier.
Dowden, Geo. C., sheep farmer, Booborowie.
Duffield, Hon. W., Parra Parra.
Duncan, John, sheep farmer, Wallaroo.

Duncan, W. H., sheep farmer, Oulnina.
Dunn, Andrew, stationholder, Woolmit, Robe.
Dunn, Joseph, stationholder, Palmer.
Dunn, J., J.P., Mount Parker.
Dunn, Wm., Hallett.
Edwards, Herbert, stationholder, Penola.
Edwards, J., station owner, Penola.
Edwards, M., stationholder, Swanport.
Elder, Smith and Co., Adelaide.
Elliot, M., sheep farmer, Second Valley.
Embury and Co., Port M'Donnell.
Everard, Wm., stationholder, Ashford Bay Road.
Everard, W., Marshfield.
Fallow, R. N., Woolmit, Robe.
Fergusson, A., overseer, near Mannum.
Ferrier, Peter, Encounter Bay.
Fish, W. H., Colona, Fowler's Bay.
Fisher, C. B., The Levels, Dry Creek.
Flint, Benjamin, overseer, Penola.
Flowers, James, Baldina.
Foote, H., Outalpa.
Ford, E. D., Petermooroo, Far North.
Ford, Jos., Blackwater Holes, Redruth.
Ford and Hill, Colton.
Forster, R., Allandale Station, Gillap.
Forsyth, John, East Wellington.
Forty, W. B., Bramfield, Western District.
Foster, R., Lake St. Clair, Robe.
Fowke, F. J., manager, Leigh's Creek.
Fowke, W., overseer, Leigh's Creek.
Fowler, D. and J., stock and station agents, Adelaide.
Fowler and Murray, Yarroo.
Fowler, William, Yarroo, Kulpara, Yorke's Peninsula.
Fox, Arthur, East Wellington.
French, E., and Co., Rivoli.
French, E., and Co., Port Macdonnell.
Frost and Co., F. J., Erudina.
Frost, F. J., Erudina.
Frost, Frederick J., overseer, Oladdie.
Fulford, J. H., overseer, Paratoo Station.
Glair, James, manager, Lake Victoria Station, Murray.
Gall, Charles, station manager, Mount Bryan.
Gardiner, Captain, Mingbool, via Mount Gambier.
Gardiner, R., Mount Schanck, via Mount Gambier.
Gardner, A., Mangwarry.
Gebhart, G. A., Mount Cone. Kooringa.
Geharty, James, Kukuna, Western District.
Gerner, H. J., overseer, Yartoo, Yardea.
Gerrard, W., Stud Farm, Rapid Bay.
Giffen, David, overseer, Peelawurta, Port Lincoln.
Gilbert, Jos., J.P., Pewsey Vale.
Gilbert, W., J.P., Wangalere.
Giles, C., Crafers.
Giles, H., Melrose.
Gilmour, J. G., near Mount Pleasant.
Gilmour, John, near Mount Pleasant.
Gleeson, Richard T., Yongala.
Glen, Geo., J.P., Marjura, South-east.
Glennie, W., overseer, Courtable, Port Elliot.
Gleeson, J. W., Clare.
Gleesen and Tassie, Port Augusta.
Godfree, John, South Rhine.
Godlee, Charles B., manager, Kalka, Streaky Bay.
Godlee, F. O., station manager, Peake.
Goldsworty, G., Curramulka, Yorke's Peninsula.
Gollan, D., East Wellington.
Gooch, T., Tintinnara.
Goode. C. R., J.P., Saddleworth.
Gordon and Co., W., stock and station agents, Adelaide.
Gordon, J., overseer, Kingsley, Port Macdonnell.
Gordon and Waugh, Dungalear.
Gores, William, manager, Blanchewater.
Gosden, Hiram, South Rhine.
Gosse, Henry, overseer, North-west Bend.
Gower, J., sen., Mount Crawford.
Gower, James, jun., New Brook, Mount Crawford
Graham, T. J. P., Wakefield-street, Adelaide.
Grant and Stokes, Coonatto.
Grant, G. A., overseer, Mount Lindhurst.
Gray, G. H., overseer, Beachport.
Green, W. M., Coondambo.
Greig, A. L., Mopina.
Greig and Wade, Mopina.
Greive, Charles, Greiveston, Dutton.

SOUTH AUSTRALIA. xxxv

Grice, J., and Co., Robe.
Grice, J., and Co., Kingston.
Griffin, Wm., Vallies, Nairne.
Grundy, Jos., Second Valley.
Gunn, John, overseer, Kappowanta, Port Lincoln.
Guthrie, Samuel, overseer, near Milang.
Guttine, T., Mount Graham.
Hack, Francis, overseer, Mount Templeton.
Haigh, W. F., Tiatucka, Port Lincoln.
Haigh Bros., Port Lincoln.
Haldane, Robert, overseer, Salter Springs.
Hall, Ebenezer, Joyce.
Hall, Ebenezer, Roseford, Narracoorte.
Hall, James, Point Sturt.
Hall, R. B., manager, Beltana Station.
Hallett, R., Norwood.
Handyshire, R., Penola.
Hannyside, A. D., J.P., Camayura.
Hannaford, J. E., Bonney's Flat.
Hansley, R., Cairn Bank, Robe Island.
Hanstein, Neil, overseer, Mount Burr.
Harding, C. G., Tintinarra.
Harding, J., Tintinarra.
Harding, W., Tintinarra.
Harding, W. G., Tintinarra.
Harewood, J. C., overseer, Weston's Flat.
Harris, S. A., North-west Bend.
Harris, Scarfe and Co., Adelaide.
Harrold Bros., Adelaide.
Hart, Joseph, overseer, Macumbra Peake.
Hart, Thomas, overseer, Mount Felton Station.
Hart Bros., Glanville.
Harwood, J. C., overseer, Markaranko, River Murray.
Hatten, Thomas, Astwood, Melrose.
Hawker, G. C., Parallana.
Hawker, Hon. G. C., Bungaree.
Hawson, G., sen., Polda, Western District.
Hawson, G., jun., overseer, Polda, Western District.
Hay, Alex., Nairne.
Hay, Hon. A., Linden.
Hay, Donald, Mount Graham.
Hay, James, Nairne.
Hayes, George, Bagdad, Robe.
Hayes, G. W., Lowrie's Hill, Robe.
Hayes, Thomas, manager, Richmond Park, Robe.
Hayford, Thomas, overseer, Penong, Fowler's Bay.
Heathcote and Mather, Streaky Bay.
Heathcote, J. W., J.P., Streaky Bay.
Hebard, Hy. Luke, overseer, Robe Town.
Hebditch, G., overseer, Robe.
Hegarty, James, overseer, Rocky River.
Heirns, C., manager, Flat Station, Western District.
Heirns, Thomas, overseer, Terry Station, Colton.
Helling, August, Cowarie, Lake Eyrie.
Henning, R. W. E., J.P., East Terrace, Adelaide.
Henry, P., manager, Oraparinna.
Hensley, J., Cairnbank, Lacepede.
Hensley, J., Cairnbank, Narracoorte.
Hickner and Bell, Mount Drummond.
Hiern, James, Parla, Western District.
Hiern, Maurice, manager, Yudnapinie, St. Augusta.
Higgins, H. H., manager, Mylette Springs.
Higgins, James, overseer, Yardea.
Hiles, G., McCoy's Well, Eastern Plains.
Hiles, George, Mungibbie.
Hiles, George, jun., overseer, Tetulpa.
Hill, Allen, overseer, Cape Spencer, Yorke's Peninsula.
Hobbs, Wm., Myponga.
Hodge, Francis J., overseer, Orriecoure, Yorke's Peninsula.
Hodgkiss, Hon. John, Brighton.
Hogarth, John, Strangways Springs.
Hogarth, Jos., Strangways Springs.
Hogarth, W., Strangways Springs.
Hogg, J., Waterloo Bay.
Holland, R., J.P., Turretfield.
Holloway, Charles, Compton Downs, Mount Gambier.
Holmes, Thomas, sen., Mundoo Island.
Holroyd, H., J.P., Port Lincoln.
Hooper, J., Yongala.
Hope, J., J.P., Clare.
Horn, R. A., Beefacres.
Horn, W. A., J.P., Maryvale.
Horn and Stirling, Winninnie.

Horrick, Edward, Cape Jervis.
Hosken, Wm., Chellenda.
Hoskins and Bryant, Chellenda, Streaky Bay.
Houston, W., overseer, Mayura.
Howard, W. J., overseer, East Wellington.
Howson, G., sen., Polda Station.
Hughes, H. B., J.P., Atchiney.
Hughes, C. E., station manager, Wellington.
Humphreys, Jesse, Blomfield, Koringa.
Humphries, E., Jamestown.
Hunt, John, sen., Myponga.
Hunt, M., Myponga.
Hunter, Stevenson and Co., station agents, Adelaide.
Hurd, Wm., J.P., Outalpa.
Hurst, J., Snug Cove, Kangaroo Island.
Hutchings, W., manager, Emu Belt Station.
Hutchins, J., overseer, Wirrabara.
Hutchinson and Dunn, Biscuit Flat, Robe.
Hutchison, W., Richmond Park, Robe.
Hyde, F. E., overseer, Lake Albert, Meningie.
Ibould, Walter, manager, Booleoomatta.
Ingham, Geo., overseer, Kingston.
Inglis, M., overseer, Booborowie.
Irving, Thomas, Binnum Binnum.
Jaffrey, S., Lake St. Clair, Robe.
Jagger, James, Encounter Bay.
Jagger, Robert, Encounter Bay.
James, W. B., Canowie.
Jarvis, James, Mount Gambier East.
Jeffers, J. and J., Narracoorte.
Jonas, Wm., Yongala.
Jones, B. H., Woolyana.
Jones, E., Yongala.
Jones, F. T., Mougalata.
Jones, H., J.P., Binnum Binnum.
Jones, Wm. Ourie Cowie.
Kain, John, Little Dublin, Nairne.
Kay, W., stock and station agent, Adelaide.
Kelly M., Swedes' Flat, Narracoorte.
Kelly, Michael, Mount Monster.
Kelly, Patrick, Inglis Flat, Bordertown.
Kelsh, Thomas, Moonaltinga.
Kennedy, J., Pewenna, Mount Gambier.
Kennedy, John, manager, Benara, Mount Gambier.
Kennedy, John, Pieweeny.
Kenney, Edward, Hindmarsh Valley.
Kenny, Daniel S., Colton.
Keynes, Jos., J.P., Keyneton.
Killen, G., Thalia, River Murray.
Killicoat, P. L., Kooringa.
King, Fielder, manager, Yongala.
Kingsmill, J. W., overseer, Betana Station.
Knight, Charles, Wellington.
Knowles, Thomas, overseer, Wirralpa North.
Laidlaw and McLeod, stock agents, Narracoorte.
Laidlaw, Robert, Lake Roy.
Lambert, J., Lambert Springs North.
Lammond, J., overseer, Mount Templeton.
Lander, R. S., Angus St. East, Adelaide.
Landseer, A. H., Goolwa.
Lane, John, overseer, Mayura.
Laughton and Co., E., stock and station agents, Burnside.
Lawrence, W. M., stock and station agent, Adelaide.
Leahy, Dennis, Caltowie.
Lee, Hy., Robe.
Lemon, John, Myponga Jetty.
Letchford, W. M., stock and station agent, Adelaide.
Levi and Co., P., Adelaide.
Linklater, James, Kirkala, Western District.
Litchfield, J. M., East Wellington.
Litchfield, W., East Wellington.
Lloyd, E. F., Inman Valley.
Lloyd, Geo., Mannanarie.
Lloyd, Joseph, Mannanarie.
Lloyd, T. F. F., Kangarilla.
Locke, John, Port McDonnell.
Logan, John, Keyneton.
Long, G. P., overseer, Blanchewater.
Lord, N. A., and Co., Port Macdonnell.
Love, J., Caynustta.
Love, James, Woodforde, Magill.
Love, J. and R., Mount Wedge.
Lovegrove, J. D., near Meningie.
Lovegrove, L., near Meningie.
Low, Alex., Yakelo.
Lowther, T., sen., overseer, near Teatree Gully.

PASTORAL AND AGRICULTURAL DIRECTORY.

Lutz, Ch. A. H., station manager, Condowie.
Lyon, James, East Wellington.
Lyons and Leader, stock and station agents, Adelaide.
Macbeth, G., overseer, Bamfield.
MacCormac, J. M., overseer sheep station, Western Flat.
MacGeorge, F. T., overseer, Lake Eyre.
Mackay, J., Calca, Western District.
Madely, G. F., Port Macdonnell.
Magarey, W. J., M.P., Semaphore.
Makin, James, overseer, Mount Monster.
Malcolm, W., J.P., Gawler West.
Mansell, H. F., Moralina.
Manser, W., Highlands.
Marchant, W. L., Burnside, Strathalbyn.
Marchant, W. L., Edeowie.
Mars, R., manager, Myponga.
Martin, H., Callana, Far North.
Maslin, C. B., manager, Warrakimbo.
Maslin, Geo., Hindmarsh Valley.
Maslin, Hy., Hindmarsh Valley.
Maslin, John, Bundaleer.
Mather, C. A., J.P., Fowlers' Bay.
Matheson, J. A. P., Two Wells.
Mathieson, D., Lacepede Bay.
Melrose, James, Franklin, Harter.
Melrose, John, Franklin, Harter.
Melrose, G., J.P., South Rhine.
Miller, A., Three Lakes, Bramfield.
Miller, Charles, overseer, Stuart's Creek.
Miller, Charles, Three Lakes, Bramfield.
Milne, Sir N., Adelaide.
Mitchell, J., overseer, Spalding.
Mitchell, Thos., overseer, Wewanda, Port Lincoln.
Monaghan, Thomas, Nairne.
Monckton, J. R., Lacepede.
Moorhouse, J., Bartagunyah, Melrose.
Moorhouse, W., Bartagunyah, Melrose.
Morgan and Co., W., Adelaide.
Morphett, C. E., overseer, Baroota.
Morphett, Sir Jno., Cummins.
Morris, Hy., Kalangadoo, Tarpeena.
Morris, Hy., Parara.
Morris, H., Anlaby.
Morris, J. L., overseer, Cootabena.
Morris, J., Kalangadoo, Tarpeena.
Morris, T., J.P., Biscuit Flat, Robe.
Morris, T., Kalangadoo, Tarpeena.
Mortlock, W. R., M.P., Avenel, Medindie.
Moseley, Thomas, Coondamba.
Mugge, J. F. E., Redruth.
Mundy, D., Campbell Town.
Mundy, Geo., overseer, Fowlers' Bay.
Mung, G. W., overseer, Fowlers' Bay.
Murray, A. B., Murray-Park, Magill.
Murray, A. S., J.P., Wirrabara.
Murray, D. and W., Adelaide.
Murray, G. W., overseer, Fowlers' Bay.
Murray, James, overseer, Wirrabara Station.
Murray, Jno., Mount Crawford.
Murray, John, South Rhine.
Murray, T. H., Murray Vale.
Mustard, W. F., overseer, North-west Bend.
Myers, Robert, Lake Wangary.
McArthur, W. F., Pernalty.
McAuliffe, John, Springfield.
McBain, A., Monkoora, Mount Monster.
McBain, Alex., Ardoon, Narracoorte.
McBain, B., Messamurray, Narracoorte.
McBain, Donald, Mount Benson, Robe.
McBain, D., Messamurray, Narracoorte.
McBain, J., Messamurray, Narracoorte.
McBean, A., Baldina.
McBean, —, Baldon, Truro.
McBeath, W., near Meningie.
McBeth, H. G., Bramfield, Western District.
McBride, J. M., World's End, Kooringa.
McCallum Bros., Nepowie.
McCallum, D., Moolawatana.
McCallum, D., Strathalbyn.
McCallum, J., Whoola, Port Lincoln.
McCord, James, Strathalbyn.
McCulloch, A., J.P., Gottlieb's Well and Princess Royal, Kooringa.
McCulloch Bros., Baratta, Black Rock.
McCulloch, John, Yongala.
McDill, D., Hookina.
McDill, Robert, Mount Nor'-West.
McDonald, A., South Rhine.

McDonald, D., Penola.
McEdwards, A., Mildura, River Murray.
McEegan, Michael, Tarpeena.
McFarlane, Allan, East Wellington.
McFarlin, W., manager, Brimbago.
McGilchrist, D., and Co., Narracoorte.
McGillivray, J., Manoope Park, Penola.
McGregor, D., Illawortina.
McInnes, H., Wellington.
McInnes, John, Narracoorte.
McInnes, J., Narracoorte.
McInnes, J., c./o. Mr. Graham, Millicent, via Mount Gambier.
McInnes, Malcolm, c./o. Mr. Graham, Millicent, via Mount Gambier.
McInnes, M., Crower Station, Gillip.
McIntosh, A., Eddrotrilla.
McKay, James, Morambro.
McKeand, A., Penola.
McKeand, N., overseer, Gillop.
McKechnie, Peter, Franklin Harbour.
McKenzie and Co., Penola.
McKenzie, D., manager, Franklin Harbour.
McKinnon, A., overseer, Muricoora, Tatiara.
McKinnon, A., Kingston.
McLachlan, A., Churkutt, Penola.
McLachlan, J., Mount Scab, Lacepede.
McLean and Barker, Flagstaff, E. Plains.
McLean and Barker, Prospect Hill, North Adelaide.
McLean, D., J.P., Murbko, Murray.
McLean, D., Baldina.
McLellan, A., overseer, Yallum.
McLellan, N., Border Town.
McLeod, A., Port Macdonnell.
McLeod, J., Enfield.
McPherson, Duncan, Lake Victoria, Murray.
McPherson, Wm., Penola.
McQueen, A., Robe.
McRae, Frederick, station manager, Fowlers' Bay.
McTaggart, J., Wooltana.
McTilnes, J., Mount Graham.
McVarnish, D., near Mannum.
McWhinham and Sons, Bluche, Mount Gambier.
Napper, W., Lake Bonney.
Nelson, Thomas, Nairne.
Nesg, James, overseer, Mount Wedge, Western District.
Ness, Wm., manager, Marachowie, Port Augusta.
Newland, S., Burnside.
Newland, W., The Grange.
Nial, Mrs. Jas., Stradbrook.
Noble, G., manager, Parallana Station.
Noble, J., overseer, Bungaree.
Norris, Edward, Meadows.
Norris, Hale, Meadows.
Oakley, T., Lower Finniss.
Oastler, J. L., overseer, Strangways Springs.
O'Loughlin, P., Paddy's Plains, Truro.
O'Neil, H. J., station manager, Second Valley.
Orchard, James, jun., Port Macdonnell.
Oswald, C. E., Yarrandale, Port Lincoln.
Oswald, C. P. G., Warrata, Port Lincoln.
Parke, E. W., Ellery's Creek, McDon Range.
Partridge, J. S., Saltia.
Partridge, T., manager, Yardea.
Pata, Geo., overseer, Fowlers' Bay.
Paterson, Hugh. Narracoorte.
Patterson, H., Wongalina.
Paull, Wm. Jas., Cowarie, Lake Eyre.
Peacock and Son, W., stock and station agents, Adelaide.
Pearson, J., Mount Torrens.
Pegler, A. H., Ned's Corner, River Murray.
Pegler, H. W., overseer, Ned's Corner, River Murray.
Penny, R. J., manager, Wirrega.
Perkins, Geo., manager, Arkaba.
Peters, Robert, Torrence Dale.
Pettman, Thomas, overseer, Reed Beds Road.
Phillips, G., overseer, Merowie, Yorke's Peninsula.
Phillips, G. J.P., station manager, Moorowie.
Phillips, J. R., Kanyaka.
Phillips, T. D., manager, Arrowie Station
Pile, James, J.P., Gawler East.
Pile, W., Magill.
Pile, Wm., near Kensington.
Pinkerton, T., overseer, Robe Town.
Pitts, E. W., The Levels, Dry Creek.
Plew, Thomas, Rhynie.
Polden, R., Myponga.

Polden, Thomas, Bald Hills, Mount Crawford.
Pollack, Matthew, Narracoorte.
Pondts, F., Blumberg.
Porter, T., Glenelg.
Porter, W., O'Halloran Hill.
Potter, D., Green Hill Farm, Mount Gambier.
Powell, C. B., manager, Wilpena.
Price, H. S., Wilpena.
Price, T., Mount Pleasant, Kangaroo Island.
Pryor, W. G., manager Saltia Station.
Quigley, Geo., Lower Light, Dublin.
Ragless, A., overseer, Spring Vale, near Clare.
Ragless Bros., Government Gums.
Ragless Bros., Willochra.
Ragless, J., Yulpirri.
Ragless, J., overseer, near Clare.
Ragless, O., Minbury, E. Plains.
Ralston, R. A., Penola.
Rankin, Mundalla, Narracoorte.
Rankine, A., Rushmoor, Strathalbyn.
Rayson, W. B., Fowlers' Bay.
Reddock, J. and J., Hynam Narracoorte.
Reid, Richard, Wandillah, Kooringa.
Reid, H., overseer, Reedy Wells, Tintinarra.
Reid, J. and R. J., Boocetal.
Reid, John. Bectaleo, near Laura.
Reid, Ross T., Woodford, Magill.
Reid, W. L., St. Ann's Terrace, Glenelg.
Renfrey, R. D., Craik Farm, Mount Gambier.
Renfrey, W. H., Mount Gambier.
Reynell, W., Reynella.
Richman, W., Lake Albert.
Richman, Walter, Point McLeay.
Richmond, A. J., Pekina.
Riddoch, G., J.P., Nalang and Katnook, Penola.
Riddoch, J., Yallum Park, Penola.
Riggs, A., Mullaby, Kooringa.
Riggs, J., Eastern Plains.
Roberts and Coulls, Yaralina.
Roberts, F. C., station overseer, Fowlers' Bay.
Roberts, Peter, Robe.
Robertson, A., Laundale, Narracoorte.
Robertson, D., manager, Glencoe, Tarpeena.
Robertson, J. H., Chowilla, River Murray.
Robertson, J., Mosquito Plains.
Robertson, Robert, Brookmark, Murray.
Robertson, W., Moy Hall, Narracoorte.
Robertson, W., station overseer, E. Wellington.
Robson, Robert, Glenroy.
Rogers and Co., Portee.
Rogers, J., overseer, Kalangadoo, Tarpeena.
Rogers, S., Maitland.
Rogers, S., Yuoo, Yorke's Peninsula.
Rogers, T. W., Warooka, Yorke's Peninsula.
Rogers, W., Myponga.
Rogers, W., J.P., Sandergrove.
Rogers, Wm., Inman Valley.
Ronald, Edward, overseer, Thebarton.
Ross, A., Finniss Springs.
Ross, Henning and Baker, No. 11 Register Chambers, Adelaide.
Ross, J., Fullarton.
Ross, R. D., M.P., Highercombe.
Ross, Robert, Glen Gillion, Mount Crawford.
Rounsevell, John, Hutt Station.
Rounsevell, W. B., J.P., City Chambers, Adelaide.
Rounsevell, W. P., M.P., Glenelg.
Rouse, John, Hindmarsh Valley.
Rouse, Wm., Hindmarsh Valley.
Rowley, Giles, Myponga.
Russell, E., manager, Kappawanta.
Russell, R., station overseer, East Wellington.
Rutherford, Adam, station overseer, Katnook, Penola.
Rutherford, John, Bunnerungie, River Murray.
Ryan, W., manager, Reedy Creek Station, Gillap.
Salom and Co., M., stock and station agents, Adelaide.
Sanders, James, and Co., Canowie and Curnamona.
Sanders, J. C. and R., Warcowie.
Sandland, J., manager, Koonoona, Black Springs.
Sands, A. W., manager, Poltalloch.
Santo and Co., stock and station agents, Adelaide.
Sargeant, S., Yongala.
Sassanourski, H., Compton Downs, Mount Gambier.
Sawers, A. D., Uno, Port Augusta.
Sawyer, J., Port Lincoln.
Sayers, J., overseer, Nalang, Bordertown.

Scaife, H., manager, Wirrabunna North.
Schlinke, A., Wectra, Venus Bay.
Schlinke, W., overseer, Wectra. Venus Bay.
Schmidt, C. and J., Compton Downs, Mount Gambier.
Schmidt, J., Mount Gambier.
Schnickel, J., Mount Gambier.
Schnickle, J., Glenburnie.
Scott, Andrew, Branfield. Western District.
Scott, Hy., Purnong, near Mannum.
Scott, Hon. H., M.L.C., Mount Lofty.
Scott, J., station manager, Mount Brown.
Scott, Robert, overseer, Lake Sunday, Yorke's Peninsula.
Seeby, Jas., overseer, Mayura.
Sells, W. B., Peel-street, Adelaide.
Seymour, R., Mount Benson, Robe.
Seymour, T. D., Killamoola, Narracoorte.
Shannon, James, Eudunda.
Shannon, W. M., Yatara, Koonunga.
Shaw, Bernard, overseer, Wallaroo.
Shinkle, P., Narracoorte.
Short, H. A., and Co., Manooral, Rainura and Wirriandra.
Short, H. A., and Co., Yednelne.
Short, H. A., Bicham Grange.
Simmons, E., overseer, Lake Hodgkinson.
Simpson, D., J.P., Wirrega S.E.
Sims, J. G., J.P., Oraparinna North.
Sinclair, J., sen., Green Patch, Port Lincoln.
Sinclair, J., jun., Port Lincoln.
Sinclair, W., O. B. Flat, Mount Gambier.
Skene, T., J.P., Krongart, Penola.
Skene, Thomas, Croquart, Penola.
Smith, A., J.P., Hynam.
Smith, E. H., Blanchetown.
Smith, Frank, overseer, Panramitty.
Smith, Gideon, Binnum, Narracoorte.
Smith, Geo., Binnum Binnum.
Smith, J. C., Dalhousie Springs.
Smith, John, Magappa, Penola.
Smith, Richard, station manager, Mount Arden.
Smith, T. S., manager, Woolundunga, Port Augusta.
Smith, Wm., Myrtle Springs.
Snelling, G., Kingscote, Kangaroo Island.
Snelling, H., Middle River, Kangaroo Island.
Sprigg, H. L., Narracoorte.
Stacey, Thomas, Myponga Jetty.
Stanley, Geo., Mullenlinsey, W. P.
Stephens, Robert, near Kooringa.
Stevens, H., Millicent.
Stevens, R., Stony Gap, Kooringa.
Stewart, A., Morphett Vale.
Stewart, C., Avenue Range, Robe.
Stewart, James, station manager. Red Bluff, S.E.
Stewart, Robert, overseer, Spelwood.
Stewart, Robert, manager, Peake.
Stilling, J., and Co., Port Adelaide.
Stokes, H., Emu Bay, Kangaroo Island.
Stokes, J., Stokes Bay, Kangaroo Island.
Stokes, W., overseer, Finke Bend.
Storrid, W. and J., Adelaide.
Strong, H. A., Franklin Harbour.
Stuckey, R., Adelaide.
Sullivan, R. F., manager, Cowsrie, Lake Eyre.
Sutton, A., manager, Dismal Swamp, Tarpeena.
Sutton, J., Tarpeena.
Sutton, J. C., Tarpeena.
Sutton, J. C., Pleasant Park, Tarpeena.
Sutton, Mrs. Mary, Dismal Swamp, Tarpeena.
Swan, R., Adelaide.
Swan, W., overseer, Bangor, Melrose.
Swann, M., Bullaparinga.
Swinden, E., Woolundunga.
Swinden, J. J., Gilbert Plains.
Swinden, J. J., Riverton.
Tapley, John, Wartaka, Port Augusta.
Tarlton, Hon. R. A., Glenelg.
Tarlton, McConville and Co., Mount Nod West.
Tarran, James, Rapid Bay.
Taylor, Thomas, Willunga.
Taylor, T. J., Wirrabunna.
Telfer, A. F., Coonalpyn.
Telfer, James, Koppio, Port Lincoln.
Tennant, A., Glenelg.
Tennant, A., J.P., Willipia.
Tennant and Love, Mount Wedge.
Thomas, A., American River, Kangaroo Island.
Thomas J., Hynam, Narracoorte.

Thompson, Richard, Waitpinga.
Thompson, W., Hundred, Bray.
Thompson, W., Port Brown, Western District.
Thompson, W., Harriet River, Kangaroo Island.
Thompson, W. R., Port Brown, Western District.
Thompson, W. P., Eleanor River.
Thorold, J. A., Yednalue North.
Tinline and Murray, Myrtle Springs.
Townsend, Botting and Co., stock and station agents, Adelaide.
Tucker, R., Tarpeena, near Mount Gambier.
Tucknott, H., Tungatta, Port Lincoln.
Turbull, G. M., N. B. of Australasia, Mount Gambier.
Turnbull, J. T., stock and station agent, Adelaide.
Tym, C., Wongoia, Tatiara.
Uhlmann, C. A. W., Mount Bryan.
Umphenston, John, The Caves, Mount Gambier.
Vanse, T., West End Farm, Mount Gambier.
Venn, R. E., J.P., Kingston.
Venning, W. J., Bunbury.
Vickery, Geo., Kondoparinga.
Weddell, J., sheep farmer, Red Hill, Brighton.
Wade, W. J., sheep farmer, Mopina.
Wade, W., overseer, Pitcairn.
Waite, D., overseer, Gum Wells, Paratoo.
Waite, Peter, J.P., Glen Osmond.
Walker, Charles, overseer, Padthaway, Narracoorte.
Walker, D. manager, Edlowe.
Walker, W., Hog Bay, Kangaroo Island.
Wolbridge, A. H., Coonatta.
Warbuton, R. E., station manager, Finke Bend.
Warnes, Thomas, near Kooringa.
Warren, A., overseer, Warooka.
Warren, C., overseer, Strangways Toe.
Warren, J., J.P., Springfield, Mount Crawford.
Warwick, Alle. G., overseer, Parnaroo.
Warwick Bros., Hallett.
Warwick, Francis, manager, Bullaparinga.
Warwick, J., manager, Motpena.
Warwick, J., Hollowillina.
Warwick, R., manager, Owieandina.

Watherstone, Alexander, Port Lincoln.
Watson, Alexander, Konetta Gillop.
Watson, John, Kinnatta Robe.
Watson, Robert, overseer, Mount Schanck.
Watson, T. C., overseer, Umbaratana.
Watt, D., manager, Thurk Station, River Murray.
Wegener, August, jun., Palmer.
Werner, W., Nairne.
Whalan, D. D., Dry Creek.
Whinham and Sons, Blanche, Mount Gambier.
White, C., Fulham, Reedbeds.
White, James, M.P., Yarrowie.
Whiting, E., Coorooroo, Stirling North.
Wilkinson, Charles, overseer, Clark-street, Norwood.
Wilkinson, J. C., Gawler.
Wilks, George, East Wellington.
Williams, George, Point Lowly.
Williams, John, Mitcham.
Williams, J., Port Pirie.
Williams, T., manager, Moorak, Mount Gambier.
Willoby, W. and Co., Border Town.
Willoughby, W. M., Red Bluff.
Wills, Sam, overseer, Bendelby.
Wills, T., cattle overseer, Bendelby, Coonatto.
Wilson, C. D., Amen Beach, Kangaroo Island.
Wilson, M., Hog Bay River.
Wilson, T., J.P., Hog Bay, Kangaroo Island.
Wilson, T., jun., Hog Bay River.
Wilson, W., The Rocks, Millicent.
Winch, John, Bremer.
Witherby, A. E., manager, Mount Lyndhurst.
Woods, A. T., station manager, Newcastle Waters.
Wooldridge, A. M., Curtable.
Wooldridge, A. M., Bellevesto.
Wright Bros., stock and station agents, Adelaide.
Wright, D., overseer, Yulana.
Wright, F., stock and station agent, Adelaide.
Wyat, J., Little Para.
Yates, J., Macclesfield.
Yelland, Mrs. W., Point Sturt.
Young, G., Adelaide.
Young, W. H., Mount Templeton.

QUEENSLAND.

Abbott, John, Abbotsford, Darling Downs, Allora.
Adams, H. J., Fort Cooper South, Leichardt, Nebo.
Adams, H. J., Brian Boru, Maranoa, St. George.
Addison, William, Myall Grove, Darling Downs, Condamine.
Affleck, G., Loganvale, Darling Downs, Warwick.
Affleck, Peter, Glentanner, Darling Downs, Warwick.
Ahern, J., Bengal, Gregory North, Cork.
Ahern, J., Glanmire, Gregory North, Cork.
Ahern, J., Springfield, Gregory North, Cork.
Ahern, John, Maryvale, Mitchell, Blackall.
Alcock, T. and S., Omungul, Maranoa, Surat.
Allan, W., Lansdowne, Darling Downs, Warwick.
Allan, William, Whyenbah, Maranoa, St. George.
Allan, J. F., Mount Enniskillen, Mitchell, Tambo.
Allan, Garnett, and Cameron and Crombie, Home Creek. Mitchell, Blackall.
Allan, Wm., Woolirina, Maranoa, St. George.
Allingham, J., Hillgrove, North Kennedy, Dalrymple.
Allingham, J., and Co., Kangaroo Hills, N. Kennedy, Lake Herbert.
Anderson, Alexander E., De Grey, Northern, Lake Herbert.
Anderson, James, Kinnoul, Leichardt, Throom.
Anderson, Timms and Co., Boonoodara, Port Curtis, St. Laurence.
Anderson, W. R., Koongal, Leichardt, Banana.
Anderson, W. R., Koongal, Port Curtis, Lilyvale.
Anderson and Nichol, Manuka, Gregory North, Aramac.

Anderson and Simms, Lilyvale, Port Curtis, Lilyvale.
Anderson, Bromfield, Young and Young, Lismore, Mitchell, Aramac.
Anderson, Young and Young, Warrnambool D, Mitchell, Blackall.
Andrew and Paterson, Fernlee, Maranoa, St. George.
Anning, W. and F., Compton Downs, Burke, Dalrymple.
Anning, W. and F., Reedy Springs, Burke, Dalrymple.
Anning Brothers, Charlotte Plains, Burke, Dalrymple.
Anning and Co., Cargoon, North Kennedy, Dalrymple.
Anning and Dehan, Mount Sturgeon, Burke, Dalrymple.
Anning, Dehan and Anning, Terricks, Burke, Dalrymple.
Anning, Dehan and Anning, Mount Pleasant, Burke, Dalrymple.
Archer, Wm., Minnie Downs, Warrego, Tambo.
Archer and Co., Gracemere, Port Curtis, Gracemere.
Armytage, F. W., Whitula, Gregory North Jundah.
Armytage, F. W., Eulbertie, Gregory North, Thorgomindah.
Armytage and Galletly, Thorgomindah, Warrego, Thorgomindah.
Arndell, John, Newinga, Darling Downs, Goondiwindi.

QUEENSLAND. xxxix

Arndell, John, Newinga, Maranoa, Goondiwindi.
Ascough, W. A., Palm Tree Creek, Leichardt, Taroom.
Ashburn, John, Evora, Mitchell, Blackall.
Ashburn, John, Hoganthulla, Warrego, Mitchell.
Atherton, Esther, Mount Hedlow, Port Curtis, Rockhampton.
Atherton, J., Emerald End, Cook, Cairns.
Atherton, J., Mullera, Port Curtis, Rockhampton.
Atherton, James, Bamozea, Port Curtis, Rockhampton.
Atherton, James, Canoona, Port Curtis, Yaamba.
Atherton, John, Basalt Downs, Kennedy.
Atherton, J. T., Mira, Burnett, Gympie.
Atherton, R., Howard Park, Kennedy, Mackay.
Atkins, F., Coorada, Leichardt, Taroom.
Australasian Agency and Banking Corporation, Riversleigh, Warrego, Charleville.
Australian Joint Stock Bank, Balcomba, Leichardt, Westwood.
Australian Joint Stock Bank, Barkathulla, Warrego, Charleville.
Australian Joint Stock Bank, Boondandilla, Darling Downs, Leyburn.
Australian Joint Stock Bank, Lower Bollon East, Maranoa, St. George.
Australian Joint Stock Bank, Lower Bollon West, Maranoa, St. George.
Australian Joint Stock Bank, Kianga, Leichardt, Banana.
Australian Joint Stock Bank, Lawark, S. Kennedy, Clermont.
Australian Joint Stock Bank, Spottiswood, Leichardt, Duaringa.
Australian Joint Stock Bank, Wallan Creek, Maranoa, St. George.
Australian Joint Stock Bank, Boorimberra, Maranoa, Currawill.
Australian Joint Stock Bank, Bootle, Leichardt, Duaringa.
Australian Joint Stock Bank, Cobblecundy, Darling Downs, Goondiwindi.
Australian Joint Stock Bank, Cawarral, Port Curtis, Cawarral.
Australian Joint Stock Bank, Olive Downs, Leichardt, Nebo.
Australian Joint Stock Bank, St. Helen's, Leichardt, Springsure.
Australian Joint Stock Bank, Umbercollie, Darling Downs, Goondiwindi.
Australian Joint Stock Bank, Yatton, Leichardt, St. Lawrence.
Bailey, Thomas, Canindah, Burnett, Mount Perry.
Bailey, Thomas, Old Canindah, Burnett, Mount Perry.
Baird, Thomas, and Co., Marrawilla, Gregory North, Jundah.
Baker Bros., Boomba, Maranoa, St. George.
Baker, S., Junee, Leichardt, Blackwater.
Baker, W., South Kennedy, Bowen.
Baldwin, William, Doondi, Maranoa, St. George.
Baldwin, H., Boak, Maranoa, St. George.
Bank of Australasia, Malvern Hill, Mitchell, Blackall.
Bank of Australasia, Nive Junction, Warrego, Charleville.
Bank of New South Wales, Bathampton, Leichardt, Clermont.
Bank of New South Wales, Blair Athol, Leichardt, Clermont.
Bank of New South Wales, Brush Creek, Darling Downs, Inglewood.
Bank of New South Wales, Brushy Park, Darling Downs, St. George.
Bank of New South Wales, Cardowan, Leichardt, St. Lawrence.
Bank of New South Wales, Chatsworth, Burke, Cloncurry.
Bank of New South Wales, Clunie Creek, Mitchell, Aramac.
Bank of New South Wales, Combarngo, Maranoa, Surat.
Bank of New South Wales, Coolmunda, Darling Downs, Inglewood.
Bank of New South Wales, Corrievahn, South Kennedy, Bowen.
Bank of New South Wales, Craven, South Kennedy, Copperfield.
Bank of New South Wales, Devoncourt, Burke, Cloncurry.
Bank of New South Wales, Dunrobin, South Kennedy, Clermont.
Bank of New South Wales, East Thornby, Maranoa, St. George.
Bank of New South Wales, Fort Constantine, Burke, Cloncurry.
Bank of New South Wales, Foxton, Burke, Cloncurry.
Bank of New South Wales, Gainsford, North Kennedy, Dalrymple.
Bank of New South Wales, Hazelmount, Maranoa, St. George.
Bank of New South Wales, Hidden Vale, South Kennedy, Bowen.
Bank of New South Wales, Hollymount, Darling Downs, Dalby.
Bank of New South Wales, Lawn Hill, Burke, Normanton.
Bank of New South Wales, Imbil, Wide Bay, Maryborough.
Bank of New South Wales, Magowra, Burke, Normanton.
Bank of New South Wales, Moorabaree, Gregory, South, Tambo.
Bank of New South Wales, Oxford Downs, Leichardt, Nebo.
Bank of New South Wales, Rookwood, Leichardt, Rockhampton.
Bank of New South Wales, Saxby Downs, Burke, Hughenden.
Bank of New South Wales, Snake Creek, Maranoa, Surat.
Bank of New South Wales, Talavera, Maranoa, Surat.
Bank of New South Wales, The Plains, North Kennedy, Dalrymple.
Bank of New South Wales, Varavilie, Burke, Normanton.
Bank of New South Wales, Wagoo, Maranoa, Surat.
Bank of New South Wales, Wrotham Park, Cook, Palmerville.
Bank of New South Wales, Wycombe, Maranoa, St. George.
Bank of New South Wales and Dight Bros., Glen Prairie, Darling Downs, Dalby.
Bannon, Michael, Sutton, Port Curtis, Rockhampton.
Barber and Co., Junee, Port Curtis, Rockhampton.
Barker, Martin and Martin, Hamilton, Kennedy, Mackay.
Barker, W., Eungella, South Kennedy, Bowen.
Barker, W., Nelia Ponds, Burke, Dalrymple.
Barker, William, Barmundoo, Port Curtis, Gladstone.
Barker, W., W. H., and E. B., Carpentaria D, Cook, Georgetown.
Barnard, George, Coomooboolaroo, Port Curtis, Boolburra.
Barnard, G. and T., Coomooboolaroo, Leichardt, Duaringa.
Barry, J. H., Emmet Downs. Mitchell, Isis Downs.
Barry, Lyon and Ewart, Killarney, Gregory N., Aramac.
Barry, Lyon and Ewart, Leighford, Gregory N., Cork.
Bartholemew, J. P., Cogango, Port Curtis, Cogango.
Barton Bros., Moolboolaman, Wide Bay, Mount Perry.
Barton, R. C., Toweran, Wide Bay, Maryborough.
Barton, W. H., Kensington Downs, Bowen Downs.
Bassett and Skinner, Mount Maria, Warrego, Roma.
Bassingthwaite, Jinghi Jinghi, Darling Downs, Dalby.
Bates, E. G., jun.,
Bates, G., sen.,   } Tickalara, Warrego, Wilcannia.
Bates, J.,
Bates, W., Bompa, Wide Bay, Maryborough.
Bauman, H., Tryphinia Vale, Leichardt, Dingo.
Beak, W., Toorilla Plains, Port Curtis, Rockhampton.
Beaney, R. N., Wunnamila, Maranoa, Mitchell.
Beardmore, F., Balcomba, Port Curtis, Rockhampton.
Beardmore, O. C., Tooloomba, Port Curtis, Marlborough.
Beattie, John, Duaringa, Leichardt, Duaringa.

Beatty, T. S., Nouroomo, Cunnamulla.
Beck and Raynor, Yulabilla, Darling Downs, Yulabilla.
Becker, J., Comougin, Warrego, Thorgomindah.
Begge and Co., Mount Brisbane, Moreton, Ipswich.
Bell and Atherton, Plane Creek, Kennedy, Mackay.
Bell and Dutton, Bemira, Mitchell, Isisford.
Bell, J. and R., Riverstone, Port Curtis, Gladstone.
Bell, Hon. J. P., Jimbour, Darling Downs, Dalby.
Bell and Hyde, Camboon, Leichardt, Banana.
Bell, J., Barwou, Port Curtis, Gladstone.
Bell, J., P. J., A. and M., Westland, Mitchell, Tambo.
Bell, M. and N., Pearl Creek, Leichardt, Duaringa.
Bell, J. S., Dungaree, Port Curtis, Gladstone.
Bell and Jones, Buurabi, Moreton, Gatton.
Bell, B. S., and Co., Toowoomba.
Bell, D., jun., Tongy and Boatman, Maranoa, Roma.
Benjamin, D., jun., Dungwall, Maranoa, Mitchell.
Beujamin, D., jun., Tongy, Maranoa, St. George.
Benjamin, D., jun., Warroo, Maranoa, St. George.
Benjamin, D. and J., Tartulla, Maranoa, Surat.
Berkleman and Lambert, Listowel Downs, Mitchell, Blackall.
Bettington, J. B., Canning Downs, Darling Downs, Warwick.
Biddulph, W. J., Mount Playfair, Leichardt, Springsure.
Bignell, E. and J., Widgeegoara, Mitchell, Cunnamulla.
Billgrove, John, Roma.
Bingham, B. Y., Macpheeland, Gregory N., Cork.
Binney, R. N., Wunnumindah, Maranoa, Roma.
Birbeck, C. A. and R., Glenmore, Port Curtis, Rockhampton.
Biscoe, H. G., Warronga, Maranoa, Roma.
Black and Foott, Dundoo, Warrego, Eulo.
Black and M'Kay, Tilpal, Port Curtis, Yaamba.
Blackman, F. A., Warroo, Port Curtis, Gladstone.
Blackwood, J., and F. H. Moore, Sandringham, Gregory N., Herbert R.
Blair and Jones, Chadford, Maranoa, Yulebah.
Bloodworth and Blackett, Boogera, Maranoa, St. George.
Bloomfield, E. C., Miriam Vale, Port Curtis, Gladstone.
Bode, F. R., Groganger, Kennedy, Bowen.
Bolitho, S., Ramsworth, Leichardt, Springsure.
Booey, W., Eaglefield, South Kennedy, Nebo.
Booey, W., Lenton Downs, Leichardt, Nebo.
Bosanquet, E. B., Colston Park, Leichardt, Mackay.
Bostock, Ware and Ware, Innaminka, Gregory S., Innaminka.
Bowly, C. W., Eastmere, Mitchell, Bowen.
Bowly, C. W., Fernie Lawn, Mitchell, Bowen Downs.
Bowly, C. W., Wogodoona, Mitchell, Cameron Downs.
Bowman Bros., Maiden Head, Darling Downs, Bonshaw.
Bowman Bros., Aitken's Flat, Darling Downs, Bonshaw.
Boyce, James, Reedy Flat, Leichardt, Springsure.
Bracken, executor of F., Warroo, Darling Downs, Inglewood.
Bracken, H., Warroo, Darling Downs, Leyburn.
Bradley, M. E., Yarrawonga, Warrego, Charleville.
Bradley and Rutherford, Claverton, Warrego, Cunnamulla.
Bradley and Rutherford, Paleena Downs, Gregory North, Thorgomindah.
Bradley, W. B., Yonah, Warrego, Eulo.
Brassington, S., Reynella, Warrego, Burenda.
Brathus, H., Clifford, Leichardt, Taroom.
Brennan, Patrick, Hollymount, Maranoa, St. George.
Bridson, H., Toolongra, South Kennedy, Aramac.
Bright, Chrystal, and Co., Amby Downs, Maranoa, Roma.
Bright, Chrystal, and Co., Euthulla, Maranoa, Roma.
Bright, Chrystal, and Co., Bymount, Maranoa, Mitchell.
Broad, J. and A., Currawildi, Maranoa, St. George.
Broadbent and Williams, Widgee Widgee, Wide Bay, Gympie.

Broad, J. and A., Noodoo, St. George.
Broadbent and Co., Mondure, Burnett. and Wide Bay, Gayndah.
Broadley, G. E., Burleigh, Burke, Dalrymple.
Brodie, F. A., Raincourt, Burke, Hughenden.
Brodie, J. B., Lorraine, Burke, Cloncurry.
Brodie, J. B. and F. A., Blaney, Gregory North, Aramac.
Brodie, J. B., and F. H., Richmond Downs, Burke, Dalrymple.
Brodie, J. P., P. D., and F. A., Coleraine, Burke, Hughenden.
Brodie, W. H. and G. T., Purbrook Downs, Leichardt, Rolleston.
Broadribb and Co., Kurrawah, Darling Downs, Dalby.
Brogan, W., Hammond Downs, Warrego, Thorgomindah.
Broome, W., Woodland, Rockhampton.
Brown, A. R., Hawthorn, Gregory North, Cork.
Brown, F., Affey, Leichardt, Nebo.
Brown, J., Bridgewater, Burke, Cloncurry.
Brown, James, Wompi, Gregory North, Cloncurry.
Brown, John, Tindera, Gregory South, Thorgomindah.
Brown and Johnstone, Coianne, Wide Bay, Maryborough.
Brown, Samuel, Ingliston and Glen Prairie, Darling Downs, Dalby.
Brown, T., Blairgowrie, Burke, Cloncurry.
Brown, T., Edina, Burke, Cloncurry.
Brown, T., Agnes Vale, Wide Bay, Maryborough.
Brown, T., Herbert Downs, Gregory North, Aramac.
Brown, T., Mungerebar, Gregory North, Cork.
Brown, T. W. and Co., Blythdale, Roma.
Brown, Walsh and Walsh, Iffley, Burke, Normanton.
Browne, N. W., Barolin, Wide Bay, Bundaberg.
Buchanan, A. B., Collaroy, Leichardt, Mackay.
Buchanan, H. R., Inveragh, Port Curtis, Gladstone.
Buchanan and Mort, Glenearn, Maranoa, Surat.
Buchanan and Mort, Welltown, Darling Downs, Goondiwindi.
Buckley, M., Murweh, Warrego, Charleville.
Buckley and Monig, Coleman, North Kennedy, Specimen Gully.
Buckland and Synnes, Cardigan, North Kennedy, Charters Towers.
Bucknall, L. M. and A., Mount Morris, Warrego, Charleville.
Bucknall, A. W. and F. N., Caldervale, Warrego, Burenda via Charleville.
Butcher, G., Eva, Gregory North, Thornboro.
Butcher, G., Jimboo, Gregory North, Cork.
Bridge, D., Collabara, Warrego, Tambo.
Bullmore, E. A., Boothulla, Warrego, Oakwood.
Bundock and Hays, Pegurrima, South Kennedy, Townsville.
Bundock and Hays, Richmond Downs, North Kennedy, Townsville.
Burgess, George, Mountain Side, Darling Downs, Warwick.
Burnett, Catherine, Mount Burnett, Moreton, Ipswich.
Burne, Bullmore, and Bligh, Boathalla, Warrego, Charleville.
Burston and Corner, Bidebango, Maranoa, St. George.
Butler and Co., Clonagh, Burke, Cloncurry.
Butler, William, Kilcoy, Moreton, Caboolture.
Button, John, Canal Creek, Port Curtis, Yaamba.
Caddell, Thomas, Kroombit, Port Curtis, Gladstone.
Caddell, J. J., Ideraway, Burnett, Gayndah.
Calder, Calder and Stephenson, Eulo, Warrego, Eulo.
Caldwell, John, Woodburne, Warrego, Eulo.
Callan, A. J., Elana, Leichardt, Maryborough.
Callan, —, Yaamba, Port Curtis, Yaamba.
Cameron, E. D. and M., Foyle View, Maranoa, Mitchell.
Cameron, W. J. B., Uanda, Mitchell, Dalrymple.
Cameron and Crombie, Kensington Downs, Mitchell, Aramac.
Cameron and Williams, Wild Horse Plains, Maranoa, St. George.
Campbell, Alexander, Cooyar, Moreton, Jondaryan.

Campbell and Son, Warkon, Maranoa, Surat.
Campbell, D., Breadalbane, Gregory N., Thorgomindah.
Campbell, D., Sedan, Burke, Cloncurry.
Campbell, D., Tarridle, Gregory N., Thorgomindah.
Campbell, John, Beckford, N. Kennedy, Bowen.
Campbell, John, Barron River, Cook, Pt. Douglas.
Campbell, W., Warkon, Maranoa, Condamine.
Campbell and Hay, Strathbogie, Kennedy, via Bowen.
Campbell and Hay, Undulah, Moreton, Ipswich.
Campbell and Hay, Burrandowan, Burnett, Dalby.
Capel Bros., Gnoolooma, Maranoa, Mungindo.
Carmody, Mary, Oakwood, Darling Downs, Dalby.
Caroline, D., Fiery Downs, Burke, Normanton.
Carr and Curr, Kamilaroe, Burke, Normanton.
Carpendale and Vanneck, Grantham, Moreton, Gatton.
Cassidy, F., Jimbour, Dalby.
Caswell, H. D., Tenningering, Wide Bay, Mount Perry.
Caswell, H. D., Inston, Toowomba.
Caswell and Hughes, Crinjabulla, Jundah.
Cavanagh, James, West Haran, Maranoa, St. George.
Chanvil, C. H., Canning Downs S., Darling Downs, Warwick.
Charters, M, S. E. M., Charters Towers, Charters Towers.
Chase, H. C., Girrah, Leichardt, Lilyvale.
Chatfield, William, jun., Retro, Clermont, Bowen.
Christian, J. B., Willangie, Broadwood.
Christison, R., Lammermoor, Mitchell, Dalrymple.
Christison, T. M. K. C., Mowra, Mitchell, Hughenden.
Christison, T. and R., Cameron Downs, Mitchell, Dalrymple.
Churchill, W., Stanhope.
City Bank of Sydney, Tomoo, Maranoa, Mangallalo.
Clapperton, F. W., New Caledonia, Leichardt, Clermont.
Clarke, G., Talgai, Warwick.
Clarke, John, Mount Pleasant, Kennedy, Bowen.
Clarke, J. H., Erin Creek, South Kennedy, Bowen.
Clarke, J. H., Lornesleigh, South Kennedy, Bowen.
Clarke, Geo., East Talgai, Darling Downs, Allora.
Clarke, J. and W. D., Toomba, North Kennedy, Dalrymple.
Clark, J. and W. D., Lalworth, North Kennedy, Dalrymple.
Clarke, W. J., Portland Downs, Mitchell, Tambo.
Clifford and Courtney, Telemon, North Kennedy, Townsville.
Clifford and Courtney, Marathon, North Kennedy, Townsville.
Clynes, P. J., Mount Duren, Maranoa, St. George.
Clynes, P. J., Tallwood, Darling Downs, Goondiwindi.
Clynes, P. J., Tallwood, Darling Downs, Dalby.
Clynes, P. J., War War, Darling Downs, Dalby.
Clynes, P. J., North Guraldra, Maranoa, Dalby.
Cobb, J. S., Bullwaller, Maranoa, St. George.
Cobb, J.S., Darcel, Maranoa, St. George.
Cobb and Co., Davenport Downs, Gregory, Thorgomindah.
Cochrane, Coldham and Hislop, Wolfang, Clermont.
Coghlan, D., Bona Vista, Maranoa, St. George.
Coghlan. D. J., B. H. and F. F., Yamoo, Maranoa, Mitchell.
Coghlan, J., Delphi. Maranoa, Mitchell.
Cogle, J. and Co., Tilboroo, Warrego, Eulo.
Colless, Major. Coolullah, Burke, Cloncurry.
Colless Bros., Thurral.
Colless, M. and A., Werremah, Burke, Normanton.
Colquhoun, J. M., Bauganyah, Maranoa, Mitchell.
Collins, C. and T., Mackay, Kennedy, Mackay.
Collins, C. and T., Spring Creek, Cook. Cardwell.
Collins, J., Westgrove, Leichardt, Mitchell.
Collins, J. G, Mount Merlin, Gregory North, Cook.
Collins, J., and Sons, Mudoolan, Beenleigh.
Collins, J. R ,and M., Bot Vale, Leichardt. Mitchell.
Collins, F., Thornhill, Port Curtis, Gladstone.
Collins, R. M. and W., Wycta, Gregory North, Cork.
Collins, W. and G., Brooklands, Burke, Georgetown.
Collins, W., Warenda, Gregory. Cork.
Collins and Johnstone, Fernhill, Port Curtis, Rockampton.

Colman, W., Cooper's Creek. Thorgomindah.
Commercial Bank, Binbian, Darling Downs, Condamine.
Commercial Bank, Bonohan, Darling Downs, Chinchilla.
Commercial Bank, Cameby, Darling Downs, Condamine.
Commercial Bank, Cudygah, Maranoa, St. George.
Commercial Bank, Doondi, Maranoa, St. George.
Commercial Bank, Dulacia, Darling Downs, Condamine.
Commercial Bank, Grasmere. Maranoa, St. George.
Commercial Bank, Jellinbah, Leichardt, Blackwater.
Commercial Bank, Mugrugulla, Maranoa, Mitchell.
Commercial Bank, Ramworth, Leichardt, Springsure.
Commercial Bank, Sonona, South Kennedy, Bowen.
Commercial Bank. Trent, Maranoa. St. George.
Commercial Bank, West Tchauning, Maranoa, Condamine.
Commercial Bank, Wollan, Darling Downs, Chinchilla.
Commercial Bank, Neo Neo, Maranoa, Currawillinghi.
Commercial Bank of Sydney, Cooroorah, Leichardt, Duaringa.
Conran, T. W. and H. L., Yamala, Leichardt, Lilyvale.
Conrick, J., Nappamerry, Gregory South, Thorgomindah.
Conton and Wild, Owenyowan, Warrego, Cunnamulla.
Cook, John, Wandoo, Kennedy, Mackay.
Cook, R., Boonangar N., Darling Downs, Goondiwindi.
Cook and Ross, Balnagowan, Kennedy, Mackay.
Cooper, Horace S., Mount M'Connell, S. Kennedy, Dalrymple.
Cooper and Mytton, Oak Park, Cook, Dalrymple.
Copley, P. G., Salamis, Maranoa, Mitchell.
Cory, G. G., Cecil Plains, Darling Downs, Dalby.
Cory, Cory and Taylor, Tocal, Mitchell, Thompson River.
Costello, John, Cawarral, Port Curtis, Rockhampton.
Cotton and Malpas, Currawella, Mitchell, Blackall.
Coutts Bros., North Toolburra, Darling Downs, Warwick.
Coventry, A., Goondiwindi. Darling Downs, Goondiwindi.
Cowan and Co., Windeyer, Aramac.
Cox, A., Kilmorey. Roma.
Cox and Blomfield, Evesham, Mitchell, Muttaburra.
Cox, E. K., Evesham, Mitchell, Aramac.
Cox, J., Culeraigie, Burnett, Rawbelle.
Cox, J. W. G., Eureka, Burnett, Rawbelle.
Craig. Simmie and Fraser, Mount Hutton, Leichardt, Roma.
Craig, W., Ringwood Park, N. Kennedy, Cardwell.
Craigie, J., Lake Dunn, Mitchell, Copperfield.
Crane, Martin, Ugly Mountain, Darling Downs, Warwick.
Cramsie, J., Bowden, J. C., Palmer, W. C., and Woodfall, Naryileo Downs, S. Gregory, Thorgomindah.
Creed, J. and G., Langmore, Port Curtis, Gladstone.
Croasdill, William, Glenhoughton, Leichardt, Taroom.
Croft Bros., Cooberri, Port Curtis, Cawarral.
Cromwell and Eazy, Tahiti, Wide Bay, Maryborough.
Cronin, James, Brisbane.
Cross, Edmund, Eagle Hill, Port Curtis, Rockhampton.
Crossthwate, R., Wodonga, Gregory N., Cork.
Crossthwate and Tetley, Rocklands, Burke, Normanton.
Crosthwate and Tetley, Barclay Downs, Burke, Normanton.
Crouch, William, Mount Pleasant, Maranoa, Mitchell.
Crump and Hughes, Buralee, South Kennedy, Bowen.
Cudmore and Budge, Googra, Charleville.
Cudmore, Swan and Smith, Gooyea, Mitchell, Tambo.

Culhane, M. S., Emu Creek, Darling Downs.
Cummings, T. M., and Co., Cunnamulla, Warrego, via Sydney.
Cunningham, M. W., Rannes, Leichardt, Banana.
Cunningham and Co., Woodhouse, North Kennedy, Townsville.
Cunningham, T., Elsie Vale, South Kennedy, Bowen
Curr, M., Cardigan, North Kennedy, Ravenswood.
Curtis, G. S., Rockhampton.
Cuthbert, A., Bunda Bunda, Burke, Normanton.
Cutten, F., Cooper's Plains, Brisbane.
Daisey, M., Trinidad. Maranoa, Roma.
Daisey, M., Murilla, Maranoa, Condamine.
Dalglish, J., and J. Crawford, Hamilton Downs, Burke, Hughenden.
Dallon, Charles, Greendale, Rockhampton.
Dangar, A. A., Noorindoo, Maranoa, Surat.
Dangar and Bell, Tingin. Maranoa, Condamine.
Dangar, Bell, Bell and Ewan, Gunna Warra, North Kennedy, Cardwell.
Dangar, Bell, Bell and Ewan, Niagra, North Kennedy, Townsville.
Dangar and Bode, Bromby Park, North Kennedy, Bowen.
Davenport. F. H., Genara, N. Kennedy, Nanango.
Davenport and Fisher, Bundaleer Plains, Maranoa, Currawillinghi.
Davenport, G. H., Retreat, Darling Downs, Dalby.
Davenport and Co., O. K., Darling Downs, Toowoomba.
Davey, R., Thornby, Leichardt, Banana.
Davey, R., East Thornby, Maranoa, St. George.
Davidson, J. E., Mackay.
Davidson, R. G., Craven, Leichardt, Clermont.
Deane and Woodburne, Bluff, North Kennedy, Charters Towers.
De Burgh, Persse T., Tabragalba, Moreton, Beenleigh.
Delaney, Joseph, Cabulture, Moreton, Cabulture.
Delgar, John, Durah, Darling Downs, Dalby.
Dempsey, J., Sorrell Hill, Leichardt, Duaringa.
Dencher, G., Western Creek, Dalby.
De Salis Bros., Strathmore, Kennedy, Bowen.
Deschamps, J., Warroo, via Gingin.
Desmond, John, Edwinstorde, Mitchell, Blackall.
Devine, P., Woondoola Downs, Burke, Normanton.
Devine, P. E., Springrove, Maranoa, Surat.
Dight, Arthur, Yenda, Burnett, Gayndah.
Dight, Messrs., Billa Billa, Darling Downs, Dalby.
Dight, Messrs., Ingleston, Darling Downs, Dalby.
Dight, Messrs., Tucka Tucka, Goondiwindi.
Dight and McLeod, Terica, Darling Downs, Leyburn.
Dockrill, W., Tartha, Darling Downs, Dalby.
Donelly and Hewitt, North Branch, Darling Downs, Cambooya.
Donahoe, P. and W., South Gayndell, Darling Downs, St. George.
Donkin, F. W., Langlo Downs, Warrego, Tambo.
Donner, S. W., Balcho, South Kennedy, Bowen Downs.
Dotswood, G., Rourke, Townsville.
Dougherty, J. G. and Co., Yarrwovale, Warrego, Charleville.
Douglas, W., Brighton Downs, Gregory North, Evesham.
Douglas, W., Toolebuck, Gregory North, Cork.
Douglas, W., Urbana. Gregory North. Blackall.
Douglas, R., jun., Mount Maria, Warrego, Charleville.
Douglas, R., jun., Wyeroo, Gregory North, Cork.
Downey, G. E., Tryconnel, Maranoa, Mitchell.
Dowzer, James, The Oaks, Burnett, Tiaro.
Dreyer, E. G., Rosebrook, Mitchell, Blackall.
Drinan, P., Annandale, Gladstone.
Drinan, P., Woondoola Downs, Burke, Normanton.
Drinan, William, Village of Logan, Moreton, Beenleigh.
Duffy, James, Slatey Creek, Leichardt, Boolbarra.
Duncan, Robert, Coolarah, Port Curtis, Rochester.
Dunlop, J. H., and Co., Warwick.
Dunstan, D. W., Noogilla, Maranoa, St. George.
Durack, P., Sultan, Gregory South, Thorgomindah.
Durack, P. M., Thylungra, Gregory South, Thorgomindah.
Durrick, P. and J., Galway Downs, Gregory South, Thorgomindah.

Durrick, P. and J., Bungenderry, Gregory South, Thorgomindah.
Durrick, P. and J., Galway Downs, Mitchell, Tambo.
Dutton, C. B., Goomally, Leichardt, Duaringa.
Dutton, C. P. and A. F., Beauhinia Downs, Leichardt, Duaringa.
Eaglesfield, Barker, Rosella Plains, Cook, Townsville.
Earl, James, Butcher's Hill, Cork, Cooktown.
Earl, James. Glenlee, South Kennedy, Bowen.
Easton, F. C., Ellenton, Darling Downs, Clifton.
Easton, H. E., Billa Billa, Darling Downs, Dalby.
Eaton, John, Teebar, Wide Bay, Maryborough.
Eaton and Booker, Apis Creek, Leichardt, Marlborough.
Eaton and Booker, Clifton, Port Curtis, Maryborough.
Egan, Stephen, Rosewood, Port Curtis, Rockhampton.
Egan and Healey, Burgurrah, Maranoa, St. George.
Elliott, A. J., Landsborough Downs, Mitchell, Aramac.
Elliott, A. J., Stamfordham, Mitchell, Bowen Downs.
Elliott, Lothbridge and Elliott, Forestvale, Maranoa, Mitchell Downs.
Emmerson, D. R., Prosperine, Kennedy, Bowen.
Ensor, H., Summerhill, Darling Downs, Warwick.
English, John, Ravenswood, North Kennedy, Ravenswood.
Ewan, W. G. and Co., Waterview, Townsville.
Ewan, Alexander, Mount Hillalong, South Kennedy, Nebo.
Fairbairn. G., jun., Peak Downs, Leichardt, Emerald.
Fairbairn, G., Landsdowne, Warrego, Tambo.
Fairbairn, G., Beaconsfield. Mitchell, Aramac.
Fairbairn, S., Barcaldine, Mitchell, Blackall.
Farendon and Hammond, Winsor, N. Kennedy, Charleston.
Farquharson, J., Beta, Darling Downs, Condamine.
Farquharson. J., Undula, Condamine.
Farrendown, Thomas, Charters Towers, Charters Towers.
Faulkiner. Robert, Mount Irwing, Darling Downs, Jondaryan.
Fanning, Nankivell and Co., Tambo, Mitchell, Tambo.
Feehan, R., Kungie South, Warrego, Eulo.
Fenwick and Co., Brisbane.
Fenwick and Scott, Highlands. Mitchell, Isisford.
Ferrett, John, Bottle Tree Ranges and Wallan, Darling Downs, Condamine.
Ferrett, John, Tchanning Runs, Darling Downs, Condamine.
Ferrett, J., Wallan, Darling Downs, Miles.
Ferguson, A., Byernen, S. Kennedy, Bowen.
Ferguson, G., Carrara, Port Curtis, Gladstone.
Ferguson, James, Jersey, Mitchell. Aramac.
Ferguson, James, Springvale, Mitchell, Aramac.
Ferguson, J. T., Kangaroo Creek, S. Kennedy, Bowen.
Ferry, Thomas, Nuke, Maranoa, St. George.
Firth, Ezra, Mount Surprise, Albert Downs, Cook, Cardwell.
Fisher, C. B., Hayfields, Darling Downs, Dalby.
Fisher, C. B., Retreat, Darling Downs, Cambooya.
Fisher, C. B., Talgai, Darling Downs, Clifton.
Fisher, Davenport & Co., Condamine Plains, Darling Downs, Dalby.
Fisher and Davenport, Ellengowan, Darling Downs, Cambooya.
Fisher, Davenport and Mason, Headington Hill, Darling Downs, King Creek.
Fisher and Hill, Bullomon, Maranoa, St. George.
Fisher and Hill, Nindigulla, Maranoa, St. George.
Fisher and Hill, Cubbie, Maranoa, St. George.
Fisk, H, Albion, Burke, Hughenden.
Fitzgerald, T. L. N., Moongool, Maranoa, Condamine.
Foot, H. C., Frederic East, Prairie, Indaryan, via Brisbane.
Foot and Sons, Mount Leonard, Warrego, Charleville.
Forbes, G. E., Mount Stanley, Moreton, Walloon.
Forbes and Raff, Colinton, Moreton, Ipswich.
Ford and Slater, Retreat, Leichardt, Springsure.
Forrester, W. J., Forresters' Retreat, Mitchell, Welford Downs.

Forsyth, W., Aramac, Aramac.
Foulkes, Robt., Planet Downs, Leichardt, Springsure.
Fox, F. J., Bombardy, St. Lawrence.
Fraser, Brown and Brown, Babiloora, Warrego, Springsure.
Fraser and Co., Manero, Aramac.
Fraser, Laidlaw and Fraser, Surat Downs, Mitchell, Aramac.
Fraser, Mary, Killarney, Warrep, Mitchell.
Fraser, R., J., R. A. and T. H., Mitchell Vale, Cook, Port Douglas.
Fraser, Sydney P., Kilmorey, via Roma.
Frost, T., Glenbower, Mitchell, Blackall.
Frost, T., The Springs, Mitchell, Blackall.
Frost, W., Kilkerry Downs, Gregory North, Blackall.
Fry, Julius, Brush Creek, Darling Downs, Leyburn.
Gaden, W. H., Molangool, Wide Bay, Maryborough.
Garbut, Charles, Woodleigh, North Kennedy, Thornborough.
Gardiner and Stuart, Amby Junction, Maranoa, Roma.
Gardiner and Stuart, Mitchell Downs, Maranoa, Mitchell Downs.
Gibbs, C. H., Mentone, Warrego, Charleville.
Gibson, James, Mellingria, Kennedy, Richmond Downs.
Gibson, James, Taldora, Kennedy, Richmond Downs.
Gilchrist, W. O., Greenmount, Kennedy, Nebo.
Gilchrist, W. O., Kalongo, Wide Bay, Maryborough.
Gilchrist, W. O., Bomballera, Warrego, Cunnamulla.
Gilchrist, W. O., Listowell Downs, Warrego, Tambo.
Gilchrist and Watt, Pike's Creek, Darling Downs, Stanthorpe.
Gilchrist and Watt, Boondooma, Burnett, Dalby.
Gilham, T.W., Rookwood, Leichardt, St. Lawrence.
Gillespie, R., Allandale, Gregory North, Aramac.
Glennie, James, Thornhill, via Gin Gin.
Goggs, M., Bullaroo, Maranoa, Roma.
Goggs, M. B., Wolston, Moreton, Goodna.
Golden, G. M., Bundi, Leichardt, Condamine.
Goldsborough and Marden, The Auburn, Darling Downs, Gayndah.
Gordon and Crawford, Angellala Downs, Warrego, Burenda.
Gordon and Davis, Cooberie, Rockhampton.
Gordon and Flood, Gowrie, Warrego, Charleville.
Gordon and James, Cluden, North Kennedy, Townsville.
Gore and Co., Yandilla, Darling Downs, Yandilla.
Govett Brothers, Isis Downs, Mitchell, Tambo.
Govett and Green, Talundilly, Mitchell, Blackall.
Graham, A., Thornby, Maranoa, St. George.
Graham, J. L., Calliope, Port Curtis, Calliope.
Graham, W., Malvern Hills, Tambo.
Graham, W., Coomrinth, Darling Downs, Dalby.
Graham and Beardmore, Clive, Leichardt, Marlborough.
Graham and Williams, St. Ronan's, Gregory North, Blackall.
Graham and Williams, Wondul, Darling Downs, Western Creek.
Grambauer, A. F. W., Rosedale, Mitchell, Aramac.
Gray, R., Bowen, Burke, Dalrymple.
Gray, R. C. and M., Hughenden, Burke, Dalrymple.
Green, C. H., Rosedale, Lyndhurst Crossing.
Green, T. O. S., Craven, Leichardt, Argyle.
Grell, William, Duckabrook, Leichardt, Springsure.
Greig and Nash, Cambridge Downs, Burke, Dalrymple.
Grice, J. and J., Ruthven, Mitchell, Isis Downs.
Grieve, Wm., Wallaby Hill, Darling Downs, Dalby.
Grimes, J. W., Toowoomba.
Groom, W. H., Toowoomba.
Gunn, Donald, Pikedale, Darling Downs, Leyburn.
Gunn, Donald, Summerhill, Warwick.
Hackett, M., Dalton, Mitchell, Wombunderry.
Hamilton, A. G., Belmont, Leichardt, Banana.
Hamilton, F., Fanning Downs, North Kennedy, Charters Towers.
Hamilton, R., Culrossie, Burnett, Gayndah.
Hammond, E., Homeward Bound, Gregory South, Thorgomindah.
Hammond, E., Hammond Downs, Gregory South, Thorgomindah.
Hammond, E., Burrangong, Gregory South, Thorgomindah.
Hammond, J., Argyle, Gregory South, Thorgomindah.
Hammond, James, Tenham, Gregory South, Thorgomindah.
Hammond, M., Thiweeniah, Gregory South, Thorgomindah.
Hann, W., Maryvale, North Kennedy, Dalrymple.
Hann, W., Miall, North Kennedy, Dalrymple.
Hann, W., Tara, North Kennedy, Dalrymple.
Hannam, M., Walton, Leichardt, Duaringa.
Hannesford, S., Oak Vale, Maranoa, Womblebrook.
Hanmer, T., Talgai and Canal Creek, Hendon.
Harden and Walker, Glenlyon, Stanthorpe.
Harding, T., Galbally, Gregory North, Cork.
Harding, T., Datson, Gregory North, Cork.
Hart, G. E., Bollon, Maranoa, St. George.
Hart and Flower, Brisbane.
Hatfield, T. J., Yatton, St. Lawrence.
Hay, A. and A., Gilmore, Warrego, Eulo.
Hay, W., Tewantin, Burnett, Tewantin.
Haygarth. M. J., Koomlbyn, Moreton, Veresdale.
Haynes, J. L., Morinish, Port Curtis, Rockhampton.
Hayes and Bundock, Bletchington Park, North Kennedy, Charters Towers.
Hazard, G. R., Horan, Maranoa, St. George.
Hazard, R. and G., Balagna, Maranoa, St. George.
Headrick, J. and Co., Rockhampton.
Headrick and Livermore, Fernyside, Leichardt, Taroon.
Henness, Walter, Scrubby Land, Maranoa, St. George.
Henness, Walter, Mulga Downs, Maranoa, St. George.
Henness, W. R., Bonna Vonna, Maranoa, St. George.
Henderson, A., Invercol, Port Curtis, Gladstone.
Henderson, C. and C., Avon Plains, Leichardt, Clermont.
Henderson, J. A., Gerara, Gregory North, Jundah.
Henderson and Moore, Tantutha, Burnett, Bundaberg.
Henderson and Skim, Havilah, South Warrego, Bowen.
Hennessy, Thomas, Belrose, Warrego, Charleville.
Henning and Prendergast, Emu Plains, South Kennedy, Bowen.
Henning and Prendergast, Emoor, North Kennedy, Bowen.
Hess, G. M., Suttor Creek, South Kennedy, Nebo.
Hetzer, Martin, Temple Downs, Burke, Normanton.
Hickson, R. A., Unumgar, Ipswich.
Higgins, W., Binda, Darling Downs, Dalby.
Hill and Blackburn, Mount Morris, Langlo River, Charleville.
Hill, Fenwick, and Gore, Booth Avington, Mitchell, Blackall.
Hill, T. and A., Yarranbah, Maranoa, St. George.
Hinton, J. V. & S., Glenlee, Leichardt, Springsure.
Hinton, W. T., Cania, Gregory North, Blackall.
Hinton, W. T., Roslin, Gregory North, Blackall.
Hislop, George, Wolfang, Clermont.
Hobson and Hamilton, Bulgroo, Gregory South, Thorgomindah.
Hobson, Hamilton and Willis, Candie, Gregory S., Thorgomindah.
Hood, W. C. and W., Annandale, Gregory S., Innamincka, S.A.
Hood, W. C. and W., Annandale, Gregory N., Thorgomindah.
Hodgson and Ramsay, Eton Vale, Darling Downs, Cambooya.
Hodgson, Ramsay and Rait, Tooloombilla, Maranoa, Mitchell.
Hogarth, William, Balgownie, Darling Downs, Cambooya.
Holland, J., Wallan, Maranoa, St. George.
Hollinshead, Hazlerigg and Baker, Shotover, Leichardt, Duaringa.
Holmes, A. and E., Aberglassie, Maranoa, Mitchell.
Holmes, A. and E., Homeboin, Maranoa, St. George.

Holmes, J., Hertford, Maranoa, St. George.
Holmes, J., Strathmore, Maranoa, St. George.
Holmes, R. Y., C. T., and H., Wyaga, Darling Downs, Dalby.
Holt, Joseph, Bancory, Leichardt, Clermont.
Holt, Thomas, Salisbury Plains, Kennedy, Nebo.
Holt, F. S. E., Salisbury Plains, Kennedy, Nebo.
Holt, F. S. E., Islay Plains, S. Kennedy, Copperfield.
Holt, F. S. E., Bancory, S. Kennedy, Copperfield.
Holt, F. S. E., Wealwandangie, Leichardt, Springsure.
Holt, F. S. E., Spring Creek, Leichardt, Springsure
Holt. W. H., Glenprairie, Marlborough.
Homer, Broadbent and Williams, Moura, Leichardt, Banana.
Homsich, G. H. Van, Windsor, Gregory North, Cork.
Homrigh, H. Van, Thompson River, Aramac.
Howie, W. and J. H., Haddon, Gregory South, Jundah.
Howie, W. and J. H., St. Albans, Gregory North, Jundah.
Hooper, Geo., Hawkswood, Burnett, Gayndah.
Hope, Hon. Louis, Kilcoy, Moreton, Caboolture.
Hope, John, Costello Creek, Gregory South, Kyabra.
Hopkins, E. B., Goodan, Darling Downs, Goondiwindi.
Hopkins, J., Mount Douglas, South Kennedy, Bowen.
Hornung, G., Heidelberg Hotel, South Kennedy, Bowen.
Houghton, J. T., Stonington, North Kennedy, Capeville.
Hudson, B., Stonehenge, Darling Downs, Leyburn.
Hudson and Moore, Bindebango, Maranoa, St. George.
Hughes, H. B., Nockatunga, Gregory South, Thorgomindah.
Hughes, Shand and Co., Wombah, Wide Bay, Mount Perry.
Humphrey, T. F., Mount Debateable, Burnett, Gayndah.
Humphrey and Bullmore, Oakwood, Warrego, Charleville.
Hunter, R. M., Dubbo Downs, Gregory North, Blackall.
Hunter, H., Victoria Downs, Warrego, Mitchell.
Hutton, James, Raspberry Creek, Port Curtis, Cawarral.
Hutton, Jas. and W., Peninsula, Yaamba.
Huxley, T., Wild, Warrego, Eulo.
Hyne and Co., Rocky Waterholes, South Kennedy, Mackay.
Hyne, William, Burton Downs, Leichardt, Nebo.
Imlay, A., Comongin, Warrego, Thorgomindah.
Ivory, F. J., Eidswold, Burnett, Gayndah.
Jardine, J. R., Marlborough, Port Curtis, Marlborough.
Jenkins, —, Mangalore, Warrego, Charleville.
Jenkins, R. L., Callandoon, Darling Downs, Goondiwindi.
Jenkins, R. L., Tarewinnabar, Darling Downs, Goondiwindi.
Jenkins, R. L., Balaclava, Port Curtis, Rockhampton.
Jerrard Brothers, Scoria Creek, Port Curtis, Gladstone.
Jessop, J. S., Forest Park, Darling Downs, Goondiwindi.
Jessop, W. and G. Fox, Latus Creek, Leichardt, St. Lawrence.
Jeune, E. B., Brangan, Bundaberg.
Jockhien, William, Ben Lomond, South Kennedy, Bowen.
John, H. J., Ban Ban, Burnett and Wide Bay, Gayndah.
Johnson, W. J., Warro, Gin Gin.
Johnston, A. and A., Walla, Wide Bay, Maryborough.
Johnston, J. A., Cooroorah, Darling Downs, Dalby.
Joint Stock Bank, Leura, Leichardt, St. Lawrence.
Jones, executors of D. M., Boonara, Burnett, Nanango.
Jones, Richard, Tobermorey, Warrego, Thorgomindah.
Jones, Green and Sullivan, Bulloo Downs, Warrego, Thorgomindah.

Jones and Downing, Tryconnell Downs, Maranoa, Mitchell.
Jones, Duffy, McAllan and Flanagan, Good Hope, Gregory South, Thorgomindah.
Jones, Green and Sullivan, Dynevor Downs, Warrego, Thorgomindah.
Josephson, J. F., Moorside, Rockhampton.
Joyce and Gill, Lochaber. Burnett, Gayndah.
Kelly and Mactaggart, Glenbarr, Burnett, Maryborough.
Kelman and Robson, Swan Vale, Mitchell, Jundah.
Kelman, W., Meteor Downs, Leichhardt, Springsure.
Kelman, W., Corella Downs, Gregory North, Isis Downs.
Kenavan, W., Maroo, Gregory North, Mount Margaret.
Kennedy, Alexander, Noranside, Gregory North, Cork.
Kennedy, J., Myally, Burke, Normanton.
Kent and Wienholt, Jondaryan, Darling Downs, Jondaryan.
Kent and Wienholt, Rosewood, Moreton, Rosewood.
Kent and Wienholt, Tarampa, Moreton, Laidlaw.
Keating, Richard, Wombiana, North Kennedy, Charters Towers.
Kilgour and McKay, Bellkate, Gregory North, Muttaburra.
Kilgour, William, Surbiton, South Kennedy, Clermont.
King, G., and Sons, Gowrie, Darling Downs, Gowrie.
King, G., G. B., and H. V., Speeling, Warrego, Cunnamulla.
King, G., G. B., and H. V., Weellamurra, Warrego, Cunnamulla.
King, P. G., Corona, Mitchell, Aramac.
Kinnear, D., Canada, Gregory North, Aramac.
Kirk and Co., Edith Vale and Cardington, North Kennedy, Townsville.
Kirk, G., Mooraby, Maranoa, St. George.
Kirk, G., Wagaby, Maranoa, St. George.
Kirk, G. M., Gulnabar, Maranoa, St. George.
Kirk, W., Cardington, North Kennedy, Townsville.
Kirk and Walker, Doongmabulla, South Kennedy, Bowen.
Kirk and Walker, Ullcanbah, South Kennedy, Bowen.
Knox, E., Mundaburra, Burnett, Gayndah.
Knox and Ruthledge, Coonambulla, Burnett, Nanango.
Knox, R. W., and J T. Smith, Gumbardo, Warrego, Charleville.
Knox and Stephen, Kolan, Wide Bay, Maryborough.
Knox and McCord, Cania, Gladstone.
Knyvett and Box, Wyagee, Darling Downs, Leyburn.
Lacy, Dyson, St. Helena No. 2, South Kennedy, Mackay.
Lalor, J., Gubberamunda, Maranoa, St. George.
Lalor, W., Bengalla, Darling Downs, Inglewood.
Lalor, W., Myall Downs, Leichardt, Roma.
Lalor, W., Weeyan, Maranoa, St. George.
Lalor, W., Beebo, Darling Downs, Leyburn.
Lamb, G. T., Nebull, Maranoa, St. George.
Landy Bros., Bowen Park, Darling Downs, Dalby.
Langton and Williamson, Greenvale, North Kennedy, Dalrymple.
Langton and John, Greenvale, Townsville.
Lawless, Mrs., Boobygan, Burnett and Wide Bay, Gayndah.
Leadbetter, D. T., Maryvale, Warrego, Morven.
Leishman, H. A., Lorne, Mitchell, Tambo.
Leishman and Co., Lorne, Blackall.
Lester, L. C., Rosenthal, Warwick.
Lewis, T. W., Waverly or Cabbage Tree, Moreton, Ipswich.
Lewin, R., Luss Vale, Maranoa, Mitchell.
Lilley Bros., Boyne Island, Port Curtis, Gladstone.
Lindsay, William, Hiddon, Jundah, Mitchell.
Little, John, Redcliffe, Leichardt, Duaringa.
Little, John, Bideston, Darling Downs, Toowoomba.
Little, James, Rosedale, Port Curtis, Gladstone.

Littlejohn and Alford, Gwambagwine, Leichardt, Taroom.
Littlejohn and Alford, Taabinga, Burnett, Jondaryan.
Littlejohn and Alford, Coochin Coochin, Moreton, Ipswich.
Living, J., Memilo Plains, Leichardt, Duaringa.
Living, J., Wooroona, Leichardt, Duaringa.
Lloyd, G. H., Redbank, Burnett, Gayndah.
Lloyd, J. P., and Co., Maryborough, Burnett, Maryborough.
Logan, R., Mingoola, Darling Downs, Tenterfield.
Logan, R., Durham Downs, Roma.
London Chartered Bank, Winton, Darling Downs, Goondiwindi.
Macansh, J. D., Cooroora, Darling Downs, Warwick.
Macansh, J. D., Canning Creek, Darling Downs, Leyburn.
Macansh, J. D., Kitticarara, Gregory North, Cloncurry.
Macansh, J. D., Mantuan Downs, Leichardt, Springsure.
Macansh, J. D., Isis Downs, Mitchell, Isisford.
Macansh, Windeyer and Cadell, Cooroora, Darling Downs, Dalby.
Macartney, Mayne, Elliot and Co., Sandsborough Downs, Mitchell, Aramac.
MacDonald, C. C., The Auburn, Darling Downs, Gayndah.
MacDonald, H., Glengarry, Port Curtis, Rockhampton.
MacDonald, P. F., Yomeapps, Port Curtis.
MacDonald, P. F., Columbia, Leichardt, Marlborough.
MacDonald, P. F., Fernlees, Leichardt, Springsure.
MacDowell and Coutts, Cashmere, Cardwell.
MacGlasham, D., Bowie, South Kennedy, Bowen.
MacKay and Others, Omega, Leichardt, Clermont.
MacKay and Kilgour, Alpha, Leichardt, Clermont.
MacKay, E. H., Teirawomba, Leichardt, Nebo.
MacKay, E. H., Huntley, Leichardt, Clermont.
MacKay, Jas. Bondandilla, via Cambooya.
Mackenzie, John, Reserve, Port Curtis, Rockhampton.
Mackenzie, W., Arabella, Warrego, Charleville.
Mackenzie, Bostock and Co., Maidan, Burke, Aramac.
Mackie, R., Cobbareena, Darling Downs, Condamine.
Macleay and Beaumont, Talawinta, Maranoa, Brewarrina.
Macleod, R., Terrica, Darling Downs, Stanthorpe.
Maconochie, John, Fernlee, Maranoa, St. George.
Mailer, R., Durham Downs, Gregory South, Mount Margaret.
Malcolm and Mackinnon, Albury Downs, Maranoa, Mitchell.
Malpas, W. J., Caiwarroo, Warrego, Eulo.
Malpas, W. J., Cungabulla, Gregory North, Wilford Downs.
Malpas, W. J., Currawilla, Gregory North, Wilford Downs.
Malpas, W. J., Thorlindah, Warrego, Eulo.
Manifold and Bostock, Sesbania, Gregory North, Aramac.
Manifold and Bostock, Muttaburra, Aramac.
Mant and Littleton, Gigoomgan, Wide Bay, Maryborough.
Mark, W., G. H., J. C., and R. W. E., Byron Downs, Burke, Cloncurry.
Markey, J., Bodandilla, Towoomba.
Markwell, S., Beaudesert, Moreton, Veresdale.
Marsh, M. and H., Folkestone, Darling Downs, Stanthorpe.
Marsh, M. H., Maryland, Darling Downs, Warwick.
Marsh, W., Hillsborough, Maranoa, St. George.
Marsh, W. and T., Glencoe, Maranoa, St. George.
Marshall, S. T. and H., North Merewa, Darling Downs, Goondiwindi.
Marshall, Wm., Well, Darling Downs, Warwick.
Marshall and Slade, Glengallan, Darling Downs, Warwick.
Marlindale and Stephens, Clarke, Mitchell, Clermont.

Martel, S. A., Mount Chance, Gregory North, Cork.
Martel, S. A., Tyrie, Gregory North, Cork.
Martel, S. A., Woodstock, Gregory North, Cork.
Massy Bros., Sonoma, Kennedy, Bowen.
Matherson, D., Broadwater, Leichardt, Boolburra.
Mayne, W. C., Ghinghinda, Leichardt, Taroom.
Mayne Brothers, Peakvale, Leichardt, Clermont.
Mein, G. A. and P., Log Creek, Warrego, Eulo.
Mellow, Matthew, Gympie, Burnett, Gympie.
Melville, A. W., Doongoil, Wide Bay, Maryborough.
Melville, A. W., Maryborough, Burnett, Gympie.
Menzies, Archibald, Raglan Station, Port Curtis, Rockhampton.
Menzies, John, Raglan Station, Port Curtis, Rockhampton.
Menzies and Douglas, Eurella, Maranoa, Roma.
Menzies and Meredith, Taldora and Willungra, Burke, Cloncurry.
Mercantile Bank of Sydney, Green Hills, Mitchell, Aramac.
Meredith, Menzies, and Co., Taldora, Burke, Cloncurry.
Meredith, Menzies, and Co., Millungera, Burke, Cloncurry.
Miles, M., Mount Elise, South Kennedy, Bowen.
Miles, William, Park Head, Darling Downs, Condamine.
Miles, William, Brunell Downs, Warrego, Mitchell.
Miles, W., Kynuna, Gregory North, Cork.
Millis, James, Nanango, Burnett, Nanango.
Mills, James C., Woodleigh, Darling Downs, Yandilla.
Mills, Fletcher and Co., Dallmally, Roma.
Milson, J., jun., Corona, Leichardt, Aramac.
Milson and De Statge, Coroena, Mitchell, Aramac.
Missing, Henry, Gootchy, Wide Bay, Maryborough.
Mitchell, Henry, Iron Pot Creek, Darling Downs, Warwick.
Mitchell and Gill, Christmas Creek, North Kennedy, Dalrymple.
Moloney, J. P. and M., Bendemere, Maranoa, Condamine.
Monohan, J., Shylock, Gregory North, Blackall.
Moore, J. and J., Moorlands, Rosewood.
Moore, J. D. and W., Drumbaggan, Warrego, Charleville.
Moore, J. D. and W., Burandilla, Warrego, Charleville.
Moore, J. and H., Baramba, Burnett, Nanango.
Moore, Isaac, Tantitha, Wide Bay, Bundaberg.
Moore Bros. and Baynes, Baramba, Burnett, Nanango.
Moore, Moore and Martin, Binnerbilla, Warrego, Charleville.
Moore, P. E., Waterloo, Maranoa, St. George.
Morehead, H. B. D., Wallambilla, Maranoa, Condamine.
Morehead, J. and D., Targinie, Port Curtis, Gladstone.
Moreton, B. B. and S., Wetheron, Burnett, Gayndah.
Moreton, F. and Co., Prairie, Port Curtis, Gayndah.
Morgan, William, Mount Stewart, Leichardt, Lilyvale.
Mort, Henry, Redbank, Burnett, Hawkwood.
Mort and Richards, Franklynvale, Moreton, Ipswich.
Mortimer, I., Manumbar, Burnett, Brisbane.
Muirhead, J., and A. Brown, Albro, South Kennedy, Surbiton.
Muirhead, J., Elgin Downs, South Kennedy, Clermont.
Mundell, J., Bungabana, Leichardt, Taroom.
Mundell, J., Winterbourne, Port Curtis, Gladstone.
Mundell, J., Callide, Port Curtis, Gladstone.
Murphy, E. D., and Co., St. George.
Murphy, F. B., Max Vale, Roma.
Murphy, Sir F., and Sons, Northampton Downs, Mitchell, Blackall.
Murphy, J., Greenlands, Warrego, Ellangowan.
Murphy, J., Mount Tierney, Maranoa, Mitchell.
Murphy, J., Pine Mountain. Maranoa, Mitchell.
Murphy, J., St. Mullins, Darling Downs, Warwick.
Murray, J., Agricultural Reserve, Rockhampton

Murray, P., Mount Lookout, South Kennedy, Nebo.
Murray, Stewart, Clanmaroo, Maranoa, Dalby.
Murray and Sons, Butler Creek, South Kennedy, Bowen.
McArthur, J., Glenelg, Darling Downs, Leyburn.
McBain and Telford, Consuelo, Leichardt, Springsure.
McBain and Telford, Carnarvon Creek, Leichardt, Springsure.
McBean, L., Grenvillia, Port Curtis, Gayndah.
McBrae, Mrs. P., Mount Margaret, Warrego, Thorgomindah.
McCartney, Sir J., St. Helens No. 1, Kennedy, Mackay.
McCartney, J. A., Tamworth, Mitchell, Hughenden.
McCartney, M., Plevna Downs, Surat, via Brisbane.
McCartney, W. C., St. Helens No. 3, Kennedy, Mackay.
McCartney, W. G., Bloomsbury, Kennedy, Mackay.
McCartney and Mayne, The Nile, Gregory North, Cork.
McCartney and Mayne, Waverly, Port Curtis, St. Lawrence.
McCartney and Mayne, Afton, Burke, Hughenden.
McCartney and Mayne, Annandale, Leichardt, Nebo.
McCartney and Mayne, Bladensberg, Gregory North, Ellerslie.
McCartney and Percy, Diamantina Lakes, Gregory North, Cork.
McLean, J., executors of, Bindango, Maranoa, Roma.
McConnell, John, Durundur, Moreton, Brisbane.
McConnell, J. H., Cressbrook, Moreton, Walloon.
McConochie, J., Coomburrah, Maranoa, St. George.
McCord, W. F., Cania, Burnett, Gayndah.
McCord, W. F., Coonambula, Burnett, Gayndah.
McCord, W. F., Wigton, Burnett, Gayndah.
McCormack, James, Langton, South Kennedy, Mistake Creek.
McCormack, P., Merino Downs, Surat.
McDermott, P., Lower Laurie River, Cook, Cooktown.
McDonald, Alexander, Louisleigh, Kennedy, Bowen.
McDonald, A., Harvest Home, South Kennedy, Bowen.
McDonald, A. B., Grosvenor Downs, Leichardt, Copperfield.
McDonald, A. and P., Wildhorse Plains, Maranoa, St. George.
McDonald, G. F., Collybeen, Maranoa, Mungundi.
McDonald, J., Hidden Valley, South Kennedy, Bowen.
McDonald, Jessie, Dugandan, Moreton, Ipswich.
McDonald, estate of the late N. H., Lara, Gregory South, Thorgomindah.
McDonald, McDonald and Harding, Cores, Gregory North, Aramac.
McDonald, McDonald and Harding, Charlotte Plains, Warrego, Cunnamulla.
McDonald and Smith, Ban Ban, Burnett, Nanango.
McDonald and Smith, Mantuan Downs, Springsure.
McDonald and Coulson, Dromellon, Moreton, Veresdale.
McDonnell, J., Conway, South Kennedy, Bowen.
McDougall, A. S., Guuyan, Darling Downs, Texas.
McDougall, Hon. J. F., Rosalie Plains, Darling Downs, Jondaryan.
McDougall, M. S., Clifton, Maranoa, St. George.
McDowall and Couts, Welcome Downs, North Kennedy, Cardwell.
McFarlane and Appleyard, Bidenham, Charleville.
McGhie, Suya and Co., Cootharaba, Burnett, Gympie.
McGill and Clymont, Amamoor, Burnett, Gympie.
McGillivray, G., Berwick, Burke, Hughenden.
McGillivray, G., Eddington, Burke, Dalrymple.
McGlashan, D., Bowie, South Kennedy, Bowen Downs.
McGrath, Mount Walker, Moreton, Ipswich.
McGregor, D., Glengyle, Gregory North, Thorgomindah.

McGregor, D., Tomodonka, Gregory North, Mount Margaret.
McGregor and McLeon, Jollmont, Kennedy, Mackay.
McGuigan, Patrick, Terribooh, Gregory North, Cork.
McIlwane, Bros., Riversleigh, Charleville.
McIlwraith, T., Ayrshire Downs, Gregory North, Cork.
McIlwraith, Thomas, Gin Gin, Wide Bay, Mount Perry.
McIlwraith and Smyth, Merivale, Maranoa, Mitchell.
McIntosh, James, Blinkbonnie, Darling Downs, Warwick.
McIntyre, D., Kalara, Burke, Dalrymple.
McIntyre, D., Llanarth, South Kennedy, Bowen.
McIntyre, D., Dalgonally, Burke, Dalrymple.
McIntyre, Duncan, Lagoon Creek, Darling Downs, Oakley Creek.
McIntyre, Donald, Llanarth, Suttor River, Kennedy, Nebo.
McIntyre, Donald, Dalgonally, Burke, Dalrymple.
McIver and Curtis, Nickavilla, Gregory South, Tambo.
McIver and Curtis, Nickavilla, Warrego, Tambo.
McKay, D. F., Bandy Andy, Maranoa, St. George.
McKay and Caswell, Canindah, Gayndah.
McKay and Co., Huntley Downs, Leichardt, Clermont.
McKellar and Holt, Cotherstone, Burnett, St. Lawrence.
McKenzie, Bostock, and Co., Werna, Gregory North, Wittown.
McKenzie, J., Dulbydilla, Maranoa, Mitchell.
McKenzie, W., Authoringa, Warrego, Charleville.
McKinnon, M., Albany Downs, Maranoa, Dalby.
McLean, executors of J., Redford and Sunnyside, Maranoa, Mitchell.
McLean, Jonathan, Marivale, Maranoa, Mitchell.
McLean, M. J., Cracow, Leichardt, Banana.
McLean, Hodgson, and Greene, Goombuna, Darling Downs, Allora.
McLean, Taylor, and Co., Currawillingi, St. George.
McLennan, D., Ingle Downs, Leichardt, Lilyvale.
McLeay and Taylor, Currawillinghi, Maranoa, St. George.
McManus, W. R., Oolandilla, Maranoa, Mitchell.
McManns, W. R., Mount Lonsdale, Maranoa, Mitchell.
McMicking, R., Cashmere, Maranoa, St. George.
McMullen, J. F., Rockybank, Maranoa, Roma.
McMullen, J. F., Tarong, Burnett, Gayndah.
McMullen, J. F., Kincora, Darling Downs, St. George.
McMullen, J. F., Durham Downs, Leichardt, Roma.
McMullen, J. F., Booroondara, Leichardt, Lilyvale.
McMullen, J. F., Barwon Park, Warrego, Lilyvale.
McMullen, J. F., Wombo, Darling Downs, Condamine.
McMullen, J. F., Wimpole, Gregory North, Jundah.
McNale and Sutherland, Kyanga, Banana.
McNamara, P., Rocky Bar and Spring Vale, Darling Downs, Dalby.
McNeale, Barry, Newland, and McCabe, Naccowlah, Gregory South, Thorgomindah.
McNelly, J., South Teelba, Maranoa, Surat.
McNulty, T., Muggleton, Maranoa, Roma.
McPherson, D., Emerald Downs, Leichardt, Lilyvale.
McPhillamy, C., Sherwood, Leichardt, Duaringo.
McRae, C., Mount Margaret, Gregory South, Mount Margaret.
McTaggart, Executors of J. D., Kilkivan, Wide Bay, Kilkivan.
McVicar, Dugald, Wombunderry South, Gregory South, Thorgomindah.
National Bank of Australasia, Cotherstone, Leichardt, Clermont.
Neil, Hugh, Galloway Plains, Port Curtis, Gladstone.
Nelson, H. M., Myra, Darling Downs, Dalby.
Nelson, H. M., Louden, Weimbilla, and Malara, Darling Downs, Dalby.
Nelson, H. and W., Da.by.
Nichol, Davidson, Windeyer, Mitchell, Tambo.

Nicholson, John, Haste, Maranoa, Mitchell.
Nimmo, J., Junee, Maranoa, Mitchell.
North Australian Company, Rosenthal and South, Darling Downs, Warwick.
North Australian Pastoral Company, Woodstock, Kennedy, Townsville.
North British and Australian Company, Isla, Leichardt, Banana.
North British and Australian Company, Halliford, Darling Downs, Dalby.
North British and Australian Company, St. Ruth, Darling Downs, Dalby.
North British and Australian Company, Waterton, Leichardt, Taroom.
North, Joseph, Moray Downs, South Kennedy, Clermont.
North, Joseph, Ipswich, Moreton, Ipswich.
Norton and Marcom, Rodd's Bay, Port Curtis, Gladstone.
Nott and Mair, Banana, Leichardt, Banana.
Nutting and Doyle, Chastleton, Warrego, Thorgomindah.
New Zealand and Australian Land Company, Cardbeign, Leichardt, Springsure.
New Zealand and Australian Land Company, Chinchilla, Darling Downs, Dalby.
New Zealand and Australian Land Company, Greendale, Mitchell, Tambo.
New Zealand and Australian Land Company, Willshot, Tambo.
New Zealand Loan and Mercantile Agency Company, Cashmere, Maranoa, St. George.
New Zealand Loan and Mercantile Agency Company, Wallinderry, Gregory South, Mount Margaret.
Oriental Bank, Cawaroo, Surat.
O'Brien, D., Dalby.
O'Brien, Denis, Yalebone, Maranoa, Surat.
O'Brien, M., Wallabella, Surat.
O'Brien and Wilson, Green Hills, Cook, Georgetown.
O'Brien, P., Georgetown, Burke, Georgetown.
Officer, John, Humeburn, Warrego, Eulo.
O'Reilly, F. H., Samford, Moreton, Brisbane.
O'Shannassy, K., Werebone, Maranoa, Surat.
O'Shannassy, Sir John, Mount Howitt, Gregory South, Thorgomindah.
O'Sullivan, O'Roughlee, Leichardt, Roma.
Paine, C. H., Collaroy, Port Curtis, St. Lawrence.
Pain, T., Bowra, Warrego, Charleville.
Pallisier, M., Palestine, Maranoa, Bollon.
Palmer, Hon. A. H., Beaufort, South Kennedy, Clermont.
Palmer, Hon. A. H., Cambridge Downs, Hughenden.
Palmer, H. and E., Conobie, Burke, Dalrymple.
Parker and Ward, Retreat, Mitchell, Isisford.
Parr, B. C., Chiverton, via Warwick.
Parbury and Lord, Cockatoo Creek, Leichardt, Taroom.
Patterson, Andrew, Glen Hill, Darling Downs, Warwick.
Patterson, A., Rosenthal, near Warwick.
Patterson and Jones, West Hill, St. Lawrence.
Patterson, W., Wonomo, Gregory North, Cork.
Paterson, Andrew and Ord, Fernlie, St. George.
Paterson, R. L., and Co., Monte Christo, via Rockhampton.
Paterson, R. L., Monte Christo, Port Curtis, Gladstone.
Patton, Robert, Wellshot, Mitchell, Isis Downs.
Parker, E. W., Lanark Downs, Clermont.
Parker, Langlow, and Co., Barcoo, Barcoo River via Rockhampton.
Paxton, W. H., Mackay.
Pearse, John and William, Junction Station, Darling Downs, Condamine.
Pearce, M., Wondoo, Leichardt, Banana.
Peberdy, W. K., Headingly, Gregory North, Cork.
Peberdy, W. K., Cooroorah, Port Curtis, St. Lawrence.
Peberdy, W. R., Jellintal, Blackwater, Rockhampton.
Peel River Company, Coona Downs, Aramac.
Pender, M. L. and W. A., Lake Pare, Gregory South, Thorgomindah.
Peppin and Webber, Bargie, Gregory South, Thorgomindah.
Peppin and Webber, Abbotsford, Gregory South, Thorgomindah.

Peppin and Webber, Cottesmore, Gregory South, Thorgomindah.
Peppin and Webber, Cunnavella, Gregory South, Thorgomindah.
Peppin and Webber, Monkira, Gregory North, Jundah.
Peppin and Webber, Kyabra, Gregory South, Thorgomindah.
Perry and Horam, Wild Horse Plains, Maranoa, St. George.
Perese, De, B. F., Buckingham Downs, Gregory North, Cork.
Perese De, Birgh, Conemara, Gregory North, Jundah.
Perese, De, B., Laington, Gregory North, Normanton.
Peterson and Rolfe, Dillalah, Warrego, Charleville.
Picot, P. H., Brisbane.
Picton, C., Mungun, Maranoa, Mungindi.
Pierce, J. and W., Junction Station, Toowoomba.
Piper and Collins, Cyprus Downs, Maranoa, St. George.
Piper and Collins, Kenilworth, Maranoa, St. George.
Place and West, St. Helens, Darling Downs, Cambooya.
Plant and Jones, Pomona, Kennedy, St. Herbert.
Pollock Bros., Mangalore, Cunnamulla.
Pollock, James, sen., Nerrigundah, Warrego, Charleville.
Pope, R., Wallumbilla, Roma.
Porter, A. E., Strath Almond, Darling Downs, Leyburn.
Porter, Francis, Grampian Hills, Moreton, Ipswich.
Porter, H. A., Spring Mount, Moreton, Toowoomba.
Pott, G., Burnt Foot, South Kennedy, Bowen.
Powell, J. W., Parlands, Gregory North, Cork.
Powell, J. S., Lower Doongal, Wide Bay, Maryborough.
Powell, Thomas, Traverston, Wide Bay, Gympie.
Powell, W., Maryborough, Burnett, Maryborough.
Primrose, F. A., Emu Creek, Moreton, Murphy's Creek.
Prior, T. L. M., Bully Creek, South Kennedy, Bowen.
Prior, T. L. M., Moonbago, South Kennedy, Bully Creek.
Prior, T. L. M., Pullen, Moreton, Ipswich.
Pritchard, E. R., Brisbane.
Pritchard and Tebbutt, Powlathanga Lake, North Kennedy, Charters Towers.
Prout and Galvin, Diamantina, Gregory North, Cork.
Province, T., Roslyn, Burnett, Mount Perry.
Province, Thomas, Bannia, Burnett, Mount Perry.
Pryde, Thomas, Glenmourie, Moreton, Walloon.
Queensland National Bank, Carraba, Leichardt, Taroom.
Queensland Investment and Land Mortgage Company (Limited), Hogauthulla Downs, Warrego, Mitchell.
Queensland National Bank (Limited), Ardoch, Warrego, Thorgomindah.
Queensland National Bank (Limited), Junction, Darling Downs, Western Creek.
Queensland National Bank (Limited), Kilcummin, South Kennedy, Clermont.
Queensland National Bank (Limited), Kilworey, Maranoa, Mitchell.
Queensland National Bank (Limited), Millbank, North Kennedy, Thornborough.
Queensland National Bank (Limited), Mungy, Burnett, Maryborough.
Queensland National Bank (Limited) Myall Grove, Darling Downs, Condamine.
Queensland National Bank (Limited), Yabber, Wide Bay, Jimna.
Rait, W., Anniston Vale, Gregory North, Blackall.
Rates, Francis, Hendon, Darling Downs, Hendon.
Rawson, Brothers, Shamrock Vale, Kennedy, Mackay.
Rawson, C. F., Abington, Kennedy, Mackay.
Raymer, D., Ribble, Condamine.
Rayne, David, Moraby, Condamine.
Read, J., Alice Downs, Warrego, Morven.
Reid, A., Wombunderry, Gregory South, Thorgomindah.

Reid, Reid and Paterson, Geo lwood, Gregory, Cork.
Reid and Strathorn, Darr River Downs, Mitchell, Aramac.
Reid, Walker and Co., Rockhampton.
Reid and Palmer, Mitchell River, Cook, Palmerville.
Reppel, F., Hillside, Maranoa, Mitchell.
Reynolds, T., Feather Bed, Cook, Kingsborough.
Rezold, M., and Co., Middle Creek, Darling Downs.
Rice and Turner, Mount Spencer, Leichardt, Nebo.
Richards, R., Cawildi, Maranoa, Balonne.
Richards, W. H., and Co., Springsure, Leichardt, Springsure.
Richardson and Campbell, Wigugomrie, Gregory South, Thorgomindah.
Richardson, Nutting, Charters and Campbell, Muncoonia, Gregory South, Thorgomindah.
Richardson, T. G., and Co., Toowoomba.
Richardson, W., Tugurnum, North Kennedy, Specimen.
Richardson, W. W., Morinish, Gregory South, Thorgomindah.
Richardson, W. W., Congie, Gregory South, Thorgomindah.
Richardson, W. W., Nundramundoo, Gregory South, Mount Margaret.
Ridler, R. B., Yarrol, Burnett, Mount Perry.
Ridler, R. B. and J. C., Cania, Burnett, Mount Perry.
Rivers, C., Bloomfield, Blackall.
Roach, T. W., Dalby.
Robertson Brothers, Taunton, Port Curtis, Gladstone.
Robertson and Edkins, Roxborough, Gregory North, Cork.
Robertson and Hopkins, Moselle Downs, Burke, Dalrymple.
Robertson, J., and Co., Yandilla, Darling Downs, Yandilla.
Robertson, J. H., Nelson No. 1, North Kennedy, Charters Towers.
Robertson, John, Teeswater, Maranoa, Mitchell.
Robertson, R. R. C., Baliandean, Darling Downs, Stanthorpe.
Robertson, R. and T., Baffle Creek, Port Curtis, Bundaberg.
Robertson, Thomas, Bingera, Wide Bay, Bundaberg.
Robertson, W., Bunalbo, Warwick.
Roberts and Taylor, Brewarrina, North Kennedy, Caperville.
Robinson, H. F., Mount John, Townsville.
Roche, F. H., Rochdale, Gregory North, Georgetown.
Roche, F. W., Runnymede, Maranoa, Dalby.
Roche, F. F., Fermoy, Mitchell, Muttaburra.
Rocke Brothers and McDonald, Fermoy, Blackall.
Rodgers, A., Willarie, Maranoa, Roma.
Rodgers, James, Belle, Warrego, Burenda.
Roff, G., and Co., Brisbane.
Rolfe, J., Apple Forest, South Kennedy, Clermont.
Rolfe, J., Bowlee, No. 1, South Kennedy, Clermont.
Rolfe, J., Pioneer, South Kennedy, Clermont.
Rolfe, J. R., Castle Vale, Leichardt, Springsure.
Rolleston, C., Albinia Downs, Leichardt, Springsure.
Rome Brothers, Terrick Terrick, Mitchell, Tambo.
Rome, C., Terrick, Mitchell, Blackall.
Rome, T., and Co., Welford Downs, Mitchell, Isis Downs.
Rook, E. H., Box Forest, Darling Downs, Dalby.
Ross, D., Roslin, Maranoa, Surat.
Ross, Jessie, Oberina, Maranoa, Roma.
Ross, Thomas, Kilkeven, Burnett, Gympie.
Rotheray, E. W., Nardoo, Leichardt, Springsure.
Rourke, Henry, Watershed, Kennedy.
Rourke, Henry, Rockwood, Mitchell, Bowen Downs.
Rourke, J. H., Dotswood, Kennedy North.
Rouse, George, Culloden, Aramac.
Rowan, D. and Co., Durra River Downs, Mitchell, Aramac.
Royds, C. and E., Jundah, Leichardt, Condamine.
Royds, E., Isis Lagoons, Blackall.
Ruff, Robertson and Co., Mount Stanley, Ipswich.
Rudgers, S., Willaineri, St. George.
Rule, John, Arcturus Downs, Springsure.

Rushbrook, F., Weranga, Darling Downs, Dalby.
Russell, Thomas, Wonolah, Mitchell, Tambo.
Rutherford and Robertson, Cunnamulla, Warrego, Cunnamulla.
Ruthorpe, R., Mexico, Mitchell, Blackall.
Rutledge and Palmer, Eureka, Wide Bay, Maryborough.
Ryrie, J. C., Vergemont, Mitchell, Isis Downs.
Sadlier and Brooke, Werle Ela, Warrego, Ewlo.
Sadlier and Brooke, Bingara, Warrego, Cunnamulla.
Sadlier and Brooke, Bundilla, Warrego, Eulo.
Salisbury, R. J., Spattiswood, Taroom.
Sandeman, Gordon, Authoringa, Charleville.
Sandeman, Hon. G., Nurenda, Mitchell.
Sandeman, S., Durenda, Charleville.
Sandiman, M., Banksea, Rockhampton.
Saunder, D., Cattle Creek, Dalby.
Sawtell Bros., Byrimine, Burke, Cloncurry.
Sayse, J. N., Tieryboo, Darling Downs, Condamine.
Scanton, J., Springfield, Gregory South, Thorgomindah.
Scarr, Frank, Lake Nash, Burke, Roxborough Downs.
Schofield, Caroline, Perwell, Maranoa, St. George.
Schofield, R., Bendee, Maranoa, Surat.
Schollick, E. J., Ondooroo, Gregory North, Aramac.
Scottish Australian Invest. Company (Limited), Avoca, South Kennedy, Springsure.
Scottish Australian Invest. Company (Limited), Bowen Downs, Mitchell, Bowen Downs.
Scottish Australian Invest. Company (Limited), Western Creek, Darling Downs, Dalby.
Scottish Australian Invest. Company (Limited), Texas, Darling Downs, Inglewood.
Scottish Australian Invest. Company (Limited), Nive Downs, Warrego, Ellangowan.
Scottish Australian Invest. Company (Limited), Mount Abundance, Maranoa, Roma.
Scottish Australian Invest. Company (Limited), Mount Cornish, Mitchell, Aramac.
Scottish Australian Invest. Company (Limited), Dyke Head, Burnett, Gayndah.
Scott, Andrew, Euroombah, Leichardt, Taroom.
Scott, A., Goongarry, Leichardt, Taroom.
Scott Bros., Valley of Lagoons, Kennedy, Valley of Lagoons.
Scott Bros., Vale of Herbert, Cardwell.
Scott, G. A. and W. J., Vale of Herbert, North Kennedy, Cardwell.
Scott and Gibson, Cloncurry, Burke, Cloncurry.
Scott and Gordon, Vindex, Gregory North, Aramac.
Scott, Gordon, and Crawford, Maxwelton, Burke, Hughenden.
Scott, James Hall, Iverdon, Kennedy, Bowen.
Scott, Walter, Taromeo, Moreton, Ipswich.
Scott, William, Glenmoral, Leichardt, Banana.
Scraggs, W., Marra Marra, Darling Downs, Condamine.
Scrivener, G. H., Caiwarra, Cunnamulla.
Sevenson, J., Ravensbourne, Blackall.
Shanahan and Jennings, Westbrook, Darling Downs, Drayton.
Shand and Buchanan, Wombah, Burnett, Mount Perry.
Shannon, John, Salt Bush Park, Leichardt, St. Lawrence.
Sharpe and Atwell, Holme Park, Darling Downs, Leyburn.
Sharplee, Sharplee, and McKay, Thurraggai, Maranoa, St. George.
Shaw and Co., Rawbelle, Burnett and Wide Bay, Gayndah.
Sherwin, J. P., Canoona. Port Curtis, Yaamba.
Shindan, R., Oaklands, Leyden.
Sidley, K. A., St. Paul's, North Kennedy, Ravenswood.
Sidley, K. A., Charters Towers, Charters Towers.
Siebenhausen, Charles, Glen Farm, Darling Downs, Clifton.
Simpson and Campbell, Bellevue, Moreton, Ipswich.
Simpson, G. M., Bon Accord, Darling Downs, Dalby.
Sinclair, Guthrie, Knockbreak, Burnett, Gayndah.
Singleton and Menzies, Langton, Peak Downs, Clermont.

Singleton and Menzies, Langton Downs, Clermont.
Skehan, D., Newcastle, Gregory South, Thorgomindah.
Skuthorpe, J. R., Locharoch, Gregory North, Cork.
Sloane and Jeffrey, Taldora, Burke, Cloncurry.
Sloane, William, Kurrangera, Burke, Cloncurry.
Sly and Moreton, Mungy, Burnett, Gayndah.
Sly, W., Degilbo, Burnett, Maryborough.
Small, A., Glenmore, South Kennedy, Clermont.
Smith, Barnes, and Smith, Lyndhurst, Cook, Dalrymple.
Smith, G., and Bros., Stewart's Creek, Maranoa, Roma.
Smith, H. S., Afton Downs, Burke, Dalrymple.
Smith, J. and S. C., Mungulla, Maranoa, Mitchell.
Smith, Mrs. Isabella, Texas, Darling Downs, Texas.
Smith and Thomas, Kirrelah, Warwick.
Smith, W. S., Randoin Downs, Maranoa, Mitchell.
Smith, W. S., Bomballera, Maranoa, Cunnamulla.
Soloman, Maurice, Gum Valley, Leichardt, Springsure.
South, B., Bindebango, Maranoa, St. George.
South, W., Yunermun, Maranoa, St. George.
South, W., Theodore, Maranoa, Mangullala Creek.
Spencer, M. A., Arwadilla, Maranoa, Mitchell.
Springer, W., Charles Creek, Mitchell, Aramac.
Stratham, R., Bonus Downs, Maranoa, Mitchell Downs.
Staunton, W. C., Coolbah, Condamine.
Steele, James, Glenroy, Rockhampton.
Stent, W. F., Bundoona, Warrego, Eulo.
Stevens, Thomas, Crow's Nest, Darling Downs, Murphy.
Stevens, E. J., Tintinchilla, Warrego, Tambo.
Stevens, H., and Co., Toowoomba.
Stevenson. J., Ravensbourne, Mitchell, Tambo.
Stephenson, J., Forest Hills, Mitchell, Tambo.
Stevenson. Reid and Palmer, Gamboola, Cook, Palmerville.
Stephenson, W. L., Mona, Maranoa, St. George.
Stewart, S., Eddystone Vale, Maranoa, Mitchell.
Stewart, Robert, Marathon. Burke, Richmond.
Stewart, Robert, Southweek, Townsville.
Stewart, R., Telemon, Burke, Dalrymple.
Stewart, R., Southwick, North Kennedy, Dalrymple.
Stirrat Bros., Alma, Port Curtis, Gladstone.
Storck, P. J., Comet Downs, Leichardt, Springsure.
Stouber, Stephen, Hanover Square, Rockhampton.
Strathdee, R. D., Coranga, Kennedy, Dalby.
Stratford, F. A., Talgai, Darling Downs, Clifton.
Strurer, F., Pine Creek. Darling Downs, Leyburn.
Stuart, C. J., Coogoon, Maranoa, Roma.
Stuart and Co., Killoogie, Kennedy.
Stuart, Mackay and Mackay, Templeton Downs, Gregory North, Glenormiston.
Stubley, F. H., Eve Lynn, North Kennedy, Wittown.
Stubley, F. H., Charters Towers, Charters Towers.
Suell, J. C., Edwinstone, Darling Downs, Cambooya.
Suler, Clans, Ravenswood, Kennedy, Ravenswood.
Sutherland, George, Jinghi Inghi, Darling Downs, Dalby.
Swanson, J., Yabba, Gympie.
Swayne, H. W., Llandilo, Leichardt, Copperfield.
Symes, Joseph, Fairmount, Darling Downs, Dalby.
Tait, George, The Glens, Maranoa, St. George.
Tait, George, Murra Murra, Maranoa, St. George's Bridge.
Talbot, P., Byfield, St. Lawrence.
Taylor, Alfred, Millay, North Kennedy, Capeville.
Taylor, George, Merino Downs, Roma.
Taylor and Peak, Coomrith, Dalby.
Taylor, James, Dunmore, Darling Downs, Dalby.
Taylor, James, Goodar, Darling Downs, Yandilla.
Taylor, J. J. W. and G., Louisa Downs, Mitchell, Blackall.
Taylor, J. J. W. and G., Mount Marlon, Mitchell, Tambo.
Terry, A. J. W., Eton Vale, Kennedy, Bowen.
Thomson, James, Calliope, Rockhampton.
Thomson, J. H., The Auburn, Burnett, Gayndah.

Thompson. J., Rupert's Creek, Burke, Normanton.
Thompson, J., Mount Emu Plains, Burke, Dalrymple.
Thorne and Frazer, Apex Downs, Mitchell, Aramac.
Thorn, Charles, Rosebrook, Moreton, Ipswich.
Thorn, executors of late G., Warra Warra, Darling Downs, Dalby.
Thorn, executors of late G., Normanby, Moreton, Ipswich.
Thorn, George, Warra Warra, Darling Downs, Dalby.
Thorn, J. and George, Cowley Plains, Warrego, Bechel.
Thorn and Co., Nuckinenda, Moreton, Ipswich.
Thorne, J. W., Currajong, Leichardt, Lilyvale.
Tidswell, H. E., Wigton, Burnett, Gayndah.
Tilley Bros., Milton, Dalby.
Tilley and Thomas, Chiverton, Darling Downs, Warrick.
Tobin, A., Marion Downs, Gregory North, Diamantina.
Tom, H., Mount Moffat, Maranoa. Mitchell.
Tom, H., Chesterton, Warrego, Mitchell.
Tooker, M. and H., Leura, Rockhampton.
Tooth, executors of W. B., Clifton, Darling Downs, Clifton.
Tooth and Holt, Brucedale, Maranoa, Surat.
Tooth, W. B., Tallavera, Surat.
Tourle, Morse and Co., Banksie, Burnett, Cawarral.
Towns and Bonton, Burrandowan, Burnett, Gayndah.
Towns and Stewart, Calliangal, Port Curtis, Westwood.
Townshend, John A., Inkerman, Kennedy, Bowen.
Tozer and Craigie, Richmond, Mitchell, Blackall.
Tozer, W. P., Delta, Mitchell, Blackall.
Tozer, W. P., Tooleybuck, Mitchell, Aramac.
Travers and Blundell, Pastorale, Leichardt, Lilyvale.
Travers and Gibson, Aramac, Mitchell, Aramac.
Travers, R., Malvern Downs, Leichardt, Emerald Downs.
Travers, S. S., and Blundell, H. J. D., Gordon Downs, Leichardt, Lilyvale.
Travis, R., Knockbreak, Burnett, Gayndah.
Travis and Blundell, Gorden Downs, Clermont.
Treweeke, W. J., Tingun and Minimie, Goondiwindi.
Trimble and Anderson, Yambora, Burke, Normanton.
Tucker, H. C., Blenheim, South Kennedy, Bowen.
Tucker, W., Exmoor, South Kennedy, Bowen.
Tully, P., Ray, Gregory South, Thorgomindah.
Turf, A. J. M., Eton Vale, South Kennedy, Bowen.
Turnbull, G. E., Medway, Leichardt, Springsure.
Turner, Francis, Avoca, Kennedy, Springsure.
Turner, J. A., Coomrith, Darling Downs, Dalby.
Turner and Missing, Milton, Port Curtis, Gladstone.
Turner, trustees of late W., Helidon, Moreton, Helidon.
Tyler, E., Thyra, Mitchell, Specimen Gully.
Tyrrell, E., executors of, Burga Burga, St. George.
Tyson, James, Widgeegoora, Warrego, Cunnamulla.
Tyson, James, Felton and Beauraba, Darling Downs, Cambooya.
Tyson, James, Newlands, Mitchell, Jundah.
Tyson, James, Carnavon, Warrego, Springsure.
Tyson, James, Carella Downs, Mitchell, Isis Downs.
Tyson, William, jun., Paroo West, Warrego, Eulo.
Tyson, William, Mrs., Mount Alford, Warrego, Cunnamullah.
Urquhart, Urquhart and Fraser, Kalidawarray, Gregory North. Congylake.
Union Bank, Fort Cooper North, Nebo. Nebo.
Union Bank, McKinlay Downs, Isisford.
Vanderheidt, Peter, Mount Walker, Moreton, Ipswich.
Vanneck, Walter, Burdekin Downs, North Kennedy, Dalrymple.
Vanneck, Hon. W., Lake Clarendon, Gatton.
Verner, E. W., Womblebank, Maranoa, Forest Vale.
Vernon, Robert, Warra, Coranga Creek.
Vickery, E., Daaudine, Darling Downs, Dalby.

Vickery, E., Kooroon, Maranoa, Dalby.
Vignolles, F. D., Western Creek, Darling Downs, Toowoomba.
Voss, W. W., Glendower, Burke, Dalrymple.
Wade—Browne, C., Bolingbroke, Leichardt, Mackay.
Wafer, M., Charleyvue, Leichardt, Duaringa.
Wafer and Cook, Tanders, Leichardt, Duaringa.
Waite Bros., Crystal Brook, Kennedy, Bowen.
Wales, Charles, Nanango, via Brisbane.
Walker, A. C., Lower Bungera, Burnett, Bundaberg.
Walker, John, Lynd Water, Kennedy, Cardwell.
Walker, P., Dalby.
Walker, S., Cowan Downs, Burke, Dalrymple.
Walker, S. D., Sorghum Downs, Burke, Normanton.
Walker, S. D., Leonard Downs, Burke, Normanton.
Walker, Thomas, Tenterfield, Darling Downs, Tenterfield.
Walker, Thomas, Burenda, Warrego, Burenda.
Walker, Thomas, Glenlyon, Darling Downs, Leyburn.
Walker, W. T., Townsvale, Moreton, Logan.
Wallace, J. T. J., Killarney, Leichardt, St. Lawrence.
Wallace, James, Irvingvale, Dalby.
Waller, W. N., Cheshunt, Warrego, Thorgomindah.
Waller, W. N., Norley, Warrego, Thorgomindah.
Walsh, Brown and Walsh, Granada, Burke, Normanton.
Walsh, John, Cootah Downs, Burke, Normanton.
Walsh and Mullet, Monduran, Wide Bay, Maryborough.
Walton, W. F., Harcourt, Leichardt, Banana.
Walter, T., Portland Downs, Isis Downs.
Want, W., Moroco, Maranoa, Surat.
Ware and Scott, Morney Plains, Gregory South, Jundah.
Ware, George, Juarungea, Warrego, Thorgomindah.
Warner and Holland, Woodlands, Maranoa, Mitchell Downs.
Watson, S. G., Gregory Downs, Burke, Normantown.
Watson, S. G., Punjaub, Burke, Normanton.
Watson, S. G., Upper Gregory Downs, Burke, Normanton.
Watt and Gilchrist, May Downs, Leichardt, Broadsound.
Watt and Gilchrist, Noorama, Warrego, Cunnamulla.
Watt and Gilchrist, Glenprairie, Port Curtis, Marlborough.
Watt and Gilchrist, Stanton Harcourt, Wide Bay, Marlborough.
Watt and Cunningham, Rannes, Rockhampton.
Watt, J. B., Yerilla, Burnett, Gayndah.
Watt, J. B., Proston, Burnett, Gayndah.
Watt, J. B., Leichardt Downs, Leichardt, St. Lawrence.
Webber and Peppin, Bingie Bingie, Warrego, Thorgomindah.
Webber and Peppin, Korangoola, Gregory South, Thorgomindah.
Webber, T. and J., Dulwerton, Gregory South, Thorgomindah.
White, William, Maryborough, Burnett, Maryborough.
White, W. D. A. and E., Beaudesert, Burke, Dalrymple.
White, W. D., and Sons, Bluff Downs, North Kennedy, Dalrymple.
White, W. D., and Sons, Nindooimbah, Beenleigh.
White, W. D., and Sons, Bluff Downs, Townsville.
White, — Tallegulla, North Kennedy, Dalrymple.
Whitman, W., Hampton Court, Gregory North, Cook.
Whitman, W., Tarran, Warrego, Tambo.
Whitman, W. and J., Teddington Lock, Gregory North, Bulln, via Cork and Wittown.
Whittingham Bros. and Davidson, Alice Downs, Mitchell, Blackall.
Wienholt Bros., Fassifern, Moreton, Fassifern.
Wienholt Bros., Maryvale, Darling Downs, Warwick.
Wienholt Bros., Blythdale, Maranoa, Condamine.
Wienholt, E., Dalgangal, Burnett, Gayndah.
Wienholt, E., Saltern Creek, Mitchell, Blackall.
Wienholt, E., Goomburra, Hendron.
Willdash, F. J. C., Stradbroke Island, Moreton, Southport.
Wilkinson, J. H., Baroon Park, St. Lawrence.
Williams Bros. and Commercial Bank, Cuongoola, Warrego, Cunnamulla.
Williams, Charles, Dalganal, Burnett, Gayndah.
Williams and Conn, Boondoon, Warrego, Bechel.
Williams, D. L., Glenlee, Springsure.
Williams, D. L., Silsoe, Mitchell, Westland.
Williams, H., Culburra, Cook, Thornborough.
Williams, James, Bendena, Maranoa, St. George.
Williams, J. F., Ambatala, Warrego, Charleville.
Williams, Williams and Dreyer, Bierbank, Warrego, Cunnamulla.
Willamson and Thornton, Tower Hill, Mitchell, Aramac.
Wills, C. S., Cullin, Leichardt, Springsure.
Wilson, D., Raglan, Port Curtis, Rockhampton.
Wilson, H. and N., Currawinga, Warrego, Eulo.
Wilson, H. and N., Salmonville, Gregory South, Thorgomindah.
Wilson, Hon. W., Pilton, Clifton.
Wilson, L., Bluff, Warrego, Wilcannia.
Wilson, James, Ullathorne, Darling Downs, Warwick.
Wilson, John, The Glen, Darling Downs, Warwick.
Wilson, J. G. H., Orion Downs, Leichardt, Springsure.
Wilson, Mrs., Nanango, Burnett, Nanango.
Wilson, N. H., Currawinga, Thorgomindah.
Wilson, R. S., Dunbern, Darling Downs, Warwick.
Wilson, Samuel, Diamantina, Gregory North, Cork.
Wilson, Samuel, Elderslie, Gregory North, Cork.
Wilson, Sir Samuel, Logan Downs, South Kennedy, Clermont.
Wilson, Wm., Palton and Haldon, Warwick.
Winton, James A., Bogarella, Warrego, Forest Vale.
Withycombe, James, Woolamut, Warrego, Mungindi.
Witham, J. D., Fairfield, Leichardt, Springsure.
Wolseley and Parker, Melton, Maranoa, St. George.
Woodburn and Dean, Spring Creek, Charters Towers.
Woods, William, Ashton Grove, Darling Downs, Dalby.
Wood, E. G., Rockhampton.
Wormwell, Pinkney, Eagle Farm, Rockhampton.
Worthington, J., Turkey, Gladstone.
Wright, A. A. and F. W., Avon Downs, South Kennedy, Clermont.
Wright, A. A. and F. W., Nulalbin, Leichardt, Duaringa.
Wright, Haydon and Wright, Rio, Leichardt, Boolburra.
Wright, Haydon and Wright, Vena Park, Bourke, Normanton.
Wyndham, F. and A., Winton, Darling Downs, Goondiwindi.
Yonge, A. K. D., Tarawinaba, Darling Downs, Dalby.
York, A. C., Broadmin, Dalby.
Young, W., Mount Larcom, Port Curtis, Gladstone.

WESTERN AUSTRALIA.

Abbey, D., Newtown.
Abbey, J., Busselton.
Abbey, N., Quindalup.
Abbey, T., Newtown.
Adams, C., Newcastle and Toodyay District.
Adams, H., Greenough, Victoria District.
Adlam, James, jun., Greenough, Victoria District.
Ager, J., Javis, Upper Blackwood.
A'Hern, — Greenough, Victoria District.
Alcock, J., York.
Aldridge, I., Irwin and Dongarra.
Ali, James, Bunbury, Wellington District.
Allender, F., Greenough, Victoria District.
Allington, G., Northam.
Allnutt, John, Blackwood.
Anderson, D., Swan.
Anderson and Grant, Merlyie, De Grey.
Anderson, J., De Grey River, North West Coast.
Anderson, J. W., De Grey River, North West Coast.
Anderson, Thomas, Greenough, Victoria District.
Anderson, W., Swan.
Andrews, W., Narring Lakes, King George's Sound.
Annice, J., Nowancrup.
Annice, J. and J., Albany.
Anstey, G. and T., Toodyay District.
Arber, J., Albany.
Armstrong, A., Albany.
Armstrong, Charles, Serpentine.
Arthur, F., York.
Ashworth, E., York.
Ashworth, R., York.
Atkinson, J., Victoria Plains.
Atkinson, Thomas, Northam.
Austin, W., York.
Ayscough, J., Greenough.
Bagshawe, J., Beverley.
Bailey, A. T., Beverley.
Bailey, Job, York.
Bailey, Joseph, Williams River.
Baldwin, B., Serpentine.
Baldwin, J., Serpentine.
Barndon, J., Northam.
Barron, Edward, Williams River.
Barron, J., Arthur River.
Bartlett, E., Williams River.
Bartram, H., Beverley.
Bartram, J., Beverley.
Bashford, W., Dandurga.
Bates, Thomas, Victoria Plains.
Batt, A., Hotham River.
Batt, D., Canning.
Batt, W., Murray.
Bayles, J., Gingin.
Beacham, J. J., Pinjarrah.
Beard, M. and Co., Northam.
Beard, W., Toodyay.
Beardman, W., Toodyay.
Beere, E. B., Williams River.
Beere, E., Newcastle.
Beere, F. W., Newcastle.
Beeson, J., Greenough, Victoria District.
Bell, J., Rockingham, Fremantle.
Bell, J. and W., Greenough, Victoria Distr
Bell, R., Williams River.
Best, G., Toodyay.
Betts, R., Guildford.
Bibra, F. L. Von, Perth.
Bingham, W., Williams River.
Bingham, W. H., Williams River.
Birch, A., Pingarrah.
Bird, T., York.
Bishop, G., Victoria Plains.
Bishop, John, Mininup.
Bishop, Thomas, Greenough.
Blake, W., Northam.
Blechynden, John, Bridgetown.
Blechynden, Edwin, Beverley.

Blechynden, Hy., Beverley.
Blechynden, Mrs., Beverley.
Blechynden, W., Blackwood.
Blizzard, H., York.
Blythe, Joseph, Lower Blackwood.
Boddington, H., Arthur River.
Boirlee, F. P., C.M.G., Governor of Honduras, Warren.
Bone, J., Greenough.
Bone, Wm., Greenough, Victoria District.
Bourk, J., Toodyay.
Bourke, M., Toodyay.
Bourke, R., Canning.
Bourke, Thomas, York.
Bowen, M., Toodyay.
Bowram, J., Beverley.
Boxhall, W., Victoria Plains.
Boxham, W., Guildford.
Boyle, G., Black Pool, York.
Brady, J., Greenough.
Brand, A., Greenough.
Braud, D., Dongarra and Irwin.
Brandon, R. W., Greenough, Victoria District.
Brennan, J., Busselton.
Brennan, Thomas, Newtown.
Bresnahan, D., Northam.
Brett, J., Newcastle.
Bridges, Geo., Busselton.
Bridgeman, J., Greenough.
Broad, R., Victoria Plains.
Brockman, Charles, Irwin and Dongarra.
Brockman, E., Guildford.
Brockman, E. R., Henley Park and Seabrook, Northam.
Brockman, F., Vasse.
Brockman, H., Cheriton, Gingin.
Brockman, J., Vasse.
Brockman, T., Irwin and Dongarra.
Brockman, W., Moond and Lyndhurst, Gin Gin.
Brockman and Fane, Gascoigne River.
Brooks, J., York.
Brooks, Joseph, Northampton.
Broom, W., Greenough.
Brown, C. F., Beverley.
Brown, Charles, Dongarra and Irwin.
Brown, C. F., Arthur River.
Brown, G. F., Beverley.
Brown, John, Wandering.
Brown, J. W., Avondale, Beverley.
Brown, M., Hotham River.
Brown, Maitland, J.P., Newmerker, Champion Bay.
Brown, Thomas, Wandering Brook.
Brown, Wm., Arthur River.
Brown, W. and G., Arthur River.
Browning, J., Greenough, Victoria District.
Browning, J., jun., Greenough, Victoria District.
Bryan, Samuel, Ludlow.
Buckingham, A., Canning.
Buckingham, Thomas, Canning.
Buckley, D., Greenough, Victoria District.
Buckley, J., Greenough, Victoria District.
Buckley, T., Newcastle.
Bull, J., Beverley.
Bull, W., Newcastle.
Bunbury, M., Warren.
Bunbury, Mrs., Busselton.
Burgess and Co., Andover.
Burgess, L. C., Oakabella, Champion Bay.
Burgess, M. R., Busselton.
Burgess, R., Tipperary, York.
Burgess, Samuel, Dongarra and Irwin.
Burgess, S. E., sen., J.P., Tipperary, York.
Burgess, T., J.P., The Birves, Northampton.
Burnett, J. and G., Dandarragan.
Burnett, W., Dandarragan.
Burnes, T., Northam.
Busher, Frank, Dardanap.
Busher, James, sen., Dardanap.
Busher, J., jun., Dardanap.

Busher, Richard, Dardanap.
Busher, Thomas, Dardanap.
Bussell, A. P., J.P., Vasse.
Butter, T., Fremantle.
Butter, T., Greenough.
Butter, W., Victoria Plains.
Butterley, J., Boogine, Newcastle.
Byrne, E., Gingin.
Byrne, T., Greenough.
Cage, John, Newcastle.
Cahill, E. and J., York.
Cain, T., Newcastle.
Calder, L., Blackwood.
Campbell, O., Dandarragan.
Campbell, D., Victoria Plains.
Campbell, J., Dandarragan.
Campbell, W., Dandarragan.
Cant, William, Greenough, Victoria District.
Carmody, P., sen., York.
Carmody, Thomas, York.
Carr, R., York.
Carr, W., Geraldton.
Carroll, James, Brunswick.
Carroll, M., Irwin and Dougarra.
Carrats, J., Kojonup.
Casey, N., York.
Castle, Thomas, Preston.
Chance, C., Beverley.
Chapman, Thomas, junr., Preston.
Chapman, Thomas, sen., Preston.
Chester, G., Albany.
Chevill, J., Guildford.
Chidlow, W., Northam.
Chifney, W., jun., York.
Chifney, W., York.
Chippen, Thomas, Balgarrup, King George's Sound.
Chipper, T., Koyjunup.
Chitty, C., Toodyay.
Chitty, H., Toodyay.
Chitty, J., Toodyay.
Chitty, Thomas, Toodyay.
Chitty, W., Toodyay.
Christian, J., Gingin.
Christmas, C., Northam.
Christmas, G., Northam.
Christmas, H., York.
Claridge, D., Victoria Plains.
Clark, A. S., Beverley.
Clark, R., Beverley.
Clark, T., Northampton, Victoria District.
Clarke, A., Blackwood, Wellington.
Clarke, Arthur, Busselton.
Clarke, G., Dandarragan.
Clarke, James, Brunswick.
Clarke, J., Harvey.
Clarke, W., Australind.
Clarkson, B. D., Mount Anderson, Toodyay.
Clarkson, E. W., Dongarra.
Clarkson Bros., Karratha, Roebourne and Cossack.
Clarkson, J. S., Toodyay.
Clarkson, R., Robe River.
Clayton, R., Beverley.
Cleary, James, Dardanup.
Clifton, Gervaise, Bunbury.
Clifton, J. E. M., Australind.
Clifton, M. W., Brunswick.
Clifton, R. W., Australind.
Clinch, C., West End, Dandarragan.
Clinch, James, Berkshire Valley, Dandarragan.
Clune Bros., Canterbury, Dandarragan.
Cockburn, Campbell, Sir T., Mount Barker.
Cockram, E., Canning.
Cockram, J. and E., Gingin.
Cockram, R., Gingin.
Coffey, John, York.
Cookworthy, J., Busselton.
Coles, G., York.
Collins, J., York.
Connell, D., Busselton.
Connell, Thomas, Mininup.
Connell, W., York.
Connell, W., Northam.
Connolly, Charles, Greenough, Victoria District.
Connolly, James, Greenough, Victoria District.
Connolly, Joseph, Greenough, Victoria District.
Connolly, Mrs., Greenough, Victoria District.
Connolly, R., Greenough, Victoria District.
Connor, M., Toodyay.
Connor, T., Fremantle.
Connors, M., Newcastle.
Conway, M., Beverley.
Cook, Charles, Dandarragan.
Cook, F., Newcastle.
Cook, F. H., Newcastle.
Cook, Hy., Toodyay.
Cook, H. J., Neulyine, Northam.
Cook, John, Greenough, Victoria District.
Cook, J., Dandarragan.
Cook, T., Newcastle.
Cook, W., Dandarragan.
Cooke, H. J., Northam.
Cooke, N. W., Irwin and Dongarra.
Coonan, M., Dardanup.
Coonan, P., Dardanup.
Coonan, Thomas, Dardanup.
Cooper, J. York.
Cooper, J., station manager, Murchison.
Cooper, J. and F., Murray.
Cooper, W. C., Mount Barker, King George's Sound.
Corbet, M., Irwin and Dongarra.
Corbett, James, Albany Road.
Cosgrove, J., Northam.
Cotton, James, Brunswick.
Cousins, G., Dongarra.
Cousins, J., Newcastle.
Cousins, T., Toodyay.
Cousins, W., Dongarra.
Coverly, W., Blackwood.
Cowan and Higham, Duck Creek, Ashburton.
Cowcher Bros., Hotham River.
Cowcher, H., Murray.
Cowcher, J., Murray.
Cowcher, J., sen., Hotham River.
Cox, Eliza, Newcastle.
Coyne, J. and F., Northam.
Craddock, A., Beaufort River.
Craig, J. M., sheep inspector, York.
Crampton, A., Brunswick.
Crampton, G., Brunswick.
Crampton, J., Brunswick.
Crampton, Thomas, Brunswick.
Crane, J., Hotham River.
Craney, J., Irwin and Dongarra.
Cranny, J., Murchison.
Crawford, F., Irwin and Dongarra.
Crawford, J., York.
Criddle, Henry, Greenough.
Criddle, J., Irwin and Dongarra.
Criddle, W., Dongarra.
Crisp, Eli, Newcastle.
Crisp, J., Toodyay.
Cronin, E., Canning.
Cronin, J., Dumbling Lakes, King George's Sound.
Cronin, M., Glen Cove, King George's Sound.
Cronin, M., Beaufort River.
Crouch, J., Northam.
Cuff, M., Dongarra.
Cullerton, W., Greenough.
Cunningham, James, Greenough.
Cunningham, Tim, Northampton.
Curle, M., Northam.
Curtis, Wm., Busselton.
Cusack, A., station overseer, Jones Creek.
Cusack, C., Maitland River.
Davies, T., York.
Davies, W., York.
Davis, A., York.
Davis, G., York.
Davis, J., Newcastle.
Davis, J. M., Geraldton.
Davis, J. P., Tibradden, Champion Bay.
Davis, J. R., Fremantle.
Dawson, A., Dongarra.
Dawson, E., Busselton.
Dawson, E., jun., Busselton.
Dawson, G., Busselton.
Dawson, John, Busselton.
Day, W., Rockingham, Fremantle.
Dearing, J. Dongarra.
De Burgh, H. A., Cirwalla, Moore River.
De Burgh, R., Swan.
Deer, Charles, Busselton.
Deer, W., Swan.
Delaney, Hugh, Busselton.
Delaney, J., Newcastle.
Delaney, J., Newcastle.
Delaporte, Thomas, Mininup.

WESTERN AUSTRALIA.

Delmage, J., Northam.
Dempster, A., Esperance Bay, South Coast.
Dempster Bros., Esperance Bay, South Coast.
Dempster, C. E., Esperance Bay, South Coast.
Dempster, J. P., Esperance Bay, South Coast.
Dempster, W. S., Buckland, Northam.
Denham, W., York.
Dennis, Leslie, Newcastle.
Desmond, Denis, Greenough.
Desmond, James, Greenough.
Desmond, John, Greenough.
Desmond, William, Greenough.
Devereux, J., Helena, Guildford.
Devlin, Thomas, Greenough.
Devonshire, W., Dongarra.
Dewar, Alexander, Greenough.
Dewar, J., Gingin.
Dewar, R., Gingin.
Dexter, R., York.
Dickson, W., Swan.
Dinsdale, A., York.
Dix, John, Victoria Plains.
Dixon, H., Fremantle.
Dixon, Thomas, Busselton.
Dodd, J., Albany Road.
Dodd, M., Dandarragan.
Donaher, James, Greenough, Victoria District.
Doncon, E., Beverley.
Doncon, R., York.
Doncon, Reuben, York.
Donelly, P., Newcastle.
Donovan, J., York.
Donovan. J., Busselton.
Doolan, E., Gingin.
Doolan, J., Australind.
Doolan, P., Greenough, Victoria District.
Dorgan, M., Greenough, Victoria District.
Doust, J., station manager, Murchison.
Downs, E., Dongarra.
Downes, Thomas, Dongarra.
Doyle, Jerry, Mininup.
Doyle, W., Greenough.
Drage, Thomas, Northampton.
Draper, J., York.
Draper, J., jun., York.
Drummond, J., White Peak, Geraldton.
Dudley, E., Northam.
Dunn Bros., Albany.
Dunn, J., Albany.
Dunn, P., Australind.
Dunn, W., Albany.
Dyson, George, Albany Road.
Eacott, J., Murray.
Eacott, T., Murray.
Eacott, T., jun., Murray.
Eacott, W., Murray.
Eadle, D., Brunswick.
Eakins, John, Victoria.
Easton, W., Fremantle.
Eaton, R., Northam.
Eaton. W., Northam.
Eccleston, W., Preston.
Eddie, John, 125 Mile Station, Albany Road.
Edwards, C. F., Beverley.
Edwards, E. G., Victoria Plains.
Edwards, G., Swan.
Edwards, J., Swan.
Edwards, J., York.
Edwards, J., Newcastle.
Edwards, M., Gingin.
Edwards, R. E., Gingin.
Edwards, S., Swan.
Eliot, P., Minnenooka, Champion Bay.
Eliot, R. J., Brunswick.
Elliott, T., Gingin.
Ellis, G. L., Fremantle.
Ellis, Wm., Busselton.
Elverd, J., Kojonup.
Enright, A., York.
Enright, E., Northam.
Enright, P., Northam.
Enright, T., Northam.
Evans, D., York.
Everett, G., Newcastle.
Everett, J., Newcastle.
Eves, Hy., Victoria Plains.
Ewart, Wm., Newcastle.
Fahey, W., Kojonup.
Fairbairn, J., Albany.
Fallon, J. B., Beaufort River.

Fane, C. O., Dongarra.
Fane, W., Dongarra.
Farmer, S., Northampton.
Farmer, T., Murray.
Farmer, T., Hotham River.
Fauntleroy, C. C., Guildford.
Fawcett, Theo., J. P., Murray.
Fawcett, T., Pinjarrah Park, Pinjarrah.
Fawell, W., Swan.
Fee, Forbes, Dardanup.
Fennell, W., Blackwood Road.
Fenner, Geo., Busselton.
Fergusson, A., Newcastle.
Fergusson, C. W., Swan.
Fergusson, J., Newcastle.
Fergusson, T., Newcastle.
Fields, D., York.
Fields, J., York.
Fields, J., York.
Fields, P., York.
Finnerty, A., station manager, Northampton.
Finnerty, J. M., Northampton.
Fisher, James, Mount Fisher, Roebourne and Cossacks, N.W. Coast.
Fitt, J., jun., Williams River, Albany Road.
Fitt, J., sen., Williams River, Albany Road.
Fitzgerald, J., Victoria Plains.
Fitzgerald, J., Dongarra.
Fitzgerald, R., Dongarra.
Fitzgerald, W., Dongarra.
Fitzpatrick, T., Gingin.
Flaherty, E., Bunburry.
Flaherty, J., Brunswick.
Fleay, Jas., The Dale, Beverley.
Fleay, John, Beverley.
Fleay, W., Beverley.
Fleay, W. H., Arthur's River.
Fleming, P. C., Charnwood, Vasse.
Fleming, W., Beverley.
Flindall, F. B. S., Guildford.
Flinn, H., Dardanup.
Foley, J., Dardanup.
Foley, J., Newcastle.
Foley, T., Newcastle.
Fonnell, William, Busselton.
Forbes, J., Newcastle.
Ford, P., Serpentine, Murray.
Forrest, James, Busselton.
Forrest, J. H., Preston, Wellington District.
Forrest, Burt, and Co., Robe River.
Forrest, W., Blackwood.
Forsyth Bros., Kojunup.
Forward, J., Beverley.
Forward, W., Beverley.
Foss Bros., Arrinoo, and Ningham, Irwin.
Fouracre, J., Murray.
Fouracre, R., Murray.
Fowler, J., jun., Dardanup.
Fowler, J., sen., Preston.
Fowler, R., Dardanup.
Fraser, Peter, Victoria Plains.
Fraser, R., Swan.
Fraser, R., jun., Swan.
Gale, C., Geraldton.
Gale, G., Northam.
Gale, R., Fairlawn, Busselton.
Gallop, R., jun., Milepool, York.
Gardiner, A., Brunswick.
Gardiner, B., Brunswick.
Gardiner, E., Dardanup.
Gardiner, Ephraim, Dardanup.
Gardiner, Jesse, Dardanup.
Gardiner, John, Busselton.
Gardiner, O., Dardanup.
Garner, Joseph, York.
Garratty, P., Spring Hill, King George's Sound.
Garvey, Patrick, Dardanup.
Garvey, T., Dardanup.
Gavin, W. Preston.
Gee, J. M. B., Gingin.
Gentle, S., York.
Gentle, W., York.
Gibbs, George, Fremantle.
Gibbs, N. L., Canning.
Gibbs, W., Williams River.
Gibbs, W., jun., 125-mile Station, Albury Road.
Giblet, G., Busselton.
Giblet, Jesse, Busselton.
Giblet, T., Blackwood.
Gibson, W., Bunbury.

PASTORAL AND AGRICULTURAL DIRECTORY.

Giles, J., Geraldton.
Giles, J., Eticup.
Giles, J., 19-Mile, York.
Gillbridge, J., Fremantle.
Gladwell, J., Victoria Plains.
Glass, C., Newcastle.
Glass, C., jun., Newcastle.
Glass, W. C., Northampton.
Glen, D., Dongarra.
Glover, C. A., Gingin.
Godfrey, T., Swan.
Gooch, J., York.
Goodenough, R., Beverley.
Goodwin, E., Dongarra.
Gorman, John, Newcastle.
Gorman, W., Newcastle.
Gould, E., Geraldton.
Grant, Anderson and Edgar, De Grey, Cossack.
Grant, J., Dongarra.
Grant, McKenzie, De Grey River.
Grant, T., Gingin.
Grant, W., Dongarra.
Gray, H. and C., Geraldton.
Gray, T., Beverley.
Green, Levi, Murray.
Green, Samuel, Newcastle.
Gregg, R., station overseer, Mill Stream.
Gregory, J., York.
Gregory, J. A., York.
Gregory, J. H., Northam.
Gregory, W., York.
Griffin, J., Newcastle.
Grigson, T., York.
Grigson, W., York.
Guerin, T. B., Blackwood Road.
Guerrier, C. F., Busselton.
Hackett, Phillip, Busselton.
Haddleton, Thomas, Coompatine, King George's Sound
Haddrill, T., Swan.
Haddrill, W., Swan.
Haines, J., Geraldton.
Hale, O., Beaufort River.
Hale, S., Arthur River.
Hall, A., Roeburne and Cossack, N.W. Coast.
Hall, J. A., Roeburne.
Hall, R., Bunbury.
Halligan, J., Victorian River.
Hammersley, C., Williams River.
Hammersley, E., Wilberforce, York.
Hammersley, G., Greenough.
Hammersley, H., Hill River Station, Greenough.
Hammersley, S. R., Guildford.
Hancock, G., Beverley.
Hancock, J., Harding River.
Hancock and Fisher, Andover, Roebourne.
Handy, Miles, Busselton.
Hardey, J. W., Grove Farm, Guildford Road, Perth.
Hardey, R., Newcastle.
Hardey, R. D., Guildford Road, Perth.
Hardey, T., Murray.
Hardey, F., York.
Hare, F. A., Tullering.
Harris, E., Busselton.
Harris, J., Canning.
Harris, J., jun., Canning.
Harris, Joseph, Gingin.
Harris, P., Australind.
Harris, Thos., Dongarra.
Harris, W., Beaufort River.
Harris, W., Swan.
Harrison, J., Busselton.
Harrison, T., Greenough.
Hartnell, J., Dardanup.
Harvey, D., Dardanup.
Harwood, John, Busselton.
Hassell, A., Bendenup, Albany.
Hassell, A. and A., Kendenuh, King George's Sound.
Hassell, A. G., Kendenuh, King George's Sound.
Hassell, Frank, Warrenup, King George's Sound.
Hassell, John, Albany, King George's Sound.
Hassell, J. F. T., Mount Melville, King George's Sound.
Hastings, F., Newcastle.
Hatch, W., Gingin.
Hawkins, F., Brunswick.
Hay, Thomas, Williams River.
Hayden, P., Williams River.
Hayward, Thomas, Bunbury.

Haywood, J., Newcastle.
Heal, A., York.
Heal, C., sen., York.
Heal, Henry, York.
Heal, J. and C., York.
Heelan, M., Greenough.
Hegarty, H., Beaufort River.
Hennessy, C., Newcastle.
Hennessy, J., Dardanup.
Heppingstone, Arthur, Busselton.
Herbert, H., Dongarra.
Herbert, J., Albany.
Herbert, R., Albany.
Heron, Miss, Murray.
Hester, E. G., Blackwood.
Hickney, John, Mininup.
Hicks, C., York.
Hicks, H. H., Harding River, North-west Coast.
Hicks, J., Gwanbegne, York.
Higgins, F., Mininup.
Higgins, J., Busselton.
Higgins, J., Blackwood.
Higgins, J., York.
Higgins, Mrs. C., Mininup.
Highett, H., Arthur River.
Hines, W., Beverley.
Hirvard and Co., Tallering.
Hitchcock, D., Swan.
Hitchcock, J., Swan.
Hitchcock, J., Newcastle.
Hitchcock, J., Northam.
Hodges, Thomas, York.
Hogan, S., jun., York.
Holdaway, J., Williams River.
Holgate, John, Busselton.
Hollingsworth, R., Greenough.
Holmes Bros., Murray.
Holt, J. P., Dongarra.
Hooley and New, Booraning, Williams River.
Hoops, R., Norri Lake.
Hopkins, E., Borarecup, King George's Sound.
Horton, C., Newcastle.
Horton, J., Geraldton.
Hoskins, W., Blackwood.
Hough, James, Dardanup.
Hough, Joseph, Bunbury.
House, E., Mininup.
Howard, Shenton and Co., Murchison.
Howell, Charles, Dongarra.
Hunt, W., Victoria Plains.
Hurst, Basil, Brunswick.
Hurst, Thomas, Preston.
Hutchings, —, Newcastle.
Hutchins, Frederick, Busselton.
Hutton, John, Blackwood.
Hynes, M., Williams River.
Jackson, J., Greenough.
Jackson, Thomas, Bunbury.
Jessop, B., Northam.
Johnson, A., Dongarra.
Johnson, J., Dongarra.
Johnson, W. G., Guildford.
Johnston, J., Forster, Bunbury.
Jones, D., Guildford.
Jones, J., Greenough, Victoria District.
Jones, R., Blackwood
Jones, S., Gingin.
Jones, W. jun., Swan.
Jones, W. J., Blackwood.
Jones, W. L. L., Swan.
Jordan, C., Eticup.
Joslin, D., Fremantle.
Joyce, Jno., Victoria Plains.
Jubb, G. F., Perth.
Keating, J., York.
Keenan, A., Busselton.
Keenan, R., Busselton.
Keenan, S., Busselton.
Keene, T., Murray.
Keene, W. J., Murray.
Kelly, Thomas, Victoria Plains.
Kemp, Hy., Greenough.
Kemp, J., Woodbridge, Guildford.
Kempton, J., Victoria Plains.
Kempton, J., Northampton.
Kennedy, J., York.
Kennedy, J., Newcastle.
Kennedy and McGill, Montebello, Eucla Telegraph Line.
Kerr, J., York.

WESTERN AUSTRALIA.

Kett, W., York.
Key, E., Murray.
Key, T., Murray.
Kilmurray, Jas., Dongarra.
Kilpatrick, D., station overseer, Harding River.
Kindelan, T., York.
King, Geo., Greenough, Victoria District.
King, Hy., Guildford.
King, R., Swan.
King, W., Gingin.
Kinsella, E., Busselton.
Kirk, J., Fremantle.
Knapp, J., Greenough, Victoria District.
Knapp, W., Greenough, Victoria District.
Knight, J., York.
Knight, James, Beverley.
Knott, E., York.
Knott, W., York.
Lacey, A. and E., Warra Warra, Murchison.
Lahiffe, J., Newcastle.
Lakeman, S., Murray.
Landor, J., Northampton.
Lane, J., Murray.
Larkin, Thomas, Busselton.
Larwood, J. and G., Gingin.
Latrey, J., Newcastle.
Latrey, T., Newcastle.
Lavender, W., Williams River.
Lawrence, H., Northam.
Layman, Chas., Busselton.
Layman, Geo., Busselton.
Lazenby, J., Murray.
Leake, R. B., Noorergong, York.
Lee, T., Newcastle.
Lee, S., Jayes, Blackwood.
Leeson, T., Northam.
Lefroy Bros., Jayes, Blackwood.
Lefroy, H. B., Victoria Plains.
Lefroy, W. G., Herne Hill, Guildford.
Lennard, E. B., Beverley.
Lewington, R., Fremantle.
Lilly, E., Williams River.
Little, Thomas, Murchison.
Lloyd, C., Newcastle.
Lloyd, J., York.
Lloyd, J. M., Newcastle.
Locke, Ernest, Busselton.
Locke, Eugene, Busselton.
Locke, E. C. B., Blackwood.
Locke, E. N. M., Blackwood.
Lockyer, J., Northam.
Lockyer, Thomas, Perth.
Lockyer Bros., Table Hill, Roebourne and Cossacks, N.W. Coast.
Logue, J., Murray.
Logue, Joseph, Swan.
Logue, M., Champion Bay.
Logue, T., Murray.
Long, W., Long's, Victoria Plains and Dandarragan.
Longbottom, C., Busselton.
Longbottom, S., Busselton.
Longbottom, T., Busselton.
Longman, G., Victoria Plains.
Look, H., Guildford.
Lukin, G., Newcastle.
Lukin, H., Beverley.
Lukin, L. B., Deep Dale, Toodyay.
Lukin, W., Williams River.
Lukin, W. F., Beverley.
Lynch, D. G., Beverley.
Lynch, M., Newcastle.
Lynch, P., Newcastle.
Macpherson, D., Glentromie, Victoria Plains and Dandarragan.
Macpherson, D., Irwin.
Macvean, W., Malis Island, North-west.
Maddox, Wm., Williams River.
Major and Bailey, Glengarry, Champion Bay.
Major, T., Geraldton.
Maguire, James, Dardanup.
Maguire, John, Dardanup.
Maher, J., Eticup.
Mara, J., Swan.
Marchetti, G., Greenough, Victoria District.
Mark, S., Greenough.
Markham, W., Arthur River.
Marriott, John, Brunswick.
Marriott, Thomas, jun., Brunswick.
Marriott, Thomas, sen., Brunswick.
Marsh, Wm., Brunswick.
Marshall, A., Busselton.
Martin, A., Newcastle.
Martin, Chas., Swan.
Martin, G., Northam.
Martin, H., Gingin.
Martin, H., York.
Martin, J., Northam.
Martin, M., Chittering, Swan.
Martin, R., Gingin.
Martin, Robert, Swan.
Martin, S., York.
Martin, S., Newcastle.
Martin, W., Northam.
Marwick, W., York.
Maslin, T., Blackwood.
Massingham, C., York.
Maxwell, John, Busselton.
Maxwell, W., Blackwood Road.
May, G., Newcastle.
Mayo, Mrs., Swan.
Mead, H., Serpentine, Murray.
Mead, R., Serpentine, Murray.
Mead, T., jun., Northam.
Mead, W., Rockingham, Fremantle.
Meagher, M., Newcastle.
Meares, G. M., York.
Meares, S. H., York.
Melbourn, A., Newcastle.
Meredith, G., Newcastle.
Middleton, E., Guildford.
Millard, — Newcastle.
Mills, J., Geraldton.
Minchin, A. E., Swan.
Minchin, W. A., Swan.
Minlon, W., Busselton.
Mitchell, W. B., Bunbury.
Mitchell, W. O., Preston.
Moate, M., York.
Moir, A., Eticup.
Moir, G., Albany.
Moir, G., Mungup.
Moir, J., Albany.
Moir, W. and G., Fanny's Cove.
Moloney, J., station overseer, George River.
Monger and Browne, Gascoigne River.
Monger and Co., Gascoigne River.
Monger, George, York.
Monger, S., Stanton Springs, Beverley.
Moore, A., Brunswick.
Moore, J., jun., Preston.
Morgan, Charles, Dardanup.
Morgan, John, Busselton.
Morgan, W., Greenough, Victoria District.
Morgan, W. J., Northam.
Moriarty, William, Busselton.
Morley, C., Swan.
Morley, H., Swan.
Morley, H., Gingin.
Morrell, J. and D., Northam.
Morrell, J. and T., Northam.
Morrell, J. R., Northam.
Morrell, R. E., Greenough, Victoria District.
Morris, M., Kojunup.
Morrisey, M., Geraldton.
Morrisey, M., Northampton.
Morrisey, P., Dongarra.
Morrisey, T., Northampton.
Morrison, James, stock and station agent, Guildford.
Morse, T., York.
Morse, T., jun., York.
Mort, Samuel, Busselton.
Mortimer, D. and A., Gingin.
Mortimer, S., Gingin.
Mottram, John, Busselton.
Moulton, A., Bridgetown, Blackwood Road.
Moulton, James, Beverley.
Mountain, James, Dongarra.
Muir, A., Eucla.
Muir, A., Albany.
Muir, James, Albany.
Muir, J., Albany.
Muir, T., Albany.
Munn, J., Blackwood.
Munro, J., Albany.
Murchison Pastoral Association, Murchison.
Murphy, A., Geraldton.
Murphy, F., Newcastle.
Murphy, J., Newcastle.

PASTORAL AND AGRICULTURAL DIRECTORY.

Murphy, J., Victoria Plains.
Murphy, M., Northampton.
Murphy, P., Newcastle.
Murphy, P., Victoria Plains.
Murray, D. and G., Murray.
Murray, J. G., Burnside, Pinjarrah.
McAndrew, A., Brunswick.
McAndrew, J., Brunswick.
McAttee, J., Murray.
McAttee, James, Murray.
McAttee, John F., Murray.
McAuley, J., jun., Williams River.
McAuley, J., sen., Williams River.
McAuliffe, Thomas, Greenough.
McCaffrey, —, Victoria Plains.
McCagh, James, Greenough.
McCarley, John, Greenough.
McCarthy, J., York.
McCartney, Mrs., Greenough.
McCourt, James, Mininup.
McCourt, J. T., Gingin.
McCure, R., Northampton.
McDermott, J., Newcastle.
McDonald, J., Greenough.
McGowan, Charles, Preston.
McGrath, T., Beverley.
McGregor, D., Busselton.
McGuiness, John, Greenough.
McGuiness, O., Greenough.
McGuire, J., Eticup.
McGuire, P., Eticup.
McIntosh, Ewin, Toodyay.
McKay Bros., Manduballangann, Roebourne.
McKay, D., station overseer, Yule River, N.W. Coast.
McKenzie, James, Mill Stream, Fortescue.
McKenzie, J. R., Mill Stream, Roebourne.
McKnoe, Thomas, Victoria Plains.
McLarty, E., Murray.
McLean, K., Langwell and Spinifex Park, Roebourne.
McLeod, D. N., Maitland River, N.W. Coast.
McLeod, G., Williams River.
McLeod, H., Maitland River.
McManus, —, Northam.
McNeece, W., Greenough.
McNoe, W., Newcastle.
McPherson, —, Yaudenooka, Dongarra.
McRae, M., Maitland River.
Nairn, James, Dongarra.
Nairn, Wm., Dongarra.
Nancarrow, Wm., Northampton.
Negus, J., York.
Nelson, N., Albany.
Nelson, W., York.
Nevin, J., Busselton.
New, M., Dangin, Beverley.
New, M., Williams River.
Newman, M., Albany.
Newman, Thos., Williams River.
Newport, R., York.
Newstead, N., Kojonup.
Nicolay, F., Fremantle.
Nix, Fred., Gingin.
Noble, J., Newcastle.
Nolan, M., Swan.
Noonan, N. J., Norri Lake.
Norrish, G., Kinanellup, Kojonup.
Norrish, John, Warkehip, Kojonup.
Norrish, Joseph, Eticup.
Norrish, Josiah, Tambellclup, King George's Sound.
Norrish, R., Mailiyup, Kojonup.
Norrish, T., Eticup, King George's Sound.
O'Brien, M., Greenough, Victoria District.
O'Donnell, J., Greenough, Victoria District.
O'Donnell, James, Busselton.
Offer, Hy., Brunswick.
O'Flaherty, J., Eticup.
Ogilvie, A. J., Murchison Station, Northampton.
Ogilvy, —, Port Gregory.
Oliver, James, Guildford.
Oliver, John, Guildford.
Oliver, M., York.
Oliver, R., Guildford.
O'Maley, Thomas, Greenough, Victoria District.
O'Neil, A., Newcastle.
O'Neil, T., Gingin.
Orkney, R., Fortescue River.
Oxenham, N., Northampton.

Padbury, Mark, Blackwood.
Padbury, Walter, Yatheroo, Victoria Plains.
Page, J., Williams River, Albany Road.
Parish, J., York.
Parker, E., jun., York.
Parker, E. R., Beverley.
Parker, J. T., York.
Parker, J. W., York.
Parker, S. S., York.
Parker, W. M., York.
Pascoe, H., Dongarra, Victoria District.
Pascoe, John, Dongarra, Victoria District.
Pascoe, J. M., Dongarra, Victoria District.
Patterson, W. and G., Creaton, Pinjarrah.
Payne, Albert, Mininup.
Payne, Alfred, Mininup.
Payne Bros., F. G. and A., Fremantle.
Payne, George, jun., Busselton.
Pearce, J., Greenough, Victoria District.
Pearson, Robert, Greenough, Victoria District.
Peel, T., Murray.
Pell, George, Dongarra, Victoria District.
Pell, John, Dongarra, Victoria District.
Penny, H., York.
Penny, H., jun., York.
Pennyfather, J., York.
Perejuan, John, Greenough, Victoria District.
Perks, J., station manager, Murchison.
Perrin, Arthur, Brunswick.
Perrin, Edwin, Brunswick.
Perrin, James, Brunswick.
Perrin, Jessie, Brunswick.
Pettit, Robert, Dongarra, Victoria District.
Pettit, W., Dongarra, Victoria District.
Phillips and Burges, Irwin House, Irwin.
Phillips, J., Beverley.
Phillips, S., Dongarra, Victoria District.
Phillips, S. P., Beverley.
Phillips, Thomas, Kojonup, Albany Road, Albany.
Piggott, A., Albany.
Piggott, J., Australind.
Piggott, James, Marbellup, Albany.
Piggott, R., Australind.
Piggott, S., Hay River, Albany.
Piggott, Thomas, Australind.
Pilkington, J., Northam.
Pitts, J., Northam.
Plank, D., Swan.
Plester, A., Dongarra, Victoria District.
Pollard, G., Hotham River, Albany Road, Albany.
Pollard, G., Helena, Guildford.
Pollard, J., Murray.
Pollard, J., jun., Hotham River, Albany Road, Albany.
Pollard, W., Murray.
Pollard, W., jun., Hotham River, Albany Road, Albany.
Pollitt, A., Greenough, Victoria District.
Pontin Bros. and Sharpe, Mount Dean, Eucla Telegraph Line.
Pontin, S., Mount Dean Eucla Telegraph Line.
Pontin, W., Mount Dean, Eucla Telegraph Line.
Poole, E., Greenough, Victoria District.
Poole, J., Greenough, Victoria District.
Poole, J., Greenough, Victoria District.
Pope, A. and L., Geraldton.
Pope, Wallace, Geraldton.
Postens, George, Fremantle.
Powell, W., Greenough, Victoria District.
Pritchard, R., Beverley.
Properjohn, C., Mininup.
Pumphrey, W., Hotham River, Albany Road, Albany.
Quartermaine, A., Norri, Lake.
Quartermaine, Charles, Parkering Lakes, King George's Sound.
Quartermaine, Eli, jun., Yarrabin, King George's Sound.
Quartermaine, E., sen., Yonangup, King George's Sound.
Quartermaine, H., Norri Lake.
Quartermaine, John, Moogebine, King George's Sound.
Quinn, J. W., Beverley.
Quinn, M., Williams River, Albany Road, Albany.
Ramsay, Mrs. Grace, Mininup.
Ralph, E., Newcastle.
Rayner, P., Greenough, Victoria District.
Read, W., Northampton, Victoria District.
Reading, W., Australind, Wellington District.

WESTERN AUSTRALIA.

lvii

Reeves, George, Busselton.
Regan, W., Dandarragan.
Reilly, M., Kojonup, Albany Road, Albany.
Reilly, P., Busselton.
Reynolds, J. G., Busselton.
Reynolds, P., Dongarra.
Reynolds, T., York.
Reynolds, Thos., jun., York.
Reynolds, T. F., York.
Rhodes, J., Greenough, Victoria District.
Richardson, A. R., Lowlands, Serpentine.
Richardson, J., Busselton.
Richardson and Wellard, Lowlands, Serpentine, Murray.
Richardson, R. A., and Co., The Pyramid Station, Roeburne and Cossacks, North West Coast.
Ridley, L. F., Irwin.
Roberts, C. F., Mininup.
Roberts, E., Victoria Plains and Dandarragan.
Roberts, Frederick, Mininup.
Roberts, T., Mininup.
Roberts, W., jun., Mininup.
Robinson, E. and C., Roeburne.
Robinson, W., Sunning Hill, Beverley.
Robinson, W. A., George River.
Rock, W., Gingin.
Roe, T. B., Warren.
Rogers, James, Australind, Wellington District.
Rose, Charles, Blackwood, Wellington District.
Rose, George, Busselton.
Rose, R. H., Australind, Wellington District.
Roser, W., Newcastle.
Rosevear, E., Newcastle.
Rowan, M., Northampton, Victoria District.
Rowland, J., Dongarra, Victoria District.
Rowland, R., Irwin.
Rowland, R., jun., Irwin.
Rowles, J., Newcastle.
Rudd, W., Beverley.
Rumble, J., Greenough.
Rumble, W., Newcastle.
Ryan, J., Gordon River, King George's Sound.
Ryan, J., Northampton, Victoria District.
Ryan, M., Northampton, Victoria District.
Ryan, M., Newcastle.
Sadler, T. H., Helena, Guildford.
Salvado, Right Rev. Bishop, New Norcia, Victoria Plains.
San Miguel, Rockingham, Fremantle.
Saunders, W., Geraldton, Victoria District.
Savage, J., Busselton.
Scarff, R., Geraldton, Victoria District.
Scott, H. W. and E. T., Lower Blackwood.
Scott, Jessie, York.
Scott, J., jun., Mininup, Wellington District.
Scott, R., Mininup, Wellington District.
Scott, R., York.
Scott, T., Lower Blackwood.
Scott, T., Quindalup, Blackwood Road, Wellington District.
Scott, W., Blackwood.
Scott, W., Lower Blackwood.
Scott, W., Lower Blackwood.
Scotthouse, Mrs., Preston, Wellington District.
Seabrook, J., jun., Brookton, Beverley.
Seabrook, J., sen., J.P., Brookton, Beverley.
Sermon, W., York.
Sermon, W., jun., York.
Seivwright, D., Geraldton, Victoria District.
Sewell, C., Murchison, Victoria District.
Sewell, F., Mount Stirling, Victoria District.
Sewell, G., Geraldton, Victoria District.
Sewell, H. H., Beverley.
Sewell, J., Maplestead, Beverley.
Sewell, J. E., Murchison.
Sewell, M., Mount Caroline, York.
Sewell, S., Sand Springs, Northampton.
Seymour, M., Busselton.
Shanahan, O., Dardanup, Wellington District.
Sharpe, J., Eucla Telegraph Line.
Shaw, J., Greenough.
Shaw, R., Geraldton, Victoria District.
Sheehy, R., York.
Sheen, M., Swan.
Sheridan, James, Victoria Plains.
Sherry, P., York.
Sherwin, S., Geraldton, Victoria District.
Shiers, A., Dardanup, Wellington District.
Sholl, H. W., and Co., Roeburne, North West Coast.

Sholl, A., Roeburne, North West Coast.
Sholl and Son, Roeburne, North West Coast.
Silcock, Mrs., Greenough, Victoria District.
Simmons, Thomas, Preston.
Simpson, D., Fortescue River.
Simpson, J., Greenough, Victoria District.
Simpson, J. and W., Albany.
Simpson and McIntosh, Mardie, Fortescue River, Cossacks.
Sims, Charles, Greenough.
Sims, G., York.
Skelly, R., Newcastle.
Slater, G., Goomaling.
Slattery, Patrick, Dardanup, Wellington District.
Slavin, J., Greenough, Victoria District.
Sloper, C., Dongarra, Victoria District.
Smirke, T., Fremantle.
Smith, A. and F., Beambine, Beverley.
Smith, C., jun., Beambine, Beverley.
Smith, C., sen., Roseland, Beverley.
Smith, E., Arthur River.
Smith, F., Fremantle.
Smith, F., Greenough, Victoria District.
Smith, F. W., Greenough, Victoria District.
Smith, Mrs. George, Greenough, Victoria District.
Smith, G. B., Beverley.
Smith, G. W., Helena, Guildford.
Smith, J., Dongarra, Victoria District.
Smith, James, Brunswick, Wellington District.
Smith, James, Greenough, Victoria District.
Smith, M. A., Arthur River.
Smith, M. B., Brunswick, Wellington District.
Smith, R. and J., Northam.
Smith, Thomas, Lower Blackwood.
Smith, Thomas, Greenough, Victoria District.
Smith, W., Beverley.
Smith, W., York.
Smith, W. G., Arthur River.
Snow, A., York.
Snow, J., York.
Sounness, W., jun., Albany.
Sounness, W., Mount Barker.
Spanswick, R., Arthur River.
Spencer, J., Albany.
Spencer, R., Konjonup.
Spencer, W., Bunbury, Wellington District.
Spencer, W., Bunbury.
Spice, C., Gingin.
Spice, J., Gingin.
Spice, W., Gingin.
Spratt, E., Arthur River.
Stanley, W., Northam.
Stephens, John, Greenough, Victoria District.
Stephens, W., Dongarra, Victoria District.
Stevens, J., Williams River.
Stevenson, F., Harding River.
Stewart, D. and J., Lower Fortescue River, N.W. Coast.
Stewart, J., Lower Fortescue River, N.W. Coast.
Stokes, J., Greenough, Victoria District.
Stokes, Mrs. J., Greenough, Victoria District.
Stokes, W., Greenough, Victoria District.
Stone, J., Greenough, Victoria District.
Stone, J., York.
Stone, M., York.
Stone, P., Greenough.
Strathan, J., Newcastle.
Strange, A., Beverley.
Strange, R., Beverley.
Studson, H., Swan.
Sullivan, J., York.
Summers, W. H., Fremantle.
Sutton, H., Murray.
Sweeney, J., Greenough.
Syrea, W., Newcastle.
Taylor, C., Eucla Telegraph Line.
Taylor, C., Albany.
Taylor, C., Northam.
Taylor, Campbell, Thomas River, King George's Sound.
Taylor, J., Yangendine, Beverley.
Taylor, James, Arthur River, Albany River.
Taylor, S., York.
Taylor, W., Northampton, Victoria District.
Taylor, W., Beverley.
Thomas, J., Ravenswood, Pinjarrah.
Thomas, James, Busselton.
Thomas, John, Northampton, Victoria District.
Thompson, A., Gingin.
Thompson, J., Gingin.

Thompson, James, Arthur River, Albany Road.
Thompson, P., Gingin.
Thompson, R., Gingin.
Thompson, R., Newcastle.
Thompson, Robert, Newcastle.
Thompson, Thomas, Arthur River, Albany Road.
Thompson, W., Northam.
Thorp, E., Murray.
Thorp, W., Murray.
Thurkle, —, Busselton.
Tomlinson, J., York.
Tomlinson, T., Cave Hill, York.
Tommaney, T., York.
Torrens, J., York.
Torrens, S., York.
Townsend, H., Round Swamp, Albany Road.
Townsend, H., Albany.
Treasure, E., Eticup, Albany Road.
Treasure, E., Albany.
Treasure, Edward, Martinap, King George's Sound.
Trew, G., York.
Trew, J., George River.
Trigwell, H., sen., Preston, Wellington District.
Trott, A., Blackwood, Wellington District.
Truslove, J., Esperance Bay, Eucla Telegraph Line.
Tuckey, C., Murray.
Tunney, James, Slab Hut Gully, King George's Sound.
Tunney, James, Kojunup, Albany Road.
Tunney, James, Albany Road.
Tunney, R., Albany.
Turner, E., Murray.
Twine, A. G., Goomaling, Toodyay.
Twine, A. G., Newcastle.
Twine, H. G., Newcastle.
Twine, J., Newcastle.
Vanzuilecom, J. F., Kojunup.
Venn, H. W., Dardanup Park, Vasse.
Ventura, Q., Greenough, Victoria District.
Viveash, Samuel, Indenuna, North West Coast.
Viveash, S. H., Jones' Creek, North West Coast.
Viveash and Co., Inthamuna, Roebourne.
Waldeck, H. F., Dongarra, Victoria District.
Waldeck, J., Greenough, Victoria District.
Waldeck, W., jun., Greenough, Victoria District.
Walders, Patrick, Dardanup, Wellington District.
Waldock, W., Williams River.
Walker, John, Dongarra, Victoria District.
Walkden, Thomas, Victoria Plains.
Wallace, W., Dongarra, Victoria District.
Walsh, William, Beverley.
Walters, W., Guildford.
Walton, Anthony, Canipup, King George's Sound.
Wansborough, James, York.
Wansborough, W., York.
Warburton, A., Mount Barker.
Warburton, G., Mount Barker.
Warburton, G. E., Mount Barker.
Warburton, G. G., Albany.
Warburton, R., station overseer, Maitland River.
Warburton, R. E., sheep inspector, Williams River.
Ward, A., Murray.
Ward, J., Newcastle.
Warner, W., Busselton.
Warren, E. A., Guildford.
Warrener, J., Greenough, Victoria District.
Wass, W. E., Dongarra, Victoria District.
Waters, R., Newcastle.
Waters, T., Newcastle.
Waters, W., Guildford.
Watkins, G., Newcastle.
Watson, Joseph, Dongarra, Victoria District.
Watson, W., Northam.
Watton, A., Albany.

Watton, T., Beverley.
Webb, George, Northampton, Victoria District.
Webby, Job, Dongarra, Victoria District.
Wellard, J., Whitty Falls, Serpentine.
Wellard, J., Murray.
Wellman, D., Guildford.
Wells, E., Victoria Plains.
Wellstead, J., Bremer Bay, Eucla Telegraph Line.
Wellstead and Sons, Albany.
Welsh, Mrs., York.
Welsh, M., York.
Wetherall, E., Newcastle.
Wheateley, Peter, Busselton.
Wheatfield, Peter, Blackwood Road, Wellington District.
Whitby, W., Greenough, Victoria District.
White, George, York.
White, J., Greenough, Victoria District.
White, James, Bunbury, Wellington District.
White, M., York.
White, W., Northam.
Whitehead, J., Eticup.
Whitehead, W., Albany.
Whitehead, William, Nowandup, King George's Sound.
Whitehurst, C., Geraldton, Victoria District.
Whitfield, F., Mount Kine, South Coast.
Whitfield, G., Newcastle.
Wilding, T., Northam.
Wiley, Thomas, Greenough, Victoria District.
Wilkins, J., Newcastle.
Wilkinson, C. and J., Glenavon, Toodyay.
Wilkinson, J., Newcastle.
Wilkinson, Jacob, Newcastle.
Wilks, J., Northam.
Williams, J., Northam.
Williams, H., Perth.
Williams, J., Northampton, Victoria District.
Williams, J., Albany.
Williams, R., Victoria Plains.
Williams, T., Greenough, Victoria District.
Willis, S., York.
Wills, E., Murray.
Wills and Quartermaine, Arthur River.
Wilmott, R., Greenough, Victoria District.
Wilton, John, Greenough, Victoria District.
Wilton, J. M., Greenough, Victoria District.
Wilton, Thomas, Greenough, Victoria District.
Withenell, Brooklyn, North West Coast, Roebourne and Cossacks.
Wittenoon, E., Northampton, Victoria District.
Wittenoon, E. and T., Bowes and Zuin, Northampton.
Woodley, W., York.
Wood, A., Mininup, Wellington District.
Wood, H. H., Mininup, Wellington District.
Woods, Isaac, Northampton, Victoria District.
Woods, J., Victoria Plains.
Woolhouse Bros., The Robe, North West Coast, Roebourne, and Cossacks.
Woolhouse, George, Greenough, Victoria District.
Worth, G., Beverley.
Wray, J., jun., Albany.
Wright, G., Northam.
Wright, Thomas, Mininup, Wellington District.
Wyatt, J., Newcastle.
Yates, F., Northam.
York, A., Gingin.
York, H., Beverley.
York, J., Gingin.
York, J., jun., Gingin.
York, T., Gingin.
Young, Charles, Blackwood Road.
Young, D., Albany.
Young, J., Albany.